The Vertigo Years

By the same author

*Encyclopédie: The Triumph of Reason
in an Unreasonable Age*

*To Have and to Hold: An Intimate History
of Collectors and Collecting*

The Vertigo Years

Change and Culture in the West,
1900–1914

PHILIPP BLOM

Weidenfeld & Nicolson

LONDON

First published in Great Britain in 2008
by Weidenfeld & Nicolson

1 3 5 7 9 10 8 6 4 2

A CIP catalogue record for this book
is available from the British Library.

ISBN 978 0 297 85232 2

Typeset by Input Data Services Ltd, Frome

Printed and bound in the UK by CPI Mackays, Chatham ME5 8TD

The Orion Publishing Group's policy is to use papers that
are natural, renewable and recyclable products and made
from wood grown in sustainable forests. The logging and
manufacturing processes are expected to conform to
environmental regulations of the country of origin.

Weidenfeld & Nicolson

The Orion Publishing Group Ltd
Orion House
5 Upper Saint Martin's Lane
London, WC2H 9EA
An Hachette Livre UK Company

www.orionbooks.co.uk

For Cecil
and for Chelsea, Samantha, André, Pierce, Aidan,
Martine and Lukas

Contents

List of Illustrations

Text Illustrations

Colour Plate Section

Acknowledgements

No book can come to life without conversations and discussions, and a project as ambitious as the present one is particularly dependent on friends and colleagues who help give ideas a first airing, to try them out, refine them, or occasionly drop them. In the initial stages, my agent Bill Hamilton provided a wonderful foil for shaping the conception as a whole and my publisher Alan Samson wholeheartedly supported my almost suicidal ambition.

At different stages my discussion partners who helped me focus and interlink my observations and who opened my eyes to new connections were Dr Thomas Angerer, Anne Buckley, Prof. John Burrow, Prof. Christophe Charle, Prof. Tony Judt, Dr Stephen Paterson, Dr Ulrich Raulff, Dr David Rechter, Froukje Slofstra, Prof. Jon Stallworthy and Dr Magnus Walter, as well as Victoria Hobbs, Sebastian Ritscher, Sara Fisher and George Lucas, whose tireless support is of inestimable value.

Elise Allen and Simon Kasper kindly helped me with some of my research, and the staff of the British Library, the Bibliothèque Nationale de France, the Bibliothèque de la Geneviève, the Österreichische Nationalbibliothek, the Literaturarchiv Marbach, the libraries of the universities of Leiden, the Sorbonne, Oxford, Vienna, and New York University, the Wellcome Institute, London, and the Musée de la ville de Paris were to hand with assistance and advice above and beyond the call of duty.

My particular admiration and gratefulness go to Prof. Ulrich Sieg, whose depth of historical knowledge and humanity are always crucial for my understanding of my own ideas. Once the text was finished in draft, Bernadette Buckley proved a wonderfully attentive reader and made valuable suggestions.

Last, but by no means least, there is my wife, Veronica Buckley, who has supported me with her love, an unfailingly open ear for my many over-enthusiastic soliloquies and occasional writing obstacles, and endless cups of tea provided to my desk, late at night and with infinite kindness.

Nothing is less ethical than so-called sexual 'morality'; which rests entirely on social convenience... perhaps the most important psychological fact of our time is the tension between ethics and social rules, which is growing slowly and being more and more acutely felt. On this Procrustean bed the modern soul is so overstretched, so wrenched apart in its innermost fibres and made oversensitive, that it is hard to see a parallel in all of intellectual history...

Second problem: that of modernity, how to reconcile with the soul the enormous mass of the new. The particular character of today lies in the fact that no other time had to conquer such a multitude of new elements.

– Count Harry Kessler, Diary, 7 April 1903

Introduction

They are standing on the side of a tree-lined country road; men and boys mostly, full of anticipation. The heat of the summer bears down on them. They look down the road stretching out ahead, as far as they can see. A faint humming sound becomes audible. A car appears on the straight line between the streets, small and surrounded by a cloud of dust, and growing, growing with every passing second. It hurtles towards the spectators, its powerful engine speeding it on, roaring ever more loudly, a vision of concentrated power.

One of the onlookers, a young man of eighteen, readies his camera to take the shot he has been waiting for. The vehicle is coming closer, roaring, pulsing with energy. Now it is almost there. The teenage photographer is looking intently through his lens. He can see clearly the driver and his passenger behind the huge bonnet, sees the number six painted on the petrol tank, feels the shockwave of noise and power as the engine speeds past him. He has released the shutter that very moment. Now, as the dust settles around him, he must wait to see how the photo will be.

When he sees the picture he has taken on that 26 June 1912 at the French Grand Prix, the young photographer is disappointed. The number six car is only half in the frame, the background smudged and strangely distended. He puts the photo away. He is Jacques Henri Lartigue. The image he considers a failure will be exhibited forty years later and will make him famous, showing all the rush, the energy, the velocity that were so important during the years between the turn of the century and the autumn of 1914.

Today, the period before the outbreak of the First World War is often regarded as idyllic: the time before the fall, the good old days, a *belle époque* celebrated in lavishly decorated films, a beautiful, intact society about to be shattered by the forces driving it inexorably towards disaster. After 1918, according to this reading of events, the phoenix of modernity arose from the ashes of the old world.

To most people who lived around 1900 this nostalgic view with its emphasis on solidity and grace would have come as a surprise. Their experience of this period was as yet unembellished by reminiscence. It was more raw, and marked by fascinations and fears much closer to our own time. Then as now, rapid changes in technology, globalization, communication technologies and changes in the social fabric dominated conversations and newspaper articles; then as now, cultures of mass consumption stamped their mark on the time; then as now, the feeling of living in an accelerating world, of speeding into the unknown, was overwhelming. This is why Lartigue's photo is so fitting as an emblem for its time. A boy in love with fast cars and velocity, his preoccupations mirrored those of a time during which racing drivers were popular heroes, new speed records were established and broken every week, and mass production, here in the shape of hand-held cameras, was changing everybody's lives.

Velocity can be frightening as well as deeply exhilarating, and it is this fear and rejection of change that also echoes across the century. In 1900 the most profound change of all was that in the relationship between men and women, and many indications point towards a deep anxiety on the part of men whose position seemed no longer secure. For the first time in European history women were being educated en masse, earning their own money, demanding the vote and, crucially, suggesting that in an industrial age physical strength and martial virtues were becoming useless. Men reacted with an aggressive restatement of the old values; never before had so many uniforms been seen on the street or so many duels fought, never before had there been so many classified advertisements for treatments allegedly curing 'male maladies' and 'weak nerves'; and never before had so many men complained of exhaustion and nervousness, and found themselves admitted to sanatoriums and even mental hospitals.

Today, identities are questioned in different ways and anxieties are articulated differently, but they still emerge along sexual lines, often as questioned manliness. Resentment at a perceived emasculation by the former colonial powers or the 'arrogant West' have led young Muslim men to assert themselves by taking up arms or becoming suicide bombers – another echo of that earlier time, when anarchist terrorists were blowing themselves up by the dozen in attacks on members of the Russian government.

Around 1900, men worrying about not being manly enough found evidence for their deficiency in the decline of fertility in Europe, particularly among the middle classes, while according to the polemicists of the day, the 'lower' classes and the peoples in the colonies were rapidly outbreeding 'civilized' whites. We hear echoes of this debate today in the hysterical polemics about birth rates among Muslim immigrants to Europe, much-debated forecasts about the growth of the world's population, and the decline of numbers in Europe and the USA, not to mention biological research indicating the decline of fertility among Western men.

Speed and exhilaration, anxiety and vertigo were recurrent themes of the years between 1900 and 1914, during which cities exploded in size and societies were transformed, mass production seized hold of everyday life, newspapers turned into media empires, cinema audiences were in the tens of millions, and globalization brought meat from New Zealand and grain from Canada to British dinner plates, decimating the incomes of the old landed classes and enabling the rise of new kinds of people: engineers, technocrats, city-dwellers. Modernity did not rise virgin-born from the trenches of the Somme. Well before 1914, it had already taken a firm hold on the minds and lives of Europe. The War acted not as a creator, but as a catalyst, forcing old structures to collapse more quickly and new identities to assert themselves more readily.

The Vertigo Years had much in common with our own day, not least their openness: in 1910 and even in 1914, nobody felt confident of the shape the future world would have, of who would wield power, what political constellation would be victorious, or what kind of society would emerge from the headlong transformation. By contrast, during the second half of the twentieth century the Cold War created a quite different situation: the outcome seemed uncertain, but it was perfectly clear what was at stake, and equally clear that one of two ideological systems would eventually be victorious. With the collapse of the Soviet empire, some of the openness and uncertainty of the Vertigo Years have reappeared, and today it is much more difficult to say what the future will bring for our societies.

In a large part, the uncertain future facing us early in the twenty-first century arose from the inventions, thoughts and transformations of those unusually rich fifteen yeats between 1900 and 1914, a period of extraordinary creativity in the arts and sciences, of enormous change in society and in the very image people had of themselves. Everything that was to become important during the twentieth century – from quantum physics to women's emancipation, from abstract art to space travel, from communism and fascism to the consumer society, from industrialized slaughter to the power of the media – had already made deep impressions in the years before 1914, so that the rest of the century was little more than an exercise, wonderful and hideous by turn, in living out and exploring these new possibilities.

To understand this exhilarating and contradictory time, and to see the parallels and differences between it and our present, we must approach it without teleological preconceptions, without seeing these years exclusively in terms of what would or would not lead to the Great War. Instead, we need to look at it with the immediacy of the young Lartigue as he pointed his camera at the number six racing car. If the outcome appears distorted, a subjective image catching only part of the reality, nonetheless it remains the best way to capture the swiftness, the rush, the immediacy of the experience of life during this time.

In the spirit of trying to discover this time on its own terms, I would like to invite you to perform a thought experiment: imagine that a voracious but highly selective plague of bookworms had attacked the world's libraries eating through books and photos, films and other records, and devouring all historical information dealing with the time between July 1914 and 2000; imagine you knew nothing about the Sarajevo assassination, the Somme, the Great Crash, the *Reichskristallnacht*, Stalingrad, Auschwitz, Hiroshima, the gulags, or the Berlin Wall, but that history had gently dawned into memory after the turn of the millennium. Imagine you would not see the biographies, thoughts and deeds of the people living in and around 1910 through the prism of a century of monstrous crimes and monumental achievements, but that you could remove these historical spectacles for a while. Imagine yourself looking at the years 1900 to 1914 without the long shadows of the future darkening their historical present, a living moment with all its complexity and its contradictions, its hopes and fears, and with an open future, just as it was lived by the people of that time.

1

1900:
The Dynamo and the Virgin

So, you're going to come, you are already coming, you have come, monsieur et madame, to our beautiful Exposition universelle of 1900. You are in Paris; from afar you have already seen, as in a dream, the structures of the Exposition standing out against the sky of the great city. What programme should you adopt? Where to begin?   – from the official guide book to the 1900 World Fair

A simple agonising problem should occupy all of French thought: 'How can we stop France from disappearing? How can we keep the French race on earth?' Next to this vital question all others vanish...   – Jacques Bertillon, *La dépopulation de la France*

She was monstrous, if oddly prophetic: there she stood, a buxom bourgeoise 20 feet high, right at the top of the huge Monumental Gate to the Paris *Exposition Universelle* of 1900, the very entrance to a new century. Sailing ahead with the striking aplomb of a battleship on navy day and dressed in fashionable clothes, the plaster allegory of the city of Paris looked like an imperious matron chaperoning a spoilt daughter through the Galeries Lafayette: busty, bustling, arrogant. One could positively hear her barking orders at a timid sales assistant. The critics were not kind: 'ridiculous', 'simply atrocious' and 'a triumph of prostitution' were among the descriptions used by reviewers.

The sculptor Paul Moreau-Vauthier (1871–1936), a rising star of twenty-nine, had conceived of the daring idea of showing Paris as a modern Parisienne – not as a sylphlike girl or a Greek goddess in antique drapery, but contemporary and assured, a mature woman looking forward full of confidence to a new century. He had taken the actress Sarah Bernhardt, 'the Divine Sarah', as a model and commissioned the fashion house of

Monstrously prophetic: La Parisienne *crowning the exhibiton gate,*
designed to admit 60,000 people per hour.

Paquin to design a splendid, up-to-the-minute outfit for his work, which
was to become a miraculous merging of legendary grace and metropolitan
couture.

The result was as calamitous as the official opening itself. The French
president, Emile Loubert, had been forced to conduct the solemn ceremony uniting all the grandest beards and tailcoats in the Republic amid the
mud, puddles and scaffolding of a partial building site, and the first visitors
who came streaming in to see what was the world's most ambitious fair ever
found many of the halls half empty. A contemporary cartoon shows a
bewildered crowd caught amid scaffolding and 'No entry' signs. The
caption reads 'What's on show at the World Fair'.

Over the following weeks all the remaining attractions were installed and
even the last exhibitor had found his place among the multitudes. The ticket
booths at the main gate, underneath the unloved allegory of the great city
itself, had been constructed to process sixty thousand visitors an hour, and
they were working at capacity. By the end of the exhibition period, some
50 million people had visited the 112-hectare grounds in the heart of Paris, an
average of six hundred thousand every single day during weekends.

The exhibition was a grand, outrageous extravaganza, not only a trade
fair and scientific convention, but first and foremost a gigantic fairground
for local visitors and tourists from Europe, the United States and all around

the world. Among them was Jean Sauvage, a schoolteacher from Berlin (German, despite his French name), who lovingly described every detail of his trip to Paris in an essay published in the yearbook of the Seventh Berlin District High School in 1900. Having arrived in the French capital ('a single second class ticket cost me 69 marks and a few pennies') in the early evening, the enterprising educator recounted the typical tourist experience, warning his readers of the vicissitudes of being a tourist in a foreign place: 'it is better to buy a hat over there...A hat purchased in Germany means that one is recognized as a foreigner even more quickly...and becomes the target of constant assaults by tourist guides.'

Suitably disguised as a Frenchman, Sauvage made an extended tour through the city. Sauvage by name but civilized by nature, he was determined to let no detail of daily life escape him.

> The sight of the broad, beautiful streets with their tall trees (many of them plane trees) and lively traffic makes one feel elated. A multitude of shops with their different displays animate shoppers. Many shopkeepers set out their wares on boxes, crates and wooden trestles far into the street to lure customers. Here we can see masses of clothes, there the contents of a soap shop on the pavement, and there foodstuffs; an art dealer offers *objets anciens*; here we find fresh green asparagus which people love here, there oysters and rare snails (*huîtres, escargots*).... The street is littered with innumerable scraps of paper containing advertisements for restaurants and department stores. I take some of these advertisements with me.

Sauvage was amazed by the rhythm and speed of life in the metropolis. Even cycle paths were provided:

> There are many automobiles in the streets. The velocipedists are fewer in number than in our streets; on the Avenue de la Grande Armée and elsewhere they have a beautiful asphalt lane to themselves. I noticed most of all that [the velocipedists] are less of a nuisance than in Berlin; the constant ringing of bells which makes one so nervous is hardly there at all...
>
> Tramways and omnibuses are there in plenty. The difference between Berlin and Paris is not great: there are still a few horse-powered and heavy steam-powered vehicles, but there is a beautiful electric tram towards the Bois de Vincennes.

If traffic was similar at home, the teacher found other customs very different indeed: 'I noticed the many *urinoires*, which are displayed with great lack of modesty. Even *cabinets d'aisance* [public toilets] are plentiful; close to the Palais Royal there is a whole long passage in a house with a great number of them, which are used assiduously. The *urinoires* on the Boulevards are usually situated around advertising columns, which in turn are used for advertisements: you read here: *L'extrait de viande Liebig indispensable dans toute bonne cuisine,* or *Bec Auer,* or *Tendeur pour pantalons.'* Sauvage had to admit that this arrangement had its advantages, but when he saw one of these installations right at the foot of a public monument his sense of propriety was outraged. These French were quite unlike the Germans, after all.

Moving on through the cacophony of advertisements – 'a roadside automation bears the slogan: *Electrisez-vous!'* – and still cunningly disguised in his French hat, Sauvage finally visited the object of his journey, the World Fair itself. He was stunned. 'I feel incapable of describing even a small part of this gigantic work,' he confessed.

Stretching along the Seine from the graceful newly built bridge dedicated to Tsar Alexander III at the beginning of the Champs-Elysées to the Champ de Mars and the area between the Trocadero and the Eiffel Tower (sole survivor of the previous World Fair in 1889), the huge display aimed to titillate, awe and overwhelm. France, it proclaimed, was still the world's foremost nation. The centrepiece was a group of buildings resembling a gigantic wedding cake – all turreted white icing and allegorical drapery, containing the palaces (every building was a palace here) of decoration, furniture, design and other industries.

All major nations had been given space here to create an architectural representation of their culture. Actually, not quite all – the United States had initially been left out of the first, riverside, rank in this prestigious parade of countries (though Monaco had secured a spot), and only after kicking up a diplomatic storm were the others made to give up pieces of their land to make place for the new pretender. This was only fair, it was felt, even if the defiant Ferdinand Peck, Commissioner-General of the United States, was judged to have overstepped the mark, having not only the tactlessness to remind his hosts that American trade figures were greater than those of France and Germany put together, but also the presumption to state: 'the United States have so developed as to entitle them not only to an exalted place among the nations of the earth, but to the foremost rank of all in advanced civilization.' *Eh, non!* thought his French counterparts privately, with supreme self-assurance, but they gave him almost everything he wanted.

The national pavilions bore eloquent witness to a certain image of

Dressed up in old robes: national pavilions at the 1900 World Fair.

Europe and the United States, for with the notable exception of Finland (represented by a flowing art nouveau building), all nations had chosen to represent themselves through pastiches of historic architecture: Gothic for Germany, the nation that simply had to have the highest spire of all; Renaissance for Italy; medieval Moorish for Spain. Britain was represented by a mock Jacobean building by Edwin Lutyens, modelled on the town hall of Bradford-upon-Avon. The United States plumped for Capitol classicism, a building with a dome 156 feet high, crowned by a golden eagle. Identity, these structures suggested, was made up of the distant past, be it in the old countries or in the New World.

If the past held sway on the right bank area, on the left bank it ran wild. Here was one of the exhibition's principal tourist attraction '*vieux Paris*', a fantastical and fantastically kitschy recreation of what Victor Hugo had imagined medieval Paris to have been like, complete with turrets (a hanged man swung from one of them) and wooden-framed houses, a living Quasimodo, dozens of damsels, and knights attacking each other with wooden swords. Street pedlars in historical dress sold refreshments and miniature Eiffel Towers. The theme park, it turns out, is no invention of our time.

Beneath the turrets, putti and rococo scroll work of the official Fair architecture lay a different world: a thrusting, confident modernism. Machines glistened everywhere and new engines and inventions crowded the exhibition halls. The intrepid Berlin teacher Sauvage was determined to see as much as humanly possible. He visited the great exhibition of fruits in the banqueting hall built for 25,000 people; he tried the electric moving walkway with its three different speeds; he was nearly knocked out by the mirages appearing before his eyes in the Hall of Illusions; he visited the metallurgical exhibits, saw the world's largest diamond; he inspected X-ray machines in action and marvelled at African termite mounds, was wide-eyed at the sight of the Palace of Electricity illuminated by 5,000 light bulbs, dazzled by searchlights with the power of 300 million candles, awed by a huge crane built by C. Flohr in Berlin ('another area in which German engineering still has claimed victory!') and humbled by the purring dynamos supplying all these wonders with energy: 'you look at these huge machines with great respect and also with a distinct chill running down your spine ... if this power is unchained, it will smash a tiny human being to individual atoms.'

Sauvage was not the only one to be overwhelmed by the uncanny sight of machines running almost silently and creating an unseen force that could move mountains. The most intense, most lyrical and most exalted admirer of these dynamos was the historian and novelist Henry Adams (1838–1918), in Paris on a study visit from the United States. In his autobiography *The Education of Henry Adams* he recounts his (third-person) confrontation with the machine as a religious revelation:

> To Adams the dynamo became a symbol of infinity. As he grew accustomed to the great gallery of machines, he began to feel the forty-foot dynamos as a moral force, much as the early Christians felt the Cross. The planet itself seemed less impressive, in its old-fashioned, deliberate, annual or daily revolution, than this huge wheel, revolving within arm's-length at some vertiginous speed, and barely murmuring, – scarcely humming an audible warning to stand a hair's-breadth further for respect of power, – while it would not wake the baby lying close against its frame. Before the end, one began to pray to it; inherited instinct taught the natural expression of man before silent and infinite force. Among the thousand symbols of ultimate energy the dynamo was not so human as some, but it was the most expressive.

The colonial exhibition across the river, by the Trocadero Palace, was not dedicated exclusively to French colonies (France had the second-largest colonial empire of the day), but it made sure that the British possessions did not outshine those of the host nation. Here visitors could watch the inhabitants of various remote territories carrying on their lives as if there were not thousands of pairs of eyes trained on them, and a thousand French hearts beating a little more proudly at the thought that these were their subjects, too.

This was a graceful and harmlessly exciting world. You could shop at a Cairo souk, admire Algerian craftsmen and eat in Chinese restaurants, you could visit the Cambodian pagoda and watch happy and contented natives in colourful costumes. The African inhabitants of the pavilion of French Congo were particularly well nourished and beautifully dressed. Women with large jars on their heads walked past curious onlookers amid the lush rainforest vegetation, the men looked proud yet joyful, liable to break out in song and dance any minute. There was not even the remotest indication of what was taking place in their Congolese homelands, of the largest genocide the earth had witnessed, perpetrated under the personal supervision of his Majesty King Leopold of Belgium, one of the celebrated guests of the 1900 Exhibition.

A Nation Vanishes

Most of the grand façades of this 'essence of an age', as the official commemorative twenty-volume publication called it, have long been broken up or melted down, and still the Paris Exhibition remains fascinating for its sheer gaudy wealth, for its innumerable anecdotes and curious details, for what it stated so obviously, and for what it refused to say. Away from the official speeches and reassurances of universal brotherhood and national greatness, the glitter of the exhibition was welcome and the entire display had served as a highly ornamented carpet spread over the unprecedented loss of confidence and the gaping social fissures running through France itself.

The World Fair presented a new, technological world dressed in the comforting ruffles of olden times. On the centenary of the French Revolution the 1889 Paris World Fair had boldly shone into the future, its emblem the unornamented structure of the Eiffel Tower and its legendary beam of light. In 1900 there was little appetite for daring statements. The French wanted to be distracted and entertained, not astonished or even shocked.

To many French men and women the new century was not just

uncertain, but threatening. Within a single generation, the country had lost a war to Germany. It had endured the humiliation of seeing, in 1871, its emperor Napoleon III taken prisoner and forced to abdicate, being made to cede the contested territories of Alsace-Lorraine to Germany. To cap it all, the French had witnessed the rise of a new German empire and the coronation of its emperor, Wilhelm I, in the Hall of Mirrors in Versailles, the epicentre of French royal glory. In the wake of the lost war, the Paris Commune had risen against a weak and reactionary government that had retreated to the provinces to escape the Germans. Worse still, the rebellion was brutally crushed by the French army which, after retaking the city, court-martialled and executed 20,000 of its own citizens within a single week, the *semaine sanglante*. More recently, in 1894, in the Dreyfus case, an innocent Jewish officer had been set up, accused of high treason and condemned to life imprisonment in a patently rigged trial, an affair that had split the nation down the middle and had made bitter enemies of former friends and even family members. The division was still festering like an open wound, as the *dreyfusards* were pressing for a retrial of the honest captain, who was languishing in solitary confinement on Devil's Island, off French Guyana.

The rift between Dreyfus's foes and his supporters (mainly socialist or bourgeois and progressive) was carried into the private sphere: once good friends, the Impressionist painters Degas and Pissarro would never speak again because of the affair, and Degas, an impassioned opponent of Dreyfus, even sacked a model because of her sympathies for the Jewish captain. The very air of the capital seemed to be partitioned. As feelings came to boiling point, Emile Zola's 1898 article '*J'accuse!*' in *L'Aurore* summed up the argument for the defence: 'I have but one passion, that of enlightenment, in the name of humanity, which has suffered so much and has a right to happiness. My impassioned protest is nothing but the cry of my soul. May they dare to put me on trial [for slander] so that the entire affair will come to light!' He was not put on trial, but after several days of street disturbances and threats he had to seek refuge in England until things cooled off. Four years after his return, Zola was asphyxiated in his house during the night due to a blocked chimney. The death was recorded as an accident. A roofer admitted several years later that he had worked on the house next door and had put a piece of wood over Zola's chimney to kill the writer as revenge for his defence of the Jewish captain.

Dreyfus and the Spectre of Decline

Dreyfus had become a symbol for France's malaise. Only a generation earlier, France had been the undisputed centre of the cultural universe, dictating the world's fashions and the taste in music and literature of 'civilized' people everywhere, and in 1870 the French historian Joseph de Maistre could still write with cast-iron and lavishly gilded confidence that artists across the world 'were condemned to a local reputation until Paris consented to make them famous... Perhaps nothing is properly understood in Europe until the French have explained it.'

Thirty years later this was no longer true. London had become the world's financial centre; Germany's scientists and engineers led the world. France itself had become a nation haunted by the spectre of defeat, of territorial loss, of its decline and decadence under the threat of physical extinction. In contrast to other European populations, the French head-count was stagnant. In 1891, for the first time, more French people had died than were born. If the country's population had not declined between 1850 and 1900 (it had even risen from 36 to 39 million), that was due to immigration, mainly from Belgium, Italy and Poland. During the same period, the populations of Germany and Britain had risen by 20 per cent despite considerable emigration, while the Habsburg subjects had almost doubled and the number of Russians almost trebled. France's mothers were no longer bearing enough children and, more terrifyingly still, the men of the nation no longer seemed able to beget them as they used to. France, many authors said, had become sterile; its culture and way of life would simply vanish within a hundred years. 'Next to this vital question all others disappear,' wrote the historian Jacques Bertillon in 1911, '... the death of France will be one of the crucial facts of the nineteenth and twentieth centuries.' France was being left behind, while the 'hereditary enemy' to the east, the new German empire, was forging ahead not only in population terms, but also in the sciences (German researchers received more Nobel Prizes in physics and chemistry than any other country), in armaments and in industrial development France, it seemed, was not only defeated, it was slowly dying off and fading into a shadow of its former grandeur.

Undermined by fear and shaken by an atmosphere of anxious pessimism, the French wanted a jolly, unthreatening World Exhibition, and most of all they had wanted a success. Boldness of vision was not what was required by the organizers: retrospective splendour and entertainment ruled. Everybody should be impressed by the status quo, everybody would enjoy themselves – even if the papier mâché turrets of *Vieux France* looked more like a gaudy parody of national greatness than actual proof.

Not everybody was fooled by the glorious façade: 'It remains to be seen,' wrote the French essayist Eugène-Melchior de Vogüé after the exhibition gates had closed for the last time, 'what this Exhibition has given us that is new … In 1889, steel [the Eiffel Tower] offered itself up bravely to our eyes, alone and bare; it made us appreciate its virtues as an architectural element. Since then, one has the impression that it has felt the shame of man after committing Original Sin, and has felt the need to cover itself up. Today, steel wraps itself in plaster.'

The original sin was the ever-divisive Dreyfus affair. The Jewish officer was simply the ideal bogeyman for a nation that appeared to have lost its way. Ever since Edouard Drumont (1844–1917) had published his best-selling *La France juive* in 1886 (it had reached 200 editions by 1914), anti-semitism had been commonplace among the nationalist right and became a rallying cry that united both Catholics and Republican atheists under one banner. Dreyfus was ideally suited for fables about conspiracies, foreigners and international capital. As a Jew, he was identified with international capital and the end of France's traditionally rural way of life; as a native of Alsace, historically disputed between Germany and France, he was suspect-ed of divided loyalties, of being a traitor selling his country to the proliferat-ing Germans and their innumerable children in navy uniforms. As an officer he also represented manly virtues and an army keen to cleanse itself of the whiff of defeat as history itself was threatening to overwhelm the French. If the nation's men were no longer man enough to father children in sufficient numbers, perhaps the rot had reached the very core of France's historical greatness and virility, the military caste – in his *Interpretation of Dreams*, published in 1899, Freud, who had done medical research in Paris, had taken the nexus between officers and exaggerated masculinity for granted. The captain simply had the grotesque bad luck of being everything his country feared and wanted to hate. 'For me, the Frenchmen of today – a recent crisis has made that all too clear – may live side by side, do the same jobs, partake of the same disappointments, the same pleasures, but they no longer do it with the same soul,' a character in the novel *L'Etape* by the anti-Dreyfus writer Paul Bourget recounts.

The mantra of the nationalists was *la terre et les morts*, the soil and the dead, the French equivalent to the German *Blut und Boden*. It had been formu-lated by Maurice Barrès (1862–1923), a bona fide *immortel* because of his membership in that most exclusive of old men's clubs, the *Académie française*. Barrès had started his writing career as a typical *fin-de-siècle* hedo-nist, whose programmatic novel *Le culte de moi* propagated total, solipsistic selfishness and gained him a considerable literary reputation. Later on, the professional egoist got bored with his own company and involved himself in the politics of national community.

Some of Europe's most dangerous demagogues on the political right have regarded their political role as essentially aesthetic, in the service of a higher beauty and purity, and Barrès was no exception. Like so many converts, he detested nothing more than his own past, and in particular the decadence that he had once preached. Catholic France, he believed, had been corrupted by a conspiracy of Protestants, Jews and Freemasons, destroyers of the 'organic solidarity' that should reign between members of one nation united by 'our dead and the produce of our soil'. 'Every act that distorts our soil and our dead drives us deeper into the lie that sterilizes us.' The spectre of infertility rose up again, this time in the shape of a rustic Catholic castrated by Ahasver, the Wandering Jew. 'Everything comes from the Jew, and everything comes back to the Jew,' wrote Edouard Drumont in his bestselling *La France juive*.

While antisemitism was an obvious motivation in the Dreyfus case, the population debate also played a major role. Critics such as the sociologist René Gonnard were quick to pounce on the supposed reasons for the national decline: life in the city, lack of faith, general pessimism, a decadent over-refinement among the middle classes, and other hallmarks of modern life visible especially in the big 'man-eating' cities. France, the most cultivated of nations, was particularly badly hit by this: 'it happens to be the case that our French civilization with its laws and customs exaggerates this effect, forcing one to fear a depopulation in the literal sense of the term,' Gonnard warned. France was becoming impotent, unmanly, and weak despite all measures taken to the contrary, notably a ban on abortion (which would become a capital crime during the Vichy regime) and even on advertising contraceptives – the 'Gentlemen's rubber goods' appearing in the papers of the day in other countries.

Even Dreyfus's champion Emile Zola was moved to write a novel entitled *Fécondité* (1899), in which he contrasted the fate of two couples: egotistical, rich city-dwellers who invest everything in their only son (who dies, of course), while the heroic husband and wife at the heart of the story choose the simple life and a wealth of children, resulting in love and fulfilment. Zola had been brooding on the novel for some years. As early as 1896 he had written in *Le Figaro*: 'My novel...will be an immense fresco showing how a city like Paris kills germs, devours living beings, consumes abortions to become what it is, the very place of the life of tomorrow.'

The image of the city-ogre – eyes glaring with electric light, a body of stone and steel, annihilating parasites and life alike and swallowing its inhabitants with insatiable hunger – goes right back to the crazed god Saturn making a feast of his own children: the creator who destroys, the metropolis as an evil place, sucking the blood of those drawn to it – the vampire capitalism in full flight.

This political attitude had a strong influence on the arts and their presentation at the 1900 World Fair. The Grand Palais and Petit Palais, two truly palatial exhibition halls (two vestiges of the exhibition that can still be seen in Paris) were built in order to demonstrate *la gloire de la France* by hosting displays of works of art. Most of the works shown here during the exhibition obeyed the official aesthetics of turn-of-the-century French art: heavily academic fare – heroic nudity, sentimental grandeur and chaste beauty in plaster and marble, bronze and oil. A flanking display contained a retrospective of French artists of the past. Only one smaller collection struck a different note, so different that when President Loubert attempted to enter it, a conservative art critic barred his way, crying: 'Don't enter, *monsieur le Président*, the shame of France is in there!' It was an exhibit of 'radicals', curated by the art collector Roger Marx. The shameful secret was the work of Gauguin, Seurat, Cézanne, Pissarro, Picasso, Manet and Monet, degenerate art *avant la lettre*.

Much of French art was animated by a sense of stock-taking and remembrance. Most famously, this introspective private reconstruction of a past world is embodied in *A la recherche du temps perdu* by Marcel Proust, a writer at the centre of the elegant Paris scene. Far removed from the brutality of working-class life and the anxious selfishness of the *petite bourgeoisie*, Proust and his circle led a life of enchanted, languid luxury amid a succession of elegant salons, balls, and outings to the nearby Bois de Boulogne, a universe of true sophistication (in the minds of its denizens at least), spanning only a few square kilometres between the Bois, the Place de la Concorde, the great and ostentatious Opéra and the Parc Monceau on the capital's right bank.

Another artistic project, hugely ambitious in scale, chimed with the mood of the 1900 Paris *Exposition Universelle* and its retrospective presentation. Eugène Atget (1857–1927), a photographer with a patient and lyrical eye, devoted his entire working life to the city he loved and its magic, which, he was convinced, would vanish soon, submerged by the building sites of a loud new world. Having spent three decades roaming the streets of the city with a huge camera and tripod, Atget created a magical, silent world of deserted streets, mute buildings and empty interiors, a huge, minutely detailed inventory like that of some nameless official dutifully listing every chair and every last silver spoon left behind by a dying duchess. Atget's Paris is infinitely evocative, but almost always dead, devoid of human presence, or rather of a human present, for the presence of innumerable past inhabitants can still be read in the worn steps and faded walls and in the very air around them.

This nostalgia was not innocent; it was poisoned by the knowledge that an era had passed by, while a new one had not yet shown its face. Change was everywhere, but the speed of evolution obscured the immutable values and principles many sought. Novelists chronicling the lives of gilded youth could not help but notice that they had lost their parents' robust drive and principles and that the heroic period of construction was drawing to a close. This idea of decline in literature was not limited to Paris, or to France. Novels published throughout Europe between 1900 and the beginning of the War analysed the demise of a world full of energy (manliness, again) and confidence. For almost two decades European and American bookshops were piled with elegiac or satirical stories of ruined families: the sophisticated play with lost youth in Hugo von Hofmannsthal's librettos, and the ironic analysis in Robert Musil's *Man Without Qualities* (published later but started during and dealing with the period), while Rainer Maria Rilke's nightmarish *The Notebooks of Malte Laurids Brigge* (1910) and Karel-Matej Capek-Chod's *The Turbine* (published 1916) from the Czech crown lands of the moribund Habsburg empire mark out central Europe as the richest vein of doom.

In the German Reich, Thomas Mann's implacably detached *Buddenbrooks* (1901) and *The Magic Mountain* (begun 1913, published 1924) traced the undoing of the *grande bourgeoisie* while, in a pleasing inversion, his brother Heinrich chronicled the irrepressible rise of Germany in the shape of a nasty nationalist *petit bourgeois* in *The Loyal Subject* (1919). The novel *The Flax Field* (1907) by the Belgian Flemish writer Stijn Streuvels situates the conflict in a rural context, in which a young man no longer wants to lead the life of his ancestors. Even if the young farmer comes to his senses at his father's deathbed, it is clear that this is only a temporary reprieve. In an existentialist version of the theme, the exasperated protagonist of the Spaniard Miguel de Unamuno's novel *Mist* (1914) turns on his author to demand an answer to the riddle of his existence. When he finds that the author is planning to kill him, he commits suicide as a last and futile assertion of independence. In Trieste, still part of Austria-Hungary but Italian-speaking, the young Italo Svevo's *Senilità* (1898) showed its young protagonist stricken with premature senility while falling hopelessly in love – a nightmarish image of infertility and lost self-confidence.

It is not difficult to see a social, societal parallel in these accounts of once-great families stumbling to their graves, of old nobility corrupted and men paralysed by thought or infirmity while a new generation of nasty social climbers is taking their place. Chekhov's plays are pervaded by this imagery. In Maksim Gorky's 1902 play *The Philistines* the ageing tradesman Vassily looks at his son's revolutionary sympathies with contempt, and into the future with naked fear: 'What's in store? I look around and everything is breaking up. Everything's in pieces. These times we live in? What if something really happened? Who would look after us? Your mother and I are getting older and it seems everything could ... destroy us ... People want to destroy our family. Beware of them, they want to destroy us all. And I feel it, all so close. This terrible ... terrible disaster.' Death was in the air. Emile Durkheim, one of the first modern social scientists, chose for one of his major studies (published in 1897) a subject he thought symptomatic of society: suicide.

This was a nervous generation which had lost the sure footing and sturdy gait of the pioneer. The decadent aestheticism of the *fin de siècle*, of a Wilde or Huysmans or of the young Barrès, had been based on the boredom of the sons of wealth and security who amuse themselves by rebelling against the ethos of puritan morality and public service: a wicked, world-weary elegance. The new wave of writing was different. Growing out of the speed of change and the misgivings about progress and liberal ideals, it was existential and marked by fear and decline, not decadence. It saw no way out and offered none. Whereas the nerves of the artists around 1890 had been attuned to the vibrating wings of a butterfly and wanted to rise into the air themselves, those of their successors were laid bare by the incessant rattle of factories and trains. As we will see later, neurosis became a leading idea not only in fiction ('I am a neurasthenic. That's my profession and my fate,' declares a character in a novella by Heinrich Mann) but also in medicine. The young Sigmund Freud had travelled to Etienne Charcot's Paris practice to study this phenomenon and the new scientific attention lavished upon it, and sanatoriums across Europe made a tidy living out of treating nervous disorders and mental breakdowns not only of 'hysterical' women, but increasingly of men who felt overwhelmed and undermined.

The Dynamo and the Virgin

If fear of the future was particularly strong in France and expressed itself both in the hysteria surrounding the Dreyfus trial and in the aesthetic conception of the 1900 World Fair, not everyone was afraid of the impending change. Those curious enough to think about the cultural transformation enacted by technology found their imaginations taking flight in front of the huge dynamos in the halls of machines. 'The modest debutante of 1889 has grown big and strong,' wrote Melchior de Vogüé about this strange machine.

> She has her own palace, her furniture. The little dynamo has increased in size and strength. It was a metre large, now it measures ten; it produced the power of 500 horses, now it provides 5,000 … If it can move our Métropolitain which sometimes even works [a swipe against the first Métro line, still having teething troubles] it has not yet taken possession of a locomotive on our great lines, or of an ocean liner.

The Berlin teacher Jean Sauvage had felt a chill run down his spine as he contemplated the machines. No one, though, was as prophetically perceptive as the American Henry Adams, who recognized them as the very essence of the age to come in his autobiography: 'he [Adams] found himself lying in the Gallery of Machines at the Great Exposition of 1900,

The power of a new age: the hall of dynamos at the 1900 World Fair.

his historical neck broken by the sudden irruption of forces totally new.' So far, Adams believed, the West had been inspired by the force of feminine creativity symbolized once by the power of sex, by the terrifying attraction of Venus, and neutralized by Christianity in the person of the Virgin Mary. This transition from a heathen, sexual force to Christian and finally modern womanhood had, the historian wrote, robbed culture of its vitality, especially in his own country.

> The Woman had once been supreme; in France she still seemed potent, not merely as a sentiment, but as a force. Why was she unknown in America? For evidently America was ashamed of her, and she was ashamed of herself, otherwise they would not have strewn fig-leaves so profusely all over her. When she was a true force, she was ignorant of fig-leaves, but the monthly-magazine-made American female had not a feature that would have been recognised by Adam. The trait was notorious, and often humorous, but any one brought up among Puritans knew that sex was sin. In any previous age, sex was strength. Neither art nor beauty was needed…Adams began to ponder, asking himself whether he knew of any American artist who had ever insisted on the power of sex, as every classic had always done…American art, like the American language and American education, was as far as possible sexless.

There is an echo in this critical evaluation of the French debate about sterility and the decline of population. Both Adams and his Continental counterparts felt that a cultural, creative force had been lost and trivialized, even if Adams localized the problem not in his own time but in the very beginnings of Christianity. The world of advertising and mass production might have brought forth the sexless monthly-magazine-made American female, but her antecedent was the virginal mother of God, not the procreative force of Venus. It seems significant that for many European writers the problem lay not with womanhood, but with impotence. France was no longer manly, it was effeminate and dissipated.

To Adams (and to many others, as we shall see) the answer to this perceived exhaustion of Western culture lay in the vast, brute force of technology. 'The nearest approach to the revolution of 1900 was that of 310, when Constantine set up the Cross,' he summarized, and he was quite serious. Another visitor to the exhibition who felt the same kind of awe and whose reaction is characterized by a similar mixture of impatience with the old and a religious perspective on the new was the French avant-garde poet Guillaume Apollinaire (1880–1918):

In the end you are weary of this ancient world
Shepherd o Eiffel Tower, the flock of bridges is bleating
You have enough of living in Greek and Roman antiquity

Here, even automobiles look ancient
Only religion has remained entirely new only religion
Has remained simple like the hangars of airports

The only faith possible was an amalgam of the ancient and the avant garde. The present was irredeemably vulgar, be it for Adams and his women stripped of sex by their puritan world and debased by mass-produced magazines, or for Apollinaire, who saw people burying themselves in the 'prospectus the catalogues the posters singing at the top of their voices'.

When the Universal Exhibition closed in November with a dinner given for twenty thousand French mayors from all over the country down to the smallest villages (service during this culinary extravaganza was assured by waiters zooming along the tables in motorcars), it was judged to have been a success, an ample demonstration of France's continuing might and importance, of international harmony and modern technology. What was more, it had almost recouped the huge investments made, and even though twenty times the city's population had visited, no major incident had marred the event.

La Parisienne, the fashionably dressed emblem of Paris enthroned on top of the monumental entrance to the 1900 Fair, had received a terrible press and had been seen as an embarrassment. In November she was taken down and unceremoniously packed off to the wreckers, like most of the elaborate structures and ornaments conceived and created for the Fair. Judging from contemporary illustrations, the artistic merits of the sculpture were no more questionable than those of most works of art shown during the exhibition. Perhaps the real reason for the uproar caused by *la Parisienne* was

Suddenly everything was illuminated: lightning strikes the Eiffel Tower.

precisely that she was not allegorical enough. The preoccupation with birth rates and infertility, the overtones of castration and strangulation in the antisemitic clichés of the day, and more generally the obsession with moral corruption and decline, are indicative of anxieties about another, unstoppable, development that would revolutionize society: the changing role of women. Like Dreyfus, the huge, self-assured and contemporary woman greeting all visitors embodied deep public fears. She was too real, too disquietingly powerful. Hers was too much the shape of things to come.

2

1901:
The Changing of the Guard

I lived in a closed world trying to ignore the new times and to preserve to the bitter end the old habits and illusions.

– Comtesse Jean de Pange, *Comment j'ai vu 1900*

Our ancestors kept the political power of the state in the hands of those who had property... but their successors had destroyed that system, and placed political power in the hands of the multitude, and we must take the consequences.

– The Duke of Northumberland, 1908

When the moment came, it was the grandson who insisted on closing the old woman's eyes, a last gesture of respect and admiration, accorded to him by his two uncles, her sons. He reached across with his healthy right arm to fulfil this last obligation. His left arm, withered since childhood, hung by his side. He was Emperor Wilhelm II of Germany. His grandmother, who had died on 22 January 1901, was Queen Victoria.

For many years, the empire had been ruled not from London but from Osborne House, the island estate built in European style, far away from it all on the Isle of Wight, a refuge which had allowed the ageing sovereign to live among mementoes of her late husband, to escape her subjects' incessant demands for official appearances, and her son's pop-eyed vulgarity. The Queen had become a remote presence, an invocation ('Gentlemen, the Queen!'), an unseen certainty taken for granted by everyone from Glasgow to Melbourne. Her reign had lasted sixty-four years; she was the only ruler hundreds of millions of people across the globe had ever known.

In our own day, in which every value is contested and contestable, it is difficult to understand the unshakable faith the Victorians had in themselves: their sense of purpose, of mission, of God-given entitlement. It was not the meek, but the British who had inherited the earth. Britain was the richest nation and the most powerful, producing (in 1850) half of the world's industrial goods; the British had brought the gospels and the rules of cricket to natives in the remotest rainforests and deserts, and they had managed to concentrate their phenomenal power in the drawing-rooms of a few gentlemen's clubs on Pall Mall in London, the discreet epicentre of the world's largest capital. While the governors of Europe's other great powers appeared regularly in grand, tasselled uniforms, Britain was essentially a civilian culture; while elsewhere the seat of government was an elaborate, neo-something palace, Her Majesty's prime minister resided, in quiet confidence, in a plain-fronted terraced brick house in Downing Street.

Naturally, the social conventions of the time locked 'the right' people into civilian uniforms and hierarchies that were every bit as strict as those of any regiment, with no need for sabres or helmets to signal their intent. Even the vulgarian Prince of Wales, later King Edward VII, proved unyielding in this respect: 'I thought everyone must know that a short jacket is always worn with a silk hat at a private view in the morning,' he complained when his assistant private secretary Frederick Ponsonby had negligently appeared at a Royal Academy exhibition in the wrong attire. The preoccupation with propriety extended to the remotest points of the empire and to the most unlikely occasions. Survival kits of the 1860s, packed in wooden barrels and deposited on tropical islands for use by the shipwrecked on their way to New Zealand, contained, as well as the predictably useful knife, matches, rope, and fish-hooks, a three-piece tweed suit – presumably to allow any latter-day Robinson Crusoe to welcome his rescuers with appropriate decorum.

'I believe that the British race is the greatest of the governing races that the world has ever seen,' remarked the empire's colonial secretary, Joseph Chamberlain. 'It is not enough to occupy great spaces of the world's surface unless you can make the best of them. It is the duty of a landlord to develop his estate.' And develop they did: by trade and warfare, by training armies and missionaries, by building railways and prefabricated corrugated-iron chapels for dispatch to far-flung colonies.

It had been a time of constant exploits on the most colossal scale, whose very failures seemed heroic to those in the home country. In 1854, during the Crimean War, 673 British cavalrymen with sabres drawn staged a staggeringly and knowingly futile attack on entrenched Russian artillery positions. One hundred and eighteen men were killed and 127 wounded, and the attack became a gallant myth of valour and self-sacrifice, the proverbial Charge of the Light Brigade, set in verse by the Queen's Poet Laureate,

Alfred Lord Tennyson: 'Theirs not to make reply, / Theirs not to reason why, / Theirs but to do and die: / Into the valley of Death / Rode the six hundred.' When in 1885 political dithering in London left General Charles George Gordon without reinforcements at Khartoum in the Sudan, with his troops overwhelmed by Dervish attackers, Gordon calmly dressed in his best white uniform and faced his enemies alone. They riddled him with spears. He became a martyr of empire, praised in distinctively religious language by the bishop of Thetford: 'Oh, brethren, we have known others like him, with that beautiful combination of courage and tenderness, the reflection of Him, who was and is the Lion of the tribe of Judah, and the Lamb of God.'

This was an empire built for eternity, for the eye of God: London's very sewers had been constructed with huge vaulting ceilings worthy of cathedrals and no nation could rival Britain's possessions, her navy, or her glory, which was celebrated on an appropriately grand scale, never more so than on the occasion of the Queen's diamond jubilee in 1897. It was a gigantic demonstration of imperial splendour, with 64,000 soldiers marching through the capital, including, in Barbara Tuchman's almost poetic enumeration:

> ...the Cape Mounted Rifles, the Canadian Hussars, the New South Wales Lancers, the Trinidad Light Horse, the magnificent turbaned and bearded Lancers of Khapurthala, the Badnagar and other Indian states, the Zaptichs of Cyprus in tasseled fezzes on black-maned ponies. Dark-skinned infantry regiments, 'terrible and beautiful to behold,' in the words of a rhapsodic press, wound down the streets in a fantasy of variegated uniforms: the Borneo Dyak Police, the Jamaica Artillery, the Royal Nigerian Constabulary, the giant Sikhs from India, Houssas from the Gold Coast, Chinese from Hong Kong, Malays from Singapore, Negroes from the West Indies, British Guiana and Sierra Leone, company after company passed before a dazzled people, awestruck at the testimony of their own might.

The aged Queen had been delighted. A press photographer even caught a rare image of her smiling broadly into the crowd, and the whole country lived a moment of imperial splendour as the world's undisputed superpower, God's chosen people. But in reality, the jubilee celebrations were almost as much of a valediction as the Queen's funeral would be. Not many foresaw this only four years earlier. Tuchman quotes one of the most admired but also one of the strangest homages paid to the sovereign at her jubilee, the poem 'Recessional' by Rudyard Kipling, a work of great dignity and force. If Kipling was the bard of Empire, on this occasion he produced a warning, even an obituary: 'Far-called, our navies melt away; / On dune and headland sinks the fire: / Lo, all our pomp of yesterday / Is one with Nineveh and Tyre!'

Voices such as this had been few and far between during Victoria's day, though the extraordinary public response to Kipling's poem, which was printed in *The Times*, shows that his artistic sensitivity had captured one aspect of the nation's mood. The 'Sea of Faith' which Matthew Arnold had already seen retreating thirty years earlier with a 'melancholy, long, withdrawing roar' was silently but inexorably ebbing away 'to the breath / Of the night-wind, down the vast edges drear / And naked shingles of the world'.

When life finally ebbed away from the old Queen in 1901, the empire prepared for a farewell fit not for a person but for an age: a sumptuous celebration of sorrowful glory. The ceremonies were to be so elaborate, and the list of invited royalty so long, that almost two weeks went by between her death and her funeral.

The Queen's body had been transferred from the Isle of Wight to Portsmouth on the royal yacht *Alberta*. Royal Navy battleships and cruisers, as well as vessels sent from Germany, France, Portugal, and even Japan, had provided a last escort, with the Spanish regretfully unable to fulfil this decorous duty: their ship had failed to arrive in time, and a smaller craft owned by the Prince of Monaco had been obliged to sail in as a substitute. The transfer between Portsmouth harbour and London was itself testimony to the changing age: the royal remains were conveyed by train, with tens of thousands of mourners lining the rails all the way.

When the funeral cortège finally arrived in the capital on 2 February, the Queen's body was carried (at Her Majesty's expressed wish) on a gun carriage. Like a Victorian drawing room, the coffin itself was crammed with personal mementoes and photos (including, of course, the portrait of Albert, and one of John Brown, the Queen's Scottish manservant, laid on her wrist, as she had ordained). Twenty thousand soldiers accompanied Her Majesty on her last journey, with another thirty thousand forming a guard of honour along the streets. Following the coffin were the German Kaiser, who had closed the old Queen's eyes, the kings of Portugal and Greece, five crown princes, fourteen princes, two grand dukes, one archduke, five dukes, and innumerable other, lesser, dignitaries. Writing home from his London club, the American novelist Henry James recorded: 'I mourn the safe and motherly old middle-class Queen, who held the nation warm under the fold of her big, hideous, Scotch-plaid shawl and whose duration had been so extraordinarily convenient and beneficent. I fear her death much more than I should have expected; she was a sustaining symbol – and the wild waters are upon us now.'

Arnold's receding 'Sea of Faith' and Henry James's 'wild waters' were just two of the marine metaphors used to describe a blind, dark, pulling power seemingly dragging the world to an uncertain end, or crashing over it like the rejoined waves over the biblical Egyptians. The disappearance of the supreme symbol of Britain's greatest century left the onlookers reeling, the ground shifting under their feet. 'For they have lost their rhythm, / the pulse of the sea / in their salt blood,' wrote the poet Jon Stallworthy of their uncertain successors.

With unregal rashness, the new King, Edward VII, Bertie to his friends and 'Edward the Caresser' to a contemptuous Henry James, lost no time distancing himself from his mother's fusty heritage. At Windsor Castle, 'Bertie' went on a rampage. Plaster busts and statues of Victoria's Highland servant and confidant John Brown were smashed, papers burned, mementoes of the late Prince Albert packed off into storage, and hundreds of 'rubbishy old photographs' destroyed. Smoking his cigars where smoking had never been allowed and wheezing gleefully at the symbolic carnage around him, Edward felt he had rid himself of a huge and tiresome burden. With a last sweep of the new broom, he converted Osborne House, his mother's cherished retreat and the place of her death, into a Royal Navy college for cadets, and a home for retired officers.

Where Queen Victoria had been contained and discreet, Edward was crass and demonstrative; where the mother had viewed the essence of a monarch's life as an uneventful stability, the son believed in fun. His career so far had been one long round of country house parties and shooting weekends, affairs with pretty actresses and married women, race meetings and European holidays. Apart from her two servant-cum-advisers, the Scottish Mr Brown and the Indian Munshi, the late Queen had mixed only with members of the high aristocracy, settled and solid people, like Her famously solid Majesty. Not so Edward, who preferred the company of the nouveaux riches, so much brighter, so much more sophisticated, so much more entertaining, and richer too, or at least so much readier to part with their fortunes in order to keep him amused. The King was 'always surrounded by a bevy of Jews and a ring of racing people', Lady Paget noted disdainfully, adding that he had 'the same luxurious taste as the Semites, and the same love of pleasure and comfort'. The old aristocracy and its ways were being squeezed out of the King's company.

To all but his most fabulously wealthy hosts, in fact, Edward was

A jolly monarch: King Edward VII.

nothing less than a liability. To avoid incurring his displeasure, the owners of the country's great houses had to keep a constant stock of gingerbread, French patisseries, bath salts and exotic aubergines in case the King should decide to descend upon them, in which case a vast expenditure must follow. His personal entourage included more than a dozen people – including an Arab boy to prepare his coffee. Dinner for His Majesty was generally no fewer than twelve courses, including such light entrées as *Cotelettes de bécassines à la Souvaroff* (snipe stuffed with foie gras and served in Madeira sauce). The hefty King, just five feet seven inches tall, weighed over 16 stone (102 kg).

If the dinners were ruinously opulent, the shooting parties were even more expensive. It was out of the question, of course, simply to let the hunters go out in search of prey. This was Edwardian England, after all; prey was to be provided, and in prodigious numbers. On one Norfolk estate just thirty-nine birds had been killed in 1821, yet by Edward's day the number had risen to 5,363. Such vast numbers had to be bred, and released into the wild for the occasion. Lord de Grey, a famously fast shooter who had allegedly once had seven dead birds in the air simultaneously, boasted that in his fifty-six-year career he had personally shot 250,000 pheasant, 150,000 grouse and 100,000 partridge – a proud average of more than twenty-five birds a day. Animals, too, were reared for the hunt, and shot by the hundred, if not the thousand, during a single weekend by gun-toting aristocrats and their rich middle-class imitators. Not many hosts could afford this kind of lavishness for long, even for their King.

Steam Turbines and the Defeat of the Nobility

If 'Edward the Caresser' was a famous philanderer and alarmingly greedy house guest, his louche vulgarity was nonetheless symptomatic of a long decline which had begun even during his mother's reign: the decline of the apparently still splendid European aristocracy, the hierarchical and social backbone of every monarchy across the Continent. Despite the English King's behaviour, this had nothing to do with royal manners or mismanagement on the part of the governing classes. Rather, it reflected the underlying economic circumstances of the time. Since time immemorial, the power of Europe's aristocracies had been based on their land, which allowed them to raise armies and construct great palaces, or simply to bankroll a leisured life in the country or at court. The wealth of the land, and the idea of a social structure ordained by God, were the two great keystones of aristocratic rule. But within the previous three decades, both had been fatally undermined.

Until the 1870s, noblemen had managed to preserve real power everywhere in Europe, with the exception of France (where the Revolution had swept them away already) and the small nations of republican Switzerland and the Netherlands. The latter, though nominally a kingdom, had never had a strong aristocracy, at least in part, and significantly, because it simply was not large enough in area to sustain a substantial landed class. Together with the high aristocracy of Austria-Hungary and Tsarist Russia, it had been the British nobles who had preserved the greatest land-based wealth, and unlike their Habsburg and Russian counterparts, the great families of Britain had succeeded in keeping power concentrated in very few hands. This had been mainly owing to the British law of primogeniture, which allowed all titles and possessions to pass to the family's eldest son, while daughters and younger sons received only non-hereditary courtesy titles, and importantly, no land. Whereas in Austria-Hungary or Germany, for instance, all the children of a duke would themselves be dukes and duchesses, and family lands would generally be divided between them, later to be recombined by strategic marriages, in an ever changing patchwork of ownership, in Britain the nobility had remained a small and wealthy group. *Burke's Peerage* of 1880 recorded some 580 British peers, three quarters of whom owned 1,000 hectares of land or more. In stark contrast to this, Prussia alone could count some 20,000 titled families in 1800, while by 1914 Russia had more than 250,000. In Hungary and Poland, between 10 and 15 per cent of the population belonged to the nobility.

The aristocrats of Britain had defended their pre-eminence for centuries.

The apparently swift ending of their rule, and of that of many of Europe's hereditary patricians, came not from the cannon's mouth, during the Great War, but earlier and quite peacefully from across the seas. Those with ears to hear the bell tolling distantly might have recognized the humming of new ships' turbines, making it possible to cross the Atlantic, and indeed the whole globe, faster and more cheaply. They might have heard the sounds of steady advances in agricultural technology in the American Midwest, or the grunts of the longshoremen heaving American or Russian grain onto the fast new ships.

With the invention of refrigerated ships (the first, the SS *Elderslie*, was constructed in 1884), meat and dairy products from New Zealand, Australia and Argentina opened this British market to international competition. With less than a third of its workforce in agriculture, Britain was the only European country to elect not to protect its farmers and landowners by import tariffs; in consequence, the new cheap goods hit the country's land economy with its full force. By 1905, Britain was importing 60 per cent of its basic foodstuffs and 80 per cent of its grain. The global market had become a reality: not just its benefits, which had long been clear to the British, the world's pre-eminent producers and salesmen for a century or more, but now its disadvantages. For the British landed classes, this development was devastating. A domestic market that had for so long been certain, protected by geographical barriers and unchallenged by other producers, had melted away within little more than a decade, and its profits too. Land as the power base of the aristocracy had been all but destroyed. By 1900, some 14,000 estates had been mortgaged, with only 2,800 of their owners managing to keep up their repayments. Between 1903 and 1909 alone, Britain's aristocrats sold 9 million acres of land.

There were those resourceful enough to survive, of course. They sold half their estates, reduced their debt and invested in shares, thus fuelling the engine of their downfall. A vast proportion of British investments went into lucrative new enterprises abroad, particularly in the United States, South America and Russia, thereby unwittingly helping the competition to build up an efficient and modern agricultural and industrial base while factories in Britain still operated with the mid-Victorian machinery that had once made the country great, but was obsolete now and unable to keep up with the rising pace of technological development on the international market.

If life after the slump of income from the land could be perilous for the landowning families, death often meant ruin. Death duties, introduced by the Liberal government in 1894, were initially calculated at 8 per cent of inherited wealth, but by 1909 they had risen to 15 per cent. (By 1919 they would escalate to 40 per cent.) For an already indebted family hanging on precariously with a declining income, a death in the family could be simply the last straw: 'Between the duties expected of one during one's lifetime and the duties exacted from one after one's death, land has ceased to be either a profit or a pleasure. It gives one a position, and prevents one from keeping it up,' as Lady Bracknell summarizes with inimitable aplomb in Oscar Wilde's 1895 play *The Importance of Being Earnest*.

While the sale of assets enabled economic survival for some, it was also a blow for the aristocracy's identity and self-confidence. 'A man does not like to go down to posterity as the alienator of old family possessions,' Lord Aylesbury ruefully remarked in 1911. Some peers unwilling to go this way married themselves out of trouble by hitching their old names to new, often American wealth. The later British prime minister Lord Rosebery became Mr Hanna de Rothschild; the Duke of Marlborough espoused Consuelo Vanderbilt; Lord Randolph Churchill famously married Jenny Jerome, the daughter of a New York financier, who shocked London society not only by her sassy independence, but also by sporting an elegant tattoo of a snake around her wrist. The allure of wealth made inroads on the Continent, too. In 1895 the fashionable French Count Boni de Castellane married the American Anna Gould, who brought with her not only beauty but also a useful £3,000,000 dowry, which the Count spent on a lifestyle so fabulously lavish – including the construction of a pink marble palace in the centre of Paris – that his wife found it necessary to divorce him after just three years, to rescue what was left of her fortune. (The Count eventually died in penury, leaving behind him a literary grace note, his book *The Art of Living Poor*.) One of the Vanderbilt girls accepted the Hungarian Count Széchenyi.

Novelists were quick to see the dramatic and comic potential of these matches. Thomas Mann's *Royal Highness* (1909) mocks the union of a German prince and an American heiress in an affectionate if somewhat presumptuous portrait of his own marriage to a wealthy Jewish woman, casting the writer as prince of literature. The British-Jewish novelist Israel Zangwill used the same theme in his 1893 novella *Merely Mary Anne*.

Rates of Dissolution

On the Continent, the aristocratic classes of different countries unravelled at different speeds. French nobles like the Comte de Castellane, or the sprinkling of dukes and princesses so fashionable in Paris society, had not been a political force since 1789, and resistance to republican and secular values and capitalist society came mainly from the Church. While most liberal, secular-minded Frenchmen had supported Dreyfus, practically all the Catholic factions (priests, political parties and the press) had condemned him in a sustained and ugly campaign marked by nationalist, antisemitic, and anti-republican sentiments directed against the 'Judaeo-Masonic' Republic.

In 1901 the radical president Emile Combes rolled up the heavy artillery. Using an obscure law against ideological assemblies, he decreed the dissolution of ten thousand Catholic schools (all promptly reopened with republican teachers in charge) and many monasteries and convents, most famously the monastery of Grande-Chartreuse, founded in 1084, near Grenoble in eastern France, where peasants responded to the 1902 eviction order by erecting burning barricades on the roads. The army was obliged to take axes to the monastery gates to break them down. The monks left singing and flanked by a cortège of weeping parishioners.

The Dreyfus case had catalysed the century-old battle between Church and Republic and brought it to a swift conclusion, in December 1905, with the passing of the law on the separation of Church and State. Now Church establishments were not only suddenly deprived of funds, but their very roofs would have to be rented back from the state. Neither spontaneous rioting nor a papal encyclical in 1906 could do anything to turn back the clock: the power of the Church in France was broken, its teachers expelled from the Republic's schools, its monasteries closed, its organizations all but bankrupt. The radical, republican bourgeoisie had vanquished its old enemy, and it capped its triumph on 13 July 1906 (the eve of the anniversary of the Revolution) with a full exoneration and reinstatement of the now gaunt but still dignified Captain Dreyfus.

Despite the dreams of socialists, anarchists and many members of the bourgeoisie, there was almost no possibility of breaking the hold of nobility and Church in Russia. Tsar Nicholas II was convinced that his power rested on these two pillars alone and went to great lengths to stifle democratic tendencies. The Tsar's medievalist, mystical vision of society was dazzling enough to blind him to the country's problems, but in reality his aristocracy was largely bankrupt. The emancipation of the serfs in 1861 had left many landowners at a loss: unable or unwilling to implement better administration and more efficient farming methods, they rapidly ran up crippling debts and were forced to sell out to the new money. 'With the abolition of serfdom, we soon fell into the category of landowners who did not have the means to live in the manner to which their circle had become accustomed,' noted Prince G. E. Lvov (1861–1925), who was to become, in 1917, Russia's first democratically elected prime minister.

The ring of axes chopping down the trees of a minor landed family in

Chekhov's *Cherry Orchard* (1903), in which the mansion and grounds are sold to a vulgar businessman, is the beat of this chapter of Russian history. The few aristocrats flexible enough to try new methods of cultivation, new machines and new crops almost always failed when confronted with the sheer ignorance and stubbornness of their own former serfs, conservative to the core, who preferred to sabotage new methods and destroy machines rather than accept the slightest change, as the enthusiastic modernizer Levin finds to his cost in Tolstoy's 1877 *Anna Karenina*.

Prince Lvov himself was a rare success among his aristocratic peers. Having inherited 150,000 roubles of debt, he and his family chose to work on the fields themselves, planting crops such as clover that were not traditional but were well suited to the local soil, reading new works on agriculture and implementing their recommendations, and, for a while, even living like peasants on rye bread and cabbage soup. Initially, the peasants felt sorry for them, regarding them as completely mad, but the family managed to turn the estate around, and after twenty-five years of very hard work all their debts had been paid off and the farm was producing a handsome profit. Lvov had even planted an orchard and was producing apple purée for the Moscow market – as if to refute the grim message of *The Cherry Orchard*. Most nobles, however, could no more have imagined going without their customary luxuries than they could conceive of eating cabbage soup. Once the serfs' free labour was no longer available, the fate of Russia's landowners, as a class, was sealed.

Russia and Britain's nobles had reason to envy the great families of the Habsburg empire such as the dynasties of Windischgrätz, Waldstein, Harrach, Lobkowitz, Liechtenstein, Esterházy and Palffy, some of whom owned lands the size of entire English counties. The Habsburg empire was largely rural, self-sufficient, and therefore less affected by market fluctuations. Hungary was even exporting grain, and in the globalized world of 1900 it was also the largest provider of grain to beef-exporting Argentina. Hungary's wide plains, and also its conservative rural social structures, still allowed food to be produced cheaply, a rare counter-example to most European countries, which were by now being flooded by food imports from the New World. The smaller landowners, harder hit by the overall drop in land revenues, were compensated by their Emperor Franz Josef's ingenious and unique solution: he put them all on his own payroll, not only in the army, but also in government, and particularly in the diplomatic service. A state-subsidized aristocracy may seem a ruinous folly, but in fact, given the circumstances of time and place, it allowed the Emperor to maintain it as a social force.

With the empire threatening to break apart into a collection of nationalist splinter states, and independence movements everywhere looking for leadership, Franz Josef had succeeded in binding the nobility to the Crown, not only by buying their acquiescence but by actively involving them in his policies. Theirs were no ornamental posts: ministers, section chiefs, generals and admirals were on active duty, and the labyrinthine demands of Habsburgian administration and military life ensured that they were kept busy. The ministry of war alone, which absorbed a great proportion of aristocratic bureaucrats, supervised three separate armies: the Austrian, the Hungarian, and the combined Austro-Hungarian forces. And as if this were not enough administrative effort, each of them housed a Babel of languages, all of which the officers were encouraged to learn and all of which were spoken at the ministry. The men of an army unit might be commanded in one language (commands, after all, are linguistically not very complex), but might have another *Dienstsprache* for technical expressions and a third *Regimentssprache* for use with other soldiers. Some regiments contained recruits who spoke three different native languages. One of them, containing Hungarians, Germans and Slovaks from a region of high emigration to America, even adopted English as their *Kommandosprache*. The officers had learned it at school, and the ranks had all picked up an adequate working vocabulary from America-bound friends and family members.

Around the turn of the century, this apparently impossible system worked remarkably well. Within the empire there was broad agreement that it was best (and complicated enough already) to stick with the status quo, even if it meant foregoing the game of global imperial expansion that was being played by the other major powers. The watchword in everything was moderation. 'Here one was at the centre of Europe, at a focal point of the world's old axes,' wrote an acerbically perceptive Robert Musil in his *Man Without Qualities*.

> There was some display of luxury, but it was not, of course, as over-sophisticated as the French. One went in for sport, but not in the madly Anglo-Saxon fashion. One spent tremendous sums on the army, but only just enough to ensure that one remained the second weakest among the great powers. The capital, too, was somewhat smaller than all the rest of the world's largest cities, but it was nevertheless quite considerably larger than a mere ordinary large city. And the administration of this country was carried out in an enlightened, barely perceptible manner, with a cautious clipping of all sharp points, by the best bureaucracy in

Europe, which could be accused of only one defect: it could not help regarding genius and enterprise...unless privileged by high birth or State appointment, as ostentation, indeed presumption.

In the Habsburg empire the situation was kept in hand by the noble art of controlled inertia and spasmodic improvisation, and only a prescient few saw in it the beginning of the inevitable end.

England had had its Magna Carta, the Wars of the Roses and the execution of Charles I; Russian nobles had suffered under Ivan the Terrible and risen against Tsar Alexander I in 1825; the great lords of the Habsburg empire had always had a combative relationship with their regime; Hungary in particular continued to champ at the imperial bit; the Italians had lived through their Risorgimento, the Spanish through bloody civil wars, and the Poles through a centuries-long nightmare of invasions, revolutions and power struggles. France had seen the Fronde and several revolutions. There was only one European country, right at the heart of the Continent, in which aristocratic power and monarchical rule had been accepted without challenge or interruption: Germany. No revolution had ever brought its nobles down, no regicide or German Fronde had upset the way of things, nor would it do until 1944, when a group led by Claus Schenk, Count von Stauffenberg would conspire and fail to topple the head of government, Adolf Hitler.

The rulers of the new German empire declared in 1871 emerged onto the global stage from provincial lives and put their faith in the traditional military ethos. Unlike their British counterparts, all but one of them (the eccentric Prince Günter Victor, head of the tiny, 100,000-soul statelet of Schwarzburg Rudolstadt in Thuringia) would appear in uniform on all public occasions and for official photographs. On the eve of the victory parade after the Austro-German War of 1866 the new chancellor of the Reich, Otto von Bismarck, had been made honorary chief of the 7 *Schwieren Landwehr-Reiter*, with the rank of major-general, expressly so that he could appear in appropriately military splendour. Even as the first civilian politician, he regularly wore uniform to parliamentary occasions, and always in the presence of the Emperor.

The state administration repaid its aristocracy handsomely for these continuing gestures of respect and hierarchy by protecting them from the cold winds of industrialization and global competition. Tax exemptions and tariff barriers ensured that farming remained a viable (if increasingly difficult) means of support for landowners, especially on the large East Prussian estates beyond the river Elbe. While most of the East Prussian Junkers whose military ethos formed the backbone of the Prussian monarchy were heavily mortgaged and often lived as poorly as their own servants, few of them were actually forced to sell their estates. Their revenues had declined, but the tough Junkers simply refused to give up, relying instead on a spirit of sturdy self sufficiency. Frugal, proud and independent-minded, these Protestant nobles now made thrift almost as much a sacred principle as their ancient devotion to the fulfilment of duty.

Henning von Tresckow in Brandenburg, later to become one of the aristocratic conspirators against Hitler's life in 1944, grew up on one of the many East Prussian country estates operating more or less at subsistence level. His mother, who managed the estate, kept expenditure to a minimum. 'The pleasures they allowed themselves were modest ones,' a friend later recalled. 'When Frau von Tresckow had Christmas presents to buy for the village, she travelled up to Berlin on the train third class. While she was in the city she also avoided unnecessary expenses; most of the time she stayed the night in the cheapest hospice.' Even the much grander and wealthier Counts von Dönhoff were seen travelling third class during these years. At the same time, many of the sons of the struggling lower aristocracy in Prussia were absorbed by the army, and officers' salaries often helped pay for the upkeep of Junker country estates.

The special economic status of landowners in the Reich played its part in preserving the powerful Junker class in East Prussia, and under these favourable economic circumstances there was no crisis within the German aristocracy equivalent to those elsewhere in Europe, although by 1900 there was growing vocal opposition to aristocratic privileges by the Social Democrats, the largest party in the Reichstag. They faced an uphill battle, particularly since the voting system itself gave the landowning class a disproportionately large share of parliamentary seats, and also because both army and administration were studded with noble names: two thirds of the members of the government were of noble birth, as well as three quarters of all the army officers and 84 per cent of the generals. Until 1918, all Reich chancellors (Prince Otto von Bismarck, Count Leo von Caprivi, Prince Chlodwig zu Hohenlohe-Schillingsfürst and Prince Bernhard von Bülow) were aristocrats.

His Highness Duke Ernst II of Saxony-Altenburg is a textbook example of German aristocratic life at its most secure. On an official photo, a postcard idyll, as was his little duchy in east-German Thuringia, he displays himself seated on an elaborately carved, thronelike armchair, surrounded by his adoring family: his wife, Duchess Adelheid (née Schaumburg-Lippe), and his children Georg Moritz, Friedrich Ernst, Charlotte and Elisabeth.

*Happy families: Ernst, Duke of Saxony-Altenburg
with wife and children.*

Life in these little states was often simple, and strongly paternalistic. 'My father owned a car very early on,' Georg Moritz, the heir apparent, would later recall. 'He told his traffic minister that the roads would have to be improved as the ride was far too bumpy on the potholed country roads. The minister politely informed him that there was no money for such extravagances and so my father cordially invited him for a ride in his car. The minister could not very well refuse and my father went off at full speed.' And after a little pause, he added, with quiet satisfaction: 'The roads were fixed with astonishing rapidity.'

The little duchy of Saxony-Altenburg counted some 200,000 subjects. Altenburg, its capital, with 39,000 inhabitants, held the hundredth place on the list of Germany's largest cities. The duchy's land was mainly agricultural, although there was also some coalmining, and a railway network covering 185 kilometres. The duchy's largest industrialist was a manufacturer of playing cards, still produced today under the Altenburg name, and still famous in Germany. Ernst II would be the last reigning monarch in Germany (he abdicated on 14 November 1918, five days after the Kaiser) and was to have the added distinction of being the only former German feudal ruler to live and die in the communist German Democratic Republic.

In the rigidly hierarchical world of imperial Germany, the young princes learned the subtleties of status from an early age; they would have absorbed the implications of their family's rank and its relations with other ruling families almost along with their mother's (or nurse's) milk. Their family connections illustrate the deep-rooted strength of the German aristocracy.

The Saxe-Altenburgs were closely related to the Saxe-Coburg-Gothas (Georg Moritz himself was a discouraging 642nd in line to the British throne) and to many other great European families, including the royal houses of Belgium, Bulgaria and Portugal. The Duke's sister Alexandra was married to the Grand Duke Constantine Nikolaievich Romanov, one of the sons of Tsar Nicholas I. Tsar Alexander II was therefore a cousin by marriage to the Duke, Tsar Nicholas II a cousin once removed. Another sister, Marie, had married Prince Albrecht of Prussia, a brother of Kaiser Wilhelm I and great-uncle of Kaiser Wilhelm II. All of them could trace their lineage back to the early Milddle Ages, an ancestry which included, in the case of the Saxe-Altenburgs, the medieval emperors Charlemagne and Frederick II, followed by a colourful crowd of thirteenth-century margraves: Albrecht the Proud, Dietrich the Pressured and Dietrich the Pressurer (not father and son), Albrecht the Degenerate, Friedrich the Bitten, Wilhelm I the One-Eyed and George the Bearded. In 1900, the distant descendants of these intriguing princes still had the upper hand, but only just.

If life in the provinces retained a strongly paternalistic flavour, the degree of aristocratic influence and power was very different in different parts of the country, particularly in the more urbanized areas. The powerful northern seaports such as Hamburg, Bremen, Lübeck or Danzig (all belonging to the ancient mercantile Hanseatic league) were small republics which had been ruled for centuries by citizens' senates. The Junker spirit dominant in the rural expanses of Brandenburg and East Prussia was alien to the industrial cities of the Catholic Rhineland (Cologne, Essen, Bochum, etc.), which was officially part of Prussia, but whose traditions and ways of doing things were quite different.

Far from being the grovelling subjects often evoked by historians, large sections of the German middle classes had a great deal of self-confidence and looked down on the birth aristocracy as a class of degenerate, hidebound scroungers. The German *Bürgertum*, the middle class, defined its hierarchies and values in terms of education and civil merit, not noble birth. Prominent and wealthy Germans who were offered ennoblement often refused to accept it. The steel magnate Alfred Krupp declined a title (though his son would yield, and be known thenceforth as Prince von Bohlen und Halbach), as did the great pathologist and public health campaigner Rudolph Virchow. The Breslau industrialist Oscar Huldschinsky, who had earlier been graced with an invitation to sail on the imperial yacht, refused to accept the *Kronenorden* offered him, reportedly remarking, 'if nobody has thought of honouring me for my contribution to German industry, I'm not going to accept a medal just because I've been out boating with the Kaiser.' The *Bürgertum* was not, as Mommsen had so pessimistically written, 'simply born to be ruled'.

While many middle-class people were imperialists and believed in the greatness of their culture and their fatherland, the recognition they were striving for was not the Emperor's to give. German businessmen were more interested in the title of *Kommerzialrat*, the civilian, non-noble title of 'Commercial Councillor', an emblem of dependability and honourable conduct, than in a knighthood. Medical doctors had an eye on the title *Sanitätsrat*; lawyers and judges hoped to attain the grade of *Justizrat*, and so on. This hierarchy of civilian titles, as well as the academic appellations of *Doktor* and *Professor*, were taken so seriously in Germany that even wives were addressed with their husbands' titles: *Frau Kommerzialrat, Frau Professor*, etc. Moreover, with proverbial German industriousness, these titles could be multiplied, in which case they would be used in full at every official occasion. Thus, a simple medical student could dream of working his way up to a practice, teaching at a university and receiving an honorary degree there, being eventually elected to the Reichstag and then retiring, at which point he would become known (and regularly addressed in writing) as *Herr Reichstagsabgeordneter a.D., Sanitätsrat Professor Doktor Doktor (honoris causa)*, and even further, as far as his enthusiasm for committees, exams and official posts would carry him. In a characteristically German way, the burghers had emancipated themselves from the constraints of the old hierarchy by creating a new one.

Britain's new, plutocratic nobles had no misgivings about their ennoblement and began to transform the aristocracy from within, bringing a degree of middle-class values and modernity wherever they went. They purchased country estates and installed modern plumbing and electric light – not for them the idea of genteel shabbiness. In the end they became a new kind of landed gentry, who worked in the city or in the factory towns, and only on the weekend took a train or motored out in one of the newfangled automobiles to their mansions in the country. The weekend countryman had been invented.

The great ennobled magnates of the time, men like Lord Guinness, with his brewery money, W. H. Smith, with his stationery chain, and Lord Leverhulme, with his soaps, bought land on an appropriately magnificent scale. Leverhulme, for example, was a grocer's son, born William Lever in Bolton, Lancashire, where he had established a soap factory in 1886. Aided by business acumen and novel manufacturing processes, Lever's palm oil soap bubbled into a huge fortune, and the entrepreneur went into politics. He was an avid art collector and put into practice his philanthropic intentions in Port Sunlight, a settlement built for his workers. In 1917 he was created Baron Leverhulme; five years later Viscount Leverhulme. In 1916 he bought a magnificent London palace from the Marquess of Stafford, renaming it Lancaster House. He also acquired (in 1918) several whole islands in the Outer Hebrides, and on one of them a quasi-ancestral pile, Castle Lewis.

Their new estates, however, were not much more than a bauble for these new men to play with, a welcome status symbol, but in the end, peripheral to the real business of life. During the Victorian period Benjamin Disraeli had been obliged to buy himself an estate simply in order to be considered prime ministerial material, for only the aristocracy, or at least the landed gentry, were expected to hold such positions. By 1911, times had changed so much that even the Conservative Party chose as its chairman Andrew Bonar Law, a Glasgow financier who had neither title nor estate, and who was not looking for either. For the old aristocrats, their estates had been the very reason of their existence; the homes of their ancestors, seats of their power. Now they had been reduced to a wealthy man's ornament. Power had moved into the cities.

New Titles, New Wealth

If aristocratic accoutrements were amusements for the new nobility, members of the older nobility looked enviously at the money and energy that had created the fortunes of the day. Both the English King Edward and the German Kaiser Wilhelm II adored the company of this powerful, novel breed of friends, Edward most likely for hedonistic reasons, and Wilhelm because they embodied the surging economic power of his new empire.

As Prince of Wales, Edward and his social circle had already raised more than a few eyebrows among their conservative countrymen. The London society leader Lady Paget (herself somewhat ironically born Minnie Stevens in New York) may have remarked that the King was 'always surrounded by a bevy of Jews and a ring of racing people', but the Prince had merely read the signs of the time and allied himself with the winning team, the one batting for the new order: Lord Iveagh, who brewed beer, Baron Hirsch and Sir Ernest Cassel, Jewish bankers, or Sir Thomas Lipton, he of the tea bags – all extremely rich, first-generation noblemen. When the Kaiser heard that Lipton and his sovereign were sailing together in the Cowes Regatta he remarked, with a rare flash of wit, that the King had 'gone boating with his grocer'.

All the same, despite his own obsessive quest for recognition and grandeur, the Kaiser's tastes were also decidedly nouveaux riche. While the Prussian field marshal Graf Helmuth von Moltke had enjoined his country-men to 'be more than you seem' – a statement echoed by the dictum of Graf Alfred von Schlieffen, father of the eponymous and disastrous plan: 'Great achievement, small display: More reality than appearance' – Wilhelm seemed to have inverted the rule. He spent madly and lived grandly, as his itinerary demonstrates. His court was a constant roadshow, alighting in Berlin and the Sans Souci Palace in Potsdam for only half the year. The spring was spent cruising in the Mediterranean, where Wilhelm also tried his hand at amateur archaeology (he kept a palace on Corfu), or on his estates in the Alsace and East Prussia. During the summer he would put out to sea again, this time in the North Sea and the Baltic, while during the autumn months the hunting season was far too tempting to be left to others: the Kaiser was never more proud than when photographed with interminable lines of slaughtered animals.

The court in Berlin did not approve. His Majesty's lavish lifestyle offended the sense of frugality so important in the history of Prussia, whose greatest son, the legendary King Frederick the Great, had always dressed in simple uniforms, normally taking no more than a bowl of porridge even for his dinner. His less than heroic descendant had other ideas, as Baroness Spitzemberg, a lady-in-waiting at the court, recorded in her diary with obvious exasperation during one of Wilhelm's Mediterranean sojourns, an archaeological dig in the dust of Greece: 'H. M. [His Majesty] sends page-long, terribly expensive telegrams to the Archaeological Society about every last knee [of a classical statue] he finds…Bismarck was right: "no sense of proportion".'

Full metal jacket: Wilhelm II in uniform, his crippled left hand resting on his sabre.

If the old guard was not happy about Wilhelm's spending habits, the newly rich industrialists were less fussy and much less likely to lecture His Majesty on penny-pinching and proportion. Like his Uncle Bertie (Edward VII of England), the Kaiser preferred the company of jollier, less hidebound men, among them self-made moguls such as Albert Ballin, owner of the Hamburg America Line, the biggest of the age. Ballin had worked his way up from an inauspicious start as the son of a bankrupt Jewish cloth merchant. Perhaps characteristically, given his often schizophrenic attitudes, Wilhelm, who shared the antisemitic prejudices of his time, particularly appreciated the company of successful Jews like Ballin, the bankers Carl Fürstenberg and Paul von Schwarbach, the coal mogul Eduard Arnhold, or Walter Rathenau, chairman of the powerful AEG. This imperial entourage was quickly dubbed *Kaiserjuden* (Emperor's Jews) by jealous members of the court. Other favourites included Philipp Eulenburg, a lawyer and career diplomat, the son of a former Prussian army officer. Though Eulenburg was not rich, Wilhelm enjoyed his company so much that he created him Prince Eulenburg; as we shall see later, the Prince's later exposure as a homosexual would cause the Kaiser great embarrassment.

Queen Victoria's eyes had been pressed shut by her grandson Kaiser Wilhelm, the uncomprehending representative of a new empire born out of nationalism and industrial thrust. Both he and the Queen's successor, King Edward, were obsessed with the rituals of their rank, but much preferred the convenience and fun of modern life. Both were unaware of the contradiction they embodied, neither had a vision that matched the realities of his day.

Edward Elgar's *Pomp and Circumstance* marches, composed for the coronation of Edward VII in 1902, have a brassy bluster which, even at the time, sounded like the echo of an earlier age, stretched and amplified to dignify the day. In fact, after decades of frustrated waiting in the shadow of his long-lived mother, Edward had almost failed to claim the throne at all. Only days before the coronation, appendicitis had come close to claiming the new King's life, and the event had had to be postponed. Modern medicine saved the day, and as the rotund monarch waddled down the aisle of Westminster Abbey, with his current and former mistresses (including Sarah Bernhardt and the 'delectable' Alice Keppel) in a special place of honour, a relieved nation broke into a chorus of 'Land of ho-ope and gloooo-ryyy', the Edwardian empire's new, if unofficial, hymn. The words to Elgar's sumptuous, velvet-lined tune had been written by Arthur Benson, a painfully shy former Eton housemaster and Fellow of Magdalene College, Cambridge, posthumously famous for the copious diary of 180 handwritten volumes in which he grappled with his tortured homosexuality. Elgar detested the popular new lyrics for their brashness. Benson was no unthinking imperialist himself, but the words he had written reflected one part at least of Britain's national aspirations, as well as providing an ironic commentary on the stature of the gluttonous King: 'Wider still and wider / Shall thy bounds be set / God, who made thee mighty / Make thee mightier yet.' Attending the coronation, the Kaiser approved of the expansionist sentiments, though not of expansionist Britain itself. With political power shifting to the democratized, professionalized, quantified masses, the men at the top, in their gold-tasselled uniforms, were preparing to make a last stand of their own for the old order.

3

1902:

Oedipus Rex

No understanding is possible between people, no discussion, no connection between today and yesterday: words are lying, feelings are lying, and our very consciousness is lying.
– Hugo von Hofmannsthal, *Physiology of Modern Love*

In Vienna, the capital of the Austro-Hungarian Empire, the 18th of March 1902 was one of those dirty, depressing days in early spring with uncertain, leaden skies and squally showers – ideal weather for ducking into one of the city's many cafés and making use of one of their most attractive features, the dozens of newspapers provided for patrons. One cup of coffee was (and still is) all a customer had to buy in return for the right to sit and read as long as he pleased.

On this dull day the news was very run-of-the-mill. *Das Vaterland*, a conservative paper, recorded political events at home and abroad: the Vienna parliament debating the reduction of military service from three to two years; the seventieth birthday of Prince Schwarzenberg, one of the empire's grandest aristocrats; the Hungarian deputies debating the agricultural budget. The *Pester Lloyd*, a German-speaking Budapest paper for businessmen, led with a lengthy article on developments in the prices for pork fat and bacon. News about the empire's first families: Archduke Rainer is to visit an exhibition; the confinement of Archduchess Marie Christine is progressing normally.

Developments abroad were slightly more exciting. The Boer War led the foreign pages (as it did in German and French papers, also available in all self-respecting cafés). The British army had been defeated at Tweebosch and Lord Methuen had been wounded, captured, and then sent home by the Boers, who had also thoughtfully dispatched a telegram to Lady Methuen to apprise her of her husband's return. King Edward, *Das*

Vaterland noted, was not going abroad this year but would instead cruise in British waters; Prince Heinrich of Prussia had arrived in Plymouth aboard the *Deutschland*; a demonstration in St Petersburg had been stopped by police without violence, but with about one hundred arrests; a petroleum tanker in the Suez Canal had gone up in flames, creating an oil slick; Constantinople (today's Istanbul) was covered by a thick, unseasonable layer of snow.

Official news always tends to have a familiar ring to it, and the world of this time opens up in a richer way when one turns to the small ads, the local news, and the advertisements. The *Wiener Zeitung*, the official paper of record, notes on its local pages that the schoolboy Wilhelm Sopka has run away from home and is missing; the housemaid Katharina Rybetcky has been arrested for smothering her illegitimate child; the worker 'Josefine St.' has committed suicide by throwing herself out of a third-floor window; a butcher's assistant has stolen 1,000 *Kronen* from her employer.

'Comrades, Workers and Female Workers!' the socialist *Volksbote* shouts from the front page, alerting its readers to a 'people's assembly' in the Gisela-Säle on Sunday afternoon. It also reports that after a workers' rebellion during which the military shot 'dozens' of comrades, there is still a state of war declared in Trieste; that sugar will become cheaper, even if the Austro-Hungarian 'sugar barons' have tried to prevent this; and that a sacristan in Vienna has been found to have been sexually abusing altar boys in his care. For once, there is no news about injured, sacked or maimed workers, the sad staple fare of the local pages in an age with little safety at work. On the back page, Anton Pollak & Companie offers cheap clothes for boys and men; 'a decent woman' wants to take in washing; the Circus Victor announces a performance featuring a comedian and a wrestling match; a pharmacy offers 'the best home-made Rum with finest spirits, guaranteed 96% proof' (cheap and powerful enough to knock out anyone after a sixteen-hour day in the factory); 'rubber goods' (condoms) are offered, chastely hidden among tubing and washers.

Die Bombe, a humorous weekly magazine addressed mainly to young men about town, carries very different ads: 'Gratis – Interesting Mail' promises an 'artistic studio' in Hamburg, 'Photographic Nude Studies' another. *Paris Rubber Novelties for Gentlemen, Rubber goods* are advertised by A. Kruger in Berlin and Karl Franke in Leipzig. The more respectable *Wiener Zeitung* offers much safer fare: the repertoire of all major theatres, museum opening times, and 'Singing Lessons for Ladies and Gentlemen'.

In an official announcement at the foot of page one, an historic figure appears as in a cameo role:

His Imperial and Royal Apostolic Majesty has most graciously deigned to appoint to an Extraordinary Professorship in hygiene at the University of Vienna, by Supreme Decision of 5 March this year, Private Lecturer Dr Arthur Schattenfroh, and has also through his utmost grace condescended to award the title of University Professor Extraordinary at the same university to the Private Lecturers Dr Sigmund Freud, Dr Julius Mannaberg and Dr Emil Fronz.

Freud's elevation to 'university professor extraordinary' (not the same as a full, tenured position) was a long-overdue acknowledgement, for his method of treating psychological problems – he called it psychoanalysis – had won international acclaim. It had come very late. For a long time, the medical establishment had refused to recognize the Jewish doctor or his method, and even now Freud had to use the contacts of a wealthy patient to get the ball rolling. Now he had made it. At forty-four he had finally achieved a degree of public recognition.

The Dual Monarchy, Freud's home for most of his life, has vanished from the map, and yet there are still people alive today who were born under the double-headed eagle that overlooked some 20 per cent of Europe, from Czernowitz (today Chernivtsy in the Ukraine) on the Romanian border to Bregenz on the shores of the Swiss Lac Leman, from the northern Reichenberg (today Liberec in the Czech Republic) and Krakau (today Kraków in Poland) right down to Trieste (now in Italy) and then hundreds of miles along the Adriatic coast to the small heavily fortified town of Budua, today's Budva in Montenegro. Second only to Germany in terms of population, and ahead of Great Britain with Ireland and France (45 million each), the 50 million Habsburg subjects formed not so much one population, as several different and rival ones: Germans (as the German-speaking inhabitants called themselves), Hungarians, Czechs, Slovaks, Poles, Ruthenes, Slovenes, Serbo-Croats, Italians, Bosnians and Romanians, to say nothing of national and religious minorities.

The map reveals not only the Dual Monarchy's power and extent, but also its fatal flaw: Austria-Hungary was not a country but a collection of lands belonging to the Habsburg family, a political relic from the Middle Ages. Czechs, Poles and Hungarians were demanding political and cultural independence, education in their own language, control over taxes, and ever-stronger political representation in direct competition with other nationalities, and while most people in Austria *proper* ate Bohemian cuisine for the simple reason that most cooks hailed from there, Czech-speakers would no more attend Hungarian theatres than would Germans pick up a novel written in Czech, Italian or Serbo-Croat. Prague was divided in two between the Czech and German populations, each insisting on its own newspapers, schools, football clubs, cafés, and even on separate universities. German-speaking intellectuals who had lived in the city all their lives, among them Franz Kafka and Franz Werfel, were much more likely to know Latin, ancient Greek or French than Czech. A typical case is Kafka himself, who famously learned Yiddish, the better to understand the culture of his ancestors, while his knowledge of Czech was limited to 'kitchen Bohemian', the pidgin German of its day, used to communicate with domestic staff from the provinces. Throughout the empire, the overall situation could only give the impression of stability because no single national group was large and powerful enough to assure its dominance. The immediate ancestry of Austria's foreign minister in 1914, Count Leopold Berchtold (or to give him his full name: Count Leopold Anton Johann Sigismund Josef Korsinus Ferdinand Berchtold von und zu Ungarschütz, Frättling und Püllütz), made him part German, part Czech, part Slovak and part Hungarian. When a journalist pressed him on his sense of nationality he simply answered: 'I'm Viennese.'

For many decades, the government's way of dealing with this patchwork of allegiances had been to smother national and cultural differences under the thick folds of imperial ermine, but the calls for self-determination were growing louder every day. Even the sessions of the imperial parliament in Vienna were regularly interrupted by scuffles between members, and when sensitive cultural legislation was introduced some national minority parties were known to resort to a very unparliamentarian kind of noise, produced on rattles, pot lids and children's trumpets, to drown out opposing speakers and sabotage proceedings. In response to all kinds of political unrest, the imperial administration had cultivated the noble art of formalized inertia: improvising, stalling, waiting, granting a little here and taking it away with the other hand, never facing the important questions, always hoping that the problems might simply go away if only the administration proved more patient than had history.

In this empire without a national identity, the only truly unifying idea was the Emperor himself, in this case the ageing Franz Josef I (1830–1916), whose full title was:

His Imperial and Apostolic Majesty, Franz Josef I, by the Grace of God, Emperor of Austria, King of Hungary and Bohemia, King of Lombardy and Venice, of Dalmatia, Croatia, Slavonia, Lodomeria and Illyria; King of Jerusalem etc., Archduke of Austria; Grand Duke of Tuscany and Kraków, Duke of Lorraine, of Salzburg, Styria, Carinthia, Carniola and of the Bukovina; Grand Duke of Transylvania; Margrave of Moravia; Duke of Upper and Lower Silesia, of Modena, Parma, Piacenza and Guastalla, of Auschwitz [Oświęcim] and Zator, of Teschen [Cieszyn/Český Těšín], Friuli, Ragusa [Dubrovnik] and Zara [Zadar]; Princely Count of Habsburg and Tyrol, of Kyburg, Gorizia and Gradisca; Prince of Trent [Trento] and Brixen [Bressanone]; Margrave of Upper and Lower Lusatia and in Istria; Count of Hohenems, Feldkirch, Bregenz, Sonnenberg, etc.; Lord of Trieste, of Cattaro [Kotor], and in the Wendish Mark; Grand Voivode of the Voivodina of Serbia etc. etc.

Presiding over an empire of unresolved questions, the grandly titled Emperor was a thoroughly average man, a punctilious office worker who spent endless hours, always in his cavalry uniform, at his desk in Vienna's Hofburg Palace, scribbling comments and decisions in the margins of untold files. The very incarnation of service and duty, he was as disciplined as he expected his civil servants to be, but was only really happy when he was able to take time off and visit his mistress Katharina Schratt in his villa

Peering down with watery eyes: Emperor Franz Josef I, the lynchpin of stability.

in Bad Ischl, where he liked to don local costume and go for walks in the mountains. For his subjects, the old man was omnipresent, peering from official photos with cool, watery eyes at schoolchildren, civil servants and at married couples in their beds.

While the Emperor continued to function like a mechanical doll, there was a sense of emptiness and falsehood at the heart of all this stuccoed magnificence. Only Greek myth could have produced a family more dysfunctional and more glaringly immoral than his own. Empress Elisabeth (1837–1898), more famous as Sisi, had acquired a romantic aura, but her life had been a string of tantrums, fits of anorexia, and long, erratic journeys around the Mediterranean in search of the elixir of youth. Her popularity was only rescued when an anarchist fatally stabbed her in Geneva, in 1898. The brilliant and liberal-minded Crown Prince Rudolf had broken with his father and finally shot himself and his mistress at his hunting lodge Schloss Mayerling in 1889, and his cousin, the jolly Archduke Otto (who once appeared in society wearing only a sabre), was so ravaged by syphilis that he had to wear a leather nose when appearing in public. As for the current heir, the boorish, philistine Archduke Franz Ferdinand: the Emperor cordially detested him.

The place where the empire's moral heart was supposed to beat was empty. Franz Josef himself, an ardent theatregoer in his youth, inadvertently strengthened this perception. An imperial box was reserved for the Emperor and his family in every theatre in the empire, a crowning – and crowned – centrepiece to its architecture, draped in red velvet and topped by the imperial double eagle. After the death of his wife, Franz Josef hardly ever went to the theatre. The imperial boxes from Lemberg to Trieste stood empty for decades, and instead of linking faraway cities to imperial glory, they merely served as a constant reminder of the void at the centre of the Habsburg universe.

Nature abhors a vacuum, and the Emperor's fiction of unity was not sustainable. Instead, individual and competing groups (national, social, or political) filled the Habsburg void with content of their own choosing: with manners, art, hedonism, and ideas of national greatness. All these projections were allowed, as long as nobody called the imperial bluff.

The Great Cover-up

Literally as well as metaphorically, covering up the obvious became the central principle of life in Habsburg Vienna. 'The more a woman wanted to appear a "lady", the less her natural shape was allowed to be noticeable; the entire fashion followed this doctrine and thus followed the general moral tendency of the time, which was principally concerned with covering up and hiding things,' the novelist Stefan Zweig remembered of his youth.

The imperial city itself practised what it demanded from its women. The Ringstrasse, Vienna's grand boulevard, was dressed up in splendid historicism, an expression of changing times as an affirmation of eternal values and a proclamation of greatness. Every building was erected in an historical style appropriate to its purpose, from Gothic (after Flemish citizen wealth) for the city hall, to the two neo-baroque museums of art history and natural history, the Hellenizing parliament and the neo-Renaissance university. Always under the watchful eye of the old Emperor, the turn-of-the-century city was a place of grand façades, opulence, decorum and apparent certainties. Stefan Zweig describes in his memoirs how full of faith and optimism the world appeared to those fortunate enough not to go hungry: 'Everything in our thousand-year-old Austrian monarchy seemed based on durability...Only this security made our lives worth living. Today...we know that this world of certainty was nothing but a castle in the air. And yet, my parents inhabited it like a house built of stone. Not once did a storm or even a sharp draft disturb their warm, comfortable existence.'

Historicist splendour, grand façades: the Parliament and City Hall on Vienna's Ringstrasse.

To preserve this comfort, it was necessary to accept more than a little make-believe. Politically, the Habsburg empire was beset by nationalist agitation inside it and rival powers around it. Its enormous rural hinterland lagged far behind other European countries in terms of economic development and infrastructure, while its entrenched poverty and social hierarchies would have made anything on the scale of the opening up of the American West impossible, even if there had been the will to do it. Still, the face put on this struggling body was magnificent, and for many in the Dual Monarchy this imperial *trompe l'œil* soon became the preferred version of the world. 'With the premiere of [Johann Strauss's operetta] *Die Fledermaus* in 1873,' writes Bruno Bettelheim shrewdly, 'Vienna began once again to dominate the world...not the real world, but that of operetta.'

The troubled empire was determined to forget its problems over a good time, and the joke went that Habsburg diplomacy was like a Viennese waltz: first swirling right, then left, and round and round, until one finally arrived where one had started from, always on the move and never getting anywhere.

In this world of concealed, uncertain substance, style was everything, as Hugo von Hofmannsthal (1874–1929) wrote into the libretto of his sumptuous rococo fantasy *Der Rosenkavalier* (1911, music by Richard Strauss), in which everyone acts out of pure hedonism: the Marschallin with her young lover Octavian, Octavian by courting the pretty Sophie, who is, in turn, sold to the bumptious Baron Ochs so that her father, the rich manufacturer Faninal, can gain entry to aristocratic circles. Everyone pretends to act from high moral principle and in the interest of others; only Ochs, the comic figure of the piece, is at times honest about his lecherous love. In a world of iron rules, morality was the first casualty.

As in Viennese operettas, the official rigidity had its accepted flipside. If duty and the strict façade of public morals threatened to become overwhelming, there was always a pretty shop girl to console a man (the cult of Vienna's 'sweet girls' hid a widespread practice of *de facto* prostitution). For men at least, some entertainment always beckoned in theatres, concert halls, beer halls or the many country inns dotted around Vienna, where a whole area of the city, the Prater, had been set aside as a permanent amusement park where everything from a glass of beer to a little company could be found almost around the clock.

The writer Arthur Schnitzler (1862–1931) saddled himself with an undeserved reputation as a pornographer when he combined the two motifs of casual liaisons and the never-ending circle of activity in his scandalous play *Der Reigen* ('The Daisy Chain', 1903), in which couples of different social backgrounds meet in a series of random sexual encounters, beginning with a whore and a soldier, rising up to an actress and a count, only to have count meet whore in the last scene, a succession that is meaningless, endless, and knows no social boundaries. More naughtily, the writer Felix Salten (1869–1945), the creator of Bambi, the soft-eyed fawn loved by little girls the world over and pure as the driven snow, also wrote a notoriously pornographic romp, *Josefine Mutzenbacher* (1906), which left nothing at all to the adult reader's imagination.

Duplicity had become an institution in Vienna as in other European societies – a fact very clearly exemplified by Oscar Wilde's disastrous libel trial in London or the Eulenburg affair in Germany, in which respected public figures were ruined when their homosexuality, an open secret, was made public. In the Dual Monarchy, this principle was upheld with iron strength: as long as the fiction of imperial greatness and public morality could be upheld, everybody could have a good time. The public dogma of looking the other way made the double eagle, whose heads face opposite directions, appear the perfect emblem for the state, and for the state of mind. Habsburg Vienna was certainly not the only place where a rigid code of behaviour was offset by a sphere in which different rules applied, but this fact had a particular flavour here.

The origin of this collective escape into pleasure was political and it applied not just to popular entertainment, but also to high art. Ever since Metternich's rule at the beginning of the nineteenth century and even more so after the abortive revolution of 1848, a leaden autocracy had done much to discourage the bourgeoisie from participating in politics, and the rising middle classes had found a solution which echoed that of German Romanticism almost a century before: if they could not have a national life through political participation they would recreate their freedom and their values through a vibrant cultural life, an emotional projection dissimulated into the scripts and costumes of the stage.

Throughout the Habsburg empire, in Vienna, Prague, Budapest and Lemberg, theatre, literature and music mattered as nowhere else in the world. Only here could an actor such as Joseph Kainz or Eleonora Duse become national celebrities, their careers and appearances discussed (even by people who had never seen them) in every greengrocer's shop, their signatures collected by excited schoolboys, as Stefan Zweig relates. Only here could the funeral of an artist turn into a national event attended by tens of thousands of mourners, with black ribbons on portrait photos in every shop window. A general, humanistic education belonged to the repertoire of the middle classes, and in their salons busts of Goethe and Beethoven stood directly underneath the picture of the Emperor, if not replacing it altogether, while rich industrialists like Karl Wittgenstein, father of the philosopher Ludwig Wittgenstein, made it a point of honour to be patrons of the arts.

To Dr Sigmund Freud (1856–1939), the doctor whose professional advancement had been announced in the *Wiener Zeitung* of 18 March 1902, the dichotomy between moral principle and social reality was a fact of life. He had grown up here, and he knew all there was to know about the climate of duplicity. The son of a struggling Jewish cloth merchant, Freud had worked his way up to becoming a fashionable 'modern' doctor whose reputation rested on work he had done with the great Paris psychiatrist Jean Martin Charcot and on a capacity for listening to patients without being

Family man: Sigmund Freud with his grandchildren.

shocked by anything they told him. Freud's consulting room in the Berggasse was filled with members of Vienna's good society, most of whom had ailments that could not be treated conventionally.

As a young doctor, Freud had wanted to do strictly scientific work. His earliest research was devoted to the physiology of eel testicles and his doctoral dissertation dealt with the functions of bone marrow in lower fish. From these creatures of the deep the scientist had graduated to human brains, to experiments with cocaine and to a research visit to Professor Charcot in Paris, where Freud studied the powerful effects of a psychological approach to mental illness, a diagnosis and a cure based on analysing patients' statements and trying to find emotional reasons for their symptoms and behaviour. His own interests had already led him in a similar direction, to a talking cure in which words would take the place of scalpels, cutting through uncontrollable growths of the imagination in order to eliminate them and restore a healthy constitution.

It was around 1895 that Freud had discovered the Archimedean point at which he believed he could unhinge the universe of the mind. Freud was a good listener, and he had noticed that sooner or later his patients would talk about sexual disorders, wishes or fears, and that the symbolism of their accounts pointed strongly in a sexual direction. This in itself was nothing new: among doctors treating mental disorders it was an accepted fact that sex played an important part. Freud, however, went a crucial step further, as he explained in a letter to his colleague and then close friend Wilhelm Fleiss: 'Have I already communicated the great clinical secret to you, orally or in writing? ... Hysteria is the consequence of a presexual *sexual scare*.

Obsessional neurosis is the consequence of a presexual *sexual pleasure*, which later transforms itself into [self-]*reproach*.' All afflictions of the mind, Freud implied, *were* in fact sexual, and had their roots not in recent experience but in buried memories, half recalled or strenuously suppressed. The talking cure he envisaged would therefore have to use the methods of archaeologists looking for hidden structures under metres of accumulated rubble, deep truths concealed by new façades. These truths, he was convinced, would lead unfailingly to sexual feelings deemed unacceptable, to forbidden lusts, thoughts of incest, sexual jealousy and fear.

In Vienna such a theory was bound to have a particular resonance. *La théorie, c'est bon, mais ça n'empêche pas d'exister*, theory is all very well, but that does not prevent facts from existing, Freud's teacher Charcot had said – a heretical sentence in the Viennese context. The young doctor had taken him at his word; even if theory or social convention decreed that troublesome impulses did not exist, that people were rational and moral and that honour lay in the fulfilment of duty, the outlawed impulses were nevertheless real, and their suppression must result in internal conflict. The clash between one's desires and the needs of society, of order and decency, led to repression, sublimation and displacement of wishes and emotions of which the individual might not even be aware.

The destructive conflict between conscious values and subconscious desires was fought out through dreams, Freud hypothesized in his path-breaking *Die Traumdeutung* (The Interpretation of Dreams, 1899, dated 1900):

> … the dream affords proof that the suppressed material continues to exist even in the normal person and remains capable of psychic activity. Dreams are one of the manifestations of this suppressed material; theoretically, this is true in all cases; and in tangible experience, it has been found true in at least a great number of cases, which happen to display most plainly the more striking features of the dream-life. The suppressed psychic material, which in the waking state has been prevented from expression and cut off from internal perception by the mutual neutralization of contradictory attitudes, finds ways and means, under the sway of compromise-formations, of obtruding itself on consciousness during the night.

Dreams rule the subconscious, a realm of the mind as deep and as uncontrollable as Homer's wine-dark sea. The rational mind may be filled with normative ideas and good intentions, but if reason and subconscious pull in different directions, a personality must finally be torn apart. The result may be a neurosis, a displacement of subconscious needs expressing itself through a variety of symptoms. It is the role of the physiotherapist to uncover their hidden origin through questions and careful guidance, setting the sufferer free to deal with his or her impulsions rationally:

> By the analysis of dreams we obtain some insight into the composition of this most marvellous and most mysterious of instruments; it is true that this only takes us a little way, but it gives us a start which enables us, setting out from the angle of other (properly pathological) formations, to penetrate further in our disjoining of the instrument. For disease ... does not necessarily presuppose the destruction of this apparatus, or the establishment of new cleavages in its interior: it can be explained dynamically by the strengthening and weakening of the components of the play of forces, so many of the activities of which are covered up in normal functioning.

The obvious conclusion from this theory was that all 'normal functioning' was a simple lie, exclusively designed to dissimulate an inconvenient truth, namely that the functioning of society itself rested on the suppression of the individual, on a denial of pleasure:

> In the last analysis, the motive of human society is an economic one: as there is not sufficient food to maintain its members without the need to work the number of members must be kept small and their energies diverted from sexual acts to work. This is the eternal, primordial anguish of life [Lebensnot] which is continued to this day.

Society as a great collective dream designed to force people into being useful instead of enjoying themselves and fulfilling the primary (sexual) function imposed on them by nature – in the context of Viennese politics this theory read like a comment on reality in Austria-Hungary.

As a young man, Sigmund Freud had decided not to become a philosopher but a clinician, a scientist. His interest in the metaphorical had fortunately diverted him from the laboratory, and it was the philosopher Freud whose work was truly groundbreaking and most influential; almost in passing, his analysis of personality structure and early experience denied the dominant tradition of the European Enlightenment, in which all understanding and all morality is based on reason and reason alone. Already during the eighteenth century, Immanuel Kant had claimed that we can never truly know what the outside world is like, because all knowledge of it is based on perception, and all perception based on the structure and limitations of our senses and the way in which they communicate the world to us. The only truly secure knowledge, Kant had written, must therefore be found inside the mind itself: the universal moral law governing our judgements and our actions, a law that could be discovered by reason alone.

Freud's theory of personal development flatly contradicted this noble idea. Morality was by no means universal, he argued, but a result of narcissism. As the 'narcissistic perfection' of early childhood dawns into a world full of interdictions and limitations, the loss is experienced as a personal failure, guilt sets in and, struggling to regain paradise, the ego develops norms such as conscientiousness, cleanliness and compassion. Morality itself was of sexual origin, and its structure depended on the contingencies of personal experience. In the final analysis, there was no universal law, only impulse and guilt, represented by internal metaphors: the normative Super-Ego, the rational Ego and, supporting and undermining all, the boundless realm of instinct and lust, the Id. Morality, Freud claimed, was even more radically contingent and subjective than perception. Nobody could claim to discover or to act from universal principles, as these were nothing but a projection of a neurotic failure to live up to the perfection of life in the womb.

The experience of living in Vienna, the city of competing idioms and nationalist feuds, arguably contributed to this abolition of the fiction of universal values and rational morality. Freud's textual fidelity (in his dream interpretations every word, every inflection, every detail counts and holds significance) predestined him for reading between the lines, and his insistence on the text may also be an unacknowledged legacy of methods and attitudes of Jewish learning. Freud had not been given a Jewish education, but his father had still grown up in an orthodox environment, and the parallels between Talmudic learning and Freudian analysis are striking. In both, the text (of the Bible, of a dream) is sacrosanct in all its apparent arbitrariness, language is held to cover more secrets than it revealed, and the text is to be interpreted in the light of others and of principles which can be acquired through rigorous application of scholarly observation. In both, deep structures are revealed between an apparent multitude of signs and symbols. Despite Freud's rigorously secular outlook, which made him one of his time's most eloquent critics of religion, the line dividing the medical scholar from Rabbi Freud is thin and often permeable.

From today's perspective, Freud's method has proven more useful for analysing social or literary universes than for the treatment of individual patients: even his own patients did not show the dramatic improvement the master himself claimed, and many relapsed after their sessions had been terminated. Seen from the perspective of his own time, his critique of social and personal façades was subversive in the extreme. In a society relying even more than others on appearance and convention to hide the lack of solutions to the unsolvable questions at its heart, the Jewish doctor declared all convention to be corrosive of the soul, society no more than a necessary evil, the most anarchic figments of the imagination representative of deep realities. But if a society's values are based on repression and psychological violence likely to make its members sick and to twist their minds, what then is their validity?

And what about the individual? Could it really be the case that all of culture was nothing more than a sublimation of the 'basest instincts', of things one could not possibly talk about with ladies present, things of which many young girls learned nothing before finding themselves in the marriage bed? What about the dominion of dark, unspeakable impulses in the human soul and particularly in the souls of innocent children? Was such a theory not simply an attack on public morals? In a city struggling to keep up appearances, these ideas threw up unanswerable questions.

There are obvious parallels between Freud's theories and the work of Viennese artists and philosophers. Novels described how rigid social conventions broke and distorted individuals: they tortured the eponymous hero of Robert Musil's *The Confusions of Young Törless* (*Die Verwirrungen des Zöglings Törless*, 1906), who witnesses the sadistic customs at a cadet academy training imperial officers, and they were most visible in the work of that great diagnostician of the Viennese soul Arthur Schnitzler – another Jewish doctor. In a novella named after its protagonist, Schnitzler's anti-hero Lieutenant Gustl spends a sleepless night in anguish anticipating a senseless duel he is about to fight to guard his honour because of a trivial misunderstanding. In another stream-of-consciousness novella a young woman, Miss Else, is struggling with her bankrupt father's demand that she sleep with a creditor. 'They send you to school and see that you learn French and the piano and you spend the summers in the country,' she reflects about her upbringing. 'But what's happening inside me, what is tormented and frightened inside me, have they ever been interested in that?' They had not. In the context of good society the very question was heretical.

Schnitzler, who knew and admired Freud and was in turn admired by him, made it his life's work to show these repressed and bewildered people on the page and on stage acting out their neuroses like electrons spinning around an empty core, unable to control their trajectory, propelled by unseen forces and often uncertain whether they are awake or dreaming. Any attempt to escape the rigidity of convention is immediately attacked.

In *Ruf des Lebens* (The Call of Life, 1906) a young woman, Marie, tries to let fresh air into the small drawing room, only to be reprimanded by her father who sees soldiers riding past.

FATHER: What are you doing? Are you mad? I could catch my death!

MARIE: The air is hot; and the doctor always says how stifling it is in here.

FATHER: Stifling! That's why you suddenly throw open the windows? Stifling! Do you think I don't know what you really want? There. Yes, there they are riding, proud, young, healthy...healthy and young today!...Ho! We have our flat in the middle of the city – a look around the corner – and life passes you by!

Appearances could not be trusted in a social world in which the windows of the soul had to stay firmly shut to keep out temptation. Repressed impulses will out, was one of Freud's central claims, and if they cannot articulate themselves directly they will find another way. Everything that is said, imagined, or done, will be coloured by these unacknowledged central impulses.

The conclusion to draw from this claim was that words and gestures always stood for something hidden, that there was a meaning other than what was being said, and that all action must ultimately be paralysed by internal conflict, as it famously was in Musil's *Man Without Qualities* in which the 'great patriotic action', the celebration of an imperial anniversary, becomes mired in interminable deliberations, consultations and committees. The ironist Musil was endlessly diverted by his countrymen's capacity for procrastination and dissimulation. Other writers found it more difficult to deal with the unreliability of the very words they used. The writer Hugo von Hofmannsthal, Vienna's young poetic star, was so tormented by this distrust of language that he gave up writing poems. 'Briefly, my case is as follows,' he had one of his characters say in his *Chandos-Brief* (Letter from Lord Chandos, 1902), 'I have entirely lost the ability to think or speak about anything in a coherent way.' Language had turned against the poet. 'Terms suddenly adopted such a kaleidoscopic colouring and flowed into one another' that Hofmannsthal's hero found solace only once he was alone, and silent.

Language could not be relied upon to express truth, as Freud had proved and Hofmannsthal had felt. The multilingual philosopher Fritz Mauthner (1849–1923) knew about the impossibilities of literal translation between languages and became fundamentally suspicious of what could and could not be said with words. Mauthner analysed the ability of language to transport definite meaning, after having noticed that concepts and their connotations were subtly different in every language he would use. Experience is unique and immediate, and the very moment it receives a name it loses these crucial qualities, Mauthner contended, and in his *Beiträge zu einer Kritik der Sprache* (Contributions to a Critique of Language, 1901–3) it took him three hefty volumes to explain that language was unable to convey thought content – one of the more paradoxical achievements of Western philosophy.

Mauthner's philosophical project culminated in an all-embracing but godless mysticism. Ernst Mach (1838–1916) took the opposite direction. A distinguished scientist and professor of experimental physics at Prague's German university, Mach dissected not only language, but also experience and personality. In the final analysis, he recognized nothing but a constant stream of physiological sensations; everything else was just a mass of baseless suppositions, a gigantic shoal of philosophical red herrings. Sensations were everything: 'As soon as we have perceived that the supposed unities "body" and "ego" are only makeshifts, designed for provisional orientation and for definite practical ends (so that we may take hold of bodies, protect ourselves against pain, and so forth), we find ourselves obliged, in many more advanced scientific investigations, to abandon them as insufficient and inappropriate.'

Abandoning the fiction of immutable selfhood (also a philosophical metaphor of the vacuum at the heart of the Austro-Hungarian state) had dramatic consequences, Mach argued: 'The ego must be given up. It is partly the perception of this fact, partly the fear of it, that has given rise to the many extravagances of pessimism and optimism, and to numerous religious, ascetic, and philosophical absurdities. In the long run we shall not be able to close our eyes to this simple truth, which is the immediate outcome of psychological analysis.' There was nothing but physiology, everything else was make-believe, no truth out there, no hidden reality, and certainly no creator. Man was nothing but a mass of highly unstable perceptions creating the impression of personality, a thesis that was taken up and popularized by the Austrian writer Hermann Bahr in his famous essay *Das unrettbare Ich* (The Irretrievable Self, 1907).

If language was not necessarily on the speaker's side and outside influences intruded upon the fiction of the self, then the language of music was bound to be affected. Viennese composers were at the forefront of the cultural investigation of perception, of the unreliability of language, and its underlying rules. Building on the sound world imagined by his fellow student Hans Rott (who had died, aged twenty-six, in 1884), the young

Gustav Mahler (1860–1911) created his First Symphony (1888) which, with a single *unisono* tone played by the strings and interrupted by bird calls that finally bring movement into the immobile sound, created the perfect image of a mind stirred by external impulses. Later in the piece, other gleanings from the outside world create dramatic musical conflicts: a military march (as a boy, Mahler had lived next to a military drill ground), a dance tune, nature sounds – the world mirrored as an impressionistic interior space. In his later symphonies Mahler would use the childlike simplicity of folksong texts to escape the complications and contradictions of analysis.

Mahler dramatized the conflict between direct experience and conventional (symphonic) form. Composers such as Arnold Schönberg (1874–1951) and his friends and pupils Alban Berg and Anton Webern went a step further. Like Mauthner, they investigated the structure and function of their language – music – by attempting to reduce it to its most elemental form: the series of twelve semitones making up a full octave. Rather than the romantic, richly ornamented self of the classical tradition, they trusted the unassailable truth of structures based on the simplest form possible. All of them were gifted composers in the late romantic style, but they turned away from the sweltering sweetness of Wagnerian chromaticism and towards a method of composing that offered mathematical rigour – though not always emotional satisfaction. If the self was little more than a linguistic trick, then artistic creation was best based on the solidity of rational structure.

At play: Gustav Mahler relaxing during the summer holidays.

Philosophical scepticism about language, reality, and the ability of words to communicate effectively was most famously carried to its conceptual extremes by Ludwig Wittgenstein (1889–1951), who had been educated at his father's home in close proximity to the country's artistic and intellectual elite, and who had chosen to further his studies in the congenially positivist environment of Cambridge, where Bertrand Russell and G. E. Moore were then the ruling gods of analytical philosophy. A searching spirit with the mental drive of a medieval martyr, Wittgenstein retreated to a Norwegian fjord to find the peace that allowed him to formulate, in 1913, the central thoughts of what was to become one of the century's most influential works of philosophy, the *Tractatus Logico-Philosophicus* (published 1921), in which he set out to delineate in sentences of almost mathematical rigour the extent to which language can serve as an instrument of meaningful communication.

In this environment, with its heightened attention to how things could and should be said, style and literary elegance had their very own literary guardian angel, the irascible publicist Karl Kraus (1874–1936), whose work effectively consisted of a compilation of malicious commentaries on other people's writings. 'People still think that human content can be excellent despite bad style and that one's moral disposition could be established independently of it,' wrote Kraus, 'but I hold ... that nothing is more necessary than to remainder these people like so many bad books. Alternatively, a parliament should be convened for language, and hand out rewards, as now for killed snakes, for every cliché killed.'

Nothing was more apt to make Kraus despair than stylistic carelessness, bad metaphors and empty phrases, and it is an eloquent testament to the intellectual climate of his day that a man who today might send a stream of irate reader's letters to newspaper editors had his very own journal, *Die Fackel* (The Torch), which he wrote entirely on his own. While other countries, notably the United States, built on a robust, quasi-religious trust in words and the truth behind them – the very principle of advertising which was then beginning its reign on billboards across the American continent – thinkers in the multilingual Dual Monarchy were all but paralysed by their scepticism towards the very words they used. On the other hand, this struggle with truth gave the search for it an almost spiritual importance.

The Ethics of Style

Style was a matter of moral honesty for a young generation of artists openly rebelling against inherited ways of representation. 'Life is changing,' the critic Hermann Bahr (1863–1934) wrote, 'but the spirit remained old and immobile and did not stir and did not move and now it is suffering helplessly, because it is lonely and deserted by life ... The past is great, often beautiful. We will hold solemn funeral orations for it.'

The architect Adolf Loos (1870–1933), had worked for some years in the Chicago office of Louis Sullivan, the creator of some of the world's first skyscrapers, such as the Guaranty Building in Buffalo (1895), whose strictly functionalist aesthetic set new standards for its time. The young Viennese architect was a fervent admirer of both the sceptical, Anglo-Saxon spirit and the can-do attitude he had found in the United States – a glaring contrast to the endemic inertia of Habsburg Vienna. Talented and ambitious, Loos was burning to make his mark and to bring the gospel of aesthetic purity right into the heart of the capital. He worked hard to become noticed and to acquire a reputation as a modernizer; his efforts were finally rewarded with a commission to build a bank in a uniquely privileged location in the very heart of the city, directly opposite the imperial palace's Michaelertor in all its nineteenth-century splendour of columns, Hercules statues, ornamental vases and neo-baroque putti. He knew that his chance had come.

When the scaffolding came off the new Goldman and Salatsch building in 1910 and the public could for the first time lay eyes on it, there was an outcry in the press and the city council ordered the building stopped. Right in the Highest Presence of His Majesty across the square, this was a house of almost aggressive functionality, a building with no ornament, no façade.

Imperial affront: Adolf Loos's 'House without Eyebrows'
opposite the Hofburg palace.

No nude, muscular heroes supported window frames, no winged toddlers, nymphs or flower arrangements beautified what might otherwise look offensively stark. Instead, there were straight, green marble columns at the entry and above them nothing – nothing but rows of square windows. The staggering lack of respect for the feelings of the imperial family appeared particularly shocking, Archduke Franz Ferdinand vowed never again to use the Michaelerplatz entrance to the Hofburg and the Emperor himself decreed that all curtains must be shut whenever he spent time in a room with a view of the offending building.

The architect himself was not afraid to shock and throw down the gauntlet to the old guard by confronting it directly with his ideas. Art and architecture, he believed, must emancipate themselves from the tyranny of bad taste and the inherent hypocrisy of middle-class aesthetics:

> The better someone can imitate, the more the public loves him. The reverence for expensive materials, the most certain sign for the parvenu status of our people, dictates this fact... During the last decades, imitation has dominated all our buildings. The wallpaper is made of paper, but must under no circumstances show it. It had to be printed with silk damask, gobelins, or carpet patterns. The doors and windows are made of soft wood. But as hard woods are more expensive, they have to be painted as such. Iron had to imitate precious metal with the help of bronze or copper paints. Concrete, a material of our own century, was regarded with utter helplessness. But what a splendid material it is in itself...

Stuck in a world of wordless lies, of imitation this and *faux* that, architecture and design, Loos argued, had to rediscover the honesty of form. 'This furniture lacks all style,' he had written approvingly about avant-garde chairs at a fair in 1898, 'they are neither Egyptian nor Greek, neither Romanesque nor Gothic, neither Renaissance nor Baroque. Everyone can see immediately: these are pieces of furniture from 1898. It is a style that will not last. After it, the style of 1899 will have its day, and will be entirely different.' Dishonesty and decoration were two sides of the same fake coin: ornament, Loos wrote, is crime.

> I have made the following discovery and have given it to humankind: evolution of culture is equivalent to the removal of ornaments from items of use... As ornament (a remnant of a previous, animistic culture) no longer has an organic connection with our culture, it is no longer the expression of our culture. Ornaments which are made today have no

connection with us ourselves, no connection with the order of the world. It is stuck in the past.

This was more than an artistic position; it was a political point. If Loos was the most spectacular among the architectural rebels (his building on the Michaelerplatz could only be completed in 1912 because he agreed to the installation of window boxes), the most astonishing story is probably the conversion of Otto Wagner (1841–1918), successor to the high priests of the historicist Vienna Ringstrasse architecture and one of the most important and most prolifically creative of architects in Austria-Hungary. No architect in the world had created grander and more beautiful historicist fata morganas than Wagner. In his plans for a complete restructuring of Vienna (which were never realized), visions look like Piranesi sanitized, with their lofty vaults and grand ideas, their noble columns shining in white marble, veritable masterpieces of historicist art. After this epic and highly successful spree of gorging himself on the beauty of the past came what Wagner described as his 'artistic hangover' – a result of aesthetic overeating.

Wagner was already approaching sixty, an age at which most of his colleagues thought of retiring, when he changed his own style and so, too, the course of architectural history. He had redesigned Vienna's transport system and had already proved that the needs of a modern city and elegant functional design can be triumphantly united: his Metro stations and his two Danube bridges still stand as monuments to his art, as do several blocks of apartments throughout the Habsburg capital. He had established himself as the most intelligent, most masterful, most sumptuous realizer of the backward-looking utopias of the *grande bourgeoisie*, the class into which he had been born. In his elegant flats in which no detail had been left to chance, in his neo-Renaissance splendour, every professor and banker could feel himself a Medici.

Wagner had always thought and written about form and function, about the fact that 'nothing impractical can be beautiful' and that only a profound understanding of the purpose of each architectural element could create works of true beauty. Whereas Adolf Loos had refused all ornamentation and had effectively torn down the façade of his own buildings, Wagner went a step further by revealing the aesthetic grace of well-designed constructive elements.

Entering his Postsparkasse, the Postal Savings Bank, in Vienna's central district (1903/4), it is impossible not to be exhilarated by the purity of the sweeping forms, the arched glass roof of the hall, the sense of light and austere beauty, punctuated aluminium ducts looking like pieces of abstract sculpture. Wagner's was not a sheer functionalism, as was Loos's and later that of Le Corbusier and his followers, but a more modulated symbolic union of beauty and utility which never privileged one above the other. Spaces such as this one were positions defined and occupied in the battle for the aesthetic soul of the twentieth century city. Loos believed that the stakes were high, that a civilization's morality was at stake, and many of his colleagues agreed.

No art form is more public than architecture, and none more political: one can choose not to read a book, not to enter a gallery, but it is much more difficult to avoid seeing certain buildings or parts of a city, and as the aesthetic and generational conflict between historicism and early modernity progressed it left visible traces in cities all over the world, beacons of a different way of thinking about beauty, and about human nature. In the United States, a great inspiration for innovative spirits such as Loos, new cities unencumbered by tradition, combined with the new possibilities created by building materials such as improved steel and reinforced concrete and by the perfection of the elevator, had already given birth to a new kind of structure: the skyscraper. Europe followed suit with steel-frame structures such as the Royal Liver Building in Liverpool in 1911. The modernist aesthetic asserted itself powerfully around 1910. In 1909 the architect Peter Behrens built a turbine hall for Germany's burgeoning manufacturer AEG (Allgemeine Elektrizitäts-Gesellschaft) that was also a monument to the functional design heralded by mass production, and the administrative block of the Fagus works near Hanover in Germany (1914) designed by young Walter Gropius is a building whose functionalist austerity would prove truly prophetic.

Fourteen years after the historicist orgy of the 1900 World Fair a new

Built for a new World: the AEG turbine hall in Berlin by Peter Behrens.

Hardliner: The Fagus works by Walter Gropius give no quarter to historicism.

aesthetic had arrived. Such extremes of artistic purity were not the only way forward, though, and in all art forms the development of the arts was less a question of progression than of branching out: composers such as Sibelius, Elgar, Puccini and Max Reger worked at the same time as the more obviously adventurous Schönberg and Debussy; outstanding 'conventional' painters such as Max Beckmann or Ilya Repin were active alongside rebels such as Malevich and Kandinsky. In architecture the range spread – geographically as well as artistically – from masters of organic forms like Antonio Gaudí and Josep Maria Jujol i Gibert in Barcelona to modern interpretations of traditional forms by Fedor Shekhtel and Vladimir and Georgii Kosiakov in St Petersburg and Moscow.

In Vienna architecture and painting made common cause in their fight for a synthesis of form and function. Joseph Maria Olbrich's 1898 temple-like building for the Secession artists' group proclaimed this partnership. A stone's throw away from the august neo-Renaissance Academy of Arts and its professors (who might have altered the future course of history by admitting the young Adolf Hitler: he applied there unsuccessfully in 1907), it was a statement of open rebellion against the artistic establishment.

One of the founding members of the Secession group was the painter Gustav Klimt (1862–1918), who had himself undergone an artistic conversion similar to Wagner's. Every age needs its scandalous genius, and with his long tunics, his succession of liaisons and his at times copiously explicit painterly eroticism, Klimt was the apostle of a freer life. Whether genuine eccentricity or clever ruse, the master was allowed his foibles and drew innumerable admirers as well as huge prices for his works. Like Wagner, Klimt emphasized the symbolic nature of his works, and his symbolism was dangerously suggestive. *Nuda veritas*, Naked Truth, was the motto of the group he had helped to found, and whose periodical publication *Ver Sacrum* emphasized their belief in artistic truth over academic convention. The Secession's truth was sensual and subversive, undermining Vienna's perfect social façade with its seductive appeal. Klimt's mythological portraits (some of which bear the features of women from 'good' society) abandoned the turn-of-the-century decorum that so safely enveloped bodies in unnatural forms and acres of choice fabric. The defiant lasciviousness staring from these canvases was no longer content to bathe demurely in the pool of legend, but was determined to explore hidden depths that good manners thought it prudent to deny. The nymphs of academic art had been created to titillate from a safe distance; these new goddesses confronted the viewer with his own desires and, more shockingly, with those of the women portrayed.

Bourgeoise goddess: Gustav Klimt's seductive Judith.

The Secession's claim to truth also expressed itself in a paradox. A depiction using all the illusionist skills of academic painting could end up lying to the spectator by creating an impression which, for all its realism, was false, much like the elaborate façade of a building. The Secessionists no longer trusted naturalism as the best way of depicting inner worlds. If they wanted to penetrate the inner truth (the very core of desires and experiences, they believed) they had to stylize their objects and use the flat space of mythology, showing archetypes and harking back to a past free of the stranglehold of Christian and bourgeois morality. In Klimt's poster for a group exhibition, this programme is clearly expressed. Theseus and the Minotaur, Pallas Athena with the head of the Medusa on her shield – the male and the female principle were there in their noblest and most terrible incarnations, and stylized to reconnect them with the iconic world of Greek vase painting. His most striking coup, though, and a provocation to all

Sex and the void at the heart of the matter: Klimt's Secession poster.

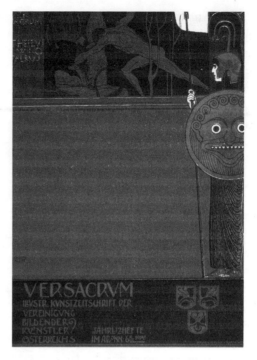

academicians and all members of the middle classes with their salons crammed to the rafters with knick-knacks and ornaments, was that the central portion of the space was simply left blank, a challenging void which, in the context of the mythological male and female, raised as many troubling questions as any of Freud's books – a void that also echoed the emptiness at the heart of Austria-Hungary.

If Klimt knew how to provoke from the safety of society's firm embrace, his young friend Egon Schiele (1890–1918) went even further in his explorations (see plate section). There was no titillation in Schiele's existentialist explicitness, no inviting curves to appeal to gentlemen of a certain age. His were angular, breathing creatures, lonely at the very moment of embrace, bereft of the protection of mythology Klimt had afforded his figures, and exposed to a vivisector's pitiless eye. Everything that had been taboo, unspeakable and unshowable – sex, voyeurism, masturbation – everything that was practised in secret but denied in public, was exposed by Schiele with sparse brush strokes, and exhibited for all to see. His angular figures looked into the world with eyes wide open, shining with fear or alive with defiance, or deep loneliness; their hands are either iconic claws or missing altogether, and even when touching someone they are little more than dead branches of an emaciated trunk. These hands do not give the warmth of human closeness, they do not grasp the world. Like the philosophers doubtful about the ability of language to communicate, to form a handle on the world, Schiele did not allow his figures to be in touch with one another.

In Schiele's works, the very last façades were ripped away, the last safe places of the soul destroyed. What the young genius (who died at the age of twenty-eight during the 1918 influenza epidemic, three days after his wife) formulated instead was a world not of despair, but of strange, stark beauty.

Schiele's art resonated with the sensualism that is a constant motif in Viennese culture, and with the desire of a younger generation to return to the bare bones of life and to construct everything anew from the first principles. A painter and dramatist, Oskar Kokoschka worked along similar lines, as did another young artist, Richard Gerstl, who would later commit suicide out of despair over his love for Arnold Schönberg's wife Mathilde, who chose to stay with her husband after a brief but passionate affair with the painter.

By 1902, Sigmund Freud had been waiting for a professorship for years. In view of his seniority in the profession (to say nothing of his brilliance as an innovator) it was long overdue, and when it finally came he greeted the news with sarcasm: 'Popular enthusiasm is huge. Flowers and congratulations are raining down on me, as if the role of sexuality had suddenly been recognized by His Majesty, the significance of dreams ratified by the council of ministers and the importance of the treatment of hysteria had received a two-thirds majority in parliament.'

Freud was particularly bitter about the fact that the appointment had not come through merit, but through influence, that very Habsburgian network between the privileged few which he had always despised. He had gained his promotion only because one of his upper-class patients had promised to donate a valuable painting to a public gallery, the pet project of the then minister of education. Had his patient possessed an even more sought-after work, Freud mused, he might have been called to a full chair at the university, after all. He was well aware of the petty provincialism that had disadvantaged him for long, and he always expressed great ambivalence towards Vienna and the Viennese. He had based his theory of the subconscious on the most recent international research, had travelled widely and comprehensively devoured scientific literature before he formulated his ideas. Despite all this (and this is true for all great leaps of science) his thought was a creature of its environment, of its time.

Every Habsburg subject was an Oedipus to the crushing father figure of the Emperor; every stroll through the city and every visit to the theatre reinforced the notion of the dangerous dichotomy between façade and structure, between external and internal life. In this world, every civil servant with sideburns as big as the Emperor's was an example of feelings sublimated; every flirtatious 'sweet girl' in a hat shop a sign that these feelings still *wanted out*. Nowhere else had Jewish culture, the Talmudic tradition of respect for the word and of close textual analysis gained such an important place in the thought of a society. Nowhere else was there quite so pervasive a smell of decay in the air, a smell that sharpened the senses and stimulated analyses into the subject's cause of death.

The naked truth was staring Viennese society in the face, and Viennese society did not like it. The intelligentsia admired and enjoyed avant-garde works (though performances of Schönberg pieces were liable to produce riots), but most of the capital's good burghers held with Crown Prince Franz Ferdinand, who, after visiting an exhibition by Secession artists, went on record as saying: 'Those rascals should have every bone in their body broken.' The Dual Monarchy, wrote Karl Kraus, was 'an experimental station for the apocalypse', and there can be nothing more sumptuously gorgeous and rich in colour than the sky during the Twilight of the Gods.

4

1903:
A Strange Luminescence

Few New Yorkers realize that all through the roar of the big city there are constantly speeding messages between people separated by vast distances, and that over housetops and even through the walls of buildings and in the very air one breathes are words written by electricity. — *New York Times*, 21 April 1912

When Maria Skłodowska (1867–1934), Manya to her friends, had come to Paris from Poland in 1891 to study she was already used to swimming against the stream, or rather, to having the stream flow against her. Born in Warsaw in 1867, she grew up in a country and a family marked by a history of occupation and revolt. Her grandfather, a patriot and a republican, had supported the 1864 uprising against Tsarist rule and had seen his career all but broken as a consequence by the brutal Russian reprisals which had culminated in the hanging of the leaders of the rebellion from the Alexander Citadel. Their bodies were left out for months, exposed to the elements, rotting and eaten by ravens, a gruesome reminder to the Poles that their Tsar was determined to crush any opposition. Manya's father, Władysław Skłodowski, was an ardent republican and atheist whose convictions resulted in a career thwarted by Russian officials who allotted him more and more humiliating, difficult and badly paid teaching jobs so that finally he found it almost impossible to support his family of four children and a wife whose tuberculosis made it necessary for her to go abroad for lengthy and expensive cures. She died in 1877, when Manya was ten. The children had known little affection from their mother. Even when she was with them, she would not touch them and would eat from separate crockery for fear of infecting them with the deadly virus.

Manya determined early that she would become a scientist, and that she would go to Paris to study there. Unable to afford the journey or her upkeep there, she made a pact with her older sister: she would work as a governess to enable her sister to study if her sister would then take her in when it was time for her to enter university herself. During these years in the provinces she already showed the determination and independence that were to be characteristic in her life: next to her official duties, she taught Polish peasant children to read and write in their mother tongue. According to Russian law this was treason, punishable with years of exile. In 1891, Manya Skłodowska boarded a train, armed with clothes, a feather mattress, food and water, and a stool for the long voyage. She was twenty-four years old. Two days later she arrived at the Paris Gare du Nord station, where she was met by her sister. Here Manya, who now called herself Marie, would be free from political oppression, here she would be able to realize her dream and study, do research. Here her life would be transformed, and here she would become world-famous as a pioneering scientist together with her husband, the physicist Pierre Curie (1859–1906). Maria Skłodowska was on her way to becoming Marie Curie.

All this has become part of the Curie legend, as have the events that followed: the years of patient study holed up in an unheated garret in the Quartier Latin (her sister's flat, she found, offered too many distractions),

Marriage of minds: Pierre and Marie Curie.

her practising for a perfect French accent and her meeting with the brilliant and completely unworldly scientist Pierre Curie, their love and their marriage, their extraordinary collaboration. Having investigated questions of magnetism, Marie Curie, as she was now, had an extraordinary intuition for scientific research. In 1897 she attended a meeting of scientists at the *Académie des Sciences* during which the physicist Henri Becquerel informed his colleagues about an interesting and unexplained phenomenon, a by-product of his research into the most fashionable phenomenon of the period, X-rays. While investigating a possible connection between the mysterious invisible rays and different luminescent materials he had noted that uranium appeared to emit a kind of radiation that was unlike X-rays and appeared to be a property of the material itself. The assembly listened and then passed to other business, consisting mainly of papers about X-rays, their nature and their possible applications.

Becquerel's observation excited Marie Curie's curiosity and she decided to investigate this phenomenon, a choice that condemned her to obscurity, for scientific interest, research grants and career opportunities lay elsewhere. X-rays were the hot topic of the day in *fin-de-siècle* Europe.

Two years earlier a mysterious discovery had been made by the German physicist Conrad Wilhelm Röntgen (1845–1923). Working on a cathode tube – a vacuum tube highly charged with electricity on the inside – Röntgen noticed that a plate coated with barium platinocyanide, used to detect ultraviolet light, began to fluoresce if placed in the path of the discharge of rays, which was itself invisible. During subsequent experiments he found out that the invisible rays would shade photographic plates and that objects interposed between cathode and plate would leave an imprint on the plate, showing denser tissues more clearly than softer ones. The dramatic effect was seen most clearly when Röntgen asked his wife to hold her hand in front of the screen. Once developed, her hand was clearly visible – her flesh a faint outline surrounding the bones and the wedding band seemingly afloat on the skeletal ring finger. The researcher had stumbled on a means of penetrating the deepest secrets of the human body without so much as cutting the skin.

Röntgen knew that he had made an extraordinary discovery, but he was cautious about publicizing it. He sent some copies of the photo to other researchers, one of whom leaked the image to the press. When the London *Standard* published the photograph on 24 January 1896, the effect was immediate and extraordinary. X-rays became a medical craze, a fashion, a miraculous panacea for all ills. Röntgen had refused to patent his invention, and X-ray machines were rapidly copied and used. It took only a year for

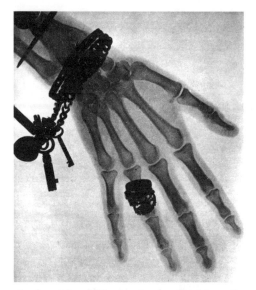

In the midst of life: the ghostly apparition of a hand under the X-ray machine.

more than thirty different designs of machine to be put on the market and employed for diagnosis, fighting infections and cancer, killing bacteria; one scientist even proposed that the invisible light might be used for 'bleaching Ethiopians' and grant Africans the light skin of their European colonial masters.

There was another, more sinister aspect to the new rays, however. In making every living body appear skeletal, they became a technological *memento mori*, a high-tech injunction whispering through the dark: *Remember you will die.* The act of stepping into one of these quasi-mystical contraptions and being subjected to the procedure with its accompanying startling noises became a surreal moment of truth for many patients. The doctor became a magus officiating in a ceremony between life and death, as described in the examination of Hans Castorp who, in Thomas Mann's novel *Der Zauberberg*, enters the 'transillumination cabinet' of the lung sanatorium to visit Joachim, his cousin:

> It smelled peculiar here. A kind of stale ozone filled the atmosphere. A separation between the blackened windows divided the laboratory into two unequal halves. One could distinguish physical apparatuses, glasses, control boards, measuring instruments standing erect, but also a camera-like case on wheels, photographic plates made of glass which covered the walls in rows – impossible to know whether this was a photographer's atelier, a dark room, or the workroom of an inventor and technical wizard ...
>
> Hans Castorp saw limbs: hands, feet, knee caps, femurs and shin bones, arms and parts of the basin. But the rounded form of life of these fragments of a human body was only ghostly and vaporous; like a mist and bleak glow it tentatively surrounded its core which appeared clearly and in exact detail: the skeleton. ...
>
> At this moment, the assistant threw the switch on the controls. For

two seconds, terrifying forces were at play, necessary to penetrate matter, streams of thousands of volts, of hundreds of thousands, as Hans Castorp seemed to recall. Barely tamed for the purpose, the powers were looking for alternative ways to regain their freedom. Discharges rang out like shots. Blue crackling surrounded the measuring apparatus. Extended lightning ran along the walls. A red light was looking on from some where like an eye, silent and menacing...Then everything fell quiet again; the light phenomena vanished and Joachim heaved a sigh of relief. It was over.

This was science bordering on the miraculous, a revelation in both the analytical and the religious sense, and while the hidden power of X-rays held the general public in its thrall, it also fascinated scientists: during the years leading up to 1900, fully 60 per cent of papers given at the Paris *Académie des Sciences* were devoted to the subject. Henri Becquerel decided to investigate one possible connection with known qualities of matter. During the production of X-rays, the vacuum tubes emitted a faint light similar to the phosphorescence of certain substances which would glow in the dark if exposed to light before. An able scientist and a pillar of the French scientific establishment, Becquerel was ideally placed for this research: like his father and his grandfather before him, he was director of the Paris Museum of Natural History and had a vast number of natural samples at his disposal. To see whether these phosphorescent substances also emitted X-rays Becquerel first exposed them to light and then put them on top of a photographic plate to see whether they would create a radiation shadow.

Using phosphorescent uranium salts, Becquerel had already set up his experiment when bad weather forced him to interrupt his research. He decided simply to wrap up the salts in their container and the photographic plate in black cloth to avoid any exposure of the plate and wait until sufficient sunlight was available. When he took out the bundle again he found to his surprise that the photographic plate had been exposed without light. Uranium appeared to emit a radiation unknown to science. Becquerel found his discovery interesting, but not significant enough to distract him from his research into the rays discovered by Röntgen.

Marie Curie, then a doctoral student in search of a project who was earning a modest living by teaching at a vocational training college for women, had listened to Becquerel with great interest. The unknown form of radiation appeared important to her, and she decided to take up the challenge. On top of her obligations as a teacher and despite having given birth to a baby girl whose care devolved largely on her herself, she found the time to enter into perhaps the most laborious and back-breaking process of individual scientific discovery the century had seen.

Curie worked under terrible conditions, as she later remembered herself:

> The School of Physics could give us no suitable premises, but for lack of anything better, the Director permitted us to use an abandoned shed which had been in service as a dissecting room of the School of Medicine. Its glass roof did not afford complete shelter against rain; the heat was suffocating in summer, and the bitter cold of winter was only a little lessened by the iron stove, except in its immediate vicinity. There was no question of obtaining the needed proper apparatus in common use by chemists. We simply had some old pine-wood tables with furnaces and gas burners. We had to use the adjoining yard for those of our chemical operations that involved producing irritating gases; even then the gas often filled our shed. With this equipment we entered on our exhausting work.
>
> [...] One of our joys was to go into our workroom at night; we then perceived on all sides the feebly luminous silhouettes of the bottles or capsules containing our products. It was really a lovely sight and one always new to us. The glowing tubes looked like faint, fairy lights.

To find out more about the mysterious radiation it was necessary to find which substances emitted it and to purify these substances, which appeared in nature only in conjunction with other elements, particularly as salts or metallic compounds. Becquerel had already discovered that air exposed to 'uranium rays' could conduct electricity. Using a complicated instrument developed by her husband for measuring very weak currents, Marie could therefore prove the presence of radiation by determining the degree to which the air in her laboratory had become able to transport an electric current.

Curie investigated all known elements and made two crucial discoveries: in addition to uranium, thorium, too, appeared to give off radiation; moreover, despite their very different chemical properties different compounds containing the two elements showed the same amount of radiation. Curie concluded that it was not the molecular structure of a radioactive substance that determined the strength of the radiation, but the amount of uranium or thorium contained in it. In other words: as uranium and thorium are specific atoms, part of the periodical table, the radiation had to be a property of the atom itself and not of the molecular structure. This was a revolutionary discovery: if atoms, until then considered the smallest possible unit of all matter, could give off rays, their structure had to be more complex than previously realized.

Of all natural radioactive substances tested, pitchblende, a uranium-rich mineral found mainly in Joachimsthal (today's Jáchymov in the Czech Republic), appeared to be the most likely candidate for further research, especially because it had a puzzling quality: it was more radioactive than pure uranium itself, an indication that it contained other, hitherto unknown, elements. Together with her husband Pierre, who abandoned his own research to work together with his wife, Marie now set out to procure large amounts of pitchblende (a generous though not disinterested donation of the ore from the Austro-Hungarian Academy of Sciences was a great help) and to break them down into their individual elements by grinding them, dissolving them in acid and crystallizing different compounds, again and again. One of these compounds stood out, and in 1898 the Curies felt confident enough to present their research claiming that 'we thus believe that the substance that we have extracted from pitchblende contains a metal never known before, akin to bismuth in its analytic properties. If the existence of this new metal is confirmed, we suggest that it should be called *polonium* after the name of the country of origin of one of us.' Later in the same year they published a second finding: barium compounds, they wrote, contained another, even more highly radioactive new element, which they named radium.

The Nobel Prize

The doctoral thesis by the young scientist Marie Curie outlining the discovery of a new element with unknown qualities caused a sensation in scientific circles. The members of the *Académie des Sciences* in Paris thought such brilliance was worth a Nobel Prize, but not to the young woman. They recommended Pierre Curie and Henri Becquerel for a joint award, and the Swedish Academy consented. Monsieur Curie was duly notified by mail – and refused to accept the award. He was honoured to be proposed, he replied to the Prize-givers, but the most important contribution was his wife's and he could not be so distinguished without her. After some hurried negotiations, the committee agreed and Pierre was allowed to share his part of the Prize with his wife, who became joint laureate in the 1903 Nobel Prize for Physics for the discovery of radium.

Marie was so much dogged by ill health that she could not travel to Stockholm for the awards ceremony, and once again her husband showed himself loyal. Two years later, in 1905, they made the journey together to accept the prize. In his acceptance speech, Pierre outlined the hopes and the fears connected with the new element:

... radium could become very dangerous in criminal hands, and here the question can be raised whether mankind benefits from knowing the secrets of Nature, whether it is ready to profit from it or whether this knowledge will not be harmful for it. The example of the discoveries of Nobel is characteristic, as powerful explosives have enabled man to do wonderful work. They are also a terrible means of destruction in the hands of great criminals who are leading the peoples towards war. I am one of those who believe with Nobel that mankind will derive more good than harm from the new discoveries.

The Nobel Prize brought international fame to the Curies and also finally allowed them to work under better conditions after Pierre was appointed to a professorship, which included his own laboratory, at the Sorbonne. Sudden fame also had its unwelcome aspects. The media were interested in the couple, in the discovery, in the extraordinary woman who had beaten the men at their game through sheer intelligence and almost superhuman perseverance. There were dinners and ceremonies, interviews, visiting journalists – all of them annoying distractions from research. With its seemingly miraculous qualities, radium had captured the public's imagination.

The Curies were happiest away from this circus, immersed in their research. Pierre even strapped a glass with uranium salts to his right arm to observe the effects and found that they produced a burn leaving a grey scar that would not heal even after six weeks; he also liked to carry around a small amount of uranium in his waistcoat pocket to illustrate its phosphorescent properties to friends. Without knowing it, the Curies were inexorably poisoning themselves with massive doses of radioactivity.

When catastrophe struck for one of science's greatest teams, however, radiation played a part only in so far as it had exhausted Pierre Curie. In 1906, on Maundy Thursday, he crossed a busy road. It was raining and his umbrella prevented him from seeing a military supply wagon coming towards him. He walked right into the horses and was thrown to the ground. One of the vehicle's rear wheels crushed his skull. A few days after his funeral, his distraught wife wrote in her notebook: 'My Pierre, I am constantly thinking of you. My head burns like fire and I feel I am losing my mind. I cannot understand how it can be that I have to live without seeing you, without smiling at the dear companion of my life.' Marie did live on, constantly pursuing her research, despite years of ill health and a wave of hostility directed against her by the French conservative press. She went on to be awarded a second Nobel Prize in 1911 for her research into radioactivity. Her death in 1934 was caused by radiation-induced leukaemia.

The Dissolution of Certainty

Science is a good place for outsiders. An unusual vantage point sometimes allows one to see things other people cannot see. Marie Curie had fought her way from her native Poland into the heart of the French scientific establishment. Another scientist of genius had begun his life on a New Zealand potato farm. A precocious boy and gifted researcher, he had studied in Christchurch and applied for a scholarship at Cambridge. Legend has it that he was out in the fields harvesting when news of his successful application came. He straightened himself and said: 'That's the last potato I've ever dug.'

Ernest Rutherford (1871–1937) investigated the phenomenon of radiation in order to understand the nature of matter itself, the structure of the atom. In experiments conducted together with the young Danish scientist Niels Bohr (1885–1962), Rutherford had observed that an ultra-thin gold foil exposed to radiation would allow most of the alpha rays (one of three kinds of radiation emitted by radioactive substances) to pass through, while a small number of alpha particles appeared to bounce off the surface of the foil. Only one explanation was possible, Rutherford thought, namely that atoms were not what they had been thought to be. Until then, atoms had, to use his own image, been imagined like plum puddings: solid and homogenous, with a few electrons scattered inside like sixpences and sultanas. No such atom, however, would let the relatively weak alpha rays pass through. This would be possible only if an atom actually was mostly empty space, more like a solar system than a plum pudding, its entire mass compressed in a sunlike core ten thousand times smaller than the orbit of the electrons circling around it and defining the volume of the atom. Matter, it turned out, was neither solid nor still, and was, at least in part, a state of energy, constantly in movement. There was, in fact, nothing stationary in the world at all – at an atomic level, everything was velocity and energy, constellations of myriads of particles swirling and hurtling through empty space, bombarding and interfering with one another, and possessed of limitless energy and electric charge.

The relationship between matter and energy, or the convergence of the two, was also the subject of the after-hours work of another scientific outsider, an 'Expert 3rd Class' at the Swiss Office for Intellectual Property in Berne, 26-year-old Albert Einstein (1879–1955). From the perspective of a theoretician, he formulated a view of the world that reinforced the findings of the likes of Röntgen, Rutherford and the Curies. His doubts, however, did not concern a mere trifle like the composition of matter, but rather, the nature of time and space itself. After Einstein, the world was simply not the same as before.

Theoretical advances and improved instruments, the observation of distant stars and of electromagnetic fields had pushed the physical concepts of the day to their limits and exposed gaps in the current scientific models of the world. One problem especially troubled scientists: to explain the movement of light and electrical waves through space, science had long postulated the existence of a medium, ether. Just as sound impulses make the air vibrate but cannot travel in a vacuum (the absence of gases), light waves and electricity, which can travel through a vacuum, must surely need the invisible ether as a propagating medium.

Detecting this ether and proving its existence therefore became one of the prime challenges of physics. The most famous of these attempts was the Michelson–Morley experiment. If the earth moved through cosmic ether in its orbit around the sun, the two scientists hypothesized, then the different velocities of the earth hurtling through the ether on its elliptical orbit (faster as it swings towards the two extremes, slower as it almost reaches them) should result in different measurements for the speed of light as seen from the earth, just as a cyclist moving against the wind would feel a higher wind speed than another cycling with the wind. Just as the two cyclists driving through the storm in opposite directions could determine the speed of the gale by meeting in a pub and comparing notes, using their variant measurements by adding or subtracting their own speeds from the wind speed they each measured during their ride to arrive at the real speed of the wind, Michelson and Morley thought that they could determine the speed of the earth relative to the ether by exploiting the differences in the speed of light measured.

Michelson and Morley's experiment had been based on one of the fundamental principles of classical physics, the so-called Galilean invariance. During the seventeenth century, the Italian physicist Galileo Galilei had postulated that the laws of physics were the same for all observers, independent of their movement through time and space. If a man fell from the tower of Pisa and was observed by a second man standing on the ground, they would both measure the same time for the fall (though the faller might have other things to worry about than to get out a watch), as time was an absolute factor for both of them.

The experiment was carried out with the most sophisticated instruments constructed especially for the purpose, but the result was always unsatisfying. Independent of the velocity of the earth in its orbit, the time of day or of year, the measured speed of light was always the same. If the speed of light, however, was independent of the speed of the planet from which it was observed, one of two things had to be true: either the experiment was flawed due to an unknown cause, or the laws of physics did not work under all circumstances as they had been defined by Newton and Galileo. Scientists had reached an impasse: descriptions of moving bodies, of the nature of space and of time were at odds with the phenomena observed Regarding the speed of light and its movement through space of time, physics had lost the ability to make accurate predictions, the very definition of a scientific proposition.

An unlikely revolutionary: Albert Einstein.

Einstein's genius lay in his intellectual courage to abstract a theory of space and time from observable reality, to dare to think the unthinkable. Albert Michelson, whose experiment proved so obstinately fruitless, had given a perfect example of the conviction of many of the day's physicists when he claimed in 1899: 'The more important fundamental laws and facts of physical science have all been discovered, and these are now so firmly established that the possibility of their ever being supplanted in consequence of new discoveries is exceedingly remote ... Our future discoveries must be looked for in the sixth place of decimals.' Six years before physics was to be thrown wide open to an entirely new understanding of the world, one of its main protagonists regarded the case as closed.

Intellectually rebellious from his earliest youth, Einstein was simply not intimidated by this orthodoxy. If Michelson and Morley had not found what they had been looking for, he realized, it was because they had been thinking too *small*, had not emancipated their analysis from the realm of human experience. Consider the unfortunate Italian falling from the leaning tower of Pisa and his friend watching him. The time of his fall might seem the same to both of them, as the distance from the ground and the speed of the fall are minute in a cosmic context, but when translated to a larger scale a very different picture would emerge.

If the faller had survived his accident but then had the bad luck to be loaded into an early spaceship and launched towards a distant star at, let us suppose, half the speed of light, something very strange would happen: while the astronaut himself would notice no difference in the passage of time, the clocks on board his ship would seem to be slower than those of an observer on the ground. Imagine a new constellation in the sky: a chain of twinkling watches set into the universe at regular intervals. The astronaut's own pocket watch (which, miraculously, was not damaged after falling from the leaning tower) would continue to mark time as usual, and a stationary observer looking at two equidistant celestial clocks would equally see them ticking steadily, showing the same time, because the light travelling from the clocks to his eye would take the same amount of time. On the spaceship, however, it would be a different story: passing one clock, the spaceship would meet the light travelling towards it from the second clock halfway (it travels at half the speed of light) and would therefore receive its signal earlier, and so for every clock along the way. For the traveller on board, the clocks outside the ship would move fast and time would elapse more quickly, while it remained constant on board.

The stationary observer would notice the opposite effect: time in the spaceship would seem dilated, an effect that would increase as the spaceship approached the speed of light. Time, in fact, is not an absolute value, with clocks ticking the same way for all of us. It is relative, depending on the movement of each observer, even though this effect only becomes relevant at very high speeds. A person falling off the tower of Pisa might not measure time differently from an observer, but a person in a spaceship would.

This elegant notion allowed Einstein to explain why Michelson and Morley had not been able to measure variances in the speed of light relative to the speed of the earth. While measured time is relative to the measurer, the speed of light is, in fact, a constant, and the dilation of time at high velocities means that the speed of light is not relative to the velocity of the observer, but is always measured with the same value: 299,792,458 metres per second. No object with mass can actually attain this speed (it would require infinite energy to do so), but the closer an object gets to it, the slower time moves relative to a slower or stationary observer, cancelling out the differential between its movement, relative to the speed of light. While the movement of the earth through space–time is vastly slower than that of light, a minimal time dilation reverses any possible variations in light speed as measured on earth.

Published in 1905 in the journal *Annalen der Physik*, the Special Theory of Relativity, as it came to be called, made the youthful patent clerk a star in scientific circles. Einstein had emancipated space and time from human experience, from old ways of understanding the world. He had chosen logical consistency over perception. Previous theories could not work, he had demonstrated, because they had been based on a wrong conception of space and time, a conception based on the small bandwidth of speeds much lower than the speed of light. What makes Einstein's contribution all the more significant is the fact that most of the mathematical and physical concepts underlying his theory were already in existence, but none of his colleagues had had the intellectual courage to go the one decisive step further, into the unknown. Scientists like the Curies and Rutherford, the German Max Planck and the Danish Niels Bohr had begun to show that the nature of matter was not what it appeared to be. Now, space and time themselves had been transformed.

There is an obvious kinship between Einstein's radical relativity of space and time and Ernst Mach's epistemological impressionism, which we encountered in the last chapter and which reduced the world and even the self to an aggregate of individual sensations which might give the impression of being solid and fixed, but are nothing of the kind. Another philosophical parallel, or precedent, for it had been published fifteen years before in 1889, was the great work *Essais sur les données immédiates de la conscience* (published in English as *Time and Free Will*) by the Frenchman Henri Bergson (1859–1941), who argued that time was being held hostage by space. Measuring time in terms of movement in space, on the face of a clock, was to make time, the duration of pure experience, of pure quality, subject to the tyranny of quantity, of counting and weighing. Pure duration as it is experienced, Bergson wrote, had nothing to do with space, or with the distance between one minute notch and another on a dial. The experience of duration was quite different, though: a constant dilation and contraction, now flashing by, now passing excruciatingly slowly:

If I follow my eyes to the dial of a watch, the movement of the hand which corresponds to the oscillations of the pendulum, I do not measure duration, as one might believe; I am limited to counting simultaneous moments, which is very different. Outside of me, in space, there is never anything but a single position of the hand and of the pendulum, because nothing remains of their previous positions. Inside me, there is a continuous process of organization and of mutual penetration of facts in my consciousness, and this constitutes true duration.

By having subjected this experience of lived duration to measurements in space, Western culture had effectively made living experience a slave to the hard, spatial culture of facts and figures, inches and tons. For the sake of success in business and science, Bergson implied, civilization was depriving itself of its most fundamental freedom.

To Bergson, consciousness had to rely on memory to create a coherent picture of the world, and in so doing the mind functioned remarkably like a movie camera, spooling off static images to give an illusion of continuous movement, of identity:

If you abolish my consciousness ... matter resolves itself into numberless vibrations, all linked together in uninterrupted continuity, all bound up with each other, and travelling in every direction like shivers ... Re-establish now my consciousness, and ... the thousands of successive positions of a runner are contracted into one sole symbolic attitude, which our eye perceives, which art reproduces, and which becomes for everyone the image of a man who runs.

Bergson would have been pleased with the following lines in Joseph Conrad's *Heart of Darkness* (1902), in which the narrator apparently sees pure, unmediated moments in the sweltering African night: 'a dark figure obscured the lighted doorway of the manager's hut, vanished, then, a second or so after, the doorway itself vanished too.' In the heat of the African night there was nothing but shapes, forms and other impressions, moulded together into a coherent world (and, according to Ernst Mach, a personality) by the workings of the mind.

As scientists smashed the object world into relative values and invisible forces, knocking over matter and time like Ming vases in an old aunt's drawing room, philosophy and the arts collected the shattered remnants and went about organizing a sumptuous funeral for them. The American philosopher William James (1842–1910), brother of the novelist Henry, pulled the rug from under his colleagues' feet when he said that truth itself was relevant if – and only if – it could be demonstrated to have a beneficial effect: everything is true that is good for you. Beyond this pragmatic definition lay mayhem and scholasticism, he believed.

If truth was nothing but a useful fiction, then so was all thought, declared the German Hans Vaihinger in his *Philosophie des Als Ob* (Philosophy of As If, 1911), who insisted that we make intellectual models of the world treating them *as if* they corresponded to a reality that is in essence unknowable. These models were essentially intellectual tools for managing the challenges of daily life, science and the arts. They had nothing to do with any reality, but they were accurate enough to be able to predict the future, to establish causalities. Ultimately however, these models – God, the soul, the atom – were nothing but mental maps, useful fictions which were valid only until better ones replaced them.

Cursing the grey weather in the German university city of Marburg where he did research, the Spaniard José Ortega y Gasset (1883–1955) broke down all knowledge and experience into individual circumstance and mutable perspective: 'this supposed immutable and unique reality…does not exist: there are as many realities as points of view.' Points of view became increasingly important, particularly to artists working with what they saw: nowhere were the splintering of identities and the fragmentation of time and space dramatised more astonishingly than in the arts, on the canvases of Picasso and Braque, Malevich, Kandinsky, Carrà and Boccioni.

Amid the weariness of reality and truth and the doubts about language itself and the multiple perspectives of experience, modernism was born. Ever ironic, Robert Musil set the tone for his *Man Without Qualities* by contrasting in the very first sentences the scientific striving for objectivity and the contents of experience:

A barometric minimum was above the Atlantic; it moved eastwards, towards a maximum above Russia, and showed no inclination to swerve to the north. The isotherms and isotheres did their duty. The air temperature was in a regular relationship to the mean annual temperature, to the temperature of the coldest and the warmest month and to aperiodical monthly temperature variations. Rise and set of the sun, the moon, the light variations of the moon and of Venus, of the rings of Saturn and many other important phenomena were in accordance with the predictions in astronomical annuals. The evaporated water in the air was at its highest elasticity and air humidity was low. In a word, which is really quite good but may sound a little old-fashioned: it was a beautiful August day of the year 1913.

Nervous Currents

While the world was attacked, ridiculed, reshaped and questioned on a conceptual, fundamental level which was understood only by a few brilliant minds, the scientific recasting of reality also had very palpable effects, reaching into the daily lives and imaginations of ordinary people. The burst of scientific discovery during the nineteenth century now pushed technology into every area of human experience. Gas lighting had conquered cities and was now itself replaced by electric light, which was cheaper, less dangerous, and free of soot. Telephones connected hundreds of thousands of households to one another, Marconi's telegraph conquered ever-greater distances through wireless transmission (the Colonial Office in Berlin directed ships off West Africa by telegraph signal); advances in technology and in the understanding of natural processes conquered the streets through automobiles, brought cheap cameras into the reach of the masses, lent colour to everyday life through the invention of synthetic pigments, paints and dyes, and put food on the table with the help of artificial, nitrogen-based fertilizers.

The protagonists of these developments became popular heroes, a race of intellectual demigods replacing the saint and the artistic genius. Just like Marie Curie in Europe, Thomas Alva Edison (1847–1931) achieved iconic status in the USA. 'If Dante, Michelangelo and Beethoven were the creative geniuses of past ages, Edison was "the wizard of Menlo Park" and of the modern age. Material as opposed to spiritual or artistic illumination was his special gift – the light bulb, the kinetoscope – though he was also the democratic-heroic inventor of waxed paper, the alkaline battery, the mimeograph, and so forth...' Other scientists such as Poincaré, Röntgen, Max Planck and Rutherford and scientist entrepreneurs like Werner von Siemens were treated as lesser gods. Some of them became household names, celebrated in newspaper articles and on commemorative postcards, their names emblazoned on automatons and machines pushing their way into doctors' surgeries, fashionable department stores and, in the form of the newly efficient light bulb, ordinary homes.

Electricity was exciting. Exhibits like the gigantic *Palais l'Electricité* were the stars of the 1900 World Fair in Paris, where millions of people flocked to see the miracle of tens of thousands of light bulbs turning night into day, and lending mysterious colours to the grand fountain in front of the building, while in the Hall of Dynamos, Henry Adams saluted the purring machines as the creative power of a new age. It was a healing power, too, or was believed to be. Ever since Mesmer's experiments on Paris society ladies in the eighteenth century, electricity had had its place in medicine, but now new possibilities and new anxieties combined: 'Come on!' shouted a typical advertisement in the French *Le Matin*:

> Get up! What cured me will cure you, too. I've taken all sorts of drugs and they all failed. But electricity has worked. Doctor MacLaughlin's Electro-Vigueur [electrical invigorator] cured me and will cure you. Every weakened man will congratulate himself on making a free trial of this great remedy, which has given health and strength to millions of people. Electro-Vigueur will make you resistant. It will heat up the blood in your veins. You will feel a wonderful energy penetrate to your very bones ... it is easy to prove that electricity restores vital forces, and that vital force is nothing else but electricity ... In the morning, when you wake up, you will feel active and vigorous, you will notice with joyous astonishment that your pains have gone ... Brochure and free consultations from 10 a.m. to 6 p.m., 14, boulevard Montmartre, Paris.

Vigour, energy, vital forces, joyous astonishment: in an age of nervous tension these words sounded like magic charms. Masculine identities were shaken and subtly undermined by women challenging their role, by constant talk about falling birth rates, about degeneration, mechanization and anxiety. Electrical baths were widely prescribed for a wide range of ailments, including digestive problems, headaches, menstrual cramps, impotence and neurasthenia (nervous exhaustion).

After the Curies and their work on radium, the range of quasi-occult medical treatments was enlarged by X-ray and radium therapies, which were equally widely prescribed, especially after radioactivity had been shown to be usable in the fight against advanced cancers. Indeed, there seemed to be no end to the beneficial properties of this new, mysterious substance. Soon the cosmetics industry seized on the public interest and produced balms and creams containing traces of thorium and radium, such as Tho-Radia, a supposedly miraculous cream produced in France. 'Stay ugly if you want to!' trumpeted the slogan of the manufacturer, whose products were wont to lend an altogether new meaning to the idea of radiant beauty.

While radioactive treatments remained a curiosity, electricity soon conquered the world as light-bringer and supposedly all-healing source of energy, all the more powerful for being invisible: 'Few New Yorkers realize that all through the roar of the big city there are constantly speeding messages between people separated by vast distances, and that over housetops and even through the walls of buildings and in the very air one breathes are words written by electricity,' commented the *New York Times* on 21 April 1912.

Miraculous but disquieting, electricity could also bring death. In 1890, newspapers in the United States had ardently followed the controversy between Edison and Westinghouse as to whether alternating or direct current was the most appropriate means of powering the first electric chair, scheduled to be used for the execution of William Kemmler, who had killed his lover with twenty-six axe blows to the skull. Edison threw himself into a series of experiments to determine the proper procedure and the current required to cause the death of a man, a process which itself resulted in the electrocution of scores of dogs and several calves and horses, strapped into electrical harnesses by the wizard's assistants. When the execution of Kemmler finally took place on 6 August 1890, the condemned man seemed calm and collected. 'Now take your time and do it all right, Warden,' he said as he was strapped into the chair, 'there is no rush. I don't want to take any chances on this thing, you know.'

The moments that followed the throwing of the switch were something that no one was prepared for. Instead of gracefully slumping over as Edison's dogs had done, Kemmler showed every sign of being in extreme agony, as his face turned dark red, blood vessels burst, and his nails cut through the skin of his palms. It took a second shock to kill him. By then the room was filled with the smell of scorched flesh. The *Chicago Evening Post* reported: 'The wretch was actually tortured to death with a refinement of cruelty that was unequalled in the dark ages.' The *New York Times* described the state of the witnesses: 'as miserable, as weak-kneed a lot of men as can be imagined ... They all seemed to act as though they felt that they had taken part in a scene that would be told to the world as a public shame, as a legal crime.'

The dark, dangerous side of the medium illuminating the world made it an ideal subject for science fiction novels, which quickly seized the new discoveries for their own purposes: the unseen power of electricity and radioactivity, of X-rays and atomic structure, was ideal to conjure up the wildest and most fascinating scenarios. Already during the 1870s and 1880s, Jules Verne had created a large readership for scientific visions of the future. Now a new generation of authors took this futuristic writing to a new level of imagination and sophistication: ray guns and microfilm, atom bombs and nuclear power, humanoid robots and gigantic airships, tape recorders and television, technological warfare, travel to distant galaxies and alien invasions, surviving dinosaurs, faster-than-light travel and human cloning can all be found in popular literature prior to 1914. Its tone, though, differed from that of earlier science fiction. It no longer had the thrusting optimism of Verne, the belief that science meant progress. The new generation of writers were often dystopians, believing or suggesting that the dangers inherent in harnessing and then unleashing the hidden force of nature might yield devastating outcomes. Change was inevitable, they wrote, but it was by no means sure that it would not lead into the abyss.

The most arresting and prophetic visions of technological futures and their many pitfalls appear in the work of H. G. Wells (1866–1946), an English novelist whose imagination seemed as boundless as it was dark. *The Time Machine, The Stolen Bacillus* (both 1895); *The Island of Doctor Moreau* (1896); *The War of the Worlds* (1898); *The First Men in the Moon* (1901); *The Land Ironclads* (1904); *A Modern Utopia* (1905); *The War in the Air* (1908); *The Sleeper Awakes* (1910); and *The World Set Free: A Story of Mankind* (1914) all describe possible transformations of the world due to physics, technology and modern capitalism, dramatizing travels into a devastated future and into space; warfare with tanks and aircraft. To Wells, the new world of science simply overwhelmed the world after centuries of ignorance:

> To electricity...mankind had been utterly blind for incalculable ages. Could anything be more emphatic than the appeal of electricity for attention? It thundered at man's ears, it signalled to him in blinding flashes, occasionally it killed him, and he could not see it as a thing that concerned him enough to merit study. It came into the house with the cat on any dry day and crackled insinuatingly whenever he stroked her fur. It rotted his metals when he put them together...There is no single record that any one questioned why the cat's fur crackles or why hair is so unruly to brush on a frosty day, before the sixteenth century. For endless years man seems to have done his very successful best not to think about it at all; until this new spirit of the Seeker turned itself to these things.

The effects of this new realm, however, were often menacing and at times catastrophic, as Wells depicted in *The War in the Air*, in which the protagonist finds himself in an air force encampment and is overwhelmed: 'The whole camp reflected the colossal power of modern science that had created it. A peculiar strangeness was produced by the lowness of the electric light, which lay upon the ground, casting all shadows upwards and making a grotesque shadow figure of himself and his bearers on the airship sides, fusing all three of them into a monstrous animal with attenuated legs and an immense fan-like humped body.' Man found himself dwarfed by science.

While Wells's utopias oscillated between benign and catastrophic, the American Hugo Gernsback (1884–1967) described life in a thoroughly technological world in the year 2660, in which the inventor hero and title character of his novel *Ralph 124C 41+* (1911) uses futuristic devices such as ray guns and space ships for very conventional ends: he saves his sweetheart. On the Continent, popular novelists unleashed new technologies on the heroes of their stories. Paul d'Ivoi (1856–1915) dramatized the findings of his compatriot Marie Curie in his adventure *La Course au radium* (The Race for Radium, 1909), while Arnould Galopin (1865–1934) used pre-Einstein physical theory to have his Doctor Omega travel race through space. Even the famous master thief Arsène Lupin was sent by his creator, Maurice Leblanc (1864–1941), to help solve the secret of a mysterious and terrifying island in *L'Île aux trente cercueils* (The Island of the Thirty Coffins, 1919). The 'divine stone' giving life as well as death which is the object of the heroine's epic search turns out to be a radium rock hidden by gigantic flowers.

In German-speaking countries, there seemed to be less appetite for futuristic adventure stories. The journalist Hans Dominik published some popular stories about space and time travel, but no novelist could make this subject his own, and no fictional hero or series of stories emerged to fill this void. Or was it a void? Is it possible that the Germans, with their fast-growing cities, their burgeoning industrialization and their almost daily news about inventions and technological records felt that they needed not more of the future but rather refuge in a simpler, more primitive life? While French, British and American readers were devouring new instalments of science fiction stories making writers such as Maurice Leblanc and H. G. Wells both rich and famous, the most famous German writer of popular adventures, Karl May (1842–1912), specialized in exotic tales set either in the Middle East or in the Wild West. His best-loved hero was a noble Apache warrior, Winnetou, who braved innumerable adventures together with his white trapper friend, Old Shatterhand. May, who had never actually set foot in the western United States which he described so vividly in his fiction (though in 1908, after having written most of his novels, he did visit New York), became one of Germany's most popular bestselling authors. His novels are still in print.

The popularity of Karl May was certainly linked to a scepticism about scientific advances, a lurking suspicion that underneath the relentless advance an atavistic world continued to exist and was waiting to burst out and sweep away the achievements of urbanized civilization. Arthur Conan Doyle's 1912 novel *The Lost World* described the discovery of live and ferocious dinosaurs on a remote South American plateau (a story echoed eighty years later in the film *Jurassic Park*), and in the same year Edgar Rice Burroughs became famous with his creation *Tarzan of the Apes* (1912, first film version 1917).

Unperturbed by cultural tremors in which she showed little interest, Marie Curie pursued her research. After her husband's death in 1906 she herself became professor at the Sorbonne, the first woman to hold such a post at France's most prestigious university. Radiation poisoning (as yet unrecognized) and her grief about Pierre had left a deep mark on her, as a journalist for *Le Figaro* recorded during her inaugural lecture: 'I look at that strange, ageless face, which seems to have read too much, or wept too much;...a face of cold serenity, of suppressed pain...And I hear behind me something which seems very true:

'– "What a career!"'

Not everyone was as admiringly sympathetic as the correspondent of *Le Figaro*. Many of Curie's colleagues resented having a woman in their midst. Their hour came five years later, in 1911, when the widow became sentimentally attached to a fellow scientist, Paul Langevin, who decided to seek a divorce. Formerly admiring of their Nobel Prize-winning star, the press now attacked Marie Curie without mercy as the 'Polack' who had ruined a good French family, the woman who did not know her place. Curie was disgusted, more so when, despite her obvious achievements, she failed to be elected to the *Académie des Sciences*. Reviled in France, the scientist found more respect abroad when she was nominated, in that same year, for her second Nobel Prize, this time in Chemistry.

'The discovery hit me with frightful force, as if the end of the world had come. All things became transparent, without strength or certainty.' So Vassily Kandinsky responded after reading about Rutherford in 1911. More than ever before, science gave answers to ancient questions, possibilities to industry and new dreams to ordinary men and women. The price for these exciting prospects was the solid, tangible nature of the old world. Certainties tumbled as possibility emerged.

5

1904:

His Majesty and Mister Morel

It was most interesting, lying in the bush watching the natives quietly at their day's work. Some women...were making banana flour by pounding up dried bananas. Men we could see building huts and engaged in other work, boys and girls running about, singing...I opened the game by shooting one chap through the chest. He fell like a stone...Immediately a volley was poured into the village.

– Captain William Grant Stairs, Congo diary, 28 September 1887

In early 1904, a thick typewritten report by an obscure civil servant in the colonial administration was filed in the London Colonial Office. Commissioned to investigate a clutch of rumours about the goings-on in an African colony sharing a border with British-owned Rhodesia, the document was not thought to be of any special importance. Yet it contained the greatest tale of horror and inhumanity the world had seen.

The author of this tale was Roger Casement (1864–1916), an Irishman who had spent two decades of his professional career as Their Britannic Majesties' Consul in various African territories. During the previous year he had been dispatched to the Congo Free State to report on allegations of mistreatment of natives at the hands of their colonial masters. What Casement found and recorded in the detached language of a seasoned diplomat was a catalogue of atrocity, mass mutilation, state-sponsored slavery and murder, and monumental greed. Whole ethnic groups, it seemed, had all but vanished:

When I visited [Lukolela] in 1887 it numbered fully 5,000 people; to-day, the population is given, after a careful enumeration, at less than 600...

... [in 1887] the population of the three towns [in another area] had numbered some 4,000 to 5,000 people ... Scores of men had put off in canoes to greet us with invitations that we should spend the night in their village. On steaming into Irebu on the 28 of July of this year, I found the village had entirely disappeared and its place was occupied by a large 'camp d'instruction' (training camp), where some 800 native recruits, brought in from various parts of the Congo State, are drilled into soldierhood ...

In addition to the wholesale disappearance of villages, the report soberly chronicled a pattern of savage floggings and mutilations, particularly the hacking off of hands:

Two cases of the kind came to my actual notice while I was in the lake [area]. One, a young man, both of whose hands had been beaten off with the butt ends of rifles against a tree, the other young lad of 11 or 12 years of age, whose right hand was cut off at the wrist. This boy described the circumstances of his mutilation and, in answer to my enquiry, said that although wounded at the time he was perfectly sensible of the severing of his wrist, but lay still fearing that if he moved he would be killed. In both these cases the Government soldiers had been accompanied by white officers whose names were given to me.

The report meticulously documented many such instances, as well as uncommonly cruel executions (in one case a man was hung head-down over a low fire, women were repeatedly raped and then disembowelled, many were whipped to death) and countless incarcerations of women and children.

The unlikely reason for this unimaginable terror inflicted on native peoples by their European colonizers was an invention made some years earlier by a genial Irish veterinarian, Doctor John Dunlop of Belfast. He had devised air-filled rubber tubes for his son's tricycle and had begun to market them. Soon the demand was so great that in 1890 he had ceased to look after horses and invested in the transport of the future. Fitted with miraculously shock-absorbent rubber tyres, bicycles became a cultural phenomenon, a symbol for the young generation and its time, for speed, freedom and physical fitness. The worldwide demand for rubber boomed.

Enter the ultimate businessman who quickly understood this demand to be an historic opportunity: King Leopold II of the Belgians (1835–1909). Through the good offices of the legendary explorer Henry Morton Stanley, the King had acquired in 1885 a chunk of the Congo as big as Europe. He wanted the territory not for his country, but as a personal possession, and from the very start he treated his colony, which he baptized Congo Free State, as a profit-making concern. There was ivory inland, and there were countless natives who could be pressed into service. When the rubber boom occurred Leopold found that his colony happened to be rich in wild caoutchouc vines and so had the potential to exercise a virtual monopoly on the world rubber market, at least until rubber plantations planted elsewhere were mature enough to go into production. The King understood that there was no time to be lost: an immense fortune could be made. He set to work, or rather, he set tens of thousands of natives to work by implement-ing a regime of systematic terror geared to deliver maximum yields of exportable rubber, regardless of the human cost. As the wild vines necessi-tated climbing into the trees of densely forested areas, the King's officials managed the men, who could not climb while in chains, by holding women and children hostage until production quotas were fulfilled. Any opposi-tion, and even any failure to meet these quotas, was punished by military expeditions which burned and murdered whole villages. As proof of execu-tion the black soldiers, who might otherwise waste precious cartridges for hunting game, were ordered to bring back their victims' hands from the campaigns, which often took several weeks, making it necessary to smoke the severed limbs for preservation. The military units involved had a special post, the 'keeper of the hands'. Soldiers who wanted to better their killing premium were given to severing the hands of the living as well as the dead, leaving their victims where they had cut them down. Forced labour, mass rape and hostage-taking, thousandfold murder and endemic brutality were key components of the rubber with which the Free State supplied a vora-cious market in Europe and the United States. In his Belgian palace, King Leopold became rich beyond his wildest dreams.

Unfair Trade

The reality of what was going on in the Congo Free State was uncovered, almost by accident, by Edward Dene Morel (1872–1924), an English ship-ping clerk, whose task it was to verify cargoes transported to and from the colony by his employer, a Liverpool shipping company. Being of French extraction and a fluent French-speaker, his duties frequently took him to Belgium, where he would supervise the loading and unloading of the Congo ships: ivory and rubber from Africa, and items of daily use as pay-ments and for trade, according to the official Belgian statistics. One day, while he was attending a meeting with the highest-ranking official in the

Belgian Congo administration, the young book-keeper was privy to a scene that aroused both his suspicions and his curiosity, as he himself later remembered with the rhetorical flourishes that would make him such a formidable journalist:

The face of mass murder: King Leopold of the Belgians. Some ten million people were killed in the Congo Free State, his personal fiefdom.

> A room whose windows look upon the back of the Royal Palace at Brussels. A gloomy room, thick-carpeted, heavy curtains; a room of oppressive shadows. In its centre a man, seated at a desk. A man thin to emaciation, with narrow, stooping shoulders; with a receding forehead, high curved nose, large ears set far back: lantern jawed, cold eyed. A face in repose passively inhuman, bloodless, petrified, all sharp bones and gaunt cavities: the face of the then 'Secretary of State' for the Congo Free State ... He leans forward and in rapid staccato accents complains that confidential information as to the last outward-bound steamer's cargo has been divulged to the press ... The paragraph is pointed out. It looks innocent enough, being a list of the principal articles on board. But that list contains an enumeration of the cases of ball cartridges, the cases of rifles and the boxes of percussion-cap guns ... That is the fault. That is the lapse from professional secrecy. As the enormity of the indiscretion is denounced, the speaker rises, the cadaverous cheeks flush, the voice trembles ... He will hear no excuses; allow no interruption. Again and again he repeats the words *secret professionnel* with passionate emphasis.

Astonished at this scene, Morel verified the records by using his company's shipping lists and found that the official statistics were pure fiction. Outgoing cargoes consisted overwhelmingly of small arms and ammunition. There was no evidence of any trading with those who produced the rubber imported from the Congo. He also noticed that the official statistics reported only a fraction of the profits made. Someone, it seemed, was very discreetly earning tens of millions of Belgian francs from the colony. Morel had enough experience with statistics and profit margins to know what this meant:

> These figures told their own story … Forced labour of a terrible and continuous kind could alone explain such unheard-of profits … forced labour in which the Congo Government was the immediate beneficiary; forced labour by the closest associates of the King himself … I was giddy and appalled at the cumulative significance of my discoveries. It must be bad enough to stumble upon a murder. I had stumbled upon a secret society of murderers with a King for a croniman.

A man of exceptional determination and courage, Morel had found his life's mission: to expose and to end the terrors of the Congo.

Morel was not the only observer to be horrified by the atrocities perpetrated in the Congo. The black American journalist George Washington Williams had already exposed Leopold's regime in the 1890s and Mary Kingsley's book-length reportage *Travels in Africa* had been popular since its publication in 1897. But Morel was by far the most effective champion of the cause. His information was always accurate, his tenacity legendary,

A true hero: Edward Dene Morel worked tirelessly to expose the crimes committed in the Congo.

his style as vivid as it was energetic, and his outrage as raw as on the day he had made his first discovery. Morel was determined to force the world to take notice, and he had a phenomenal capacity for work. At twenty-eight, he resigned from his job (turning down several offers to buy his silence), raised money, corresponded with hundreds of eyewitnesses and people in influential positions, collected information from missionaries and documents from contacts within the colonial administration, founded a newspaper in which he published the damaging information, gave speeches and lectures, wrote hundreds of articles and thousands of letters, and lobbied politicians. The brutally exploited people of the Congo found their champion in a small, mustachioed Liverpudlian with neither a steady income nor influential friends, who was en route to becoming the most persistent, most stinging antagonist of a European monarch, and who would never even set foot on the African continent.

Supplied with inside information by Morel, newspapers throughout Europe and the United States began to print damaging revelations about Leopold's regime; lecture halls were regularly crammed to bursting when Morel gave his famous talks on the colonial atrocities, and members of parliament and other decision-makers would receive letters of searing eloquence. After several years of this campaign, the Colonial Office could no longer ignore the troubling news coming from the Congo Free State and sent one of its most reliable and experienced men, Roger Casement, to investigate.

Casement had set off in 1903 and spent several months travelling through the Free State on a hired steamer – an important fact, as it made him not only independent of the concessionary rubber companies and the administration in the area, but also impossible to control. When he finally returned, he decanted his rage into a book-length report which he submitted to the foreign secretary. Casement's findings bore Morel out in every gruesome detail. It detailed a war of destruction perpetrated against Africans: 'One of the largest Congo Concession Companies,' Casement wrote, 'had...addressed a request to its Directors in Europe for a further supply of ball-cartridge. The Directors had met his demand by asking what had become of the 72,000 cartridges shipped some three years ago, to which a reply was sent to the effect that these had all been used in the production of india-rubber.'

While native women would be held in detention camps (where they were routinely raped by their guards) to ensure the return of their menfolk sent to harvest resin, the men themselves would be punished severely if they failed to return with a sufficient amount of raw materials: 'As to the condition of the men who paid by detention in the "maison des otages" their shortcomings in respect of rubber, I was assured by the local agent that they were not badly treated and that "they got their food". On the other hand, I was assured in many quarters that flogging with the *chicotte* – or hippopotamus-hide whip – was one of the measures used in dealing with refractory natives in that institution.' On page upon page, individual acts of European barbarism were painstakingly detailed, with places, dates, and names of witnesses. Several appendices supplied additional proof.

Casement's cautious and official report gained much of its quiet power from its disinterested tone. It calculated the profits made in different areas, the number of workers needed, the impact of death tolls on production, in much the same way as one would have analysed a factory. When it was published in the Parliamentary Reports of April 1904, the calm enumeration of margins realized and people tortured or killed in the process was a great boost to Morel's campaign. Soon the two men met and became firm friends, as Morel recounts:

> I saw before me a man, my own height, very lithe and sinewy, chest thrown out, head held high – suggestive of one who had lived in the vast open spaces. Black hair and beard covering cheeks hollowed by the tropical sun. Strongly marked features. A dark blue, penetrating eye sunken in the socket. A long, lean, swarthy Vandyck type of face, graven with power and withal of great gentleness. [...] I often see him now in imagination as I saw him at that memorable interview, crouching over the fire in the otherwise unlighted room... unfolding in a musical, soft, almost even voice, in language of peculiar dignity and pathos, the story of a vile conspiracy. For hours he talked on, with now and again a pause, as the poignancy of recollection gripped him, when he would break off the narrative and murmur beneath his breath, 'Poor people; poor, poor people.'

Casement was driven by the same zeal for justice and he helped the Congo campaign in whichever way he could. His own motivation for taking the side of the underdog may have been rooted in his personal experience. As an Irishman, he increasingly resented the English rule to which his country was subjected, a fact that brought him into direct conflict with his employers and presumably did nothing to further his career. A man of outstanding abilities, he was given minor, unimportant postings at the margins of the empire for his entire career, presumably because he did not belong to the aristocratic, public-school and overwhelmingly English elite (he himself had been sent to a minor school) from which the higher echelons of the service were drawn. Casement was marginal in another way: he was a homosexual. To admit to his passion was unthinkable, and so he was reduced to consuming it in countless casual encounters with young men in harbours and on remote postings, all of which he recorded in his diaries, the record of his true feelings, in which he makes no attempt to mask his emotions about the exploitation he was there to witness: 'Sunday 30 August. Spent quiet day. In afternoon saw M. Lejeune at Abir 16 men women & children tied up – from a village Mboyo close to the town. Infamous! The men were put in the prison the children let go at my intervention. Infamous! Infamous shameful system.' The entries dealing with his sexual encounters are remarkably frank: 'Agostinho kissed many times. 4 dollars'; 'Down and oh! oh! quick, about 18'; 'Tall, "How much money?"'

An outsider himself in so many ways, the charismatic Casement made it his business to defend those who could not defend themselves. His duties as a consul, which more often than not involved negotiating with the police on behalf of drunken soldiers who had got into trouble, or listening to the indignant tirades of wronged British travellers, were tiring and frustrating, and the quest for justice seemed finally worthy of his intelligence and his passion.

Boosted by his new, invaluable ally, Morel was now heading an effective international publicity campaign reinforced by first-hand testimonies like that of the Reverend John Harris and his wife Alice Seely Harris, Baptist missionaries who had come back from the Congo not only with moral outrage but also with photos they had taken themselves, as well as sad souvenirs: whips and manacles which they displayed at public lectures. As these instruments of terror made the rounds among the spectators, Reverend Harris read out reports, this one among them:

> Lined up ... are 40 emaciated sons of an African village, each carrying his little basket of rubber. The toll of rubber is weighed and accepted, but ... four baskets are short of the demand. The order is brutally short and sharp – Quickly the first defaulter is seized by four lusty 'executioners,' thrown on the bare ground, pinioned hands and feet, whilst a fifth steps forward carrying a long whip of twisted hippo hide. Swiftly and without cessation the whip falls, and the sharp corrugated edges cut deep into the flesh – on back, shoulders and buttocks blood spurts from a dozen places. In vain the victim twists in the grip of the executioners, and then the whip cuts other parts of the quivering body – and in the case of one of the four, upon the most sensitive part of the human frame. The 'hundred lashes each' left four inert bodies bloody and quivering on the shimmering sand of the rubber collecting post.

Following hard upon this decisive incident was another. Breakfast was just finished when an African father rushed up the veranda steps of our mud house and laid upon the ground the hand and foot of his little daughter, whose age could not have been more than 5 years.

The Harrises showed shocked audiences the photo to prove this very episode.

The horror: a father stares at the hands of his five-year-old daughter, severed as a punishment for having harvested too little caoutchouc.

This truly was the Heart of Darkness evoked in the 1899 novel by a Polish-British sailor and adventurer whom Roger Casement had befriended in the Congo: Joseph Conrad. It was the cancer eating away at Europe's claim to moral leadership and missionary zeal to colonize the world. King Leopold himself – dull, business-minded and possessed by epic greed – had cited humanitarian motives for appropriating the Congo, which, he had pledged, would be thoroughly studied and Christianized. He had even founded a scientific organization to carry out the research, and one of his many huge building projects in and around Brussels was a monumental museum devoted to the cultures of central Africa. Behind this philanthropic façade, the Colony was robbed not only of raw materials, but also of lives. Some ten million Congolese natives perished under Leopold's rule, murdered, maimed, or left to starve. It was the largest genocide the world had seen. The proceeds of his murderous business practices also financed endless enlargements and renovations at the royal castle in Laaken, an extensive park with architectural follies, a promenade in the seaside town of Ostend, a gallery for his favourite racetrack, a golf course and his pet project, a monumental triumphal arch commemorating his achievements. He also bought palatial properties in other countries, notably in southern France, where he liked to spend weeks with his mistress, whom he had discovered as a teenage Parisian prostitute and whom he would eventually marry shortly before his death.

The Shame of Empires

It was not difficult to hate and despise Leopold, but a vein of violent oppression ran beneath all colonial projects. However, despite the (often quite sincere) rhetoric of Christian missions and the 'white man's burden', and partly thanks to Morel's ceaseless and highly effective activism, the international press was increasingly aware of aspects of colonial policy that were absent from official documents, school lessons, and the memoirs of distinguished administrators. No event did more to sway public opinion away from an uncritical endorsement of imperial adventures than the Boer War (1899–1902), which was a constant presence in European and American newspapers.

The European press was extremely critical of Britain's cynical attempt to secure South Africa's most lucrative gold fields for the Crown, if necessary by exterminating the local colonizers of Dutch descent, the Boers. Early defeats of the British forces were cheered like great patriotic victories from St Petersburg to Paris. Always good for a foreign-policy scandal, the German Kaiser had caused a major diplomatic incident by sending President Kruger a telegram congratulating him for beating off the first British incursion, the Jameson Raid of December 1895. When the imperial forces were strengthened and went onto the counter-offensive, European papers followed the fate of individual Boer units and their commanders with daily front-page dispatches from the front, as if the fighting were occurring in the streets of Frankfurt or Lyon.

This international public outrage at the British attempt to subdue the plucky Dutch colonists and their legitimate interests was to some degree political, of course, especially in Germany, which had a strategic interest in South Africa. Much of the revulsion abroad, however, was quite sincere, and the critical voices grew into a storm of protest when the British commander Lord Kitchener adopted a policy of scorched earth, systematically destroying Boer farms and herding women and children into internment facilities dubbed 'concentration camps' – the first occurrence of this term. Twenty-eight thousand civilians, a quarter of all prisoners, died of starvation, exposure and of epidemics soon raging in the hastily improvised camps. Of these victims, 22,000 were under sixteen years of age. The satirical Austro-Hungarian magazine *Der Floh* captured the mood of many Europeans about the final peace agreement in 1902 in doggerel: 'Old England, cheers! No longer war / And now we can go to it. / We lug home all that Transvaal ore / We'll live like kings, champagne galore / And shear the Boers to do it.'

Opposition to the Boer War often came from the left. The socialist Vienna paper *Arbeiterzeitung* echoed the feelings of many on the left when it wrote about Britain's 'bloody struggle against a people of heroes'. In Britain, the thrust of the argument against big capital and its involvement in the British-owned gold-mining firms in the Transvaal often developed antisemitic overtones, as in the writings of the liberal writer J. A. Hobson, who held in a popular book that the gold business was 'almost entirely in … [the Jews'] hands' and that 'Jewhannesburg' was not worth the blood of Christian soldiers. Just as Captain Dreyfus was the perfect embodiment of French anxieties, the image of the straight-living Christian Boers being crushed under the boot of a superior power with undeniable economic motives made them an ideal symbol of a common anxiety, a rallying point for admirers of very different backgrounds.

It was relatively easy for European observers to show solidarity with the Boers; they were, after all, Europeans themselves, and dared to defy the colossus of the British empire. This was not quite a colonial war: rather, it seemed to be a war of liberation, much like the struggles for Polish independence during the early nineteenth century, a vision which accorded perfectly with the Boers' perception of themselves and their struggle. Despite their modern Mauser rifles (feared by their attackers), the staunch men with their huge beards who proudly posed for press photographs published around the world seemed like a nation of prophets defending their promised land: a pious white society which they would defend to the last drop of their blood. They fought hard for a society in which Apartheid was effectively already implemented, not for anything even vaguely resembling a society with civil liberties for blacks. When Colonel Robert Baden-Powell, later to become the founder of the Boy Scouts, armed black men for the defence of British-held Mafeking which was being besieged by the Boers, the commander of the attacking forces, General Pieter Arnoldus Cronje, was so disgusted by this act of racial treason that he sent Baden-Powell a message across the lines: 'I would ask you to pause and ... even if it cost you the loss of Mafeking, to disarm your blacks and ... act the part of the white man in a white man's war.' Baden-Powell refused to play the part and held the town, partly due to his disgraceful ruse.

For Britain itself, the Boer War was a disaster, even if her troops eventually overwhelmed the exhausted settler forces in June 1902. Victory had been won at an appalling human cost, and none but the blindest imperialist could think of it as an evenly matched and honourable conflict. The glorious British forces had been humiliated by a ragtag band of settlers who at the beginning of the conflict could rely on little else but their courage and stubborn determination (later on, material support and even volunteers arrived from France and Germany). When they had eventually forced the decision in their favour, they had done so at the price of tens of thousands of innocent civilian lives, and with very questionable motivation. The lofty principles with which the colonizers justified their empires no longer looked so pure. What had been a victory in military terms was still seen as a moral defeat of devastating proportions. 'The horrible consciousness that we have, at best, shown ourselves to be unscrupulous in methods, vulgar in manners and inefficient to the last degree, is an unpleasant background to all one's personal life ... The Boers are, man for man, our superiors in dignity, devotion and capacity – yes, *in capacity*,' noted the Fabian activist Beatrice Webb in her diary in disgust in 1900, before the concentration camps and the scorched earth.

In view of this recent history, the British government's response to the Casement Report two years later was predictably muted. Moral outrage at the brutal exploitation of an African territory would not have looked very credible. The colonial experience became none of the colonial masters, in fact. In the case of Germany, one of the most vociferous supporters of the Boers, the cancer of violence erupted that very year, when a group of tribes in German South West Africa rebelled against Wilhelm II's forces. Armed Herero warriors laid siege to the township of Okahandja, and attacked farms and police stations in the area, with the loss of some 140 German lives.

With only a small troop contingent in place, the governor of the colony turned to Berlin for reinforcements and got more than he bargained for. On the direct order of the Kaiser and against the advice of most senior officers of the general staff, Lieutenant-General Lothar von Trotha was dispatched into the area. Trotha had years of experience in the colonial service, as well as a reputation for exceptional harshness. When he found that he could not beat the rebels in open battle and instead saw himself faced with an infuriatingly effective guerrilla campaign, he turned to more comprehensive tactics and issued the following decree to the Herero:

> I, the great general of the German soldiers, am sending this letter to the Herero people. The Herero no longer are German subjects. They have murdered and stolen, have cut off ears, noses and other body parts of wounded soldiers and now they are too cowardly to fight... The Herero people has to leave this land. If they do not go, the *Groot Roor* [artillery] will force them to go. Within German borders, every Herero, with or without a gun, with or without cattle, will be shot and I no longer shelter women and children, I will drive them back to their people or have them shot at. These are my words for the Herero people. The great general of the mighty German Kaiser.

Trotha's forces, most of whom were worn out from the campaign in the unfamiliar heat and weakened or disabled by tropical diseases, were in no state to execute this brutal order. However, faced with other punitive measures such as blocked water holes, a column of some 30,000 Herero had taken flight into the arid hinterland, beyond the reach of the German forces. Their way led them into the waterless Sandfeld desert, where most cattle and some 12 to 14,000 men, women and children died of thirst. Scouts later found water holes several metres deep and surrounded by skeletons, but without water. When the order from Berlin came (accompanied by an outcry in the media) to countermand the declaration, cease hostilities and give humanitarian aid to the survivors, roughly a third of the Herero people had died, either in battle or in the Sandfeld.

Driven into the desert: surviving members of the Herero tribe.

*

If Trotha's barbaric intent and the terrible death toll among the Herero people were an isolated occurrence in Germany's short colonial history, murderous violence was frequent and systematic in the Ottoman Empire, where between 1894 and 1915 millions of Armenians perished at the hands of the army and its often Kurdish henchmen, and, to a lesser extent, in some of the Dutch colonies, notably in Java and Sumatra. Also in 1904, the Dutch Lieutenant-Colonel van Daalen mounted a penal expedition against an insurrection in the Aceh region (troubled by civil war already then), during which his soldiers burned several villages and killed 2,900 natives, 1,150 of them women. A photographer brought along to document the expedition photographed officers proudly standing over the slain bodies of villagers, one foot planted on the corpses' heads. Ten years earlier, a young lieutenant had taken part in another punitive raid. In letters to his wife he recounted the experience: 'I had to drive together nine women and three children who were begging for mercy and deliver them to death. It was unpleasant work, but there was nothing else I could have done. The soldiers killed them with bayonets.' He accepted the 'terrible duty of the colonial soldier', he wrote. The lieutenant, Hendrikus Colijn, would later become prime minister of the Netherlands. Some 2,000 natives were shot or hacked to death in the expedition in which he dutifully took part.

Media Wars

It was due to men such as Morel and Casement that atrocities like these became more difficult to hide and public pressure for change increased around the world. Morel's effectiveness was largely due to his immense skill in exploiting the unprecedented reach and hunger of the mass newspapers. More people than ever could read and afford newspapers, which had become the dominant source of information and entertainment. Only a decade before, cheaper and faster typesetting, photographic reproduction and printing technologies had revolutionized the industry and a good story always sold, especially if it involved atrocities committed by a foreign power. Morel fed the papers and fanned the flames of public outrage with an effective publicity campaign which even involved a trip to the United States in September 1904, on which he visited President Roosevelt in Washington and won the support of Mark Twain; in Europe he had already secured the support of the French writer Anatole France and the Nobel Prize-winner Björnstjerne Björnson from Norway. Congo committees and societies sprang up all over the world, ranging from regular rallies in Zurich to a series of talks given in New Zealand. Almost single-handedly, Edward Morel had made the Congo an issue that would not go away.

Newspapers had taken a new place in the public consciousness. Leopold quickly understood that the only way to counteract Morel's influence was by going to the media himself. He instituted a toothless commission of missionaries carefully selected for eminence, working in a region without significant rubber exploitation, and with inaccessible mission stations. In a systematic international campaign, he paid lobbyists to influence politicians and bribed newspaper editors to change their tack. His German agent pulled off the remarkable feat of having the Berlin *National-Zeitung*, which had previously attacked Leopold as 'the unscrupulous businessman who lives in the palace in Brussels', switch within two years to belittling reports about atrocities as 'old wives' tales'. In Britain, Leopold's agent (working on a handsome retainer) went further and sent two presentable specimens of English society on a fact-finding mission preceded by a degree of cosmetic enhancement wherever the travellers went. Both came back with glowing tales about their experiences. One of them, Viscount William Montmorres, published a gushing book about hard-working officials and cheerful natives. The other traveller, the publisher Mary French Sheldon, was shown around by officials of the concessionary rubber companies, fell in love with the captain of her steamboat and later wrote in *The Times*. 'I have witnessed more atrocities in London streets than I have ever seen in the Congo.' Leopold made sure that this message got to the right people, paying out of his own pocket for a lecture by Sheldon followed by a dinner for five hundred invited guests at the Savoy.

All this to no avail. The war about the Congo was a media war and, despite his best efforts, the Belgian King was losing. This may have been due to his strategy of targeting people he deemed important with grand free dinners or brochures entitled *The Truth about the Congo* put into the first-class compartments of luxury trains, while Morel made sure to speak to a more general public. But it may have also been simply because Leopold defended the indefensible, up to the point of disseminating stories about atrocities committed by other colonial regimes and dismissing the amputated hands of his unfortunate Congo subjects as isolated cases of malicious cancers selflessly treated by Belgian doctors. The case against him was simply overwhelming, and Belgium carried too little political weight to be shielded by other great powers for strategic reasons.

One of the lobbyists recruited by the King of the Belgians to turn around public opinion was Colonel Henry I. Kowalsky, a flamboyantly brash and fast-living San Francisco lawyer whose legendary girth once caused the mayor of San Francisco at a dinner given in Kowalsky's honour to remark: 'I shall not closely follow the text of the toast which has been assigned to me. Like our guest, it is too large a subject.' On an annual salary of 100,000 francs (the equivalent of £300,000), the novice public relations manager travelled to visit his new boss in Brussels and then moved to New York, where he installed himself in sumptuous offices on Wall Street. The 'colonel', whose rank was as spurious as his other qualifications, proved a disastrous choice. The Belgian colonial office soon attempted to marginalize the embarrassing American who was famous for his loud clothes and addressed Leopold in his voluminous correspondence as 'My dear Majesty'. When the money from Brussels dried up, Kowalsky indignantly changed sides and sold his bulky and detailed correspondence with Leopold to the newspaper tycoon Randolph Hearst.

The effect of publishing the evidence of the Belgian King's manipulation of the press and of Washington politicians was catastrophic. Once more, Leopold sought to head off the worst by instituting a commission of inquiry. This time, however, naive missionaries would not do, and despite their being carefully chosen for their views, the commission of three European judges that travelled to the Free State actually took their work seriously, proceeding to hear hundreds of witnesses. During the deposition of statements one of the judges broke down and wept. One witness, a chief who had himself been flogged and held hostage, laid 110 twigs on the commission table – one for each member of his tribe murdered in the pursuit of rubber. On hearing the first findings from the commission in March 1905, the Congo governor-general, Paul Costerman, slit his throat with a razor. Time was running out for the Congo Free State.

Despite the fact that most of the harrowing direct testimony by Congo natives was edited out of the report and buried in the Brussels state archives, and even though Leopold managed to hoodwink many international papers into publishing a 'summary' of the report which he had helpfully supplied himself and which contained no allusions to systematic atrocities, the damning findings of his own commission bore out Morel's accusations in all important aspects, and they soon became known. Leopold, who was by now a septuagenarian given to riding around the park of his palace on a tricycle and to terrorizing his court with his monumental hypochondria and his fear of germs, finally decided that his colony (much less lucrative now that other rubber producers had appeared on the world market) was not worth keeping any longer. He generously agreed to sell it to the Belgian government. For its monarch's gesture, Belgium took on 110 million francs (£330 million in today's money) of debt, agreed to finance all of the King's ongoing building projects, and pay him an additional 50 million francs 'as a mark of gratitude for his great sacrifices in the Congo'. Leopold II died in December of the following year.

After a decade of strenuous work, Edmund Morel, the clerk who dared to take on a king, had won his contest. His crusade was the first international human rights campaign, his Liverpool study the first NGO (non-governmental organization) financed by often modest private donors and carrying its pressure right into the heart of the world's greatest powers. This had been possible because the new mass media had democratized power to a degree. Even in countries such as Austria-Hungary and Russia where press censorship was still in force, the sheer volume of printed matter often rendered the censors practically redundant. Information and ideas spread like wildfire in the cities and reached even the remotest farms within a matter of days. Their power could force through change by overwhelming pressure, ultimately imposing an uncontrollable climate of opinion.

It was not only Morel who benefited from this sea change in power politics. Captain Dreyfus had been retried and exonerated due to a press campaign, though his had been a national affair, pushed forward 'from above' by powerful members of Parisian society, politics and the military. Another important example of the increasing levelling power of the press was the Beylis case in Kiev in 1913, in which a Jewish bookkeeper of a local factory, Mendel Beylis, stood accused on an absurdly trumped-up charge of the ritual murder of a Christian boy. The rabidly antisemitic Tsar had taken it upon himself to instruct the judges to find Beylis guilty and every pressure was applied on the court. Here, too, the attention given by the international press to the case ensured that the accused was promptly acquitted.

The sham trial with its bought 'witnesses' and bogus experts was followed and commented on by the whole world. It eventually collapsed under this weight. The mass media had put power on a different footing. The image of power, always paramount in politics, was no longer the domain of official artists and grand projects but was decided in newspaper offices. 'Modern' monarchs like Wilhelm II of Germany did their best to court and use the media and to project a persona invented for this purpose, but he too had to learn that this was a dance with a devil who could veer off in a different direction without any prior warning. Spin doctors in every era have known that perception is infinitely more potent than mere fact.

The Costs of Power

Morel's success illustrated the importance of winning the image war, and almost a century later the image of colonialism itself and its importance for Europe has been thoroughly reassessed by historians. There can be little doubt that colonial possessions were crucial for the self image of the great powers. The colonies were of the greatest importance for countries like Britain, Germany and France. They created a club of 'Major Powers' with substantial empires, and a sense of historical mission and national greatness.

The much-highlighted dark side of this race for global power and prestige was that colonialism left a profound and often profoundly damaging legacy for those who had been colonized. In the worst cases, such as the Congo, it bled dry a region already suffering from centuries of slavery (by Arab traders, mostly, who robbed the Congo of half a million people a year even before the Europeans arrived) and set them up for a post-colonial history of cruelty, misery, dictatorships, and civil war. In the best instances colonialism left behind largely arbitrary borders but also railway systems, schools, judicial systems and a semblance of democracy, but no home-grown elite trained to administer them. In all cases, it left behind huge questions.

For the colonizers, too, the image and the reality of colonialism split apart and a closer investigation shows how much our own perception of colonialism is beholden to the rhetoric of a century ago: the colonies were nowhere near as vital to the great powers as they would have their subjects believe. Britain, of course, was the country most influenced by the reality of empire, ruling one fifth of the world and one quarter of its population. Imperial culture reached its apogee with the gigantic diamond jubilee celebrations for Queen Victoria in 1897, which went on across the globe, and mobilized huge crowds. The empire was an important trading partner for the mother country, as well as a place for young men in search of a career and a fortune, and, to some extent, to confirm the superiority of the English race. The empire, we are told, made Britain what it was.

This is true, up to a point. If Britain played a great role in most areas of the empire (farmers in rural India who were still directly ruled by an 'approved' local ruler will have noticed relatively little of their colonial administrators), the empire played much less of a role in Britain itself. The balance of trade was in Britain's favour (not least because of London's brutal tactics in the Opium Wars and the resulting highly profitable drug-running to China), with India absorbing around a fifth of British exports and producing valuable goods such as tea, cotton and opium. But it also had a cost for the colonizers. It depressed the textile industry at home and took a great deal of money to administer. Seen from a longer-term perspective, the £270 million invested in India around 1900 also meant that these funds were not available for upgrading ageing British industrial plants and competing with European neighbours.

In addition to this, the Jewel in the Crown made it necessary to maintain the world's largest and most powerful navy, armed with successive generations of ruinously expensive fighting vessels. Falling behind the competition, notably Wilhelm's Germany, would have meant the end of empire. Securing Britain's strategic predominance also necessitated investments in much less lucrative areas of the world: without control of the Suez Canal, rule over India and its attendant trade was impracticable; without control over Egypt and Palestine there was no security for the Canal itself. And ruling Egypt (*de facto* though never officially a colony) meant securing its vast southern hinterland, including the notoriously war-torn Sudan, an area which created its own mythology by making the reputation of military 'heroes' like Lord Kitchener of Khartoum, but which also dragged the empire into endless, smouldering military confrontations and was never a profit-making proposition.

If the empire very probably created as many obligations as opportunities, it remained a source of great national pride – or did it? It depends on whom one asks. There certainly was an important colonial lobby and a widespread belief in the 'white man's burden', in Britain's historical mission, a paternalistic vision summarized by Joseph Chamberlain, the colonial secretary: as 'the duty of a landlord to develop his estate'. The presence of the empire in the everyday life of the middle classes may also be inferred from the innumerable knick-knacks cluttering Victorian and Edwardian houses, many of which had colonial overtones. The house of the composer Sir Edward Elgar, for instance, contained numerous such mementoes, heirlooms from Lady Elgar's family: some Indian brass candle-snuffers, a carved Bombay rosewood square footstool, a marble group of two elephants fighting, an elephant with howdah, a marble idol with dog, etc., etc.

This enumeration may be evidence of the presence of empire in everyday life, but making such a claim is problematic: when Max Nordau caricatured the contents of a *grand bourgeois* home in Vienna, Prague or Budapest he painted a similar, oriental picture of Turkish tassels, Persian rugs and Indian daggers, although Austria-Hungary possessed no colonies at all. The taste for exoticism was a strong force at the time, an outlet for fantasies of freedom, eroticism and primitive dignity, something akin to Edward Said's 'orientalism'; it was not necessarily evidence of colonial pride.

Colonial pride (and, latterly, shame) as embodied by Cecil Rhodes, the African Colossus and prime instigator of the Boer War, was imperialism at its most visible and at its crudest, but it was not representative of British culture, or British thought. If foreign politics and government rhetoric were at times dominated by matters imperial, these matters had, in fact, relatively little presence in people's everyday experience. Unsurprisingly enough, the historical record shows that citizens were rather more concerned with their own lives, with class, work and politics at home, than with societies thousands of miles away. News was published about the colonies in the papers, but the popular imagination was at no point particularly preoccupied with Her or His Majesty's foreign possessions. There was the *Boy's Own* culture, of course, but neither music hall songs (with the possible exception of the popular number 'The Boers Have Got My Daddy') nor West End plays, neither literature nor painting devoted much attention to the colonies.

For painters, the fashion had simply passed. The high Victorianism of Frederic Lord Leighton's English maids in obscure harems and the riotously coloured crowds and wallowing bosoms of Sir Lawrence Alma-Tadema belonged firmly in the nineteenth century. By 1900 a more sober mood had set in. The new generation of artists did not look to India or Africa but into the English countryside, or across the Channel, to France.

With the exception of Rudyard Kipling, British authors had never really exploited life in the colonies as a subject, and around 1900 the empire found very little literary resonance. From Thomas Hardy's timeless England to the utopian nightmares of H. G. Wells, the topics chosen by literary novelists stayed clear of colonial themes. *The Island of Doctor Moreau* by Wells (1896), in which a scientist attempts to transform the animals on a remote island into a humanlike 'race without malice' by surgery, then rules over them with the iron hand of a dictator, can be read as an allegory of imperialism. But it is precisely its allegorical character that makes it a comment on the debates raging about the ideas of Darwin and Malthus, and a mirror of British society itself in the tradition of Robert Louis Stevenson and Francis Bacon.

If and when the colonies or colonial figures appeared, they often did so in a subordinate role – very much like ex-Indian army Dr Watson, in fact, the faithful but never scintillating friend of Sherlock Holmes. Many of the great detective's cases have a colonial background, in fact, but this background is useful only as a repository of unusual poisons, opium, rare snakes, unexplained fortunes, and men returning to their country with their health ruined. They are a bag of tricks, not a presence immanent in everyday life. Much of what we think of today as the culture and imagery of empire – Lawrence of Arabia, Noël Coward's *Private Lives* ('I've been around the world, you know...' 'How was it?' 'The world? Very enjoyable.'), E. M. Forster's *Passage to India* (1924) – dates from after the First World War. In an amusing intellectual manoeuvre (but without humorous intent), the late Edward Said attempted to stand this argument on its head by postulating that it was exactly the absence of any reference to empire before 1914 that showed how deeply suffused Britain was by an imperial, orientalist ideology – so deeply that it was simply assumed as an implicit subtext. The historical evidence, however, does not bear this out.

In the state schools successive imperially minded observers found to their dismay that the children knew hardly anything about the colonies. In public schools, the picture was very similar: boys crammed Greek and Latin verbs, studied their Shakespeare and Tennyson. If they took modern languages, they were most likely to learn German or French. Their socialization in an institutional, often militarized context of boarding schools and cadet corps may have prepared them well for future roles in the imperial administration, but few of their essays or school debates dealt with imperial matters. The empire remained a hazy affair for many of them, despite the institution of 'Mafeking Night', a patriotic springtime anniversary celebration of the relief of the British stronghold during the Boer War, which for schoolboys was an ideal occasion, not only for burning effigies of President Kruger, but also for general mayhem and disorder. In the schoolyard children played, as Bernard Porter remarks, not 'settlers and Zulus' but 'English and Romans', before 'Cowboys and Indians' were introduced. Stanley and Livingstone were national heroes, but so were Shackleton, Scott and even Amundsen some years later, though their exploits were of no value as colonial enterprises and Amundsen was not even British. They were gallant heroes, sportsmen of a kind, adored by a nation that venerated sports.

Colonial administrators were trained at Britain's universities. Oxford was famous for its oriental studies, as was London's Imperial College. Institutions like these taught Indian and African languages and cultures, edited Sanskrit texts and studied everything from art to agriculture, but their students remained in the ivory tower or went out to govern. There was little interchange with the country's wider culture. In chapter eleven we will encounter the fascination of many artists with 'primitive' cultures as a counterbalance to the modern, hyper-civilized world and the rootlessness of life in the big cities. It is interesting, however, that hardly any of these imaginative thinkers turned to the colonies of the countries they lived in. Pablo Picasso was fascinated by objects from French central Africa which helped him discover a new aesthetic in tribal masks and sculptures, while others, like Vassily Kandinsky, who went to live with shamans in the Urals, or Igor Stravinsky, who relived imaginary rituals of ancient Russians, looked for inspiration closer to home. In Britain it was particularly William Butler Yeats who sought a truer, original spirituality, yet he turned to ancient Irish myth and the occult, not to the temples of India. 'We seem, as it were, to have conquered and peopled half the world in a fit of absence of mind,' Sir John Seely, the Cambridge Regius Professor of History, famously sighed.

The situation in France, endlessly anxious about manliness and national decline, was very different. *La gloire de la France* was inextricably linked with the fate of its empire, and had been since Napoleon. This was partly due to the fact that, according to French law, the overseas territories *were* France, and Frenchmen were expected to feel just as much *chez eux* in the jungles of Indochina and the deserts of Algeria as they were in Picardy or on the Champs-Elysées. The press did much to keep colonial themes and images before the public eye. In 1904, for example, the popular journal *l'Illustration* carried not only extensive stories about the Russo-Japanese War (with a notable admiration for the Japanese), but also long reports, serialized stories, photos, drawings, cartoons and other items on the French colonies and their populations in almost every issue. The *Petit journal*, a newspaper with a daily circulation of around a million copies, even dedicated its edition of 6 March 1910 to the 'heroes of colonial expansion'. As in French politics, there was also a vocal anti-colonial faction. The satirical *Assiette au beurre* mercilessly lampooned the colonial idea (as well as everything else), and the *Revue socialiste* polemicized furiously in the name of the 'pained cries of a violated humanity'.

La France d'outre-mer was a constant presence in French life: the Paris Exhibition of 1900 had a large colonial section complete with mock-up native villages, and it was followed by two dedicated colonial exhibitions, in Marseille 1906 (1.8 million visitors) and in Paris one year later, with 2 million visitors. Exhibitions of 'real people' in a parodic semblance of their home setting and garnished with a surfeit of exotic animals, dances and rituals were hugely popular all over Europe. It had been the business acumen of Carl Hagenbeck, the founder of the Hamburg zoo, to import living exhibits from countries as different as Finland, Ceylon and East Africa and to show them off in their 'natural habitat' in Hamburg and during extended European tours from 1874 onwards. Here, a gaping public could enjoy watching, amongst other things 'Australian cannibals, male and female. The only colony of this savage race, which is strange, disfigured, and the most brutal ever to have emerged from the interior of savage countries. The lowest order of humanity.' Some thirty of these ethnographic spectacles went through Europe before 1914, drawing hundreds of thousands of visitors.

Visitors to these shows were driven by plain curiosity. In France, however, their interest was based on a long history of orientalist exoticism reaching back to Eugène Delacroix's forceful fantasies, the languishing women painted into the harems of Jean Auguste Ingres or described in Flaubert's *Salammbô*, and further, to the Egyptomania that had seized the country after Napoleon's brief conquest of Egypt and even the *Lettres persanes* written in the eighteenth century by Montesquieu. The Orient was close to France, not only in terms of geography. Writers like André Gide, Louis-Ferdinand Céline, Jules Verne and Guy de Maupassant all followed in the creative footsteps of Victor Hugo, who had declared with characteristic megalomaniac aplomb and well-tuned sexual undertones: 'Go, peoples! God offers Africa to Europe. Take her ...'

One writer who followed Hugo's advice (in the Orient, not in Africa) in the most personal sense possible was the popular writer and French Academician Pierre Loti (1850–1923), who immortalized his love affair with a Turkish woman whom he describes in perfect orientalist fashion: 'Her eyebrows were brown, slightly curled, so close they almost touched; the expression of her eyes was a mixture of energy and naiveté; one would have said a child's look, so much freshness and youth was in it.' The writer's love for the beautiful Aziyadé became an abiding theme of his life – especially as she obligingly died after his navy duties called the young officer elsewhere. He was convinced that she had expired of a broken heart. Loti, who liked to sport a fez in his portraits, fed the public's appetite with exquisitely written sentimental tales set in exotic locations, which he adored. His house in Rochefort, on the Atlantic coast, is an orientalist fantasy turned to stone, with Turkish and Arabic rooms, intricate ornaments and arches, sumptuous fabrics and the soft murmur of fountains.

The colonial empire had a considerable hold over the national imagination – no doubt also motivated by a will to compensate for the traumatic loss of Alsace and Lorraine to Germany after the Franco-Prussian War of 1870–1. The popular French politician Léon Gambetta even seriously speculated about exchanging the regions for some French colonies. But what was the real importance of the colonies? Were they as crucial for the national economy as they were for national pride? Certainly not. For a start, France did not have a population surplus that could be made to settle the colonies, a major motivation for Britain and Germany, where it was hoped that if sufficient workers could be made to emigrate, the constant spectre of social unrest could be held at bay. With a population kept stable only by immigration into the *Hexagone*, a policy of settling foreign territories was meaningless for France. Economically, the French Congo was exploited almost as ruthlessly as the Free State next door, and there was exchange with Tunisia and Algeria (especially imports of cheap wine into France) and with Indochina, but nothing on the scale of Britain's trade with her colonies.

For Germany the possession of a colonial empire was simply a question of keeping up with the neighbours, an exercise in global power politics with no economic significance. Among the ruling classes the colonies were a source of considerable national pride, but even here enthusiasm for a German empire was far from unanimous. There was support from the conservatives, most importantly from the powerful *Flottenverein* (Fleet Association) pressing for a large navy and therefore also a more important international and colonial role, but the impeccably conservative Reich Chancellor Bismarck regarded the whole idea as a costly folly and did everything he could to prevent it, until political expediency made him a convert to the colonial idea in 1884. The socialists were split on the issue: the majority opposed it on humanitarian grounds, while a minority was in favour, hoping that it would help 'civilize' the natives and thus make them potential socialists themselves, and that the inevitable oppression in the colonies would hasten the world revolution.

Despite the symbolic importance of the empire, it counted for little in political life. Walter Rathenau, then an industrialist trying to break into politics, won his spurs in 1907–8 by travelling to German South West Africa on a fact-finding mission. He made it clear, though, that the post of colonial secretary was not sufficiently interesting for him; he wanted an 'important' ministry. Baroness von Spitzemberg, that unfailing chronicler of the political elite at the Berlin court, wrote at length in her diary about the Russo-Japanese War, relations with the great powers, the meltdown of the Ottoman empire, and the Morocco crisis. The colonies are mentioned only in passing; the only sentence devoted to them between 1900 and her death in 1914 is one of exasperated criticism: 'How wrong the German way of colonization is, which immediately introduces our bureaucracy and our authoritarianism ... the English leave much more individual freedom.'

Among the populace at large the colonies had even less cultural presence. Greengrocers' shops selling exotic fruit were called *Kolonialwarenläden*

(Colonial Wares Stores) until far into the twentieth century, but there was almost no popular or middle-class cultural expression of the colonial pride the government sought to instil, and very few Germans had ever visited the colonies. Germany's colonial power was praised in school books, but essays were set on European themes – Siegfried or Thucydides were much more likely to make a schoolboy sweat than exploits in German South West Africa. One example from 1900: the inventory of essay topics, books for the school library and practical exhibits received during one year by a Berlin secondary school contains no reference of any essay, map, book or specimen that was specifically colonial. The furthest afield these pupils were led was ancient Greece.

By contrast with the French, very little serious German literature was devoted to colonial themes. There were successful novels about the empire, especially after the 1904 uprising. *Peter Moors Fahrt nach Südwest* (Peter Moor's Journey to South West Africa) by the former priest Gustaf Frenssen (1863–1945) even became a runaway bestseller, with 200,000 copies sold before 1914. Despite the presence of colonial images in literature, other exotic locations were more popular with adventure writers, particularly Karl May, who created worlds of intrepid explorers, noble natives and cruel bandits for millions of young readers; his settings, however, were almost exclusively the Middle East and the American Wild West. Boys played with toy soldiers, but their leaden enemies were French or Russian or 'Red Indians', not African. Children were dressed in sailor suits, not khaki. The colonies were almost absent not only from their rooms, but from the drawing rooms as well. Very few people worked in the colonial administration or in army units abroad, and if contemporary novels and newspapers can be believed, the colonies were hardly ever the subject of conversation. If Germany had become a colonial empire, that fact had made little impression on public consciousness.

Why was this so? Perhaps the notoriously unstable sense of national identity that had been modified yet again by the foundation of the empire in 1870 left little room for new definitions. Perhaps, also, the fact that most of Germany was landlocked and had historically been occupied fighting off invasions, rather than invading others, may have had something to do with it. Empires were for maritime nations such as Britain, the Netherlands, Portugal and France. Powers such as Austria-Hungary and Russia, whose access to the oceans was compromised by foreign-controlled Gibraltar and Suez for the former and by ice for the latter, made no serious attempts to establish a colonial empire.

Economic reasons were never at the heart of Germany's colonial policy, and the critics were right to point out that the colonies and the immense expansion of the German navy lost the country money and set it on a dangerous collision course with the overseas interests of Britain and France. The Kaiser was attached to the colonial idea for reasons of prestige. To be a major power, one simply had to have colonies – a perception which also led Italy to pour millions into the sands of Libya in search of national glory in 1911.

Imperialist culture and orientalist imagination are not the same. The latter was a significant part of European culture around 1900. Its function, though, was not so much to represent imperialism, as to provide an escape from the dizzying speed of modern life. The Orient was projected as being everything the Occident was not. Men lusted after the supposed sexual freedom symbolized by the 'ethnographic' photos of nude African girls (as well as the occasional boy) and their descriptions in literature – sensual, naive, but vibrating with energy and endowed with lips like ripe fruits, just like Loti's beloved Aziyadé – promised pleasures that bourgeois marriages rarely offered; indeed, the popular repertoire of images such as the strong but animalistic negro, the all-enduring Asian and the sexually potent Arab with his harems and endlessly available women symbolized the very life force which many thought was dying in the West. The fascination with the Orient was also a fascination with a sensual world of 'natural' and strong emotions, of an erotic paradise untouched by the withering hand of the Church, or the perversion of the big city.

There was another strong attraction to the world of Orientalism. Its sense of timelessness, the mirages of deserts, of tropical forests and remote plateaus (which, as Conan Doyle imagined, might harbour entire prehistoric worlds of dinosaurs and dragons), and of ancient cities in which ancestral customs governed the lives of fatalistic inhabitants, was the very antithesis to the driven, technological lives that modern cities forced on their own denizens. Even opium and hashish, the drugs imported from this enticing world, promised the sweet embrace of forgetfulness and a few moments of bliss outside of time and space. If speed was the poison of modernity, the Orient was its antidote.

One of the artists who felt this connection was the great Russian poet and novelist Andrei Bely. The protagonist of his novel *Petersburg*, Nikolai Apollonovich, the son of a rationalist senior civil servant whose greatest ambition it is to transverse the Nevsky Prospect 'at maximum speed' every day in his carriage, has opted out of the hectic life of modernity at a young age. Having abandoned his studies he now rises late, wears a dressing gown from Bukhara (in Uzbekistan, Russian Central Asia), a little skull cap and Persian slippers and has transformed his salon into an Orientalist stage set:

> the Bukhara dressing gown was continued by a stool in dark brown tones; it was embellished by intarsia made of fine strips of ebony and mother of pearl; the dressing gown was continued by the negro shield manufactured of the thick leather of a rhino killed at some point and by the rusty Sudan arrow … and finally the dressing gown was continued by the colourful leopard fur, stretched out at their feet with gaping mouth; on the stool were arranged a dark blue water pipe and a three-legged incense burner in the form of a crescent; but the most amazing object was a colourful cage in which small green parrots fluttered their wings every now and then.

As in Loti's house in France, all continents, all Orientalist tropes are jumbled together in this room, a cell of resistance against the tyranny of modernity. The Orientalist imagination thrived on these fantasies, even if the realities of life away from industrial civilization bore no resemblance to these scenarios of sweltering seduction. Important to politicians as symbols

Beautiful, proud, and bristling with virile force: Ludwig Deutsch's Nubian Guard, *a fine specimen of Orientalist art.*

of power and prestige (but certainly not as sources of profit), the colonies also mattered because they carried the promise of a different life.

This gap between perception and the reality of the colonial empires is most cruelly striking in the case of the Belgian Congo. As they marvelled at tribal masks and newly built museums, the Belgians could read in the newspapers about the good that was done in Africa in the name of the country's *mission civilisatrice*. The reality behind this carefully maintained screen, however, was not only horrifying, its secret balance sheets tilt the whole wicked operation towards the grotesque. Hugely profitable for the short while during which Leopold effectively held a world monopoly on the rubber trade, the Congo Free State made the King an immensely rich man, but the business of murder on a gigantic scale also created its overheads. The Belgian historian Jean Stengers has estimated that up to 1908 the Congo yielded a profit of some 60 million francs to Leopold, with a further 24 million after the handover to Belgium. Administration, defence and transport, however, cost King and country some 210 million altogether, a net loss of 126 million francs.

If the human cost of Leopold's regime was unspeakable, it is not inestimable. Without accurate population statistics, it is impossible to determine exactly how many people were murdered in the Congo Free State, but a mosaic of sources has given historians a good idea of scale. According to the change in population patterns, the reports and estimate of missionaries about the people in their areas, and recent historical analyses it is probable that between 1885 and 1908 more than 10 million people (more than those killed during the First World War) were either murdered directly by Leopold's henchmen, or died as a consequence of famine and disease as they were prevented from cultivating crops or attending to their animals, driven out of their homes, or left to starve in hostage camps or in the jungle.

Even with its unprecedented ruthlessness, the exploitation of the Belgian Congo was profitable only for a few short years. If Leopold managed to make a killing – in both senses of the word – out of his colony it was simply because he pocketed the profits directly and passed on both his debts and the bulk of the administrative cost to his country, in return for which he graced streets from Brussels to Bruges with ostentatious and self-aggrandizing building projects. Leopold had murdered in the Congo and stolen from the Belgians, to whom he left a landscape gratefully commemorating a great monarch. Many of the statues are still standing today.

Neither Edmund D. Morel nor Roger Casement was to have

monuments erected in his name, and neither died a peaceful death. Morel, one of the 'few people whom I could deeply admire', according to the philosopher Bertrand Russell, fought for pacifism and was almost universally vilified by the press. Finally he was incarcerated in Pentonville Prison, where he was held in solitary confinement and made to sew mailbags during the day in total silence in 1917. When he was released he was physically broken, but continued working, eventually becoming an MP in Britain's first Labour government.

Knighted in recognition of his services, Sir Roger Casement became increasingly involved in Irish nationalism. He travelled to the United States to collect funds from Irish-Americans for the purchase of black market firearms to be used in an anti-British insurrection and then took a steamer from New York to Germany to make an offer to the Kaiser's government: in exchange for support for Irish independence, Casement proposed forming a brigade of Irish freedom fighters from prisoners of war held by Germany, a unit that would battle on the Germans' side. On his return to Ireland he was arrested and brought to London, where he was held in the Tower.

Friends and supporters swiftly organized a campaign for Casement's defence; among those giving money or writing appeals for clemency were the United States Negro Fellowship League and the writers Arthur Conan Doyle and George Bernard Shaw. After the trial and the guilty verdict against Casement, all efforts to commute his death sentence into life imprisonment were quickly and discreetly scotched by the police, who made sure that influential figures in Parliament and in London's clubland were shown the incriminating (and often very explicit) entries about homosexual encounters in Casement's diaries, which had been

'The best thing was the Congo', Roger Casement, hero and traitor.

found during house searches following his arrest. Treason, it seems, was a grave offence, but to be a homosexual was unforgivable. The appeals for clemency were rejected.

Sir Roger Casement was hanged in Pentonville Prison (in which Morel would serve his sentence only a year later) on the morning of 3 August 1916. A few days before his execution he wrote to a friend: 'I have made awful mistakes, and did heaps of things wrong and failed at much – but... the best thing was the Congo.'

6

1905:
In All Fury

—The storm! Soon will break the storm!
The bold storm finch proudly flies between the
lightning and the frothing anger of the sea;
now screams the prophet of victory:
Let the storm burst forth in all fury!
 – Maksim Gorky, *The Song of the Storm Finch*

On the morning of Sunday 9 January 1905, one of those clear, mild winter days on which St Petersburg looks at her most serene, Sergei Yulevich Witte, a tall man of fifty-five years, got out of bed and stepped to the window of his grand apartment to look out onto the boulevard. 'I...saw a crowd of workers, *intelligenty*, women, and children marching along Kamenno-Ostrovskii Prospekt, carrying church banners, pictures and flags,' he wrote. 'As soon as this crowd, or, rather, procession, passed by, I went to my balcony, from which I could see Troitskii Bridge, toward which they were marching. I got to the balcony just in time to hear shots, a few of which whizzed close by. One of these killed a porter at nearby Tsarskoe Selo Lycée. Then came a series of salvoes. Within ten minutes a large crowd came running back, some of them carrying dead and wounded, among them children.'

The people who had assembled for the procession, countless masses, perhaps a hundred thousand strong, had been in a festive mood and dressed in their Sunday best as they set out to the Winter Palace to see their Little Father, the Tsar. They were singing religious hymns. Some had fasted and prayed the night before. Others, less optimistically, had written farewell letters and even made their wills. This day was going to be important in the history of Russia, an unprecedented act of love and loyalty: a people asking its sovereign directly to hear them in their need. They had prepared a petition to give to their Tsar. 'We workers and residents of the city of St

Petersburg...have come to Thee, Sire, to seek justice and protection,' the document read. 'We have become beggars; we are oppressed and burdened by labour beyond our strength; we are humiliated; we are regarded, not as human beings, but as slaves who must endure their bitter fate in silence...' The Tsar, these workers thought, had no idea of their hardship. He must be told, and then he would set about punishing the capitalists, the bureaucrats, and all oppressors of the Russian people. They would go as adoring people to 'cry out their sorrows on his shoulder', carrying with them their holy icons and their hopes. 'Save Thy People, O Lord,' they sang, their breath forming steam in the cool air. People on the roadside crossed themselves; the church bells tolled.

The different columns converging on the Winter Palace were soon faced with roadblocks on all major thoroughfares: at Mytninskaya, on the Neva Embankment (close to where Witte stood watching); on Vasilevskii Island. When the main procession reached the magnificent beaten copper façade of the Narva Gate, built to commemorate Napoleon's defeat, a squadron of mounted Life Guard Grenadiers charged the crowd with sabres drawn and retreated again. An infantry regiment was taking aim beside a small bridge on the left. There was a moment of silence after the first confusion. The demonstrators joined hands and sang louder. They were massed around an orthodox priest in his long cassock, a young, charismatic man. Then the bugle sounded, the signal to fire. A police officer shouted: 'What are you doing? How can you shoot at a holy pilgrimage holding the portrait of the Tsar?' He was one of the first to fall. All around the priest his companions collapsed under the hail of bullets. Icons and banners clattered into the dirty snow. Then the crowd fled.

On Vasilevskii Island it was the Finnish Life Guard Regiment that stopped the petitioners. Envoys with white handkerchiefs went over to the soldiers, attempting to explain that they had come for, not against the Tsar. When they saw the soldiers' rifles pointed at them, some of the marchers bared their breasts and dared their brothers in uniform to shoot. Orders were shouted and salvoes of shots rang out; cavalry cut down those too slow to get away. There is a surviving photo of the scene: a line of soldiers in their long winter coats are taking aim at a crowd at the other side of a brilliantly white square. The demonstrators are scrambling to safety; uncertain dots in the distance. A sole, isolated figure is standing in the no man's land between the lines. At the end of this Bloody Sunday, as soft snow was covering the city, 130 demonstrators had been killed and 299 wounded according to official estimates. Foreign journalists recorded that there were up to 4,600 casualties.

There Is No God!

'Bloody Sunday', as it was to become known, was widely seen as the day the Tsar set his army upon his own people. The outrage it caused sparked months of revolutionary unrest and marked a turning point in Russia's history. 'There is no God, there is no Tsar!' the tall priest at the front of the procession at the Narva Gate had cried in despair when the shots were ringing out over the square and he saw his comrades falling around him. His name was Father Gapon, and his cry would echo to the far corners of Siberia.

In many ways, town and country were connected more intimately in Russia than in any other major country. The fifth largest economy in the world, Russia's cities were modern and industrialized, but only about 20 per cent of Russians lived there. The overwhelming majority laboured and thought almost exactly as they had done for centuries, far, far away from the great transformation gripping the country's western neighbours. Any understanding of Russia and of the 'little revolution' of 1905 must set out from one of thousands of dusty village squares surrounded by the low huts in which most of the Tsar's subjects lived out their lives.

Peasant villages, *derevni*, derived their name from *derevno*, the Russian word for wood, the main building material used for the dwellings, which were usually erected and dismantled (if fire did not destroy them first) within a few days. Large families of several generations lived together in a single house, often in a single room with a stove on which they slept, a table by which they ate, and the shrine with the house icon, a world of 'icons and cockroaches', as Leon Trotsky put it, bolted behind its inhabitants in more than just a metaphorical sense: 'The doors are kept vigorously closed, windows are hermetically sealed and the atmosphere cannot be described,' a desperate English Quaker wrote in a letter home. 'Its poisonous quality can only be realised by experience.'

Behind these 'vigorously closed' doors, life went on as it had done since time immemorial. Most villagers were illiterate until the end of the nineteenth century; until 1917, there was no compulsory education in Russia, even at primary level. In 1901, only one in five children of school age was in school. While roughly a third of village schools were run by the Orthodox Church, the priests had little influence on their flock. They were themselves hardly more than peasants and were deeply ignorant; studying theology and doctrine was the domain of the robed 'black clergy' in the monasteries, who fulfilled no pastoral duties. Knowledge of Christian doctrine was therefore minimal, as Maksim Gorky heard from a Kazan peasant, who said that God 'cannot be everywhere at once, too many men have been born for that. But he will succeed, you see. But I can't understand Christ at all! He serves no purpose as far as I'm concerned. There is no God and that's enough. But now there's another! The son, they say. So what if he's God's son. God isn't dead, not that I know of.'

Peasant life was a law unto itself, in the most literal sense. Finance minister Sergei Witte estimated that there were ten thousand policemen for a hundred million peasants in Russia, and justice of a sort was meted out according to caprice and custom – usually in the form of communal humiliations or floggings by peasant courts. The most vicious punishments were reserved for adulterous women and horse thieves. Women accused of betraying their husbands would be stripped naked or have their skirts tied together over their heads and then be beaten or dragged round the village behind a cart. Horse thieves had even worse to fear: they were often castrated, flogged, branded with irons, or hacked to death with sickles. The violence of daily life was extreme, especially for women, who could be beaten by their husbands without any protection of the law. 'The more you beat the old woman, the tastier the soup will be,' said a Russian proverb. 'Beat the fur, and it's warmer; beat your wife, and she's sweeter,' ran another. During the wedding ceremony, the husband's new authority over his wife was symbolically affirmed when the young woman's father handed the groom a whip. Village feasts usually turned into drunken brawls, and it was accepted as part of the fun that some of those joining in the fighting would never get up again.

The real face of Russia? Peasant men in the provinces.

It is perhaps a measure of the muzhik's medieval mind that despite these miserable conditions and despite the constant hunger and famine in the countryside there was hardly any emigration from rural Russia. Seventy per cent of the 3 million of the Tsar's subjects who left their country between 1897 and 1916 in search of a better life were either Poles or Jews. Life outside the village was almost inconceivable.

Borrowed from the Village

Almost but not quite. As land holdings for individual families in village communes grew smaller and families larger than before, hundreds of thousands went to the city to work in factories and formed an urban underclass that never became anything like the industrial proletariat that Marxists expected to see. In contrast to other countries, most Russian peasants who took work in the city eventually returned to their villages. The industrial proletariat of Manchester, Milan or Essen was an urban constituency in the proper sense of the word. Russian factory workers were only borrowed from the village.

Men, especially, were often married and so sent money home, returning to their families when they could afford it. Women had a much harder time. Back from their stint in the 'godless den of sin' they were considered compromised, less virtuous, less marriageable. Many therefore had to remain in the cities, eking out a precarious life between factory work, domestic service and prostitution.

Workers who returned brought with them inexorable change. One would recognise them at once: they wore their shirts inside their trousers and might even have a jacket, they had shaved off their beards and no longer had their hair cut under a bowl. They brought money and consumer goods, ready-made clothes in city fashions, books and political ideas. They had seen the world and wanted more independence than those who had stayed at home. Even the women who had done factory work seemed 'distinguished by a livelier speech, greater independence, and a more obstinate character'.

As the city began to infiltrate the village, so the village carried its brutality and hardship into the expanding slums and factory dormitories of Moscow and St Petersburg, where the workers would live almost like animals, many to a room without running water or sanitation, and with hardly any heating – just enough to sleep the sleep of exhaustion after a thirteen-hour working day, six days a week. Even the water from the public wells was not safe to drink and whole districts were all but drowned in a combination of industrial and human waste. As late as 1909, a cholera epidemic claimed 30,000 victims in St Petersburg.

Once again it was the women who suffered most. Pregnancies, numerous childbirths and mistreatment from drunken husbands or lovers cost them dearly: 'A woman worker of fifty sees and hears poorly, her head trembles, her shoulders are sharply hunched over. She looks about seventy. It is obvious that only dire need keeps her at the factory, forcing her to work beyond her strength. While in the West, elderly workers have pensions, our women workers can expect nothing better than to live out their last days as lavatory attendants,' a doctor reported in 1914:

> ... they are remarkable for the fact that with very few exceptions and despite the cold and frozen wet snow they appear practically without clothes on ... Unfastened trousers, some rags instead of a shirt, and literally not one of the necessities of ordinary human apparel. Here, also, some questionable women with hand baskets even carry on a lively trade in these horrible rags and worse. People undress under the nearest gate and even right on the street, in full view, without attracting any special surprise or curiosity. Obviously this is a common business.

Another observer, the journalist Aleksei Svirskii, had written in 1905:

> Three days and two nights I passed among people who had fallen out of life. They are not living, these people, but moldering like charred logs left scattered after a fire. In the gloomy half-light of the dirty dives, in crowded, bug-infested flophouses, in the tearooms and taverns and the dens of cheap debauchery – everywhere where vodka, women and children are sold – I encountered people who no longer resembled human beings.

The Pugilist at Court

The steep rise of Sergei Witte from provincial clerk to head of government is exemplary of the frustrations and opportunities Russia presented to its abler inhabitants. Witte's stupendous advancement was possible only because he was a technical man whose expertise was needed: he was hardworking, he was competent, and he was in railways, a key element of the country's economic modernization. Unlike his ruler, the pragmatic and foresighted Witte understood from the beginning that such a partial overhaul of the country was not only unjust, it was impossible: 'it is a general rule that if a government refuses to meet the demands of the people for eco-

*Admitting defeat: Sergei Witte leaving the peace
negotiations with Japan.*

nomic and social reforms, the people will begin to demand changes in the
political structure. And if a government does not meet such demands...
revolution will break out.'

Witte came as an outsider to the political establishment. Born in Tiflis,
in the Caucasus, his family was probably of Baltic German stock, a constituency that had brought forth many of the country's most able professionals and administrators. His father was a senior civil servant and the boy
grew up in a climate of precarious privilege. Later he was sent to Odessa for
his studies. At university the tall and awkward young man (he never
acquired a metropolitan gloss and was to be famous for his rough manners
and provincial accent, as well as for his habit of chewing gum) found a
world in which privilege was allowed in the form of debauchery and brothel
visits, but any political or civic engagement was severely discouraged: 'You
professors can meet among yourselves, but only to play cards. And you students remember that I will look with an indulgent eye on drunkenness but
a soldier's uniform [i.e. a twenty-five-year conscription into the army]
awaits anyone who is noted for free thinking,' the director of Kiev
University had reminded the assembled faculty.

Witte's political temperament was like Bismarck's: instinctively conservative and quietly pragmatic. His time at university had coincided with the
high point of an intellectual debate about the future and the nature of
Russia that would set the tone for decades to come, and possibly up to the
present day. While one party, the modernists, argued vigorously that the
country had to shake off its 'semi-Asian' backwardness and do its utmost to
become a modern, Western state, their Slavophile opponents held that this
would spell the nation's doom. Russia, they argued, was different, was

inherently half European and half Asian, a special people put on the earth by God to fulfil a unique task according to a vision of life that was uniquely Russian, tied to the soil, the primitive piety of the peasant, and the grandeur of Church and Tsar. Needless to say, this approach left little room for democracy, industrialization, secular education, or for accommodating the different national cultures of the empire – one third of the Tsar's subjects were neither Russian nor Orthodox – for Poles and Mongolians, Muslims, Finns and Jews.

A young engineer with bold ideas and plenty of energy, Witte rose quickly through the ranks of the embryonic railway service (in 1853 the Russian empire, the world's largest country, had had a total of 650 kilometres of tracks), and he soon attracted the attention of the government hierarchy, especially after he made himself unpopular by going against his superiors on a safety issue concerning a particular line. His warning was ignored, an oversight that almost cost the life of the Tsar, whose train was derailed while he was on board.

Sped on his way by this event, Witte soon found a post in St Petersburg, first in the ministry of transport and in 1892, aided by energetic ideas about expanding the rail network and attracting foreign investment, as minister of finance. The 43-year-old imperial minister was an exception in many ways. The custom of awarding appointments in the administration strictly according to seniority had the inescapable consequence that the most responsible posts were held by men in their declining years, out of touch and unable to understand the challenges facing them. Promotion was governed by a table of ranks introduced by Peter the Great, a fourteen-rung ladder that not only afforded officials wonderful forms of address like 'Your High Ancestry', but also brought an automatic rise into the hereditary nobility. The table also guaranteed an equivalence of rank across the civil service, army and navy. This allowed senior officers going into retirement from army posts to enter the civil service at equivalent rank, which meant that a whole province could suddenly find itself led by a doddering colonel who had never done much more than hang around in the officers' club and bellow at recruits, and whose only practical experience might stem from his young days in the Crimean War, or from stringing up peasants after local revolts. Any kind of reform was the very last thing on the minds of these men; the quality of many imperial administrators was accordingly dismal.

Witte was an exceptional figure in the St Petersburg government, a body usually composed of princes, bureaucrats risen through the ranks, and a sprinkling of university professors in the more technical and less prestigious posts. He was robustly disdainful of the camarilla of grand dukes and generals at court, a feeling that was mutual. While the aristocratic faction viewed him as an uncouth upstart, intent on upsetting their comfortable lives with reforms and other demands, the minister had a good deal to say about the officials appointed by the Tsar. A governor sent to pacify the rebellious duchy of Finland, Prince Ivan M. Obolenskii, a member of one of Russia's most eminent families, seemed ideal for the job in the eyes of the court, as Witte remarked. He had 'distinguished himself as governor of Kharkov by his successful suppression of peasant riots, in the course of which he had personally supervised the flogging of rioters...That the prince had peasants flogged severely was taken as proof of his youth and decisiveness: "what a solid young man", "what a fine fellow", "who else but he should become governor-general of Finland".'

Of the governor of Kiev, General Kleigels, Witte wrote that although he was 'undoubtedly better than those who succeeded him, that [was] no recommendation. He was a very limited man, poorly educated, with a greater knowledge of horses than of men,' a rather complimentary assessment compared with the verdict on the viceroy for the Far East, Admiral Alexeev, 'a man with the mentality of a sly Armenian rug dealer', who had made his career, Witte alleged, because he had once rescued the young Grand Duke Alexis Aleksandrovich from public embarrassment when the latter had misbehaved in a Marseille brothel (after having been sent abroad to forget a mistress he had become rather too infatuated with). Alexeev took responsibility for the sordid incident in front of the French police, and ever after, the Grand Duke promoted his advancement.

If Witte had little sympathy for the upper echelons of the imperial government, his view of the Tsar and his family was, if anything, more grim. First, of course, there was the Emperor, Nicholas II, whom Witte judged to have a personality like 'an average guards colonel of good family', amiable but utterly ineffective and deluded. 'Emperor Nicholas II is very unlike his father: he is well bred (more so than any man I have ever met), is always dressed to the nines, never uses rough language, never behaves in a rough manner,' was the kindest thing he had to say about his sovereign.

The heart of the Russian empire was a void, the 'character, or lack of character' of an Emperor who was utterly dominated by his German wife Alexandra Fedorovna, whose 'dull, egotistical character and narrow world-view' was evident in the Tsar's political opinions. 'She might have been a suitable wife for a German prince or for a Tsar with a backbone,' Witte reflected maliciously, 'but sad to say, this Tsar has no will.' The result was a little world of autocratic hypocrisy and ignorance completely insulated from reality: 'the Empress...and her spouse [!] immure themselves in fortresses – the palaces at Tsarskoe Selo and Peterhof. From their fortresses they send telegrams of condolence to the wives of men who have fallen at the hands of foul revolutionary assassins, praise the fallen for their courage, and declare "my life does not matter to me as long as Russia is happy".'

The court was almost entirely sequestered in a parallel world in which the Tsar still considered himself to be presiding over a mystical union between Old Rus and its eternal God, a vision all the more comically inappropriate because the Russian credentials of Nicholas II himself were weak at best. The French ambassador Maurice Paléologue calculated that even according to the most optimistic genealogical analysis, the monarch, who looked so similar to his cousin King George V that even members of their entourage could not tell them apart if they donned each other's uniforms and who had imitated his forebears by taking a German wife with whom he corresponded in English, could not possibly be more than 1/128th part Russian, and that if rumours were true that Catherine the Great's son Paul was sired not by her husband but by a count who had been one of her many lovers, Nicholas was not Russian at all. In his mind, though, Nicholas was the father of Russianness itself, the divinely appointed guardian of the Slavic soul, which he was determined to defend against the corrosive effects of modernity and the insolent challenges of liberalism.

A pragmatic reformer at a deeply reactionary court, Witte had to tread carefully, and he was skilful at tailoring his message to his addressee. When the notoriously antisemitic Tsar Alexander III, the father of Nicholas II, asked his then finance minister whether it was true that he 'liked Jews', Witte, who did not like Jews, responded himself with a question. 'I asked if he could drop all the Jews of Russia into the Black Sea. If he could, the Jewish problem would be solved. But since that was impossible, the only choice as a means of solving the Jewish question was the gradual elimination of all discriminatory laws against the Jews.' In fact, Witte was at once clear-sighted and intensely prejudiced. He had little time for 'insolvent yids' – (*zhidy*), but he saw that the 'Jewish question', as it was then called, was a problem of Russia's own making. 'Anti-Jewish legislation, arbitrarily interpreted, reinforced by the negative influence of the Russian schools, helped drive the Jewish masses, particularly the youth, to become extreme revolutionaries,' he noted, referring to the appallingly inhumane conditions to which the overwhelming majority of Jews in the empire was reduced by legislation limiting the movement and the professions they could follow, and imposing special taxes. As Witte saw, these burdens fell 'on the poorest Jews, for the richer the Jew, the easier it is for him to buy his way out'. His attitude remained contradictory: given to ranting about 'yids' pushing their way up in Petersburg society, Witte chose to endanger his entire career by marrying Matilda Lisanewich, a Jewish divorcée, against the scandalised opinion of all of 'good' St Petersburg society, which lost no time in ostracizing the couple. By all accounts he was a devoted husband.

Dangerous Ideas

Tsar Nicolas was never able to resolve the question of how to run a medieval state supported and financed by a modern, industrial economy. Such an economy relied on an educated class, and while the Tsar sought the practical, technical expertise of a professional middle class he was fearful of its unruly liberal ideas. Any attempt at innovation or reform, any flirting with liberal ideals, the faintest whiff of revolutionary thought, would invariably be dashed, either by the almighty bureaucracy or by the more ruthless methods of the secret police. Nor were there any other instruments of democratic participation apart from the zemstvos, the local assemblies which quickly became rallying points for reformers. There was no national parliament, no official political party, and the press was as strictly controlled as ever.

It was dangerous to be seen to be interested in ideas. At best it might ruin one's career in the civil service; at worst it would cost one's life. In 1849, Fedor Dostoyevsky had been subjected to a mock execution for reciting a subversive poem. The oppressive atmosphere, however, only made the appeal of liberty all the more irresistible. Revolutionary ideas were discussed behind closed doors and imported between the covers of clandestine journals and books, which were then copied by hand and widely circulated. Occasionally, even the imperial censor took his eye off his desk for a crucial moment. Marx's *Capital* had been authorized because the censor could not conceive of anyone actually wanting to read so dull a work of economic theory. In 1862, one of his colleagues had a particularly bad day when he was so overcome with discouragement at the wooden style and clunking plot of *Chto delat?* (What Is to be Done?), a novel by one Nikolai Chernychevsky, that he authorized its publication. The hero of this novel survives terrible ordeals, steeling himself for the revolution, and ends up eating only meat and sleeping on a bed of nails to strengthen his dedication to the cause. An entire generation of disenchanted young Russians, amongst them Vladimir Ulyanov, who was to become known as Lenin (1870–1924), regarded Chernychevsky's work as an inspiration for their own subjugation to the revolutionary ideal. Many no longer believed in the possibility of constitutional reform and of a peaceful evolution.

Intimidated, bullied and threatened by the state, they turned to other means. In the very year of the publication of *Chto delat?* another student revolutionary published his vision of things to come:

> Soon, very soon, the day will come when we shall unfurl the great banner of the future, the red flag, and with a mighty cry of 'Long Live the Russian Social and Democratic Republic!' we shall move against the Winter Palace to exterminate all its inhabitants ... we shall kill the imperial party with no more mercy than they show for us now. We shall kill them in the squares, if the dirty swine ever dare to appear there; kill them in their houses; kill them in the narrow streets of the towns; kill them in the avenues of the capitals; kill them in the villages. Remember: anyone who is not with us is our enemy, and every method may be used to exterminate our enemies.

The apparent hopelessness of their cause had radicalized an entire generation of revolutionaries and turned them into jihadists of the revolution. The weapons of choice in what was the modern world's first wave of terrorist suicide attacks were revolvers and home-made bombs which would be used at close range, often taking with them both the target and his assassin. The campaign had proved cruelly efficient: some 17,000 people were killed in terrorist attacks during the twenty years leading up to 1917, including two prime ministers and several provincial governors. If one adds to this the many local rebellions, particularly in Poland and Finland, where they were viciously suppressed, the many peasant revolts and the mass strikes in the cities, the picture that emerges is that of a constantly simmering civil war whose outbreaks of insurrection and reprisal punctuated a fragile stalemate in the state.

A Victorious Little War

Given the situation in the Russian empire, with its brutalized and ignorant peasant majority, its viciously suppressed minorities, a frustrated middle class and the often staggering incompetence of its administrators, it seems a miracle that a large revolution did not occur much earlier. When it finally happened, it arose from a cause as stupid as it was unnecessary: the disastrous war with Japan.

Eager to extend his empire into south-east Asia and to ensure an ice-free port in the Pacific, the Tsar had been looking for ways of consolidating his influence in Manchuria and Korea. He had managed to strong-arm Japan into ceding its northern possession of Sakhalin Island and to pressure

China into leasing to Russia the strategically valuable harbour town of Port Arthur (Lüshun), a natural harbour in the bay formed by northern China and Korea. As soon as the lease was signed, Russia proceeded to fortify the port and to strengthen its army bases in the east, a task made simpler by the Trans-Siberian Railway, one of Witte's pet projects, which was nearing completion and whose purpose was obviously military, rather than economic.

All this had infuriated the Empire of the Rising Sun, which had quietly but solidly prepared for war by investing in Prussian military advisers and British warships. In January 1904 Japan began to urge Russia to accept a treaty of mutual territorial guarantees in Manchuria and Korea, and as there was no response from St Petersburg for several weeks, the Japanese Emperor withdrew his ambassador. Admiral Alexeev, the Viceroy of the Far East, who happened to be in Tokyo, telegraphed the Tsar to tell him that Japan was bluffing. They would never attack, and even if they did, Prime Minister Vyacheslav Plehve thought that Russia's domestic situation could be improved no end by a 'victorious little war'.

In the late evening of 8 February 1904, Japanese battleships and torpedo boats encircled Port Arthur and opened fire on the Russian fleet helplessly moored in the harbour. With much of the fleet in the Pacific destroyed, damaged or hemmed in, the Tsar's generals had to watch as Japan landed troops in Korea and marched on Russian positions. In St Petersburg, the general staff flew into a panic. There were not nearly enough forces in the east to counter a Japanese advance; the Trans-Siberian Railway consisted of a single track and was still unfinished around Lake Baikal, a body of water roughly the size of Switzerland. Rails had to be laid on the ice to transport troops to the theatre of war, while construction of the route around the lake was driven forward at maximum speed. Within months it would transport 410,000 soldiers, 93,000 horses and 1,000 heavy guns to Manchuria.

As the news from the east worsened during the ensuing weeks, panic sowed disorder and gave rise to hare-brained schemes. The Baltic fleet was ordered to relieve the trapped forces in the Japanese sea and began to make its agonizingly slow way past Denmark and towards Africa and the Cape of Good Hope. Confusion and paranoia were so intense among the Russian military that the Tsar's navy almost provoked a war with Britain when it sank a British fishing trawler at Dogger Bank off the Norfolk coast, thinking that it might be a Japanese torpedo boat. Russian ships even fired on each other.

True to his early choice, Nicholas II had made his viceroy also the supreme military commander of the war, a decision noted caustically by

Real carnage: Russian casualties in a press photograph.

Sergei Witte: 'The admiral was as qualified for his new post as I. He knew nothing about the army and little about the navy.' Refusing to listen to his advisers and relieve Alexeev from his post, in order to save the military situation the Tsar resolved to send a second commander, General Kuropatkin, an experienced and competent officer whose task was made impossible by contradictory orders and the constant interference of the vainglorious viceroy. Horrified by these developments, Sergei Witte spoke to Kuropatkin before his departure, imploring him to have Alexeev arrested immediately upon the general's arrival and sent back to St Petersburg under guard. Kuropatkin 'burst out laughing and, as he left, said "You are right".' The next day he left for Manchuria, 'with great pomp, as if he were certain of victory'.

Over the following months, it became abundantly clear that there was to be no such victory. In May Russia suffered heavy casualties at the battle of the Yalu River; a breakout attempt of the Russian fleet at Port Arthur ended in disaster in August; and in February 1905, after a massive and costly battle, the Japanese forced Kuropatkin to retreat from his headquarters at Mukden (Shenyang), 400 kilometres north of Port Arthur. The Russian forces were badly equipped, badly trained, and uncoordinated, and intelligence-gathering was so rudimentary that the army was forced to rely on the London *Times* for accurate news about troop movements. In an attempt to boost the morale and sense of mission of his troops fighting the 'Yellow Peril', the Tsar had a large shipment of icons, including the Holy Mother of God and various Orthodox saints, sent to the front, an initiative that many saw as typical of the priorities and the blindness of central power. 'The Japanese are beating us with machine guns,' General Dragomilov remarked, 'but never mind: we'll beat them with icons!'

The guns proved stronger. When the Baltic fleet finally made it to its destination in May 1905 after having circumnavigated the globe, the Japanese admirals had all the time in the world to choose a place of engagement. They gave battle to Russia's forces off the island of Tsushima, between Korea and Kyushu, sinking eight battleships and effectively ending the 'victorious little war' Plehve had wished for. In an attempt to salvage what he could of Russia's badly shaken prestige as a great power, Sergei Witte was dispatched to the United States to sue for peace.

If Russia's government had badly overestimated its military prowess, it had fatally misjudged the internal situation. The little war had turned into a huge disaster; instead of silencing critics, it caused a storm of protest which soon linked the decision to go to war to the general incompetence, ignorance and arrogance of the government. On 15 July 1904, Russia's ruthless but able minister of the interior, Vyacheslav Plehve, was assassinated with a 16-pound bomb by a young revolutionary socialist. No one mourned the unpopular hardliner. In Warsaw people danced in the streets when the news of his death arrived, and the Austro-Hungarian ambassador Count Aerenthal reported home that several men he had spoken to had voiced the opinion that 'further catastrophes similar to Plehve's murder will be necessary in order to bring about a change of mind on the part of the highest authority'.

The sudden power vacuum at the heart of government was hurriedly patched up by the Emperor, who appointed Pyotr Dmitrievich Sviatopolk-Mirskii, one who he hoped would calm the troubled waters, as Mirskii was widely seen as a man of integrity and a moderate. How grave the Tsar's views of the situation was can be gathered from the fact that he promised his prospective interior minister 'several months' leave each year' if he accepted the job, which Mirskii had tried to turn down, pleading weak nerves. Mirskii set out on what he hoped would be a slow campaign to change the Emperor's mind and prepare him for the inevitable and long-overdue reforms demanded with increasing confidence by the liberal press, notably a national zemstvo assembly, the precursor of a central parliament. Soon, however, he had to admit that he had set himself an impossible task, as the Tsar, entirely out of touch with political reality, at one point even appeared to agree with his minister about the desirability of a national zemstvo assembly, but added: 'Then they will be able to look at the veterinary question' – a classic case of closing the stable door after the horse has bolted. When Mirskii warned that otherwise there would be a revolution, Nicholas simply maintained a polite silence.

As the regional zemstvo assemblies – long a focal point of the force for change in the country – mounted their pressure on the interior minister to allow a general reunion of all zemstvo councils in the capital, Mirskii reached a compromise with their representatives. He could not possibly authorize an official meeting openly discussing constitutional reform and the institution of a legislative assembly, he told them, but nothing could prevent them from coming to St Petersburg on private business and meeting socially 'for a cup of tea' in the houses of their friends. Nothing said there would be any of his business. This very political tea party was held from 6 to 9 November 1904 in the residences of various St Petersburg grandees, among them Vladimir Nabokov, whose son, the future writer, observed the goings-on.

In November, the news went from bad to worse. The besieged harbour of Port Arthur capitulated to the Japanese, an act widely seen as yet another example of cowardice and incompetence among the Tsar's military commanders. Inside the country, the activists of the local zemstvos held a series of 'professional banquets' for democracy, following the example of the revolutionary banquets held before the French Revolution of 1848. This show of force by the bourgeois camp resulted in a unique situation, as the imperial censors were ordered to allow the debate to play itself out in the newspapers, obviously in the hope that this would prevent it from spilling out onto the street. A torrent of articles on constitutional reform and open attacks on the government now appeared, and it quickly became clear that the battle for public opinion had been lost, and that the new openness had spiralled out of control.

The cries of defiance even punctuated the high walls of Tsarskoe Selo, where Nicholas liked to spend his time. With his back to the wall not only in moral but also in military terms (should a rebellion break out at home, his general had told him, the government forces were too heavily committed in Manchuria to keep control in the Russian cities), the Emperor passed the poisoned chalice to Count Mirskii, asking him to draft an imperial decree concerning necessary reforms. When presented with the draft, the Tsar struck out those parts most wanted by the liberals. 'I will never agree to the representative form of government because I consider it harmful to the people whom God has entrusted to me,' he stated. Mirskii had understood, and despaired of being able to achieve anything. 'Everything has failed,' he said to a colleague, 'let us build jails.'

A Useful Priest

To control this groundswell of discontent, S. V. Zubatov, the chief of the Moscow Okhrana, or secret police, had developed a novel strategy of which he was particularly proud. Rather than suppressing all workers' clubs and trade unions, he had helped create patriotic workers' associations which were tolerated (as well as constantly spied upon) by police. These organizations were designed to absorb some of the workers' demands while inspiring loyalty to state and Emperor through a message carefully drafted upon the precepts of Russian Orthodoxy and which was calculated to appeal to the supposed piety of recent arrivals from the countryside. Meetings began with the Lord's Prayer and ended with hymns.

The strategy worked extraordinarily well, as initial reports showed. The Workers' Society of Russian Factory and Plant Workers in St Petersburg was led by the charismatic young former prison chaplain Father Georgi Apollonovich Gapon (1870–1906). It soon reached a membership of 30,000. Gapon was a gifted organizer, and within a few months he set up a network of lending libraries, reading rooms, insurance plans and social activities. While active socialists saw the priest as a police stooge and were weary of his motives, many of the workers appreciated the atmosphere at the clubs, with their inspirational speeches and readings from conservative, state-approved newspapers. Gapon himself was a fluent speaker and communicator, but politically deeply naive and driven by great personal ambition.

Even during the summer of 1904, Gapon openly showed his filial trust in the Tsar. A worker at the Putilov steel plant later recalled a speech in which the priest told workers: 'Though the Tsar is far away and God is high in the heavens and although there is much which the authorities do not know, we will bring the situation of the working people to the attention not only of the factory owners but of the powers that be.' The Father of the People would be dismayed to learn of his children's hardships and would punish those whose greed and cruelty had created the workers' misery, the priest assured his audience.

Father Gapon was an intelligent man who clearly detested the conservatism of the official Church and had chosen active social engagement. He knew the daily struggle for existence of the workers who came to him and was familiar with their miserable living conditions, the constant danger of accident and penury, the hunger, the alcohol, and the illness dogging their lives. He agreed with the socialists in believing that the situation had become untenable. Unlike the revolutionaries, however, Gapon was sure in

'There is no God!' Father Gapon surrounded by supporters.

the knowledge that if only the Tsar in his goodness were not misled by his duplicitous advisers, everything could be changed. Capitalism was a blight on Russia's soul because it interjected a pernicious layer of officials and rich entrepreneurs that sundered the age-old bond between the Tsar and his people. The solution was therefore a simple one: the Little Father would have to be told, personally, away from the influence of the wicked men around him.

Father Gapon's workers' ministry developed far more momentum than expected by the authorities who had allowed his organization and influence to grow. He began to hold meetings with intellectuals, political activists and businessmen, and together with an inner circle he started work on a petition to be presented to the Tsar in person as soon as an opportunity should arise, possibly on the occasion of another great military defeat – a moment at which the Tsar could not but listen to his people. The opportunity came sooner than even Gapon had expected when four railroad car workers were summarily dismissed from the Putilov plant. All four were members of Gapon's organization and so, perhaps also to prove his credentials in the world of real work, he took it upon himself to intercede for their jobs. The management was intransigent, pointing out that the workers in question had been lazy and unreliable, and in the tense general situation some 12,500 workers at the plant went on strike in support of their colleagues on 5 January. Gapon backed their action and suddenly found himself at the head of a huge wave of strikes that swept through the city like wildfire. On 4 January the workers of the Franco-Russian Machine Plant joined in, one day later 16,000 at the Neva Machine and Shipbuilding works, 2,000 at the Neva textile factory, and hundreds more in smaller plants. Within three days, some 140,000 workers in 380 factories were refusing to work.

At Father Gapon's headquarters, the mood became one of hectic optimism. Meetings succeeded one another across the city until deep into the night as the organization realized that the strike gave them an unprecedented power base. If the Tsar was to be made to see the desperate condition in which his humblest subjects found themselves, this was the moment to speak. A peaceful march to the Winter Palace was decided: a workers' pilgrimage to the centre of power, imploring His Majesty to listen. Aware of the dangers this project entailed, Father Gapon personally wrote to Interior Minister Mirskii, requesting permission for the march to go ahead and enclosing a copy of the petition to be presented to the Emperor in front of the palace gates. All members of the organization were asked to appear on the morning of 8 January in their best clothes, with icons and other religious symbols – and sober.

The petition, which has already been quoted, was couched in the most respectfully subservient terms but ended with an almost menacing flourish of praise for the Emperor: 'Thou wilt thus make Russia both happy and famous, and Thy name will be engraved in our hearts and those of our posterity for ever. And if Thou dost not ... respond to our pleas we will die here in this square before Thy palace. We have nowhere to go and no purpose in going.' It may have been the undertone of threat and determination contained in this otherwise innocuous document that determined the government not to authorize the march and to post flyers throughout the city, warning that any large gatherings would be dealt with 'by the appropriate measures'.

The Tsar himself had shown not the slightest inclination to play the workers' game and had stayed at Tsarskoe Selo, outside the capital, where on 8 January units of infantry and cavalry were posted around strategic routes. The workers, meanwhile, continued with their preparations. There were rumours that they would not be allowed to march, but there were always rumours of one kind or another. The plain-clothes policemen who in any case were present at all their assemblies listening to their speeches gave no indication that there might be a problem. If they were to meet a cordon of soldiers with bayonets, they would simply go up to the soldiers and say 'Brother, do you really want to shoot me?' an old man said, to general approval.

An eerie quiet lay over St Petersburg on the morning of 9 January. The weather was mild and the steps muffled by the freshly fallen snow; normal traffic and activity had almost come to a standstill in the striking city as first hundreds and then thousands of workers assembled at various points around the city to begin their march. They were not sure what fate would await them, but foreseeing the worst, they had put able-bodied men at the front. A worker addressed the crowd waiting at Vasilevskii Island: 'You know why we are going. We are going to the Tsar for the Truth. Our life is beyond endurance ... Now we must save Russia from the bureaucrats under whose weight we suffer. They squeeze the sweat and blood out of us. You know our workers' life. We live ten families to the room. Do I speak truth?' Voices from the crowd assented, puffing their warm breath into the winter air. 'And so we go to the Tsar. If he is our Tsar, if he loves his people he must listen to us ... We go to him with open hearts. I am going ahead in the first rank and if we fall the second rank will come after us. But it cannot be that he would open fire on us.' Then the crowd said the Lord's Prayer. Sobs were heard among the mumbling voices. The march began.

Among the demonstrators slowly making their way towards Troitskii Bridge (overlooked at this very moment by a sleepy Sergei Witte from his salon window) was Maksim Gorky, who later described the killing of one worker in the crowd by Cossack cavalry:

> The dragoon circled round him and, shrieking like a woman, waved his sabre in the air ... Swooping down from his dancing horse ... he slashed him across the face, cutting him open from the eyes to the chin. I remember the strangely enlarged eyes of the worker and ... the murderer's face, flushed from the cold and excitement, his teeth clenched in a grin and the hairs of his moustache standing up on his elevated lip. Brandishing his tarnished shaft of steel he let out another shriek and, with a wheeze, spat at the dead man through his teeth.

As they were fired upon and attacked by Cossacks with sabres drawn, the protesters' bitter disillusionment struck more terribly than the soldiers' bullets. 'There is no Tsar, there is no God!' Father Gapon was heard crying, as his comrades fell around him and holy icons fell into the snow from their lifeless hands. As the crowd scattered into the surrounding streets, the priest managed to escape to Gorky's flat, where he was admitted by the million-aire revolutionary industrialist Savva Morozov, who amused himself by playing bodyguard to his writer friend. ('He scurries before the Revolution like a devil before the dawn,' in Chekhov's words.) 'Give me something to drink! Wine. Everyone's dead!' cried Gapon, who was blue in the face and stared around in wild bewilderment. Gorky tried unsuccessfully to calm down the priest, who was shaved and disguised in civilian clothes to avoid arrest. It was a priority to prove to the workers that their hero was not among the victims (there were already rumours that he had been one of the first to die) and so Gorky summoned the director of the Art Theatre, Asaf Tikhomirov, to come over to the flat and make up the traumatized priest to give him a semblance of vigorous life. Vodka had to do the rest.

In the evening of Bloody Sunday, Father Gapon appeared in front of a crowd of workers and *intelligentii* at the Free Economic Society. When he appeared next to Gorky on the stage, a small, clean-shaven man looking 'like a shop assistant in an elegant store' and wearing strange clothes, an excited whisper ran through the crowd. Gapon's message was as unfamiliar as his garb: 'Peaceful means have failed. Now we must go over to other means!' he shouted, and pronounced a 'pastor's curse' on the 'traitor Tsar who ordered the shedding of innocent blood'. Later that night, Gapon, now a revolutionary, fled to Finland, and from there to Zurich, where he met Lenin.

Even the monarch himself was more than usually moved by the day's events. In his diary, which usually carried faithful weather reports and numbers of animals shot during the hunt, he noted: 'A terrible day. Troops had to fire in many places of the city, there were many killed and wounded. God, how painful and awful. Mama came straight from the city to mass. We lunched together. Walked with Misha. Mama is staying with us for the night.'

Into Chaos

Reactions to Bloody Sunday were swift. A general strike was called and life in St Petersburg ground to a complete standstill as railway workers joined en masse. Armed 'workers' protection' groups began to roam the streets and fought skirmishes with the police. The situation was deteriorating fast, with strikes and unrest now also flaring up in other cities, particularly in Moscow. The Tsar's response to this impending catastrophe was to appoint General Dimitrii Trepov, a tough cavalryman and, in Witte's words, 'a sergeant major by training and a *pogromshchik* by conviction', as new governor of St Petersburg, commanded to restore order with an iron hand. Trepov presided over the collapse of civil order, busily clapping in jail the very democratic activists who might have been able to alleviate the situation on the streets, while the monarch proceeded to do nothing at all.

At this point, even the most conservative of his admirers expressed their despairing disillusionment with their ruler. Ilya Repin, painter of portraits to high society, wrote to a friend on 22 January: 'How good that for all his base, greedy, predatory thieving nature he [the Tsar] is at the same time so stupid that perhaps he will soon fall into a trap to the general happiness of enlightened people'; Leo Tolstoy commented that the Tsar 'listens to his uncles, his mother… He is a pitiful, insignificant, even unkind person.' Another observer, Count Bobrinskii, wrote in his diary: 'The Tsar sleeps. He sleeps on a volcano,' and then: 'The Tsar is still without will – he sleeps. The Tsar and the Tsarina sit behind locked doors at Tsarskoye Selo. The Grand Dukes are absolutely terrified.'

'An average guards colonel of good family': Tsar Nicholas II.

The result of this paralysed fear was the replacement on 20 January of the well-meaning Count Mirskii as minister of the interior with Alexander G. Bulygin, who could be relied upon to follow orders rather than give them. Even the new minister, however, insisted that concessions would have to be made. 'One would think you are afraid a revolution will break out,' the Tsar remarked critically, only to be told: 'Your Majesty, the revolution has already begun.' Finally, on 18 February the Tsar issued a manifesto promising a consultative Duma elected according to a new formula which, as liberal journalists calculated, would allow less than 1 per cent of the potential electors of St Petersburg to cast their vote. In other regions, the percentage of eligible voters would be even smaller. It was, in Witte's words, 'a body modelled on Western European parliaments in all respects but the essential one, the power to enact laws'.

The Bulygin Duma was in no way enough to satisfy the demands of the revolutionaries on the streets. But were they truly revolutionaries? Did the uprisings of 1905–6 amount to a revolution? Perhaps not in the strict sense of the word. There was no coordinated effort and no transfer of power. Still, after a year of strikes and sporadic outbreaks of civil war in some cities, the 'little revolution' brought a complete breakdown of Russia's fragile civil society and an almost total suspension of the rule of law. Strikes went on throughout the year, with numbers reaching from some 36,000 striking workers in the relatively quiet month of September, to the height of the revolt in December, when some 418,000 men and women in 13,000 factories downed tools. Universities across the country were the scenes of angry mass protests by students and were closed for the remainder of the year. In the larger cities, marauding mobs became a common sight. In Nizhni Novgorod they attacked at will anyone who looked well dressed, injuring more than seventy people in a single day; in Moscow children of ten years were accused of 'sedition' and beaten by angry mobs under the eyes of the police, in Mogilev the policemen themselves went on the rampage, while the governor of Kishinev in Bessarabia feared that the city was turning into 'an arena of civil war'. The frequent intimidation by groups of workers met with counter-terror: the Black Hundreds, a rightist organization with a long history of counter-revolutionary violence, launched attacks on those they deemed responsible for the breakdown of order. Believing the Jews to be behind all disloyalty and leftish agitation, they began a campaign of pogroms and individual attacks on Jews throughout the empire.

The situation in the countryside, some of it beyond the reach of the law at the best of times, deteriorated into general anarchy as peasants organized rent strikes, began illegal logging in the landlords' woods and attacked the manor houses themselves. Everything that smacked of the decadent, Westernizing luxuries of the ruling classes was smashed, hacked to pieces, or simply plundered and divided up among the villagers: porcelain, clothes, entire libraries. In one instance peasants even broke up a grand piano and shared out the ivory keys. By early 1906, some 3,000 manors had been looted or burned down.

The government had already lost control over large areas of its territory. A state of siege had been declared in Warsaw after the bloody suppression of a demonstration involving some 100,000 during which soldiers fired into the crowd and killed 93; Finland was in the grips of a general strike; and western Georgia was effectively ruled by the Marxist national liberation movement. Only 80 miles from Moscow itself, Sergei Semenov, a peasant admirer of Tolstoy, established the Markovo Republic, refusing to acknowledge the authority of the Russian state and governing a region comprising several villages, through a system of democratic councils. The republic addressed demands to the St Petersburg government, including a national legislative assembly, civil rights for the peasantry, free and universal education, freedom of movement, and an amnesty for political prisoners. Only when these demands were met would the citizens of the Markovo Republic pay taxes to the Tsar, or obey his authority in any way. Semenov was president of this courageous impromptu state, whose brief story ended for its leaders in Moscow prison cells in 1906.

Overwhelmed by the breakdown of order throughout the empire, the authorities knew that they could not rely on the armed forces to restore order. Often peasants themselves, who had been pressed into the army for many years and were forced by their pitiable pay to mend their own boots and grow their own vegetables and livestock ('an army of cobblers and farmers', Orlando Figes calls them), the soldiers began to disobey orders when asked to put down revolts in the countryside.

The most technically demanding branch of the armed forces was the navy, which also had on its list the largest proportion of literate men and of socialists. Discontent was high among sailors, and was raised still higher by Admiral Alexeev's pitifully incompetent waste of ships and men at Port Arthur and Tsushima against a numerically inferior but vastly better trained Japanese navy. It took nothing more than a piece of rotten meat to cause a full-scale rebellion on one of the navy ships still lying in the Black Sea, the battleship *Potemkin*. When the ship's doctor decided on 14 June that a side of beef crawling with maggots could and should be eaten by the crew, the men protested and the captain ordered the muster of armed marines against the sailors. Fearing a summary mass execution of their leaders the sailors rushed the officers, killing seven of them, while one of their own number, Grigori Valenchuk, also fell. Now in the hands of the insurrectionaries, the *Potemkin* raised a red flat and set course for the harbour of Odessa, where striking workers and government forces had been fighting running battles for the past fortnight.

The *Potemkin* episode sent a clear signal to the government. Even the Tsar could no longer deny that the situation had escalated beyond the usual rebellion that could be put down with a few hundred floggings and a handful of imprisonments, and even the most reactionary of his closest advisers urged him to create a State Duma and give in to the main demands of the liberal opposition. Otherwise, they argued, the powerful but scattered strikes would sooner or later become coordinated and would create an unstoppable movement for revolution. The choice was between loosening his grip on power or risking not only his crown, but also his life, they argued in front of the Emperor, who at first remained unimpressed: 'I'm not afraid for my life,' he commented. 'I believe that God has a plan for all of us.'

The Tsar was at a complete loss as to how to react to the mounting pressure upon his reign. In his despair he turned to a man he distrusted and disliked: Sergei Witte, who had just achieved a remarkable result at the negotiating table in New York, where he had managed to secure advantageous peace with Japan. On 9 October 1906 Witte was summoned to the Tsar and asked his opinion of the situation. He informed the Emperor that the proposed Bulygin Duma had failed to satisfy the demands of the revolutionaries, and the country was now on the brink of revolution. There were only two possible courses of action left: to grant constitutional reform and hold elections for a Duma, a state of parliament with universal suffrage, or to appoint 'a reliable person with virtually dictatorial power to employ ruthless force against disorder of whatever variety'. The second option, Witte warned, would be very bloody, and its success uncertain because the troops might side with the insurrectionaries. Time was of the essence, he insisted: the hitherto spontaneous strikes in the major cities were now being coordinated by the leaders of the socialist movement who had come out of their exile to organize and command a proper revolution, and the situation might become impossible at any moment. The Emperor vacillated, reflected, listened to his uncles, and changed his mind.

Sergei Witte, now Count Witte in recognition of his success at the negotiating table, was exasperated at this procrastination. 'His Majesty does not tolerate those whom he does not consider mental inferiors nor those whose opinions differ from those of the court camarilla, i.e., his household slaves,' he moaned. 'Being a weak man, he believes above all in the use of force... to destroy his real or fancied enemies, and he considers those who oppose the unlimited, arbitrary, serf regime to be his personal enemies.' As the strike movement gathered renewed force, even the arch-reactionary Grand Duke Nicholas Nikolaevich advised his nephew that the troops in the capital were too few even to guard the railways, let alone put down a full-scale revolution. The Tsar finally gave in and signalled that he might be willing to allow a Duma, despite rumours assiduously spread by members of his entourage that the constitutional option was a bid for power by Witte himself, who already fancied himself president of a Russian republic.

On 10 October a well-organized general strike paralysed the country. There were no railways and no trams, no newspapers and no electricity, nor telegraphs and telephones, and the Russian troops fighting in Manchuria no longer received ammunitions and supplies. From drosky drivers to the ballet dancers of the Marinskii Theatre, from doctors and stockbrokers to some 40,000 factory workers, the stoppage brought Russia to a complete standstill. No country had ever seen a greater demonstration of force by its working population. Faced with general insubordination, the police had all but ceased to operate, and bands of men roamed the streets, pillaging, robbing and looting what they could. Cut off from all communication in his Siberian headquarters, General Kuropatkin, commander in chief of the army, was unsettled by reports from agents of the Russian-Chinese Bank who told him that parts of the army had joined the revolutionaries, that Moscow was burning, fighting in St Petersburg had cost thirty thousand lives and the Tsar and Tsarina had fled to Kronshtadt and Denmark respectively.

On 17 October the Tsar finally sacked his interior minister, Bulygin, and issued a decree calling for the free and universal election of a State Duma the following May. It was not a decision he had taken lightly. Two days later he wrote in a letter to his mother: 'you can't imagine what I went through before that moment... From all over Russia they cried for it, they begged for it and around me many – very many – held the same views... There was no other way out than to cross oneself and give what everyone was asking for.'

There were celebrations in the streets when the decree was published. To the liberals, 17 October was the beginning of a new democratic era. The power of the autocracy was broken (it would be quickly regained), and Russia could now take her place among the modern nations. But there was more bitterness to come. Moscow suffered the hot breath of civil war when the funeral of a worker murdered by a group of Black Hundreds activists turned into a mass demonstration attended by some 200,000 people and resulted in street fighting between demonstrators, Black Hundreds militias, and the army.

Barricades were thrown up and several plants, particularly the Schmidt furniture factory and the Prokhorov textile factory into which the workers had retreated with their families, were shelled by the army. Just under a thousand people were killed in Moscow by bombs and bullets before the insurrection was finally put down. Nikolai Pavlovich Schmidt, the twenty-year-old owner of the Schmidt factory and revolutionary sympathizer, was arrested at his house at 16 Novnsky Boulevard. Had the police bothered to look in his basement, they would have found cases of rifles and revolvers, 'still in shipping transport grease'. As it was, they interrogated the young man whose fortune had helped support the insurrection, deprived him of sleep and food for eight days and threatened to execute him. Schmidt finally signed a confession. On 12 February he wrote to his sister saying that the night had been terrifying and that he feared the next one. He was found the next morning lying in his cell, with cuts to his neck, hands and lower arms and bruises to his face. The police recorded suicide as the cause of death.

Seizing Control

As the bourgeois camp threw itself excitedly into the business of creating political parties and electing a parliament, support for the strikes faltered and collapsed. Order slowly returned to the country, or rather, it was imposed with brutal force, as the government embarked on a long series of reprisal missions. The Semyonov and the 16th Lettish regiments were particularly notorious for their indiscriminating brutality as they moved through towns and villages throughout the empire in an orgy of summary executions, rapes, floggings and destruction. Villagers were herded together and beaten until they delivered the leaders of local rebellions, who were hanged from nearby trees without a trial. Drunken Cossacks were allowed to go on a rampage, and tens of thousands of buildings were burned.

Between October 1905 and April 1906, an estimated 15,000 peasants and workers were hanged or shot, a further 20,000 injured, and 45,000 sent into exile, while in the cities 5,000 revolutionaries were sentenced to death and another 38,000 punished with prison or penal servitude. *Cela ma chatouille!* (That tickles me!) exclaimed a delighted Tsar Nicholas on hearing news of the successful punitive expeditions and other reprisals by rightist forces as the settling of accounts began. A wave of savage pogroms against Jewish populations swept the country. Once more, the Tsar was firmly in the saddle. The disturbances were regrettable, but his world-view had remained intact, as he wrote in a letter to his mother:

> The people are indignant at the insolence and the audacity of the revolutionaries and the socialists and since nine-tenths of them are Jews all the hatred is directed against them. Hence the pogroms against the Jews. It is astonishing with what *unity* and how *simultaneously* these occurred in all the cities of Russia and Siberia. In England, naturally, they write that these disorders were organized by police. But this is already a well-known fable. Not only have the Jews suffered – also engineers, lawyers and all other kinds of bad people. What has happened at Tomsk, Simferopol, Tver and Odessa clearly shows what can happen in a storm of fury – the houses of the revolutionaries were surrounded and set afire. Those who were not burned to death were killed as they emerged. I have received very touching telegrams from everywhere with thanks for the gift of liberty but also with clear declarations that they wish autocracy to be preserved.

It was all the fault of the Jews. Now calm had been restored. It was, as Friedrich Schiller had put it almost a century before, 'the calm of the graveyard'.

As an iron hand reimposed a semblance of order, the ferment below only intensified, indeed, the revolution was already beginning to devour its children. Father Gapon, unwitting instigator of Bloody Sunday and the ensuing revolt, had made several attempts to establish himself as a revolutionary leader. Unable to hold his own among the socialist theoreticians, he had returned to Russia and left again, been sighted in Monte Carlo, and finally attempted to set up a new workers' organization in St Petersburg. His political bumbling and popular following made him a target for both revolutionaries and secret police. Sergei Witte's long arm involved Gapon's name in plots and betrayals to discredit him, and in a shady plot involving a notorious double agent, the amateur revolutionary Gapon was lured to a cottage near the Finnish lake resort of Ozersky for secret consultations. The true reasons for what followed remain unclear but an account survived: a handful of men awaited Gapon in the hut to sit in judgement over him. They voted unanimously that he deserved to die and began to tie his hands. 'Brothers, darlings, stop! Give me a last word!' cried the terrified priest as they strung him up on a hook on the wall which was so low that one of the assailants had to sit on Gapon's shoulders until he had choked to death.

Everyone Feared Something

The experiences of 1905 imbued Russian society with a sense of dark foreboding. Every rational path forward out of its catastrophic stagnation seemed blocked by autocratic rule, a door so conclusively bolted shut that only an explosion could blast it open. Feeling oscillated between despondency and rage, between impotent frustration and a fatalistic certainty that another, far more bloody apocalypse would only be a matter of time. The youngest generation of artists powerfully articulated the hopelessness of this vision of life. In Ivan Bunin's story *A Gentleman from San Francisco* (1910), an ocean liner steams across agitated sea, its passenger's hostages to fortune. Dancing in the ship's elegant salons, they are unaware of the inferno of the flamelit boiler rooms and the murderous seas outside, and unable to influence their own fate.

In his great novel *Petersburg*, Andrei Bely, too, evoked the haunted sense of his generation. Bely had happened to arrive in the capital on Bloody Sunday, and the events of the day had made such a deep impression on him that he wrote a novel set against the backdrop of the disturbances. Throughout it, the city is frightened by the spectre of the red domino, a ghostly appearance blown out of all proportion by the sensationalist press and in reality nothing but the son of a high official in a theatre costume. The hero's predicament, though, is as terrible as it is absurd: having promised a terrorist to throw a bomb, he has discovered that his victim is to be his own father. Horrified, he has nevertheless primed the device, which is ticking away inside a sardine tin as he agonises over what to do. Amid the splendour of the classicist palace mayhem and destruction are only hours away.

It is not only the protagonist who finds himself in a murderous dilemma; the entire city is gripped by a sense of menace:

> In the workshops, in print shops, in hairdressers', in dairies, in squalid little taverns, the same prating shady type was always hanging around. With a shaggy fur hat from the fields of bloodstained Manchuria pulled down over his eyes, and with a Browning from somewhere or other stuck in his side pocket, he thrust badly printed leaflets into people's hands.
>
> Everyone feared something, hoped for something, poured into the streets, gathered in crowds, and again dispersed.

The fields of bloodstained Manchuria were the theatre in which Russia had played out its foolish war with Japan, a 'primitive' force from the east now threatening to engulf civilization:

> As for Petersburg, it will sink.
>
> In those days all the peoples of the earth will rush forth from their dwelling places. Great will be the strife, strife the like of which has never been seen in this world. The yellow hordes of Asians will set forth from their age-old abodes and will encrimson the fields of Europe in oceans of blood.

This sense of fear and farce became all-pervasive in Russia after 1906. The Tsar clawed back powers from the Duma as soon as it was opened, and Witte was sent into bitter retirement once again. As the court retreated ever further into obscurantism and isolation while mystics and madmen like the thoroughly debauched monk Rasputin gained power over an imperial couple losing its last connections with reality, the Tsar looked over his country with eyes bleary from incense and alcohol. Meanwhile Russian culture exploded in an angry and radiant creativity. Nowhere in the world was the sense of precariousness more urgently felt than in this stifled society torn apart by the ineluctable forces of change, and nowhere was this clearer than in the works of many artists for whom their vocation was a continuation of revolution by other means – or a flight away from this absurdly downtrodden world into a realm of pure, mystically inspired symbolism.

We have come to think of Paris and Vienna as centres of artistic innovation around the turn of the century, but surely Moscow and St Petersburg after 1906 cannot be far behind. Fuelled by wild dreams, an entire generation of artists set about to shape a new vision of the world – savage and strange, brutally mechanical, dark, and incomprehensible. The young Igor Stravinsky translated the bloody spasms of the revolution into the *Sacre du printemps*, a cruel ritual sacrifice of youth in ballets whose choreography used tutus for simple smocks and pirouettes for pounding rage; Alexander Skriabin made his sense of dislocation audible in piano pieces floating loosely between tonalities and in orchestral poems combining sound and light into overwhelming hallucinations; Kandinsky brought to his canvases the primeval symbols of shamanic rituals in restless and disjointed geometrical compositions; Kasimir Malevich found the uncompromising power of abstraction, and the painter Mikhail Larionov reproduced his view of a fractured, often frightening world in ragged shapes very similar to those conceived by Braque and Picasso. The old values were dead. 'The genius of our day: trousers, jackets, shoes, tramways, buses, airplanes, railways, magnificent ships. We deny that individuality has any value in a work of art,' declared Larionov. Around 1905 his work evolved from tender and lyrical expressionist compositions to an uncompromisingly childlike primitivism with saturated colours and rough-hewn features. Having scraped off the thin veneer of civilization, Larionov found himself amid half-men and savage women, carousing lowlifes, Turks and circus performers who smoked and sat with parted legs. Other painters, such as Robert Falk, Piotr Konchalovsky and Larionov's companion Natalia Goncharova underwent a similar development.

The deep vein of darkness and absurdity that runs through the Russian imagination came to the surface in literary works for the period, and nowhere more so than in Valery Bryusov's poem *The Pale Horse*. This took its central image not only from one of the Horsemen of the Apocalypse, but also from the Bronze Horseman, the strutting statue of Peter the Great on a rampant stallion in St Petersburg which had dominated the minds of Russian writers ever since Pushkin's poem by the same name. The Horseman rode through the nocturnal capital in Bely's *Petersburg*, his steed reappeared, in bloody crimson, in paintings by Malevich and Kuzma Petrov-Vodkin, and it thundered into Bryusov's fearsome description of a brutal apparition that flashes through the bustling city of St Petersburg much as the revolution had ripped through the fabric of life some years before:

The street was like a storm. The crowds passed by as if pursued by inevitable Fate. Cars, cabs, buses roared amid the furious endless stream of people. Signs whirled and sparked like changing eyes high in the heavens from the terrible heights of the 30th floor. Wheels hummed proudly, newsboys screamed, whips cracked. Suddenly amid the storm – a hellish whisper. There sounds a strange dissonant footfall, a deadening shriek, a tremendous crash. And the Horseman appears. The horse flies headlong. The air still trembles and the echo rolls. Time quivers and the Look is Terror. In letters of fire the Horseman's scroll spells Death.

Bryusov's life was just as stormy as his morphine-sped imagination and he spent some years locked in an unhappy love triangle with Andrei Bely and the disturbed, delicate Nina Petrovskaya. The two men could only just be persuaded not to fight a duel over her.

Like the revolutionaries who wanted to blast society away to start afresh, many artists of the avant-garde believed that there was nothing worth saving about the status quo. Mikhail Larionov, Natalia Goncharova, Vladimir Mayakovsky and others went about Moscow with painted faces and wooden spoons or radishes in their lapels instead of flowers. Their clothes were adorned with letters and signs. Vasily Kamenskii claimed that much like anarchist terrorists they wanted to 'throw a bombshell into the joyless, provincial street of the generally joyless existence', while Larionov and a friend wrote in one of their Futurist manifestos: 'We paint ourselves because a clean face is offensive, because we want to herald the unknown, to rearrange life.'

A Slap in the Face of Public Taste was the title of a manifesto issued by a group of artists in 1912; it appeared that the members of the avant-garde tried to be as offensive, blasphemous and crude as they could. In Russian peasant lore, authority was nothing but the power to subdue by force. The writings of Russia's young artists echoed this sentiment: 'Wherever you look, the world lies before you in utter nakedness, around her tower beskinned mountains, like bloody chunks of smoking meat. Seize it, tear it, get your teeth into it, crush it, create it anew – it's all yours, yours!'

Avant-garde artists in Moscow and St Petersburg oscillated wildly between utopian hopes and utter despair, mad erotic entanglements and celibacy (never for too long), empty gestures and moments of sheer brilliance. In Bryusov's astonishing story 'The Republic of the Southern Cross' he describes an artificial city state in Antarctica, protected from the elements by a gigantic roof. This pivotal achievement of human engineering houses the earth's most advanced community, a magnificent, democratic society with overhead roads, comfortable houses, free education, libraries, fine food, and the most refined amusements. In truth, it is a sinister utopia some of whose traits have become familiar to those living a century after the text was written:

It must be said that this democratic exterior concealed the purely auto-cratic tyranny of the shareholders and directors of a former Trust. Giving up to others the places of deputies in the Chamber they inevitably brought in their own candidates as directors of the factories. In the hands of the Board of Directors was concentrated the economic life of the country... The influence of the Board of Directors in the international relationships of the Republic was immense. Its decisions might ruin whole countries. The prices fixed by them determined the wages of millions of labouring masses over the whole earth. And, more-over, the influence of the Board, though indirect, was always decisive in the internal affairs of the Republic. The Law-making Chamber, in fact, appeared to be only the humble servant of the will of the Board.

Bryusov's secretly diseased ideal city is finally destroyed by an outbreak of 'contradiction', an illness that makes sufferers rebel against all that is reasonable:

The stricken, instead of saying 'yes,' say 'no', wishing to say caressing words, they splutter abuse. The majority also begin to contradict them-selves in their behaviour: intending to go to the left they turn to the right, thinking to raise the brim of a hat so as to see better, they would pull it down over their eyes instead and so on. As the disease develops, contradiction overtakes the whole of the bodily and spiritual life of the patient, exhibiting infinite diversity conformable with the idiosyncrasies of each. In general, the speech of the patient becomes unintelligible and his actions absurd.

Overcome by this sudden attack of senselessness and destruction, the city sinks at last into ruin and desolation.

While many fashionable artists like Bryusov, Bely and the mystical poetess Zinaida Gippius wrote much of their work in the 'perfumed pastures' of symbolist language and tried to grasp a higher reality with the help of spiritualist seances, others chose a confrontational approach to the unbearable reality. Leonid Andreyev created a scandal when his novel *The Seven Who Were Hanged* was passed by the censor and published (a clear indication of how times had changed), giving bewildered readers a pitiless journalistic depiction of a night spent in prison by seven condemned terrorists awaiting execution in the morning. They are kind, thoughtful people driven to an extreme act (a failed assassination) by extreme circum-stances. The novel retells the trial, gives the reactions of the parents – respectable people all of them – and reveals the conversations between the prisoners, as well as their lonely thoughts:

He has been transformed into an animal waiting to be slaughtered, a deaf-mute object which may be taken from place to place, burnt and broken. It matters not what he might say, nobody would listen to his words, and if he endeavored to shout, they would stop his mouth with a rag. Whether he can walk alone or not, they will take him away and hang him.

And if he should offer resistance, struggle or lie down on the ground – they will overpower him, lift him, bind him and carry him, bound, to the gallows. And the fact that this machine-like work will be performed over him by human beings like himself, lent to them a new, extraordinary and ominous aspect – they seemed to him like ghosts that came to him for this one purpose, or like automatic puppets on springs. They would seize him, take him, carry him, hang him, pull him by the feet. They would cut the rope, take him down, carry him off and bury him.

As grimly as it began, Andreyev's novel ends with the dead bodies being laid into cheap coffins.

Nothing like this had been published in Russian before, and readers were disturbed not to be able to see these young people as terrorists. Their motives, the grief of the old officer paying a visit to his son before his execution, the noble young woman who comforts others – all this was far removed from official propaganda. Values like justice and truth appeared to crumble under the novelist's cold, concentrated stare. Other authors discarded values altogether. In Mikhail Artsybashev's erotic novel *Sanine*, the hero prowls through life like a modern Marquis de Sade, totally amoral, totally indifferent, looking for nothing but the gratification of his lust. The joyless sex is described as graphically as the censor would permit, and almost all protagonists end badly. 'What a bad joke is man!' exclaims the protagonist at the end of the work.

'One can say without exaggeration that all Russia echoed to the *cri de coeur* that "it is impossible to live this way any longer",' Sergei Witte had written about these years, during which Russia's culture took on all the traits of advanced schizophrenia, a time of violence violently crushed rather than of peace. Things could not end well, that much was clear. How and when the catastrophe would happen was still unsure, but as the students in *The Seven Who Were Hanged* keep saying to each other, 'It won't be long now!'

7

1906:
Dreadnought *and Anxiety*

We will glorify war – the world's only hygiene – militarism, patriotism, the destructive gesture of freedom-bringers, beautiful ideas worth dying for, and scorn for woman.

> – F. T. Marinetti, *Futurist Manifesto*

Almost all the grand houses around the Champs-Elysées and the Parc Monceau are in Jewish hands; sometimes through an open window, one heard in the solitude echoes of some concert: some Jew who is treating his neurosis.

> – Edouard Drumont, *La France juive*

Portsmouth, 10 February 1906 With a soft but resonant 'plonk' the bottle of Australian wine made contact with the huge steel hull, but a garland of flowers prevented the bottle from breaking. Swinging from a long rope, the bottle was fished out of the air and His Majesty King Edward, wearing the uniform of an admiral of the fleet complete with plumed hat and still visibly puffing from the exertion of climbing up to the platform, let go once again. This time the bottle obligingly cracked and spilled its contents over the grey expanse of steel dominating the scene and dwarfing the attending crowds. 'I christen you *Dreadnought*,' the monarch declared. He then took a small mallet and began tapping away at the last rope holding the newly named vessel in its dry dock. The colossus started sliding down the ramp: 'The ship diminished sharply before one's eyes,' the *Manchester Guardian*'s correspondent noted. 'Then a crash of waters aroused one's other senses. There came a roar of hurrahs, the first sounds of the band playing "God save the King" and tugs blowing their horns and the perfume of spilt wine and of flowers.'

Even for a King who was an old hand at cutting ribbons, smashing bottles and tapping ceremonial mallets, this was not an everyday occasion. The launch of the 18,000-ton, 527 feet, all-big-gun HMS *Dreadnought*, a ship faster, more powerful and more destructive than anything afloat, was the beginning of a new era. In honour of this special moment, the Royal Navy had pulled out all the stops: the bishop of Winchester had begun the service with the 107th Psalm ('They that go down to the sea in ships, that do business in great waters; these see the works of the Lord, and his wonders in the deep') and had blessed the ship, a boy's choir had sung hymns, thousands of workmen, seamen and holidaying onlookers jostled to catch a glimpse of the huge steel structure crowned by four triumphal arches, and on the water, military ships and innumerable pleasure craft added dash and colour to the spectacle.

The launch of a big ship is always an emotional, exhilarating sight. No flag-waving little boy, though, could match the excitement of the First Sea Lord, Admiral John Arbuthnot 'Jackie' Fisher, who was standing next to the King, inundating him with a spate of technical data and enthusiasm, with top speeds, fire power, range, armament, manoeuvrability, and other details the monarch politely feigned interest in. For Fisher, this was the culmination of a campaign that had taken many years to accomplish, a personal crusade to reform the British navy and forge it once again into the efficient, awe-inspiring fighting force it had been at Trafalgar, a hundred years before. The *Dreadnought*, supreme symbol of Britain's naval might, was all he had dreamt about for well over a decade.

Fisher's uncompromising and steely determination was both the outcome and the continuation of an international arms race that brought European countries to the brink several times before 1914, fuelled in part by one man's nostalgic childhood memories of seaside holidays. Kaiser Wilhelm II was not shy about admitting this very personal motivation for his fleet-building programme. 'When I was a little boy,' the Emperor told his uncle, Edward VII, during an official dinner, 'I was allowed to visit Portsmouth and Plymouth hand in hand with kind aunts and friendly admirals. I admired the proud English ships in those two superb harbours. Then there awoke in me the wish to build ships of my own like these someday, and when I was grown up to possess as fine a navy as the English.'

The relationship between the German monarch and Britain with its navy showed the Emperor at his most maddeningly narcissistic, insecure, and ambivalent. Born to an English mother, the Empress Victoria (who was always homesick for her native country, and detested heel-clicking, officious, military Prussia from the bottom of her soul), the ambivalence was planted early in the boy's mind. 'She delivered judgement on everything and found everything wrong with us and better in England which she habitually called "home",' Wilhelm would write in his memoirs. To the young prince, his mother's 'beloved England' became a reference point in many ways, all the more so because it was almost impossible for him to excel at the skills valued and admired at the Potsdam court. A medical blunder at his birth had left his left arm withered and almost useless, making riding, hunting and other aristocratic pastimes an ordeal for him. Riding, especially, was to be the terror of his childhood. His mother judged it 'intolerable' that the heir to the throne should not cut a good figure on horseback and instituted a harsh training regime, which involved hauling the weeping eight-year-old onto a horse without stirrups and making him gallop. 'He fell off continually; every time, despite his prayers and tears, he was lifted up and set upon his back again. After weeks of torture, the difficult task was accomplished: he had got his balance,' his tutor noted with obvious satisfaction.

In England, when visiting his grandmother, Queen Victoria, Wilhelm was away from these torments and from his drill-like education with lessons from 6 a.m. to 6 p.m. every weekday. He breathed more freely in the comparatively informal atmosphere of Osborne House, where he could play with other children and watch the grand navy battleships gliding by silently into Portsmouth harbour. Later, the ambitious prince took to sailing during the Cowes Week regatta at the Isle of Wight and had a luxury racing yacht, the *Meteor*, built for the express purpose of beating his uncle Bertie, heir to the British throne. Much to his fury, Wilhelm lost year after year, despite the flood of complaints about handicaps and regulations which he unleashed on the committee of the Royal Yacht Squadron, complaining of unfairness to him and him alone.

Wilhelm was desperately eager to belong to the languidly elegant Cowes set, the perfect embodiment of British aristocratic life. While there, he wore civilian clothes, spoke English almost like an Englishman and would host sumptuous dinners on his imperial yacht *Hohenzollern*, but it was his uncle who held all the attention: 'He wore a white yachting cap, smoked large cigars and always carried an ebony walking stick. His prominent eyes were china blue and kindly... He was always followed by an entourage of intimate friends;...the beautiful Mrs. George Keppel, the notorious Mrs. Langtry, and sometimes his wife, Queen Alexandra, who seemed to me the most beautiful of the ladies,' one eyewitness remembered.

Wilhelm could not escape his uncle's shadow. It was Edward who proposed his nephew for membership in the exclusive Royal Yacht Squadron;

it was he whom the Queen designated to supervise and control him. This duty was much resented by Bertie, whose mind was on other things, particularly as, despite the British blood he was so proud of, the young Prussian proved simply unable to enter into the spirit of the event, which was in effect one large garden party garnished with splendid boats. As a racer he tried too hard and was obsessed by winning, a cardinal sin. As a participant, his habit of appearing with his yacht off the coast, surrounded by what looked like half the imperial battle fleet, attracted amused comments from the in-crowd. As a socialite, he was often too jovial, too loud, making gentlemen cringe under his back-slapping and familiarity. At other times, he would sulk at not being given due respect and complain loudly about matters that every public schoolboy could have told him were best left alone. In short, the forward prince made a nuisance of himself. Eventually, in 1895, he declared that the handicaps were unfair and he had decided not to race at Cowes again.

Still eager to outdo his uncle, the Kaiser founded his own racing week at Kiel, which he intended to be altogether grander than its British equivalent. The setting was magnificent, but once again, the officers and soldiers standing stiffly to attention amid the sound of military bands could not match the laid-back style of Cowes. Kiel became a very personal concern, as the monarch's brother, Prince Heinrich, remarked: 'There's no doubt about it, our people buy yachts and race them only to please my brother...Half of them have never seen the sea. But if they go to the seaside and read about the Emperor's yacht...and if the wealthy merchants who know nothing of the sea become yachtsmen to please the Emperor, then it stirs up interest and we can get money for the navy.' In a country without a strong recent naval tradition, the Kaiser's regatta week became a playground for the newly rich. Wealthy Americans liked to come over to rub shoulders with the aristocracy. Guests were put up in luxury ocean liners chartered for the purpose as floating hotels. Wilhelm was happy here, and during some races he even tried his hand at taking the helm, though not very well. 'If the Kaiser steered himself, he regularly hit the buoy,' as Chancellor Bülow, always effusive with praise to his employer's face, remarked with acid effectiveness.

Germany's aggressive naval policy also had a less personal, more properly political purpose. The Reich's burgeoning industrial success and rapidly rising population put its politicians into an expansionist mood. As the country acquired colonies and prepared to use its power abroad, global aspirations faced a dilemma: with harbours in the Baltic and the North Sea, Germany's ships had to circumnavigate Britain, either via the Channel or around Scotland, to reach open waters. In view of the overwhelming British naval force which could blockade these exits at any moment, Germany was effectively a colonial power at Britain's mercy. Had the country contented itself with Continental and economic power, and had the imperial navy accepted the impossibility of breaking this stranglehold, this geographic conundrum would not have mattered. That, however, would have meant giving up any aspirations of becoming a serious colonial power and relying instead on its traditional strength, its formidable army, to establish prestige and security. Wilhelminian Germany, though, was determined to play a global role similar to, and eventually perhaps greater than, those of Britain and France. 'Our future is on the water,' the Kaiser declared. In the long run, conflict was inevitable.

Germany's proposed way out of Britain's ring of naval steel was formulated by Admiral Alfred von Tirpitz and was as simple as it was elegant: apart from Germany, Britain's immediate rivals for naval superiority were France and Russia, both of whom also had expansionist naval policies. Germany would have gained independence if she could just build a navy strong enough to make defeating it too costly for the British forces, which would itself sustain heavy losses and be therefore unable to guarantee the defence of her coasts, her trade routes and her colonies against her other rivals. Simple as this policy was, it shackled German dreams of greatness to a pharaonically expensive naval construction programme.

Like the Kaiser, Tirpitz, whose daughters were sent to Cheltenham Ladies' College, was an anglophile who spoke excellent English and read English novels and newspapers. Like his employer, the young officer had learned to admire the British navy while stationed in Plymouth, which the fledgling German navy used as a supply base: 'Here we felt ourselves almost more at home than in the peaceful idyllic Kiel, which only grumbled at Prussia,' he would later remember. 'Our tiny naval officers' corps looked up to the British Navy with admiration ... We grew up on the British Navy like a creeping plant. We preferred to get our supplies from England. If an engine ran smoothly ... if a rope or a chain did not break, then it was certain to be not a home-made article but a product of English workshops ... in those days we could not imaging that German guns could be equal to English.' Like Wilhelm, Tirpitz was also acutely sensitive to being patronized by British naval officers, and passionate about Germany's role in the world.

It was Tirpitz who gave the Kaiser's naval enthusiasm its decisive form. The question was strategic: Germany needed a strong navy, but for what purpose and with what strategy in mind? Propelled by his bitterness about having to stand on the sidelines in the Boer War, Wilhelm wanted a fleet of agile, long-range cruisers suited for becoming a global player, to apply pressure abroad and protect German shipping. Cruisers, though, stood little chance against more powerful battleships with long-range artillery able to sink their adversaries before they themselves got close enough to open fire. Tirpitz therefore convinced the Kaiser that what he needed first and foremost were battleships to guarantee open sea routes and to counter any attempt at a naval blockade. 'For Germany, the most dangerous naval enemy at the present time is England,' as he bluntly put it in a memorandum in which he asked for a fleet of nineteen battleships to be ready by 1905 at a cost of 408 million marks. Battleships had heavier armament and therefore a shorter operational range; using them to protect German interests on the high seas was out of the question. They made sense only if Germany expected to fight a powerful enemy close to its own coast. Building them sent a clear signal to London.

Ruling the Waves

One man who heard this signal was Admiral Jackie Fisher, who had made it his mission to modernize the British navy. During his own early career on British training ships in China and in the Mediterranean, Fisher had come to know the fleet as anything but an effective strike force: its ships and guns dated from the time of the Crimean War, and its strategies were still modelled on Nelson's victories, with broadsides exchanged, and weekly cutlass training for close combat after boarding enemy craft. The wooden three-decker ships of the line, with their muzzle-loading brass cannon that brought Britain victory at Trafalgar, remained the Admiralty's ideal. HMS *Victoria*, the last of these ships to be built, was launched in 1879. In the age of steel ships and modern artillery with a range of several miles, all this was obsolete, but the hierarchy clung to tried and tested ways. The ambitious Fisher had no time for such preconceptions of glorious combat, or for the social ethos of the officer corps. He himself had risen through the ranks by merit: his father had been a colonial officer in Ceylon (now Sri Lanka), who had ruined himself with a coffee plantation and sent his son into the navy at the age of thirteen. The boy had never seen his father again.

During the later nineteenth century the position of the world's first maritime power fell to Britain by default: only the French maintained a navy powerful enough to mount a challenge to Queen Victoria's. This lack of competition had made the British forces complacent, and the main preoccupation of the officers was to run a ship that was polished, holystoned, painted and burnished to perfection. Holystoning, the scrubbing of the wooden decks with pumice stone, was a daily ritual for the seamen, who would make wooden surfaces gleam like mirrors, only to have them soiled by the next splash of sea water. It kept the men busy, orthodox opinion ran. The rule was similar to that of the French navy: Salute everything that moves and paint everything that doesn't. Other aspects of navy life were reminders of the most brutal aspects of the bad old days. 'The day I joined as a little boy, I saw eight men flogged – and I fainted at the sight,' Fisher commented.

The navy was slow to reform, and those who thought to innovate often found themselves frustrated and their careers in peril. When the enterprising Captain Sir Percy Scott took command of the *Edinburgh* in 1886, he found that not only was the standard of gunnery abroad deplorable, but the seamen also resisted the idea of training, which might tarnish their immaculate craft. 'We were twenty years ahead of the times,' he recalled later, 'and in the end we had to do as others were doing. So we gave up instruction in gunnery, spent money on enamel paint, burnished up every bit of steel on board and soon got the reputation of being a very smart ship. She was certainly very nice in appearance. The nuts of all the aft bolts on the aft deck were gilded, the magazine keys were electroplated and statues of Mercury surmounted the revolver racks.'

For Admiral Fisher, such niceties had no role to play in the navy's future, nor in his country's. Having once himself been given a ship to command that was so decrepit that it could hardly survive a storm, never mind an engagement with the enemy, Fisher was determined to reform the navy from the bottom up, a mission he regarded as far too important to let social niceties stand in his way: 'On the British fleet rests the British Empire. Only a congenital idiot with criminal tendencies would permit any tampering with the maintenance of our sea supremacy,' he trumpeted, driving home the message that modern warfare between floating forts with heavy artillery was likely to be decided with terrible suddenness. 'Once beaten the war is finished,' he explained. 'Beaten on land, you can improvise fresh armies in a few weeks. You can't improvise a fresh Navy; it takes four years.'

As Germany's naval building programme began heating up, Fisher revised Britain's strategy, which had so far targeted France as its most likely enemy. Driven with tyrannical rigour by Admiral Tirpitz, who was famous for his histrionics, Germany's parliament ratified one naval bill after the next, pledging ever more millions to its supremacy on sea, and shipyards working around the clock soon produced a growing and increasingly alarming

Ruling the waves: Admiral Jackie Fisher was the driving force behind the Dreadnought *race.*

number of modern, efficient battleships with more and more tonnage and guns. Fourteen large battleships (with an average of 11,000 tons of displacement) came off the docks from 1893 to 1903. During the following decade, twenty-two new-generation battleships would follow, this time with displacements rising from 12,000 to 28,000 tons, monsters roughly half the size of the *Titanic* (an ocean liner) and consisting of powerful turbine engines, 12-inch guns, and steel armour plate. In addition to this, German docks built some seventy cruisers, torpedo boats and other, smaller war craft.

Fisher was determined not to risk Britain's naval pre-eminence. Aided substantially by his friendship with King Edward, he cajoled, threatened and begged the government to give him money for more and more stronger ships. His intention was not so much to play Germany's game, as to raise the stakes. The ship Fisher planned in 1904 would simply make the entire German fleet obsolete. It would be faster, larger, and more heavily armed. It would blow the *Kriegsmarine* out of the water before they could even come close. The ideal of the suddenness of war which he had preached for so long had found its perfect embodiment: HMS *Dreadnought*. Like other visionaries, Fisher had the perverse satisfaction of being treated both as a fool and a lunatic by his adversaries, but with the King's support he persevered. With the help of two squadrons of *Dreadnought*-class battleships, Britain's navy would simply impose its own new rules for wars at sea: British rules.

Critics pointed out the new class of battleship would not only make Germany's but also the Royal Navy's older craft obsolete – as far as large battles were concerned, the largest war fleet in the world would effectively become scrap iron overnight. More dreadnoughts would be needed, even larger ones, to keep pace with the Kaiser's forces. Fisher was undeterred. On 22 December 1904, he convened a committee to design the vessel, following the recommendations of an Italian engineer and the experience of the battle of Tsushima, during which British naval observers had observed the operation of Japan's newly built and uncompromisingly modern maritime forces. Abroad Admiral Togo's flagship, one of them reported home: 'when 12 inch guns are fired, shots from 10 inch guns pass unnoticed, while, for all the respect they instill, 8 inch or 6 inch might as well be pea shooters.'

On board the *Dreadnought* industrial efficiency was all, in both its construction and its operation. The decision to have only one calibre of gun, for example, was motivated by the reasoning that only a single type of ammunition would have to be used and the crews could be trained to operate all guns with equal efficiency. Identical cannon with identical ammunition would be much more easily ranged in on a target, as they should all hit the same spot if fired at the same angle. Fisher was exultant: 'Suppose a 12 inch gun to fire one aimed round each minute. Six guns would allow a deliberately aimed shell with a huge bursting charge every ten seconds. Fifty percent of these should be hits at 6,000 yards. Three 12 inch shells bursting on board every minute would be HELL!'

Taking the industrial logic further, Fisher moved with phenomenal speed. Pre-produced steel plates were stacked in the Portsmouth shipyard even before the ship's keel was laid on 2 October 1905, and from then on the vast form could be seen to grow by the day. Within two months the hull of the world's largest battleship was towering menacingly over the shipyard and being painted. On 9 February 1906, the launch took place in the presence of the rotund King, who was visibly affected not so much by emotion, as by breathing problems. During the following months, the ship was fitted out in record speed: boilers in March, turbines and six coats of paint in May, guns in June and July. In September, HMS *Dreadnought* was commissioned and ready and soon steamed off to the West Indies to undergo a batteries test. A weapon of unheard-of proportions had been constructed in a fraction of the normal time.

The naval arms race, the biggest the world had ever seen, soon became a global phenomenon. France and the United States, Russia, Austria-Hungary, Japan, Italy, the Ottoman empire and several other nations each built their own all-big-gun battleships, which were in turn superseded by even larger ones. Military expenditure swallowed just over a third of national budgets in France and Russia, a little less in Britain and almost a quarter in Germany and the Austro-Hungarian empire.

Manly Strength

The Dreadnought race was symptomatic of its time. Whole societies were in the thrall of uniforms and military strength. Russia alone kept a standing army of 1.4 million men and operated a system of ranks applying to the armed forces, as well as to its civil administration. The Russo-Japanese War had shown the army and its leadership to be woefully inefficient, but it had always been an important element for internal control. The universal draft had nominally existed since 1874, but in practice most young men could sneak or buy their way out of being drafted, leaving the poorest peasants to shoulder the burden of a twenty-year army service term, often begun with a ritual mock funeral conducted by the priest of their home village, as they were not expected to be seen again alive. Feared and loathed especially in the countryside, the army's presence hung over people's lives like a dark cloud.

In France, too, army and society were strongly interlaced. The country has a long tradition of military men as head of state, reaching from Napoleon to Marshal MacMahon in 1873, Boulanger in 1888 and Pétain in 1940 right up to General de Gaulle. As always torn between two visions, one Republican and one conservatively Catholic, the French could not agree what the civic function of their army was. While the conservative establishment saw it as an instrument of national glory (one that had been badly tarnishes by the defeat in 1870), the Jacobin tradition regarded it most of all as a school of the nation, mixing social classes and instructing recruits in the values of Republican citizenship and national solidarity, a vision famously articulated by the socialist leader Jean Jaurès in his book *l'Armée nouvelle* (1907), in which he postulated that a short draft was both democratically and militarily more advantageous than a smaller professional army, which would always pose a danger to the constitutional order. This was no empty theorizing: in 1889 General Boulanger had been within a hair's breadth of marching on the Elysée Palace, surrounded by enthusiastic supporters.

The Dreyfus case had laid bare the anxieties of society as a whole and the army in particular, a bitter divide between those who saw the army's role in hushing up a flagrant miscarriage of justice as proof of its reactionary, royalist tendencies and those who, on the contrary, viewed the Jewish officer as guilty by default, the epitome of everything they hated about the way their country was going. Endlessly argumentative, the French saw their army with equal measures of pride, suspicion and aggression. As Theodore Zeldin relates, cadets of the prestigious Saint-Cyr military academy were advised to go out in their civilian clothes to avoid incidents in some parts of Paris, while one officer complained: 'Among the masses, we were considered the enemy, *les payots*. In bourgeois circles, we were considered imbeciles.'

If the army's identity was insecure, there was one thing all sides agreed upon: for better or for worse, it was a 'school of subordination, of the virile spirit, of male pride', as the French *NCO's Manual* (written in 1893 and reprinted until 1913) put it. 'When one is not a soldier,' one peasant recruit's mother told him, 'one is not a man.' Real men fought, and those with honour, particularly military honour, to defend, often considered it their duty to fight on the slightest ceremonial pretext. Duelling became all the rage in the 1880s and continued far into the twentieth century.

It was not only army officers who were in the habit of challenging one another. Marcel Proust was particularly proud of having challenged a literary critic, Jean Lorrain (who had hinted publicly at the writer's homosexuality), and survived to tell the tale, and in 1908 he challenged a young friend of his who did not even know what he had done to cause offence. As it transpired, the young man in question, nineteen-year-old Marcel Plantevignes, had heard a lady make a remark about the famous poet's 'unusual morals' without springing to his defence. The intensely asthmatic Proust was considerate enough to give the youth's father the choice of fighting in his son's stead, as well as the choice of arms. At the father's adamant insistence, the matter was cleared up without violence, but it is obvious that Proust thought he could not allow even the slightest aspersion to be cast on his robust manliness – a comical idea for all who knew him. Still, more than mere appearances were at stake: 'my seconds in duels can tell you whether I behave with the weakness of an effeminate man,' the writer confessed in a letter to Paul Souday.

Deadly serious: duelling increased around 1900, though most confrontations ended with a symbolic drawing of blood.

Not even committed and progressive peace-lovers like the socialist politicians and writers Léon Blum (later to become prime minister) and Jean Jaurès hesitated to pick up a weapon to defend their honour. The last known sword duel in France was fought by Gaston Defferre and René Ribière, both deputies in the Assemblée Nationale, in 1967. President de Gaulle had thought it prudent to formally forbid his government ministers to act as seconds. Georges Clemenceau (1841–1929), '*le tigre*', prime minister from 1906 to 1909 and again from 1917 to 1929, fought twelve duels: seven with pistols, and five with swords. He was a terrifyingly fine fencer, as the American journalist Wythe Williams reported of one of the prime minister's duels:

> The adversaries who dared face the point of his sword had no chance. He delighted in first disarming them with a flashing but terrific *coup de seconde*, the most powerful blow in swordplay, almost paralyzing the arm. The Tiger would laugh mockingly, and bow while waiting for the weapon to be retrieved. Then he would flick his opponent in a part of the anatomy of his own choosing. He would perform the operation delicately, with just enough damage for the satisfaction of honour, and the termination of the affair.

The leader of the Radical party, Clemenceau did not hesitate to challenge political opponents who, he felt, had gone too far. In 1892 he fought a pistol duel with the antisemitic writer Paul Deroulène in front of a huge crowd controlled by police officers. Six years later, his championship of Dreyfus made him fight the notorious author of *La France juive*, Edouard Drumont. The opponents missed both times, very probably intentionally, as it was considered 'bad form' to hit an adversary with firearms. Duels with sabres or épées, however, were fought at least to first blood and often resulted in serious, sometimes fatal injuries. The duel was perceived as a healthy tonic against the sluggish, decadent life of modern times, 'the first tool of civilization, the only means man had found to reconcile his brutal instincts and his ideal of justice', in the words of Anatole France, who was to receive the Nobel Prize for Literature in 1921.

Military Virtue, Military Vice

The byword for a society ruled by uniformed, mustachioed and heel-clicking officers was of course, Wilhelm II's Germany. Nowhere else in the world was the link between state and army, between army and national history, so close. It was the army that had transformed Prussia from a sandy nowhere without natural resources or natural borders into a world power, a miracle worked through the pact between Prussia's kings and their aristocracy. Prussian generals and soldiers had opened the way into the Hall of Mirrors in Versailles after the victorious war with France in 1870; Prussian discipline and manpower were the foundations of the new German empire. It was at least partly true that the empire had been 'forged in the white heat of the battlefield', to use a cliché of the time.

Not all Germany was Prussia, of course, and the excesses of drill-ground mentality and goose-stepping silliness were laughed at not only abroad but also in Stuttgart, Hamburg and the Prussian but Catholic Rhineland. Prussia was, however, the most powerful partner in the federation of states making up imperial Germany, and Prussian culture was imposed through schools and universities, through the army itself, and in a stream of propaganda engulfing all areas of life: 'People drank from cups adorned with symbols and pictures of different kinds of ordnance, with farewell scenes [of soldiers leaving for the front], propaganda slogans and Hohenzollern profiles; they ate from plates with battle scenes, and beautified their homes with military knick knacks: porcelain soldiers, miniature castles, music corps, guards regiments, monuments and cannon, with tin soldiers in battle formation; and "reservist beer mugs" ...' as two later German historians described the scene in many households. Under the Christmas tree, that symbol of German domestic bliss, boys hoped to find what a popular seasonal song had promised them: 'Tomorrow comes Father Christmas, he comes with his presents: drums and pipes and a gun, flag and sabre and even more, yes, a whole army corps is what I want!'

Drill and military spirit surrounded the nation's children as soon as they entered school. A popular manual for primary schoolteachers gave young educators helpful hints on what orders to use: 'Sit up straight! Quiet! Shut your mouth! Pens straight! Hands up! Show exercise books! – and after the revision Out! ... Obedience to an order must be trained, so that it will be second nature to a teacher to command and to a pupil to follow the orders immediately.' If the primary schoolteacher was to be the nation's drill sergeant, professors at the *Gymnasium*, the secondary school, moved about in a cloud of magnificence, reflecting not only a profound respect for education but also the total hierarchization of society. Badly paid, shabbily dressed and often too poor to marry, even the lowliest of them had a right to be addressed as *Herr Professor* by pupils who stood to attention when speaking to him – a world memorably evoked by Heinrich Mann's novella *Professor Unrat*, later made into one of Germany's classic black and white films: *The Blue Angel*, starring Marlene Dietrich as a dance girl leading an ageing *Gymnasium* teacher astray and causing his social universe to collapse. The world into which boys at a German *Gymnasium* were introduced had very little connection with the political reality of the day, as Hans Kohn, then a Prague schoolboy, would later remember: 'Politics – Austrian, European, Turkish or Asian – meant little to us and we knew nothing about it. People did not travel as they do today and our horizon was largely defined by our classical education and the German language. The neighbouring world of the Slavs was unfamiliar to us, although we devoured the fashionable novels by Dostoyevsky and other Russians.'

All too often the state educated its citizens without educating them to become citizens. With characteristic intuition, the young Thomas Mann had articulated the sense a German child could have of the society he lived in : 'As a boy, I personified the state in my own imagination and pictured it as a wooden figure in tails, with a black beard, a star on his chest, and equipped with a military as well as academic mixture of titles, which demonstrated to perfection his power and dependability: *General Dr von Staat.*'

The military ethos was an integral part of society, or of a certain kind of society. In order to have access to the highest echelons of the administration, the judiciary, and even industry, an ambitious young man did well to be one of the 120,000 Prussian reserve officers. If he was an academic and wanted to make even more effort for his future success, he would join a *Burschenschaft* or student fraternity, most of which were thoroughly reactionary, antisemitic and nationalist, and devoted to drinking, singing, more drinking – and duelling with sabres. These were duels without real cause. Honour was not at stake, but could be gained. The use of pistol or light épées (as was the custom in France) was disdained as 'girls' fighting'. German fraternity students were made of sterner stuff. They would strip to the waist and then, in a *Mensur*, a ritual regulated to the smallest minutiae, lay into each other with heavy sabres. Combattants were made to stand at regulation distance and were not allowed to move their feet, defensive swordplay was disdained and the fight was stopped by heavily padded umpires when the first nasty gash had appeared on a cheek, forehead or chin. Several times, student duellists' noses were lopped off. To the fraternity students it was worth the risk: the scars on their faces would be certain passports to promotion by sympathetic superiors, who had themselves been in fraternities.

If student duels in the fraternities were a *rite de passage*, creating their own, strongly corporatist class with scars as their outward sign of manliness, courage and belonging, duelling for honour was also widespread. There was a national peculiarity, however. Only officers and university graduates –

and, in many cases, non-Jews – were regarded as *satisfaktionsfähig*, that is, socially acceptable for a dispute about honour. Others, it was implied, simply had too little honour to worry about. A man's honour was by necessity a virtue best symbolized by a uniform, and uniforms were omnipresent in public life. Officers and simple soldiers appeared in public in the Kaiser's cloak, civil servants had uniforms for ceremonial occasions; businessmen and even academics often chose to wear the uniforms of their reserve grade; policemen were everywhere on the streets; members of the government wore uniform, and the Kaiser himself had a passion for elaborate military apparel and would travel long distances just to have the chance to wear his Admiral's uniform, or one of the many officer's outfits belonging to the foreign regiments of which he was an honorary member. He appeared on mugs, paintings and postcards now with an eagle helmet, now with a shining cuirass, now in the simple blue tunic of his guards' regiment, but always with his right shoulder turned towards the viewer, his crippled left arm discreetly draped in a pocket or resting on his sabre.

Just how far the respect for uniforms and military bearing could go was shown on 16 October 1906, when an army captain in the capital commandeered a platoon of soldiers on their way to their barracks, put them all on a train and marched them into the town hall of Köpenick near Berlin. There he arrested the mayor and sent him to Berlin under escort, confiscated the town's cash register, wrote out a receipt, ordered the soldiers to remain at their post, walked away, and was not seen again. When the culprit, one Friedrich Wilhelm Voigt, was arrested six weeks later, it turned out that he was not, nor had ever been a military officer. He had spent twenty-nine years of his life in prison for various instances of petty theft and fraud and had simply assembled his uniform (that of a captain in the Ist Foot Guards Regiment) from local pawn shops, after a fortnight's search. Once glorified by epaulettes, the petty crook had become a god. Seeing an officer enter his bureau, the hapless mayor of Köpenick had jumped to his feet, stood with his fingers at his trouser seams and followed orders. When Voigt found the town hall's police guard asleep he had reprimanded him sternly and in the rasping tone of a true officer, making the guard quake in his boots and promise to take more care in future. The soldiers had followed the unknown captain without so much as a raised eyebrow. Voigt had obviously enjoyed the entire spectacle: after having made off with more than 4,000 marks and dispatched his prisoners to Berlin by train, he could not resist going there himself, installing himself in a café opposite the police station and watching the prisoners with their guards arrive and the station erupt in general confusion.

Voigt was sentenced to four years in prison but was soon pardoned by the Kaiser himself, who had the grace to be hugely amused by the incident. The *Hauptmann von Köpenick* became a phenomenon. A biography appeared, thousands of postcards were printed, and after being released from prison the former trickster made a good living appearing at fairgrounds and in night-clubs, telling his story and signing photos of himself. He even went on a tour of Dresden, Vienna and Budapest. In London, the paying public could admire his wax figure wearing a captain's uniform at Madame Tussaud's.

If Voigt's daring prank was sensationalized to Europe's universal amuse-ment, this was made possible by the already existing market for images of heroic virility and its chief icon, the Kaiser himself. No ruler before had exploited the media with such gusto, and no other monarch so assiduously projected an image of heroic masculinity as he. The aged Habsburg Emperor Franz Josef was usually shown uniformed but unarmed and with few medals, an image of authority due to his white whiskers and steady gaze; Edward VII, jolly and famously promiscuous, was hardly ever seen in uniform at all; while diminutive Nicholas II revelled in his love for tassels, gold braid and military decorations. Not even the Tsar, though, could rival the grand attitudes struck by his German cousin.

William the Sudden

A self-styled embodiment of martial masculinity, the impulsive 'Wilhelm the Sudden' would regularly drive his officials to despair with his uncon-trollable urge towards grand, flamboyant rhetoric whenever he found himself in front of a crowd, as he frequently did. According to Christopher Clark, between 1897 and 1902 the Kaiser made at least 233 visits to at least 123 German towns, and would always seize the opportunity to make an impromptu speech, brushing aside the safe text prepared for him by his cabinet. Chancellor Bülow spent a good deal of his time editing overblown phrases out of his master's utterances before they reached the press, only to find himself accused of having 'left out the best bits' by the Kaiser. These 'best bits', excised from the official versions made available to newspapers, usually came straight from the Emperor's heart and said more about his personal mood than about political priorities. In 1890 a preoccupation with the dangers of socialism led him to remind recruits of a Guards regiment that they would have to be prepared 'to fire on their fathers and brothers if he ordered them to do so'. In 1900, when seeing off the expeditionary force sent to subdue the Boxer Rebellion in China, he famously exhorted his sol-diers to be like Huns: 'there will be no mercy, prisoners will not be taken.

Just as the Huns one thousand years ago ... made a name for themselves in which their greatness still resounds, so let the name of Germany be known in China in such a way that a Chinese will never again dare even look askance at a German.' In 1907 he promised an audience that the German eagle would 'spread its wings once again over Europe', a phrase amended in the official version to 'over the German Empire'.

The Kaiser's gung-ho rhetoric did not reflect the thinking of German politicians, and their exasperation reached a peak in the wake of the *Daily Telegraph* affair, kicked off by an interview with Wilhelm which was published in Britain in 1908. The monarch had spent some weeks at Highcliffe Castle, which he had rented from its owner, Colonel Edward James Montague Stuart-Wortley. Glorying in the role of British country gentleman, His Majesty had given his host generous insights into the imperial mind during long fireside chats, and Stuart-Wortley had taken these remarks as the basis of an 'interview' he offered to the *Daily Telegraph*. The text had been cleared with the German chancellery, but this time it was allowed to appear – whether through negligence or calculation – including the Emperor's customary offensive remarks, which on this occasion attacked Britain, much to the dismay of diplomats in London and Berlin who were engaged in a round of delicate and elaborate talks sounding out the possibility of avoiding conflict over their countries' naval programmes. The Kaiser's clumsy bravado hit German–British relations like a bomb: 'You English are mad, mad as March hares ... To be forever misjudged, to have my repeated offers of friendship weighed and scrutinized with jealous, mistrustful eyes, taxes my patience severely. I have said time after time that I am a friend of England, and your press ... bids the people of England refuse my proffered hand and insinuates that the other holds a dagger.'

It was not only the opposition that shook with rage. The Berlin courtier Baroness Spitzemberg noted in her diary: 'This is the most shameful, the lowest, most indiscreet and the most worrying thing the Kaiser has ever been guilty of ... [He] ruins our political position and makes us the laughing stock of the world ...! One can only clutch one's head, uncertain about whether this is a madhouse!' More public voices were hardly less chiding, particularly among elected politicians furious at seeing their efforts dashed yet again by their reckless ruler. Ernst Basserman, a national liberal politician, rose to his feet in the Reichstag to vent his 'feeling of bottomless astonishment, of deep sadness'. The Social Democrat Paul Singer spoke of 'legitimate rage, a deep shame amongst the German people', and even the Prussian arch-conservative Ernst von Heydebrandt und der Lasa vented his feelings of 'an accumulation of concern and resentment that has been gathering for years, even in circles whose loyalty to the Kaiser and Empire has hitherto been unquestioned'.

'I wish I could put a padlock on his mouth for all occasions where speeches are made in public!' the Kaiser's exasperated mother had already exclaimed in 1892, but her son's swaggering impetuosity was uncontrollable, despite the efforts of those closest to him, including his most trusted adviser, Count (later Prince) Philipp zu Eulenburg (1847–1921). The Count alone dared speak openly to his monarch, and the ministers of state would often address themselves to Eulenburg to make his imperious master see sense. Eulenburg was 'Ambassador of the German Government to the Kaiser', members of the Reichstag quipped, and he was more than content with this unofficial leverage. He was shrewd enough to know that he owed his extraordinary influence over the Emperor to the fact that he had always remained outside the realm of official power. 'Whenever he came into our Potsdam home,' the Kaiser noted, 'it was like a flood of sunshine in the routine of life.' Several times the Kaiser invited him to join his government, and the Prince always refused, politely and with gentle self-mockery, preferring instead the much more modest post of Prussian ambassador to Vienna and later Prussian representative in the German cities of Oldenburg, Stuttgart and Munich: 'A poor barndoor fowl like me, cockered up into an eagle. I can hear myself cackling instead of clawing, and see myself laying an egg instead of sitting with flaming eyes on the gable of 76 Wilhelmstrasse [the foreign ministry]. The thing is out of the question.'

To the Kaiser, Prince 'Phili' Eulenburg, a man twelve years his senior whom he had met on a hunting visit to friends in 1886, was not one of those bustling and grovelling Berlin officials constantly telling him what he could not do and what the Reichstag would not pass or pay for. Rather, he was a pure, disinterested friend whose country house at Liebenberg was a secluded paradise. There the Kaiser enjoyed days spent out hunting, uncomplicated companionship, long conversations, and evenings with friends clustered around the piano, with the host playing his own compositions, and Wilhelm himself eagerly turning the pages. It was an atmosphere that was the absolute opposite of Wilhelm's own upbringing at court and at the hands of his strict preceptor, Hintzpeter. At Liebenberg the Kaiser would relax in a circle of like-minded men with the Prince and the cultured Count Kuno von Moltke and could admire his friend Phili's talent for telling amusing and sometimes risqué anecdotes, as well as for music and for literature – after all, Eulenburg was not only a career diplomat but also an ambitious composer whose *Rosenlieder* song cycle had sold 500,000 copies, as well as a playwright whose works were professionally produced. Every now and then, Eulenburg's wife and children would be allowed to join in and the daughters would sing their father's songs, then the men would be left alone once more.

Wilhelm was intoxicated by the Liebenberg atmosphere and by the Prince, whom he described to Hintzpeter as 'my only bosom friend,' and it appears that Eulenburg, too, was genuinely enthusiastic about the qualities of the personable but erratic young Crown Prince, as he wrote in a letter to Wilhelm, describing their friendship as 'a radiance in my life'. Many observers commented on this close relationship. Returning from the peace negotiations after the Russo-Japanese War, former Russian prime minister Sergei Witte paid the Emperor a visit at the country estate of Rominten. He was met at the train by Prince Eulenburg and spent the night with the imperial family. During the evening's conversation around the fire, Witte noted, 'I was particularly struck by the Emperor's attitude toward Prince Eulenburg. He sat on the arm of the prince's chair, his right hand on Eulenburg's shoulder, almost as if he were putting his arm around him.'

So admiring was Wilhelm of his older friend that he treated him with a consideration not shown to anyone else. An inveterate and crude practical joker (the King of Bulgaria once departed from Berlin 'white with hatred' after the Kaiser had jocularly slapped him on the bottom in public), Wilhelm would often amuse himself on his Baltic cruises by summoning all guests for morning gymnastics on deck and then giving a well-judged push to one of the generals puffing on their hands and knees so as to enjoy the hilarity as they collapsed in a heap. But never Eulenburg. 'The Emperor has never touched me,' the Prince stated simply, 'he knows I would not suffer it.'

If Eulenburg's tempering influence was largely positive and helped steer the Kaiser away from some of his more disastrous ideas, it is also true that the Prince exploited his power and was not above mounting elaborate intrigues to ensure that a candidate he approved of was appointed to an important post. On one occasion, Friedrich von Holstein, the *éminence grise* of the foreign ministry and a long-time ally, requested that Eulenburg ask the Russian ambassador to Bavaria if he would ask the Tsar to recommend a particular diplomat as German ambassador to St Petersburg to his cousin the Kaiser. Eulenburg then earnestly counselled his monarch that it would be a grave insult to go against the personal and spontaneously expressed wish of Nicholas II, and the appointment was duly made.

Phili's Fall

Eulenburg had always avoided the exposure of government in order to retain a steady and all the more pervasive influence. Eventually, however, his considerable power antagonized even his closest allies, who mounted their own intrigue to rid themselves of him, a campaign that began with private insults but soon spiralled into the biggest scandal the Kaiser's Germany had ever seen. The trigger for this chain of events was a resignation letter meant as a sign of hurt pride, but not to be taken seriously. The man who had written it was Eulenburg's ally, Friedrich von Holstein (1837–1909), first councillor to the foreign ministry at Berlin's Wilhelmstrasse, known to his enemies as the 'monster of the labyrinth', who had effectively been running much of the country's foreign policy (and been responsible for some of its disastrous failures) from the anonymity of his wood-panelled office. Like Eulenburg he was suspicious of official power and had repeatedly refused promotion, arguing that the social obligations and diplomatic receptions attached to a high position would be a waste of time. A former protégé of Bismarck and reclusive to the point of ducking out of the back door of his office whenever the Kaiser visited the ministry, he preferred quietly working in his office, twelve hours a day every weekday, surrounded by silent messengers who entered, bowed, left their paper on his desk and left without saying a word. He did not accept invitations to fashionable houses; he lived alone; he even dined alone, in a room kept for him at the Borchardt restaurant, which he entered through a side entrance after a short walk from the office. Chancellors and foreign secretaries had succeeded one another in the limelight, but his work and quiet, iron grip on policy remained the same.

For all his dedication and ability, Holstein was a notoriously touchy man, quick to take offence and very slow to forgive even the smallest lack of respect towards him, even on the part of his superiors, whom he would regularly frighten by threatening to resign if anyone opposed his opinions. His vindictiveness and tantrums were tolerated, as Count Eulenburg noted: 'Holstein's great talents [were considered] to be indispensable. No one could replace his understanding of complex questions of international importance … In the Emperor's and the Government's interests, he had to be humoured, as one humours a bad-tempered, erratic, positively dangerous sporting dog for the sake of his good nose.'

In 1906 the expensive luxury of an uncontrollable and obscure but brilliant presence at the heart of the foreign ministry seemed an indulgence too far in the eyes of the new state secretary there, Heinrich von Tschirschky. Holstein had been involved in Germany's latest foreign policy disaster, the 1905 Morocco crisis which had risked an unnecessary and profitless war with France and Britain. Now his superior, von Tschirschky decided to put the monster of the labyrinth on a tighter leash. Holstein reacted as he had often done before: he submitted his resignation. This time, however, he had overplayed his hand. Chancellor Bülow, his long-term political ally, forwarded the resignation to the Kaiser, with a recommendation to accept. After decades in the diplomatic service, Holstein was out of a job, and fuming.

Who could have plotted against him? Who could be brazen enough to attack the brain of the foreign ministry? Holstein let his friends and enemies pass before his mind's eye. Bülow, he calculated, was too loyal, too old an ally to betray him. On the very day of the Kaiser's signing his resignation, however, Eulenburg had lunched at the imperial palace. It was his inscrutable, nefarious toady who had poisoned Wilhelm's mind, Holstein decided in a rare but comprehensive misjudgement of the political situation. Eulenburg had the Emperor's ear, Eulenburg had worked against him; Eulenburg must be destroyed.

Holstein knew at once what to do. Having been on friendly terms with Eulenburg for decades, he, like everyone at court, knew the open secret that the Prince, the father of eight children from a detested marriage, was not, in fact, interested in women and that behind all his culture and male cama-raderie lay a crime punished, according to German law, under the infamous article 175 of the penal code. In an angry letter, he wrote to his former friend: 'My dear Phili – you needn't take this beginning as a compliment since nowadays to call a man "Phili" means – well, nothing very flattering. You have now attained the object for which you have been intriguing for years – my retirement ... I am now free to handle you as one handles such a contemptible person with your peculiarities.'

Even to the gentle and unmilitary Philipp zu Eulenburg, this letter allowed only one course of action: he challenged Holstein to an exchange of pistol shots 'until disablement or death'. Horrified by the prospect of a duel fought by two elder statesmen, Secretary von Tschirschky embarked on a whirl of intra-governmental diplomacy and succeeded in extracting a grudging apology from Holstein, but this additional humiliation only made the slighted diplomat look for other, more devastating means of bringing Eulenburg down. He found an unlikely but devastatingly effective ally in Maximilian Harden (1861–1927), an investigative journalist, editor of the newspaper *Die Zukunft*, and long-time thorn in the government's side. Supplied by Holstein with confidential government documents, Harden mounted a comprehensive attack, accusing Eulenburg and other members of the Liebenberg circle of homosexuality first by innuendo, then openly.

Harden's main interest in the story (his own monumental ego aside) was political. Eulenburg was emblematic of the undemocratic, unaccountable and personalized style of government that Wilhelm so loved and the democratic opposition so despised. A ruthless journalist with a gift for controversy, Harden understood that this was his chance of showing that the Kaiser was open to the dark, unhealthy influences of a decadent, perverted coterie secretly ruling over one of the world's foremost countries. Eulenburg's social ruin was a price the journalist was only too willing to pay.

In Wilhelminian Germany (as, indeed, in other European countries) the mere suspicion of homosexuality was enough to wreck lives and careers, even – and perhaps especially – in the highest reaches of society. Only a few years earlier, the Austro-Hungarian Archduke Ludwig Viktor ('Luzi-Wuzi'), the brother of Emperor Franz Josef, and known for his propensity to turn out in public in women's clothes, had had to go into exile in provincial Salzburg after an affair with a masseur. In Germany in 1902, none other than the Continent's richest and most powerful industrialist, Fritz Krupp, committed suicide at his grand Villa Hügel in Essen after being publicly accused of holidaying in Capri not so much for the sun, as for the younger sons of the island.

Harden had no proof that Eulenburg was homosexual, but he piled article upon article: 'I am pointing my finger at Philipp Friedrich Karl Alexander Botho Fürst zu Eulenburg und Hertefeld, Graf von Sandels,' his first salvo read, 'who is … whispering in the Kaiser's ear that he alone is called to rule … At least the insidious working of this man must no longer be in the dark.' The following year he became more explicit. The Liebenberg circle, he implied, had taken the manly strength out of Germany's foreign policy and made the Kaiser back down where he should have stood firm. The result was a policy of effeminate indecision, as the circle no longer 'dreamt of burning worlds' because they were 'already warm [German slang for homosexual] enough'; a little later, he wrote openly about Eulenburg's 'unhealthy *vita sexualis*'.

If part of the accusation was that a 'court camarilla' of unelected noblemen and hangers-on kept the Kaiser isolated from reality, then Wilhelm's reaction itself provides the best illustration: the first time he heard of the entire affair was on 3 May 1907 when the Crown Prince confronted his father with a copy of *Die Zukunft* containing one of the damaging articles. Chancellor Bülow and other court officials had thought it wiser not to burden His Majesty with such details. The Kaiser was flabbergasted but acted quickly to dissociate himself from any damage the revelations might cause. One of those accused, his friend of long standing, Count Kuno von Moltke, was immediately dismissed. The very next day, the Kaiser wrote to Eulenburg, asking him not only what steps he intended to take against these accusations, but also whether he felt 'beyond reproach regarding certain allusions'. At the end of the month, Wilhelm set his formerly much adored mentor an ultimatum: sue Harden or get out of the country, 'avoiding all publicity'. The two men would never meet again.

Eulenburg was deeply hurt by the 'revolting vulgarity' of the Kaiser's reaction, the end of an intense twenty-year friendship. During the following year, a succession of libel cases was followed by the German public with rapt attention. Eulenburg brought a case against himself and was cleared of all charges. Kuno von Moltke challenged Harden to a duel. When the journalist declined, von Moltke brought a case against him in the provincial court. Over the following weeks, prosecution and defence cited one witness after the other, and each of them contributed another scandalous facet to the case. The Kaiser, it was revealed, was called *Liebchen* (sweetie) by his Liebenberg friends, and a whole rogue's gallery of rent boys, past and present, testified to having known the gentlemen in question. Von Moltke lost the trial and he appealed the verdict. 'I never did anything dirty,' he simply affirmed, and, with a different judge presiding, he was acquitted and Harden sentenced to four months in prison.

Harden took revenge by engineering another trial, this time defending himself against a newspaper article libelling him, but secretly commissioned by him. Freshly prepared and with renewed energy, he presented the Munich district court with the milk merchant Georg Riedel and the fisherman Jakob Ernst, both of whom claimed to have had love affairs with Eulenburg as young men: 'Whenever we went on an outing, we did the dirty thing,' Ernst claimed. For Eulenburg, who had already suffered one heart attack under the stress of the trials, this was the end. The judge had him remanded in custody and transferred to Berlin's Charité hospital under guard. His old friend the Kaiser twisted the knife by ordering the Prince to return his Order of the Black Eagle, the empire's highest decoration. A disillusioned and disgusted Eulenburg sent it back, together with all other medals he had ever received. His health deteriorated further and he had to be carried into court on a stretcher every day.

When his prey could no longer leave his sick room at all, Harden had 145 witnesses (most of whom had a criminal record or a history of mental illness) pile past the bed, stare at the broken man and pronounce that yes, they had indeed been intimate with him. Eulenburg's failing constitution eventually put an end to this farce. The trial was suspended in 1909 and never reopened. Eulenburg died, bitter and isolated, at his Liebenberg estate in 1921. 'These things are unutterably sad because the social annihilation [of Eulenburg and von Moltke] is so total,' sighed Baroness von

Spitzemberg in her diary, 'but morality and moral consciousness demand a boycott, a total exclusion of such sinners.'

Faced with the debris of the campaign he had conducted, even Maximilian Harden would have second thoughts about whether he had been right to use a prejudice he himself did not share to destroy a political opponent. While the journalist was mulling over the morality of wrecking a man's life for political gain, Kaiser Wilhelm himself was cruelly reminded of his abandoned friend in 1908, when his boyhood comrade, General Dietrich Hülsen-Haeseler, chief of the military cabinet, was entrusted with cleansing the Prussian officer corps of homosexuals in the wake of the Eulenburg affair. Hülsen-Haeseler appeared before the guests of a hunting party in the Kaiser's honour dressed 'in pink ballet skirts with a rose wreath and began to dance to the music'. Having finished his performance, the Count bowed to the applauding audience, and collapsed. General chaos ensued among the guests. Princess Fürstenberg, the hostess, wept uncontrollably and the agitated Kaiser was seen pacing up and down, but the doctor who had been hastily summoned could do nothing more than declare the performer's death by heart failure. When attention finally turned back to the general, rigor mortis had set in and it proved very difficult to get the late chief of the military cabinet out of his tutu and into more seemly military attire.

Being Uranist

Many great scandals of the two decades leading up to the First World War involved the army and accusations about homosexuality. Oscar Wilde's trial in London pitted the outrageously homosexual poet against the Marquess of Queensberry, an army officer and boxing fanatic; during the Dreyfus case, resolved in 1906 with the full pardon and reinstitution of the Jewish captain, the undertones had been antisemitic as well as sexual; in the Eulenburg affair Kuno von Moltke, the military commander of Berlin, had represented the armed forces and paid the price; the Austro-Hungarian traitor and double agent Colonel Alfred Redl was forced to commit suicide by his superiors in 1913 after he had sold military secrets to Russians, who had blackmailed him over an affair with another officer; and evidence of Roger Casement's homosexuality during his trial would be enough to hang him in 1916.

As well-oiled machinery was taking over from muscle power, making masculine strength less valuable in the work space, and the changing role of women raised fundamental questions about the relationship between the sexes, men felt less sure of themselves, of who they were supposed to be, and what space would remain for the traditional male virtues – courage, honour, strength – in an industrialized society. Amid these insecurities, homosexuality had become a worrying spectre, liable to break lives and certain to grab the headlines.

Homosexuality was still a crime in all European countries, and an accusation, even anonymous, could result in social ostracism and lengthy prison sentences. But, as Freud has shown, societies with such strong prohibitions in the face of human passions can never exist without an operational degree of hypocrisy. In Berlin, for instance, there was a flourishing gay scene, lovingly described by the early sexologist and psychiatrist Magnus Hirschfeld (1868–1935) in his reportage *Berlins drittes Geschlecht* (Berlin's Third Sex, 1904). The big city, Hirschfeld wrote, allowed identities to thrive away from neighbourly control, and the result was there to see for all with eyes to see it: 'Those who are in the know see on the streets and in various Berlin cafés not only men and women in the conventional sense of the word, but also frequently persons whose mannerisms and even their physical appearance can be different from others. It is almost as if there were not only a male and a female sex, but also a third one.'

Using a then fashionable appellation (whence the notorious pun in Wilde's *Importance of Being Earnest*), Hirschfeld described a 'uranist' scene of astonishing frankness in Berlin, a barely hidden and extensive subculture of cafés, pubs, beer gardens, clubs, gyms, swimming pools and even social occasions such as dances almost exclusively frequented by gays: 'One has seen homosexuals from the provinces who have come to such spots for the first time crying with profound psychological shock,' Hirschfeld commented about the liberalizing effect of such a scene on those who had been 'deprived of rights and humiliated' all their lives.

Sandow the Magnificent

Being a man meant different things in different countries. German Chancellor Bülow regarded it as a point of honour and great pride to gallop past his Emperor at the head of his old regiment, the King William I Hussars, a feat rewarded with a commission as major general immediately afterwards. It would be impossible, the historian Robert Massie rightly points out, to imagine British prime ministers Salisbury, Balfour, Campbell-Bannerman or Asquith engaging in any such antics. Britain was calm, measured and civilian, and looked askance at its neighbours' martial posturing. The underlying preoccupations, however, were much the same,

A perfect man: Eugene Sandow's displays of strength were followed by huge audiences.

as a look into any newspaper of the time shows: the same advertisements here for tinctures promising to cure 'male exhaustion', the same pills for 'manly vigour' and hidden corsets to fight middle-aged spread – only in London or Manchester the figure of the hero was less likely to be encased in a uniform than in leopardskin shorts.

The shorts in question draped the extremely muscular loins of Eugene Sandow (1867–1925), a strongman, fitness prophet, businessman and international phenomenon. Sandow had been born plain Friedrich Wilhelm Mueller in the east Prussian enclave of Königsberg and had set himself the goal of developing a perfect body. After a stint displaying his feats of strength at provincial fairs, he was snapped up by the legendary showman Florenz Ziegfeld and soon became a star in the Anglo-Saxon world. His shows were sellouts from Chicago to Invercargill in New Zealand; crowds would cheer their hero and demand autographs, women would go backstage and pay three hundred dollars to touch his steely muscles, and his books, with titles like *Sandow's System of Physical Training, Strength and How To Obtain It*, and *Body-Building* were bestsellers. 'Such a scene of excitement has never before been witnessed in any Australian theatre,' wrote a breathless reporter in Perth. 'The audience went absolutely frantic at Sandow's Marvellous Performance, and recalled him no less than fifteen times.'

Not content with imitating Greek statues and lifting impossible weights on stage, Sandow also believed he had a mission to improve humanity's puny lot by founding a series of twenty fitness studios, a magazine dedicated to physical strength and a mail order business for merchandise ranging from Sandow cigars to Sandow dumb-bells and exercise books in order to enable other, lesser, men to attain his miraculous proportions. His success was extraordinary. George V and Sir Arthur Conan Doyle were among his friends, and the 1901 finals of his Great Competition, the first official beauty contest for well-muscled men, attracted a crowd of 15,000 spectators at London's Albert Hall.

It is possible that British men were less worried than their Continental counterparts about their modern identities – the industrial revolution, after all, had taken place much earlier here than in the rest of Europe, and urban life and culture more established in a country with a rural population that was the lowest of any developed country (only 8 per cent of Britons of working age were employed in agriculture in 1911, three times more in Germany and four times more in France); but if the visibility of the army in public life was so much smaller in Britain than across the Channel it is also worth remembering that its importance in British history had been much smaller. A fraction of the size of those of its Continental neighbours, and constantly engaged in far-flung regions of the globe, the British army was respected, but remote. Britain, after all, was famously an island and a marine empire not invaded for centuries and it had given its navy, the key to its abiding power, pride of place. The Dreadnought race was not just a military matter; it was a defence of a national self-image. Britannia, all politicians and newspapers agreed, simply had to rule the waves. Toting the biggest guns was a simple necessity.

The British were proud of their essentially civilian culture, but the military enthusiasm of their neighbours bared underlying anxieties. Who could say whether they would withstand an invasion attempt? Who could say that they still had the mettle, the sheer moral force, to defeat an enemy at home? Was it not possible that Britain was already being undermined by foreign spies? Ever on the lookout for a sensational story, the English *Daily Mail* thought it wise to advise its readers: 'Refuse to be served by an Austrian or German waiter. If your waiter says he is Swiss, ask to see his passport.'

The spying waiter, the overly curious hairdresser with a suspicious accent, the cabbie who was more ear than mouth – these figures became commonplace. Most foreigners, the novelist William Le Queux (1864–1927) warned the British public,

> were Germans who, having served in the army, had come over to England and obtained employment as waiters, clerks, bakers, hairdressers, and private servants, and being bound by their oath to the Fatherland, had served their country as spies. Each man, when obeying the Imperial command to join the German arms, had placed in the lapel of his coat a button of a peculiar shape with which he had long ago been provided and by which he was instantly recognized as a loyal subject of the Kaiser.

An important shift occurred in this form of popular paranoia. Ever since William the Conqueror, and certainly since Napoleon, the traditional enemy had been France. Around 1900, however, the threat was increasingly perceived to be Germany. Terrifying numbers were bandied about in public. Lord Roberts, himself a military hero, speculated that there were 80,000 trained German soldiers living in Britain, while the Conservative MP Sir John Barlow claimed to know of 66,000 German army reservists living in and around London alone. Popular novelists were quick to capitalize on this idea. In the wildly successful *The Riddle of the Sands* (1903), the writer Erskine Childers lets two young Englishmen stumble upon a dastardly plot by the Kaiser, for whom one of the protagonists expresses great admiration:

> I did know something of Germany, and could satisfy his tireless questioning with a certain authority ... I described her marvellous awakening in the last generation, under the strength and wisdom of her rulers; her intense patriotic ardour, her seething industrial activity, and, most potent of all, the forces that are moulding modern Europe, her dream of a colonial empire, entailing her transformation from a land-power to a sea-power. Impregnably based on vast territorial resources which we cannot molest, the dim instincts of her people, not merely directed but anticipated by the genius of her ruling house, our great trade rivals of the present, our great naval rival of the future, she grows, and strengthens, and waits, an ever more formidable factor in the future of our delicate network of empire, sensitive as gossamer to external shocks, and radiating from an island whose commerce is its life, and which depends even for its daily ration of bread on the free passage of the seas.

In the manner of a *Boy's Own* story, the two heroes eventually come to realize that the inexplicable movements they have observed on the German coast point to an enormous danger: 'I understood at last. I was assisting at an experimental rehearsal of the great scene, to be enacted, perhaps in the near future – a scene when multitudes of sea-going lighters, carrying full loads of soldiers, not half-loads of coal, should issue simultaneously, in seven ordered fleets, from seven shallow outlets, and, under escort of the Imperial Navy, traverse the North Sea and throw themselves bodily upon the English shores.' The problem, or so one of the novel's protagonists claimed, was that the English had grown soft: 'We've been so safe so long, and grown so rich, that we've forgotten what we owe it. But there's no excuse for those blockheads of statesmen as they call themselves, who are paid to see things as they are ... By Jove, we want a man like this Kaiser, who doesn't wait to be kicked, but works like a nigger for his country and sees ahead ... We aren't ready for her [Germany].'

Other authors agreed, both with the sentiment and its overt racism, and Lord Northcliffe found the matter important enough to have his *Daily Mail* serialize a novel by William Le Queux, *The Invasion of 1910*, in which Britain is overrun by a German horde close to the one Kaiser Wilhelm must have had in mind during his infamous 'Huns' speech. Looting, burning, raping and killing, they make their way towards the capital, which they at first succeed in taking, but must inevitably lose again, submerged by a tidal wave of British outrage and stubborn courage. To launch the novel, sandwich men wearing blue Prussian uniforms and spiked helmets marched up and down Oxford Street. The novel sold over a million copies, even if Le Queux found to his disgust that in the German translation it was the Kaiser who triumphed over the empire he had so long been jealous of.

It is one of Britain's greatest charms that its citizens refuse to take anything very seriously, even and especially their own great symbols; it is one of her greatest weaknesses that they pay as much attention to the subtleties of class as a German would have to epaulettes. This lesson was learned somewhat painfully by the admiral commanding HMS *Dreadnought* in 1910, when he received the Emperor of Abyssinia on board, or thought he did. The visit had been announced by telegram and the navy had pulled out all the stops: red carpet, honour guard, flags waving, bands playing, the entire crew standing to attention in their best uniforms. Given the short notice, no Abyssinian flag could be found, and the flag of nearby Zanzibar was flown instead. Undisturbed by such details, the imperial delegation was shown around the ship, a translator whispering into His Majesty's ear. They were astonished at the ship they saw. An electric light switch first startled and then delighted them. During the visit, they also requested prayer mats and bestowed military honours of their country on some of the officers.

It took a few weeks for the visitors to be properly identified in a sensational article in the *Daily Mirror*, to which members of the delegation had sent a group photo taken at the occasion. They were, in fact, a group of English friends, made up with grease paint and false beards. Among the delegation were Duncan Grant and the young Virginia Stephen (adorned with a fetching black beard), who was to marry Leonard Woolf. During the visit they had conversed with one another by using a few words of Swahili learned on the train and adroitly mixed with fragments from Virgil's *Aeneid*, half remembered from school. The 'interpreter' and the fake Foreign Office representative of the visit had appeared undisguised. He was Horace de Vere Cole, the mastermind and financier of the operation, and a man who devoted a good part of his life to conceiving and executing elaborate practical jokes. He was an old hand at disguises: at his Cambridge college he had appeared dressed as the Sultan of Zanzibar, and in middle age he had capitalized on his resemblance to Ramsay MacDonald by arranging for the Labour leader to be temporarily 'lost' in a taxi in the London traffic while Cole went to a meeting of the Labour Party in his stead and gave a speech, telling the workers to work more for less.

Madmen and Muscle Jews

The worship of manly strength could bring forth strange blossoms, perhaps none stranger and more symptomatic of the period's preoccupations than Max Nordau's glowing invocation of the Muscle Jew as the physical and spiritual goal of Zionism. Nordau's woolly but influential bestselling tome *Degeneration*, had made him one of the main voices critical of everything he saw as the enfeebling and debilitating influences of modern life and art. The threat to civilization was grave, Nordau claimed, and it came from:

> ...a contempt for traditional views of custom and morality...a practical emancipation from traditional discipline...unbridled lewdness, the unchaining of the beast in man...disdain of all consideration for his fellow-men, the trampling under foot of all barriers which enclose brutal greed of lucre and lust of pleasure...to all, it means the end of an established order, which for thousands of years has satisfied logic, fettered depravity, and in every art matured something of beauty.

Nordau did not pull any punches when he went against the perceived excesses of the new, menacing, speeding machines, or the degeneracy of contemporary art. Of the legendary nineteenth-century poet Paul Verlaine, he wrote: 'We see a repulsive degenerate with an asymmetric skull and a Mongolian face, an impulsive vagabond and dipsomaniac, who, because of crimes against morality, was placed in a penitentiary;...a dotard, who displays the absence of any definite thought in his mind by incoherent speech, meaningless expressions, and frizzy images.' The creature of this life of mechanical enfeeblement and immoral over-excitation was an aberration: 'physically, sick and feeble; morally, an arrant scoundrel; intellectually, an unspeakable idiot who passes his days choosing the colours of things to drape his room artistically, observing the movements of mechanical fish, sniffing perfumes, and sipping liqueurs...A parasite of the lowest level.'

A doctor himself, Nordau knew that parasites had to be exterminated, and he had no hesitation in applying this scientific principle to society:

The weak, the degenerate will perish; the strong will adapt themselves to the achievements of civilization or will subordinate them to their own organic capacity. ... The art of the twentieth century will connect itself at every point to that of the past, but it will have a new task to fulfil: to bring a stimulating variety to the uniformity of cultured life, an influence that probably only science, many centuries later, will be in a position to exert over the great majority of humankind ... Whoever believes with me that society is the natural organic form of humanity, ... whoever considers civilisation to be a good that has value and deserves to be defended, must mercilessly crush the anti-social vermin [*Ungeziefer*] under his thumbs.

For its author, this violent rhetoric was little more than a pose. Born in Pest (later a part of Budapest) in Hungary in 1849, Nordau was the son of an orthodox rabbi by the name of Südfeld. Estranged from religion, the young Maximilian Südfeld changed direction, not only in life but also in his surname, in which he swapped *south* for *north* and *field* (Feld) for *meadow* (Aue), and Doctor Max Nordau was born, a self-made publicist who finally opened a practice in Paris and published a succession of books on cultural topics. Like the Viennese foreign correspondent Theodor Herzl, Nordau was deeply disgusted by the wave of antisemitism rising in France during the Dreyfus affair, and soon the two men began to discuss their ideas about the future of the Jewish people. Nordau became one of Herzl's most ardent supporters, but his vision of a Jewish renaissance carried connotations different from Herzl's. While the latter's vision was largely pragmatic, the author of *Degeneration* fused his two preoccupations, the decline and decadence of Western societies and the future of his own people, into a curious but influential amalgam: heroic Jewishness, a race of new Jews with 'clear heads, solid stomachs, and hard muscles'.

Nordau's message fitted perfectly into the anxieties of Jewish emancipation, eager to distance itself from the antisemitic stereotypes of the pale and feeble inhabitant of the ghetto with eyes reddened from study, his emaciated body pallid, the very blood in his body dull and lifeless, part of a dirt-poor flood of strangers transformed into capitalist exploiters of honest muscle work. Jew-hating authors like Richard Wagner's British son-in-law, Houston Stewart Chamberlain (1855–1927) had peddled this message far and wide, and Nordau accepted this diagnosis:

Microbiology teaches us that microorganisms that are harmless as long as they are living in the open air turn into terrible, disease-causing pathogens if one deprives them of oxygen and, to use the technical language, transforms them into anaerobes. Governments and people had better beware of making the Jews into anaerobic beings. They could have a high price to pay, regardless of what they do, to get rid of these Jews whom they turned into pests [*Schädling*] by their own guilt.

To Nordau, Zionism was not just a political necessity, it was a call for spiritual rebirth, and many of his readers found themselves agreeing that Jews could be really free only if they were masters not only of their own countries, but of their own healthy bodies. Jewish sports clubs sprang up, often with names reminiscent of biblical warriors: the Bar Kochba (1898) and the Maccabi Union of Jewish Sports Clubs (1902) in Berlin, the Hakoah ('the force') in Vienna (1909), and dozens more across Europe. The movement had its own magazines, its own championships and its own idols. How important it was deemed to be may also be seen from the fact that the universal strongman Eugene Sandow chose to publish an article about Jewish body culture in the first issue of his *Sandow Journal*.

For the leopard-skinned Sandow, as for the proud new Jews, manliness was of prime importance, as Nordau stated with a flourish:

Our new muscle Jews have not yet regained the heroism of their forefathers ... to take part in battles and compete with the trained Hellenic athletes and strong northern barbarians. But morally speaking, we are better off today than yesterday, for the old Jewish circus performers of yore were ashamed of their Judaism and sought, by way of a surgical pinch, to hide the sign of their religious affiliation ... while today, the members of Bar Kochba proudly and freely proclaim their Jewishness.

Nordau was only too happy to accept the role of prophet of the new kind of Jewishness that was so enthusiastically supported by Zionist youth across Europe. Nothing, however, was more hateful to him than to have prophets next to himself. His special venom was reserved for a man who had been, he wrote, 'obviously insane from birth' and whose influence on Western civilization had been entirely negative. 'From the first to the last page ... the careful reader seems to hear a madman, with flashing eyes, wild gestures, and foaming mouth, spouting forth deafening bombast ... So far as any meaning at all can be extracted from the endless stream of phrases, it shows, as its fundamental elements, a series of constantly reiterated delirious ideas, having their source in illusions of sense and diseased organic processes.' This madman was, of course, Friedrich Nietzsche.

Anxious Virility

The struggle against the enfeebling slavery of convention and the desire to become a 'superman' were Nietzsche's dreams, and an entire generation had dreamt them after him. Every single educated person at this time would have been conversant with his work. Some of his books, such as *Thus Spake Zarathustra*, were read over and over, passed from hand to hand, and discussed as great prophetic utterings, particularly among the younger generation. Of great intellectual subtlety and depth in their ensemble, some of his more declamatory sentences were fatally liable to being quoted out of context. This and the devastating editing work of his sister, Elisabeth Förster-Nietzsche (later a passionate admirer of Hitler), after his descent into madness, made his legacy ambivalent and the thinker himself into a prophet claimed by movements as different as the nihilists of the late nineteenth century and the National Socialists.

What Nordau so despised about Nietzsche was his determination to overthrow all bourgeois values in order to return humanity (or those few who had the strength in them) to a pre-modern paradise of instinct mastered by spiritual force. Nordau, an assimilated Jew, did not want to do away with the blessings of civilization, with discipline and order; he merely thought they were threatened by decadence and wanted to cleanse them by methods carrying unmistakably Darwinist overtones. There is an irony here, of course, which Nordau, with a profound blindness given only to those who will not see, does not appear to have appreciated: dreams of power were much like those dreamed earlier by Nietzsche, and his ideal Muscle Jews were effectively misunderstood Nietzschean supermen with a 'surgical pinch', as Nordau himself put it. Nordau's physical Zionism as well as his wider cultural critique were effectively a weaker second serving of the older man's revolutionary ideas. The Zionist writer was not alone in suffering this indignity. The cult of strength and manliness that was such a dominant feature of pre-1914 culture was celebrated everywhere in Nietzsche's shadow.

Eugene Sandow and Kaiser Wilhelm, Dreadnought battleships and duelling, body-building, sailor suits and grand military parades all played their part in the cult of virile strength that was, in part at least, a reaction to the spreading uncertainty about masculine virtues and manliness itself. A new time seemed to demand new models, new identities, and it was true that men appeared to be overwhelmed by the demands placed on them. That, at least, was one of the conclusions French writers drew from the decline in birth rates, and it was certainly one of the reasons for the wave of male neurasthenics washing into the sanatoriums from Switzerland to Scotland.

Writing in 1904, the feminist writer Rosa Mayreder analysed this phenomenon. 'The "strong fist", which under other conditions was crucial and formed the legal foundation of his dominion, has become entirely superfluous.' Those men who, in the face of unforeseeable change, could think of nothing better than clinging on to outdated moral codes were woefully ill equipped for the rush of life in the modern cities:

> Modern man suffers from his intellectualism as from an illness ... is it not significant that men, educated to be critical in all questions, remain uncritical for longest when it comes to analysing masculinity? To be masculine ... as masculine as possible ... that is the true distinction in their eyes; they are insensitive to the brutality of defeat or the sheer wrongness of an act if only it coincides with the traditional canon of masculinity.

This canon was on its way out. Women like Rosa Mayreder were not demanding only the vote and better working conditions; as we shall see in chapter 9, some of them were openly challenging the very cultural values the West had been built upon: the relation between men and women, notions of honour, property and physical courage, patriarchy itself. Even the suffragettes who refused to go that far pushed into male domains and showed themselves determined and effective and in no ways angels in the house. In the early media age, these arguments and their often outrageous protagonists were a daily presence in newspapers and conversations. Cases like the various suffragette trials, the hunger strikes and speeches given by Emmeline Pankhurst and the activism of women like Anita Augspurg caused international media interest, as did strong female figures such as Sarah Bernhardt, Jenny Churchill and Lady Astor.

Male culture reacted to this threat to its supremacy by glorifying manliness in its most traditional form, from the Kaiser's love of uniforms and the Tsar's fetishism for detail of military dress to the avant-gardist Guillaume Apollinaire and his sexually charged fast machines, the exuberant, flashy energy of the Futurist Filippo Marinetti, and the place of the military in public life. Never before had so many uniforms and moustaches been worn on the streets of Berlin, Paris and St Petersburg; never before had so many devoured at home openly misogynist expositions of male greatness such as the bestselling works by Otto Weininger and Julius Möbius. All the strutting, parading, twirling of moustaches and polishing of large guns, however, could not disguise the fact that the game was up. Something new would have to replace it – a new form of living perhaps, a new vision of the world.

8

1907:
Dreams and Visions

Extinguish all your days and nights!
Eliminate all foreign pictures from your house!
Let rainy darkness fall upon your soil!
Listen: the music of your blood will rise inside you!
                                             – Ernst Stadler, c. 1910

The 256 delegates from forty-two countries, most of them elderly men, who assembled for the opening ceremony of the International Peace Conference in The Hague on 15 June 1907, had only one thing in common: they were not interested in peace treaties which, most of them privately thought, were nothing more than a nuisance and a hindrance to the healthy development of nations. They had simply had to come and sweat it out in their stiff collars, morning suits and uniforms, shut away from the world in the Ridderzaal (normally the gathering place of the Dutch parliament) because popular opinion was excited about woolly ideas, and no state could very well be seen to be against peace *on principle*. So here they were, the most hard-bitten veterans of international diplomacy, in their pockets a mandate from their rulers not to give anything away and above all, never to agree to any binding initiative that might involve limits on their governments' actions. Invited to talk peace, they were prepared for battle.

The top brass of the major powers had not been troubled for the occasion, and negotiations on behalf of Russia were left in the hands of the obscure and aged Mikhail Nelidov, whose frequent bouts of ill health confined him to his rooms for the greater part of the negotiations. The United Stated were represented by 75-year-old Joseph Hodges Choate, Britain by Sir Edward Fry, eighty-two, and Sir Ernest Satow, who was merely in his sixties, as was Baron Marschall von Bieberstein (a perfect Prussian complete with twirled moustache and duelling scars), Germany's former ambassador to Constantinople and now the emissary of Wilhelm II. Constrained by protocol and public opinion to put peace on the agenda, the delegates grudgingly discussed the topic during a plenary session – for a full twenty-five minutes. The remainder of the four-month period of consultations was taken up with a formalization of the rules of war, including regulations governing the use of mines on land and on sea, the treatment of enemy merchant ships during times of war, the rights of neutral countries, and so on. When the final declaration was signed by all participating powers on 17 September, the cause of world peace had not been advanced an inch. On the contrary, behind the scenes secret agreements had been reached between some of the great powers. While the attending governments declared themselves satisfied with the results of the conference, other, non-governmental participants were seething with anger and frustration. For one of them especially, the indefatigable Nobel Peace Prize Laureate Baroness Bertha von Suttner, this was an historic chance missed, a tragedy for humankind.

Baroness Suttner (1843–1914) was a remarkable woman. Born Countess Kinsky in Prague, she belonged to one of the Habsburg empire's most illustrious families. Her father having died before her birth, Bertha's childhood was dominated by her nervous and impulsive mother, whose addiction to gambling soon squandered the remnants of the family fortune. The young countess was forced to earn her living, even though her aristocratic upbringing had prepared her for little more than life in elegant drawing rooms. Enterprising from the start, she attempted to make a career as a singer and then as a music teacher. But despite her accomplishments at the piano it was difficult to make ends meet, and so the young woman chose the only alternative left for one of her class: in 1873, aged thirty, she became a lady companion at the house of Baron von Suttner in Vienna. What followed seems to have sprung off the pages of a romantic novel. The young, poverty-stricken noblewoman fell in love with Arthur von Suttner, her employer's son. Faced with stiff parental opposition, she fled temptation and moved to Paris where she answered a newspaper advertisement for a position as private secretary to a 'wealthy elderly gentleman' whose melancholy, cultured personality enchanted her. He was Alfred Nobel, the industrialist and inventor of dynamite. After a few weeks, however, passion got the better of reason and the Baroness travelled back to Vienna and eloped with Arthur.

Penniless, the couple were in no position to choose their place of exile and went to the Caucasus (today Georgia), where a friend of the family had a country estate. Twelve years of hardship followed, during which Bertha tried to earn money by penning occasional pieces for Viennese newspapers

Apostle of peace: Bertha von Suttner, the first woman to be awarded the Nobel Peace Prize.

and Arthur contributed his part by giving French conversation and riding lessons. During the Russo-Turkish War of 1877–8, Bertha was appalled to see the misery of war in wounded soldiers and civilians, and she turned her home in Tiflis into a makeshift hospital. The impression was so deep that she resolved to devote the rest of her life to promoting peace. By 1885 the couple's financial situation and relations with the von Suttner family were sufficiently stabilized to envisage a move back to Vienna, where Bertha threw herself into writing an autobiographical novel, *Die Waffen nieder!* (Put Down Your Arms!), which appeared in 1889 and was an immediate bestseller. Her description of anguished wives and mothers and massacred soldiers, of lives and hopes destroyed in the name of glory and fatherland, touched hundreds of thousands of readers, and suddenly Bertha von Suttner was a household name. More than thirty novels followed.

Inevitably, Baroness Suttner's fame was controversial. Bourgeois morality often saw war not as a tragedy or even as a necessary evil, but as a healthy, invigorating mechanism of historical progress. A hundred years earlier, the German philosopher Friedrich Wilhelm Hegel had provided the rationale for this view: history is a continuous ascent towards enlightenment and freedom, and this progress manifests itself through the struggle of conflicting ideals whose collision creates something new and better. Peoples were the carriers of these ideals, the way that the *Zeitgeist*, World Spirit, chose to assert itself in history. Wars were therefore necessary for the progress of humanity, as a stronger, healthier, more advanced people imposed its culture and created new civilization, until its inevitable demise at the hands of another, even more advanced incarnation of the World Spirit.

This view was deeply rooted in bourgeois morality, which judged a call to put down arms as nothing else but cowardice before the enemy, and before history. Enemies were as necessary to progress as night was to day. The crusading Baroness was ridiculed in the press: her earnest emotional appeals made an easy target, her constant lecturing and the stream of articles and novels from her pen made her look not so much a peace dove but a broody hen, busily laying literary eggs. She was an amateur. She did not understand. She was overwrought by grand ideas. She was hysterical. She was, after all, only a woman.

At a time when social Darwinism and arguments from 'natural law' were all the rage, it is unsurprising that not only the opposition against Suttner, but also the arguments themselves were sexualized. Men were from Mars; women were from Venus. 'Theoretically speaking,' wrote the Austrian socialist leader Rosa Mayreder, 'war is the utmost, terrible extreme of manliness, the last and most horrifying consequence of absolute masculine activity.' Lida Gustava Heymann, a contemporary German suffragette and peace activist (a frequent combination at the time, as we shall see in chapter 9), took the logic one step further: women were from Venus, but they were trapped in servitude on planet Mars: 'the male, destructive principle is diametrically opposed to the female, constructive one, which is based on mutual aid, on grace, on understanding and dialogue. In the modern, male, states, women have not only been deprived of any possibility of expressing their essential nature, they had to submit to the male principle, they were forced to recognize it, they were raped.'

Undeterred by sexual politics, criticism and caricature, Baroness Suttner continued her campaign. Her platonic affair with Alfred Nobel had not ended with her flight back to her lover, and she had kept up a steady correspondence with the older man, who had become a father figure to her. 'I wish I could produce a substance or a machine of such frightful efficacy for wholesale devastation that wars should thereby become altogether impossible,' he had told his secretary during her brief stint of employment with him, and his interest in peace and international arbitration was genuine. Conceived for use in engineering, in building tunnels, mines and roads, dynamite had also transformed warfare, and Nobel was acutely aware that a part of his fortune rested on destruction. He therefore resolved to devote his profits to the promotion of peace. In 1892 the two hatched the plan of awarding a prize in Alfred's name to peace activists. Nobel died in 1896. In his will he bequeathed his entire fortune to a foundation to award prizes in Physics, Chemistry, Physiology or Medicine, Literature and Peace.

In 1905 the Nobel Peace Prize was awarded to Bertha von Suttner, who painted an apocalyptic portrait of conflict in the age of industrial warfare. In a future war, she claimed,

> all states [will be] ground to dust, all work will cease, all domestic hearths will be upturned, and only one cry will echo from border to border. Every village will be a holocaust, every city a pile of rubble, every field a field of corpses, and the war will rage on: beneath the waves torpedo boats are shooting to drag mighty steamers into the deep, in the very clouds armed and manned airships will rise against other airborne troops and mutilated warriors will fall from six thousand feet like bloody snowflakes.

A Strange Champion for Peace

If the pre-War years were a time of rampant militarism, they were also a period of intensive activity for peace. Suttner's appeals were heard by a great number of people nervous about the accelerating arms race between the great powers and appalled at the 'uncivilized' spectre of wholesale slaughter. As the world appeared to be hurtling faster towards catastrophe with every passing year, there were important counter-cultures searching for or proclaiming different visions of society. In every county and every city there were peace activists, often (but not always) also supporters of women's suffrage and socialism. The contrast between public warmongering and peace activism was strongest in Germany, which boasted the largest and most active peace movement in Europe. The Deutsche Friedensgesellschaft (German Peace Society), founded by Bertha von Suttner and the journalist Alfred Hermann Fried, counted 10,000 members in Germany alone and was growing steadily, but the real support was much wider. Almost the entire following of the Social Democratic Party (which polled 35 per cent of votes for the German Reichstag in 1912) saw war as little more than a convenient way for the bourgeoisie to keep the workers down. A peace march in Berlin to protest against Germany's hard-line stance in the Morocco Crisis in 1911 (one of many flashpoints for a possible world war) brought 100,000 people into the streets of the capital, with similar rallies in all major German cities. In September that same year, a huge crowd of 250,000 people assembled in Treptow Park in Berlin to demonstrate against war. At government level the Interparliamentary Union, almost exclusively made up of socialists, had 3,640 members in 1912, belonging to forty parliaments on three continents, including 157 German deputies, 141 from Russia and 516 from France, including such key political figures as Jean Jaurès.

Despite the novels, the pamphlets and lectures, the congresses and agitation, the international peace campaign seemed unable to change the martial climate of European politics and even had to witness its rhetoric being used for the furthering of very different political goals. In 1898 the cause of world peace had received a helping hand from the most unlikely of allies: Tsar Nicholas II. In an unprecedented gesture, the ruler of all Russians had summoned the powers of the world to a peace conference to be held at The Hague the following year. The young monarch waxed lyrical about his newly espoused cause. Peace was an historic goal, he pointed out, and at the moment the great nations were getting no closer to it: 'The ever-increasing financial charges strike and paralyse public prosperity at its source; the intellectual and physical strength of the nations, their labour and capital, are for the most part diverted from their natural application and unproductively consumed; hundreds of millions are spent on acquiring terrible engines of destruction ... National culture, economic progress and the production of wealth are either paralysed or perverted in their development.' Neither Bertha von Suttner nor Karl Marx could have put it more eloquently.

For all its florid enthusiasm, the Tsar's appeal had a history that is nothing short of farcical. It had all begun with a solid piece of Russian espionage, through which General Alexei Kuropatkin, later tragic commander of the Russian forces in the Russo-Japanese War, and in 1898 minister of war, had learned that Austria-Hungary was planning to invest in rapid-firing field guns with a rate of fire six times higher than that of Russian ordnance. A glance at the depleted coffers of the war ministery made it abundantly clear that Russia would not be able to compete. Kuropatkin therefore hit on the felicitous idea of proposing an arms moratorium to the Austrians, Russia's chief rivals. He submitted his cunning plan to finance minister Sergei Witte (then at the height of his powers), who pointed out with characteristic pragmatism that there was little in his deal to interest Habsburg's ministers and that it would only serve to 'reveal our weakness to the whole world'. Trying to console the soldier and his ally, foreign minister Count Muraviev, Witte spoke a little about modern ideas of peace and international negotiation, about the successive attempts at creating an international council of arbitration, and the call for an international peace conference. Ideas like these were little discussed among Muraviev's aristocratic acquaintances and the prospect appeared entirely new to him. An international peace conference would not only solve Russia's financial quandary, it would make Russia appear a benefactor of humankind.

It would be almost impossible to convince the Tsar of the benefit of this strategy, Muraviev knew. Russia was governed through the military and Nicholas was never happier than when surrounded by soldiers. However, the Count was helped by the publication of *The Future of War*, a huge six-volume study written by a Polish Jew, the industrialist Ivan (Jean) Bloch (1836–1902). Having made a comprehensive study of military and technological developments and their strategic implications, Bloch had come to the conclusion that the classic war of the nineteenth century – army confronting colourful army on the battlefield in great, set-piece conflicts won by daring cavalry charges and individual bravery – was a thing of the past. After interpreting countless statistical data, national capacities and factors (down to the range and cost of artillery shells and the price of uniform buttons), Bloch was convinced that war would be industrialized and would depend on overall production capacities, railway lines and logistics, and all-engulfing conflict between national economies that could be won only once the opponent was economically exhausted, as all participants would be. Any military victory would also be national suicide, bringing collapse and revolution in its wake. The prospect of an inevitable socialist revolution in the event of war was enough to shake even the Tsar temporarily out of his dreams of glorious victory, and he decided to become a champion of international peace. An invitation by him would be impossible to refuse.

The 1899 First Peace Conference at The Hague had taken place among great public excitement and profound scepticism on the part of the diplomats, as expressed in the words of a disgusted Count Münster, leader of the German delegation: 'The Conference brought here the political riffraff of the world. Journalists of the worst type…baptized Jews like Bloch and female peace fanatics like Mme de Suttner…All this rabble, actively supported by Young Turks, Armenians and Socialists into the bargain, are working in the open under the aegis of Russia.'

Other delegates saw a more positive, even prophetic picture. Could this assembly of nations not be a first step towards a permanent structure – a federation of the states of Europe perhaps, or a league of nations? Could arbitration not result in establishing an international court of justice at The Hague, the place chosen for the Peace Conference? For the moment, these were distant visions, generously augmented by a public imagination running riot over proposals for world peace. 'The queer letters and crankish proposals which come in every day are amazing,' recorded the hard-bitten American ambassador, Andrew D. White. 'It goes without saying that the Quakers are out in full force…The number of people with plans, schemes, notions, nostrums, whimsies of all sorts, who press upon us and try to take our time, is enormous.'

As the conference bogged down in realpolitik and negotiations about the minutiae of modern warfare and ethical slaughter, utopian schemes quickly receded into the background. Germany and Russia would not hear a word about limiting their armies ('the German people is not crushed beneath the weight of armament expenditures...They are not hastening towards exhaustion and ruin!' the German Colonel Gross von Schwartzkopf exploded at one point, puncturing the Tsar's grand rhetoric), America would not agree to any limitation of naval ambitions, and Britain had taken the precaution of sending Admiral Jackie Fisher to prevent anything that could endanger the precious Dreadnought programme. Fisher distinguished himself as an outstanding dancer during social occasions. In committee, however, he alone insisted on giving the beat: 'Thanks to the energetic attitude and persistent efforts of Sir John Fisher all provisions of the original articles which were likely in any way to fetter or embarrass the free action of the Belligerents have been carefully eliminated,' a relieved First Lord of the Admiralty recorded.

By the time that the conference drew to a close in July, it became apparent that all attempts at peace and disarmament had suffered shipwreck on the rocks of governmental intransigence. 'Cold, cold are all hearts – cold as the draft that penetrates the rattling windows. I feel chilled to the bone,' wrote a disillusioned Bertha von Suttner, always present at The Hague, in her diary, shivering, despite the mild summer weather. The Second Conference of 1907, called once again by Tsar Nicholas II, this time in an attempt to regain international prestige after the disaster of the Russo-Japanese War, was similar in outcome. 'It was not a conference about peace, but about the customs of war,' Suttner would lament, and she was right.

Dionysus in the Tower

The pacifist movement, working against the prevailing culture of war, military drill and compulsory manliness, was only one way of imagining different societies, different ways of living together. Every society has its dropouts, and every wealthy, rigid society (witness 1968) has its alternative cultures – usually predicated on the security they profess to despise. As the societies of Europe and the United States were struggling to cope with the explosive change transforming their lives, a vast number of alternative movements, prophets and fads sprang up, ranging from the admirably far-sighted and profoundly scholarly to the eccentric and plain dotty.

The original prophet of all these apostles of the New Life had come from

Russia. Count Leo Tolstoy (1828–1910), the writer and social reformer, had been fortunate to be able to enjoy both a simple life and peasant's smock, and a large landed estate and income from his world-famous novels. Tolstoy's vision of a life in harmony with nature was often criticized, but also very seductive to readers encountering his liberal ideas, amid the myriad strictures of middle-class life.

These newfangled designs for living were often intertwined with bohemian lives and with one another, an ever-shifting landscape of spiritual leaders and assorted hangers-on, of mystics and scholars, charmers and charlatans. In Tolstoy's own country this enchantment with the occult had penetrated the very heart of power in the person of Rasputin and the sway he held over the Tsarina and her circle, but outside the walls of Tsarskoe Selo there were other, more subversive groupings. On a popular level, there were charismatic Christian figures like Father Gapon; while in the political sphere the greatest excitement and debate were caused by the secular messianism of the socialists, communists and anarchists.

But there were also more profoundly subversive figures, whose vision it was not just to change the political order, but to alter people's very mode of feeling and the way they lived their lives. The most famous of these was Vyacheslav Ivanov (1866–1949), a brilliant classicist who had slipped out of the academy and into a world of his own devising. As with Bertha von Suttner's, his story begins with an elopement – a significant fact, perhaps, for those wishing to flee bourgeois values. In his case it was a meeting, in 1893, with Lydia Dmitrievna Zinovieva-Annibal, a poet and translator who was, like Ivanov himself, married at the time. The couple settled first in Athens and then in Geneva, making numerous journeys to Palestine, Egypt and Italy, where the scholar became fascinated with the tragic, excessive and dark god, Dionysus. The result was a conversion to pagan mysticism which Ivanov documented in his first important book, *The Hellenic Religion of the Suffering God* (1904).

In 1905, the Ivanovs returned to St Petersburg, where they encased themselves inside a turreted building known to all and sundry as 'the Tower'. Inside the Tower, the rigid rules of contemporary Russia no longer applied. The huge apartment had no walls at all, but was divided by low bookcases and adorned with oriental artefacts. Heavy carpets, lilies dispersing their thickly sensual scent and candles lighting the dusk of this strange kingdom completed the ensemble. There were no clocks, and no fixed times. Ivanov himself would often go to bed at eight in the morning and wake in the late afternoon, ready to receive his many guests, whom he would ply with large quantities of tea, wine and mysticism for as long as they cared to stay.

Some of his young admirers took him at his word. Andrei Bely, author of the groundbreaking novel *Petersburg*, once remained in this sacred grove for a full five weeks; others, like his friend Emil K. Metner, did not manage longer than two days. As the guests arrived for evening sessions there would be endless discussions about philosophy, religion, literature, poetry and art. Ivanov expounded his vision of a religion of the future that would fuse Christ and Dionysus, redemption and ecstasy, the conquest of the next world and the enjoyment of the present one in one great cultic mysterium, complete with orgiastic rites: a rebirth of culture out of the hidden impulses of antiquity. Late in the night, when most visitors had left, remaining groups would continue their discussions, while others would discreetly pair off in couples and seek out one of the more private areas to continue their exchange without much talking.

Dionysus and Christ appeared remarkably often in the visions of those preaching new forms of life. Nietzsche had brought the Greek god back from mythological death, and the ecstatic, irrational dimension that was his appealed strongly to a young generation whose childhoods had been dominated by rigid notions of discipline, control, reason and self-sacrifice. It is significant that the epicentre of this explosion of alternative ways of living lay in Germany and Austria-Hungary.

Bohemians and Barefoot Prophets

Prophets of all shades and flavours abounded particularly in Vienna and Munich, the two poles of this little universe. Some were simply eccentric socialists or Catholic missionaries who had got carried away by their sense of mission, but others had more radical, more individual visions. Home of the German *Bohème* and of an artists' colony in the Schwabing district, among Munich's denizens were luminaries like the writers Thomas Mann and Frank Wedekind, the satirical journal *Simplicissimus*, the painters Vassily Kandinsky, Franz Marc and Gabriele Münter. Schwabing was a laboratory for designs of living.

One of the most emblematic figures of this set was Countess Fanny von Reventlow (1871–1918), whose short, difficult and rich life burned itself out in misery, but left us one of the funniest and most perceptive analyses of the Schwabing universe, *Herrn Dames Aufzeichnungen* (Mr Dame's Note Books, 1913). Born into an aristocratic family in northern Germany, the young Fanny had soon rebelled against the conservative values at home. Marriage appeared to be a way out (she was pregnant by another man as well), but the young woman found this too constraining. Not yet thirty and already divorced, the passionate *bohémienne* moved to Munich to study painting, only to find that she had no talent for it. During the following years, the rebel countess made a precarious living as a translator, journalist, cook, secretary, decorative glass painter and insurance agent while she pursued her dream of becoming an artist and was herself pursued by several of Schwabing's literary lions. She responded enthusiastically and had liaisons with several of them, episodes that later found their way into her *roman-à-clef* about her Munich years.

Bohemian beauty: Fanny von Reventlow was a canny chronicler of the experiments in living in Munich.

Reventlow's novel not only caricatures the florid goings-on amid the Schwabing set, but also elaborates on the theme of male anxiety in a changing world. The hero is Herr Dame, 'Mister Lady', who continuously excuses himself for his ridiculous surname and is convinced that he will never be able to find a woman willing to be called Mrs Lady. Branded an outsider by his very name, Herr Dame observes the artists, prophets and imposters who make up the local pond life and notes down their absurd parties and conversations, dripping with mysticism, neologisms and dark murmurings. 'I feel as if I had to take my brain apart and reassemble it anew,' the hero complains. 'The way it has been functioning till now and the trains of thought I know and am used to are no longer useful – I want to switch them off, take them out of service until I am able to move more securely amid all this novelty.'

The group's incessant talk about matriarchy, Dionysian rites, ancient religion and pagan rituals leads to the project of celebrating a Bacchanal, an episode that was modelled (like the rest of the novel) on a real party given at the house of one of Schwabing's local philosophical demigods, Karl Wolfskehl. Half ritual, half orgy, the proposed celebration promises something exciting and new and members of the circle throw themselves into preparations for the grand occasion: 'we went to buy tricot fabric [for suitable outfits] and went through countless shops until we found red vine leaves for wreaths and symbolic dewdrops made of glass.' When the great occasion finally arrives, slightly marred by the fact that one of the revellers has misunderstood the idea and turns up dressed as Pierrot, the result is another comical challenge to upstanding manliness.

> Delius [a man] had arrived dressed in the black cloak of a Roman matron; on his head he wore a black veil, and in his hand was a metal triangle, which he struck melodiously with a little rod. And the professor, too, as Indian Dionysus in a purple tunic with vine wreath and long, golden staff. During the dance he hurtled about wildly and his eyes rolled and I remarked that he was quite a beautiful man with his mighty frame and dark beard. He appeared to please quite a few women, too, and he kept staring at them with ecstatic eyes and thought them all beautiful beyond words. There was no lack of enthusiasm and he lived his role to the full, if I can put it that way. Only during one scene he became annoyed – in an animated moment, Maria tried to climb his enormous golden staff – he looked at her gleefully and mindlessly offered his staff, and the staff snapped off in the middle.

It was not easy for a man to be equal to the task the historical moment demanded of him. Mr Lady and the professional Dionysus with his staff broken in half by a female reveller were two examples of this quandary.

While the Schwabing bohemians were having fun by talking grandly, smoking too much and dressing up, Munich also attracted more radical prophets. There was the imposing figure of Wilhelm Diefenbach, bearded, long-haired and shrouded, if dressed at all, in long, flowing robes, a painter who created a community of twenty-five devotees to nudism and a strict vegetarian diet. To the endless amusement of the local press, Diefenbach spent almost more time in court than anywhere else, as he and his followers insisted on walking naked at least within the confines of their property: 'His pupil,' recorded the *Münchner Post* with obvious delight, 'the patissier's son Hugo Höppeler from Lübeck, a splendid youth with purple cheeks and luscious black locks ... is supposed to have committed the sin of

*Barefoot prophet: on his wanderings through Italy Gusto Gräser
was taken for Christ.*

having shown himself in Adam's costume on the sunny lawn, his posterior pointed disrespectfully towards the heavens.' The youth in question defended his action as 'pleasing to God' but his barefoot appearance in court earned him an additional two days in jail for gross indecency, the judges having found that the group's behaviour was simply a *Schweinerei*. A skilful and prolific artist, Diefenbach was finally brought down by local politicians who made it almost impossible for him to exhibit his paintings and earn a living. He died, of pneumonia, in 1913.

Hugo Höppeler, who had appeared in court as a follower of the wayward artistic genius, was himself destined to become, as Fidus, one of Germany's most famous painters. He maintained his interest in beautiful bodies, nudism, and alternative ways of living, as his interests turned to supposedly ancient Germanic rites, grand designs for sun temples and a series of hugely popular paintings and graphic works heaving with erotic charge.

There were other 'barefoot prophets', as they were called: the disturbingly Christlike Gustav Nagel, who combined a well-groomed moustache with hair falling down to his bare shoulders and who lived in a cave, roaming the vicinity on foot to proclaim his gospel of Christian naturism; the itinerant prophet and life reformer Gusto Gräser, who threw away a secure bourgeois existence including all his clothes and walked to Italy, barefoot, bearded, and with hair down to his shoulders, a true hippie *avant la lettre*. On his way peasants bared their heads and cried *ad venit Christus!* Constantly

Hail the New Age: a seeker for truth at the Monte Verita colony in Italy, which also attracted the young Hermann Hesse.

arrested and thrown out of the cities he visited to give friendly talks, recite his poetry and distribute leaflets about the New Life, Gräser eventually founded the nature community Monte Verita in the name of universal love. Among his early devotees were Fanny von Reventlow, disillusioned by life in Munich, and the young Hermann Hesse, who would later win the Nobel Prize for Literature with novels strongly tinted by fantasies of escape into a world of delicate mysticism, a time before or beyond the bourgeois morality that had crushed his spirits growing up as the son of a sternly Calvinist pastor in Switzerland. There were many, many others setting up experimental communities and rebelling against the Wilhelminian morality and conventional decency of property arrangements.

This rebellion and the search for a simpler, more natural life also came with a more acceptable façade. Founded in 1896, the *Wandervogel* movement in Germany attracted tens of thousands of young people. Unlike Baden-Powell's Boy Scouts in Britain, with their emphasis on discipline, survival and paramilitary education, the young 'migratory birds' had had enough of uniforms, drill and discipline. They wanted to roam free, to go for long cycle rides through the countryside, and generally to escape from the strictures of bourgeois anxiety into a world without constraints, happily singing around the camp fire. Predictably, this was a volatile mix. Boys and girls together, close and unsupervised in God's open air after a long and exhilarating cycle ride – the idea was abhorrent to good Wilhelminian minds, and with some reason. The nights spent listening to a guitar being strummed by a camp fire probably did more to change German society in the long run than any number of debates in the Reichstag. The volatility, though, also proved to be intellectual. The movement split and fissured in spectacular fashion, parts of it absorbed into environmentalism and naturism, while others were to be subsumed into the Hitler Youth.

Sharing the earthbound enthusiasm of the *Wandervögel* and the Nietzschean will to transform all values and create a New Man, were exponents of one group who had for long been on the outside looking in: the Zionists. Born out of the venomous nationalist debates of Austria-Hungary and the ruthless oppression in Tsarist Russia, Zionism was a largely political movement aiming for no more than normalizing the situation of the Jews by giving them a state, as every other people had. Some Zionists, however, went much further in their goal, hoping for nothing less than a spiritual rebirth of Jewish culture and of the heroic strength of Samson.

The Voice of the Blood

One of the most striking examples of spiritual Zionism was a student fraternity in Prague, a collection of young men from Jewish bourgeois homes who had called their group Bar Kochba after the legendary anti-Roman rebel in second-century Palestine. They were far from the only Jewish fraternity (excluded by their 'Aryan' fellow students, many Jewish academics founded their own fraternities; some of them even duelled with sabres), but their correspondence with each other and with well-known philosophers whom they invited to give talks are a valuable record of their ideas.

The prophet to whom these enthusiastic young men addressed their high hopes was the appropriately bearded Martin Buber (1878–1965), the grandson of a great Talmudic scholar. Having made his career first as a poet (treating Jewish as well as non-Jewish themes), the young scholar had become interested in resurrecting Jewish culture out of the living traditions of the Hasidic Jews, whose emphasis on irrationality and mysticism strongly complemented his own interest in the mystical traditions of Asia and the West. His publication in 1908 of the *Legends of the Baalshem* and *Rabbi Nachman's Stories* had brought him to the attention of a wide Jewish reading public. The young Prague students had grown up in an entirely assimilated environment. They would never have exchanged a word with an orthodox Jew on the street and would have had no language in which to communicate with him, one knowing only Yiddish and Hebrew and perhaps a little Russian; the other German and possibly French, Latin and Greek. In Buber's writings, they saw the possibility of breaking out of their double ghetto of antisemitism and 'foreign' culture and of rediscovering the inner voice of their Jewish selves, which Buber encouraged them to do in a series of speeches:

> the hour in which one discovers the succession of generations, of fathers and mothers which had led to the presence ... the confluence of blood ... will make one feel the immortality of the generations and the community of the blood ... In addition ... he will find in the discovery of his blood the rooted, nourishing force in each individual, the discovery that the deepest layers of our being are determined by blood, that our thought and will are coloured by it.

Ideas like these situate Buber in an unexpected context: that of German neo-Romantic nationalists such as Paul de Lagarde and the publisher Eugen Diederichs, who published Buber's books, as well as others proclaiming the spiritual revival of the German *Volk* out of the nobility of their ancient blood such as Julius Langbehn's hugely popular tome, *Rembrandt as Educator* (1890), which portrayed the Dutch genius as a living embodiment of the German ideals of inwardness, creativity and honesty. Other books on his list carried titles like *The New Mysticism*, *The Germanicization of Christianity*, and *Elective Affinities of the German Blood*.

The Jewish students of the Prague Bar Kochba listened eagerly to the voice of blood and augmented its message with reading of their own. They enthusiastically read and swapped books by Nietzsche, the virulently antisemitic Paul de Lagarde, the arch-racist Houston Stewart Chamberlain, the conservative French Catholic writer Paul Claudel and the French philosopher and apostle of the unthinking *élan vital*, life force, Henri Bergson. Paradoxically, the emphasis on the community of the *Volk*, of blood, soil and irrational life forces, did not free the Jewish students from the bondage of assimilation but assimilated a European and particularly German intellectual world of racial thought that was to be a direct ancestor of National Socialism. The seductive power of this rhetoric seemed inescapable.

The cult of life and the idea of a true community, of free spirits not subjected to the rules of society, and the vision of a rebirth of truths long lost, fascinated German artists too. In the case of the thoroughly bourgeois Richard Strauss, this fascination expressed itself in his choice of topics for his orchestral pieces, ranging from the heroic hermit Zarathustra to the leg-

Dangerous subversion: young Wandervogel *activists of both sexes enjoying nature.*

endary medieval mischief-maker and radical outsider Till Eulenspiegel (who is hanged by a court not sharing his sense of humour) to the protean passions of Don Juan. Texts chosen by Gustav Mahler conjure up a love of nature and naiveté whose burning intensity illustrate the artist's longing for a full communion with nature and a return to life in a primitive community.

No other artist went quite as far in the cult of community as the conservative poet and aesthete Stefan George (1868–1933), whose disdain for the humdrum lives of ordinary people was matched only by his twin loves of beautiful texts and beautiful young men. A despotic and idealist adorer of the German soul who liked to be referred to as 'master', George acquired a considerable following during the many years he travelled through the country, moving his court from city to city, ever careful never to be polluted by the banality of having to earn a living. His poems were highly thought of at the time, but his real influence was exercised by the group of intelligent and good-looking youths he attracted wherever he went. One of these, a boy by the name of Max Kommerell, died young, and his memory became a veritable cult to the poet, who resurrected the handsome memory in his poems as 'Maximin'.

Echoes of George's swelteringly homoerotic circle of ephebes can be found in the aristocratic Liebenberg circle around Prince Eulenburg, a reflection throwing further light on Wilhelm II's fear of becoming entangled in the scandal around his friend and adviser. The wrath shown by the persecutors of Eulenburg and von Moltke in the press, the judiciary and at court was also a reaction against the subversive culture of alternative, community-based visions of life which many upstanding burghers felt was threatening to undermine the foundations of Wilhelminian society. The tension between elective communities seeking to realize a particular vision of life and of society, and belief in an imposed community with a rigid morality, was a strong presence in German society and art. Already in 1887 it had been articulated by Ferdinand Tönnies in his book *Community and Society*, in which he contrasted two radically different modes of social organization and their implications, arguing that society is always prone to suppress the charismatic ferment of communal visions.

Troubling Visions

Trouble loomed wherever alternative visions collided with official institutions. As we have seen in chapter 3, the Vienna Secession movement of young artists itself contained a strong element of creating an alternative way of living and of seeing the world, and no one expressed this desire for difference more eloquently than Gustav Klimt. Habitually dressed in clothes of his own design and similar to Tolstoy's peasant frocks, famously unkempt and unwashed and endowed with an apparently superhuman capacity for attending to the wishes of female admirers, as well as to his permanent mis-

Flowing robes: Gustav Klimt in clothes of his own design.

tress Emilie Flöge, Klimt was practically a one-man alternative universe. His was more than the bohemian attitude habitually cultivated by artists. Klimt's anarchic, Eros-centred view of life translated directly into his work. This directness was to cause the greatest artistic scandal in pre-War Vienna.

It had all begun with a highly official pat on the back in 1894, when the young painter Klimt, already famous for his gorgeously writhing, grand historicist tableaux on the Ringstrasse, received a commission from the ministry of education for three panels to adorn the hall of ceremonies in the newly built neo-Renaissance university building. The three works were to be part of an ensemble showing the Triumph of Light Over Darkness and Klimt was to represent three of the four university faculties: Medicine, Philosophy and Law – classic nineteenth-century allegorical fare, to be executed in the most dignified and exotically charged manner possible. The painter took his time to tackle this prestigious assignment, a period that coincided with a complete artistic reorientation. He had made good money with his sumptuous processions and architectural fantasies, but he had lost confidence in this way of representing things. The true nature of things, he felt, was darker, more archaic and more sensual, and had to be represented in a radically different manner.

When Klimt finally delivered the panels to the university in 1902, the works bore witness to his evolution from the merely suggestive to the downright outrageous – stages of an artist's vision of society. The first panel, depicting *Philosophy*, was disturbing in its dark voluptuousness. At the bottom of the surface, a mask-like Sphinx stared at the beholder, while above there was a whirl of obscure matter and a torrent of bodies, descending from early childhood via two pairs of lovers to the despair and loneliness of old age – an existential vision gravely at odds both with the rationalist optimism of the Enlightenment and with the analytical, positivist predictions of the Viennese school of philosophy. *Medicine*, the second panel, showed the stern figure of Hygiena in the foreground, an unapproachable, richly adorned female form holding a snake and a beaker. The remainder of the canvas, however, pursued the idea of hopeless entanglements and fundamental loneliness like a Schnitzler drama staged by a deranged orientalist. A cloud of nude figures to the right, each isolated in his or her own despair, clustered around a skeleton whose sightless eyes were turned towards a single female figure on the left, provocatively seen frontally and from below, an image of desire lost in space. The naked truth was staring the beholder in the face.

Most stylistically advanced and most provocative was *Jurisprudence*, on which Klimt worked intermittently until 1907. In this panel, the frigid spectre of Justice had receded into the far distance, taking up no more than a quarter of the height of the composition, an insignificant and impossibly distant figure flanked by two dreamy companions, Law and Truth. The canvas was dominated, however, by Klimt's own vision of hopelessness: trapped in a terrible, submarine realm and ensnared by a gigantic, pitiless octopus, a naked male figure – middle-aged, stooping, and with sagging, egregiously unheroic features – bowed its head in the expectation of an inevitable punishment. Surrounding him were three naked female furies, seductive but unreachable in their bloody-minded vindictiveness. This 'erotic nightmare in a clammy hell', in the words of Carl Schorske, promised no justice, but only suffering under the judgmental stares of the disembodied, pitiless faces surrounding the tiny trinity, like a parody of baroque putti in a country church. The bourgeois order of things, the young painter proclaimed, held no promise for him. Kafkaesque terror and existential isolation were all that was to be expected from the empire's great institutions and their morality.

The professors of Vienna University were outraged. Eighty-seven of them signed a petition against the paintings, arguing that they represented 'unclear ideas through unclear form' and were nothing more than 'gloomy phantasms' illustrating the chaos and confusion in the mind of the artist. While the conservatives were livid about this attack on public morality and decency, more progressive critics found to their embarrassment that they agreed with people they would not have greeted on the street. The well-known liberal philosopher Friedrich Jodl, for example, grounded his own opposition to the paintings in the fact that, with so much obscurantism and occultism threatening the achievements of an enlightened, rational society, the last thing the chief university of the Habsburg empire needed was a group of paintings dramatizing the darkness of the soul and the impotence of reason.

Egged on by Klimt's own martial stance (a friendly journalist relates that at the end of an interview he took a revolver out of a drawer and told her to go as he now had to wait for his enemies), the rejection of the Faculty paintings caused a furious public debate about the nature and purpose of art itself, and catapulted the painter into a position of prominence as *artiste à scandale*, provider of wickedly beautiful images and the best-paid artist in Austria-Hungary.

Isis Unveiled

Alternative visions of reality and of a better future could take many forms, none richer in personality and pungent detail than the most important movement to reject all apparent truth and to postulate, instead, a spirit world directing the earthly realm of illusion: the occult teachings of theosophy and anthroposophy. The ancestor and inspiration of this world-view was Helena Blavatsky (1831–91), a cousin of that arch pragmatist, the Russian prime minister Sergei Witte.

'Madame Blavatsky', as she became universally known, had lived through a rather turbulent early career that led her to flee an unhappy marriage to an uninspiring bureaucrat after only three months. She boarded a steamer bound for Constantinople and nothing certain can be said about her whereabouts for the next ten years, which she claimed to have spent travelling throughout the spiritual centres of the world and especially Tibet, where, according to her accounts, she had been inducted into ancient initiation mysteries by Buddhist monks. Almost by way of an afterthought, she had also worked as a circus rider, toured in Siberia as a concert pianist, opened and managed an ink factory in Odessa, worked as an importer of ostrich feathers in Paris, and been an intimate of the French Empress Eugénie. After a passionate affair with an opera singer and a stint in Cairo, Blavatsky materialized in 1873 in New York. There she had decided to settle, having returned, as she would later write, from a failed attempt at making a new life in the West, and after a dramatic spell that had included meetings with Egyptian cabbalists, a shipwreck off the Greek coast, fighting for Garibaldi in Italy, and meetings with Indians at the inland frontiers of 1860s America.

Blavatsky's arresting appearance – her deep, mournful, knowing eyes, incessant smoking, her hair 'crinkled like a negro or a Cotswold ewe' and fantasy robes – made a deep impression on the people she met. Having worked in New York first as a seamstress and then as a medium and author of the occult magnum opus *Isis Unveiled* (1877) Blavatsky and her companion Henry Steel Olcott presided over a court of seekers after deeper truths.

*Glowing eyes, prophetic beard: Madame Blavatsky
with her companion.*

Their quest was directed by letters from the spirit world in gold ink on green paper, delivered to the followers by the medium herself and usually containing stipulations advantageous to her. Together with Olcott she founded the Theosophical Society, moved to India and from there to Würzburg in Germany and London, where she died in 1891.

Madame Blavatsky's brand of occult, Indian-inspired initiation teaching found a lively following, particularly in Britain, Germany and Russia. Science, she claimed, was simply too limited a way of seeing the world, as it excluded the reality of the spirit world. This had been the chief error of Darwin (while in New York, Blavatsky had kept a stuffed baboon with a copy of *The Origin of Species* under its arm in her rooms), who could have been a great scientist if only he had been more open-minded, and whose errors she had come to correct. Physical reality was a mere distraction from the spiritual truth, Blavatsky went on to write, and only through meditation and initiation was it possible to turn attention from the earthly body and towards the astral body, which mankind, the first species to inhabit planet earth, had possessed long before their physical bodies.

Blavatsky fascinated and intrigued intellectuals in London. The mystical quest of the Irish poet W. B. Yeats brought him to her doorstep, the Fabian socialist George Bernard Shaw wrote an account of her life and developed mystical ideas closely related to her own, and the architect Edwin Lutyens was one of her movement's most enthusiastic patrons and followers, as was the extravagantly duplicitous Charles Webster Leadbeater who, much like Madame Blavatsky, pretended to have lived through a multitude of exotic and occult adventures before turning to theosophy and eventual initiation.

Leadbeater's undoubtedly real enthusiasm concerned the young boys he cultivated, allegedly to find a pure soul who would be the next Great Teacher. In India, he believed he had found this extraordinary individual in Jiddu Krishnamurti, a handsome but by all accounts intellectually backward youth who, together with his brother, soon came to live with Leadbeater to follow a rigorous programme of special tuition and teaching of universal mysteries, including close supervision of the boys' meals and wash times. Eventually, Leadbeater (who had let it be known that in 40,000 BC he had been the wife of Annie Besant while their common child had been Krishnamurti) moved to England to pursue his educational plans for the boys. They followed him with a guarded blessing from their father, who may or may not have known that his sons' guardian had already once, in 1906, been excluded from the Theosophical Society over accusations of pederasty involving two American boys to whom, he claimed, he had only mentioned the matter of masturbation as part of a healthy upbringing. This defence looked somewhat thin after the discovery of a coded letter to one of his many charges which read: 'My own darling boy ... Twice a week is permissible, but you will soon discover what brings the best effect ... If it comes without help he needs rubbing more often, but not too often, or he will not come well ... Glad sensation is so pleasant. Thousand kisses, darling.'

By 1911 British theosophy had blossomed into a substantial movement. It had 16,000 members, was organized in local lodges and enjoyed the camp pleasure of elaborate rituals held in ceremonial robes, uniforms and special jewellery. At the heart of it all stood the semi-divine figure of the boy saint Krishnamurti, who was sullen and subdued in the unaccustomed lightless grey of his new English surroundings. He would stay true to his calling, remaining a spiritual teacher until his death in 1986.

Even outside their small circles there was a considerable interest in mythology in Britain. The Scottish anthropologist Sir James George Frazer's bestselling *The Golden Bough* (1890, republished and greatly enlarged 1905–16) was influential among the middle classes, but Frazer's sober exposition did not lend itself to spiritualist fantasy. On the contrary, in putting Jesus next to Buddha and analysing the reasonances of diverse mythologies in Christian belief, the anthropologist and scholar did much to demystify religion.

The middle-class fashion for alternative beliefs also, as so often, went hand in hand with ideas of a change in sexual mores. The activist and former curate Edward Carpenter (1844–1929) embodied this all-purpose attitude with a very personal mélange of homosexual liberation, nudism, organic farming, Anglicanism, vegetarianism, socialism and poetry. One of the first men of his class to dare to live openly with his male partners, Carpenter published *The Intermediate Sex* in 1908, in which he also expounded on the subversive potential of sexual and spiritual liberation:

> Eros is a great leveller. Perhaps the true Democracy rests ... on a sentiment which easily passes the bounds of class and caste, and unites in the closest affection the most estranged ranks of society. It is noticeable how often Uranians [homosexuals] of good position and breeding are drawn to rougher types, as of manual workers, and frequently very permanent alliances grow up in this way, which although not publicly acknowledged have a decided influence on social institutions, customs and political tendencies.

Carpenter's 'uranian' proclivities and political activism made him many enemies, and when he founded the Independent Labour Party together with George Bernard Shaw, he and his followers drew the bile of George Orwell, who was to complain that 'every fruit-juice drinker, nudist, sandal wearer [and] sex maniac' now thought that he had a political message. While serious socialists like Orwell were appalled at Carpenter's apparent frivolity, others were encouraged by his example. The novelist E. M. Forster took Carpenter as inspiration for his novel *The Longest Journey*, and the young poet Rupert Brooke, just out of Cambridge, merrily formed a 'neo-pagan' circle whose rituals consisted mainly in nude river bathing by moonlight with equally adventurous friends such as Virginia Stephen.

These experiments by Britain's incipient artistic and intellectual *Bohème* were only the beginning. The assortment of visions, experimental schools, artistic movements and avant-garde publications that shook up British culture were to flower after the War. After all, the most important focus for this counter-culture, the Bloomsbury Group which developed around the sisters Virginia and Vanessa Stephen (later Virginia Woolf and Vanessa Bell), was only just coming into existence. There was the prolific and blazingly promiscuous Augustus John, a painter resplendent in gypsy clothes and endowed with truly titanic libido and decidedly unconventional morals, but he spent a great deal of his time in Paris during these years, where he found more congenial spirits among the Paris *Bohème*.

In Germany, meanwhile, one member of the Theosophical Society had begun to go his own way. Rudolf Steiner (1861–1925), the son of a station-master in rural Styria, in Austria-Hungary, was a curiously charismatic prophet of Spiritual Truth whose legacy endures to this day. A brilliant literary scholar with a thorough knowledge of philosophy, history and natural science, Steiner had studied in Vienna and Rostock. At the age of twenty-seven, he had been invited to edit Johann Wolfgang von Goethe's scientific writings. This project was based in Weimar, where the researcher remained for eight years, fascinated not only by Goethe's poetry but also his scientific ideas which, though discredited by natural scientists, seemed to him to herald a higher knowledge of nature.

Having lectured to the Theosophical Society chapter in Berlin, Steiner was appointed leader of the German and Austro-Hungarian chapter in 1904, but he soon found the Buddhist emphasis of the Blavatsky school too limited and so founded a rival organization, the Anthroposophical Society, whose teacher and pivotal figure he would remain through years of manically productive work. A true polymath, Steiner was much more than just the founder of a 'spiritual science' designed to develop hidden organs of perception to perceive the spiritual world. His literary output was gigantic, compromising 6,000 lectures and dozens of books. On top of his writing and his constant travelling and lecturing across Europe, he found time within the twenty-one years remaining to him to found schools and design their entire curriculum, and to work with farmers on a system of husbandry in tune with the cosmos which was to become known as biodynamic agriculture. He also managed to sculpt, paint and write occult mystery plays; to inspire forms of expressionist dance, plus a school of architecture based on his own designs for seventeen buildings; to develop a medical method akin to homeopathy, as well as a new school of economic thought and a kind of cooperative bank and, after the First World War, to found a religious community based on a mixture of Catholicism and expressionist aesthetic.

Steiner appeared indefatigable, a fact his many followers ascribed to mystic powers. In 1913 he decided to build a spiritual centre for the movement: the Goetheanum in Dornach near Basel, Switzerland, a building devoted to the cult of spiritual truth and its apostle Goethe, constructed entirely of wood and designed down to the smallest detail by 'the doctor', as his followers called him (and still do to this day). With his monastic bearing, his darkly glowing eyes and his mysterious utterances, Steiner was successful in attracting a better kind of crowd than did the theosophists. His seeming intellectual rigour and wide reading were impressive, and his system had the twin advantages of sophistication and coherence, especially as he always impressed on his

pupils the importance not just of believing what he told them, but of using his teachings as a way of discovering the truths of the spiritual world themselves, according to an elaborate and 'scientific' system of spiritual sensibilization and mediation.

Anthroposophical teachings, which relegated the harsh, rigid social reality to an insignificant secondary plane, and explained the world in terms of a mystical struggle between Christ and the forces of evil incarnated by Lucifer and the Persian godhead Ahriman, were an attractive way of fleeing social constraint and the loss of orientation that many people felt during this time. The rush of technology and fast machines, after all, was nothing but

Sad prophet: Rudolf Steiner, one of many visionaries of the day.

Ahriman's materialistic way of bringing immortal souls into his power. Anthroposophy had an answer to everything, and many intellectuals with a mystical bent who remained unsatisfied by wordly knowledge found its attraction irresistible. Andrei Bely fell under Steiner's spell (his friend, the glorious Viacheslav Ivanov, succumbed to the crusty spiritual charms of Madame Blavatsky), and his influence extended into the works of the German poet Christian Morgenstern, the Russian composer Alexander Skriabin, the Swedish Nobel Laureate Selma Lagerlöf, the conductor Bruno Walter and the painter Piet Mondrian. Another, more distant admirer was Bertha von Suttner, the peace activist, who mentioned Steiner in several publications. For several years Steiner was based in Berlin, where his connections extended deep into the heart of Wilhelminian society. He was a personal friend of the chief of the general staff, Count Helmuth von Moltke (a cousin of the disgraced former governor of Berlin, Kuno von Moltke), and admired by members of the Kaiser's government, such as its last chancellor, Prince Max von Baden.

With its ideas of historic destiny and its racist overtones, Steiner's teaching was congenial not only to those seeking a higher truth beyond rationality, but also to the thinking of men with a conservative German background. Behind all the pyrotechnics of reincarnation, Christology and spirit realms, his philosophy of history was solidly Hegelian, a vision of progress through struggle, culminating inevitably in the dominance of a Christian, European, Aryan and, more particularly, German civilization. Along with dialectics and determinism Steiner had also imported Hegel's ideas about the merits of other races, which were seen as representing previous stages of human development.

Opinions like these showed Steiner to be not so much a genuine initiate as a true child of his time and of his rural Austrian background. Some of his works appeared original and innovative, while others were trite and clearly borrowed. His artwork, held in the greatest reverence by his followers, was atrocious. The anthroposophical system was based on a generous amalgam of Indian mysticism, a sublimated Catholic Christianity, an expressionist aesthetic and an almost animist idea of a natural world inhabited by hidden forces close to the German, Nietzschean cult of life. All this was heavily seasoned with Hegel, with Goethe's grandeur and rhetoric, plus a sprinkling of Kantian methodology.

Sceptical minds attending his lectures found this stew unpalatable. Hermann Hesse declared them to be 'indigestible'; Franz Kafka reflected after one of Steiner's lectures that he was 'very good with words' but also had 'the makings of a pied piper'; and Albert Einstein scoffed: 'the man has never heard of non-Euclidian geometry! Extra-sensual experiences! What nonsense! You have to use at least one of your senses to experience anything!' Even a more sympathetic observer and former friend, the socialist Rosa Mayreder, wrote with obvious puzzlement: 'I cannot understand the effect he has on people. He appears, dressed like a priest, black, buttoned up... and speaks monotonously with too much pathos and overblown effect, like a preacher. What he says can be classified in three categories: witty aphorisms taken from his wide reading, empty talk based on stock phrases, and incomprehensible hints at extra-sensory capabilities...'

The School of Life

Surveying the European scene, it is striking how unequal the interest in alternative visions of life and future was. Intense in Germany, Austria-Hungary and Russia, it was much smaller in Britain and almost non-existent in France. The spread of alternative education is a case in point.

Once again, Germany with its relatively uniform, state-controlled education system, tops the table. Wilhelm's Reich was a fertile breeding ground for methods of raising and teaching children. The phenomenally influential book *The Century of the Child* by the Swedish educationalist Ellen Key appeared in 1900 and was quickly translated into several languages. By 1909 it had sold more than 30,000 copies in Germany alone. Key saw children differently from most teachers and educators. Children had a right to a loving and honest upbringing without hypocrisy, constraint and physical punishment, she wrote, to an education in independence and freedom of judgement. 'The fundamental condition for the shaping of an individual consciousness is... to give a child the certainty of conscience to go against a general opinion, a common custom, or a familiar emotion.' Current education, Key continued, was 'murdering souls', moulding children's spirits into cowards by brutalizing and boring them. In a world in which many schoolmasters behaved like drill sergeants and the role model for schools was the army, this claim rang out like a cannon shot.

Calls like Key's were heard by diverse educational reformers in the Reich. The conservative Hermann Lietz founded no fewer than four schools in Germany, while his pupil and later rival Gustav Wyneken made many enemies with his pamphlets against the teaching of classics and established canons, and created an experimental school based on the idea of a 'youth culture' of honesty and comradeship. Inspired by a similar disgust with the inhuman rush of modern life, Paul Geheeb founded two schools, the second of which, the Odenwaldschule (1910), proved extraordinarily influential. In other European countries, similar initiatives included the

1907 opening of the Casa dei Bambini by the Italian Maria Montessori, an anarchist Modern School founded in 1901 by Francisco Ferrer in Barcelona, and the orphanage Dom Sierot in Warsaw, a project of the wise and courageous Janusz Korczak. The orphanage was administered by the children themselves, who made all decisions – ranging from budgeting and curriculum to discipline – in their own, democratic parliament. In 1942, despite being offered false papers to flee the country, Korczak was murdered in Treblinka together with 'his' children, whom he would not abandon.

One of the most successful and most forward-looking of these school projects was the private girls' school founded by Eugenie Schwarzwald (1872–1940) in the heart of Vienna. Wealthy, full of self-confidence and a true intellectual (she held a doctorate from Zurich University), Schwarzwald wanted to offer children an inspiring alternative to her own dreary education and so created a curriculum reflecting the world-view of Vienna's artistic avant-garde, whose main exponents frequented her famous salon, and some of whom she persuaded to teach at her school. Adolf Loos taught architecture here; Arnold Schönberg lectured the children on music. Only the painter Oskar Kokoschka presented a problem with the authorities. He did not possess an official teaching licence and was therefore barred from teaching by the ministry. When Schwarzwald protested that he was a genius, the minister coolly replied: 'Genius is not allowed for by regulations.'

A wealthy and intelligent woman participating energetically in Vienna's intellectual life raised the hackles of several men, particularly the caustic and misogynist Karl Kraus, pilloried her mercilessly and almost obsessively in his journal *Die Fackel*. In the small world of the salons the two often crossed paths, and a conciliatory Eugenie once remonstrated with Kraus that he never seemed to remember her and would never greet her. 'You must excuse me, Madam,' came the reply, 'I thought you were that dreadful Schwarzwald woman.'

In Britain the situation was much more sedate. For those in a position to choose, there had always been private schools, but the ethos enforced in these institutions fostered anything but a new, utopian world. For those with diverging ideas about education, there was a selection of faith-based schools such as those run by Quakers and Catholics. Closest to the reform movement on the Continent, and indeed an inspiration to many later schools, was Abbotsholme, founded in 1889 by the Scotsman Cecil Reddie, and Bedales, founded in 1893 by John Haden Badley as an answer to Victorian educational strictures.

The brilliant Stephen girls who were to become the epicentre of the

Bloomsbury circle had, incidentally, never been to school at all. They were educated at home by their father, who gave them the run of his library, one of the finest in the country, which fact provides another small insight as to why there was a lack of utopian gurus and groups in England. The English alternative vision of the future, it seems, was essentially private and domestic. Grand Answers were viewed with amusement and distrust. Both Yeats and Shaw, the two London intellectuals most implicated in a mystical way of seeing the world, were Irishmen.

If a comparison with France is not really possible with regard to education, this fact is in itself significant. There were no private experimental schools in France for the simple reason that they were illegal. In 1905 and 1906 the country lived through the climax of its long battle between Church and Republic, which had ended with a near-fatal knockout for the former. Until then, many schools had been financed by the state but administered by the Catholic Church. With the passing of the bill of Separation of Church and State, however, this situation changed overnight. All schools in the Republic were now financed and administered by the state and staffed with reliable teachers trained according to Republican ideals. Alternative visions of education had no place in this new world.

Compared with its neighbour across the Rhine, France showed generally remarkably little enthusiasm for social, educational or spiritual utopias. The socialists were an important force (the pacifist engagement of Jean Jaurès springs to mind) and Paris was an obligatory station on the itinerary of every prophet and charlatan who lived, but life reform, naturism, occultism and anthroposophy had only a small following among the French themselves. Perhaps the bitter social divisions of the preceding generation go some way towards explaining this. The brutal suppression of the Paris Commune in May 1871 had not only given the conservative government an opportunity to round up ideological enemies of all stripes and either imprison or exile them, it had also left a deep scar in the nation's psyche, a wound torn open again by the Dreyfus case. Now healing and unity under the banner of the Republic were required.

Not everybody went along with this, of course. Paris still had its legendary *Bohème,* a magnet for artists and eccentrics from around the world, but a gaggle of unconventional people did not add up to a vision of the future. Even those who genuinely sought alternative ways of life did so as an aesthetic or intellectual project, not as a rejection but as an adornment. André Gide through his hedonistic homosexuality, Anatole France through closely argued humanistic tracts and novels, the novelist Pierre Loti, perhaps, through celebration of life as an orientalist fantasy. There was not a single barefoot prophet or vegan redeemer of the world in sight. A vegan in Paris? The thought seems blasphemous.

The turn-of-the-century visionaries had in common that they found the present wanting not in superficial aspects but in a fundamental way which only a total rethinking of civilization could address, a radical reimagining of society and what it meant to be human. By turns joyful and cruel, Dionysus rose against the suffering Christ, Life against Science, Nature against Convention, the voice of the blood against the voice of reason, and sex against anything that would stand in its way. Inherited structures could no longer provide adequate answers to the rush of life, to the new social realities created by urban, industrial societies, consumerism, and the new self-confidence of women.

9

1908:
Ladies with Rocks

At every opportunity they [men] insist on their superiority over women, cling to this fearful idea – it is the last resort of the poor wretch at the bottom of pile – for, if woman were not more stupid than he himself, who would be?   – Grete Meisel-Hess

The women on the steam launch moored opposite the Houses of Parliament were in a boisterous, defiant mood as they issued their invitation to the members of the House having tea on the terrace. 'Hyde Park 21 June' read one of the posters held up for the parliamentarians to read. 'Members of Parliament Specially Invited' another. By megaphone the issuers of the invitation promised the bemused men that there would be no arrests made and that they would have plenty of police protection.

Their kind invitation fell upon deaf ears. A police boat unsuccessfully attempted to catch the intruders, and it is unlikely that any of the men on the terrace of the House of Commons even considered having a look at the goings-on on that June day. They missed a gigantic spectacle: approximately half a million people, more according to some sources, the largest physical gathering of people recorded so far, a vast sea of bodies massed in the centre of the capital. Here, on the ten platforms erected throughout the park, speakers were addressing the crowds under the watchful gaze of the organizer of the event, 'General' Flora Drummond, resplendent on horseback and in uniform, while forty matching bands played throughout the area to entertain the crowds. It was much like any official Edwardian occasion, but there was also one important difference: the majority of the half-million people (including the formidable General Drummond with her epaulettes and riding crop), the speakers, the members of the bands, the orderlies and organizers, were women, and they had come to demand the vote.

It was an occasion designed to impress and silence critics. The organizers, members of the Women's Social and Political Union (WSPU), were experts at staging events guaranteed to attract publicity. In addition to the forty female bands in their grand outfits with double-breasted uniform jackets and drum majors, tens of thousands of women had appeared dressed in the Union colours of white, green and purple. They had made their way to Hyde Park in seven orderly processions from Euston Station, Trafalgar Square, the Victoria Embankment, the Chelsea Embankment, Kensington High Street, Paddington and the Marylebone Road, carrying 700 banners of 8 x 3 feet, as well as ten huge silk banners and thousands of flags. Shop windows had been decorated in WSPU colours and displayed posters demanding votes for women, buses had been transformed into mobile advertising platforms, and among the marchers converging in London were Labour leader Keir Hardie, George Bernard Shaw, the novelists Israel Zangwill and Thomas Hardy, and Amy Catherine Wells, the wife of another visionary writer, H. G. Wells. The London *Daily Chronicle* estimated the crowds at about 300,000; *The Times* at 250 to 500,000; and the journal *Votes for Women* trumpeted triumphantly: 'It is no exaggeration to say that the number of people present was the largest ever gathered together on one spot anywhere in the world.'

Not all those who had chosen this warm Sunday afternoon to come to Hyde Park were devoted to the cause of women's suffrage, indeed, many – and perhaps most – were out for a good time, as the suffragist speaker Helen Fraser recorded in her diary: 'The 21st was very wonderful. It was successful and yet not entirely satisfactory – the crowd was about half a million ... at three platforms there was much rowdyism ... At mine, we had a splendid hearing. It seemed to me, however, that the vast mass of people were simply curious – not sympathetic – not opposed. Simply indifferent.'

Politically appealing or not, the Hyde Park meeting had succeeded beyond the suffragists' wildest dreams. Prime Minister Asquith had long dismissed calls for women's suffrage with the argument that he simply did not believe that many women were interested in it and it would be ridiculous to make so important a change just to appease a handful of radicals. Women, he had claimed, were simply not meant for the cut and thrust of political power: 'their natural sphere is not the dust of politics, but the circle of social and domestic life ... The inequalities ... we should fight against and remove are the unearned privilege and the artificial distinction which man has made ... not the indelible differences of faculty and function by which Nature herself has given diversity and richness to human society.' Not so, the suffragists had angrily riposted, and set themselves an ambitious goal: if 67,000 men congregating in Hyde Park in 1867 had been sufficient to topple a Reform Bill aimed at suppressing the right of political assemblies on public spaces, then they would double that number to demonstrate widespread support for their campaign.

The Vote and Working Women

The 1908 Hyde Park meeting came at a turning point for the British suffragist movement, not the largest but certainly the most spectacular of all women's rights pressure groups in Europe and the United States. After more than a decade of patient work, of handing out flyers, lobbying MPs, collecting tens of thousands of signatures, submitting petitions, fundraising, marching and holding meetings all over the country, frustration and fury were taking over from principled enthusiasm. The movement reached its spectacular apex in pre-War London, but it was not born in the capital. It descended upon the seat of government from the mill towns in the North.

The votes for women campaign had its roots in women's rights activism and writing, from Mary Wollstonecraft in the late eighteenth century onwards, but it was the spinning and weaving industry in and around Manchester, Huddersfield, Bradford and Salford that gave these demands the necessary social weight to grow into a popular movement. More than any other industry, textile manufacture employed a high proportion of women, often in excess of half of the workforce. Around 1900, for example, three quartets of unmarried women in Blackburn, Burnley and Preston were employed, and one third carried on after marriage – a picture that contrasts starkly with northern English mining areas in which most work was done by men and was better paid than factory jobs, a pattern accompanied by a much more conservative outlook among the workers, who liked their wives to stay at home, and who typically had the largest families of all working people.

While miners' wives had little political involvement and were only marginally represented in the women's rights movements of the time, the working lives of the Lancashire spinners and weavers necessarily fostered a spirit of independence and even revolt. Women had their own wages to take home (always less than men's, usually about three quarters of full pay for a man); they worked and discussed their problems with other women at the factories; they organized themselves in reform clubs, associations, co-operative stores and trade unions such as the Women's Trade Union League and the Co-operative Guild.

If women (and often their children aged ten and over) were instrumental in earning the family pay, they also bore the brunt of the workload. Coming home from a twelve-hour day surrounded by noisy looms and spinning machines, they were faced with heavy household chores (no labour-saving machines for them, and certainly no maid to help) and the care of their children, often six or more – always under the erosive tension of money worries, which forced some families to pawn their Sunday best from one weekend to the next. Caught in the struggle for respectability and cleanliness, and constantly menaced by the descent into debt and the poor-house, working women were locked into a grid of unrelenting rigidity, as the tailoress Lavena Saltonstall described: 'In my native place the women, as a general rule, wash every Monday, iron on Tuesdays, court on Wednesdays, bake on Thursdays, clean on Fridays, go to the market or go courting again on Saturdays, and to church on Sundays. There are exceptions, of course, hundreds of exceptions, but the exceptions are considered unwomanly and eccentric people.' Lavena was under no illusion as to what would happen to such radicals:

> Should any girl show a tendency to politics, or to ideas of her own, she is looked upon by the majority of women as a person who neglects doorsteps and home matters, and is therefore not fit to associate with their respectable daughters and sisters. If girls develop any craving for a different life or wider ideas, their mothers fear that they are going to become Socialists or Suffragettes – a Socialist being a person with lax views about other people's watches and purses, and other people's husbands or wives, and a Suffragette a person whose house is always untidy.

It was scrubbing, cooking, working and childbearing all the way. How grindingly hard this life could be is illustrated by the account of one woman, Hanna Mitchell from Ashton-under-Lyne, who remembered the birth of her first (and only) child:

> One Friday, having done my weekend cleaning and baked a batch of bread during the day, I hoped for a good night's rest, but scarcely had I retired before my labour began. My baby was not born until the following evening, after twenty-four hours of intense suffering which an ignorant attendant did little to alleviate... My baby was brought into the world with instruments and without an anaesthetic... Only one thing emerged clearly from much bitter thinking at the time, the fixed resolve not to bring any more babies into the world. I felt it impossible to face again either the personal suffering, or the task of bringing a second child up in poverty.

Despite their low status in the household, women were taking decisions for themselves, and the campaign for women's suffrage flowed almost naturally out of their discussions and concerns. Unlike most of the women she would have lived and worked with, Hanna Mitchell decided not to have any more children and found an understanding partner in her husband. She also became devoted to women's suffrage. Other women also decided to make a change from the pattern that had been set for their mothers and grandmothers.

The historian Jill Liddington has unearthed the biographies of working suffragettes from Lancashire and has given us a vivid image of who these women were and what motivated their decisions to involve themselves in politics. There was Mary Gawthorpe, born 12 January 1881 in Leeds, whose childhood in a red-brick terraced house, typical accommodation for workers at the time, is described vividly by Liddington:

> Downstairs, in front of the fireplace stood the heavy wooden tub (later replaced by a zinc bath), in continuous use on Saturday evenings. The floor was covered with coconut matting and a home-made rug; her mother's invaluable sewing machine, also always in use, stood to the left of the fire to catch the best light. Upstairs were two bedrooms. Four daughters and a son were all born in the big bed; they appeared at regular intervals over a dozen years, 'controlled entirely by Nature's rhythm'. Lacking indoor toilets, the bedrooms contained 'the sanitary indispensables for night use' – the alternative being a dark walk up Melville Street to fearsome communal outdoor closets.

Mary's mother had worked in the mills since the age of ten. Her father was an active Anglican who spent much of his time in church and canvassing for the Conservative Party. Indeed, he partly owed his job as a foreman to the fact that his employer, who also happened to be the local MP, valued his campaigning skills. The constrained propriety of Home, Church and Party, of cleanliness and godliness, began to crack when the father had an affair and went off the rails, losing interest in his religious faith as quickly as he had found that his political convictions could be most usefully discussed in the pub. To the mother, committed to temperance, this came as a shock, as Mary would later recall:

> I am standing by the fire. Mother is also standing there. Father has just come in – he is late for tea, the evening meal. He is explaining himself and Mother says 'Stop maudlin!' ... Mother looks at me. Something *that can be felt* drops into me and I know that Father, whose teetotalism I

have strenuously maintained in the school yard, for no beer is drunk in our house, is not teetotal, as indeed someone has said.

Looking backwards I see that as the moment of transformation when I was first led to take, silently, Mother's side...

A clever girl, thirteen-year-old Mary had been allowed to stay at school longer than most other girls, who had either already gone into the factories as 'half timers', working six-hour shifts in the mornings and then catching up on much-needed sleep at school in the afternoon, or had taken positions as tailoresses or domestic servants. Now she was given the opportunity of avoiding life as a housemaid by becoming a pupil teacher, a kind of teacher's apprentice. 'One day I was a pupil,' she commented. 'Next day I was a pupil teacher.'

As the girl thrived in school, her mother faltered under the dual strain of an unreliable husband and a workload she could no longer shoulder. By the age of forty-five, she had lost all her teeth and struggled to keep up with the demands of daily life. By now an assistant teacher earning £50 per year, Mary took the decision to liberate herself and her mother from the alcoholic father and husband. She accepted a live-in job at Beeston Hill and as she was the major family breadwinner by now, the family had to follow her. Her father refused to move, which may have been part of her plan in an age when divorce was still a stain on the family name. The mother, Mary and brother Jim went on their own. '*We left him...* The work was done. We had left Father.'

There is a photo, small, damaged by damp and almost erased on its right half, a photo that shows Mary during this period, a pretty girl with sparkling eyes and self-confident demeanour, her hair gathered in a knot on the top of her head and wearing a dark cotton dress with three white bands of embroidery running down the front. A young woman full of energy and intelligence, sure of herself and nobody's fool. Her school work brought her into contact with the ideas of the Independent Labour Party and the Leeds Arts Club, run by an eccentric and gifted teacher and Nietzsche devotee who was interested in anything from socialism to theosophy. Here Mary encountered a whole world of ideas, a wealth of perspectives and horizons unknown in the household of her hard-working parents or in the drill-like school curriculum. It was at the Arts Club that she heard her first talk on women's suffrage, and the idea set her on fire. From now on, she vowed to herself, she would dedicate herself to bringing about the vote for women.

During this period, around 1904, the first wave of the suffrage movement headed by the Manchester activist Emmeline Pankhurst (1858–1928) and her daughter Christabel had passed through its first, almost timidly respectable phase of giving talks and collecting signatures and moved on to more direct means of creating pressure on politicians. So far, they had gathered nothing but polite assurances and patronizing sermons. Asked during a political meeting in Leeds when he would grant the vote for women, Home Secretary Herbert Gladstone had opined that 'the Parliamentary machinery (six million votes) was "already" large and cumbersome, and that if women were enfranchised, they would be "eligible for all offices" etc, just as men', a fact he obviously found distasteful to contemplate. Not all of his male colleagues were taken in by so much Victorian obfuscation. Victor Grayson of the Independent Labour Party recorded drily: 'The placing of women in the same category, constitutionally, as infants, idiots and Peers, does not impress me as either manly or just.'

'We left him ...' *Mary Gawthorpe was one of many working-class pioneers of women's rights.*

Voices like Grayson's remained exceptional. Faced with a largely stolid and unmovable opposition, the suffragettes finally decided to go further. 'The newer and more revolutionary ideas and methods are gradually supplanting the older and more subservient ones, for women are beginning to realise what freedom really means!' a suffrage activist had told an Independent Labour Party protest meeting, and Mary was to be at the vanguard of this new breed of protesters. 'Those who are really in earnest,' she wrote, 'must be willing to be anything or nothing in the world's estimation, and publicly and privately, in season or out, avow their sympathy with despised and persecuted ideas, and their advocates, and bear the consequences.' Together with like-minded activists, she went to political meetings to disturb the proceedings by heckling the speakers and demanding votes for women, a practice that would invariably result in their being thrown out, and would often involve them being roughly treated and insulted by stewards and the public alike. Mary was not discouraged. She became a central figure in the suffragette movement and would be instrumental in the next and more spectacular stage of its campaign. Every meeting, every demonstration and every instance of hostility she encountered seemed to stiffen her resolve.

Among the young women drawn in by this promise of escape from lives of rightlessness and Dickensian poverty, torn between work, respectability and constant pregnancies, was Lavena Saltonstall, born near Hebden Bridge in 1881. The Saltonstall family was struggling to cope with the father's pay from the dye works and constantly on the move between cheap lodgings whose damp ruined their health: Lavena's five-year-old sister died of tuberculosis, her brother, aged nine, of the same illness. Less fortunate than Mary Gawthorpe, Lavena herself worked in a factory as a 'half timer' from the age of ten. Life was closing in upon the vivacious girl, who would bitterly reflect:

> As I am a tailoress many people think it is my bounden duty to make trousers and vests, and knit and crochet and sew, and thank God for my station in life.
>
> I am supposed to make myself generally *useless* by ignoring things that matter – literature, music, art, history, economics, the lives of the people round me and the evils of my day. They think I ought to concern myself over clean doorsteps and side-board covers – things that don't matter so much...

'What mattered' was always dictated from the outside, and not just for working women. Society had its expectations of women, pressures that were all but impossible to escape.

Among the established political forces, the Liberal Party had looked most likely to introduce a universal suffrage bill in Parliament, but after their 1906 landslide victory it soon became clear that Prime Minister Henry Campbell-Bannerman was in no hurry to include a reform of the electoral system among the raft of changes his government pushed through. Having campaigned for the Liberals and feeling entitled to a share in their triumph, the suffragettes felt angry and betrayed. Quiet, respectable and lawful measures, it seemed, were no longer enough, and the activists decided to change tactics.

Already on 13 October 1905, the suffragists Christabel Pankhurst and Annie Kenney had interrupted a speech by Sir Edward Grey at Manchester Free Trade Hall by constantly shouting: 'Will the Liberal government give votes for women?', only to be first ignored, and then dragged away by police. The constable was rough and the two young women gave as good as they got, kicking, screaming and spitting at the officer, an act of defiance

Anguished impotence: Egon Schiele's self portrait without hands or feet.

Exploding verbiage:
Carlo Carrà.

Like a bullet: Luigi
Russolo's *Dynamism
of a Racing Car.*

Delaunay's Eiffel explosion: nothing was solid anymore.

Above Grim Reaper: Malevich's peasant figures have the rough-hewn solidity of tree trunks.

Right Dazed and confused: overwritten and swamped by symbols Malevich's city dweller is a sorry creature.

Above left Invasion: Umberto Boccioni showing the overwhelming dynamics of city life.

Left The good life: Matisse's utopia is set in a warm, pagan world.

Primitive power: the whores in *Les Demoiselles d'Avignon* by Picasso combine the stare of a sphinx and the force of African masks.

Dangerous innocence: Klimt forces his viewers to admit the inadmissible.

Yes, we have bananas: Giorgio de Chirico's graphic comment on new women.

Hopelessly inadequate: André Derain's little soldier has nothing to offer to his partner.

that landed them in court, where they were fined five shillings each. They refused to pay, preferring to go to prison instead. The case created a sensation in the British press. Women who were violent – young middle-class women from respectable families who were jailed not only for their decidedly unladylike comportment but for their political opinions – all this touched a deep chord with the British public and it inspired suffragettes like Mary Gawthorpe:

> The clarion note ... was sounded when Christabel Pankhurst and Annie Kenney were first arrested ...
>
> I heard and answered that call instantly, as soon as the news that the two women were submitted to imprisonment rather than pay a fine was reported in the press, next day. According to my opportunities, I said, writing to Miss Pankhurst in Strangeways Prison, if it was necessary to go to prison in order to win the vote, I was ready. That declaration brought me into direct contact with Christabel ... She now followed me up with a barrage of press cuttings.

Mary had not been the only woman to volunteer, and after the disappointment with the Liberals in 1906 it soon became apparent that a new generation of suffragettes was coming of age, a generation for whom demure fundraising teas and decorous, military-looking marches were no longer enough. Lavena Saltonstall was part of a group of women who decided that only the press coverage accorded to spectacular events could sway public opinion and put pressure on politicians. They decided to present another petition for voting rights – this time, however, not to a senior politician in the privacy of his office, but on the floor of the House of Commons. They did not wait for an invitation but planned to march on the House, intending to force their way into the debating chamber. They put their plan into action on 11 February 1908, and were arrested and brought before a judge, where Lavena simply remarked that she had nothing to say other than that the constable 'resisted me in the execution of my duty'. She was sentenced to six weeks in prison. Others were sent to Holloway with her.

Violence

The suffragette campaign grew increasingly violent. Stones were thrown at shop windows in Oxford Street and at the windows of MPs and government ministers and, in 1912, at 10 Downing Street. The women who were arrested were often brutally handled and always chose prison over fines or being bound over to keep the peace. The government became nervous. Stories of violent policemen manhandling ladies and factory girls alike were exploited for all their worth by the press. Soon, another development made the situation even more acute. In June 1909, one of the imprisoned suffragettes refused to take food, and the idea of being held responsible for a woman starving herself to death for being denied the vote was too much for the Home Office. It was therefore ordained that women on hunger strike should be forced to ingest food, a measure that turned into an even greater public relations disaster. Newspapers published detailed reports of women being pinned down on chairs by several prison guards while doctors inserted rubber tubes into their stomachs through their noses, through which liquid food would be administered. This was a long and tortuous procedure which proved almost fatal for at least two women who had porridge forced into their lungs instead of their stomachs and nearly died of septic pneumonia.

*Carried by conviction: Emmeline Pankhurst during
a demonstration.*

Leonora Cohen was one of these extreme rebels for the cause of women's suffrage. Born in Leeds in 1873 as the daughter of an artist and stonemason with progressive ideas, she had married jeweller Henry Cohen, in itself an act of rebellion, as her prospective husband's parents, Jewish immigrants from Russia and Prussia, were appalled at the idea of their son's marrying out of the faith and so cut him off. Leonora was certainly no working girl. Her husband's business went well, their son Reginald was sent to boarding school and Mr Cohen was one of the pillars of the Leeds and County Liberal Club. Having been happily immersed in running the house and looking after her son (a daughter had died of tubercular meningitis), Mrs Cohen began to develop her political interests. Aged thirty-eight, a mother and the wife of a respected local businessman, Leonora's situation was difficult, as her first forays into activism soon showed. Of all her friends and acquaintances, only her husband Henry supported her regardless: 'He stuck all that for my sake,' she would later write, 'I lost every friend I had... My name was mud.'

By now, the suffragettes' attempts to storm Parliament had become a public spectacle, with crowds of onlookers and reporters waiting for the women to appear, as a reporter for the *Yorkshire Post* related somewhat breathlessly:

All the roads adjacent to the Houses of Parliament were blocked by sturdy men in blue, who stood in steady lines waiting for the feminine onslaught... Plain clothes men hung about furtively under lampposts; ambulance men paraded with self-importance... We found little to suggest that the Palace of Westminster was about to be disturbed...

But a sudden change came over the scene. The flash-light of the photographer announced the approach of the enemy from Caxton Hall [the Suffragist assembly point]... The Scotland Yard officers had the pale set faces of men who knew they would have to go through with it. From the Clock Tower the hour of eight was boomed out by Big Ben...

This time, as on several other occasions, Leonora Cohen was in the middle of the fray, trying to break the police lines and make a dash for the House, but the women were repelled. In the ensuing battle, she was 'thumped on the jaw with [the] clenched fist of [a] policemen, and knocked down under a mounted policeman's horse', as she later claimed. She got up and aimed a stone at the offices of the Local Government Board and hit a window. The missile was wrapped in paper, on which was written in green ink:

Votes for women
    This is my Protest against the Liberal Government for its treachery and torture of the Suffragettes of Great Britain who claim the right to have a Vote and become recognized Citizens.
    Signed, Leonora Cohen
    Leeds

As had been the case with other activists, Leonora Cohen was sentenced to prison, an experience that made her determined to take her protests further. Amid a climate of increasing radicalism, of arson attacks on empty buildings and letter boxes and even a letter bomb addressed to Prime Minister Asquith, Cohen had understood that this kind of warfare was symbolic and therefore had to be directed against symbols. 'I went to London,' she later recalled, 'and bought a guide book. I searched through it looking at art galleries and goodness knows what. Then I got to the "T"s. The Tower of London. I thought, that's the place. They've never had a woman there before causing trouble.'

And cause trouble she did. At ten thirty, 11 February 1911, armed with an iron bar, Leonora entered the Tower on a tourist ticket. Having waited for the patrolling Beefeaters to move away, she flung the bar at a display cabinet in the room containing the Crown Jewels. 'What did you do that for?' a guardsman demanded, after arresting her. 'It is my protest against the treachery of the government against the working women of Great Britain,' she answered. Again she appeared in court, though this time she had to be released on a technicality. Another time, after another window-smashing, things took a serious turn for her as she refused food and drink in prison and had to be released under the 'Cat and Mouse Act' (which allowed the police to re-arrest hunger-striking women released for health reasons, after they had regained their strength). Her health was so badly damaged that for several days she was between life and death. She lived, and lived long: she died in 1978, aged 105.

During the last, desperate period of the suffragettes' struggle, their campaign degenerated into a guerrilla war of arson, sporadic attacks on members of government (usually with umbrellas, not grenades as in Russia) and dramatic hunger strikes. The police retaliated with increasingly close supervision, even going so far as to take secret photographs of imprisoned suffragettes for police identification. On one of these stolen pictures one of the most radical activists, Lillian Lenton, can be seen walking through the prison yard, her hair falling over her shoulders (hairpins were forbidden in jail)

My Protest: Leonora Cohen symbolically attacked the Crown Jewels.

and wearing a light jacket, her face gaunt and worn but quietly determined, an image all the more striking as her informal appearance makes her look like a woman of today.

The radical phase came to a sad climax when on 4 June 1913, Emily Wilding Davison attempted to stop the King's horse during the Epsom Derby by running onto the racetrack. The animal collided with her and she died of her injuries three days later. Her funeral became one last occasion for the movement to display the pomp and circumstance, now draped in sumptuous black, that they had so memorably orchestrated five years earlier during the Hyde Park rally. War would soon overshadow all domestic concerns, and many of the suffragettes channelled their energies into war work. Emmeline Pankhurst, the leading

Dangerous women: suffragettes' photos were taken clandestinely by police photographers, here the radical campaigner Lillian Lenton.

figure of the British suffragette movement, even toured the country anew, this time to give flaming patriotic speeches. At the same time, however, the War would prove a mighty catalyst for change, here as elsewhere: a growing proportion of women replaced men in factories and mines, thus demonstrating in practice a competence denied to them in theory. This changed the balance of opinion, but still women had to wait until the hostilities were over to be acknowledged as full citizens. British women over thirty were given the franchise in 1918; equal and universal suffrage was introduced only in 1923, long after New Zealand (1893), Australia (1902), Finland and Norway (1908), and Canada (1917).

Between Tolstoy and Autocracy

The lives of Mary Gawthorpe, Lavena Saltonstall and Leonora Cohen are exemplary for thousands of women who worked and campaigned tirelessly for the cause of women's suffrage, which took on an air of high political drama in Great Britain far more than in other European countries. It is an historical orthodoxy that the women's movements on the Continent failed to achieve their goals, but that would be taking a decidedly short-sighted view. The reality was, as it always is, a good deal more layered and complex.

Feminism in Russia before the October Revolution was certainly a clear and comprehensive failure. With only a small middle class and battling overwhelming chauvinism and male prejudice, women could do nothing more than make a few symbolic gestures, which was all the more tragic because Russian working women often lived under conditions of unspeakable hardship. In the cities, the only way to make ends meet for many of them was prostitution. There were between thirty and fifty thousand street girls and luxury whores in St Petersburg around the turn of the century (figures for Vienna and Paris were similar), a number that speaks volumes about the emotional and psychological conditioning of the society in a city of 1.4 million inhabitants: there was roughly one prostitute for every ten adult men in the city.

This legal prostitution, however, was only the tip of an iceberg of depravity and misery. A 1906 government report drew the authorities' attention to the growing problem of child prostitution, in which children as young as five years old were offered to drunken men, for a few kopecks, often chloroformed before being handed over to their 'clients'. There was also a trade in Russian child sex slaves that delivered to markets as remote as Istanbul and Argentina.

Russian girls had very few opportunities. As late as 1907 there were only 120,000 girls enrolled in Russian secondary schools and a year later the imperial education minister, A. M. Shwarts, attempted, and failed, to convert all girls' schools into institutes of home economics training. Faced with solidly reactionary ideas about a woman's role in life, ideas made more fashionable by Tolstoyan anti-feminism and its insistence on women's total subservience, Russian feminists such as the formidable Anna Filosophova (1837–1912, the aunt of both the philosopher Dimitrii Filosovof and the entrepreneurial choreographic genius Sergei Diaghilev) and Anna Nikitichna Shabanova (1848–1932) could hardly do more than work locally and otherwise look on in impotent frustration as girls and women continued to be treated as second-class citizens.

The one breath of hope in this situation came with the events of Bloody Sunday 1905. In the chaotic and utopian aftermath of the massacre, the women's movement gained new impetus, and various associations and clubs were formed. Following the English example, Russian suffragettes, too, attempted to enter their parliament, the newly constituted and short-lived Duma, only to be stared at by unsympathetic or outright hostile deputies who felt that they had other fish to fry. A bewildered Bernard Pares, a conservative member, described in his memoirs the Duma lobby 'raided by suffragettes, short-haired young ladies in spectacles, most of them puny-looking', and an older peasant deputy kindly took one of the women aside, telling her: 'Look here, let me give you a piece of advice. You get married. Then you'll have a husband and he'll look after you altogether.' Another peasant representative saw the intrusion as symptomatic of the ills of the city. 'Our women are not concerned with universal suffrage,' he exclaimed indignantly, 'our women look after the household, the children, and the cooking.'

Despite having a declaration in favour of women's suffrage signed by 111 deputies, feminist activists soon found that even the liberal Cadet Party was of the opinion that they should attend to a myriad other problems before they could make universal suffrage their priority. Worse was to come. As the state recovered from the chaos, and repression set in once again with renewed ferocity, the 'newfangled' ideas of the suffragists were among the first to be forgotten. In 1906, the largest feminist organization, the Women's Union, counted 8,000 members. One year later, the membership had shrunk to one tenth of this, as meetings were prohibited and journals closed down. At the same time, the National Women's Council in Denmark counted 80,000 members. As women elsewhere were getting organized, the Russian movement was all but stamped out.

One result of this impossibility of changing one's lot, of improving a condition that was obviously intolerable, was what the historian Richard Stites called 'Oblomovism' on the part of Russia's women – a deep indifference and resignation, even among those financially privileged enough not to have to work. Wondering what to do with her life, one young middle-class woman wrote in her diary:

> I do not have the preparation, the zeal, or the perseverance for serious study. And now I am old it is too late. You do not begin studying at twenty-five. I have neither the talent nor the calling for independent artistic creation. I am unmusical and understand nothing about it. As for painting, I have done no more than study a few years as a schoolgirl. And literature? I have never written a thing except this diary. So only civic activity remains. But what kind? Fashionable philanthropy which is held up to ridicule in all the satirical journals? Establishing cheap dining rooms? That's like trying to patch up a piece of crumbling, rotting flesh. Opening up literacy schools when it is universities that we need? I myself

have jeered at these attempts to empty the sea with a teaspoon. Or perhaps I should turn to revolution? But to do that, one has to believe. I have no faith, no direction, no spiritual energy. What is left for me to do?

Some women, however, did believe, did have direction, and did turn towards the revolution. As a legitimate articulation of their grievances became all but impossible, a surprising number of young women joined the ranks of anarchist terrorists and socialist revolutionaries. In Odessa in 1905 a woman was hanged for her involvement in terrorism, while another threw a bomb at a government official and shot herself. Six further women were held on terrorism charges. Zina Konophyanikova, a village schoolteacher who had killed the brutal 'pacifier' of the Moscow insurrection of 1905, was hanged at the Schlüsselberg Fortress, as was Lidiya Struve, a Bolshevik student involved in the killing of Justice Minister Shcheglovitov. Before she went out to meet her death, she asked her father to contribute ten roubles to a fund for poor students. Her story was the inspiration for the figure of Musya in Leonid Andreyev's harsh novel *The Seven Who Were Hanged*. The only encouraging example, amidst all these wasted and brutalized lives, was seen in the case of Mariya Spiridonova, who shot one of the butchers of the 1906 reprisal campaigns, General Luzhemovsky, directly in the face on a railway platform. The soldiers who arrested her beat her savagely, tore her hair out and stubbed out cigarettes on her breasts, a treatment so uncommonly despicable that it caused an international outcry when it was reported in foreign newspapers. Under the glare of European correspondents, the Spiridonova incident had an unusual outcome: Mariya was not executed but condemned to ten years of exile in Siberia, from which she would eventually return in triumph.

Outrageous Women

It is astonishing to see the differences in style and intensity of the various European feminist movements before 1914. Women in Finland and Norway won the vote early and participated actively in politics already. In France, the mother country of revolutions, there was a good deal of activism but little effective organization. Public opinion, it seemed, was still exhausted from the Dreyfus affair and split over the government's radical division of Church and State, too preoccupied in any case to give much attention to women's rights. There were some associations devoted to the cause, books being written both for and against it, there were large conferences and smallish suffrage marches and several journals. Marguerite Durand (1864–1936), an actor and journalist, was converted to the cause after she had been sent to a feminist congress to write a disparaging article for Le Figaro. Convinced by the arguments she heard, Durand founded La Fronde, a newspaper written, typeset and printed entirely by and for women, with the purpose of advocating feminist demands ranging from women's admission to the Ecole des Beaux Arts to enlisting them into the regular army. As if to underscore her serious intent, Durand strolled on the streets of Paris accompanied by a pet lion.

Madeleine Pelletier (1847–1939) was far more extreme and uncompromising in her convictions than British activists. A psychiatrist by training and the first woman doctor to work in a state insane asylum, Pelletier wore her hair cropped short and dressed in men's suits and bowler hats, the very image of female defiance of male con-

Striking an attitude: Madeleine Pelletier, an early French activist for abortion and lesbian love.

vention. She claimed women's political rights but also went into far more controversial territory by agitating for free abortions and radical changes in girls' education, a catalogue of demands documented in the titles of her books: *La femme en lutte pour ses droits* (Woman Struggling for Her Rights, 1908), *Idéologie d'hier: Dieu, la morale, la patrie* (Yesterday's Ideology: God, Morals, the Fatherland, 1910), *L'émancipation sexuelle de la femme* (The Sexual Emancipation of Women, 1911), *Le Droit à l'avortement* (The Right to Abortion, 1913), and *L'éducation féministe des filles* (The Feminist Education of Girls, 1914).

Pelletier was at the 1908 Hyde Park women's meeting as part of a French suffrage delegation. An inveterate campaigner, she was also active in the anarchist movement and a founding member of the unified French socialist movement (the *Section française de l'Internationale ouvrière*, 1905), as well as one of the country's first female Freemasons. Her multiple enthusiasms ultimately made her a tragic figure, as her fellow travellers in the different movements had little understanding of her ideologically promiscuous tastes and distanced themselves from her. Ultimately, her political commitment became her down-fall: insisting on openly practising abortion (still forbidden in France, as across Europe, except for medical emergencies), she was arrested in 1939 and sent to an asylum, this time forcibly and as an inmate. She died within a year.

Despite flamboyant advocacy, political feminism remained a marginal concern in France. Even the liberal President Georges Clemenceau, himself married to a decidedly progressive woman, was firmly opposed to it, for a reason entirely typical of the French debate: having fought for and finally won, in 1906, the elimination of the Church as a major power in education and in society, he was convinced that women, especially in rural areas, would vote overwhelmingly for clerical parties and so undo the achieve-ment he regarded as among the most important of his career. This attitude was rooted in the robust misogyny of the Jacobins and remained entrenched in France: universal suffrage was introduced in 1944, while women in the French department of Algeria had to wait until 1956.

Another reason may have contributed to the weakness of French femi-nism in the public debate: the presence of independent and sometimes scandalous women in public life may have made it seem a less urgent concern. The great scientist Marie Curie had been awarded two Nobel Prizes; Sarah Bernhardt was an actress whose fame spanned the Atlantic; the sculptor Camille Claudel was considered an artist in her own right, second only to her long-time lover and mentor Auguste Rodin (who, however, always downplayed the importance of her hand in his own work). The novels of Colette were literary sensations. and other female writers also succeeded in making a name for themselves: Natalie Clifford Barney, Renée Vivien and, behind protective pseudonyms, Colette's one-time lover, Missy (Mathilde de Morny), and the satirical novelist Gyp (Sibylle Gabrielle Marie Antoinette Riqueti de Mirabeau). In addition to these, there were wealthy women who very publicly lived according to moral ideas that owed nothing to patriarchal morals and everything to strong-willed independ-ence: Winaretta Singer, Princesse de Polignac (an American heiress), Hélène van Zuylen, the young Gertrude Stein (another transatlantic import), and the poet and society hostess Anna de Noailles, a centre of Proust's social circle. No other country in Europe had so strong a female presence in public life, so many stars whose bohemian morals and personal scandals became not the source of their downfall, but a part of the glory of the French capital itself, of its mythology and appeal.

Things went very differently in the two German-speaking empires. There were hardly any militant suffragists such as in Great Britain, no anarchist terrorists as in Russia, and precious few openly emancipated women such as those adorning Paris. Despite this appearance of passivity, however, German feminists were often so ambitious in their goals that the world had to wait another two generations until some of their ideas would resurface during the 1970s.

The English suffragettes were spectacular in their determined action, but their demands largely concerned becoming enfranchised Edwardian women who wanted access to society – without seeking to transform the basis on which this society was built. A good number of German-speaking feminists, however, wanted the vote only as a prelude to much more deep-seated changes, as Anita Augspurg (1857–1943) argued: 'The question whether the fundamental relationship of men and women needs reforming must not only be answered in the affirmative, we can even say that it must be revolutionized in its very foundations.' Marriage and sexuality, free love, homosexuality, family planning and abortion – everything was analysed in tracts, speeches and debates, up for grabs and awaiting a Nietzschean trans-valuation of all values. In Great Britain, such ideas were treated with scepti-cism or outright hostility, as they were thought to undermine the respectability of the suffrage movement. Millicent Garrett Fawcett, one of the main forces in the suffragist WSPU, was scathing of any attempt 'to link together the claims of women to citizenship and social and industrial independence with attacks on marriage and the family'.

This was perhaps the greatest difference between British and German-speaking feminists. While most feminists' activities consisted in classic activism and lobbying against prostitution and for temperance, for women's voting rights, for access to education and equality before the law, there was a branch of radical feminism and intellectual ferment that sought to change the foundations of society. We have already quoted Anita Augspurg, one of the most eloquent and uncompromising advocates of women's rights in Germany. Her life story was inspirational for the many women who felt suffocated by the conventions of male-dominated society and the social expectations of young girls. Born as the youngest daughter of a barrister in a provincial town, Augspurg attended the usual school for *höhere Töchter* ('higher daughters', i.e. middle-class girls), learning the skills that would be useful for a life as a wife and mother. Augspurg's later lover and long-time companion, the feminist activist Lida Gustava Heymann, gave a vivid sketch of the frustrations of such a girlhood, which the young Anita would have felt as well: 'Already as a youngster ... I was disgusted by the self-overestimation and the hauteur of men. Their condescending and disdainful way of treating women, especially their own wives – all this

Cropped short and ready to face the world: Dr Anita Augspurg.

disgusted me. When I had become an adult I swore to myself that I would never allow a man to limit my personal freedom – as far as that is possible in the given circumstances, in a men's state.'

Augspurg, too, began her professional life in a men's state: she helped in her father's law practice while following a teacher training course. Soon, however, this very conventional trajectory seemed dispiritingly bleak. She took acting classes and worked in theatres in Germany and the Netherlands but was discouraged by the obvious expectations of acting roles according to established patterns. Abandoning her stage career, she moved to the bohemian Munich of Fanny von Reventlow fame, where she and another woman, Sophie Goudstikker, took a flat together, ran a photo studio and gloried in the scandalous reputation they quickly acquired:

> The fact that two women in their early thirties were living together, were successful in business and claimed their independence, two women with short hair – think of it, in the eighties of the last [nineteenth] century – that they kept stimulating, interesting company in their home and publicly fought for women's liberation; two women who engaged in sports, rode horses and bicycles, went rambling and generally lived as they pleased – all this caused great consternation in Munich.

The photo studio, Atelier Elvira, soon became a magnet for the Munich *Bohème* and for a time it was the most fashionable place to have oneself photographed. Even the Bavarian heir apparent chose to have his portrait taken here. Augspurg, however, was feeling restless once more. Her relationship with Sophie Goudstikker was coming to an end and she was hungry for new challenges. In 1893 she moved to Zurich, home of the only German-speaking university that granted full degrees to women, and read law, graduating four years later and becoming Germany's first female legal scholar and *doctor iuris*.

By this time, Augspurg was already a seasoned political activist who had worked for causes ranging from girls' education to the regulation of legal prostitution. She moved to Berlin, where she set up house with Lida Gustava Heymann to continue her political work, editing the newspaper *Zeitschrift für Frauenstimmrecht* (Newspaper for Women's Suffrage). Augspurg's activism reflected her admiration for the British suffragettes, which she also expressed by attending the Hyde Park meeting in 1908.

Augspurg had long understood that rational arguments were falling on deaf ears among Germany's power elite. So she chose provocation to make her message understood. In 1905, for instance, she publicly called for a marriage boycott, arguing that no self-respecting woman could abide the loss of legal rights to property and self-determination that occurred when she signed a marriage contract: 'her urge for self-preservation, her self-respect and her claim for respect from her husband make common-law marriage the only option,' she declared, enumerating the obstacles making it all but impossible to live as a self-determined woman: 'You want to rent a work space for your professional work and the landlord asks for your husband's consent and wants to conclude the contract with him... You go to a bank where you want to pay in your earnings or take out money, and people have the effrontery to demand your husband's signature.'

In deciding on key issues for their campaigns, the activists were spoilt for choice. A Swedish art student arrested as a prostitute for walking unaccompanied by a man was one case they publicized (Augspurg managed to get herself arrested by a suspicious policeman just to prove the point); another was the truly horrifying case of a fifteen-year-old housemaid who had been gang-raped by four young men on an island in the river Elbe. The rapists were tried by a Hamburg court and acquitted because the judge found the girl was 'no longer innocent', having already had sexual relations with one of her assailants on a previous occasion. Augspurg's angry public denunciation of the judge as 'a brutal beast' resulted in a fine for insulting a court of law.

Like many radical feminists later in the century, Augspurg regarded sex almost exclusively as a form of male oppression, a 'sexual slavery weighing directly on some and indirectly on all women', an analysis that drove her to adopt a position not far removed from that of the Catholic Church: 'Sexuality is designed by nature exclusively for the purpose of maintaining and improving the race, but in our culture it has become a purpose in itself... it has become depraved and depraving, ruining and destroying our race.'

While Augspurg and Heymann were middle-class women claiming their rights not only to full citizenship, but also to full personal, intellectual and sexual self-expression, the problems facing women looked different from a working-class background. German socialism had embraced women's emancipation ever since socialist leader August Bebel had published his study *Die Frau im Sozialismus* (Woman under Socialism, 1879), which sold more than 150,000 copies before the War.

Bebel's insight that 'woman became a slave before the first slave existed' was a challenge to society and defined the approach the German socialist movement would take on this question. It would not be enough to fight for women's rights in isolation, for: 'the true nature of society and its laws, which are at the bottom of this development, must be understood before a movement for the elimination of these unjust circumstances can be envisaged with any chance of success.' The emancipation of women, in other words, was only a detail of the great class struggle, and to follow it too single-mindedly was nothing but a bourgeois distraction from the central question. The socialist activist and labour leader Clara Zetkin (1857–1933) followed Bebel's analysis. Socialism, she said, demanded first a classless society which would quite naturally bring about the emancipation of women. Zetkin dismissed feminist activists as bourgeoises, clinging on to their class privilege instead of joining the fight for universal justice, but her own engagement for women's rights and fairer women's legislation and her position at the head of the 175,000-strong socialist women's movement made her the leader of Europe's largest feminist organization in all but name.

While the political effectiveness of feminists in the German Reich was hampered by the split between women's campaigners and socialist thinking on women's rights, feminists in Habsburg Vienna were able to push the boundaries of debate even further. Despite considerable opposition, feminism flourished in Austria-Hungary. The culture of the Danubian empire was characterized by an unusual intensity of debate, and Viennese society (much like its Paris equivalent) gave more prominence and cultural presence to extraordinary women, be it the peace activist Bertha von Suttner, the scandalous and scandalously attractive Alma Mahler, the feminist novelist Rosa Mayreder, the educationalist Eugenie Schwarzwald, or intellectual hostesses and patronesses such as Berta Zuckerkandl – not to mention Eleonora Duse and other stars of theatre and opera who were followed with almost idolatrous fervour.

The feminist thought growing out of this climate was often radical, and directed not only against women's social, economic and legal inequality but also against their ideological preconceptions. The spirited writer Grete Meisel-Hess (1879–1922), for instance, took the fight to the opposition by attacking the two gods of anti-feminists, Otto Weininger and Friedrich

Nietzsche. Born into a wealthy Prague family and trained (as a guest student, the only possibility open to women) at Vienna University, Meisel-Hess took the fight to the opposition by analysing male attitudes. The more questionable passages in the works of Nietzsche, whose hatred of women had had a profound effect throughout Europe, were given short shrift: 'Even great minds have an experience no more than five fingers broad; directly next to it, thinking stops and the indefinite empty space of stupidity begins.'

A capable philosopher, Meisel-Hess attacked the pillars of anti-feminist received opinion. She wasted no time in deconstructing the often deranged mixture of anti-

Spirited opposition: Grete Meisel-Hess had little trouble taking apart Weininger's bestselling rant.

semitism, misogyny and pseudo-science underpinning Otto Weininger's *Sex and Character*, and launched into her own ambitious analysis of sexuality in Western society. Weininger and Nietzsche were prime witnesses, if not in the sense they themselves would have wished. 'The greater part of civilized humanity,' she wrote in her path-breaking study, *Die sexuelle Krise* (The Sexual Crisis, 1909), 'suffers... from this laborious suppression of a natural emotional state... Sexual psychosis is thus also the most widely spread pathological consequence of our sexual misery.'

Western culture, Meisel-Hess argued, had steered humanity away from a natural approach to sexual impulses untainted by power and property relations. The same system, teaching children humanist values and moral purity, yet separating emotion from action, also forced women into sexual slavery or abstinence. At the same time, it pushed men into sexual relations with prostitutes, which were not only dangerous to their health but also morally barren. All sexual relations were thus tainted by the logic of possession and the suppression of women, and even the act of creation itself was turned into dead lust: 'Capitalism permits the young man to save up a few marks to be able now and then to go to the prostitute and pour his healthy, live-giving seed into her artificially sterilized womb... [Capitalism] quite simply emasculates the citizens of this society.'

Like Gretel Meisel-Hess, the feminist writer Rosa Mayreder (we have encountered her already) thought that the resolution of the 'sexual question' lay in overcoming modern stereotypes. This would result in full sexual emancipation for women and men who were each, in their way, victims of a harmful and unnatural moral system. Mayreder was the daughter of an innkeeper who was wealthy enough to send his children to good schools and who encouraged his precocious girl to study with her brothers. A striking photograph shows the sixteen-year-old girl in a conventional 1880s studio pose, standing between the unavoidable potted palm complete with ornamental muse and a monstrously historicist writing table, her body strapped into a dark velvet dress and turned away to display her hip-long hair, chastely woven into a plait. Her face radiates inquisitive intelligence. Mayreder's own artistic interests – she was an accomplished watercolourist and wrote several novellas as well as the libretto for an opera by the Viennese composer Hugo Wolff – quickly led her to realize the strictly limited circle of activities allowed to a bourgeois girl, whose ambitions might be indulged, but never taken seriously. Her energetic engagement in both socialist politics and the women's movement soon made her an important exponent of both, and her articles in national newspapers established her as a fierce debater.

In 1905, Mayreder published *Kritik der Weiblichkeit* (Critique of Femininity) in which she summarized her thinking on female and male sexual identities. While Mayreder's eloquent analysis of the social and sexual subjugation of women and their necessary emancipation followed a conventional pattern, her understanding of the role given to men made her argument all the more controversial. The present situation, she argued, let men have the whip hand, but at the price of distorting their emotional life to a terrible degree and forcing them, and ultimately all society, into a blind veneration of a long-superseded, heroic masculinity: 'Like an old divine idol which is still publicly venerated and honoured with the necessary sacrifices even if it has long since ceased

With the power of reason: Rosa Mayreder, one of the most lucid critics of male values.

to perform its miracles, the concept of masculinity still holds its place in our modern culture. The conceptual content connected with this idol is filled with remnants of past times, with leftovers of former circumstances.'

Men, Mayreder wrote, were selectively blind when it came to analysing this feature of their minds: 'many outstanding men, whose spiritual tenden cy is usually liberal, are Philistines when it comes to women. The reasons for this lie in the nature of a particular kind of masculinity; it is an eroticism [i.e. a sexual, gender identity] which is conducive to normative violence.' Man the warrior was simply no longer needed in a modern society, in which even manual labour often required little physical prowess, and yet men were required to adhere to an ideal they could no longer fulfil:

> Even the work of a man has been replaced by the machine. The machine worker is a mere executor of a particular movement, which could just as well be done by women and children ... The 'strong fist', which under other conditions was crucial and formed the legal foundation of his dominion, has become entirely superfluous. But even while modern life is restricting the effectiveness of primitive masculinity more with every passing day ... the barbaric evaluation continues to exist in our morals and social norms. The military is still regarded as the first social order.

> To be masculine ... as masculine as possible ... that is the true distinction in their [men's] eyes; they are insensitive to brutality of defeat or the sheer wrongness of an act if only it coincides with the traditional canon of masculinity.

> We will only know what women really are once we stop imposing on them what they are supposed to be.

Civilization feminized men by making the lives of men and women more alike: 'culture and education close the gap between men and women, feminize men, make him anti-virile. The more culture grows and grows sophisticated, the more the anti-virile influences are on the increase.'

Mayreder evoked the worst nightmares preached by the philosophers of degeneracy and the theoreticians of male strength: 'civilization – almost exclusively the work of male intelligence – has been a process in which men themselves worked for the destruction of masculinity,' she concluded, and connected this analysis with the sickness of the day: 'The office, the workplace, the professional practice, the atelier – they are all coffins of masculinity. But the monumental mausoleum is the city itself ... all influences of city life are conspiring to increase the sickness most opposed to the character of masculinity: nervous exhaustion.'

Backlash

Society is never static, and the balance of freedom and power between the sexes has swung throughout history, from the relative independence women enjoyed in the Elizabethan age, to their almost total repression two centuries later; but never before had so much changed so suddenly and with such force. It was a transformation that was as sweeping as it was pervasive, affecting the personal relationships and lives of each and every one, and all the more powerful as it was not immediately and conveniently conceptualized within traditional frameworks of reference. It did not express itself in the rise of a new religion, a new state or a new prophet; instead, it transformed societies and individuals from within, and all the more lastingly.

This hidden revolution had occurred with astonishing speed, accelerating the pull into the cities and the creation of new social realities that had begun in the middle of the nineteenth century and had become an entirely new force towards the 1890s and the early 1900s. Within less than a generation, most received truths about the social order and the roles of the sexes had been invalidated. Among the millions of women who did not become feminists or who were even hostile to feminist ideas, there was hardly one whose life was not affected, whether by taking a job, by having access to a rudimentary education, or by choosing to have fewer children than their mothers and grandmothers had.

There was a backlash, of course. The number of anti-feminist tracts and associations (some of them actively supported by women) was legion, and many careers were made by raging against the new 'unwomanly' breed of women, against a loss of traditional values, against modernity in all its forms. In the eyes of its opponents, women's emancipation became associated with other perceived ills of the new order.

The main exponent of the scientific line of attack on women's newly awakened ambitions was the German psychiatrist Paul Julius Möbius (1853–1907), whose magnum opus *Über den physiologischen Schwachsinn des Weibes* (On the Physiological Imbecility of Women, 1900) went through several editions before the War. Relying on measurements of male and female brains and their different parts, Möbius claimed that nature herself had created women exclusively for birth and childcare, rendering their little brains so feeble in other respects as to be almost useless. This argument was hardly new, but its scientific discourse and the depth of supposed proof was greeted as a breakthrough by those who wished to consign women to Home and Hearth.

The most vicious opposition to women came from Vienna. We have already encountered the misogyny of the brilliant journalist Karl Kraus and his resentment against Eugenie Schwarzwald, but it was as nothing compared to the mania of Otto Weininger (1880–1903), a Jewish doctoral student who one day (probably in 1902) appeared on the doorstep of the Jewish doctor Sigmund Freud and asked him to read a manuscript, a book based on his dissertation. Freud was shocked by what he read and counselled the young man never to publish his work. Weininger published the book anyway, under the title *Geschlecht und Charakter* (Sex and Character, 1903). His chaotic and hate-fuelled diatribe became an instant bestseller.

Weininger's 'scientific' reasoning had an enormous contemporary resonance because it made explicit what had been implied in cultural debates for years: the identification of Jews and women as the two main enemies of individuality and manhood: 'The real Jew and the real woman, both live only as part of their species, not as individuals,' Weininger claimed, and proceeded to season his argument with lengthy statistics and analyses. Neither of them, he argued, was capable of creative and original work, both were corrupting and low by nature. Apparently driven by sexual paranoia, he had formulated a crucial insight into the culture of his time: women and Jews caused trouble, and they caused the same, sexual, trouble.

In chapter 1 we encountered the French debate about fertility, the Dreyfus case, and the role played in both by antisemitism. Capitalism, city life, newspapers, stock markets and other aspects of modern life were strongly identified with Jews, who flourished in this environment for reasons partly to do with their long-overdue legal emancipation and subsequent assimilation, and partly with their culture of learning and international, entrepreneurial outlook, after centuries of exile in a world that had closed its doors to them.

As the industrial bondage of factory work was often equated with an uprooting, a theft of identity and a symbolic castration (witness the role declining birth rates played in this debate), antisemitic stereotypes effectively portrayed Jews as effeminate city people luring virile peasants away from the fields and into their factories, where these true men and carriers of the national soul were turned into emasculated machine slaves.

The same fear is visible in many arguments against and perceptions of suffragettes, who (when not accused of being depraved and sex-crazed harlots) were regularly described as mannishly unattractive or as 'short-haired young ladies in spectacles, most of them puny-looking', as a Russian deputy to the Duma had put it. Some exponents of feminist activism, such as Anita Augspurg or Madeleine Pelletier, with their suits, riding crops and bob cuts, invited such criticism, but even the most ladylike of feminists were not immune from having their sexuality and their womanliness called into question. These creatures were not considered 'real' women at all, but monstrous hermaphrodites, freaks of nature. They disturbed the natural order, which was divided into men and women, each within their clearly defined sphere.

Once Weininger's rant had drawn attention to it, the parallel with women was obvious: they, too, flourished and came to new prominence in the environment of the modern city, they took jobs and educated themselves, they encroached upon male rights and male domains – and they bore fewer children. The ghetto Jew of newspaper cartoons was weedy, pale, unmanly, if not positively effeminate. The stereotype of the suffragettes saw them as mannish, thrusting lesbians. Women, it appeared, were conspiring with Jews to upset the ancient order of the sexes, to create a weird and threatening third sex, not man, not woman, a freak creature of the modern city.

Weininger had little time to enjoy the triumphant success of his book, which influenced not only right-wing thinkers but also truly interesting minds such as those of Robert Musil, Elias Canetti and Ludwig Wittgenstein. An archetypal self-hating Jew, as well as a pathological misogynist deeply troubled by his own sexual impulses, the student author became overwhelmed with revulsion at his own existence. Shortly after publication of his book he took a room in the house in which Beethoven had died and shot himself with one last, pathetic gesture. He was twenty-three.

Reality had changed for women, as for men, as Rosa Mayreder analysed so perceptively. Old values no longer reflected reality, even if the ruling elite in most countries was determined to cling on to the martial, chivalrous ideal of manhood that was a survival of a pre-industrial age. Masculinity defined as muscle power had become all but worthless in a world dominated by machines and specialized technocrats, brawn was losing out to brain, and the latter was not, despite the protestations of anti-feminist scientists, the sole dominion of men. Within economic life, muscle power was now associated with the lowliest and worst-paid of occupations, if not relegated entirely to the fairground.

Confusing the visible agents with the invisible causes of change, both antisemites and anti-feminists directed their hatred against a group they perceived as corrupt and sexually abnormal. It was a group they saw as threatening traditional manliness either with insatiable depravity (an alternative charge levied at both Jews and emancipated women), or by symbolizing a dangerously unstable sexual identity that could seemingly lurch in the blink of an eye from primeval rootedness to asexual immorality. Both Jews and women came to symbolize the male fear of being unmanned through being turned into the soulless subject of the machine. Men worried about the inhuman pace of life, sure to erode the nerves of even the strongest man and to plunge him into a shadow life, far from the laws of nature which, incidentally, decreed that his place was at the top.

If mannish women and effeminate men were among the ogres haunting the imagination of anti-modernists around 1900, the image of androgyny and other games with sexual identity had a powerful appeal to many artists. Giorgio de Chirico wickedly satirized his fellow men's fears with his 1913 canvas *The Uncertainty of the Poet* (see plate section). In this work a female torso, the ultimate sex object in its headless, armless pose with pert breasts and inviting buttocks, is situated behind a bunch of ripe bananas, a whole hord of phalluses seemingly sprouting from her loins, the ultimate man-woman with more than a nod towards the supposed virility of the 'savage' African men in their natural splendour. Just to drive home the point, a steam train in the background ejaculates white smoke as it rushes across the horizon line. De Chirico was anything but subtle. In a variant on this motif, *le rêve transformé*; the head of a sad patriarchal god, Zeus or perhaps Poseidon, gazes at a bunch of bananas in front of him, impotently jumbled in front of a testicle-like pair of pineapples, while the steam train still rushes behind. Both works show disjointed, composed figures in the convention of classical civilization confronted with the brute force of nature and the exuberant force of technology, and both show sexual identities as being essentially and hopelessly out of kilter.

The Frenchman André Derain simply held his camera-like eye steady on reality. In his *Bal des soldats à Suresnes* (1903) he shows a soldiers' ball at which everything is going awry. Three uniformed men stand impassively in the background, two of them with their enormous sabres planted in front of their crotches, while one soldier is being led by a woman on the dance floor, haplessly clinging to her and planting a possessive hand on her hip, without impressing her in the slightest. She is tall, confident, and obviously bored, while he tries to swivel her away from the centre of the canvas which is cutting through them like a knife. He has no chance. He is a stunted member of an inferior species, vainly trying to assert himself over a latter-day Amazon.

As sexual identities were losing themselves in the ambiguities of social construction and free will, feminine boys and boyish women invaded the imagination of writers and painters alike. They can be found in works ranging from Kokoschka's early *Dreaming Boys* (1903) to Thomas Mann's novella *Death in Venice* (1912), in which an ageing writer develops an overwhelming passion for a beautiful adolescent boy; from Ulrich's incestuous relationship with his gaminish sister Clarisse in Musil's *The Man Without Qualities* to the feminized boys in the paintings of the Russian Kuzma Petrov-Vodkin. The same images are seen in Picasso's early scenes and those of eccentric artists like Edith Sitwell, as well as in the lanky beauty of the young Anna Akhmatova, and the ambivalent appeal of Sarah Bernhardt. This androgyny also found its expression in Isadora Duncan's famously flagrant interest in both women and men.

This ambivalence was not the lush, decadent eroticism of the symbolist *fin de siècle* with its languid youths – it was a dangerous sensuality, a threat had invaded the images and phantasms of the early twentieth century. It bore not the promise of seduction into a luxurious beyond, but the menace of selfhood undermined by the endless possibilities of hidden impulses. No man could be certain that his nervous constitution or his moral universe could resist the barrage of temptations of the modern city, or that the corseted, long-frocked appearance of a woman did not conceal a wild-eyed fury, red in tooth and claw, and ready to tear apart the thin layer of civilization: a savage, sexual animal like the ecstatic dancers painted in the rural witches' sabbath by the German Emil Nolde. Even on canvas, women would no longer just lie down demurely.

10

1909:
The Cult of the Fast Machine

> It has to be said … that automobilism is an illness, a mental illness.
> This illness has a pretty name: speed … [Man] can no longer stand
> still, he shivers, his nerves tense like springs, impatient to get going
> once he has arrived somewhere because it is not somewhere else,
> somewhere else, always somewhere else …
>
>   – Octave Mirbeau, *La 628 E-8*, 1910

'I am alone. I can see nothing at all. For about ten minutes I lose all orientation. It is a curious situation: without guidance, without compass in
the air, above the Channel. My hands and feet rest lightly on the levers. I
let the plane choose its own course. And then, twenty minutes after having
left the French coast, I see the cliffs of Dover, the castle, and further to the
west the point where I should have landed.'

A few minutes later, at 5.13 in the morning of Sunday, 25 July 1909, the
pilot landed on a golf course close to Dover Castle. Louis Blériot
(1872–1936), a French engineer, had become the first person to fly across the
Channel and claim the *Daily Mail*'s £1,000 prize. The crossing had taken
him thirty-one minutes. Removing his leather flying cap and clambering
out of the cockpit of his self-constructed machine, nursing his right foot,
which had been severely burned during a flight only one month earlier (the
pioneering pilot had already survived more than fifty crashes, making it
necessary for his tailor to cut his suits to his deformities), he was ready to
receive the reporters and the military honour guard who came running as
soon as they had located him. When the first soldiers arrived at the plane,
Blériot greeted them courteously. 'Would you be so kind as to hand me my
crutches?' he asked, in English. The Channel flight was the sensation of the
day. The aviator was received in Dover by huge crowds; later in the day he
made a triumphant entry into London, where the powerful media baron

Flying into history: Louis Blériot crossing the Channel.

Lord Northcliffe awarded him his prize. Newspapers all across the world put the Frenchman on their front pages. 'England No Longer an Island!' trumpeted *Le Matin* gleefully.

The record had almost been snatched out of Blériot's hands by his rival Hubert Latham, who had attempted a Channel flight eight days earlier. Midway across, his motor had given up the ghost and he had to be fished from the sea. But Blériot, despite his injury, had pressed on in order not to lose his chance. He had scheduled his flight for 23 June, but bad weather had delayed him. Then, at 4.35 on the morning of 25 June, he had limped to the fragile flying machine supposed to carry him across *la Manche*. With 17 litres of petrol on board he battled head winds that made the engine hard to control in the poor visibility; in little more than half an hour he saw the famous white cliffs rising out of the thin cloud. Shortly afterwards, the plane's two bicycle wheels touched down, carrying with them the first human being ever to come to Britain through the air.

Blériot was not the first aeronautic pioneer, of course – there had been Otto Lilienthal in Germany and the Wright brothers in the United States, as well as several lesser-known inventors – but he was the first to mark the symbolic milestone of flying an engine-driven plane across open water, and between countries. He had shown that aeroplanes could do more than fly for a few hundred metres over a long field on a beautiful day, as the inventors of so many experimental models had proved. Now planes could actually be used as a means of travel.

Those Magnificent Men

Flying was glamorous, dangerous, irresistible. It realized an ancient dream, captured in legend by the Greek artificer Daedalus. The gods had punished him by sending his son Icarus to a youthful death by making the wax in his wings melt. Now, almost three thousand years later, humanity had broken the monopoly of the skies previously held by Olympians and birds. The gods still plucked young pilots from the air and let them perish in the flames of their contraptions – the 1912 issue of the French popular magazine *Je sais tout* featured an impressive group portrait of dozens of aviators killed in test flights over the past five years – but the barrier had been broken. From now on, it would be technological progress, not myth, that would dictate the pace of events.

Not only pilots exerted a magical attraction on the public at large. Car racers, rally drivers and cycling champions became popular heroes. Every step of their careers was followed in the papers; new records were broken and recorded every week. Racing was one of the obsessions of the age; speed was its drug of choice. And speed there was, nowhere more so than in burgeoning Germany, whose engineers led the world. Already on 28 October 1903 the German company AEG had tested an electric locomotive that reached 210.8 kilometres per hour (130.5 mph), becoming the fastest man-made vehicle ever. Only a week earlier, a similar locomotive produced by rival manufacturer Siemens had reached 206 kph (128.5 mph).

Within a single generation, the country had transformed itself from a flyblown patchwork of feudal statelets into an industrial giant, ready to take on all comers. She had beaten the arch-enemy France, had become an empire, acquired colonies. From the sandy flatlands of Prussia came soldiers and administrators; the rural south had become a world leader in chemical industries and precision engineering; the seaports in the north teemed with wares from all over the world, as well as goods 'Made in Germany'; while on its western flank Europe's largest urban conflagration, the Ruhr area, was pumping out coal and steel faster than anyone else in the old world. This unprecedented expansion had made the country rich in many ways. More and more people could afford a middle-class life and buy a classical, non-vocational education for their sons. German banks poured vast sums of money into the educational system. Universities created the most productive and original elite in the humanities and sciences the world had ever seen (more Nobel Prizes went to Germany than anywhere else), and the country sported the world's greatest density of theatres and opera houses, fine libraries and museums, as well as a roaring market in books and newspapers. No other nation, apart from the United States, had come so far so quickly.

Swept along by this rush of development, an increasing sense of speed was a major preoccupation, a public love affair, a deep fear, and the pulse driving millions of lives. The great machines in Krupp's plants, the chemical works of Bayer and BASF, the electrical appliance giants AEG and Siemens or the burgeoning Daimler Benz swallowed up hundreds of thousands of miners, engineers, unskilled workers and foremen who clocked in every weekday, their work counted and punctuated by the dead hands of watches and factory whistles and turning them into mechanical dolls that repeated their tasks with mind-numbing regularity. Women in telephone exchanges rapidly created connections amid the clicking of contacts and the constant hum of voices, secretaries took dictation from impatient superiors at a hundred words a minute while pneumatic messages whizzed through tubes over their heads, and telephones short-circuited the decorous ways of correspondence. Illuminated shop signs and advertisements on huge poster walls were instant messages, rushing past travellers' eyes. The railways prided themselves on being swift and, above all, punctual; electrical trams had been running in Berlin since 1879; the cranes in Hamburg's free harbour moved in a carefully timed ballet of loading and unloading with not a minute to lose; the giant wheels of pit-head towers rotated round the clock as one shift of workers after the next was lowered into the darkness. For industrial workers, the threatening vision of Charlie Chaplin's *Modern Times* had become a reality long before its future creator was out of his short trousers.

The messiah of this gospel of saving time at the workplace was Frederick Winslow Taylor (1856–1915), an American engineer who had devoted his life to rationalizing working practices by analysing the movements of every worker, down to the smallest gesture, dismantling the actions and reassembling the process in the most time-saving way. He came from a Quaker family and had received part of his schooling in Germany. During the steel crisis of the 1880s he had observed workers and had come to the conclusion that the old way of working – governed by a craftsmanlike application of rules of thumb and independence, and by workers dragging their feet – would no longer do. From now on, every movement was to be scientifically analysed and responsibility for practices and schedules was to be given exclusively to managers. 'In the past,' he wrote, 'Man has been first. In the future the system must be first.' Only rigorous analysis could increase working speed and efficiency, Taylor demonstrated, using the example of a fictitious worker whom he reassuringly named Schmidt. He applied his principles to many branches of industry, increasing efficiency in a bicycle works so that 'thirty-five girls did the work formerly done by one hundred and twenty. And that the accuracy of the work at the higher speed was two-thirds greater than at the former slow speed.'

Henry Ford (1863–1947) was the first car manufacturer who famously understood that he could make more money by selling hundreds of thousands of cheap cars at low prices to people with modest incomes, than by selling a few hundred expensive ones to the rich. His most revolutionary insight was to make the unit travel to the appropriate worker, rather than making specialized workers go to every unit. Thus the assembly line was born. Introduced in 1908, Ford's Model T car cost $825 and was the first one to be affordable for the masses, especially as efficiency gains in the works were immediately translated into price drops. By 1916, a factory-new Model T sold for $360. Everything about these cars was calculated to maximize speed and efficiency of production. Even their black paint had been chosen because it dried fastest. 'Any customer can have a car painted any colour that he wants so long as it is black,' Ford famously observed. It is entertaining to imagine what might have happened if pink paint had dried more quickly.

The ideas of Ford and Taylor were not widely implemented in pre-1914 Europe, but they were hotly discussed, and 'Taylorism' became a shorthand for efficiency among the bosses, and for the mechanized exploitation of workers among trade unionists, who put up determined resistance against all 'Taylorist' initiatives. Still, far-sighted Europeans were immensely attracted by the American approach to work, to life, and to the present. 'History is more or less bunk. It's tradition. We don't want tradition. We want to live in the present, and the only history that is worth a tinker's damn is the history we make today,' Henry Ford had exclaimed. Faced with the hidebound societies and practices of Europe, some of the Continent's most innovative minds – among them the car manufacturer Louis Renault, the later Austro-Hungarian steel magnate Karl Wittgenstein, and the architect Adolf

Loos – travelled to the United States to observe the workings of a society untrammelled by tradition. They returned with the conviction that Europe must be streamlined, dusted, and thoroughly sped up.

Speed had become a physical experience. Four times faster than a pedestrian, the bicycle propelled its rider out of the confinement of his own life and into the countryside, away from the drawing rooms and towards a life free from social convention. Moralists were scandalized by the effect these anarchic vehicles would have on public morals, most especially on women, who pedalled along gleefully, having discarded their corsets and put on more practical clothing, including trousers. Meanwhile scientists gravely warned that the sheer rush, as well as their position – boldly astride the saddle – would stimulate women beyond endurance and reduce them to infertility, hysteria or worse, wanton creatures without any restraint.

The novelist Maurice Leblanc (creator of the famous gentleman thief Arsène Lupin) made entertaining use of this public fear in his 1898 novel *Voici les ailes!* (Here Are the Wings!) in which he described a cycle tour by two young couples. On the first day, one of the men remarks that nothing evokes speed more strongly than the hum of the wheels on the road, and the riders' senses become more acute, allowing them a new experience of landscape. Meanwhile, the women begin to unbutton their blouses. Day two sees the women without their corsets, and on day three they remove their blouses altogether, riding through the countryside as modern-day Amazons. Finally, the two couples discard all convention in an orgy of free love.

The nexus between velocity and sexual excess was reinforced by Alfred Jarry's novel *Le surmâle* (The Superman, published 1902), in which the cyclist hero first wins a 10,000-mile race against a steam train and then throws himself into paroxysmal love-making ('This is not a man, but a machine,' another character comments) which leaves him dead, exploded by his own energy and expired from lust. On a provincial railway track in New York State, far away from the lofty realms of avant-garde literature, the dream of man outracing a train had already become a reality. In 1899 the racing cyclist Charlie Murphy rode a mile in under a minute in the wind shadow of a train engine, gaining on it as he did so. Murphy almost died from exhaustion in the attempt and was badly burned by flying debris from the speeding locomotive, but for a few seconds, sheer human muscle power had propelled him faster than a steam train.

Technology and speed created a new kind of artificially enhanced superman, the precursor to the bionic heroes of our own day. In *La Locomotion à travers le temps, les moeurs et l'espace* (Locomotion Through Time, Customs and Space) Octave Uzanne rhapsodized about the 'fever of speed' in 1912: 'The citizen is a mole with his undergrounds; he is an antelope, a thunderbolt, cannon ball with his automobiles; he is an eagle, sparrow, albatross with his airplanes.' In the journal *Je sais tout*, an anonymous author calculated in 1905 how much 'taller' people had grown through technological enhancement. He calculated the 'effective physical size' of a traveller by comparing how quickly a cyclist could cover a set distance, as compared to a pedestrian. His assessment showed how tall the pedestrian would have to be to walk at the cyclist's pace: the hypothetical pedestrian would have to be fifteen metres tall. Comparisons with other forms of transportation showed that in a fast train, a voyager would be effectively 51 metres tall, while the chauffeur of a racing car would almost dwarf Notre Dame Cathedral in Paris. Technology had created a new race of giants – in both senses of the term – and it changed the experience of space and time itself. Greater speed made distances shrink and travel seem trivial. While space shrank, however, time expanded dramatically, making smaller and smaller intervals matter more, from Taylor and his system to newspapers printing events from around the world, complete with photos of scenes which had occurred just hours earlier, and sportsmen winning or losing by tenths of seconds.

At the Races

Every weekend, hundreds of thousands of people sought the exhilaration of speed by going to the races. Formerly this had been the domain of thoroughbreds and of high society, but the new bicycle and car races brought the thrill of fast machines to a mass audience. The indoor racing stadium the *Vel d'hiv* (*Vélodrome d'hiver*) in Paris opened in 1900, the Tour de France was first held in 1903 and the Berlin Sportpalast was inaugurated in 1906. Car races and rallies were already well established and newspapers were full of breathless reports about those magnificent men in their flying (or racing) machines.

Recording sporting achievements relied on another piece of technology that was now asserting its universal grip on humanity: whereas previously only the rich could afford watches, industrial manufacturing and the needs of an increasingly sophisticated economy now brought pocket watches to the masses. The historian Karl Lamprecht has estimated that some 12 million pocket watches were imported into Germany alone around the turn of the century. The first stopwatches with hands showing tenths of seconds came on the market in 1900. Sporting records, which had until then been matters of anecdote and estimate, now received the dignity of being documented fact.

The race was on. The mind of modern man, the French writer Octave Mirbeau thought, was an endless racetrack: 'His thoughts, feelings, and loves are a whirlwind. Everywhere life is rushing insanely like a cavalry charge, and it vanishes cinematographically like trees and silhouettes along a road. Everything around man jumps, dances, gallops in a movement out of phase with his own.' Marcel Proust was fascinated by cars and even decided to spend 27,000 francs on an aeroplane for his chauffeur and current idol Alfred Agostinelli, who fancied becoming a pilot. Before Proust could complete his purchase his young friend crashed into the Mediterranean and drowned. Proust was distraught at his loss.

Not only writers enthused about technological playthings. While there were some 3,000 automobiles in France around the turn of the century, the number had risen to 100,000 by 1914, and an automobile exhibition in Paris attracted 500,000 visitors in 1903. Other, less industrialized areas meanwhile were virtually car-free: Budapest counted 159 in 1905. America was a different story altogether. Ford's legendary Tin Lizzie, the Model T, assembled in only twelve hours and eight minutes, was sold in vast numbers. In 1914 alone, Ford's factory produced and sold 308,162 cars. The rather more frugal Germans owned only 55,000 automobiles by 1914. Even so, the visibility and prestige of cars were high. The Kaiser himself was an enthusiastic driver, as well as the patron of the highly exclusive Allgemeiner Automobil Club with its grand headquarters in the centre of Berlin. Most senior members of the government and junior members of the high aristocracy were also members of the club.

The speed of this new automotive traffic was hardly breathtaking by today's standards. In 1904, the speed limit in Britain was 20 miles per hour on public highways, while the inner-city limit in Germany was 15 kilometres an hour – 25 for the fast-living capital. These trundling conveyances, however – often quite intimidating with their bulk and shining metal – were irrelevant to a public imagination dominated by press accounts of daredevil races, speed records and intrepid explorers. In 1902, the *Deutsche Zeitung* ran a long feature about two adventurers, one British and one German, who had equipped a car especially constructed by Panhard-Levassor in France to drive around the globe. They got as far as Nizhni Novgorod before their car broke down. Little setbacks like this, however, only lent these motorized exploits an air of daring, of danger. Journals carried regular reports about sporting events and records, as well as long individual articles about the Tour de France; aircraft pilots and aircraft designs; the future role of military aviation (including Trafalgar-like air battles between fleets of zeppelins); fast, motorized postal services; the chaos caused by private cars in Paris (a situation requiring the attention of *several* police officers); the 'incredible speed' of wireless telegraphy; record-beating sportswomen; and a curious new automobile fad, *le camping*

Even disasters had become part of this acceleration of the world. The 1898 novel *Futility* by Morgan Robertson imagined a huge, 'unsinkable' ship, 'the largest craft afloat and the first of the works of men', racing for the coveted Blue Riband for the fastest Atlantic crossing, but hitting an iceberg, with far too few lifeboats on board. Robertson had called this imaginary craft *Titan*. The hero recognizes 'this wanton destruction of life and property for the sake of speed', but can do nothing about it. Robertson's novel was prescient: fourteen years later the famous iceberg collision of the record-chasing *Titanic* shook the world. Early reports reached the newspapers within hours, and special editions were rushed out. There was no time to lose, especially not to the competition. News had become a part of life, and only the latest news was of any interest.

In 1865, the *Great Eastern* had laid the first telegraph cable across the Atlantic, connecting Europe and the United States at the grand speed of eight words per minute. Since then, hundreds of thousands of miles of telegraph and telephone cables had been laid, and it was now practically taken for granted that news from anywhere in the world would arrive within hours. The reports 'hot off the wires' showed a new world. Where correspondents would have previously collated and shaped the stories they posted to their head offices, events were now related as they were unfolding day by day, fragmentary and immediate, an effect that was accentuated by the famous 'telegraphic style' journalists adopted when dictating their stories: using shorter sentences, fewer adverbs, and simpler grammar to avoid confusion at the other end.

Advances in photographic reproduction showed a more immediate, less edited picture of the world. Events no longer had to be reproduced in the standardized, heroic style of an engraver or a draftsman, but could be captured in the raw. War and crime reporters now showed not artists' reconstructions but images of real explosions, destroyed cities, and victims of violence, particularly those of the Russo-Japanese War in 1904–5. There were still the usual pictures of grave, bearded politicians and generals carefully posed for the camera, but the same technology was now used to give a strikingly anarchic image of the world: crowds and corpses, victims of catastrophes and common soldiers, as well as sporting heroes and film stars, all sharing the same few pages, and all photographed days or hours before.

During the late eighteenth century, idealist philosophers had told a stunned world that what we know is only a function of what we perceive, that the only revelation we can rely upon is within the closed universe of our senses – a deeply disturbing thought in a religious age. One century later, in the 1870s, enterprising photographers had driven home this point by fixing instants far too short to be registered by the human eye. In America, Eadweard Muybridge had made multi-image motion studies of people and animals, arresting their progress in a series of individual images over a very short time. The resulting series made a single person (naked for better accuracy and all the more evocative of classical antiquity) look like a sequence of cloned humans while at the same time it lent statuesque dignity to even the most modest tasks. The most stunning aspect of these photos was, however, that they could make visible what had been invisible before: patterns and fleeting instants. Soon cameras were fast enough (exposure times were down to 1/1000 of a second around 1880) to photograph even more ephemeral things, and in 1886 the Austrian physicist and philosopher Ernst Mach had even photographed a bullet in flight, clearly showing the airflow streaming from it. And photography could do still more: instead of showing only what was too distant or too fast to see with the naked eye, the camera could also expose what was invisible to the naked eye. The novel X-rays could reveal the skeletons inside the living – a small anticipated death. Human senses were clearly not acute enough to take in the rush of the world; technology had outstripped and supplemented them.

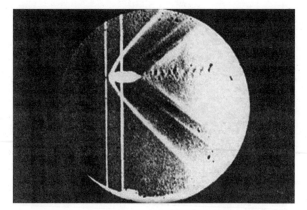

Frozen speed: Ernst Mach's photograph of a bullet in flight.

Small and cheap mass-produced cameras with fast exposure times and commercial film made the miraculous eye of photography available to non-professionals. The snapshot was born. After receiving his first camera at the age of nine in 1904, the Parisian Jacques Henri Lartigue could hardly contain his delight at the dash and excitement of it all. Born to wealthy parents, this wonderfully gifted child found he could document the world around him, and what he chose to photograph (not surprisingly for a boy) was often the sheer surge of exhilaration produced by speed. A racing car hurled around a curve, its shape distorted by its velocity and followed by a cloud of dust; reckless friends came zooming down hills on home-made go-carts; the horizon of a racing driver captured the road as seen from a car surging ahead at full throttle; a boy jumping into the water was caught floating over the still smooth surface of the water in full, incongruous flight – even a grown woman was seen as a blurred shape, hurrying indecorously across a square.

Nowhere, however, was the rush of the world more evident than in the new medium of cinema, as we shall see in chapter 12. Movies enjoyed huge popularity. Newsreels could show important developments as fast as a reel of film could be transported. For the investiture of the Prince of Wales at Carnarvon in 1911, a film made of the occasion was put on a special express train equipped with a darkroom in one of the carriages. The film was developed during the journey and shown in London on the same evening. The ceremony, witnessed hundreds of miles away only four hours after it had taken place, was not quite as stately as the live version: as usual, the projection was speeded up and showed the Prince and his entourage moving with the jerkiness of robots.

Cinema could do more than just record what had taken place, whether staged or not: it changed the way stories were being told. Silent and beyond verbal wit, and exuberantly exciting in their effects and in their greed for speed and thrills, films soon defined their own aesthetic repertoire. Cuts could startle audiences and move the story along, closeups were used to intensify emotions, insets could provide silent commentaries, fast-forwards could dazzle an entire auditorium. Flowers would burst into bloom before the public's unbelieving eyes; a caterpillar would build its chrysalis and emerge from it as a splendid butterfly. What took weeks in nature was here the work of a mere minute. The theatre could not compete. Speculating about the demise of melodrama on the stage, a critic observed of the cinema: 'The swiftness develops the breathlessness and excitement [that] the melodrama proper fails to evoke.'

Capturing the Moving World

Artists were fascinated by this accelerated reality and its possibilities, by its fragmentation into thousandths of seconds and individual frames of film, its forces pulling it around and twisting it, by the sheer energy and sexual charge of speed and its technological agents. The cult of speed and technology was an important element of the pessimistic vision of H. G. Wells and his monstrous future worlds. In his hands, machines became not exhilarating, quasi sexual devices, but engines of destruction. *The Land Ironclads* (1906) describes a trench war with almost uncanny prescience, with soldiers bogged down in indecisive bloodshed, a war suddenly and cruelly transformed by the arrival of ironclad vehicles with mechanical guns rolling over the enemy entrenchments. A young officer has just been busy explaining to a war correspondent why the enemy could not possibly win:

> Their men aren't brutes enough; that's the trouble. They're a crowd of devitalized townsmen, and that's the truth of the matter. They're clerks, they're factory hands, they're students, they're civilized men ... but they're poor amateurs at war. They've got no physical staying power, and that's the whole thing ... Our boys of fourteen can give their grown men points ...

The ironclads, however, have no difficulty overcoming the heroic resistance of the 'burly, sun-tanned horsemen' defending the trenches. The young officer's regiment falls under the rapid fire of the attacking 'few score young men in atrociously unfair machines', leaving the journalist stunned: '"Manhood *versus* Machinery" occurred to him as a suitable headline ... He strolled as near the lined-up prisoners as the sentinels seemed disposed to permit, and surveyed them and compared their sturdy proportions with those of their lightly build captors. "Smart degenerates," he muttered, "Anaemic cockneymen".'

To other British authors the rush of velocity seemed otherwise far away. With the keen eye of an admiring outsider, the young T. S. Eliot captured an attitude towards the future that had nothing to do with enthusiasm or great confidence:

> And indeed there will be time
> To wonder, 'Do I dare?' and, 'Do I dare?'
> Time to turn back and descend the stair,
> With a bald spot in the middle of my hair –
> ...
> Do I dare
> Disturb the universe?
> In a minute there is time
> For decisions and revisions which a minute will reverse.

In cautious, polite London this kind of laconic response might have made sense, but the scandalous young artists of the Russian empire took an opposite view. Disturbing the universe was their very *raison d'être*. Mayakovsky & Co did their utmost to land 'A Slap in the Face of Public Taste', as their 1912 manifesto was called. They wanted speed, danger, destruction, as Mayakovsky wrote in one of his poems:

> Soldiers I envy you!
> You have it good!
> Here on a shabby wall are the scraps of human brains, the imprint of
> shrapnel's five fingers. How clever that hundreds of cut off human
> heads have been affixed to a stupid field.
> Yes, yes, yes, it's more interesting for you!
> ...
> Today's poetry – is the poetry of strife.
> ...
> When you tear along in a car through hundreds of persecuting enemies,
> there's no point in sentimentalizing: 'Oh a chicken was crushed under
> the wheels.'

If the young radicals in Moscow and St Petersburg longed for a disruption of the stifling calm of autocratic rule, the prize for the most speed-besotted artistic nation must surely go to Italy, where an entire movement, Futurism, was devoted to the worship of cars, velocity, technology and violence.

Futurism was the brainchild of one man, Filippo Tommaso Marinetti (1876–1944), an Italian poet who loved being photographed in visionary poses and startling the world with extraordinary gestures and wild rhetoric. Born in Alexandria in Egypt and educated mostly in Paris, the young Marinetti had caught the French fascination with the car and with technology and speed in general, and he carried this gospel home to his own country. Futurism is probably the world's only movement to be born out of a car crash. The key ideas, Marinetti would write, occurred to him when he drove his shining automobile into a ditch, survived, and saw the car rescued, 'like a beached whale'. Henceforth, he decreed in 1909, when he proclaimed Futurism:

1. We intend to sing the love of danger, the habit of energy and fearlessness.
2. Courage, audacity and revolt will be essential elements of our poetry.
3. Up to now literature has exalted a pensive immobility, ecstasy, and sleep. We intend to exalt aggressive action, a feverish insomnia, the racer's stride, the mortal leap, the punch and the slap.

4. We affirm that the world's magnificence has been enriched by a new beauty: the beauty of speed. A racing car whose hood is adorned with great pipes, like serpents of explosive breath – a roaring car that seems to ride on grapeshot is more beautiful than the Victory of Samothrace.

5. We want to hymn the man at the wheel, who hurls the lance of his spirit across the Earth, along the circle of its orbit.

The surge forward had become the essence of life for those who understood, in Marinetti's words, that 'Time and Space died yesterday. We already live in the absolute, because we have created eternal, omnipresent speed.' Nothing would be suffered to bar the way of this glorious new time. 'We want to free this land from its smelly gangrene of professors, archaeologists, ciceroni and antiquarians. For too long has Italy been a dealer in second-hand clothes. We mean to free her from the numberless museums that cover her like so many graveyards.' Instead, the world would be galvanized by a great, manly cleansing: 'We will glorify war – the world's only hygiene – militarism, patriotism, the destructive gesture of freedom-bringers, beautiful ideas worth dying for, and scorn for woman...Art in fact, can be nothing but violence, cruelty and injustice.'

Today it is impossible not to see an infernal stew of machine worship, badly digested Nietzsche (never an author for weak stomachs) and incipient fascism in these words, first published by *Le Figaro* on 20 February 1909, but they worked like a tonic on readers throughout the Western world. Finally the old guard and their values were called into question – not in a small literary magazine or a privately printed book of poems, but by a mass-circulation newspaper, for everyone to read. Marinetti and the friends who had joined him, though, had no intention of going into politics. They were preoccupied with seeing the world through the prism of speed and dynamism and with attempting to capture their impressions in works of art, wondering how movement (a process) could be rendered in a static image to show the true nature of an object and the energy driving it.

Futurist painters experimented with fragmented or blurred images which borrowed heavily from Cubism. Where Picasso & Co had produced static scenes, however, their Italian followers used the shattered outlines of their subjects to suggest rapidity and force. Paintings with names like *The Dynamism of the Automobile, Rhythms of a Bow, Speed of a Motorcycle* or *Abstract Speed* (all painted between 1909 and 1914) were testaments to their determination. One of the most gifted painters of this circle was Giacomo Balla, whose *Dynamism of a Dog on a Leash* (1912) is a wonderful transformation of a very bourgeois motif. Painted from the perspective of a casual photographer or a passer-by, and coloured almost like a sepia photograph, the feet of the pet and its owner are shown in all phases of movement, with those of the dog creating a much busier, more intensive fan-like pattern. With true Futurist disdain for normality the painter was interested not in subjects themselves, but purely in their motion, in the very fact that their passing marked nothing but a moment of fleeting anonymity. Look away for one moment, the image suggests, and the canvas is empty.

Other Futurists celebrated the speed-induced death of individuality and middle-class life. Umberto Boccioni (1882–1916) attempted to paint pure states of mind, before devoting himself to portraits showing the very instability of what was in front of him. In his *The Street Enters the House* (1911), a woman looks over her balcony into a town square (see plate section). She is seen from inside the room, but neither she, nor the balcony, nor the square can defend themselves against the irresistible energy of the building site outside. Outside and inside, person and background become mingled in an infernal dance. The scaffolding erected by busy workers sticks like hairpins in the woman's hair, a cart is driving straight through the cast-iron railing of the balcony, and four horses, escaped from the cart and from classical legend, clamber through the screen and out of the picture, while the figure of the woman itself is invaded by the colours and shapes of the town. Even the buildings surrounding the square, typically the guarantors of upright respectability, stand disjointed and inclined, as if bowing to the force of the workers. Bold, repeated diagonals give an impression of exploding strength.

An Italian Nobel Prize-winner, Luigi Pirandello (1867–1936), was also the first writer to make a technician, a cinema projectionist, the hero of a novel. *Shoot: The Notebooks of Serafino Gubbio, Cinematograph Operator* (1915) is the account of a man whose function makes him see the world in a different light – from the stare of the projector's eye. 'I also know the external, mechanical contraptions of life which are always in thunderous, vertiginous motion, without a break. Today it is this and that, one thing or another that must be done; you've got to run, watch in hand, to be there on time.' Gubbio knows that his function is only that of a second-rate machine, and that a clever mechanism could replace him altogether, and he suspects that machines may be after more than just his job: 'A machine is made to act, to move, and it needs to gobble up our soul, to devour our life. And how could they could give us back our soul and our life, with their centuplicate and continual production?' It is obvious that Pirandello did not share the Futurists' boundless enthusiasm for the machine age. For his hapless character, the question is not so much that the battle lines are drawn, but that the war is already lost: 'From long habit, even my own eyes and ears have begun to sense everything in the guise of this rapid, quivering, ticking mechanical reproduction.' At the end of the novel, Gubbio is as much invaded by the machine age as the woman in the Boccioni painting. He no longer knows where his body ends and the machine begins, and he capitulates before the ceaseless, remorseless efficiency of the machine. 'I cease to exist. It walks now, on my legs ... I form part of its equipment.'

After 1914, an even more rueful, fearful note crept into writings about the speed of life, nowhere more than in the long essay *Some Aspects of the World's Vertigo* by the French novelist Pierre Loti, which was published in 1917:

> Having been knocked off balance by our knowledge, today we know that underneath us there is nothing but emptiness ... an emptiness that falls vertiginously, the emptiness into which everything is falling without hope. And, at certain hours, one grows heavy with the thought, it becomes an anguish to realize that never, never we or our ashes, our last dust, will be able to repose in peace on something stable, because stability no longer exists and we are condemned, after life as during it, to career around in that dark void ... we have no point of reference which would not be caught up in the vertigo of movement, and this frightening speed can only ever be evaluated relative to other moving things, to other poor little things ... which are also falling.

While artists were very much alive to the possibilities and dangers of a technological future, in Europe's most thrustingly dynamic economy, imperial Germany, the idea of speed and of an all-conquering era of dynamism was regarded with deep scepticism and so found almost no resonance in the arts. Amid the roar of a rapidly expanding economy, of increasing urbanization and modern technologies, the writers who defined the period were aesthetes like the young Thomas Mann, Hugo von Hofmannsthal and the notoriously delicate Rainer Maria Rilke – swan songs for a dying kind of bourgeoisie the Futurists had vowed to destroy. More radical, engaged artists such as the graphic artist and sculptor Käthe Kollwitz or the playwrights Gerhart Hauptmann and Frank Wedekind chose social criticism over aesthetic proclamations.

If technology did make it into German artistic works it was often included as a warning: Musil's *The Man Without Qualities* begins with a car crash, and in *The Loyal Subject*, a novel by Heinrich Mann, the grovellingly monarchist protagonist 'meets' his Kaiser by running alongside his car and shouting, 'Heil! Heil!' again and again, almost fainting with breathless hysteria. Expressionist poets and painters showed a world in turmoil, using techniques that borrowed (visually and verbally) from telegraph style and the fast images of cinema.

American Nervousness

The growing speed of daily life, of news and work and play, was a fetish of artists and industrialists alike, as well as an important factor of everyday experience. Not everyone proved equal to this pace, and in Germany this effect was especially marked. Never before had so much social change occurred so quickly. At the same time, an illness of epidemic proportions crept up on those who lived life in the fast lane. From factory workers to heads of state, from telephonists to high-school teachers, people complained of having 'shattered nerves'; overwhelmed and disoriented, tens of thousands were treated in psychiatric hospitals and sanatoriums which shot up like mushrooms.

The symptoms of this mysterious condition had first been described in 1869 by George Miller Beard (1839–83), an American doctor with a penchant for spectacular therapies, who observed in an alarming proportion of his patients a malaise that he called 'neurasthenia' – an exhaustion of the nerves. Beard's treatments for this mysterious disorder ranged from cannabis and caffeine to wine, 'particularly claret and Burgundy', and to electrodes applied to the bodies of his patients. 'American Nervousness' reached across the Atlantic. Beard's work was translated into German in 1881 and his diagnosis became a convenient shorthand for a cluster of symptoms that doctors were observing more and more in their patients.

'There is a large family of functional nervous disorders that are increasingly frequent among the in-door classes of civilized countries,' Beard wrote. 'The sufferers from these maladies are counted in this country by thousands and hundreds of thousand; in all the Northern and Eastern States they are found in nearly every brain-working household.' The patriotic doctor could not suppress his pride at this state of affairs. Neurasthenia, after all, was the disease of an advanced civilization, and 'no age, no country, and no form of civilization, not Greece, nor Rome, nor Spain, nor the Netherlands, in the days of their glory, possessed such maladies'. Hard-working and increasingly productive, America was indeed the most advanced country on earth. In 1901 the writer John Girdner suggested a different name for this mystery sickness: Newyorkitis, a special inflammation of the nerves resulting from life in big cities.

Towards the end of the nineteenth century, Europe had an ever-growing

number of large cities of its own, and with them came a wave of neurasthenic patients. What shocked the medical establishment (and no doubt
added urgency to the problem) was that this wave of nervous exhaustion
had nothing to do with the hysteria that male doctors had long diagnosed
in women. Grown, professional men were collapsing. Judges, lawyers,
teachers and engineers were suddenly unable to cope with their lives. The
historian Joachim Radkau has analysed the patient files of several German
mental hospitals during the years of the *Kaiserreich*, imperial Germany. The
patients' testimonies paint a vivid picture of the symptoms they were
experiencing, as most of them were only too happy to talk. One even had
prepared a 55-page dossier on himself.

A 21-year-old man at a private sanatorium told a fairly typical story:

> The nervousness had already come in my earliest childhood. I can
> remember that I often fainted and that the whistle of a locomotive could
> shake me to my foundations ... I was always excited and would explode
> at the slightest provocation. If I had to be in a crowd, I felt dizzy. I
> would involuntarily feel my heart and be convinced I was suffering a
> heart attack ... For years I suffered from thinking that I would not be
> good enough at my job, an idea that made my heart race every day.

Another patient, a Junker from East Prussia, was judged in 1905 to be 'Very
irritable. Since 5 to 6 years always at work, many honorary posts, etc., a
large effort, also constantly looking to increase his fortune, overworking on
his estate. Since the birth of his last child, the patient has only the idea to
make more money, even though wife and child are excellently looked after.
Sexually very excitable, also in his marriage. Always a heavy smoker, 30–35
cigars a day.'

Overwork was a common theme in the patients' histories. In fact, the
condition seemed to target those who were most successfully living the lives
of modern people – mobile, professional, hard-working, often with university degrees. One man had built up a business in London and was earning
well, when he broke down. 'Overwork given as the reason for heavy fits of
vertigo, unconsciousness, mad babbling and convulsions,' notes the doctor.
The patient went to his native Germany to recover for two years, and then
picked up his London life. 'Here he began to feel drawn to a *puella publica*
[prostitute: doctors liked to veil morally contentious references in Latin]
and thought of marrying her. When she emigrated to America, the patient
developed depressions, a constant pressure in his head, constant thoughts of
suicide, nervous pains in back and arms.' Another businessman who had
gone to Argentina, where he came to be called 'the nervous man of Buenos

Aires', had a similar story to tell: hard work and hard play, irritability, 'sexual overextension', breakdown and shattered nerves. The relationship between sexual activity and neurasthenia was a common motif. 'I am 26 years old,' relates a patient at the Ahrweiler clinic in 1907. 'During the last years, my mother suffered terribly from neurasthenia. During the 16th year of my life I began with my onanism. My first neurasthenic symptoms date from that time: a tiredness of the brain, a functional debilitation of my lower spine, broken sleep, dejection, depressed spirits, etc.' Later he sought relief by taking up smoking and visiting a prostitute, but his condition deteriorated.

Who, then, was neurasthenic? A survey of one mental hospital in 1893 found that among nearly 600 cases, there were almost 200 businessmen, 130 civil servants, 68 teachers, 56 students and eleven farmers (there were no manual workers at this clinic). Neurasthenia, the overheating and exhaustion of nerves, affected mainly white-collar workers, overwhelmed by the demands placed on them.

During a switch to a new system of telephone wiring in Berlin, one observer noted how the challenges of technology could be too much for workers who were only just coping. The changeover had its hitches, and the women on the telephone exchange were finding it difficult to cope:

> Many calls were not connected, a large number of connections was impossible, the acoustic signals did not work properly and the callers became impatient. This provoked our workers all the more, and finally one burst out in compulsive shouting, and before long most workplaces were affected and the telegraph director, who happened to be in the room ... wrung his hands, crying 'My poor girls! my poor girls!'

After 1900 an increasing number of workers began to complain about nervous exhaustion even if they remained in the minority, and treatment for members of their class was rare. 'As my work was done with machines, with the rollers used in the ovens, which now employ 80–100 people,' a metal worker told his doctor, 'well, you can see, if you work for forty-two years in this roaring and noise, how that can wreck an old man's nerves. I sweat all day, I feel afraid. I often cry like a young child, I cannot sleep at night ... Several other workers have the same disease. One was pushed so far that he slit his throat.'

People at the frontiers of technology – telephone operators, typesetters on new, faster machines, railway workers, engineers, factory workers handling fast machines – and those at the heart of the rapidly growing economy such as businessmen and administrators were most vulnerable to the symptoms that were grouped under the name neurasthenia, or extreme stress, as we might call it today. One German doctor called illnesses of the nervous system 'the pathological signature of the time in which we are living'. The American doctor Margaret A. Cleaves simply stated: 'The work of the world is largely done by neurasthenes.'

Nonetheless, the dimensions of the problem were frightening. In Germany, 40,375 patients were registered in mental hospitals in 1870. The number rose to 115,882 in 1900 and 220,881 in 1910. Over the same period, the proportion of patients admitted to general hospitals for 'illnesses of the nervous system' rose from 44 to 60 per cent. While these numbers include those suffering from many and varied mental conditions, not just neurasthenia, they do not include the huge number of sufferers who preferred going for cures or long stays in private sanatoriums, spas or other paramedical establishments in which a doctor would look after the guests – as in the one described by Thomas Mann in *The Magic Mountain*. Nor do they include those neurasthenics who simply consulted a doctor. There is, however, one more interesting number to report. While hysterics were overwhelmingly female, some 68 per cent of neurasthenics were (according to the figures of one specialized institution at least) men.

Was neurasthenia an illness of successful middle-class men? Of course it was not as simple as that. But workers who were institutionalized for 'shattered nerves' usually complained about the pressure of piecework and the noise and danger of the large machines they operated, while a large proportion of the women treated broke down under the strain of working, studying and trying to win a place in the world. These are conditions that today's doctors would diagnose as different from the feelings of inadequacy and the battles with their sexual selves that were related by the overwhelming majority of male patients from the worlds of business, academia or government. Neurasthenia was a condition that illuminated the emotional constellations of its time.

Sex, Lies, and Early Cinema

Over the past decades, research into the history of women has revealed a dimension of historical reality that had long been neglected. The high incidence of nervous diseases among men, however, shows that the turn of the century was also a difficult time in which to be a man. Squeezed between what many saw as the relentless demands to perform and the changing role of women, male identities were under threat. It is therefore not surprising that the anxieties expressed by neurasthenics almost always had a sexual component.

Sex had become more available. At the same time it had become a problem, a threat. Expectations and opportunities had changed, particularly in the cities, and particularly among the young. Cheaper coal for heating and functional apartments meant that there was more privacy. The younger members of a household were now more likely to have a bed or even a room of their own. Students often lived in rented digs. Technology and science also fostered a different relationship to the outside world, and to sexuality. Freud's theses on the omnipresence of sexuality had found their way into polite drawing rooms (not in front of the servants, of course), and publications linking sexuality and 'natural' or 'primitive' environments flourished, as is shown by the runaway success of popular science books like Wilhelm Bölsche's *Das Liebesleben in der Natur* (Love-Life in Nature, 1898–1902) or the many, sensitive and sensible sexological treatises by the British doctor Havelock Ellis.

The city itself presented a multitude of temptations and erotic possibilities among the anonymous crowd, and with it a host of perils, real and imagined. Boulevards attracted night birds, and inns offered easy and inebriated acquaintances; theatres, cinemas and revues excited their audiences by showing as much flesh as possible; pornographic photographs were sold on street corners (as well as through newspapers by mail order); stag films were shown during all-male celebrations and there was a large enough intake of young, single and usually poor women to ensure an unlimited supply of prostitutes. Unmarried men were tacitly expected to seek their pleasure in this milieu, as long as they settled down by the time they married.

At the same time, sex was danger. Many neurasthenics thought about their illness as the 'consequence of their youthful follies' – an unmistakable allusion to syphilis and to the allegedly devastating effects of masturbation. The fear of a steady descent into madness and a slow, agonizing death through syphilis was a constant presence in the West, and even a moderately hypochondriac disposition could be enough to make a mature adult who had 'seen the world' terrified at the slightest symptom that might be an indication of this cruel souvenir of early ardour.

'Manliness,' wrote Ernest Monin in 1890, 'very probably originates from the incessant reabsorption of sperm [into the blood] ... The abuses of coitus or of masturbation, the loss of sperm, etc., bring on a depletion of seminal secretions, and with it neurasthenia, phobias, etc.' Sexual activity, especially activity not destined for procreation, resulted in an inevitable decline and degeneration of the enfeebled individual. Even Sigmund Freud believed that the neuralgic pains he suffered from were the result of 'incomplete intercourse' with his wife, and doctors everywhere gave parents serious advice on how to prevent their children from masturbating, ranging from avoiding licentious remarks and spicy foods to having cold showers, injections, and even cauterizing the genitalia of girls – all in a good cause.

The world had grown more exciting, the pervasive capitalist ethic invited people more strongly than before to be masters of their own lives, to work hard and play hard and to decide who and what they wanted to be, but it was almost universally agreed that giving in to this excitement would have the gravest consequences. While 'manliness' was a cardinal virtue, sex was still a mortal sin. 'The bed is the real battlefield of the neurasthenic,' one German patient remarked.

The transformation of the role of women was an added stress to men and their identities. Now that suffragettes were demonstrating for their rights and more women were gaining a measure of independence by earning their own money and going to university, men, it seemed, had to be stronger, more manly than before. Confronted with this cocktail of constant energy, temptation, demonized sexuality and a new, strong kind of woman, male feelings of inadequacy were inevitable. 'Every female creature,' wrote a twenty-year-old German student to his father from a mental institution, 'is a dagger in my heart: you are abnormal, you are abnormal! *You cannot have intercourse!* You are a perverse sadist!'

For medicine, neurasthenia also had a very gratifying characteristic: as an illness, it was vague enough to become a canvas on which to paint many a picture of society's preoccupations. In Russia, psychological research was very advanced and active, and many researchers found themselves intrigued by the illness, before becoming disillusioned with the terminological ragbag in their hands. Beyond the medical establishment, the 'civilization disease' elicited very different responses. To those wishing to Westernize the empire, it was an essential part of modernity and therefore almost a welcome sign: 'At present we Russians will hardly find rivals in other nations when it comes to the enormous number of neurasthenics in our homeland. Might one therefore not be justified in calling neurasthenia the Russian illness?' asked Pavel Kovalevskii, himself certainly no modernizer. His own answer was damning: 'Lacking God within them, [the Russian people] rushed to embrace Mammon...The pursuit of profit required extreme exertion of energy and effort: countless sleepless nights, excessive mental exertion, lack of means, frequent bargaining with one's conscience – this could not help but devastate the nervous system.'

Civilization in the image of Paris and London had created unRussian creatures without morals, urban degenerates, who were, according to the writer Sergei Aksakov, guilty of 'contemptuous lack of faith in one's own strength, firmness of will and purity of intentions – this epidemic of our age, this black impotence of the spirit that is alien to the healthy nature of the Russian, but that is visited upon us for our sins'. The perceived impotence of the nation was as much of a threat to Mother Russia as literal impotence was to many individual sufferers, and it was a threat that came from the cities: 'In Petersburg there is no sun,' commented Kovalevskii in 1903.

> You could charge admission for showing the Petersburg sun, it's such a rarity. In Petersburg there is no air. In Petersburg there is no light, no space, no life... There is only vegetative existence. People have turned day into night and night into day... In Petersburg people work beyond their strength, but they blabber even more... Given such a life, can we really expect health, the continuation of our race, the strengthening of society?... Never – degeneration is its fate.

In different terms, this debate was mirrored in the very country that the believers in Holy Russia were most disgusted by: in France. If in the Tsar's empire the idea of neurasthenia conjured up the eternal debate between Slavophiles and Westernizers, in France the ideas of speed and nervousness elicited not only the enthusiasm of Apollinaire and the patient art of the self-confessed neurasthenic Proust (whose father was a doctor who had published on the illness), it also summoned the spectre of national decline and infertility. Many of the motifs of this debate belong in the context of the Dreyfus trial and the concerns about sinking birth rates, but neurasthenia reinforced and focused them. A few young artists and metropolitans might be having fun with fast cars, but for others the speed of the age was a sign of degeneracy and moral failing. Writing in 1901, Louis Bally delivered an angry attack on 'a generation of playboys and pleasure-seekers, anaemic and neurasthenic, bereft of both will and courage... the impotent and the tubercular, who lie about... in café concerts and fashionable brasseries'. Neurasthenia, which was as endemic in France as it was in Germany, was seen predominantly as a moral failing, induced by the 'unhealthy' life of the cities. 'No wonder our boys are becoming neurasthenics,' commented an outraged Virgil Borel, because all conditions conspired to 'annihilate individual initiative, force of will, moral energy and firmness of character'.

Like their avant-garde counterparts who saw speed and energy as erotic forces, they were mainly preoccupied with sex. Neurasthenia was a matter of modern egoism, of men seeking pleasure in the fever swamp of the capital instead of devoting themselves to the nation. Already the school books told children that illness was evidence of moral weakness. 'It is necessary to resist [illness], be strong and the disease will not vanquish us. But if we are not strong, it is our own fault. We deliver ourselves up to our vices and they kill us.' Syphilis was a direct consequence of moral degeneracy, and nervous exhaustion was often held to be the same: men who were too 'selfish' to settle down and have plenty of children and preferred to 'waste themselves' by indulging in pleasures of the flesh. Men who, like masturbators, were 'squandering their seed' wound up exhausted, wrecked, and spent.

In Austria-Hungary the disorientation was viewed with interest, rather than fear. The reason for this may lie partly in the fact that in the more rural, less industrialized Habsburg empire, neurasthenia was experienced by a smaller circle of people, mainly among the middle classes of cities like Vienna, Prague, Budapest and Lemberg. The condition was even intensified by the constant rivalry between ethnic groups and the fragility of social identities.

Schiele's portraits, Klimt's disquieting sensuality, the social and erotic entanglements of Arthur Schnitzler's stage characters are all shaded by neurasthenia, and Gustav Mahler's life reads like a case study: from his search for erotic fulfilment in the arms of his young wife Alma (he was not a good lover, she would later state) to his obsessive work schedule, his humble background and lack of confidence, his nervous crises and his need for solitude. He even consulted Sigmund Freud about his problems, and the doctor met him in Leiden, in the Netherlands – a great compliment to the composer, as Freud usually refused to treat mere neurasthenics, thinking there was nothing hidden to be discovered in their dreams and fantasies, which bored him. Mahler's grand symphonic gestures, ranging from the morbidly introspective to the maniacally grandiose, are musical illustrations of the condition: the constant intrusions of the outside world (the military band, the banality of dance music puncturing the delicate mood in the scherzo of the First Symphony, for instance), the mechanical rushes, the occasional sentimentality, the constant, undercutting irony and the overwhelming longing for transcendence and for peace, are expressed in texts of childlike simplicity.

There was a pervasive sense in Austria-Hungary that neurasthenia was *culture* (witness Freud's fondness for literary and mythological examples) and it is not surprising that the most vociferous and vituperative conservative critic of his time, the Zionist Max Nordau, inverted this equation. To him, contemporary culture was itself a symptom of disease and degeneration. The physician, he wrote, 'recognizes at a glance in the *fin-de-siècle* disposition, in the tendencies of contemporary art and poetry, in the conduct of men who write mystic, symbolic and "decadent" works, and the attitude taken by their admirers and aesthetic instincts of fashionable society, the confluence of two well-defined conditions of disease ... degeneration and hysteria, of which the minor stages are designated as hysteria.' Culture itself was diseased by an excess of sophistication and urban life. 'The inhabitant of a large town ... is continually exposed to unfavourable influences which diminish his vital powers,' he wrote.

Habsburg art, then, was positively flamboyant in its often fascinated investigation of neurasthenia and its psychological dimensions. In Britain's medical establishment, the response to neurasthenia was mainly a stiff-upper-lipped disapproval of histrionics. Not that anyone doubted its existence, as one of the most famous practitioners, Sir Thomas Clifford Allbutt (who also held the wonderful title of Commissioner for Lunacy), noted: 'not only do we hear, but daily we see neurotics, neurasthenics, hysterics, and the like: is not every large city filled with nerve-specialists, and their chambers with patients.'

'Neurotics, neurasthenics, hysterics, and the like' had become part of the medical landscape. Extensive theorizing about the condition, however, was left to Continentals. Allbutt himself was certainly not interested in elevating sufferers to the status of brain-working, fast-living modern antiheroes. Neurasthenia, he wrote, 'is common enough also in the wage-earning classes of England; it is frequent in West Riding, especially, I think, among colliers ... The truth is that neurasthenia is found no more in the marketplace than in the rectory or in the workhouse; no more in busy citizens than in idle damsels.' While degeneration of national strength was a concern as everywhere else, there was little or no indulgence of foreign fancies. Some people were simply nervous; their complaint would be made worse by overextension, and better by cool baths, rest cures, sexual abstinence, healthy activity like riding, entomology or apiculture, and a little dose of blood-enriching arsenic.

This expert dismissal, however, did not lessen public concern. Popular newspapers were full of advertisements for nerve tonics and health resorts. Much stronger than in the official debate, the old concerns about sexual exhaustion and general inadequacy resurface in these texts. Beechams Pills, Tidman's Sea Salt, Ambrecht's Coca Wine and Odo-Magnetic Apparel – hundreds of products were advertised for the treatment of 'nervous exhaustion and enfeebled constitution'.

Germany and Nervous Tension

If neurasthenia was the illness of the age it also quickly became a way of life for modern men like the Kaiser. Like no monarch before him, 'William the

Traveller' or 'William the Sudden' as his entourage called him behind his back, had embraced technology, speed and the media; like millions of his subjects, he too suffered from the vertigo brought on by this fast ride.

Notorious for his explosiveness, irritability and short attention span, the Kaiser exasperated those around him. 'He always wanted something to happen, always wanted new impressions, new images,' recounted the erstwhile Reich chancellor, Bernhard Fürst von Bülow. The monarch found it simply impossible to stand still; rather, he raced through his life like someone 'who is driving downhill too fast and has difficulties controlling his vehicle', wrote the diplomat Friedrich August von Holstein to Prince Eulenburg, who replied: 'the poor Kaiser makes everyone nervous, but that can no longer be changed.' The Protestant theologian Friedrich Naumann had an interpretation that was at once more positive and more general: 'Wilhelm II is the first virtuoso of the modern traffic age. He participates in life everywhere, listening by telegraph and talking at the same time,' he wrote in 1905, concluding: 'he is an incarnation of the electrical tendencies at work in all of us.'

The Kaiser loved speed and was always in a rush. When he was late for the funeral of Queen Victoria 1901, he ordered the train driver in Portsmouth to stoke the locomotive with every ounce of coal on board, and he did, pushing the engine to 145 kilometres per hour, an unheard-of speed which almost sent the imperial party hurtling off the rails. Throughout his reign, Wilhelm kept up a constant and prodigious travel schedule. In an average year, he would not spend more than four months in Berlin. It is hardly surprising that a veiled satire on the Kaiser, Ludwig Quedde's 1894 novel *Caligula* (which quickly went through 34 editions), describes the Roman Emperor 'hurrying endlessly from one task to the next, caught in nervous haste'. Like his fictitious counterpart, the German Emperor would get excited about an idea and then try to push it through come what may, never more so than when they gave him an opportunity to show strength, modernity, might. 'Never has a temptation excited the Kaiser's nerves as much as the fleet project,' noted Holstein.

Speed and energy – not always well directed – were declared the watchwords of the day. So universal was the feeling of pressure that the respected and conservative paper *Deutsche Rundschau* could run a story about a high-school boy who had contracted a fatal meningitis from learning the gerundive of the Latin verb *amare* (to love). One has to admire the journalist for finding a story that included all ingredients: the rigidity of society represented by the school, the pressure of having to work hard in order to get on, and the devastating confusion resulting from any confrontation with sex – even or especially in the gerundive.

At the Paris Exhibition of 1900, Henry Adams had worshipped at the altar of the dynamo, with its quiet force and velocity. In Germany, it appeared to many that the dynamo had taken over. It was not only the Italian Futurists who saw energy as a virtue in itself. Mechanical energy became the very opposite of the decadent, degenerate culture of neurasthenia. 'Where "energy" became the highest virtue, a world-view emerged in which there was no longer "good" and "evil", not even "right" and "wrong", but only "energetic" and "neurasthenic"; "forceful" and "limp",' writes the historian Joachim Radkau.

Thomas Mann famously wrote about the 'almost unbearable nervous tension' of these years, and it was his genius to condense the motifs of the neurasthenia debate and of an entire era into his novel *The Magic Mountain*, in which Hans Castorp, a young engineer, visits his sick cousin, an officer in the German army, in a Swiss sanatorium. The short visit becomes a seven-year stay in a place whose most important characteristic is the suspension of all speed, of time itself. Days, months and years flow into one another as the rules of the world 'down there' seem suspended, and after a while Hans falls in with the residents and even loses interest in his only book 'up here', *Ocean Steamships*. The counterpart to the engineer and his fast machines is his cousin Joachim Ziemsen, the tubercular officer, whose greatest terror is being thought of as 'limp' and unable to do his manly duty 'down in the plains'. Disguised as an institution for the treatment of sick lungs, the sanatorium is in fact a neurasthenic cosmos in miniature, a refuge for people no longer able to keep up, a universe saturated with anxiety and morbid sensuality – all the more so as the ferocious and Freudian Dr Krokowski is given to lecturing on topics such as 'Love as an Illness-Inducing Force'.

Speed was fascinating *because* of its inherent danger, because machines embodied the thrusting force of modernity. When Henry Adams had proclaimed the end of the age of the Virgin and the beginning of the age of the Dynamo he had equated the quiet force of the generator with a female principle; the male equivalents were aircraft and racing cars, which transformed every pilot and chauffeur into a mechanically enhanced, bionic superman whose potency was measured in horsepower. Fast cars, as Apollinaire had suggested, were sexually charged, and the men of the 1900s needed more of them – or so they thought.

The alternative to hitching a ride in the cockpit was being run over. Those who could not adapt fast enough, those who were paralysed by the gulf between public morality and personal impulse and those who did not have the strength to hold on to the vehicle were left by the wayside, bruised and bloodied by the encounter. Despite the new horizons opened by it, the new world was a merciless place, dividing humankind into those who coped and those who did not. The battle for the mind of the twentieth century was fuelled by technology, but it was fought over sex.

11

1910:
Human Nature Changed

We have ceased to ask 'What does this picture represent?' and ask instead, 'What does it make us feel?' We expect a work of plastic art to have more in common with a piece of music than with a coloured photograph.   – Clive Bell

One evening in 1923, a strikingly elegant woman with a face of severe, almost classical beauty stood in front of a group of Cambridge students to deliver a lecture about modern literature, built around a sentence that was as arresting as she was beautiful: 'in or around December, 1910, human character changed.' The author of this grandiose claim was speaking about novels, but her statement applied to all the arts, and she was uniquely qualified to make such a statement, because already in 1910 she had been at the heart of one of Europe's most conspicuous artistic groups. She was, of course, Virginia Woolf.

The change in human character which Woolf believed she had observed was subtle and difficult to grasp: 'I am not saying that one went out, as one might into a garden, and there saw that a rose had flowered, or that a hen had laid an egg. The change was not sudden and definite like that. But a change there was, nevertheless, and, since one must be arbitrary, let us date it about the year 1910.' Instead of occurring outside and with the gratifying obviousness of a definite flowering or the production of something useful, the transformation happened inside, at home, and in people's heads:

In life one can see the change, if I may use a homely illustration, in the character of one's cook. The Victorian cook lived like a leviathan in the lower depths, formidable, silent, obscure, inscrutable; the Georgian cook [i.e. under George V] is a creature of sunshine and fresh air; in and out of the drawing room, not to borrow the *Daily Herald*, but to ask advice about a hat. Do you ask for a more solemn instance of the power of the human race to change?

A ruddy-cheeked kitchen maid with a fashionable hat may not be the most obvious symbol of a revolution, but Woolf was adamant that she represented nothing less: 'All human relations have shifted – those between masters and servants, husbands and wives, parents and children. And when human relations change there is at the same time a change in religion, conduct, politics, and literature.' A writer herself, Woolf was interested in this last, and the change she described here – obvious in the 1920s but originating around 1910 – was one that was all the more fundamental for not being fully understood. Until that point, she claimed, novelists had been able to describe the world more or less as it was, whether they concentrated on character and story or chose to use their characters as examples of larger ideas. Now, however, the tools of narration seemed inadequate for fixing on the page the feelings and nature of people and events. Once sophisticated and exact, language had become 'the sound of breaking and falling, crashing and destruction'. It was no longer possible to capture the world in simple sentences; conventions, roles and expectations were changing so fast and so thoroughly that the metaphorical web of language had trouble keeping up. The contract between writer and reader, a silent agreement similar to those of polite conversation, had broken down and left both sides squirming in the attempt to say anything meaningful:

> At the present moment we are suffering, not from decay, but from having no code of manners which writers and readers accept as a prelude to the more exciting intercourse of friendship. The literary conversation of the time is so artificial – you have to talk about the weather and nothing but the weather throughout the entire visit – that, naturally, the feeble are tempted to outrage and the strong are led to destroy the very foundations and rules of literary society. Signs of this are everywhere apparent. Grammar is violated; syntax disintegrated; as a boy staying with an aunt for the weekend rolls in the geranium bed out of sheer desperation as the solemnities of the sabbath wear on. Their sincerity is desperate and their courage tremendous ... but what a waste of energy!

The consequence of this reinvention of language was twofold: on the one hand, the creative energy invested in words made new writing wonderfully rich and colourful; on the other, however, too little was left to drive along the text, to convey a minimum of assurance even to the most daring reader. Reading T. S. Eliot's poetry, Woolf herself explained, she found herself at once admiring and exhausted: 'As I sun myself upon the intense and ravishing beauty of one of his lines, and reflect that I must make a dizzy and dangerous leap to the next, and so from line to line, like an acrobat flying from bar to bar, I cry out, I confess, for the old decorum and envy the indolence of my ancestors who, instead of spinning madly through mid-air, dreamt quietly in the shade with a book.' So much effort had gone into devising new narrative tools, a new language and a new style, that the text itself was sapped of vital force, as if the very words were suffering from neurasthenia: 'if you compare [Lytton Strachey's historical masterpiece] *Eminent Victorians* with some of [the Victorian historian] Lord Macaulay's essays, though you will feel that Lord Macaulay is always wrong and Mr Strachey is always right, you will also feel a body, a sweep, a richness in Lord Macaulay's essays, which show that his age was behind him; all his strength went straight into his work; none was used for the purpose of concealment and conversion.'

In or around 1910, everything had become difficult for writers, Woolf claimed. The changes that occurred were too powerful to be ignored, too swift to be fully assimilated, and they had left language itself behind. The consequence was a difficult season in the arts, a kind of art demanding of its public to 'tolerate the spasmodic, the obscure, the fragmentary, the failure'.

Talking of Copulation

Daring as it was to fix 1910 as a key date for humanity, for Virginia Stephen, the later Virginia Woolf, it was a year of powerful biographical resonance. After the death of their father in 1904 (their mother had died almost ten years earlier), the four Stephen siblings had moved into a large house at 46 Gordon Square, Bloomsbury, an area of faded gentility far away from the social world of their childhood. Their decision to live together, without any matronly figure to watch over their virtue and without a chaperone for Virginia and Vanessa, raised eyebrows, but they were determined to live their own lives free from the constraints of Edwardian upper-middle-class respectability.

For Virginia this was a period of beginnings. Aged twenty-two, she wanted to write, and she began by penning reviews for literary magazines. The death of her father had precipitated a severe mental crisis for her, the first of many, and in her new home she began to construct an adult personality for herself. Her determination was tested once again when her adored brother Thoby died of typhoid during a trip through Greece in 1907, but she inherited from him a circle of Cambridge friends who would still come to the Stephens' bohemian residence with its airy interiors, Indian scarfs draped over walls and furniture, and piles of books everywhere. There they would drink strong coffee and smoke cigarettes and discuss every topic under the sun, even scandalous, unspeakable things. The liberating blow had been struck in 1908 by one of Thoby's friends, as famously retold by Woolf:

> The long and sinister figure of Mr. Lytton Strachey stood on the threshold. He pointed his finger at a stain on Vanessa's white dress.
> 'Semen?' he said.
> Can one really say that? I thought & we burst out laughing. With that one word all barriers of reticence and reserve went down. A flood of the sacred fluid seemed to overwhelm us. Sex permeated our conversation. The word bugger was never far from our lips. We discussed copulation with the same excitement and openness that we had discussed the nature of good. It is strange to think how reticent, how reversed we had been and for how long.

Strachey (1880–1932), the flamboyantly homosexual later author of *Eminent Victorians*, had a particular gift for finding the right phrase at the right time. When in 1914 he became a conscientious objector and had to appear before an army panel, he was asked by the officers what he would do if a German soldier raped his sister. 'I would endeavour to come between them,' was his reply.

After Vanessa's marriage to the painter Clive Bell, the bohemian Stephen household changed and Virginia moved, together with her brother Adrian, into a house close by, where the life of books, discussions and designs for living continued unabated. In 1910, aged twenty-eight, Virginia was ready to confront the world head-on. Three events that year, each one characteristic of a different aspect of the time, accentuated this determination. In February she was involved, at the last minute, in a practical joke designed to explode the grand 'Britannia rules the waves' rhetoric that was prevalent at the time: as Prince Mendax she participated in the Dreadnought Hoax, face blackened and with a false beard stuck to her chin. During the year, Woolf also became involved in the suffragette movement, whose campaign was reaching its high point. Her personal involvement did not go beyond stuffing and addressing envelopes in a local office of the NWUSS, but it involved taking a stand, even if Virginia found that she herself was not made for political movements and agitation.

The third event in 1910 that sharpened Woolf's sense that something new was happening and that human character and outlook were no longer the same as they had been was an exhibition of 'post-Impressionist' painters, curated by another member of their circle, the painter and art critic Roger Fry.

Oh, for a time when art still had the capacity to shock! Into the genteel world of James Abbott McNeill Whistler and John Singer Sargent, into the lives of a middle class whose heads were filled with works by Victorian dream merchants such as Dante Gabriel Rossetti and John Everett Millais, burst the new wave. A public taste marked by English landscapes was invaded by the primeval emotional intensity of Vincent van Gogh, the quasi-abstract grandeur of Paul Cézanne, and the primitivist sensualism of Paul Gauguin's Tahitian canvases. The effect was extraordinary. Overwhelmingly hostile, reviewers called the works 'hysterical daubs', 'crude intolerable outrages' and 'childish rubbish'. Predictably van Gogh's work was attacked as the ravings of an 'adult maniac', Gauguin's for his 'crude savagery' and Cézanne's unveiling of geometries in nature was seen as 'sterile' and 'unmanly', while the exhibition itself was criticized as a collection of 'sickening aberrations' created by 'morbid', 'diseased minds', a symptom of 'the last degradation of art'. This, many critics agreed, was not art, but an attack on all that is beautiful, true and sacred in civilization.

Some of their colleagues across the Channel were altogether more understanding of the energies at work in these canvases. In his book *Modern Art* (published in English translation in 1908), the German critic Julius Meier-Graefe perceptively and characteristically explained the message of a Gauguin in terms of disease and civilization, health and nature, virility and femininity:

'Your civilization is your disease,' he says, 'my barbarism is my restoration to health. The Eve of your civilized conception makes us nearly all misogynists. The old Eve, who shocked you in my studio, will perhaps seem less odious to you one day... Only the Eve I have painted can stand naked before us. Yours would be shameless in this natural state, and if beautiful, the source of pain and evil.'

The English art world had been largely sheltered from new developments in European art and was, in effect, a generation behind its time. The work of Picasso and Klimt, Schiele and Malevich, the Fauves and the Futurists had passed almost entirely unnoticed (even by avant-gardists like Fry himself), and so it was the previous generation of searchers and provocateurs that brought a shocked public to realize that art could be many things it had not yet seen or understood. Woolf followed the vituperations by the press and by an establishment that left her feeling increasingly alienated. The way of seeing the world that she and her friends were cultivating, she realized, was in effect at war with the aesthetics, the politics and the morals of the Edwardian establishment and its public expressions. She saw a society refusing to accept that something had come to an end with the death of Queen Victoria, that something new was happening, a different way of seeing the world, of being in the world.

Yet another convenient date helped Woolf to pinpoint the date of the transformation. On 6 May 1910, George V ascended to the throne after his father Edward the Caresser had wheezed his last in a hotel in Biarritz. Making a clear division between the old Edwardian days and her own time, Virginia Woolf would refer to this period as 'Georgian', hoping perhaps that this second Georgian period (a term which has not survived into history writing) would bring as much innovation and social change as had the first, two hundred years earlier.

If there are several convenient pegs with which to fasten Woolf's perception of radical change to the year 1910, we must not forget the less obvious but more ubiquitous shifts in outlook and behaviour which punctuated daily life. Woolf herself points in this direction by taking, with more than a little ironic snobbery, 'one's cook' as the only and supreme example of her grand claim. Formerly banished downstairs, the said cook is now confident enough to breeze into the sitting room to ask her employer's advice about a hat – speaking as if she were among equals, behaving like someone who has a life away from her vocation and her preordained role, someone who wants to look feminine, to enjoy herself, perhaps to find a man, to have a family – someone who feels entitled to ask all that of life, and to ask it in the face of her social betters. She was not alone. The suffragettes were on the streets, miners in Wales were on strike and Ireland was demanding Home Rule. To many this was a dangerous symptom of modern degeneration that had to be fought with all means possible, just as the post-Impressionists were nothing but barbarians poisoning the wells of civilization. Others, however, saw these changes as necessary and concluded that not only society but the very way of perceiving the world and of feeling would have to give way to something new, and that art had to respond to this new fact.

While in 1910 the London art world was reeling from the shock of encountering the French avant-garde of the 1880s, this was a crucial time for artistic renewal throughout Europe. The artistic mainstream was still conservative.

In music, it was just moving out of romanticism (a whole generation had just vanished from the scene: Tchaikovsky had died in 1893, Bruckner in 1896, Brahms in 1897, Verdi in 1901 and Dvořák in 1904) and was cautiously trying to get to grips with the harmonic and formal innovations Richard Wagner had brought. The first decade of the century was a fruitful period in the work of well-established late Romantics – the landscapes of the Finn Jean Sibelius, the tragic heroism of Edward Elgar, the folkloric sounds of Nikolai Rimsky-Korsakov in Russia, the elegant textures of Gabriel Fauré and the academic grandeur of Camille Saint-Saëns in France, the compositions of Max Bruch in Germany, of Manuel de Falla in Spain, of the Dane Carl Nielsen and of Ferruccio Busoni's richly seasoned tone poems. Eclipsing them all in success were the operas of Giacomo Puccini, whose sure-fire trio of *La Bohème* (1896), *Tosca* (1900) and *Madame Butterfly* (1904) played to full houses the world over and who would finally give a nod to his own century with the American emigrant opera *La Fanciulla del West* (1910). All of these artists were of a conservative, tentatively searching disposition, and all of them were outstanding in their way. It is the way of history to be particularly interested in change, in fissures, in seminal works and new developments, but it does not do to let this interest obscure our view of the fact that art can be great without being radically new or creating a new school.

Europe's bookshops were already selling sentimental trash, self-help books and science fiction, and for the more discerning or more socially ambitious they stocked the decadents of the late nineteenth century (Wilde, Baudelaire, Maeterlinck) as well as the more recent, avowedly realist social fiction of Emile Zola and the German Gerhart Hauptmann, of George Bernard Shaw and the ageing Thomas Hardy, or the self-consciously outrageous Italian Gabriele d'Annunzio. In a gallery or a museum of modern art, one could see canvases painted by the popular Russian portraitist Ilya Repin, by the German late Impressionist and wit Max Liebermann (asked how he would paint the then chancellor of Germany he answered: 'Bismarck? I'll pee him into the snow!'), the expressionist fantasies of Edvard Munch, the cloying sumptuousness of Sir Lawrence Alma-Tadema and Frederic Leighton – Britain was still recovering from the exquisite artistic sins of the Pre-Raphelites.

This is the background against which we have to see the artistic revolution Virginia Woolf described. Often these experiments were focused on groups like the Bloomsbury circle. Imagining the new is easier when ideas bounce back and forth. In Paris, the American Gertrude Stein became a focal point for artists who came to her house to have a hot meal, to talk about art, or to sell her their work in order to pay the rent for another month; in Germany, Munich's Schwabing circle and groups in Darmstadt or the north-German village of Worpswede or the group Die Brücke (the bridge) fulfilled this function; in St Petersburg, the ecstatic goings-on in Vyacheslav Ivanov's Tower were a focus for artists and philosophers alike (as well as for the usual colourful band of hangers-on); Milan was the head quarters of the Italian Futurist movement; the Secession and the salons of Eugenie Schwarzwald and Bertha Zuckerkandl the focus for Vienna's new generation of artists; and countless smaller and often short-lived communities. It is interesting to notice how distinct from one another these groups were. There were no Cubists in Vienna, no Futurists in Berlin or Munich, and twelve-tone music was not composed in St Petersburg or Paris. Despite the availability of art magazines and photographic reproduction, it appears that there was simply no great interest among the individual artistic movements, among journalists or among the reading public to widen the scope of artistic appreciation beyond national, or even city borders.

Immediately, one exception springs to mind: 1909 was the year of the publication of Marinetti's *Futurist Manifesto* in the Paris newspaper *Le Figaro*. We have already encountered this text in the previous chapter, but in the light of Woolf's claim it is important to recall his demand for 'the complete renewal of human sensibility brought about by the great discoveries of science. Those people who today make use of the telegraph, the telephone, the phonograph, the train, the bicycle, the motorcycle, the automobile, the ocean liner, the dirigible, the aeroplane, the cinema, the great newspaper (synthesis of a day in the world's life) do not realize that the various means of communication, transportation and information have a decisive influence on the psyche.' Most did not, perhaps, but there were some who were acutely attuned to this change.

Conservative circles were alarmed by such talk and what they considered its disastrous consequences for public morals. In 1910 Pope Pius X even went so far as to introduce a compulsory oath for all priests, forswearing modernism and its values. The wave of change that had been on the rise since the late 1890s had finally reached its high point, and art became a central battlefield in the age-old but newly embittered war between the ancients and the moderns.

1910 was a year during which the whiff of change and of intellectual experiment was particularly pungent. You could smell it, and while some felt in their nostrils an aroma of freedom and discovery, others thought they detected the stench of decadent Europe's rotting corpse. The generation born and educated during the prosperous and relatively peaceful 1880s and 1890s was now reaching maturity and began to articulate its own vision of life, its own rebellion against its fathers, coloured by a childhood that had been, for the first time in history, increasingly determined by a culture of professionalized administration, standardized education and mass consumption. Not for them the perfumed decadence of *l'art pour l'art*, the sensualist literalness of the Impressionists. Not for them the confident naturalism of Thomas Hardy, Theodor Fontane and Gustave Flaubert or the earnest campaigning of Emile Zola. Their view of things was shaped by reading about races in fast machines and in children's magazines, by overhearing adult whispers about nervous breakdowns and fast women, by a daily life increasingly dominated by cities, newspapers and an intense relation to the future, whatever it might bring. Their imagination was alert to the fact that an age had ended and a new one – by turns a promise and a menace – was bursting onto the scene, visible as yet only in flashes and fragmented visions. Their work was jagged, shot through with undigested rushes of information pushing their way into art as noise, collage or quotation; by splintered faces, swirling shapes and imploded personalities whose very essence turned out to be nothing but a wild conflagration of geometrical shapes, an exploding supernova of raw verbiage, a screech hurled from the stage.

Had human character changed? Could it ever change? These were the main questions asked by the artistic avant-garde. In view of the revolutionary execution of the works used to ask questions and give answers to them, the artists' response is perplexing, but only at first: No! they stated firmly, it has not, there is nothing new under the sun. Artists did not deny that something radically novel had occurred, that society had been transformed, or that their own lives had changed; their argument was at once more subtle and more forceful. Nietzsche had taught this generation that Christianity had been nothing but a perversion, making free people into slaves and bowing them under the yoke of theology and self-abnegation. It was this yoke the young artists were eager to throw off, the ties of a civilization whose galloping pace seemed to them nothing but a technologized continuation of the slave life of old. Human character had always been different: savage, primeval, mythological. The bourgeois individual was nothing but an ape dressed up in Manchester twill. Take away his suit and you discover the underlying nature of all things – take it away or go directly where no suits have ever been worn, and you will see that the human mind exists in its ancient, primordial form. Look for the deepest patterns, and you find yourself on a journey into the interior of humankind, a return to the sources, a search for the primitive, for ritual and myth.

Ritual, Myths and Masks

Even in an art world still capable of being scandalized, no outcry was so great as that erupting in 1913 during the first Paris performance of a ballet by a young Russian composer, Igor Stravinsky (1882–1971), who had already made a name for himself with two innovative virtuoso scores, *The Firebird* and *Petrushka*.

The ballet had been commissioned by Sergei Diaghilev (1872–1929), who had created the Ballets Russes company by an act of sheer will. Without any money himself, the young Russian had secured the financial backing of one of France's richest men, the banker Comte Greffulhe, whom he had persuaded to invite a whole ballet company, including all stage sets and costumes, to Paris. He reasoned that the project might be costly and might even make a loss, but that French banks had huge investments in Russia and that after the disastrous Russo-Japanese War and the subsequent revolution with its bloody suppression, French investors needed to be reassured that Russia was a civilized nation; a nation of great culture, a safe bet. Greffulhe was convinced and went to other bankers. Diaghilev got his money and threw himself into commissioning scores and stage decorations and generally spending huge amounts of his backers' funds on anything that took his fancy.

The first season of the Ballets Russes in 1909 was a success not least due to the brilliantly innovative and daring choreography by Michel Fokine, who had already made a name for himself in St Petersburg. From then on Diaghilev took his dancers on a European tour every year. The company was known for its innovative dance styles and sets, even though most of the ballets performed were traditional and were danced to music by established composers such as Alexander Borodin, Anton Arensky and Nikolai Rimsky-Korsakov. Stravinsky's first two ballets had been well received, but soon the composer and the impresario decided that something more daring was needed, something that would really capture the imagination.

Stravinsky had an idea: an 'old Russian' spring ritual, a sacrificial dance around a virgin who was to dance herself to death in a pagan welcome of the new season, with old men and women in ancient costumes, and with bands of young people erupting into ecstatic movement. He threw himself into the composition, working hard on the score while following the ballet company to oversee the performance of his other pieces. In 1912 the young Russian received fair warning of the Paris public's reaction to music it deemed scandalous. Diaghilev had allowed Nijinsky to perform an original choreography on the poem by the French composer Claude Debussy

(1862–1918), *L'Après-midi d'un faune*, a superbly impressionistic scene evoking a lazy afternoon spent by a Greek faun in pursuit of an adored nymph of whom he can capture no more than a veil left behind. The decoration by the company designer Léon Bakst took its cues from Greek vase painting, and the faun was danced by the company's star male lead, Vaslav Nijinsky. 'Nijinsky as the faun was thrilling,' recalled Lydia Sokolova, the only English member of the troupe.

> Although his movements were absolutely restrained, they were virile and powerful and the manner in which he caressed and carried the nymph's veil was so animal that one expected to see him run up the side of the hill with it in his mouth. There was an unforgettable moment just before his final amorous descent upon the scarf when he knelt on one leg on top of the hill; with his other leg stretched out behind him. Suddenly he threw back his head, opened his mouth and silently laughed. It was superb acting.

The public, however, was less concerned about the quality of the acting, than about that 'final amorous descent', during which Nijinsky draped himself over the scarf and mimed a very public, explicit act of masturbation in front of the Paris audience.

Outrage! Even during the performance people left the hall, and the reviews were overwhelmingly hostile. 'We have had a faun, incontinent, with vile movements of erotic bestiality and gestures of heavy shamelessness,' wrote Gaston Calmette, the powerful editor of *Le Figaro*, who described the mythical creature as 'an ill-made beast, hideous from the front, and even more hideous in profile', a description piqued by the fact that, to emphasize his character's intent and nature Nijinsky had chosen not to wear anything underneath his speckled costume tights, making the performance all the more explicitly virile and obscene. The 'too-expressive pantomime of the body' he had performed on stage really left very little to the imagination. 'These animal realities will never be accepted by the true public,' Calmette opined, no doubt identifying true taste with that of the Paris set.

Stravinsky, meanwhile, was working like a man possessed. He completed his own highly intricate score by the end of the year. 'Today 4/14.IX.1912 Sunday with an unbearable toothache I finished the music of the Sacre. I. Strav. Clarens, Chatelard Hotel,' he had scrawled in his notebook. If he himself was convinced that this was great music, music that had never been written before, not everyone else was equally enthusiastic. The designated conductor, Pierre Monteux, was more than sceptical when the composer demonstrated the piece to him:

Stravinsky sat down to play a piano reduction of the entire score. Before he got very far, I was convinced he was raving mad. Heard this way, without the colour of the orchestra, which is one of its greatest distinctions, the crudity of the rhythm was emphasized, its stark primitiveness underlined. The very walls resounded as Stravinsky pounded away, occasionally stamping his feet and jumping up and down to accentuate the force of the music. Not that it needed much emphasis... My only comment at the end was that such music would surely cause a scandal.

The conductor's scepticism was echoed by the orchestra's. The incessant time changes, discordant keys played concurrently and dissonant motifs clashing in all instrumental groups made them unsure whether their parts were correct. During the rehearsals, some of the musicians simply laughed. Seated at the piano, Stravinsky furiously defended his music, playing, counting, shouting instructions to the singers, and insisting on every detail, every rhythmic complexity.

Then came the performance. The art nouveau auditorium of the newly built Théâtre des Champs-Elysées was filled to capacity, and the public was in a good mood, comfortably settled in for an evening's worth of beautiful dancing after a pleasant first piece, danced on point and in classic white tutus. When the music of the *Sacre* started, however, it was clear from the very first bars that this was something unheard of. A high-pitched melody floated through the air, played on a bassoon, an instrument designed for a much lower range. In the audience, the composer Camille Saint-Saëns, a superb craftsman but never known as an avant-gardist, jumped up and left his seat. 'If that's a bassoon I'm a baboon!' he hissed to his neighbour as he got up. Shortly afterwards all hell broke loose. 'During the first two minutes the public remained quiet,' Monteux later recalled, 'then there were boos and hissing from the upper circle, soon after from the stalls. People sitting next to one another began to hit one another on the head with fists and walking sticks, or whatever else they had to hand. Soon, their anger was turned against the dancers and especially against the orchestra... Everything to hand was thrown at them, but we continued playing.' The chaos was complete when members of the audience turned on one another, on anyone supporting the other side. A heavily bejewelled lady was seen slapping her neighbour before storming off, while another one spat in her detractor's face. Fights broke out everywhere and challenges to duels were issued.

Monteux had been firmly instructed to keep on playing, no matter what was happening behind him, but soon the ruckus was so loud that the dancers could no longer hear the orchestra. A panicked Stravinsky left his seat in the stalls and ran backstage, where he found the work's choreographer, Nijinsky, hanging precariously from one of the wings and yelling instructions to the dancers in Russian. To keep Nijinsky from falling onto the stage, the delicately built and myopic composer held on to his coat tails while the music unfolded, almost drowned out by the rioting audience. Meanwhile Monteux and the musicians were concentrating desperately on the complexities of the score, playing as if their lives depended on it.

The *Sacre du printemps* was a revolutionary piece, not only in its orchestration and its use of instruments, but in its entire conception. Traditional structure had been abandoned. Instead, different motifs and passages assailed the listener with unexpected force. There were drumming, stomping rhythms for which percussion and strings formed a block of terrifying sounds; woodwinds that were by turns discordant, plangent and archaically stern; aggressive and often brutal interruptions from the brass, then sudden total silence. Meandering flutes and shimmering shoals of trills led to insistent, almost ecstatic sections during which the entire orchestra was strained to the limits of its capacity: a heaving mass of precisely calculated cross-rhythms, moments of strange beauty and eerie calm followed by eruptions of tremendous force, folk motifs and pilgrims' choirs hard on the heels of feverish syncopations, a pitiless ritual during which the visceral force of the dance was as audible as were birdsong and the victim's shrieks. Music would never be as it had been before. Gaston Calmette, who had already criticized Debussy's faun, now railed against 'the strange spectacle of a laborious and puerile barbarism', another critic called the piece *le massacre du printemps*. Even the most progressive journalists were politely shocked: the artsy journal *Excelsior* commented daintily: 'the most interesting guests do not always lead to happy finds: this seems to be the case for the new pantomime created at the Théâtre des Champs-Elysées by the troupe of M. Serge de Diaghilev. One has to pay homage to his inventive audacity: one can go no further.' One young listener, Jean Cocteau, noted with genuine enthusiasm that he felt 'uprooted' by the piece. 'Beauty speaks to the guts. Genius cannot be analysed any better than electricity. One has it, or one does not. Stravinsky does... The Russian troupe has taught me that one must burn oneself up alive in order to be reborn...' To Cocteau's perceptive mind, the genius which uprooted him from his thoroughly bourgeois identity was an electric phenomenon, a shock to the nerves that burned up everything old in order to make a new culture rise from the ashes.

Stravinsky's fascination with archaic ritual was shared by other artists, particularly in his native Russia, and while the composer himself had been content to crib folk motifs for his music from an anthology of songs edited by his teacher Rimsky-Korsakov, others went further in their search for authentic folk art and for a mythological way of thinking. In 1889, the legal scholar Vassily Kandinsky (1866–1944) had joined scientists on a journey to the Urals in order to study the customs of the Komi people. There he had developed a fascination for their shamanic rites and the abstract religious symbols used to decorate ritual items and objects of daily use. When Kandinsky decided to abandon law and to turn to painting in 1896, the symbolic language of the Komi shamans became the driving force of his work. He moved to Munich, where he met another gifted painter, Gabriele Münter (1877–1962), who not only became his lover, but also moved in with the Russian, who was still married at the time.

During the next fifteen years, Kandinsky moved away from a somewhat soupy late Impressionist style and found a much more individual and archaic visual language, in which the rattles and drums of the shamans, with the figures of birds and snakes used in their incantations, resurfaced on the canvas, creating a graphic universe that went beyond the conventions of painting, or rather, pre-dated them. These symbols held universal significance, Kandinsky felt: they had the power to stir collective memories of an existence before electricity and cars, before cities, before civilization itself. The critical reaction to works like these was overwhelmingly hostile, as some of Kandinsky's German colleagues discovered after an exhibition in 1911. A reviewer for the *Kölnische Zeitung* gave them a broadside of conservative aesthetics:

> The pictures are impossible to supersede in the uselessness of their design and are nothing but garishly coloured games played by these cannibals. Looked at as painting they are the end of art, a prank. But they show a more nefarious side. The modern phrase that the object of art is indifferent, is abused here in a truly malevolent way ... What is presented to us breathes the poison breath of the darkest places of vice of the big city and shows the constitution of the artists, which can only be understood in terms of pathology.

Elsewhere, things were hardly better. London critics scoffed at the post-Impressionists presented to them by Roger Fry; in 1905, a Paris reviewer coolly concluded of an exhibition by Matisse: 'He has thrown a pot of paint into his public's face,' and the French Fauvist painters got their group name when the journalist Louis Vaucelles spotted an Italianate-looking and very tame bronze of a nude woman surrounded by the avant-gardist canvases and exclaimed: *Donatello chez les fauves!* (Donatello among the savages!) The name stuck.

Although Kandinsky had chosen to settle in Germany, his development towards what might be called shamanic abstraction had strong parallels in Russia, where a whole generation of young artists sought different ways of approaching and portraying nature. In Moscow, Mikhail Fyodorovich Larionov (1881–1964) created strong, simplistic figures inspired by Russian folk art – figures like prehistoric cave paintings, reduced to the very essentials, and speaking, not without irony, of the essentials of life: sex, food, man, woman. His lover Natalia Sergeeva Goncharova (1881–62) was equally enthralled by peasant art and created vivid tableaux as well as archaic portraits. Nobody, however, moved as fast and as far as Kasimir Severinovich Malevich (1878–1935), who assimilated all artistic currents of his time and arrived at the most austere of abstractions (see plate section). To Malevich, the world and imagery of peasant art and imagination was a touchstone of authenticity and a way out of the oversophisticated imagery practised by the previous generation of painters. His portraits of peasants and wood-cutters show figures like tree trunks, monumental and tubular, like gods from a lost mythology, grown out of the soil of Mother Russia. After completing a series of these canvases, Malevich turned to his own time and the life of modernity. If he had reduced peasants to figures of primeval force, his city people were splintered up in countless fragments, unrecognizable behind bits of writing and shreds of images, half covered by curious symbols (a fish, a sabre, a wooden spoon), powerless against the vortex of information and speed sucking them into its dark core.

Malevich's technique and stylistic development were mirrored almost exactly by those of a painter from the other extremity of Europe, the young Catalan Pablo Picasso (1881–1973), who also discovered the force of primitive forms and the disintegration of the subject as means of artistic expression. Malevich, however, drew his inspiration from Russian peasant art, while Picasso was influenced by a very different aesthetic world. For the young painter (his magnificently Catholic full name was Pablo Diego José Francisco de Paula Juan Nepomuceno María de los Remedios Cipriano de la Santísima Trinidad Clito Rula y Picasso), the move to Paris had been an escape from what he felt to be the provincial narrowness of Barcelona. In his new home, his exuberant talent exploded in a multitude of forms and styles. Picasso drew inspiration from everywhere: from predecessors like Cézanne and from advertising, from travelling circuses and from curiosities sold in junk shops. Among the latter were African carvings brought back by troops stationed in West Africa and sold in the harbours for a few drinks. Nobody thought of them as possessing any value, either aesthetic or financial, and while those who had served in the colonies might put them on the

*Eat Drink Man
Woman: Mikhail
Larionov reduced
life to its most
primitive
elements.*

wall together with Berber carpets, hunting trophies and selected sabres and pistols, nobody gave them another thought.

Picasso did. He was startled by them and bought as many as his meagre earnings would allow him. Their rough-cut shapes, irregular symmetry and powerful simplification seemed to him the only possible answer to the over-refined aesthetics of bourgeois taste with its floating nymphs, art nouveau girls and dainty plants, its endless allegories and innocent nudity, its beauty and its mind-numbing technical perfection. Totally indifferent to what these African items might have meant in their own culture, what their significance and symbolism were, Picasso used the formal repertoire of tribal art for his own ends. In the masks he recognized the unchanging structure of the human condition, underneath what appeared to be personal; an individual reduced to a sign, a cypher stripped of anything unique.

This new and profoundly sceptical vision of civilization was first and most fully realized in his *Les Demoiselles d'Avignon* (see plate section), a large canvas of brutal and disturbing bluntness which, much like Stravinsky's *Sacre du printemps*, did everything to hide its underlying technical and compositional virtuosity. Created in 1907, the scene is the interior of a brothel, with naked prostitutes posing for a client. The women, though, are unlike anything that had been seen before in art. Their exposed bodies are reduced to geometrical components, barely hinting at arm and leg, breast and crotch. The faces consist of nothing more than black lines on the colour of the flesh. The woman to the right seems to have an African mask growing out of her skull, while the figure in front, squatting, is completely disfigured, her eyes at different heights, her nose grown into a line at once monstrous and abstract – a reminder, perhaps, of the terrible ravages of syphilis.

Both Picasso and his friend and colleague Georges Braque (1882–1963) found this technique of dissolving fluent shapes into seemingly archaic elements a powerful means of appropriating reality and articulating their response to life in metropolitan Paris. While it could be used to reduce individuals to archetypes, and quotidian reality to myth, breaking down complex forms into simple constituents could also do the opposite: it could show what modern life was like by looking at it with ancient eyes. Until well into the Middle Ages, a painting has been understood to represent more than just a single moment; it was seen to represent a spiritual essence. Thus an altar could depict the entire process of Christ's passion, all twelve Stations of the Cross with the figure of Jesus in them, on a single panel – a progression in time seen as a progression through space. Following on where Cézanne had left off, Picasso and Braque's 'Cubist' paintings now applied the same principle to modern, secular subjects. By showing a face or a figure from several different angles at once they destroyed the formal coherence of their subject as well as any sense of a particular moment or place. But in so doing, they hoped to capture an essence, to see all its facets from all sides, to perceive something more profoundly true than what is possible for one chained to one perspective and one spot in time and space.

At the same time the language of Cubism was a powerful way of conveying another message: in the modern city people were no longer in one piece, as Malevich's monumental peasants were. They were composite, splintered and pasted figures, made up of scraps of this and parts of that, not a fully grown entity but an almost random conflation of elements and disparate points of view. The very opposite of his explosive friend Picasso, Georges Braque was a methodical, intellectual man who worked slowly and deliberately. He was sensitive to the theoretical implications of painting, to the fascinating paradoxes implicit in recreating a three-dimensional world in two dimensions, in the tension between illusion and symbolic representation, in depicting a mere moment out of the work of months, and of artistic creation in a world increasingly dominated by industrial design, utilitarian shapes, advertising and mass reproduction. The son of a decorative painter and furniture restorer, Braque used wood imitations in his paintings, more by way of an open question to the viewer than with any intention of deceiving the eye. He was particularly fascinated by violins, no doubt not simply because of their rounded shape and the contrast of the straight lines of the strings and the curves of sides and scroll, but also because the violin was an instrument designed to be heard and not seen, the challenge to the painter being essentially one of translating the language of sound into that of vision. In his *Man with Violin* (1912), Braque reflects on several of these ideas. Hovering above the multi-faceted shape of the violin, the figure of the player is a mere ghost, the idea of a player hinted at with the outlines of robotic eyes, mouth and nose. The man seems stunned, submerged by the sounds swirling around him in the shape of fragmentary

Invaded and fragmented: Braque's Man with Violin
cannot defend his contours against outside forces.

musical notations. It is not so much a portrait of a person as of an experience, and a disquieting one, as the human form is the least certain element of the composition, dissolved as it is in the shapes and sounds of its surroundings.

This fragmentation of identities was further reinforced by contemporary influences such as cinema. As effective cutting and trick photography became standard features of the movies, the way people were thinking about stories changed. Writers and painters began to imitate the rapid shifts of perspective and the disjunction found in films. Ortega y Gasset's epistemological claim that the only possible way of seeing the world was that of a multitude of individual vantage points began to sound like a theory of cinema, and the floating enchantment of the stream of consciousness in authors like Luigi Pirandello, Arthur Schnitzler and Andrei Bely sees the world through the eye of a camera, recording random details and impressions and letting them merge into vivid ideas. The self, Ernst Mach had claimed, was nothing but an accumulation of sensations and experiences.

Influenced by the sequential photography developed by Eadweard Muybridge and Thomas Eakins, which split up a single movement into its constituent parts, the French painter Marcel Duchamp (1887–1968) anatomized human sensation with his path-breaking *Nude Descending a Staircase*

Leapfrog, sliced: Sequential photographs such as this one by Thomas Eakins were a source of inspiration for avant-garde painting.

Number 2 (1912), which showed a classic subject of painting, a female nude, fanned out into the many facets of a moment, half analytical, half romantic, and wholly ironic. The work was regarded with suspicion by colleagues like Picasso and Braque, who sensed that it represented an independent departure from the Cubist creed. One year later, in 1913, the nude was presented at the Armory Show in New York and it succeeded in stirring up considerable scandal. Like the Italian Futurist Giacomo Balla, Duchamp had incorporated the passage of time into a single canvas, pointing again to an age-old paradox of painting, the relation between a depicted instant and the time it takes to create a work, between being true to life and true to art. Duchamp's canvas showed that being true to empirical experience changed not only what was seen, but also how it could be translated into feelings and experiences. The work challenged viewers to ask how one can fall in love with a series of moving shapes and how moments of sensation become experience or personality.

In the real world, the fragmentary, episodic nature of existence went hand in hand with the rush and inconstancy of fashion and the imperious

Conquering time:
Duchamp's Nude
Descending a Staircase
captured a sequence of
movement on a single
canvas.

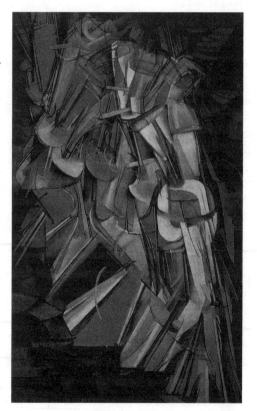

demands of industrial developments, sweeping away with an iron broom everything that was not up-to-the-minute. Despite rising life expectancy and increased choice, life had never felt more transient, more fragile. To many of those who felt this fragility, those struggling for respectability, the past suddenly seemed like a promised land of stability and belonging.

Let us return to the fascination of the primitive. Henri Matisse (1869–1954) did not have the existential drive of a Picasso or Braque's analytical bent. His work shows that he was simply too glad to be alive to waste much of his energy on intellectual analyses of things that seemed so clear to him under the vivid Mediterranean sun of his southern French retreat. But while Matisse's mind was not set on analysing modernity or taking an axe to the human form and cutting it out of the colours as one might carve a canoe from a tree, his own paradise was definitely set in an archaic world – one long and languid *après-midi d'un faune*, with a kinder look at humanity and its potential. The nude figures in his large canvas *Bonheur de vivre* (see plate section) breathe the aestival ease of an imagined meeting between the sensuality of Greek gods and the simple joys of life during prehistoric times. The goats to the right are like remnants of cave paintings from Altamira (a Spanish cave whose ancient carvings had been recently dated as 15,000-year-old masterpieces), while the gesture and manner of the young goatherd is inspired by Greek vase painting.

Searching Far and Near

Like many artists, Matisse saw beauty and happiness in a pre-civilized state of man, a return to his roots. Civilization and modernity stood for speed and neurasthenia, for questioned identities, feeble minds and unsound bodies. Matisse dreamt himself into a colour-saturated Eden in which such a happy life before the fall could become true. Others were not content to dream; a small but steady stream of artists set out to find this earthly paradise, whether in artists' colonies and communities or on voyages abroad, where they could study cultures unsullied by European modernity, and perhaps could throw off the shackles of bourgeois morality. French artists had the great advantage of French Algiers and French-dominated Morocco on their doorstep (sub-Saharan Africa was too remote, too foreign), and many made use of this enticing opportunity.

The German painter August Macke (1887–1914) and the Swiss Paul Klee (1879–1940) travelled to Tunisia in 1914 and came back with sketchbooks full of vivid colour and semi-abstract shapes; Matisse had been in Tangiers in 1912 and richly profited from seeing the colours, the traditional crafts and decorations, and the apparently simpler life of the North Africans. For those who could not make the journey themselves, an exhibition of Islamic art held in Munich in 1910 brought a new aesthetic universe into one of the nerve centres of the European avant-garde.

Many artists followed the call of a more 'natural' life abroad, partly in the footsteps of the pioneers of the previous generation. Paul Gauguin, one of the stars of the 1910 London post-Impressionist exhibition, had shown the joys of the South Seas to European art lovers. Embarking on an almost mystical quest to redeem himself through passion and lucidity, the sensualist French novelist André Gide had found the courage to follow his amorous instincts during repeated stays in Algiers. Gide loved boys, and many men of independent means chose north Africa or southern Italy to indulge their forbidden passions: the German photographer Wilhelm von Gloeden in his villa in Taormina in Sicily; Friedrich Alfred Krupp in Capri. In all cases, the travellers' interest was aroused not only by a different attitude to sex – homosexual or otherwise – in different cultures, but by a different attitude to sensuality and to emotions, as Gide himself had written in his autobiographical account *Si le grain ne meurt* (If It Die, 1926, transl., 1927):

> In the name of which god, which ideal do you forbid me to live according to my nature? – And that nature, where would it take me, if I simply followed it? Until then I had accepted Christ's morality... In order to force myself into submitting to it I had wound up with a profound disarray of my entire being.

The search for a primordial, 'natural' morality did not necessarily have to lead its adepts abroad either physically or in their imagination.

The largely rural and often underdeveloped, almost medieval ways of living preserved in Eastern Europe offered a foreign country within national borders to many in search of authenticity. In 1905 the composers and musicologists Béla Bartók (1881–1945) and Zoltán Kodály (1882–1967) travelled through the hinterland of their native Hungary in an attempt to document Magyar and gypsy folk melodies. The music resulting from this expedition into a rural world outside of classical tonal systems and formal constraints resulted in a new musical aesthetic expressed in their own composition; a music with jagged edges, as unfamiliar to the ear as were Stravinsky's sounds. Theirs was not the gentle folk concert paraphrases and orchestral music made popular by Liszt and Brahms, Dvořák and Tchaikovsky during the late nineteenth century. This music, as well as that of the Czech Leoš Janáček (1854–1928), did not seek to adorn elaborate high art music with subtle and exotic touches. Rather, the composers wanted to change art music, to reform ways of hearing by reverting to the often stark, unfamiliar and dissonant sounds of folk music which, they surmised, was as yet untouched by the sickly gloss of Western life.

The search for a national culture with ancient roots had political aspects, of course. Throughout the nineteenth century, folk motifs in music and painting, folk stories, fairy tales and little-used languages had been used as means of proclaiming a national identity, and artists vied in their championship of the national idea, famously in the case of the Czech composers Smetana and Dvořák, whose national styles divided the Czechs into two musical camps but united them in their defiance of Vienna. Now the political edge of national revival grew sharper, particularly when it went in search of a prehistoric past. German-speaking artists of the avant-garde were singularly uninterested in the Germanic past. Painters such as Emil Nolde (1867–1956) and Max Pechstein (1881–1955) created canvases depicting ecstatic dances by groups of girls and women which had all the energy of a spring sacrifice or even a witches' Sabbath, but it was impossible to say whether they hailed from German forests or a Tahitian beach.

The tension between the alienation of urban life and the nostalgia for an idealized, simpler past was particularly acute for many assimilated Jews, who found themselves caught between a Western world in which they did their utmost to excel and be accepted, and the seemingly timeless way of living of the shtetl, which was still in the memory of older members of their family. For most Jews the memory of poverty in the ghettos was still too recent to be romanticized; the pull of full citizenship in Western society too strong. It is significant that many Jewish artists and intellectuals from this time had the heightened sensitivity of the outsider and were eager to seize on questions of custom, class and origin, but with exceptions such as Marc Chagall and Martin Buber they rarely ever did so by invoking the Jewish past their families had left behind. Gustav Mahler used Austrian folk tunes, military music and German folk poems in his symphonies and songs, not klezmer tunes. Sigmund Freud would later write about Moses, but he drew the mythological archetypes of his psychoanalytic work from Greek mythology, not from the Bible.

The God of Ecstasy

Freud was one of many intellectuals at the time who tried to draw refreshing water from the deep fountains of ancient Greece. What better remedy for a tired civilization clogged by a legacy of stifling Christian values than to resort to its pre-Christian founding myths? What impulse could be more natural for a generation educated in Latin and Greek at humanist schools, a generation who knew more about the Peloponnesian wars than about any other conflict in history? Nietzsche, that great prophet of renewal and an author every single self-respecting person of intelligence had read, had been a professor of classics, of course, and he had demanded that the ecstatic, often destructive Dionysian element be given a higher place in culture, as a counterweight to the cold crystal stare of Apollo and Athena.

Among those who revisited the Greeks and cast them in their own image was the Austrian essayist and dramatist Hugo von Hofmannsthal. Begged for a new challenge by the German star actress Gertrud Eysoldt, he had turned to Sophocles' tragedy *Electra* as inspiration for a play by the same name. Work progressed well, and after only three weeks of writing, a delighted Hofmannsthal could dispatch a manuscript to the actress who was known for her daring roles, and for giving her all in every performance. Her reaction was immediate and intense, as she confessed in an appropriately dramatic letter to him:

> Tonight I have taken home your Electra and I have just finished reading it. I am lying here broken – I am suffering – I cry out oppressed by this violence – I am afraid of my own strength, of the torture that awaits me. I will suffer terribly [while playing Electra] … You have written with my own burning life – you have formed from my blood the possibilities of wild dreams – and I have been living here suspecting nothing … this *infinitely inflamed* will of my blood [*all dies* unendlich brünstige *Willen meines Blutes*].
>
> I recognize everything – I am terribly shocked [by my recognition] – I am horrified. I am struggling – I am afraid.

What was the actress so afraid of? Hofmannsthal had indeed written a shocking drama, a 'bloody furor with style', as the famous critic Alfred Kerr put it after its first performance in 1904. Electra's entire existence is centred on revenging the murder of her heroic father Agamemnon, killed by his own wife (Electra's mother) and her lover. Like Hamlet, she wants to right a wrong, but unlike Hamlet she is entirely consumed by her own murderous feelings and has sacrificed her entire life's hopes in her determination to slay her mother and her mother's lover: The public was shocked to see a woman baying for blood, a woman torn by overwhelming emotions – not of hysteria, or loyalty or the defence of girlhood purity. From ancient myth, Hofmannsthal had created a new kind of woman: dangerous, forceful, and devastatingly passionate – everything, in fact, that women were not supposed to be; and he had gone further. In the Greek original, Electra had been the instrument of divine revenge and the real drama and the responsibility for human acts were thus played out on Olympus. In the new version, however, this reassuring dimension had been erased and all passion, all madness and all lust had been put into the minds and souls of the protagonists themselves. Electra is neither a tool of higher forces nor a woman on a righteous quest; she is a woman tortured by violent, bloody urges over which she has lost all control:

> I have sowed darkness
> and harvested lust over lust.
> I was a black corpse
> among the living, and this hour
> I am the fire of life and my flame
> burns up the darkness of the world.
> My face must be more white
> than the white-hot face of the moon.
> When one looks at me,
> he must receive death or must
> perish with lust.
> Do you see my face?
> Do you see the light I radiate?

The real scandal was the rage and the lust: a woman as an agent and not one acted upon, a woman of strong, indomitable passion. The effect on the public was extraordinary, electrifying. Within four days of the first performance at the avant-garde Berlin Kleines Theater under Max Reinhardt's direction, twenty-two other German theatres asked for permission to stage *Elektra* and three editions of the text were sold out within weeks.

Hofmannsthal was adamant that his Greece was not the whitewashed utopia so dear to the nineteenth century, but a much darker place without 'historicizing banalities', as he made clear in the stage directions: 'The character of the set is marked by narrowness, inevitablility, enclosedness. The stage painter will aim in the right direction ... if he lets himself be led by the atmosphere of a densely crowded city house ... instead of conventional temples and palaces.'

The piece's shattering effect was intensified when the composer Richard Strauss (1864–1949) asked Hofmannsthal to adapt the text for an opera. When the resulting work was premiered in Dresden in 1909, the result was unparalleled scandal. Instead of softening the impact with the voluptuous texture of his late-Romantic tone poems, Strauss put his music entirely at the service of amplifying the emotional charge, thus making it all the more frightening. In the very first scene a cry rang out throughout the theatre as the orchestra worked like a hundred-armed machine designed to magnify murderous madness; there were no conventional arias, only a seething mass of soaring emotion, a music that dramatized a woman's passion without condemning it (Electra's meeting with her long-lost brother Orestes in the third act contains some of the most lyrical, most intimate operatic moments written in the twentieth century), only to tip once more into the frenzy of revenge. The public was not comforted by easy beauty. Electra's emotional chaos filled the evening.

Reviewers were outraged at the artists' temerity. 'The noble images of these women, which classical poets drew with eternal traits, have been distorted and perverted by these "modernizers",' complained one, while others predictably accused Hofmannsthal's Electra of being 'a sadistic megaera [one of the three Furies in Greek mythology], almost a lesbian'. The fears articulated in the face of this wild woman are obvious, particularly the accusation of lesbianism levelled, then as now, at female strength. It is man's ultimate fear: his total sidelining, becoming superfluous. The Viennese essayist Hermann Bahr had understood this, and more: 'The tragedy wants nothing different from those two doctors [Sigmund Freud and his mentor Josef Breuer]; it reminds a people diseased by its own culture of things the people does not want to be reminded of, of its evil effects which it hides, of earlier, savage man still lurking and grinding his teeth beneath the façade of the educated person.'

The mythological monster threatening the orderly appearance of civilized humanity was often a topic for art. But while painters of the nineteenth century had often used motifs from mythology as a convenient excuse for exotic drapery and a little tantalizing flesh, the new generation wanted to expose not only the body, but also the hidden corners of the mind. Vienna's fragile truce between dream and reality became an ideal stage for fantasies of this kind: Oskar Kokoschka's illustrated poem *Die träumenden Knaben* (The Dreaming Boys, 1908) created a dangerous reverie suspended between Arcadian innocence and sexual tension; Ferdinand Hodler's canvases seemed to record ancient pagan rites; the poet and graphic artist Alfred Kubin showed Mars, the god of war, as a blind and savage giant with Greek helmet and shield, crushing armies under his monstrous, rock-like boots.

Nobody went further in this reinterpretation of Greek mythology than Gustav Klimt, whose Greek goddesses radiated a dangerous erotic charge. No classic equilibrium, no Olympian calm here. 'All art is erotic,' Klimt

Suspended reverie: Kokoschka's dreaming children are isolated and charged with tension.

had proclaimed, and the obvious sensualism vibrating in his forms and colours seems a fitting tribute to the sex-obsessed deities of Greek myth. Klimt's panels fot Vienna University's great hall had caused outrage. Their iconography and composition flatly contradicted everything a public institution was seen to represent. His aim was not to use classical drapery for modern efficiency; on the contrary, even when faced with the most modern motif, he wanted to strip away the veneer of convention and emotional containment, to expose the primeval passion underneath.

In its effort to expose the primeval in the everyday, Klimt's impertinent gaze, at once that of a satyr and a philosopher, stopped at nothing. His portrait of nine-year-old *Mäda Primavesi* (1912) probes deeply into the observing mind itself (see plate section). The image shows a pretty child surrounded by her toys, but as the eye fastens on the detail, invisible cracks open all over the canvas and the spectator is drawn into a vortex of disturbing force. First there is the girl's face. Is it not too old, too knowing for a nine-year-old? It is, rather, the face of a grown woman who has seen everything, who anticipates and invites everything. She challenges the spectator with her insolent stare, her right hand on her hip, and her feet set far apart. The onlooker becomes accomplice to the immoral artist. He is the observer

The god of death: Kubin's visionary work shows the dangers of exaggerated manliness.

who looks into his own outrageous soul, even as he views what is in front of him. Klimt sees the future woman in the child and his gaze is subtly salacious, scandalously probing her growing girlhood and his own response. Like Röntgen's X-rays, his eyes undress the girl while the spectator looks on, and from her feet a line, barely visible, traces the outline of the thighs until it reaches the point, above the ruffles in the dress, where the sex is clearly visible through the white gauze. Nothing is innocent here. The dress of conventional morality is little more than a titillation to the senses of those who have learned to see through it, to see pink, naked flesh underneath the starched propriety.

Did human character change, after all, in or around December 1910?

A large part of the European avant-garde answered resoundingly that no, human character had not changed, nor could it. But it had been diverted from its true course temporarily by the emotional repression imposed by Christianity, by two thousand years of denial and combat against passion, against eros, against all that is authentic and unconstrained within the human mind. The result, wrote anthropologists and psychoanalysts, philosophers and poets, was the alienation of the human mind from its own emotions, of head from heart; the result as painted by Picasso and Klimt, Malevich and Braque, was the cowed life of the urban professional and the slaves of industry, castrated by the huge engines of capitalism; the result, said Stravinsky and Bartók, was the need to reacquaint the tired ears of modern audiences with the harsh vitality of archaic sounds from an imagined age of truth.

Human character, then, had not changed. A new generation of artists and intellectuals was trying to recapture what they felt had always been there: the undying essence of humanity which had been obscured underneath the teachings of Christian morality and its legitimate, if secular, successor, the bourgeoisie, as described in 1904 by the German sociologist Max Weber (1864–1920). A man of immense intellectual power whose manic-depressive nature did not allow him to publish the *opera magna* he attempted to write, Weber was a perfect example of his class and age: hard-working and highly professional but constantly beset by sexual anxieties and 'neurasthenic' episodes which paralysed his capacity for work so badly that he had to abandon a brilliant university career. Living on the emotional knife edge of his time, Weber was sensitized to seeing and understanding the mechanism that kept society functioning. Weber's most seminal work was somewhat uninspiringly entitled *Die protestantische Ethik und der 'Geist' des Kapitalismus* (*The Protestant Work Ethic and the Spirit of Capitalism,* 1904–5). It created a framework for the understanding of modern society and the way in which human character had been changed by it. Having demonstrated the disproportionate success of Protestant and particularly Calvinist societies and individuals (and, we might add, of Jews) in economic life, Weber explained this fact with a stroke of analytic genius: whereas Catholicism forced the faithful into asceticism and the sublimation of their desire for salvation in the next world, the Calvinist doctrine of divine grace given to or withheld from the individual from the beginning conveniently interpreted success in this world as implying godliness. Success in business became proof of divine grace. At the same time, however, indulging human weakness by displaying wealth and living in luxury was seen as debauchery and decadence. Money, therefore, must be earned to be sure of God's blessing, but it must not be spent. It is to be invested and grown; thus capitalism is born. Workers may be exploited; the very fact that they live in miserable poverty is a strong indication that divine grace has been withheld from them.

A specifically 'citizen' economic ethic had grown up. With the consciousness of standing in the fullness of God's grace and being visibly blessed by Him, the citizen business man, as long as he remained within the bounds of formal correctness, as long as his moral conduct was spotless and the use to which he put his wealth was not objectionable, could follow his pecuniary interests as he would and feel that he was ful-filling a duty in doing so. The power of religious asceticism provided him in addition with sober, conscientious, and unusually industrious workmen, who clung to their work as to a life purpose willed by God.

Weber's spirit of capitalism admirably describes the mind-set of the stereo-typical capitalist exploiter, of the striving middle classes, of money breeding money. It also, however, shows a system based on asceticism, on repression of emotions for the sake of a higher goal.

It is easy to see how Freud's analysis follows on from Weber's: the sup-pression of natural urges is a necessary precondition for capitalist success, but while it is productive for the group and its wealth, such an approach will eventually exact its revenge on the individual. Emotions locked away since early childhood could not be exorcized according to the model of a Christian education (centred on beating the Devil and the legacy of original sin out of the child). The suppressed elements were still there, festering in the dark, and would eventually erupt in a series of dreams, psychoses and physical symptoms, making their way to the surface in the only way they could. Salvation, psychoanalysis taught, lay in becoming aware of these denied impulses and according them their place within the mental whole. This, too, was a return to the source, to a view of humanity before repression, man before the Fall.

Have we moved too far from Virginia Woolf and her ruddy-cheeked cook bursting into the living room with a new hat? Not at all. Woolf had written that in Victorian times the cook 'lived like a leviathan in the lower depths, formidable, silent, obscure, inscrutable', and is this not the perfect image for a life force suppressed in the economic organism of the bourgeois house? If the new generation of cooks were creatures of 'sunshine and fresh air' they were also (Woolf's irony aside) creatures of a new time in which life forces were let out, corsets fell from fashion, nature and light were wor-shipped as never before. What better image for psychological liberation (and its attendant perils) than Leviathan dragged out of the darkness and exposed to sunshine and fresh air? To Woolf, human character had changed simply because it was beginning to revert to a more natural, more ancient form of expression.

What Virginia Woolf wrote about writers in the 1920s as heirs to 1910, 'grammar is violated; syntax disintegrated', was already true for painters and composers before 1914. If they wanted to depict both the reality of life in the nerve-racking metropolis and the possibility of a return to an earlier way of being, they needed to adapt their language to the challenge. The many-faceted, artificially composed, industrially clothed, ideological and politicized self of a modern city-dweller could be portrayed only by mirroring this fragmented state, by holding a shattered mirror up to personalities constantly on the verge of shattering themselves. To evoke what might have been and what might be possible again, artists needed to find an idiom radically unlike that of the Western tradition which had, after all, also been the tradition of repression, of Christianity and of capitalism. Raw and dissonant sounds, extreme passions, rough-hewn figures and rigid masks were needed to expose and then smash through the polite sophistication of the bourgeois self immured in its rules and prohibitions. Not so much changed as freed, human character would certainly never be quite the same again.

12

1911:
People's Palaces

Here comes the New Man, demoralizing himself with a halfpenny
newspaper.   – George Bernard Shaw

Reality seems valueless by comparison with the dreams of fevered
imaginations.   – Emile Durkheim

The search for archaic authenticity in art was the obsession of a brilliant
few. Meanwhile, many millions of people rushed into the arms of an
age of unprecedented comforts and excitements, of things previously
beyond their reach. Intellectuals might dream of a rejuvenation of culture
from its ancient roots, for ways out of capitalist society, but most of their
contemporaries were looking for a way in: to get enough to eat, better lodgings, a decent job, a good wage, a suit, a car, a novel entertainment. And
they got entertainment, nowhere more accessible than in the rapidly developing movie theatres that went from little backrooms and converted cafés
and pubs to great palaces, temples of popular diversion.

The greatest of these was a converted hippodrome in Paris, the
3,400-seat Gaumont Palace on the place de Clichy, which opened its doors
to the awed public in 1911. The excitement was captured by Abel Truchet, a
genre painter who specialized in Paris and Montmartre street scenes.
Wonderful contrasts are at the heart of this image: the greatest sanctuary of
film as the subject of an oil painting; the façade illuminated by electric
lighting; the horse-drawn cabs unloading their passengers; the black of the
streaming crowd against the sulphur tones of the brightly lit cinema.
Through the large windows in front one can almost see the sky-blue
decoration of the vast audience hall with its long curved rows of seats and
its enormous balcony, its orchestra pit in which a full complement of
musicians not only played during intermissions, but also accompanied the

The façade of cheap dreams: the Gaumont Palace cinema in Paris, the largest in the world.

films, and with sound effects produced by specialized *bruiteurs*, or noise-makers.

Léon Gaumont (1864–1946) and his competitors, the Pathé brothers, were the biggest players in French cinema, and, in fact, the biggest world-wide producers of films and photographic equipment, as well as the owners of the largest chains of cinemas. Before the War, cinema – a newfangled entertainment that quickly developed an audience in the tens of millions – was almost exclusively French. Moving pictures had been invented and developed in several places, and in parallel: Edison's kinetoscope had been presented in Chicago in 1893, the *cinématographe* designed by the brothers Lumière, and the bioscope constructed by the Skladanowsky brothers in Berlin had astonished their paying public in 1895. For a year or so, this new scientific attraction had thrilled those who had money enough to pay, but as more projectors and more reels were produced, these first cinemas had quickly become a working-class entertainment with an itinerant existence, setting up in cafés, music halls or fairground stalls to show short films for an entry fee of a few pennies. Film was a kind of animated magic lantern –

a brief glimpse, a few minutes only, of people in movement, people like the workers (mostly women) seen streaming out of the Lumière factory in Lyon – hardly a subject of great drama, but an astonishing sight, nonetheless. Soon, humorous episodes, such as a man drenching himself by looking into a garden hose that suddenly comes to life, Edison's *Fred Ott's Sneeze* (1894) and magic tricks joined the repertoire. Other reels showed music hall performers, boxers or circus artistes, and for a decade or so, the ragtag world of cinema projection was regarded as a kind of vulgar reality peep show for the uneducated masses.

The main attraction of these early movies had been movement itself, but the attraction soon wore off (prompting the enterprising Louis Lumière to the exasperated sigh, 'Cinema has no future') as the audience began to demand films with more plot, more elaborate décor, more spectacle, an entertainment beyond sprinklers and sneezes. To survive against competing fairground offers, film would have to become more exciting, and more expensive to produce, leaving the field to the few larger players with enough money to pay for a director, professional actors, an elaborate set, special effects and throngs of extras. Gaumont and Pathé-Frères had developed mainly as producers of technical equipment such as cameras, projectors and film, and had established a healthy dominance in a rapidly expanding market.

These early silent movies seem curious to us with their theatrical, hammed-up acting, the frightening makeup, the obvious sets, and particularly because of the famously wooden, jerky movement with which early movie stars, troops and crowned heads stagger, puppet-like, across modern screens (almost inevitably accompanied by jolly ragtime piano). Even so, the sped-up, manic atmosphere of old films would have been familiar to contemporary audiences around 1910: while producers tended to slow down the rate even further in order to save precious film stock, projectionists and cinema owners often sped up their reels in order to cram in more people more quickly, and in the last showing many cinemas were notorious for their extra jerkiness, as bored staff cranked the handles faster to get home earlier. Very probably, the world as it appeared on the screen was a frenzied, overexcited affair, and even projectionists with the best of intentions would have to be artists in order to be faithful to their material. In an age before effective standardization, every film and every cameraman had his own, individual speed.

The rise of Pathé-Frères, the larger of the two competitors, is exemplary of these early years. Having begun by importing Edison's phonograph and then producing their own rip-off version of his kinetoscope, the wily brothers were selling 200 cameras and projectors per month as well as 12,000 metres of film per day in 1905. In 1906 they were already selling 40,000 metres of film a day, producing a dozen short movies a week at 75 copies each, and were in the process of creating a worldwide distribution network for their films. Pathé-Frères agencies opened in Moscow, New York and Brussels in 1904; in Berlin, Vienna, Chicago and St Petersburg in 1905; and in Amsterdam, Barcelona, Milan and London in 1906, and were soon spreading throughout the world along colonial routes to India, South-east Asia, Central and South America, and Africa. By 1908, 200 copies of each Pathé film were shipped to the United States alone, and an empire of 200 cinemas in France and Belgium ensured control of the home market. In or around 1910, cinema had become a million-franc industry with huge audiences and an even bigger potential. In the United States, the nickelodeons, cheap cinemas, had quickly become a popular phenomenon, an anarchistic cut-throat industry that took off practically overnight, as an American journalist observed in 1907:

> Three years ago there was not a nickelodeon, or five-cent theatre devoted to moving-picture shows, in America. To-day there are between four and five thousand running and solvent, and the number is still increasing rapidly. This is the boom time in the moving-picture business. Everybody is making money … The nickelodeon is tapping an entirely new stratum of people, is developing into theatregoers a section of population that formerly knew and cared little about the drama as a fact in life … Incredible as it may seem, over two million people on the average attend the nickelodeons *every day of the year*, and a third of these are children.
>
> The nickelodeon is usually a tiny theatre, containing 199 seats, giving from twelve to eighteen performances a day, seven days a week. Its walls are painted red, the seats are ordinary kitchen chairs, not fastened. The only break in the red color scheme is made by half a dozen signs, in black and white, NO SMOKING, HATS OFF, and sometimes, but not always, STAY AS LONG AS YOU LIKE …
>
> As might be expected, the Latin races patronize the shows more consistently than Jews, Irish or Americans. Sailors of all races are devotees … The enterprising manager usually engages a human pianist with instructions to play *Eliza-crossing-the-ice* when the scene is shuddery, and fast ragtime in a comic kid chase. Where there is little competition, however, the manager merely presses the button and starts the automatic going, which is as apt as not to bellow out, *I'd Rather Two-Step Than*

Walz, Bill, just as the angel rises from the brave little hero-cripple's corpse.

Europe had its own wave of small, fly-by-night cinemas, but this craze was already dying out. A new generation of movie theatres spread like wildfire. In 1912, London counted some 500 cinemas and Manchester 111, and 350 million movie tickets were sold annually in Britain alone. Even rural Hungary had 270 cinemas, 92 of them in Budapest, and European movies were watched as far away as Rangoon, Shanghai and Melbourne. 'The age of cinema had dawned, a new cult, penetrating Europe and conquering the world,' wrote René Doumic in 1913. This was the time of the rising empires, particularly Pathé-Frères and Gaumont, giants who lured audiences with longer, more spectacular films and with ever-bigger cinemas in which screenings were no longer anarchic and uncontrolled, but grand and grandly decorated people's palaces, a communion with a world of glamour and of aspiration, with heroes down on their luck and stars in the social stratosphere. The 3,400-seat Gaumont Palace in Paris was the biggest and most spectacular of these.

The last chapter has shown how artists reacted to this feeling of fragmentation in general, but there are also direct parallels between cinema and other arts. As nickelodeons were drawing in millions of curious punters every day, newspapers began to react to the demand for quick, punchy, graphic stories by publishing comic strips. Krazy Kat, the Katzenjammer Kids and the Teenie Weenies became regulars in American newspapers and developed their own expressive vocabulary.

POW! Krazy Kat, one of the first cartoons, throwing a trademark brick.

Starstruck

The new breed of screen heroes soon captured the popular imagination, and none more so than Max Linder (Gabriel-Maximilien de Leuvielle, 1883–1925), the archetype of the French cheeky chappy, whose adventures were followed with rapt delight across the globe. The cheerful, mustachioed Max did his utmost to succeed in life, but he was surrounded by chaos. If he sat by the fire his shoes would go up in flames; his stiff collars would be impossible to do up; every situation into which he got himself would inevitably end in social ruin and hilarious embarrassment. In 1912 alone, Linder made thirty-four films, and this headlong rush of slapstick netted him a salary of one million gold francs.

In the soup: the Frenchman Max Linder, the first movie star,
in one of his films, 1907.

This was stardom of a new dimension, and it functioned differently from old-fashioned fame. During the nineteenth century, if you wanted to partake of the legend of the great Sarah Bernhardt (1844–1923), *la divine*, who was already a star before the 1900s, you had to buy a ticket in an expensive theatre in Paris, or in the United States, St Petersburg or London, during one of her tours. If you wanted to see her after the turn of the century, still playing young roles at over sixty years, you only had to wait until one of her new movies came out and you could experience what was thought to be the summit of theatre – no matter whether you were in the capital, in a village in the Pyrenees, or in a back street in Lisbon, Cracow or San Francisco. Bernhardt's fame originated in the nineteenth century, aided by her tempestuous performances on and off the stage, but it grew larger in the twentieth, fuelled mainly by her off-stage notoriety – and it had all the ingredients of fame that the fans expected.

No star before Bernhardt (whose career apogee coincided with the appearance of mass-circulation newspapers and photographic reproductions

such as postcards) had been as present in the public eye with personal
details, idiosyncrasies, and all the delicious ingredients of private mythology.
Bernhardt's occasional habit of sleeping in her coffin (and having herself
photographed in it) attracted as much comment as her exotic menagerie,
which included, at different times, a lion, a lynx, a baby alligator which was
accidentally killed by being fed too much champagne, a boa constrictor
which committed suicide by swallowing a sofa cushion. The exotic colours
of her animals, however, paled before the star's notoriously slight figure and
princely train of life, and before her countless and highly publicized affairs,
pursued with almost missionary zeal, and later embroidered and further
embellished through rumours and biographical accounts. 'You know, she's
such a liar, she may even be fat!' quipped the French novelist Alexandre
Dumas fils. Among her scores of lovers were Edward, Prince of Wales, the
artist Gustave Doré and the Italian novelist Gabriele d'Annunzio, the French
writer Pierre Loti, and, as Robert Gottlieb put it, 'the ultra-homosexual
Robert de Montesquiou, Proust's Charlus, whom she mischievously

*The power of seduction: the many lovers of actress
Sarah Bernhardt were legend, among them was
Edward VII.*

initiated into heterosexual sex, reducing him to twenty-four hours of vomiting'.

These fleeting affairs were only minor roles played out between more substantial engagements, notably with the famously virile Jean Mounet-Sully ('Up to the age of sixty I thought it was a bone,' he was heard musing in his old age) of the Comédie-Française and with a handsome young Greek, Artistides Damala, whom she worshipped and married, and who cheated her out of her fortune. He might have ruined her altogether, had he not had the grace to die of a morphine overdose. Bernhardt mourned him as grandly and as theatrically as she had loved him. All this was part of the legend that had grown around Sarah Bernhardt, the great tragedienne, the great ambassadress of France, the incarnation of French art, of dramatic art, of womanhood of the most scandalous and grandest kind. Her personal motto had always been *Quand-même*, despite everything, very much the spirit in which she appeared as Hamlet in French on the London stage, prompting one of her harshest critics, George Bernard Shaw, to call her 'a worn out hack tragedienne'. Shaw was part of a very small minority who did not admire her, writing acerbically, 'I could never as a dramatic critic be fair to Sarah B., because she was exactly like my Aunt Georgina.'

Unlike the aunt-hating Shaw, newspaper editors loved Sarah Bernhardt. Any story about her boosted circulation, as people obsessively wanted to know more about 'their Sarah', about her beauty, her makeup tricks, her predilection for trouser roles and her spectacular death scenes, her spend-thrift habits and devotion to her illegitimate son Maurice, the truth about her lovers – and later the tragedy of her amputated leg and her courage in reciting poetry to soldiers at the Front. Bernhardt was consumed by her millions of admirers – they devoured the newspapers and magazines that featured her, flocked to her films, bought photographs, fashion and fans associated with her, and wrote to her for autographs; they hung Alphonse Mucha's famous posters of her as Hamlet or Gismonda on their walls. Long after she had conquered the stage, the divine Sarah was a media celebrity.

Fame on the scale of a Max Linder or a Sarah Bernhardt was the symptom of a new kind of culture that was rapidly transforming both the public sphere and the nature of personal experience. Until the advent of mass communication, of cinema and gramophone, each and every experience had been unique. You could go to the opera or to a music hall, knowing that (in fact, not even questioning whether) tonight's experience was unique and unrepeatable. Another evening would be different, with other vocal inflections, gestures and reactions. Life was a precious good slipping through one's hands, and nothing in the world could stop time even for a moment. The new media changed people's relationship to experience. Enrico Caruso, the miraculous tenor of the century, or the great soprano Amelita Galli-Curci might sing differently every night at New York's Metropolitan Opera or at La Scala in Milan; they might be in form or not, might give a new nuance to a tried-and-tested interpretation. But on their gramophone recordings they sounded the same every time. Caruso's spectacular 1907 recording of the aria 'Vesti la giubba' from Leoncavallo's opera *Pagliacci* was the world's first gramophone record to sell a million copies. A new market was born, and with it a new way of appreciating art. It was no longer necessary to be in an opera house, with all the social baggage that implied, to appreciate the singer. Instead of forking out for a ticket, you only had to buy a cheap disc. You could sit in your shirt sleeves and listen to the maestro at home, when you liked and as often as you liked – and every time the great man would be in top form, and every time you would feel that familiar thrill at the same points in the recording. Cinema and recordings made experience repeatable.

Another innovation had a different, almost magic quality: it could stop time itself, freeze experience. First introduced in 1900, George Eastman's simple Brownie camera, little more than a cardboard box with a lens, was sold for just one US dollar. The six-exposure films cost 15 cents. Within one year of their launch Kodak, the inventor's firm, had produced and sold

The tenor Enrico Caruso was the star of the Metropolitan Opera and produced the first record selling more than a million copies.

150,000 of these little cameras, cheap and easy enough for a child to use. Professional photographers and well-heeled amateurs had been producing pictures for more than a generation, but the wave of cheap and simple cameras around 1900 changed the entire game. Everybody could now be photographed – not only formally, in a studio and surrounded by large drapes, painted backdrops and fussily decorated furniture to lean upon, but outside, during their daily lives, in the most casual and unexpected situations. We have already encountered the boy photographer Jacques Henri Lartigue and his love of speed, and tens of thousands of (mostly less gifted) amateurs shared his fascination. Moments that last but a flash were preserved here, their energy still vibrating in their hazy light. Reproduced in newspapers with editions of up to a million copies (in 1913, 16 million newspaper copies were printed every day in Germany alone), press photographs gave immediacy to realities otherwise so remote that they might as well be fairy tales. Photos made the world a smaller, faster place, and at the same time they carried the enchantment of time suspended in full flight.

Not everyone was comfortable with this new and formidable power to change experience with the click of a button or the throwing of a switch. As the French priest abbé Mugnier, the confessor of *le tout Paris*, grumbled in his diary in 1910: 'One is no longer at home with oneself today. It is only going to get worse. X-rays will penetrate you, Kodaks will photograph your passing, phonographs will engrave your voices. Aeroplanes threaten us from on high.' Mugnier was only one among many across the Western world who perceived the rapidly changing popular culture as a threat. Another observer, Louis Haugmard, analysed cinema and the effects on viewers, and came to the following, remarkably prescient conclusion:

> Through it [cinema] the charmed masses will learn not to think anymore, to resist all desire to reason and to construct, which will atrophy little by little; they will know only how to open their large and empty eyes, only to look, look, look… Will cinematography comprise, perhaps, the elegant solution to the social question, if the modern cry is formulated: 'Bread and cinemas'? …
>
> And we shall progressively draw near to those menacing days when universal illusion in universal mummery will reign.

The Beauty of the Masses

Members of the elite might rage, but the great majority of people eagerly embraced the democratization and globalization of the ways they entertained

Taking the curve: Jacques Henri Lartigue celebrating the excitement of speed.

Rushing ahead: a photo taken from a racing car, by Jacques Henri Lartigue.

318

and informed themselves, of how they thought and what they found beautiful.

The avant-garde had proclaimed a new kind of beauty – but their strident voice was heard by only a few thousand people around the world. Their paintings were shown (if at all) in smallish galleries away from the mainstream; their novels were often published privately and with print runs of a few hundred copies. Visionary as they may seem today, they were only very rarely noticed, and much less understood. The great majority of people in the West, those who could afford to choose for themselves, lived in surroundings largely disguised under the cloak of history. The prints on their walls and the plaster busts on their piano might be mass-produced, but their ornamental twirls and uplifting messages breathed the easy air of times gone by, for the print was in a gold frame (factory-made, of course) and showed a work by an old master (usually a heliotype, a newly perfected printing technology for colour reproductions). And the composer or poet's bust in every self-respecting German household celebrated (depending on the household's progressiveness) Beethoven, Goethe, Friedrich Schiller or perhaps even Heinrich Heine (a poet, an ironist, and a Jew) or Richard Wagner (a nationalist and antisemite). French households of a certain kind might pay homage to Napoleon or might instead display a crucifix (France, the polarized), while their British counterparts glorified Shakespeare.

Now being produced in large factories, furniture usually imitated the styles of other periods. There were those who set out to produce innovative designs, such as Charles Rennie Mackintosh in Glasgow and Adolf Loos and the Wiener Werkstätte in Vienna, but their work was eyed suspiciously by the European middle classes, who much preferred the solid dignity of historicism or the soft, feminine lines of *Jugendstil* design. Often elegantly sumptuous, feminine and playful, household furniture was decorated so as to soften the blow dealt to bourgeois pride by mass production. The natural forms, the flowers and nymph-like virgin girls, the climbing plants, enticing blossoms and dripping leaves and the very lushness of its execution made the happy owner overlook that these were objects designed to be mass-produced and assembled in factories, little more than a mock re-enchantment of industrial form. *Jugendstil* and art nouveau sang softly of natural beauty and the flow of life, but most of their designers worked in modern offices and drew objects to be produced in bulk.

Jugendstil and art nouveau and their various national forms or antecedents such as the Arts and Crafts movement were creatures of the nineteenth century, emerging from an artistic response to the encroaching reality of mass production and industrial aesthetic, and soon overtaken by commercial interests. They had been an attempt to re-enchant an increasingly prosaic world by giving it new beauty, but even they faced determined opposition. Outraged by the Viennese culture of façade in emotional economy as in architecture, Loos had declared ornament a crime. Only Gaudí in Barcelona could still summon the courage to build animist architecture writhing with gargoyles, mysterious beasts and symbolic forms. The new design was the product of a world without spirits, a world that had lost or freed itself of animism; it was preoccupied not with the evil eye but with functionality, mechanization, production processes and costs; it belonged to a different, industrial world. How elegant it could be was demonstrated by the functional simplicity of the Thonet Brothers' steam-bent wooden furniture. But even though the Thonet factory produced more than 2 million units in 1912 alone, and despite their grace and comfort, the pure lines of Thonet's objects made their way into ordinary households only slowly. People simply preferred the dignified look of historical quotation.

Palaces of the People?

Items produced in huge quantities needed outlets, and the new tribe of urban consumers needed places to shop. The hour of the department store had struck: huge smooth selling machines whose commercial engine rooms, lift boys, chic terrasses and multi-storey elegance had more than a passing resemblance to fashionable ocean liners.

Shopping at Selfridges
A pleasure – A pastime – A relaxation

promised posters alerting Londoners to the 1909 opening of the city's latest big-selling establishment, in which nothing had been left to chance: exhausted husbands could be entertained in a separate, reassuringly club-like smoking room.

The Paris *grands magasins* (Bon Marché and Louvre, Printemps and Galeries Lafayette), Macy's in New York, London colossi like Harrods, Whiteleys and Derry and Toms, Moscow's Muir & Mirrilees, Innovation in Brussels, Holzer and Fischer in Budapest, or Wertheim, Schocken and Tietz in Germany: these were no mere shops, but shopping experiences striving to offer everything customers might conceivably desire from food to live animals, from clothes to massages, from cars to perfumes and stationery. And they did everything in the name of customer service and convenience. As early as 1894 the Paris Bon Marché, one of Europe's oldest and most elegant department stores, had a mailing list of 1.5 million addresses for its catalogues. Ten years later its owners presided over an expanding empire with branches in Brixton, Southport and Gloucester and a total of 7,000 employees. In 1905, Harrods established a 24-hour telephone ordering service. The great Paris stores delivered to Trouville and other fashionable beach resorts so loved by their clientele during the summer months, and Muir & Mirrilees in Moscow dispatched its wares throughout the Russian empire. Settled unhappily in Yalta, Anton Chekhov was so dependent on their quality goods that he named his two dogs Muir & Mirrilees.

Mixing the thrill of buying with the greater promises of creating a new reality that was at once exciting and convenient, commercial centres and events attracted huge crowds. When the 1904 *Salon de l'automobile* opened its doors in the Paris Grand Palais, 40,000 people visited the sales exhibition on the first day (compared with 10,000 who had attended the opening of the *Salon de la peinture* that year). What they had come to see, however, was not just a collection of new cars, but a new vision of things, new and exciting possibilities, as one journalist explained:

> You must come at nightfall. Come out into the world from the entrance to the Métro, you stand stupefied by so much noise, movement, and light. A rotating spotlight with its quadruple blue ray, sweeps the sky and dazzles you; two hundred automobiles in battle formation look at you with their large fiery eyes... Inside, the spectacle is of a rare and undeniable beauty. The large nave has become a prodigious temple of Fire; each of its iron arches is outlined with orange flames; its cupola carpeted with white flames, with those fixed as it were solid flames of incandescent lamps: fire is made matter, and they have built from it. The air is charged with a golden haze, which the moving rays of the projectors cross with their iridescent pencils...

Flooded with light from 200,000 light bulbs, the Grand Palais dominated the city like a gigantic jewel.

Another Paris institution combined commercial splendour with social prophecy. Georges Dufayel (1855–1916) offered a department store with a difference. The grand palace of commerce that Dufayel had erected close to Montmartre (at prodigious cost) in 1895 symbolized consumer dreams and the very universe of commerce. 'On entering Dufayel's store by the main door it seems as though you are entering a palace rather than a shop,' wrote one visitor, suitably impressed by the three supreme symbols on the façade: two statues to either side of the monumental door represented Credit and Publicity, the pillars of this empire, while high above, a gigantic clock reminded everyone that time is money. On the inside the reality of commerce was adorned by 200 statues, 180 paintings, ornamented pillars, shining figures in bronze holding brightly lit candelabra, painted glass and a grand staircase leading up to a theatre seating 3,000 spectators and encasing them in white and gold, in silk curtains and a sea of light reflected into infinity by gigantic mirrors. In the basement, a Cinematograph Hall offered a four-hour programme to 1,500 visitors. At night, the glass cupola of the building was illuminated with the power of 10 million candles, a landmark visible for twelve miles and rivalling the legendary searchlight of the Eiffel Tower.

Putting on a front: the Magasin Dufayel in Paris, a palace of commerce and credit.

Dufayel was different from other department stores: customers only had to make a downpayment of 20 per cent of the purchase price and could pay the rest in weekly instalments against a commission of 18 per cent. Around 1900, the firm had 3 million customers on its books and 3,000 clerks administering the system. The statue of Credit by its entrance door was there with good reason.

The goods sold by Dufayel through an empire of 400 branches in the French provinces targeted not moneyed society folk, but people of more modest means. Imitating the taste of the rich, these stores sold simulacra of wealth and success. Mass-produced silk dresses for women and prefabricated suits for men; rabbit pelts processed to look like precious furs; extravagant feather arrangements imitating rare and exotic birds; electroplated tin tableware made to look like solid silver; brilliantly coloured artificial flowers; soft furnishings with sumptuous velvet; and machine made book cases filled with cheap, gold-embossed editions of classic literature, all these combined to create a world of pretended wealth.

Many observers threw up their hands at so much vulgarity, but not all dismissed this new reality as decadence. The historian George d'Avenel (1855–1939) made it his life's work to analyse this fascinating new phenomenon and its social implications. Self-appointed aesthetes who deplored the lowering of standards had simply missed the point, he argued: 'Each time [industries] extend their reach, the life of a great number of individuals gains a new satisfaction; they allow the pale and illusory but sweet reflection of opulence to penetrate even to the humble. These vulgarizations are the work of our century: they honour it greatly.' If there was no spark of individual genius in this appearance of wealth and individuality, this new, mass-produced happiness still represented progress: 'The character of the new luxury is to be banal. Let us not complain too much, if you please: before, there was nothing banal but misery. Let us not fall into this childish but nevertheless common contradiction which consists of welcoming the development of industry while deploring the results of industrialism.'

The results of industrialism were most strongly felt in the United States, where no different legal systems, customs and national borders obstructed the flourishing consumer market. Sophisticated distribution networks and consumer research encouraged new, rationalized ways of selling goods, and allowed businessmen like John Hartford to carpet the country with his A & P chain stores. Between 1912 and 1915 a new store would be opened every three days. Mail-order catalogues allowed even isolated farming families to partake in the blessings of mass-produced comforts, and brought modern consumer goods even to the remotest pioneers. Sears Roebuck & Company, the most famous of these mail-order firms, produced tomes of almost biblical proportions, and in prodigious numbers: their 500-page illustrated catalogue of commercial promises of a better life through consumption had reached a circulation of a million copies in 1904, and rose by a further million or so every year. Together with the Bible, the Sears catalogue was America's most widely read and distributed book. Its short texts and lively illustrations even made it a favourite reading primer for small-town schools, where children would learn spelling from the product descriptions and arithmetic by adding up orders.

An early advertisement for Kellogg's.

This new consumer world of statistics standardized not only production, but also consumers. With measuring tape, slide rule and statistics, researchers plotted the standard human body and its most common sizings so that manufacturers could produce ready-made clothes efficiently. As the number of life insurances rocketed throughout the West, actuaries, trained mathematicians, were hired by insurance firms to calculate the likelihood of injury and death to their clients and therefore the repayments and conditions. Traffic planners and urbanists used statistical evidence to work out everything from roads to sewage systems, tramway seats and prison capacities. In this modern world, men and women were numbers first, individuals second.

Few people lost much sleep over their numerical existence. The result of the modern way of planning and producing things gave ordinary people unprecedented opportunities to improve their circumstances, or that, at least, was what advertisements stated with a loud and incessant voice, as Kellogg's, Singer sewing machines, Kodak, Quaker Oats and Coca-Cola (advertising budget in 1900: $100,000) became household names. For most people, the attraction of this society of convenience and supposedly endless possibility was irresistible, though here and there a preacher or an artist might see the pitfalls inherent in it. Upton Sinclair's 1906 novel *The Jungle*, for instance, which describes the cruel working lives of recent immigrants in the Chicago meat industry, warned of the dehumanization by mechanized production that was to become one of the leading themes of the twentieth century:

> The carcass hog was then again strung up by machinery and sent upon another trolley ride; this time passing between two lines of men ... upon a raised platform, each doing a certain single thing to the carcass as it came to him. One scraped the outside of a leg; another scraped the inside of the same leg. One with a swift stroke cut the throat ... Another made a slit down the body; a second opened the body wider; a third with

a saw cut the breastbone; a fourth loosened the entrails; a fifth pulled them out … There were men to scrape each side and men to scrape the back; there were men to clean the carcass inside, to trim it and wash it. Looking down this room one saw creeping slowly a line of dangling hogs … and for every yard there was a man working as if a demon were after him.

Chicago's new-found assembly-line efficiency was to be one of the inspirations of the automobile assembly lines in the factories of Henry Ford. It is hard to escape the impression that it also presaged the mechanized slaughter of two world wars.

In his 1895 movie *Charcuterie méchanique* the film pioneer Louis Lumière had demonstrated not only the surprising effects of trick photography (in this case a backward screening), but also the tenuous and increasingly convoluted relationship between the living individual and mass production. In the sequence, sausages vanish into the meat grinder and eventually reconstitute themselves into pork halves and, finally, a happy, living pig. Mechanized convenience and individual life somehow appeared to be at opposite ends of the spectrum in which most people's stories played themselves out. This dichotomy created fear, and hordes of prophets preached against 'Americanization', vulgarity and the decline of good taste.

Other, sharper observers caught sight of underlying problems that were all the more serious for being obscured by the sheer dazzle of it all. The surface of things had never been more dazzling than during that great celebration of the culture of consumption at the dawn of the century, the 1900 Paris World Fair; Maurice Talmeyr (1850–1933), a journalist for a Catholic periodical, described the virtual reality of the fair in a series of articles. What the visitor saw, Talmeyr wrote, was no representation of anything known, but rather the result of a striving for maximum effect and entertainment. The 'Hindu temples, savage huts, pagodas, souks, Algerian alleys, Chinese, Japanese, Sudanese, Senegalese, Siamese, Cambodian quarters … a bazaar of climates, architectural styles, smells, colours, cuisine and music' had nothing to do with life in any of these countries, and everything with the organizer's desire to see more tickets sold. In the Indian section, visitors could see a group of stuffed animals including a trumpeting elephant, a flock of hens, a wild boar, and a serpent ready to strike, and, close by, a jaguar family and a rose ibis that was 'evidently surprised' to be surrounded by so many different animals. Reality was being effaced by commercially inspired fantasy:

The notion of such an India, of an India-warehouse, so magnificent and so partially true as it may be, is true only partially, so partially as to be false, and all these overflowing rooms...speak to me only of an incomplete and truncated India, that of the cashiers. And the other? That of the famine? For this land of enormous and sumptuous trade is equally that of frightening local degeneracy, of a horrifying indigenous misery. A whole phantom-race dies there and suffers in famine. India is not only a warehouse, it is a cemetery.

Wherever Talmeyr looked in the colonial exhibition, he found nothing but 'nullity, buffoonery, gross alteration, or absolute falsity', impressions made to titillate and to fulfil stereotypes, but never to present something genuinely new. Instead, everything had become stagework, nothing was as it seemed:

> We are here, it seems, in the most legendary Spain, and this time there is indeed a well-done reproduction of great fidelity and delicacy. I feel, in these old walls, in this broken well, in these small columns which are crumbling, in a coat of arms that is obliterated, five centuries of mystery and sunshine...Then I look, I observe more closely, and I notice, above the door, in the patina of the stone, the tracing of Gothic letters...I approach , and what is it I make out?
> Simply: *Menier Chocolate*...

To Talmeyr, the world of mass consumption was necessarily a world of economically motivated lies, and it would be absurd to ask anything else of it. Entering the grounds of the World Fair meant agreeing to its rules, just as entering a department store entailed, or rather allowed, a delicious suspension of disbelief that made all shoppers rich and free of troubles for a little while:

> An exposition must, above all, be an exposition, which is to say a certain type of didactic banking whose first goal is to attract, to hold, and to attract and to hold by the exclusive means of the bank...Truth, history, common sense, will be arranged afterward as best they can. So...why, in English India, do the panther, wild boar, partridge, elephant, monkey, ibis and serpent present themselves all in a family and form this touching commune? Because this fable gathers them together, and what matters, above all, is to gather them together. And why is starving India incarnated in well-coiffed, well-nourished, well-clothed Indians? Because famine is not and never can be an attraction...And why does Andalusia – in the time of the Moors – recommend Menier Chocolate to us? Because the authentic Moors and the Authentic Andalusia do not,

according to all appearances, sufficiently allow for advertisements, and an exposition is not going, never has gone, and never will go without advertisements.

If the World Fair brought the world to the capital, new means of transport brought the inhabitants of the big cities into the wider world. Vienna's *Sommerfrische*, Trouville, Biarritz and other seaside towns in France; cheap hotels and workers' holiday homes throughout the rural regions in Germany and the Baltic Sea resorts – they all allowed Europeans to leave the haste and intensity of the city behind for a few days or weeks.

Earlier industrialized, and more open to developments from across the Atlantic such as Coney Island (the legendary place of relaxation in which New Yorkers exchanged the heat of the city with the heat of the amusement park), Britain was the unquestioned champion of seaside holidays. The railways brought the sea within everybody's reach, and the piers in Blackpool and Brighton with their spectacular architecture, music halls, theatres and other popular entertainments were only the largest in a quasi-interminable list of more or less famous seaside resorts from Bognor Regis to Westward Ho. Blackpool alone was host to some 3 million visitors around 1900, 4 million by 1914 – roughly one in ten Britons visited the seaside town that year. Many more went to alternative destinations. Agreeable as it was to many, the invasion of the masses was perceived by some as an affront to good manners, but it was a necessary part of the whole, as Georges d'Avenel pointed out:

> [It] would doubtless be more pleasant for each Parisian to own the Bois de Boulogne all by himself, or with a small number of friends, rather than share its enjoyment on holidays with 500,000 other proprietors. But it is precisely the glory of Progress to have created this congestion in making accessible to all an outing which used to be very remote.

The world itself, it seemed, was coming closer, and it became increasingly difficult to flee the crowd, the speed and strain of city life, the din of traffic, and the persistent visual assault of advertising.

The cultures of consumption and of industrially produced convenience and entertainment, of 'bread and cinemas', were one of the key aspects of the age of the masses. Where slowly evolving traditional structures – regional origin, religious faith, guilds and the estates – had been the main factors delineating identities since the dawn of civilization, other constructions were now taking over, powerfully aided by urbanization and the mass media. A man who thought of himself as a Protestant from a village in Provence, a wine-grower like his father, might see no future in the rural life, and so might decide to pack up and become a factory hand in Paris. In his new life he might become a loyal reader of *Le Matin* who particularly enjoyed the sports section and serialized novels, a fan of the novel series of *Fantomas* crime movies, a socialist, a member of an allotment gardening association, and a supporter of the Paris Football Club – an identity composed of individual choices. He might also be married to a woman from the overwhelmingly Catholic Brittany and proclaim the family's social ambitions by giving their children traditional French names, or turning for inspiration to the French Revolution, Greek mythology, sports heroes, or popular stars.

The engine of these choices, industry and its mass-produced goods, had asserted itself in people's daily lives with discrete but formidable force, often transforming not so much the appearance of things as their very fabric; literally so in the case of the ready-to-wear clothes and shoes people wore. The taste of Mr and Mrs Average might have changed little since the 1870s – indeed it might have been driven further into historicizing neo-Renaissance or neo-medieval fantasies by the insecurities engendered by social change – but the availability and price of their objects of desire had. Many could now afford modest luxuries and make personal choices in catalogues or department stores, they could buy newspapers and cinema tickets, and could take the family for a week's holiday at the seaside. By going about their day-to-day lives, they made themselves part of a fully globalized economy, the last link in the chain: they read the same papers as millions of their peers, ate meat imported from New Zealand and Argentina, wheat from Russia and Canada, and had milk delivered by industrial dairies and tea and coffee from the colonies.

New Tribes

People's world-views, their hopes and aspirations and their loyalties, were no longer what they had been a generation earlier. Political ideologies transmitted themselves via large party networks and newspapers. Hundreds of thousands organized themselves in trade unions and in political parties corresponding to the social realities of industrialized societies. Women's organizations defended women's interests, socialist and communist parties made themselves champions of the working poor, conservative parties defended the interests of the haves against those of the have-nots, and the liberal movements in Europe expanded from enlightened Whiggism to an emphasis on economic freedom and reform in the French radical mould.

Young people organized themselves in sports clubs and associations like the German *Wandervogel* movement and conquered the world in bands of teenagers cut loose from society at large – a first recognition of youth as a world in itself and not just a kind of deficient adulthood, a group demanding recognition, entertainment, identity.

Their demands were heard only dimly: youth culture as such, a world of 'cool' with its own clothes, customs, music and consumer goods, would not exist for another sixty years. For the time being, youth was accorded little or no value, as the Austrian writer Stefan Zweig recalled:

> Someone wanting to advance [his professional career] had to use every masquerade imaginable to appear older than he was. Newspapers recommended patent medicines to make beards grow faster, young doctors of twenty-four or twenty-five, just after their exams, wore mighty beards and golden glasses even if they had no need of them, just to give their patients the impression of being 'experienced'. One wore long, black frock coats and walked slowly, if possible with a slight *embonpoint*, to incarnate that desirable settledness; and the most ambitious tried to disown their real, suspiciously unsolid age...

Young people as consumers were a resource largely untapped by industry; they had not yet become a commercial, urban tribe. There were no special clothes for the young once the boys had outgrown their short trousers. There were no cultural events for them alone; no places where they could meet away from school. Children's magazines catered for the tastes and excitement of young teenagers and there were popular novels for juvenile audiences, but none of these constituted anything like a youth culture. The foundations for the later changes, however, were laid already: the changing status of women and the first stirrings of a sexual revolution, a longer youth for middle-class children because of time spent in secondary and tertiary education, the formation of clubs and associations and, of course, the explosive energy of young artists from the German expressionists to the young people around the Stephen sisters in London's Bloomsbury.

New tribes needed new rituals, new ways of common living, demonstrations of cohesion and power such as the communist Mayday marches which regularly attracted hundreds of thousands of participants in Europe's large cities, and moments of collective communion such as soccer matches, in which the life-and-death struggle for existence was played out vicariously on the central turf. In Britain alone, 12,000 football clubs with 300,000 players were registered with the Football Association in 1910, and an event like the FA Cup Final could attract more than 100,000 spectators. Other sports events, such as the tennis championships at Wimbledon or important cricket matches, also drew large crowds, and at the turn of the century twenty-five London newspapers were entirely devoted to sport.

These new tribes were a central fact of the emerging social order. A realignment of identities was taking place everywhere, leaving most people suspended between their traditional communities (religious faith, regional origin and customs) and new communities – half chosen, half imposed – of life in the modern city. As villages close to industrial sites or mining operations boomed into urban prosperity, they created whole cities with their own civic culture, often centred on popular pursuits rather than the preoccupations of the elite. There was more likely to be a first-rate football ground, with stands for tens of thousands of visitors, than a first-rate public library or opera house. In addition to this, political rallies, workers' education clubs, sports clubs, trade unions and co-operatives provided additional focal points for social life. Democratic choices about culture were powerfully asserting themselves.

The choices offered by mass society were particularly marked for women. Decent, cheap dresses in fashionable fits and colours were now available on every high street. Wearing reform clothes instead of corsets meant that they could breathe freely and no longer be subject to picturesque fainting fits, that they could function as social equals to men, and that they could enjoy and demonstrate their independence by playing sports. Bicycling women in baggy trousers, a scandalous sight to many, were one of the iconic motifs of the popular press.

The availability of things, the lure of the possible satisfaction of all dreams, increased both the range of possible experiences and the psychological pressure. Looking at the advertising sections of newspapers in France, Austria and Germany (less so under the more restrictive obscenity laws of Britain and Russia) that were mainly directed at male audiences – satirical journals, sports papers – one is struck by the predominance of sex. Pages are filled with ads for condoms, for 'interesting photographs', erotic literature, remedies for impotence and 'sexual neurasthenia', hair and beard tonics, tinctures, pills and electric belts to improve virility and make men more impressive, more masculine. Sex and the cult of masculine force were more publicly present than they had ever been a decade earlier, as recorded in a Berlin reportage by the pioneering journalist Hans Ostwald:

In front of a shop window. Inside, rows and rows of books. Many show a lascivious female head. Several carry a wrapper:

'Interesting! Formerly forbidden!! Really fascinating! Revelations about the fast set!!'

An early example of female independence.

Others [books] offer information about marital issues. Flagellation books with revolting illustrations on the cover. And at the very front of the window are photographs with banderoles:

'Formerly confiscated!'

And in front of it: young and old gentlemen, and very young boys and girls, looking at this strange world with eyes wide open.

'Yea – man – I'm gonna buy that,' says a twelve-year-old boy to his neighbour.

Communities of Consumption

The new communities of consumption, the new tribes, were communities of fears as well as dreams. At the centre of these fears was the trade-off between certainty and opportunity at the heart of the new tribal society (others call it 'the modern project') itself. If ideologies could be chosen like dress styles and furniture, this freedom came at the price of an established identity, of protection from tradition, Church, and established principle. Looking in the mirror, people found a face of almost Cubist facets staring back at them. Given more opportunities than ever before, and exposed to the growing rush and clamour of a myriad different voices, people found they were no longer made of one piece, that there was no single perspective that described them adequately. They had become many things, unfamiliar things. Not everyone who saw this fragmentation in his inner looking glass could live with the resulting image.

One of the most perceptive contemporary observers of the interchange of destruction, transformation and construction around him was Georg Simmel (1858–1918), a German-Jewish scholar whose financial independence allowed him an intellectual freedom that a university career would not have afforded him – a fact he discovered to his cost when a lecture he gave at the university of Berlin in order to become eligible for a professorship (the *Habilitation* in the German system) was boycotted because the young philosopher had dared to contradict a senior professor in public.

A Jewish boy born in the very centre of bustling Berlin and who had lost his father as a young child, Simmel was in many ways predestined for close observation, an outsider looking in. He spent his working life at the margins of the academic establishment and published a series of books and articles that brought him international renown. The titles of many of his essays read like seismographic records of his time: *Two Forms of Individualism* (1901); *Spiritual Life in the Metropolis* (1903); *The Philosophy of Fashion* (1905); *The Philosophy of the Sexes* (1906); *The Fragmentary Character of Life* (1916): 'The characterization of life as a fragment can claim reasons,' Simmel wrote in this last work, '… often individual life is experienced thus [as fragmentary], as if in a hidden layer or in God's eye there were a perfect whole… from which innumerable parts break off as soon as it comes into our empirical reality.' Being alive in the modern world entailed damage, fragmentation.

A central paradox governed the relationship between the individual and his or her new power to choose in a consumer society: while mass production furthered not only membership of a tribe, but also personal, individual choice as an assertion of personal preference and taste, industry itself depended on looking at people not as individuals, but as types, as averages. For managers and product planners no individuals existed, but only budgets, sizing charts, bell curves, fashions, markets. Marketing and advertising worked to close this gap. They associated perfectly anonymous products with faces, gave them a personal appearance, a little homely warmth.

Amid the growth of the new, old things suddenly seemed more precious, motivating people to document vanishing worlds and ephemeral moments. The photographer Eugène Atget haunted the streets of Paris to preserve what he saw and what could not last; August Sander made his first great portraits of Germans at work; the Russian Sergei Mikhailovich Prokudin-Gorskii (1863–1944) took an astounding series of vivid colour photographs (using a camera produced according to his own designs) of monuments and peoples of the Tsar's empire; and the Briton Benjamin Stone founded the National Photographic Record Association in 1897. Preservation was the order of the day. Founded in 1895 and devoted to preserving country houses and other sites of historic interest, the National Trust in Britain was recognized by law in 1907. The Dürerbund in Germany, 1902, aspired to fulfil a similar role, while in France sites identified as *patrimoine national* were protected by a law passed in 1905, and Austria gained a highly official 'Imperial and Royal Monuments Commission' in 1911.

We have moved away from the cinema, but its luminous revelation was a key sign of the times. It provided not only entertainment but a race of demigods appearing to their devotees in a blaze of light, the apotheosis of the individual. More than ever, technology had now taken control of people's dreams, and authors and engineers competed to innovate and expand the technical and aesthetic possibilities of film.

There was another cinema-related event in 1911, though it went all but unnoticed. The great French firms had quickly found that it was best to install their studios in the bright and sunny south of the country, where natural light could be used instead of expensive and accident-prone high-voltage lighting. In October 1911 the American David Horsley, thinking along the same lines, went to California to open the first cinema studio there, the Nestor Studios. As a convenient location he chose a hilly suburb of Los Angeles, a village by the name of Hollywood, where he set up shop on the dusty but grandly named Sunset Boulevard.

13

1912:
Questions of Breeding

The man who is thoroughly healthy in every respect simply cannot act badly or wickedly; his actions are necessarily good, that is to say, properly adapted to the evolution of the human race.

— Hugo Ribbert

Seven hundred men and women from across the civilized world crowded together in the corridors and lecture halls of London's University College to hear speeches and to participate in seminars and discussions led by some of the most distinguished experts in the world. They were doctors and university professors, politicians and biologists, theologians and feminists, social reformers, philosophers, statisticians, anthropologists and eminent natural scientists, and they had all come to debate the one idea that most of them considered the chief foundation of a better future: the genetic improvement of the human race.

The 1912 First International Congress of Eugenics was held from 24 to 30 July and it received blessings from high places. Its president was Major Leonard Darwin, chairman of the British Eugenics Society and son of the founder of the theory of evolution. Among the honorary vice presidents were the first lord of the Admiralty, Mr Winston Churchill; Sir Thomas Barlow, president of the Royal College of Physicians; Lord Alverstone, the lord chief justice; Charles Gore, the lord bishop of Oxford; the eminent German biologist Friedrich Weismann; the famous Swiss pathologist Auguste Forel; Alexander Graham Bell, inventor of the telephone; the Munich professor Max von Gruber and the German eugenicist and prophet of Nordic racial superiority Dr Alfred Ploetz, president of the International Society for Race Hygiene; David Starr Jordan, the chancellor of Stanford University; and Charles W. Eliot, president emeritus of Harvard.

Formerly the reserve of cranks and eccentrics, eugenics had risen to the highest scientific honours. It was discussed at universities and in learned journals, in bestselling books and parliamentary debates. Laws enacting eugenic measures such as forced sterilization were passed, political leaders across the ideological spectrum espoused its goals, and scientists everywhere thought of it as the salvation of the human race, while philosophers and writers sang its praises. None of this would have been possible without two scientific discoveries that would prove seminal to all biological thinking and research in the twentieth century and beyond.

The first of these breakthroughs had occurred decades earlier without attracting any notice. It was the fruit of the experiments of a reclusive Austrian monk, Gregor Mendel (1822–84), who had followed the distribution of inherited traits throughout several generations of common peas. A particularity like the yellow husk of one of the parent plants would reappear only two generations down the line, and then only in 25 per cent of the cases. Mendel concluded that the inherited information must be passed on in two strands of information, a dominant and a recessive one, so that recessive characteristics would be expressed only if two recessive strands came together, while otherwise the dominant strand would be expressed.

In 1866 Mendel had published his findings in a scientific journal and sent his article to prominent scientists, among them Charles Darwin, but his findings had been ignored – an intellectual tragedy, not only for the monk but also for Darwin himself. His theory of natural selection demonstrated that organisms could adapt to their surroundings, but the mechanism was a mystery even to Darwin. Here, Mendel held the secret, and the British scholar had the solution right under his nose: a copy of Mendel's article lay, unopened, on his desk for years. The findings of the Austrian monk received wider attention only after their rediscovery by the Cambridge biologist William Bateson (1861–1926), who finally understood their implications. Bateson published his findings in *Mendel's Principles of Heredity* (1909). A later book by him, published in 1913, bears a word that he coined to describe the nature of Mendel's discovery: *Problems of Genetics*.

Another crucial discovery had been made by one of the vice presidents of the First Eugenics Congress, the Freiburg zoologist Friedrich Leopold August Weismann (1834–1914). The son of a provincial high-school teacher in Germany, Weismann had worked hard and had become not only a professor at the prestigious university of Freiburg but also a central figure in the debate about how organisms could adapt to their environment. Until now, many scientists had followed the theory put forward by the French zoologist Jean-Baptiste Lamarck (1744–1829), who had claimed that characteristics were learned or imposed by an environment, and would then be transmitted to following generations. Thus the giraffe had a long neck because every generation tried to reach ever higher branches in the savanna and thus, by implication, generations of human refinement and intellectual endeavour would create people specifically adapted to ruling over other, more brutish ones.

Weismann had little time for Lamarck's theory and proposed a very different scenario. He had identified the 'germ plasm' of individual cells (roughly what we today would understand by DNA) and postulated that this innermost core of every individual was passed on to the next generation without being affected by the parent's experiences or acquired characteristics. Weismann argued that only this could explain otherwise inexplicable facts like the existence of infertile animals such as worker or soldier ants, whose parents could not have passed on their specialization to them. This idea elegantly and easily solved many discrepancies between theory and observation in nature, but it created a new problem, namely how to answer Lamarck: if acquired characteristics cannot be inherited, then how do organisms adapt to their environment and how does evolution bring forth new and better-adapted species?

The grand theory of evolution has been carried by humble vehicles. Mendel made his discoveries with peas, Weismann loved to work with sea urchins, and the missing piece of the evolutionary adaptation puzzle (the greatest discovery in genetics until the unveiling of the double helix in 1953) was contributed by a single white-eyed fly, or rather by an American researcher who himself had eyes sharp enough to spot the tiny creature. The Columbia University biologist Thomas Hunt Morgan (1866–1945) advanced science by a giant leap by looking at fruit flies, *Drosophila melanogaster*, beloved or hated by biology students to this day. *Drosophila*'s life cycle (egg to adult) of little over a week made it an ideal candidate for research spanning many generations. The significance of the white-eyed fruit fly which Morgan discovered in 1910 was that it came from two pure lines of red-eyed ancestors. And therefore could not have inherited the trait. The animal's genetic code must therefore have changed spontaneously; it had mutated. If mutation was not only possible, as had been advanced by several scientists, but could actually be observed, it held the explanation for adaptation without a transmission of acquired traits from one generation to the other. In an infinite number of random changes, some would provide evolutionary advantages while others would condemn their carriers. Evolution was occurring as scientists looked on.

Published under the title *The Mechanism of Mendelian Inheritance* in 1915, Morgan's observation and its theoretical framework provided the basis of a modern understanding of evolution – as well as a comprehensive refutation of eugenics, a theory built on the belief of the possibility of inherited traits and an otherwise unchanging inheritance. If some populations actually had been improved and others enfeebled or ruined throughout history, it might indeed have been sensible to accept the eugenics theory, but if random mutations intervened in both populations, and if genetic change was exclusively due to random change and not to acquired characteristics, then the whole edifice of eugenics was a nonsense. Mutation is at once the great creator and the great leveller of the organic world.

Scientific debates only ever seem clear in retrospect. For those who sought the truth about heredity and evolution, the issue was clouded in a thick fog of competing ideas and flawed theories and experiments. Science has the charm of operating with models, and it is always possible to find a defect in a theoretical construct, or to reject either its premises or the interpretation of its outcome. Indeed, when following the debates about eugenics around 1910 it is important to remember that the mechanism of mutation and the recombination of individual genes had not yet been understood, that the structure of genetic material – Watson and Crick's double helix – was not yet known. It was therefore both rational and scientific to keep an open mind about questions such as the possibility of inheriting acquired characteristics. Its role in such features as intelligence or alcoholism had still not been settled, and it was quite possible to argue that the genetic material of entire populations did indeed degrade or improve over the generations. This was still regarded as good science, and, with the best of intentions, those who subscribed to it proposed solutions based on this idea.

While all elements of a fully fledged theory of genetic inheritance and mutation were in place around 1910 there was a lively and often acrimonious debate among scientists as to which theory was the most valid. Before the discovery of a genetic code, the mechanism of inheritance remained obscure. Were traits developed by an individual, such as intelligence or brutality, manual dexterity, moral refinement, alcoholism or tuberculosis, inheritable by a next generation? Here, science had made few advances since the followers of Carl von Linné and the comte de Buffon had clashed during the eighteenth century. Traits could be observed, but it was almost impossible to distinguish nature from nurture, physical inheritance from environmental effects.

Superior Stock

The most august of all researchers into hereditary traits was Francis Galton (1822–1911), one of the great polymaths of Victorian science in Britain. Galton was the author of more than 300 scientific papers and the discoverer of, among other things, fingerprinting, meteorological high-pressure areas and their effect on weather, and statistical psychology (as well as the scientific principles of brewing a perfect cup of tea, a publication in which the question of whether milk should be added before or after the tea is poured into the cup was settled once and for all – in favour of the latter).

Using the *Dictionary of Men of the Time*, Galton had done some of his early research on the prevalence of men of ability – scientists, artists, high civil servants, politicians, military men and princes of the Church – among Britain's prominent families. As most of them were related to one another (fittingly, Galton himself was a nephew of Charles Darwin), he concluded that their inherent qualities must be better than those of the rest of the population. But if the first families of the land produced more eminent men because they were of superior stock, then it was important to protect and foster this potential and not allow it to be swamped by the lesser genetic qualities of the lower classes, whose higher birth rates threatened the power of their betters.

This classic case of *post hoc, ergo propter hoc* reasoning seems comical today, but it became the foundation of Galton's career. From the ancient Greek for 'well-born' he formed the word 'eugenic' and he publicized his findings with energy only a Victorian could muster (as Virginia Woolf recognized when comparing Lord Macaulay and Lytton Strachey). In innumerable lectures and publications, Galton propagated the idea that humanity could attain a higher level of civilization only if valuable individuals were given precedence over weak, degenerate or diseased ones. Eugenicism was born.

Galton published his research in a book with the simple title *Hereditary Genius* (1869, republished 1892), in which he proposed a method for creating a race of supermen:

> it is easy ... to obtain by careful selection a permanent breed of dogs or horses gifted with peculiar powers of running, or of doing anything else, so it would be quite practicable to produce a highly-gifted race of men by judicious marriages during several consecutive generations. I shall show that social agencies of an ordinary character, whose influences are little suspected, are at this moment working towards the degradation of

human nature, and that others are working towards its improvement. I conclude that each generation has enormous power over the natural gifts of those that follow, and maintain that it is a duty we owe to humanity to investigate the range of that power, and to exercise it in a way that, without being unwise towards ourselves, shall be most advantageous to future inhabitants of the earth.

In choosing the English upper class as the focus of his work, Galton had only acted pragmatically, he claimed: 'I should have especially liked to investigate the biographies of Italians and Jews, both of whom appear to be rich in families of high intellectual breeds. Germany and America are also full of interest. It is a little less so with respect to France, where the Revolution and the guillotine made sad havoc among the progeny of her abler races.' In writing this, Galton demonstrated one of the central political implications of eugenics: it led to the creation of a new and stronger kind of aristocracy. Not all eugenicists believed that the European noble houses did hold a superior genetic reservoir – many prominent eugenicists were socialists – but the idea of a ruling class of any description naturally entailed political fault lines, along which the debates of the following years would be fought.

Supported by painstaking statistical research and endless tables and graphs illustrating Britain's genetic decline, Galton's vision was luminous, and attracted more and more followers. 'If a twentieth part of the cost and pains were spent in measures for the improvement of the human race that is spent on the improvement of the breed of horses and cattle, what a galaxy of genius might we not create!' he wrote in *Macmillan's Magazine* in 1865. 'We might introduce prophets and high priests of civilization into the world, as surely as we can propagate idiots by mating cretins. Men and women of the present day are, to those we might hope to bring into existence, what the pariah dogs of the streets of an Eastern town are to our own highly-bred varieties.'

These thoroughbred supermen would assume the world leadership as of right:

The feeble nations of the world are necessarily giving way before the nobler varieties of mankind; and even the best of these, so far as we know them, seem unequal to their work ... We want abler commanders, statesmen, thinkers, inventors, and artists. The natural qualifications of our race are no greater than they used to be in semi-barbarous times, though the conditions amid which we are born are vastly more complex than of old. The foremost minds of the present day seem to stagger and halt under an intellectual load too heavy for their powers.

The fear was that Britain herself was turning into a feeble nation, a spectre that seemed especially threatening after the Boer War, during which the world's greatest army did not only appear to have found its match in a handful of farmers with rifles, but which had also shown that in industrial centres like Manchester, 403 out of every 1,000 recruits were unfit for medical service on account of their bad health. The national anxiety had been amplified by researchers who had ventured into the slums of London and had come back to paint a disturbing picture. One of these intrepid explorers was the American novelist and journalist Jack London, who had published an account of his own experiences in 1902 after having disguised himself as a homeless man and visited the East End (he had first approached Thomas Cook, who had refused to organize a tour there, claiming never to have heard of the place). In London's ringing prose, the condition of the poorest of the poor seemed worse than even Victorian missionaries would admit:

> The unfit and the unneeded! the miserable and despised and forgotten dying in the social shambles. The progeny of prostitution – of the prostitution of men and women and children, of flesh and blood, and sparkle and spirit, in brief, the prostitution of labour. If this is the best that civilization can do for the human, then give us howling and naked savagery. Far better to be a people of the wilderness and the desert, of the cave and the squatting place, than to be a people of the machine and the abyss.

London's picture was corroborated by the philanthropist Charles Booth, who, after a tour of the slums, had written about their inhabitants: 'Their life is the life of savages ... From them come the battered figures who slouch through the streets and play the beggar or bully. They render no useful service, they create no wealth; more often they destroy it.'

What, then, could be more natural than to end this misery by limiting its reproduction? Eugenics, Galton told an adoring audience during one of his many lectures, would be 'introduced into the national consciences like a new religion', ensuring that 'humanity shall be represented by the fittest races. What nature does blindly, slowly, and ruthlessly, man may do providently, quickly, and kindly.' To arrange for this providential hand to create a better society, Galton unleashed a plethora of activities, writing scholarly publications and even a novel to promote his ideas (it was rejected by his publisher and later burned by his niece, who was shocked at the 'indecent' nature of the work). He was the *éminence grise* behind the Eugenics Education Society (founded in 1907), which counted among its ranks men as brilliant as the economist John Maynard Keynes, whose friend, the young Virginia Woolf, would herself note in her diary on 9 January 1915: 'On the towpath we met & had to pass a long line of imbeciles. The first was a very tall young man, just queer enough to look at twice, but no more; the second shuffled, & looked aside; & then one realised that every one in that long line was a miserable ineffective shuffling idiotic creature, with no forehead, or no chin, & an imbecile grin, or a wild suspicious stare. It was perfectly horrible. They should certainly be killed.' Another admirer of Galton's teachings was the dramatist George Bernard Shaw, who wrote: 'There is now no reasonable excuse for refusing to face the fact that nothing but a eugenic religion can save our civilization from the fate that has overtaken all previous civilizations.'

Not only intellectuals were convinced of the movement's merits. Karl Pearson, Galton's assistant and general amanuensis, cheerfully wrote in a letter to the master that his ideas were beginning to be regarded as common sense: 'I hear most respectable middle class matrons saying, if their children are weakly, "Ah, it was not a eugenic marriage!"' On his appointment as home secretary in 1910, Winston Churchill secretly proposed the sterilization of 100,000 of Her Majesty's loyal but less fortunate subjects. The eugenics movement was now a real social and intellectual force, and Galton could congratulate himself on being the father of a rapidly growing movement, dedicated to good breeding. With the air of a benevolent visionary, his profile gleamed on every participant's badge of the First International Eugenics Convention.

The most significant and portentous developments of the apparently rational utopias of this period took place at the very intersection of science and philosophy. The second prophet of this new world-view was the German anatomist and writer Ernst Haeckel (1834–1919), a jellyfish specialist whose popular works on evolution and biology were among the greatest bestsellers in Wilhelminian Germany. His most successful book, *Welträthsel* (Riddles of the Universe, 1899), sold 400,000 copies before 1914.

Haeckel came to prominence as a science writer around 1900, but his career was a product of the prodigiously energetic and optimistic nineteenth century. Like several scientists of his time, he immersed himself totally in his work – much to the chagrin of the second Mrs Haeckel, who felt sorely neglected by the intellectual giant. Having read *The Origin of Species* around the time of its publication in 1859, Haeckel, then a student without any firm professional plans, had immediately recognized the book as the most important of his life and he had dedicated his entire career to spreading its message and bolstering its scientific claims. On several extended research journeys he collected specimens and worked on those that colleagues brought back from their own expeditions. He named and described literally thousands of new species, 3,500 alone after the Challenger expedition to the Polar Circle. A gifted draughtsman, Haeckel also made beautiful illustrations of his specimens.

Haeckel was cut from a very different cloth from Galton or his idol, Darwin. His intellectual patron saints were Goethe, a poet and a scientist, and another German, that great universal genius Alexander von Humboldt, who during the first half of the nineteenth century had put all his energies into creating a unified vision of the world, a grand synthesis reaching from cosmology to geology, botany, zoology and human history and thought. Standing in this German Romantic intellectual tradition, Haeckel was a scrupulous researcher, but the results of his studies were to be material for a deeper understanding of the world, a new ethics, based on the thought that all matter was invested with the same universal spirit.

The art of nature: Ernst Haeckel's successful work
showed an aestheticized nature.

One of Haeckel's most successful books, found on every good middle-class bookshelf in Wilhelminian Germany, was *Kunstformen der Natur* (Artistic Forms in Nature, 1904), in which he described the aesthetic beauty of different creatures and natural phenomena in 200 sumptuously drawn illustrations. It is fascinating book. Not only are the plates expensively produced and lovely to look at, but they are also subtly stylized, more like *Jugendstil* fantasies than scientific work. These are not real plants and animals in a random world, but animated moments of grace, indicators of a higher order, a cosmic mind which Haeckel, who finally officially distanced himself from the Protestant Church in 1910, believed to have recognized in evolution itself.

The real task of humankind, Haeckel felt, was learning to live in accordance with the rules of nature, which at the moment were being flouted everywhere by the philistines in power:

> The higher culture, which we are only beginning to construct, will always have to keep in mind the task of creating a happy, i.e. contented existence...Many barbarous customs and old habits which are thought indispensable will vanish: war, duels, forced adhesion to churches...The main interest of the state will no longer be the creation of the strongest possible military force, but the most perfect education of its youth based on the most extensive care of the arts and sciences. The perfection of technology with its inventions in physics and chemistry will satisfy the needs of all; artificial synthesis will deliver foods rich in proteins. A rational reform of marriage will create happy families.

It is possible that Haeckel had his own, copiously unhappy family life in mind when he wrote these last lines, but to his scientifically trained eye the future was bright because the solution was so clear: Politics, he wrote, was nothing more than applied biology.

Haeckel was often critical of his contemporary Nietzsche, whom he reproached for underestimating the power of sympathy and pity, but his own understanding of these qualities was idiosyncratic. He was a pacifist and an admirer of Bertha von Suttner, but at the same time his notions of pity took on a decidedly active tone. 'Rationally speaking,' he wrote in 1904, 'the killing of a crippled newborn child...cannot be subsumed under the notion of murder, as our modern law books would have it. Instead, we must see and approve of it as a sensible measure, both for those concerned, and for all society.'

It was this mixture of natural, almost pantheist piety, strict scientific thinking and social engineering that attracted a host of followers, many of whom seized particularly on the eugenic aspect of Haeckel's works, on the chance of building a new, purer, better society out of the shambles that was reality. These men, a new generation, hardened the eugenic ideas and pushed them into a particular direction. Science was becoming politics, and one of Haeckel's protégés, Wilhelm Schallmayer (1857–1919), propagated this political slant: 'The principle of natural selection is what made evolutionary theory important,' he wrote in 1910. 'Only as a result of the union of the descent theory and the theory of selection did evolution become a force which, despite strong opposition, old prejudices and powerful interests, continues to pave new roads...' If evolution reigned supreme, then an individual's value lay only in its usefulness to the species:

> It appears as if the individual exists only to perform a function for the species and is not an end in itself; individuals no longer of worth to the maintenance of the species are blessed with an early death. As Weismann had demonstrated, the duration of life of every species is regulated to fit its needs.... Death itself is, according to Weismann, a service to the species at the expense of the individuals. This law of nature, the total subservience of the interest of the individual to that of the species, must also hold true for human development.

Schallmayer was in no doubt that civilization was working against natural selection and was creating a 'crushing and ever-growing burden of useless individuals' with the inescapable result of 'a decline in the average hereditary qualities of a people such that its overall fitness with respect to the demands necessitated by the struggle for survival is diminished'. Convinced of the urgency of his task, the writer had very little patience with those too decadent and short-sighted to perceive the inexorability of the impending catastrophe:

> If the flabby views and comfortable habits for which Neo-Malthusians [who believe populations are too large already] and feminists make propaganda become dominant among the white civilized nations, the white race will not only not expand over the earth, but will doubtlessly... sooner or later either be militarily defeated by the tough and rapidly growing portion of the yellow race and then be gradually replaced by its reproductively superior competition until it [the white race] disappears, or, if hostilities are avoided by all sides, the peaceful immigration of the fecund Asiatics... will lead to exactly the same result.

Measures would have to be taken, measures outlined by another of Haeckel's pupils and one of the vice presidents of the International

Eugenics Convention in London, Alfred Ploetz (1860–1940). With supreme Prussian application, he wrote in his 1895 work *Die Tüchtigkeit unserer Rasse und der Schutz der Schwachen* (The Excellence of Our Race and the Protection of the Weak) that procreation must not be left to 'some accident, an hour of inebriation, but regulated according to fundamental principles established by science'. If such dutiful copulation resulted in a malformed child, 'the college of doctors ... will give it a kind death with a small dose of morphine'.

The founder and tireless propagator of the German Society for Race Hygiene, Ploetz was by no means more extreme than other writers, all of whom published successful books and articles. 'We do not approve of any *false humanity,*' wrote the avowedly racist eugenicist Theodor Fritsch. 'Whoever seeks to preserve the degenerate and depraved, limits space for the healthy and strong, suppresses the life of the whole community, multiplies the sorrows and burdens of existence and helps rob happiness and sunshine from life. Where human power cannot triumph over sorrow, there we honour death as a friend and redeemer.' Fostering the strong would get nowhere without killing the weak, it was believed, and here Nietzsche was used to give ammunition to those who wanted to kill to be kind: 'Even the most careful selection of the best can accomplish nothing, if it is not linked with a merciless elimination of the worst people ... Zarathustra preaches: Do not spare your neighbour! ... Therefore this means becoming hard against those who are below average and in them to overcome one's own sympathy.

A New Manliness?

There is an obvious correlation between eugenic thinking and social issues which we have seen throughout the preceding chapters. Declining birth rates, especially among the middle classes, raised fears of being swamped by those further down the social scale, and called into question – illogically yet forcefully – the manliness of husbands who fathered fewer children. The relationship between men and women had been sufficiently questioned to raise the spectre of a decadent social disorder in which people no longer knew the place allotted to them by nature. Scandals like that surrounding Prince Eulenburg and the suicide of Friedrich Wilhelm Krupp, a convinced eugenicist, because of his rumoured homosexuality had created an impression of moral degeneracy among those in positions of power. In addition to this, the wave of nervous illnesses and neurasthenia, the rise of psychiatry and the free discussion of sexual pathologies had all contributed to a feeling of destabilization, of an enfeeblement of human stock. The spectre of decadence, weakness and unmanliness rose everywhere, and behind it loomed a machine-powered dystopia, in which the masses of the weak and unfit were lulled into artificial sleep by mass entertainments and industrial levelling of all distinctions, all merit and all values. Eugenics appeared to offer a solution to these fears.

If eugenic thinking was strong in Germany and Britain, it was widely discussed in all industrialized nations. Historians have, for obvious reasons, given German eugenicism a great deal of attention, but recent research on other countries has shown that the debate there was every bit as intense, and the ideas no more moderate.

In France, the heritage of Lamarck and his doctrine of inheritable acquired traits was still dominant around 1900. In addition to this, the widespread fear about the collapse of the French population due to low birth rates tended to dissuade scientists from neo-Malthusian positions proposing a further limiting of births among those whom they believed to be of inferior stock. While the sense of needing to build a future (industrial, political and intellectual) was palpable, and eugenics became one aspect of this feast of utopian social engineering, French writers tended to be more sceptical about the future of their nation, and hence perhaps less inclined to imagine such a future.

Positive eugenics (in effect, selective breeding) was not high on the agenda, but when it came to weeding out the unfit, France was equal to other European nations. In a debate about the abolition of the death penalty (quickly rebutted by the higher ranks of justice and turned into a dispute between the relative merits of the guillotine and hanging), many experts published their views about punishment in general, and about social justice. The Italian criminal pathologist Cesare Lombroso worked on biometric measurements to define what he called the 'born criminal', a kind of person from whom nothing good could come, a class of degenerates that was best contained from birth or done away with immediately. In France, this view found enthusiastic support from the psychiatrist Emile Laurent, who argued simply and forcefully:

> If your beloved dog catches rabies you kill him despite everything this cruel act might cost you. But you also kill him to protect him from injury and to spare him unnecessary suffering. And then, all around you, nature applies the death penalty on an immense scale in its hecatombs of the weak and the vanquished, with its storms, its famine, by the claw and tooth of those flesh-eaters that are its hangmen. Kill them! says nature to society. Kill them! says the past of humanity to the present through a hundred voices in history.

Another expert, a retired military doctor, praised the efficacy of execution because of a beneficial side-effect: 'it takes out of circulation the mad procreator [of future children] and is therefore a powerful factor in the amelioration of our race [...] through the avoidance of potential, vice-infected [*viciées*] conceptions.'

Not only the conservative legal establishment took an interest in eugenics. Socialists of all countries had long proposed eugenic measures for creating a healthier proletariat. This somewhat surprising face of eugenic thinking was represented in France in the educationalist and activist Paul Robin (1837–1912). Robin was a born revolutionary. Son of a conservative naval officer, he had moved to Belgium and chosen to become a teacher. Living off private lessons, he became involved with socialist education and ideas, and spent a decade between Geneva, London, Paris and Belgium, always involved in political activism, through which he met and collaborated with luminaries such as Prince Kropotkin in Geneva and Karl Marx in London. Eventually, however, Robin tired of the ceaseless factional infighting in the International and plunged instead into practical work as director of an orphanage, where he could put his very liberal educational ideas to the test. There was no corporal punishment, boys and girls were taught together and learned a variety of trades as well as academic subjects. Astonished visitors saw all the principles of education flouted and yet had to remark on the remarkable cleanliness of both orphanage and children, and on the pupils' cheerfulness and confidence. His reformist attitude, though, was too much for his superiors, who sacked him after fourteen years of service, in 1894.

Towards the turn of the century, Robin turned more and more towards eugenic teaching, or neo-Malthusianism as it was known in France. He founded the *Ligue de la régénération* and published a journal in which he argued for eugenic measures. During his years working in popular education and as a socialist activist, he had seen his share of misery and injustice. The conclusions he drew from his experiences, though, were surprising: 'public assistance is most often addressed to those inferior people who were born like this or became such through circumstances and will remain like this,' he wrote in 1902.

> In the worst case they will haphazardly produce numerous children who will have no chance of triumphing over their difficulties and will tax all assistance beyond what is possible or imaginable. What is more, it allows the worst degenerates to live, particularly the weak of mind ... which the former state of nature or of public assistance would have allowed to perish. All these degenerates which are now allowed to live under great

sacrifice, but a life of which nobody would want even a week, and to which all of us would prefer death.

Societies, Robin believed, could not allow themselves to be burdened with such a load. 'The millions spent by all nations in order to help the inadequate, the scrofulous, the syphilitic and the alienated result in nothing but an amelioration hardly sufficient to make their miserable path in life,' he thundered, '[and] are an impoverishment of the race. It is the organization of public decline.'

Sweeping measures would have to be taken to prevent a slide back into barbarism, Robin wrote, particularly through a directive as to who should or should not produce children. Workers brought part of their own misery upon themselves by producing great numbers of children who would soon be their competitors in the workplace, and having fewer children was therefore in their interest, he believed, adding that for 'the worst incurable degenerates ... there is no other remedy than artificial sterilization'. Having never abandoned his secular principles, Robin also drew another consequence from this necessity of limiting births, for while procreation by the wrong people was a danger to society, the joys associated with it were unquestionably good and healthy, as he argued in 1902:

> Let us establish the principle that the nervous vibrations corresponding to sexual enjoyment [*volupté sexuelle*] are just as positive as other vibrations, which nobody refuses to esteem. It is just as honourable for a person to give and to receive sexual pleasure as it is to create something beautiful, useful, good, or to look with admiration at a beautiful landscape, a beautiful monument, a beautiful statue ... to listen to beautiful music, enjoy the perfume of a rose, or a violet, or of jasmine, or to eat an apple.

National stereotypes are always annoying and sometimes dangerous, but they can also be very diverting. Where the German Dr Ploetz proudly proclaimed that the sexual act would no longer be a haphazard occurrence due to a drunken moment (poor Mrs Ploetz!), the Frenchman Robin convinced his compatriots that one of the positive aspects of his neo-Malthusian brand of eugenicism was the emancipation of sexual desire from necessary procreation. Despite the jolly reputation of the French capital as Europe's foremost place of pleasure, however, Robin's robustly sensual views on sex scandalized his contemporaries and repeatedly brought him into conflict with the authorities. Emancipating sexual enjoyment from procreation and openly calling for contraception, the socialist was questioning the fundamental values of good society. Paul Robin had become a feminist: 'A woman must be able to dispose freely of her own body and to decide for instance, when she is pregnant, whether or not to keep the child she carries. The freedom of woman is the *conditio sine qua non* of regeneration. Women's liberation, freedom before the law, in morals, before public opinion is in itself... will be the veritable regenerator of humankind.'

Robin remained a rationalist to the very end. When, in 1912, he felt that his threescore years and ten had been exhausted and he was now, aged seventy-five, himself becoming one of the infirm and the scrofulous, he swallowed a large dose of morphine. Even while dying, he attempted to make notes about the symptoms of poisoning until he was overtaken by unconsciousness.

At Home with the Kallikaks

While the French were gripped by national malaise and unsure of their future, the citizens of the Land of the Free had no such misgivings. In the world's greatest place of immigration, planning populations was an obvious concern shared by, among others, Andrew Carnegie and John D. Rockefeller, two of the richest and most powerful men in the land. Their financial support allowed Charles Davenport (1866–1944), a leading Harvard biologist, to create, in 1904, the Eugenics Records Office at Cold Springs Harbor, New York, as a laboratory for research into heredity and natural variation.

American eugenicists put heavy emphasis on scientific proof and evaluation scales, most importantly those developed by Henry Goddard (1866–1957), the director of an institution for mentally retarded children in Vineland, New Jersey. Goddard had standardized the measurement of intelligence by proposing a scale entitled Intelligence Quotient (IQ) and designed by a German colleague, mapping a progression from *idiot* to *imbecile* and *moron* and from there on to more favourable adjectives. Putting his work into practice, Goddard analysed the family tree of one of the young women in his charge, 'Debora Kallikak', whose feeble-mindedness he traced back to a male ancestor's dalliance with 'the nameless feeble-minded girl' who, according to the doctor, was the cause of generations of mental trouble within the family. *The Kallikak Family: A Study in the Heredity of Feeble Mindedness* (1910) was received as a sensation by fellow scientists, as was Goddard's revelation that according to research performed by him at the Ellis Island immigration station, 83 per cent of Jewish, 80 per cent of Hungarian, 79 per cent of Italian, and 87 per cent of Russian immigrants were 'feeble-minded'. Severe cases, Goddard believed, admitted of only one rational course of action: sterilization. Only like this could a 'pure, American, superior' race be created.

Pressure from scientists and acquiescence from high-placed politicians such as Theodore Roosevelt (who was himself convinced that African Americans were 'as a race and in the mass... altogether inferior to whites'), as well as lobbying by wealthy businessmen such as the health-food manufacturer and eugenics enthusiast John Harvey Kellogg, created a public climate for Goddard's ideas to find their way into legislation. There had been repeated attempts to introduce compulsory sterilization laws in several states (Michigan 1897; Pennsylvania 1905), but the first of thirty-three successful state laws was passed in Indiana in 1907 and applied to 'confirmed criminals, idiots, rapists and imbeciles' held in public institutions. Several sterilization laws remained on the statute books for many decades, resulting in an estimated 65,000 forced or surreptitious sterilizations (the latter often during the course of other surgical procedures) in the United States. The last forced sterilization was performed in Oregon, in 1983.

The intellectual climate and preoccupations in Russia were very different from those in Western Europe and the USA. While in Western Europe the bourgeoisie saw itself threatened by an ever-growing army of the working poor, the main problem of Russian bourgeois thinkers was that they were excluded from power by an autocratic regime whose legitimacy was built on the Orthodox Church. In this situation, a different strategy emerged: instead of arguing against the rise of the lower classes and for an increased measure of control over them and their procreation, the Tsar's subjects had more interest in proving that all creatures were evolved from the same original slime, that there was a rational explanation to creation, and that consequently no group of persons could claim to have a divine right to power, as the sociologist Nicolai Mikhailovskii argued:

> The folk tradition of all peoples ascribes a more or less high origin to man. Darwin is perfectly correct in asserting that the folklore imputation of a divine or semidivine descent of man is only an illusion that does not flatter the human species; what flatters man immensely more is the idea that he has risen from lower spheres – from the depths of nature. In fact, this is the only viewpoint that allows for the advancement of man; all other views assume that man has fallen and disgraced his ancestors.

In pre-revolutionary Russia, Darwinism offered more argumentative scope than eugenicism. This would change only after 1917, when the demand from those in power was to create a new man. Russian intellectuals and scientists had accepted Darwin with huge enthusiasm. Research scientists in laboratories throughout the empire set about supporting Darwin's hypothesis, producing not only a forest worth of scientific papers, but also what was perhaps Europe's largest Darwinist scientific community, whose research and methods were often ahead of those of their Western colleagues, notably in research laboratories. One such laboratory was led by Professor Ivan Pavlov (1859–1936), who was to attain international fame with his experiments on the behavioural conditioning of dogs.

If behaviourism was a central focus of research in Russia, social Darwinism was hotly contested. Darwin's most remarkable Russian critic was the anarchist philosopher Prince Petr Aleksandrovich Kropotkin (1841–1921), who was then living in exile in London, but was being avidly read and discussed in his homeland, and was certainly one of the great intellects of his generation. Kropotkin's eventful life had taken him from an elite cadet school and a post as *cadet de chambre* to Tsar Alexander II into the steppes of Siberia, where he had joined a Cossack regiment in order to escape the stifling life at court. It was there, during long days spent at leisure and on excursions into the surrounding wilderness, that the young man observed something which apparently contradicted Darwin's idea of the struggle for existence:

> I recollect myself the impression produced upon me by the animal world of Siberia ... We saw plenty of adaptations for struggling, very often in common, against the adverse circumstances of climate, or against various enemies ... ; we witnessed numbers of facts of mutual support, especially during migrations of birds and ruminants, but even in the Amur and Usuri regions, where animal life swarms in abundance, facts of real competition and the struggle between higher animals of the same species came very seldom under my notice, though I eagerly searched for them.

The idea of mutual support, of interested altruism in nature and in society, became a central tenet of Kropotkin's social philosophy, which he finally published under the title *Mutual Aid* in 1902. Far from teaching the relentless, Hobbesian battle of all against all, the princely anarchist concluded, nature teaches that animals are most successful if they organize themselves around common interests:

> The animal species, in which individual struggle has been reduced to its narrowest limits, and the practice of mutual aid has attained the greatest development, are invariably the most numerous, the most prosperous, and the most open to further progress. The mutual protection which is

obtained in this case, the possibility of attaining old age and of accumulating experience, the higher intellectual development, and the further growth of sociable habits, secure the maintenance of the species, its extension, and its further progressive evolution. The unsociable species, on the contrary, are doomed to decay.

Kropotkin raised his voice at the First International Eugenics Congress in London. Who was more valuable to the species, he asked: proletarian women who bore and nursed children as best they could, or society ladies who went to great lengths not to produce children? His interventions were not appreciated by delegates who were still reeling from an unpleasant incident at the grand inaugural banquet of the congress, hosted by Her Grace, the Duchess of Marlborough, the lord mayor of London, and the American ambassador Whitelaw Read. The speaker at this occasion had been Arthur Balfour, one of the most eminent men in the kingdom, a former prime minister and according to Austen Chamberlain, 'the finest brain that has been applied to politics in our time'. As the 500 invited guests were mellowing over a glass of after-dinner port, the great man had given an address that made many of them sit up in astonishment. Having applied his brain for once not to politics but to science, he presented the eugenicists with some unexpected conclusions. 'We say that the fit survive. But all that means is that those who survive are fit,' Balfour had launched at his audience, and then: 'The idea that you can get a society of the most perfect kind merely by considering certain questions about the strain and ancestry and the health and the physical vigour of various components of that society – that I believe is a most shallow view of a most difficult question.'

There were other critics of eugenic thought. The British doctor and sexologist Havelock Ellis raised a troubling question of the future the eugenicists wanted to create: 'Animals are bred for specific purposes by a superior race of animals not by themselves . . . It is important to breed, let us say, good sociologists; that, indeed, goes without saying. But can we be sure that, when bred, they will rise up to bless us?' Max Nordau, who had made a career as a cultural sceptic looking forward to a brighter future peopled by superior men and women, also thought that eugenicists fell at the conceptual hurdle towards improvement:

It is clear that we cannot apply the principle of artificial breeding to man . . . There is no recognized standard of physical, intellectual perfection. Do you want inches? In that case you would have to exclude Frederick the Great and Napoleon I who were undersized; [former French President Aldolphe] Thiers, who was almost a dwarf; and the Japanese as a nation . . .

Few of these objections cut much ice, needless to say, amid the excitement of founding an international movement courted by men of state and great aristocrats. The Eugenics Conference ran its course, closed with grand speeches and declarations, and brought forth, after a gestation of only a few months, a litter of eugenics societies throughout Europe. The time was ripe for action, it seemed, not for cautious argument.

New Men, New Women

Galton's approach was very Anglo-Saxon in its emphasis on utilitarianism and level-headed statistical analysis, and eugenicists like Davenport and Goddard worked at experiments and theoretical models. But many followers of the eugenic idea looked at Galton's ideas from a different horizon – a mountain range, to be precise: the dwelling place of Zarathustra. Here, intellectuals (including some British and American ones) huddled up, exposed to the cold winds of uncertainty, but glorying in their courage and their daring. They had found their teacher, they believed, and they had found eugenics.

Wherever we have turned until now, at some point we have encountered the legacy of Friedrich Nietzsche. It was the protagonist of Nietzsche's *Thus Spake Zarathustra*, 1883–85, of course, who received such grand ovations on his mountain top. 'For my generation he was the earthquake of the age,' wrote the German expressionist poet Gottfried Benn (1886–1956). Nietzsche's rebellious stance towards authority and Christian morality had already exerted a tremendous pull on the generation of the 1890s, and his dangerous appeal had lost nothing of its magnetism by 1910. This was in part due to the very obscurity that so annoyed some of his British readers like Bertrand Russell, who quipped: 'Nietzsche's superman is very like [Wagner's] Siegfried, except that he knows Greek.'

Others were attracted by the very mixture of the classical and the mythical which so disgusted the logician Russell. With almost prophetic sensitivity Nietzsche had sensed and given shape to many of the concerns his contemporaries and their children found particularly pressing in the pre-War years: the slave morality of the Church and of its capitalist heirs; the destabilizing changes in the relations between men and women; the will or need to overcome the spiritual smallness of consumer life in industrialized societies and to create something altogether more magnificent, based on self-knowledge and the renunciation of the inessential.

It was this sensitivity that gave Nietzsche's works such a ring of truth, and it was perhaps little more than desperate overcompensation that gave them their bravado. At his best, though, Nietzsche put his finger right into the wounds of his time, a ringing voice, by turn angry, funny and apocalyptic, hurling curses into the faces of the plaster busts admired by the sages of official culture. His rhetorical gesture was more that of a poet than a philosopher. Nietzsche, in other words, could be seen to contradict himself, and imposing a system on his thought was no more possible than it would be to deduce a single and coherent vision of life from the plays of Shakespeare or the works of Shelley or Rabelais. To his followers, this was all part of his appeal. Not for them the sterile intellectual exercises of Kant and Hegel, Augustine and Aquinas.

The son of a Lutheran pastor, Nietzsche rejoiced in the idea of a future in the sign of Dionysus, the god of ecstasy and the irrepressible force of life and death, dance and destruction, a savage vivacity to sweep away all pietist oppressiveness and the cowering morality of the Protestant pulpit. True life and human value, Nietzsche claimed, expressed itself not in submission to a man-hating god of suffering, but in the will to power: 'Life is appropriation, injury, conquest of the strange and weak, suppression, severity, obtrusion of its own forms, incorporation, and at least, putting it mildest, exploitation.'

Nietzsche appeared an ideal prophet for eugenics and, later, for all forms of totalitarianism. He claimed that the coming century would be dominated by 'that new party of life, which will take into its hands the greatest of all tasks, breeding humanity to a higher level [*Höherzüchtung der Menschheit*], including the merciless destruction of everything that is degenerate and parasitical' – but in the passage in question he is actually writing about music after Wagner, about artistic renewal and a new Dionysian culture, not about politics and populations. Nowhere in his works does he show any admiration for eugenicists, and he generally treated the rationalist optimism of a Galton with contempt. Only the bile he poured over antisemites and racists could turn his sentences even more bitterly sarcastic. Antisemites, he wrote, were 'moral masturbators', little 'men of resentment, physiologically unfortunate and worm-eaten,' whose outbursts sickened him. Describing himself as the 'anti-antisemite', he laconically ended one of his last letters 'I am just having all antisemites shot.'

The attainment of a 'highest level' brings us straight to the infamous *Übermensch* who was to be reinterpreted as a terrifying parody of himself, one of the master race. Nietzsche's concept has neither racial nor brutal traits. It simply takes an individual who has overcome the banal self-destructive narcissism of the 'herd people' of the plains and has discovered, on his spiritual mountain, that values are there to be revalued, that the pure life force must be pursued beyond dogmatic thinking. Superman is not a ruler but a seeker, whose greatest challenge is to overcome himself.

Such niceties of interpretation paled before the idea of Nietzsche as the walrus-mustachioed prophet of a new and brutal kind of vitalism – dressed up, according to ideological requirements, in Nordic furs, Aryan robes, or the white coat of the scientist. The poet-philosopher was kidnapped a hundred times over, a victim of overly literal readings and of the very Will to Power he had enjoined his readers to discover.

Racists and Mystics

We have already seen how porous were the walls between biology and ideology in the scientific writings of this period. As soon as the argument moved out of the academy, however, these walls simply collapsed.

Prophets, philosophers and sages of all descriptions and nationalities despoiled science of isolated facts and theories and manipulated ideas like Nietzsche's to suit their various needs. While some of these utopians of race and heredity, such as Galton, Haeckel, Davenport, were part of the establishment and wrote from a scientific consensus, others sought more radical and darker truths which they claimed they could discern in the runes of ancient civilizations, in the stars, or in mystical documents. Most of the mystic authors, Madame Blavatsky and Rudolf Steiner among them, were racists who camouflaged their disdain for darker hues of skin under incense and initiation. Steiner particularly made it his sacred task to spread the gospel of race during his hundreds of lectures throughout Germany. According to his teaching of what is essentially a spiritual variant of evolutionism, Africans were at the very bottom of the scale while Europeans (Germans to be precise) stood at the pinnacle. The very comparison was absurd, he thought, between 'an uncompleted snail or amoeba to a perfect lion'. The 'negro race', in any case, 'does not belong to Europe', and Steiner declared himself shocked by the 'terrible cultural banality of implanting black people into Europe, a dreadful thing the French are doing to others [other Europeans]. It will have a worse effect on France herself. It has an incredibly strong influence on the blood, on the race. That will further French decadence. The French people as a race is thrown back [in evolution].'

Regarding the 'strong sexual drive' of 'negroes', the mystic explained that it was due to the sun, to light and warmth, which changed the metabolism of Africans, boiling them from the inside and heating up their affective lives, an effect that also explained their appearance. 'This is because mercurial forces are boiling and simmering within the lymphatic system … This [appearance] is caused by their boiling over [*auskochen*], which converts the general, similar human form [to that of a European] into the special one of the Ethiopian race, with black skin, woolly hair, and so on.' Seen in this context, the Jews could count themselves fortunate that the doctor claimed only that: 'Judaism as such has long outlived itself, has no justification in the community of peoples, and if it has survived nevertheless, it is a mistake of world history whose consequences followed by necessity. We are not speaking about the Jewish religion alone, but particularly about the mind of Jewry, about the Jewish way of thinking.'

Utopian visions often had a political and racial tinge in central Europe. Constantly buffeted by nationalist controversies between the German, Czech and Hungarian populations (to say nothing of the Jews and of smaller minorities), the self-anointed seers of the Habsburg empire were not content with free love and nut cutlets. A grander, more radical solution to the world's problems was needed, and amid the cacophony of voices and cultural traditions, racial purity seemed to provide an answer, and heredity the necessary instrument. Race had been a wide term, commonly used by people of all political persuasions and capable of denoting anything from breeding or class, to family background or biological predetermination and descent. It was about to acquire a narrower meaning that made it a weapon in the arsenal of the revolutionary right.

Foremost among these conservative racial mystics was the novelist Guido von List (1848–1919; the noble 'von' was awarded by himself), who discovered a world of hidden truths after a period of temporary blindness, during which he saw occult aspects of the world in a series of visions. Having recovered from his illness, he penned a memorandum about his findings and sent it to the Austrian Academy of Sciences, only to see it returned without comment. Embittered by establishment enmity towards his genius and higher perception, von List published his books himself and devoted the remainder of his life to extolling the virtues of Aryanism and the purification of the Nordic master race and the fight against 'herd peoples', dark races and Jews.

Like Steiner, List was influenced by the writings of Madame Blavatsky and, like Steiner, he believed that the German culture had a historical mission willed by ancient mythical forces. List believed he had found this truth through his studies of Germanic runes, whose interpretation, he held, unlocked the secrets of the universe, particularly the historical greatness of the Aryans as symbolized by the most powerful of runes, the swastika. Christianity had strangled the human spirit by alienating it from the ecstatic, the sensual, from true spirituality, List taught, and the answer to the limitations of his time was to return to an earlier form of spirituality – in his case, what he believed to be a Germanic, Aryan religion. One can hear echoes of other critiques of modernity in his writings. Christianity, he thought, was about to destroy the 'noble race of heroes', the Germans,

> and breed a people of slaves, which will descend to the level of Australian negroes in its dull shamanic rites... As the people of our contemporary age cannot deny the primeval natural laws despite being caught in a religious system which is negating the life force, a crooked morality has developed, spreading *hypercritical semblance of reality over hidden doings, showing all those sick phenomena of modern life which are beginning to disgust us in their hollowness and putrification.*

Modernity, List argued, had not discovered but lost the principle of selective breeding. The goal of all right-thinking people in German lands had to be to reclaim the national, racial foundation of their culture as expressed in Germanic mythology, but this project had a powerful adversary: 'Today's Jews – the poor rascals, we know why! – are born internationals and therefore from the beginning "decided enemies" of any attempt to ground a culture in a national soil.'

In List's grand vision, members of 'inferior races' would have no citizenship rights and would be prevented from owning land or businesses, or receiving a higher education. All this would help the Aryan to re-emerge from the shadows and assume the historic place he had so long been denied by a conspiracy of Jews, Freemasons and Catholic clergymen. Then, and only then, could Germans of purified blood and unsullied ancestry rise 'toward the ancient heights of pure-blooded German heroism, toward the Holy Grail, toward Aryo-Germanism'. As the mystic seal of this quest, List used an old Germanic and Indian symbol, the swastika. It comes as little surprise to learn that the young Hitler was one of List's most ardent readers.

While List liked to stylize himself in his photographs as prophet, with beard and velvet beret, one of his pupils, the defrocked priest and hysterical antisemite Baron Dr Johann Lancz de Liebenfels, preferred the pseudo-medieval cloak of a knight with a Maltese cross on his chest, an incongruous outfit, given his bald patch and wire-rimmed glasses. Liebenfels worked on the fault line between scientific heredity and Manichean mysticism. During the ancient Babylonian empire, he claimed, the superior Aryan race had committed bestiality with an extinct race of animals who were similar to pygmies and who carried evil in them, a sin that brought into the world the non-blond, non-Nordic races. In his 1905 book, fancifully entitled *Theozoologie oder die Kunde von den Sodoms-Äfflingen und dem Götter-Elektron* (Theozoology, or On the Little Monkeys of Sodom and the Electrons of the Gods), Liebenfels argued that higher men were contaminated to various degrees by primeval animalism and wickedness, which still lived on as barely understood feelings in the different races:

> Just as every Aryan feels overwhelming repulsion at the sight of a Mongol's distorted mug or a Negro's grotesque visage ... so the eyes of any member of an inferior race flare up in age-old vicious hatred at the sight of a paleface. One feels his own superiority and recognizes his divine origins, and the other still has the feelings of the untamed, savage ape which at such moments awaken as the inheritance from the ancient past.

This gnostic world-view, the eternal struggle of good against evil, was further seasoned with 'proofs' from recent scientific discoveries such as radioactivity, X-rays and electrical phenomena.

Such brutalist racial thinking was not the domain of mystical cranks. The respected pathologist Hugo Ribbert, who held successive chairs at famous universities, claimed: 'The man who is thoroughly healthy in every respect simply cannot act badly or wickedly; his actions are necessarily good, that is to say, properly adapted to the evolution of the human race, in harmony with the cosmos.' The Vienna member of parliament and philosopher Bartholomaeus von Carneri, a personal friend of Ernst Haeckel's, claimed: 'Entire human tribes stand lower than the animals ... the mental activity of the elephant, the horse, and the dog [is] significantly better developed than the lowest human species.' Such statements from within the scientific and literary establishment were numerous, while on the margins of academic respectability the likes of Otto Weininger and Houston Stewart Chamberlain attracted huge readerships with their racially motivated pseudo-scientific bestsellers.

At the intersection of Catholicism and ethnic strife, Austria-Hungary produced a particularly mystical form of the racist ideas which had become a fixed part of debate throughout the West. Maurice Barrès in France, Francis Galton in Britain and Russian Slavophile thinkers such as Vladimir Soloviev were every bit as racist as their German and Austro-Hungarian counterparts, but their racial thought articulated itself along different lines, following different national cultures of debate.

The intellectual corner-posts of eugenic and racial thinking nevertheless corresponded to certain general preoccupations of the period. Acceptance of traditional religious models was in decline (witness the separation of Church and State in 1905), and science increasingly replaced religion as the dominant paradigm for understanding the world. At the same time, the banality and anonymity of life in an urban, consumer society created a need for new models, in response to change and to the annihilation of old certainties. Any theory pretending to offer a solution to the perceived degeneracy of modernity had to use the vocabulary of science: explaining life in terms of evolutionary mechanisms and even electricity. At the same time, it had to address what was perhaps the most deeply felt change on a personal level: the shift in the relationship between men and women, male and female social roles. Darwinist thinking and theories on heredity were ideal vehicles for this, as they put sexual roles and mechanisms at the very heart of human history.

Thanks to Darwin, the world, its ills and goals could be explained in terms of sex. The levelling impact of a democratized culture of education and entertainment, as well as the rise of socialism, found its match in the perceived menace of 'lower races' taking over a high culture that was cast as originally European. The claims for universal human rights and Bertha von Suttner's peace movement could be countered by arguing in terms of a struggle for survival that was not a mere cultural construct, but part of the Darwinian, natural, order of things. Changing moral norms could be demonized 'scientifically' in terms of a degeneration of racial purity; individualism rejected by putting the needs and future of the race before concerns about personal happiness. It was science, after all: objective fact, unassailable by sentiment or more trivial concerns. Waking up in a disenchanted world, eugenicists and racial theorists sought to rob those they despised of the last of all human rights, the right to live.

14

1913:
Wagner's Crime

Today humanity...sees its evolution accelerating too furiously, just as all long falls into the abyss accelerate.
— Pierre Loti, *Quelques aspects du vertige mondial*

How I hate the man who talks about the 'brute creation', with an ugly emphasis on brute. Only Christians are capable of it. As for me, I am proud of my close kinship with other animals. I take a jealous pride in my Simian ancestry. I like to think that I was once a magnificent hairy fellow living in the trees and that my frame has come down through geological time via sea jelly and worms and Amphioxus, Fish, Dinosaurs, and Apes. Who would exchange these for the pallid couple in the Garden of Eden?
W. N. P. Barbellion, *Diary*, 22 July 1910

On 4 September 1913 Ernst August Wagner, aspiring author and conscientious headmaster of a provincial elementary school in Swabia, southern Germany, woke up in the early morning, got out of bed, took a bludgeon and a knife and butchered his wife and four children. He then mounted his bicycle and rode to a nearby railway station, not forgetting to order three pints of milk for the next day. He visited his brother's family and enjoyed a pitcher of beer with his sister-in-law. One of his nephews showed him his new rabbit hutch. After riding a considerable distance and posting some letters, Wagner arrived in the little town of Mühlhausen, where he had been teacher some years earlier, around eleven at night. He set fire to four houses, produced two Mauser handguns from his travel bag, and shot all men who happened to be in the street, killing eight and wounding another twelve, before being overpowered by a police constable and several local men. He was severely beaten in the struggle, and left for dead. When the police realized that he was still alive they arrested the injured murderer, who regained consciousness and refused to make any statement.

Before launching into his bloody frenzy, Ernst Wagner had, to all intents and purposes, been a normal, even an exemplary citizen, a German success story. Born into an impoverished farming family in 1874, as one of twelve children, the bright and lively boy had made it to teachers' college and had held a succession of junior teaching posts before rising through the ranks and becoming assistant teacher at a good provincial school at the age of twenty-seven. He had written poetry and tried his hand at historical drama. In 1903 he had married the daughter of an innkeeper who was comfortably off. By now a senior teacher with his own small school, he had been a solid family man, a valued member of the community.

His life story can be narrated very differently, though. He had lost his father at the age of two, and his mother had not been able to keep her huge hungry family afloat. She had struggled to build up a small shop, and failed, had sought refuge in the arms of a succession of different men, had married again, then divorced. Her sensitive son had seen all of this and had retained a powerful ambivalence towards women, towards trust, towards sex. As a young adult, he was suspicious of everyone. Unable to work due to 'extreme nervous excitability', he had spent six months travelling through Switzerland, desperately trying to regain his calm, his zest for life.

On his return, nothing was gained. He was distrustful, arrogant, irritable. Humiliated by his position as assistant teacher, and overwhelmed by lonely lust and self-disgust, he took out his sexual urges on farm animals. He devoured all kinds of literature he could find and lived in a dream world; only a few beers at the local would relax him and make him friendlier – so much so that one of the innkeeper's daughters had fallen pregnant to him. He was transferred to a smaller school as punishment. Now headmaster, he felt compelled to marry the young woman who was carrying his child. He despised her, along with his colleagues, his pupils, everyone. To escape the drudgery of teaching the ABC to farmers' children, he read more than before, spending a quarter of his annual salary on books. After his crime, the police found a collection of hundreds of titles, from ancient Greek authors, Shakespeare and the German classics to works by Maksim Gorky, Ernst Haeckel, Hendrik Ibsen and Friedrich Nietzsche. He had also written stage works on biblical themes and on the life of the emperor Nero. When he could find no publishers for them, he had paid for the publication out of his own pocket. He was convinced that he was destined for greatness.

The young teacher had become notorious for his edginess and

megalomania. At the local inn he was heard to shout: 'Goethe? Schiller? *I* am the greatest German dramatist!' He wore extravagant clothes and yellow shoes. In a region famous for its hard-working but provincial citizens he, a local man, insisted on speaking high German instead of Swabian dialect. Unbeknown to those around him, he often carried a concealed gun. He was certain that people were laughing about him behind his back, ridiculing him, plotting to harm him. He had planned the murders for years, carefully buying up ammunition and weapons, going into the forest for shooting practice, scouting out locations and planning his every move on that decisive day. He had finally settled on a day in late September, at the end of the summer holidays, as if he had expected to resume teaching a few days later.

The sensational murder of thirteen people was headline news in Germany and beyond. The French paper *Paris Midi* found it a wonderful vehicle for attacking the old enemy, Germany: 'Life is not a pleasant affair. If you add the misfortune of being born a German, one could call it terrible ... Is this man mad? What does it matter if he is a monster? Kill him! It would be too much honour to talk about him even for two days.' Newspapers all over Europe reported, screamed, speculated – not least (journalistic intellectual shortcuts haven't changed much) about the similarities between the teacher and Germany's other remarkable Mr Wagner, with his apocalyptic fantasies.

The murderer himself, meanwhile, had been transferred to a psychiatric hospital, where he was examined by an eminent doctor in the field, Robert Gaupp of Tübingen University, who was very surprised by his patient's appearance and bearing: 'I had expected a fearsome, vicious man of animal brutality and had therefore taken special precautions ... [But] when he was led into my examination room I immediately saw that I had been wrong. A serious man stepped forward, crooked with sadness and with a dignified air about him; polite, ready to go along with anything, and in his entire comportment an educated man.' Gaupp had the task of deciding whether or not Wagner would be facing the death penalty, but the psychiatrist's report quickly made clear that the criminal could not be held responsible for his acts. The case against Wagner was closed and he was incarcerated in the Winnetal mental asylum.

Ernst Wagner was not only a brutal paranoiac but also a remarkably articulate man, a fact which allows us to gain insight into his motives even today. The mail he had posted during the afternoon of that bloody September fourth contained three letters justifying his actions. He had also written, apart from his plays, a lengthy autobiography. This revealed that his plan had been much more ambitious than was immediately realized.

His original project had been to kill all men in the village of Mühlbach and then to kill his brother's family ('I shall be like the angel of death in his house, the angel of mercy'), and to drive to the nearby town of Ludwigsburg in a hijacked train: 'I kill. Into the castle. I kill. I burn and am burned. [...] And I can burn myself in the bed of the duchess. That's why I wished the duchess were young.'

But what had forced him to create the apocalypse in the heart of rural Swabia? Wagner's own letters and the account of his life throw light on his motivation and draw a picture of a child of his time in the worst and saddest sense. One of the letters posted on the day of the murders was addressed to 'My People'.

> There are far too many people [on earth]. Half of them should be beaten to death immediately. They are not worth feeding, because they are of rotten body. Of all of man's creations, man himself is the worst. If I were not stopped from doing so by looking at my own lamentable likeness, I would tell you how much I am disgusted by all these ugly, weedy, sick people.
>
> Whence does this misery come? Nobody, I believe, is better suited to explaining this than I. It comes from sexual abnormality. Today's generation suffers from their sex [*Das heutige Geschlecht leidet am Geschlecht*].

The killing of his family, Wagner claimed, had been necessary to protect them from his own persecutors, a measure of pity towards his innocent children who would otherwise be in the hands of his torturers. As for the men of Mühlbach, he had wanted to purge his shame and wreak revenge for the shame of having been forced to marry a girl he did not love and for being sent away to a different school, a smaller village. He closed the letter by writing: 'Finally I permit myself to remember myself in a friendly way and to come to the following judgement about myself: Subtracting the sexual element from my life, I have been of all the people I know the best by far.'

What was 'the sexual element' that must be subtracted from his life to show his moral purity? This Wagner elucidated in his memoir:

> So that I can get rid of this confession immediately: I am a sodomite. It's happily out and I don't want to talk of it any more; your lecherousness is not worth one minute of despising myself. My self despisal and sadness have turned me grey, and I am only 34 years old. This is how long I have suffered. I ask you: Take the Nazarene down from his cross and pin me to it, I am suffering turned flesh. Yes, when I think of the sacrificial lamb at Golgotha, I can only smile.

Unsurprisingly, Dr Gaupp immediately fixed his attention on this aspect of his patient's personality. Was he a homosexual? Was it true that he had repeatedly committed bestiality? His search for incontrovertible proof yielded nothing. People in the village kept silent. Only his one-time maid stated that his boots had sometimes been very dirty 'as if he had stepped into cow pats' and that she had once found short, red hairs like a cow's on the front of his jacket. The psychiatrist thought this was enough to come to the conclusion that Wagner had subconsciously wanted to punish his mother: 'This is how dirty you are. This is sexuality, so deeply dirty, so filthy. [...] This is what you, my mother, are doing with men, now that father is no longer alive.'

Whether or not this diagnosis was accurate, it is certain that Wagner's own surviving writings, a collection of aphorisms veering between insane rants and extremely pertinent observations, are pervaded by revulsion against his own sexual desire: 'the misery of the nerves [i.e. neurasthenia] is not due to alcohol, not to the workings of the great cities, not even to the haste and worry of commercial life; its main reason is sexual vice, sexual degeneration of every kind.' He was obsessed by his urges, and so revolted by them that he could not bring himself to write them down: 'everything in me is desire and lust'; 'the "derailment" [bestiality] ... has not been without trace on me. As little as the other one, onanism. I am of too weak a nature, my conscience can't stand for it.' 'It is strange: I, who have committed quite a few swinish acts, I am so embarrassed to think about it that I cannot bring myself to analyse [this] a little.' His lust was an illness, rotting him from the inside 'You know, I am guilty of my own illness. I am very ill, have been for seventeen years [i.e. since the age of fourteen], sick beyond healing. It seems, however, that my illness is not lethal. I have to help it along, otherwise it will not finish with me.'

When not wallowing in self-revulsion, he unleashed terrible scenarios of revenge and bloodshed in his head. In his dreams he was a Roman emperor ('I would certainly have made history'), and more, a cosmic monster:

> I wish I were a giant as big and tall as the mass of the universe. I would take a glowing pike and would poke it into the body of the earth. From pole to pole, from the earth's brow to its feet I would penetrate it. I would tap the belly of the equator; I would squeeze the punctured body of the earth and the lava would come gushing from all holes, I would not mind if I burned my hands. Do you hear me, old Jehova? Have I magnified you in vain? Do you not hear how the brood of philistines is laughing at me? Make the hairs of my strength grow like the longest comet's tail...

The crude sexual imagery of this passage is typical of Wagner's writings. Everything, after all, was touched by Eros ('I almost forgot that even electricity is sexual and its elements create connections.'), everything diseased. 'A comprehensive reform of humanity is imperative. And just as ruined houses and streets are pulled down in old cities ... I have a sharp eye for everything sick and weak. If you make me the executioner no bacillus shall escape. I can take 25 million Germans on my conscience without it being even one gram heavier than before.' 'Pity! – I have read my Nietzsche, of course, and I have read him with the pleasure a gourmet of the mind feels faced with such a text. ... pity with the weak, the sick, the crippled is crime, is first and foremost a crime against those who are pitied themselves.'

Wagner was not so blind to his own failings as to exclude himself from this universal indictment. 'I am at the head of my own [death] list,' he calmly noted, adding that he wanted to take 'the entire death-ridden neurasthenic horde' with him. In his calmer moments, he was even an excellent analyst of his own predicament: 'the feeling of impotence gives birth to strong words, and the most dashing fanfares sound forth from a horn named paranoia.' Then, however, darker thoughts would cloud his brain again, though he himself experienced it as quite the opposite: 'More and more I understand the mysterium of blood sacrifice, it cleanses and "maketh us pure from all sin". Murder seems a kind of worship, not in servitude to insanity, but at the temple of reason.'

Headmaster Wagner lived another twenty-five years in the seclusion of the Winnetal asylum. He wrote a drama entitled *Wahn* (Madness) about the delusional world of Bavaria's tragic King Ludwig II and kept up a steady correspondence with the psychiatrist whom he trusted and regarded as a friend. In later years, he seemed quite sane and declared himself horrified at his deed and his insanity. Having shaved off the handlebar moustache of a petty official, he looked kindly, more like a local curate than a mass murderer.

The Inverted Judge

Insanity holds up a warped mirror to its time. Individual elements are bloated, grotesquely out of proportion, while others appear to vanish altogether. In Ernst Wagner's case, sexual anxiety and an acute feeling of self-loathing were dressed up in all the costumes his time could provide: eugenic 'weeding out' of the weak and the diseased; a pseudo-Nietzschean cult of power; a conception of the scientific universe as sexual (electricity with its positive and negative, male and female poles, and Wagner also referred to women as 'negative people'); a diagnosis of neurasthenia and degeneracy (the two intellectual leitmotifs of the pre-War years) in terms of ungoverned and ungovernable lust. Independently of what he was contemplating, everything eventually became sexual, a reflection of his self-loathing and insufficiency as a sexual being. The violent megalomania engendered by his revulsion was explained best by the patient himself: 'the feeling of impotence gives birth to strong words.'

Another memoir of a psychiatric patient, a man at once very different from and yet similar to the murdering schoolmaster, made its author the subject of the most famous case of its kind in pre-War Germany. Daniel Paul Schreber (1842–1911) was highly articulate and highly educated, a successful man and a pillar of society. The son of a well-known pediatrician, Schreber had studied law and had become president of the Court of Appeal in Leipzig in 1893, at the then relatively young age of fifty-one. Already nine years earlier, when he had unsuccessfully stood for parliament, Schreber had suffered a mental breakdown. Now, with a demanding new job forcing him to work even harder in order to prove himself, his nervous troubles resumed, in a classic case of professional neurasthenia. He was unable to sleep and began to hallucinate. Soon, he was admitted to a mental hospital, where his real martyrdom began.

Deprived of any visits or outside contact, the eminent judge soon began to live in a private world of supernatural beings, whispered messages, visions, and intermittent states of intense arousal. He was made a ward of court and transferred to another hospital, where his condition seemed to improve somewhat – so much so that he demanded to be released and began writing lengthy petitions to the relevant courts. He also set about writing a meticulous account of his beliefs, his sufferings, and his world-view, initially only to allow his wife to understand what was happening to him, but then also with a view to publication. After a protracted battle, his case was heard by a new judge who decided that, while Schreber's world-view was obviously so eccentric as to be called insane, everybody had a right to his private insanity. Schreber was judged a menace neither to himself nor to other people, and was duly released. In 1903 he succeeded in publishing his memoirs, which he had entitled *Denkwürdigkeiten eines Nervenkranken* (Engl. Edition: *Memoirs of My Nervous Illness*).

Schreber's revelations are all the more fascinating as they are the attempt of a highly rational, punctilious man to analyse the hallucinations and sensations which, as he realized, were seen as symptoms of an illness, but which to him seemed entirely real and reasonable. In twenty-two lucid chapters with copious footnotes, appendices and cross-references, and judiciously seasoned with quotations in French and Latin, the learned judge attempted to order his inner universe and to explain to the world that he had been chosen by God to play a key role in its salvation, so much so that the weather and other external events were influenced by him or sent by God only to give him signs: 'as I am writing this I am quite conscious of the fact that other people might be tempted to take this for a diseased imagination on my part; for I know full well that especially the tendency to see everything in relation to oneself is frequent among the insane. In this case, however, the case is quite simply reversed,' he remarked drily as he explained the salient facts.

The human soul, Schreber explains, resides in the nerves, and it is through these nerves that any human being (indeed, any being) communicates with God, the purest, most intense form of nervous energy. A life in purity makes human nerves white and radiant; an impure life lets them turn black and finally deadens them. On earth, this phenomenon manifests itself by an increase in general nervousness and moral degeneracy, which must finally become a danger to the divine realms themselves. Once most of humanity has degenerated, blackened nerves, God has no choice but to create a catastrophe and to start again with a handful of chosen, pure individuals.

Schreber's second, decisive bout of insanity had begun one morning when, still in bed, he was suddenly gripped by 'the idea that it really must be very nice to be a woman submitting to sexual intercourse'. This idea had not left him. In the new beginning of the world, he believed, he was destined to be a woman who would be impregnated by God and bear children, a new mankind. In preparation for this event, the process of emasculation (*Entmannung*) had already begun through rays of divine nervous energy. Lying in his bed, Schreber felt waves of 'female lust' flood through his body and felt his sexual organs retreating into his body, his breasts swell, his very body shrink to be closer to a woman's height – a miracle that was invariably 'reversed' in the morning due to a pollution by darker nervous energy.

There were dark powers, of course – one of their emissaries was the doctor treating him – and there were also illusory and confusing beings sent to bewilder him, most commonly the 'hastily cobbled-together men' (*flüchtig hingemachte Männer*) and 'little men' (*kleine Männer*), who were nothing but ephemeral spirits in body form, the former apparently of normal size, the latter only millimetres tall. Other traumatic adversities in his epic fight for a new world included his being used 'like a female whore' by patients and warders, being called 'Miss Schreber' by mocking voices, and experiencing the conflict between his own voluptuous femininity and the revulsion of his male pride against the progressing emasculation.

When Schreber was released from the clinic, he was convinced that he was becoming a woman. Wearing women's clothes was therefore nothing but sensible preparation for his future role. 'Since that day, I have consciously made it my business to take care of my femininity and will continue to do so, as far as consideration for my surroundings makes this possible; may other people, to whom the transcendental reasons are obscure, think about me what they will. I would like to see the man who, confronted with the choice of being either a stupid man with male appearance or a spirited woman, would not prefer the latter. This, and *only this*, however, is the question.' After several years living peacefully at home, the former presiding judge suffered a stroke and spent the remaining miserable and haunted months of his life in yet another mental hospital. He died in 1911.

Much has been written about the Schreber case, not least by Sigmund Freud, who in the year of Schreber's death published an essay to the patient in which he argued that Schreber's desperate wish to be loved by his overwhelming father (whom, according to Freud, Schreber equated with God) resulted in his attempt to become a woman in order to be loved by him in the most literal sense. It is likely that Freud was right to assume that the relationship to a strong father had a part to play in Schreber's illness, but the analysis seems too smooth, too simple. There are traces of paternal maltreatment in Schreber's hallucinations – one of the phenomena experienced by him, the 'miracle of chest constriction' during which he had the feeling that his rib cage was crushed by an external force, is disturbingly reminiscent of a childhood experience.

Schreber *père* was a child educationist whose fanatical belief in disciplining children and controlling their 'crude nature' was the overwhelming influence on his children's upbringing. 'The idea should never cross the child's mind that his will might prevail,' wrote Moritz Schreber. In books such as the popular *Der Hausfreund als Erzieher und Führer zu Familienglück und Menschenveredelung* (The Domestic Friend as Educator and Leader to Family Happiness and Ennobling Men, 1861) he advocated contraptions to 'correct' children, their physical stand and their behaviour: bed straps, chin bands, and an apparatus to ensure a straight back. His son Daniel was regularly forced to submit to being strapped into this torture implement, to make him sit upright during dinner. All, of course, was done in his own best interest. One is reminded of young Wilhelm II's boyhood martyrdom, with mechanical devices, animal carcasses and endless riding lessons to steel the sickly boy and force his stunted arm to grow.

Moritz Schreber was not only the great tyrant of Daniel's childhood. He was also universally revered as a scientist and a sage for having founded a

medical institute, being a prolific author, and having pioneered a movement of vegetable garden allotments for worker's children, the
Schrebergärten. The influence of a cruelly dominating father certainly was
an important element in Schreber's illness (his brother committed suicide
in his thirties) but there appears to be another important cause, undoubtedly linked to the godlike and inhibiting father figure. Like Ernst Wagner,
Daniel Schreber was obsessed by his own sexual inadequacy. He and his
wife had not had any children, a continuing and pervasive sadness in his
life. Some passages in his memoirs hint at impotence.

His world, like that of the mass murderer Wagner, was a sexual world,
though under different auspices. Whereas Wagner hallucinated about all-
powerful manliness, about being a Caesar and a cosmic giant penetrating
planet earth (the goddess Gaia of Greek myth, as he would have known)
and killing everyone weak and diseased, including his pitiful self, Schreber
had gone in the opposite direction. Unable to shoulder his role as a man
and the social and professional responsibilities that went with it – both of
his bouts of insanity were caused by overwork and external expectations,
once as a prospective member of parliament, once as president of the Court
of Appeal – he had retreated into what he conceived to be the truer and
easier identity: a woman's body.

Men on the whole are not very impressive in Schreber's writings. The
'hastily cobbled-together men' whom he visualized in the hospital wards
and later in the streets were little more than a sign that men themselves
were ephemeral, liable to dissolve into thin air, figments of (women's)
imaginations. In a period of changing social models and therefore of changing male identities, Schreber did not believe that he and others could
survive as men. Becoming a woman appeared the obvious solution.

There are more similarities between the murdering schoolmaster and the
gentle judge. Both cast their imaginings in scientific terms, and both
believed that the end of the world would be brought on by the twin evils of
nervousness and moral degeneracy. Nerves were the central concept in
Schreber's theology, and they were central to the wider public discussion
and scientific thinking about the effects of modern life. Neurasthenia was
an illness which disproportionately affected not only technology workers
such as train-drivers and telephonists, but also middle-class professional
men like Schreber. In the same vein, other patient reports showed the overwhelming issue of sexual anxiety and 'deviance' (masturbation, homosexuality) as driving factors of many patients' troubles. From the convalescents
on Thomas Mann's Magic Mountain to rioting suffragettes, sex and
'nervousness' were always there, just under the surface.

The Influencing Machine

Two men, two German professionals, are anything but a representative sample of insanity and its imaginings around 1910. What did a woman imagine when her mind was deranged? One answer at least is given in the case of Natalija A., a Russian student of philosophy, who was examined by the Freudian psychiatrist Victor Tausk. In her hallucinations, another facet of the period reveals itself: the pendant, perhaps to male ideas of omnipotence or total impotence. Dr Tausk noted:

> She declares that for six and a half years she has been under the influence of an electrical machine made in Berlin. ... It has the form of a human body, indeed, the patient's own form, though not in all details ... The trunk has the shape of a lid, resembling the lid of a coffin, and is lined with silk or velvet. ... She cannot see the head – she says that she is not sure about it and she does not know whether the machine bears her own head. ... The outstanding fact about the machine is that it is being manipulated by someone in a certain manner, and everything that occurs to it happens also to her ... At an earlier stage, sexual sensations were produced in her through manipulation of the genitalia of the machine.

Risky as it may be to extrapolate from one case to a general condition, the case of Natalija A. nevertheless shows traits discernible in other women's writings, such as the childhood memories of Lida Gustava Heymann quoted earlier. There were numerous autobiographical accounts of young girls feeling shut in, as if buried alive, controlled by outside forces, and resenting this control. In A.'s mind, this sensation has become a concrete metaphor of the age of mechanization and central control: she is immured in a coffin-like machine, manipulated from elsewhere, and experiences every kind of touch as disgusting, disturbing her self-possessed activities such as thinking, reading and writing. While men felt out of control, women like Natalija A. and the early feminists felt they could not escape the faceless coercion dominating all aspects of their lives.

The great influencing machine experienced by Natalija A. was not unique to her, indeed it was not even unique to women. In the controlled, controlling environment of the modern city, remote control had become a fact of life. Another psychiatric patient, Robert Gie, made drawings of the machines controlling him, a perfect image of its time. Part god, part emperor and part industrial plant, the central, all-controlling head with its frightening teeth is attached to a machine with regulator, chimney, and reservoir. From his mouth and forehead emanate cable-like connections with the underlings, depicted with the archaic force of a Maya temple frieze. It is their intestines and their heads which are being controlled according to currents apparently measured out by a metric table to the left. They all hold weapons and are striking aggressive poses. One impulse of the central mechanism will suffice to set everything in motion.

Apaches and Other Hooligans

Les aliénés, the alienated, is the French term for the mentally ill. As a new and industrial society was emerging throughout the West, a society whose workings were based on professional expertise (on engineers and chemists, civil servants, statisticians, doctors and lawyers), those who were not and perhaps could not be integrated into this new, rational and orderly commonwealth became a special concern. At a moment when science appeared to promise a solution lying almost within reach of civilized mankind, for every ill and evil, outsiders – the insane and the criminal in particular – were not only inconvenient, their very existence threatened the validity, the self-image, of rational civilization.

Parallel to the phenomenon of neurasthenia in Europe and the United States, the rise of violent crime also became a constant preoccupation in the popular imagination. The world was becoming an increasingly dangerous place, the argument went, and particularly younger criminals were becoming more reckless and more brutal with every passing year. Newspaper stories of famous and gory misdeeds were one expression of the public fascination with crime and violence. The million-selling *Petit journal* in Paris devoted around 12 per cent of its print space and many of its illustrated title pages to stories on murders, muggings and rapes, and from the London *Daily Mail* to Austria's *Wiener Zeitung* sensational crime was omnipresent.

No gang and no horror story was more beloved by the popular press than the spectacular apaches stalking the streets of Paris. A loose conglomeration of rival youth gangs, the apaches and their leaders became famous for their ruthless and violent muggings and gang fights at the heart of the French capital. 'Their' streets in the Marais and in the outlying workers' areas had become no-go areas for the police, and at night their rule of the urban territory appeared complete. The young gangsters had come to prominence in 1902, after a bloody spate of warfare between competing groups.

It was Victor Moris, a journalist, who had named these youth gangs 'apaches'. War had broken out between two groups after the beautiful prostitute Marie-Hamélie Hélie had changed protectors and allied herself to a young man nicknamed Leca, the chief of the Popincourt apaches. Her slighted former boyfriend embarked on a campaign of retribution. The two clans clashed and several members were knifed before the two protagonists could be arrested and sentenced to banishment in Cayenne. By then, however, their war had become a piece of urban legend. The Paris theatre Les Bouffes du Nord put on a revue show featuring the apache story and offered the main role to the real-life Marie-Hamélie Hélie, who almost became the protagonist of her own story on stage – but she was never to appear in this role. The police prefect forbade her appearance, on reasons of public morality.

The apaches, the 'last rebels against industrial discipline', were becoming a symbol of everything that was perilous in France. 'All of France is at the mercy of the apaches', headlined the *Journal de Roubaix* in 1907, while the socialist *Humanité* complained in 1910 that 'the apaches are masters of the street. They injure, brutalize, and hurt passers-by [with impunity]'. The mass-circulation *Le Matin*, meanwhile, offered a solution in a dramatic appeal to Mother Guillotine herself: 'She is profoundly asleep, lethargic… wake up! This is the cry of all juries in France, the clamour of the popular classes, exasperated by the recent crimes!'

The newspapers were quick to create a whole apache folklore, detailing the lives and characters of their leaders and even particular methods of committing robberies, like the *coup de père François*, a tactic that involved asking a well-to-do passer-by for the time and then calmly going through his pockets while an accomplice who had approached the victim from behind was strangling him with a silk scarf.

By 1910 the original apaches were overtaken, in the French public imagination at least, by a new Paris gang whose leader, Jules Bonnot (1876–1912), quickly came to national notoriety as the country's most brutal criminal. Bonnot, who ironically had once during his chequered career worked as chauffeur for Arthur Conan Doyle, was perfect for the role of public enemy number one. A committed anarchist and a mechanic who stole cars for use in his spectacular and bloody robberies, he was the ideal incarnation of public fears.

It was the first time that cars were used as getaway and drive-by vehicles in crimes, and the public response was extraordinary. As Bonnot and his accomplices launched into a crime spree unprecedented in French history, the country's newspapers followed his every step.

The 21st of December 1911: a young money courier was attacked and severely injured in the rue Ordener; 31 December: surprised during an attempted car theft, Bonnot and an accomplice killed the car's chauffeur and a night watchman; 3 January: two members of the gang killed a wealthy couple during a break in; 27 February: a policeman was shot dead after an argument about a ticket for speeding in front of the Gare Saint-Lazare; the next morning the gang attempted to steal the contents of a safe, but were forced to flee; 25 March: the gang attacked and killed a car driver and owner before deciding to break into the Société Générale in Chantilly, where they shot three employees before escaping.

This campaign of violent crime had been more than enough to send the French press into a frenzy, particularly after one of the gang, Octave Garnier, coolly wrote to *Le Matin* to issue a public challenge to the police: 'I know very well that I will be overwhelmed and that I am the weaker party, but I will make you pay a heavy price for your victory.'

On 28 April 1912 the gang's luck finally ran out. Holed up in a house in Choisy-le-Roi, close to Paris, the wounded Bonnot and an accomplice were betrayed and encircled by fifteen policemen, soon joined by local men with hunting rifles. Having tracked the criminals for more than six months, the prefect of police, Louis Lépine, was not going to take any chances. A regiment of artillery with a heavy machine gun was dispatched on his order. Soon, hundreds of armed men were participating in the siege.

News of the siege had spread rapidly throughout the capital, and tempted by the chance of watching bloody history in the making, thousands of Parisians took the train to Choisy-le-Roi to watch the events for themselves. By mid-afternoon, thirty thousand spectators were watching the siege and the sporadic exchanges of gunfire. From a safe distance, they observed a courageous lieutenant sneak up to the house, protected by a cartload of hay, and place sticks of dynamite outside it. Two detonations shook the building, which was stormed by police soon afterwards. Inside, the attackers found Bonnot bleeding heavily and protected by two mattresses. He had waited for the attack. With the cry '*Salauds!*' ('Bastards') he emptied the magazines of his guns and was fatally wounded in the shootout.

By now almost all members of the gang had been killed or arrested. The two survivors still at large, both young men in their early twenties, were shot in May after a second siege, even more dramatic than the first and involving a battery of machine guns, two regiments of soldiers, hundreds of policemen and 40,000 spectators. In the pockets of one of the criminals, the publicity-seeking Octave Garnier, was a note: 'Our women and our children are crammed together in slums while thousands of big houses stay empty. We are building palaces and we live in hovels. Worker, develop your life, your intelligence, your strength. You are a sheep; the cops are dogs and the bourgeois are the shepherds. Your blood pays for the luxuries of the rich. Our enemy is our master. Long live anarchy.' Arrested before the sieges, three remaining members of the 'automobile apaches', as the press were quick to call Bonnot's men, were condemned to death and executed by guillotine on 21 April 1913.

The fame of the apaches spread throughout Europe and became a byword for a new, particularly violent kind of crime, seen in Vienna as much as in St Petersburg and London. But was there, in fact, a wave of new crime? There is no clear indication that there was, though any attempt to answer this question invariably becomes mired in questions about statistics. The brief answer is that statistics show not crimes committed, but charges brought and sentences passed, and that some increase in these was certainly due to more efficient policing, changing sentencing policies, and to the general rise in population. On the whole, there was even a slight decline in crimes against property in France, Britain and Germany, while violent crime rose slightly.

There was one spectacular exception to this rule. In Russia, and particularly St Petersburg, a wave of 'hooliganism' put even the Nevsky Prospect out of bounds after nightfall for all but the bravest. Imperial St Petersburg, always precarious with its mixture of tough repression and utter lawlessness in certain quarters of the city, had felt this crime wave from the early 1900s, when journalists noticed a marked rise in violence and insolence on the part of youth gangs: 'every passerby risks attack by hooligans. Demands for money and assaults on those who refuse to comply have already been reported in the [crime] chronicle. People are afraid to walk the streets alone. ... Hooligans do not ponder consequences – if need be, they are quick to use their knives and other weapons.'

Newspapers were full of reports about random violence. Street stabbings, in which the assailants left their victims bleeding on the ground, became an almost daily event, and there were other disquieting facts. The criminals were often as young as twelve, and they were not just disgruntled workers, as the *Peterburgskii listok* reported in 1903: 'They are a motley lot, and not only in external appearance. On the contrary, their social diversity is no less sharp. Here one finds everything: government scribes, telegraph clerks, post office and customs agents, metalworkers, printers, apprentices, tavern and café waiters.'

In the aftermath of the 1905 revolution, Russian society appeared to plunge towards disintegration, and the young hooligans (some newspapers called them 'Russian apaches') were the most conspicuous symptom of this tendency. The newspapers brimmed with horrifying reports:

On May 27 at 8:00 P.M. two extremely drunk hooligans were walking along Nevskii Prospekt. Every minute they knocked into a man or offended a women. One of them, brandishing an iron pole, threatened to break open the skull of each passerby. The other was swearing unrestrainedly…Cries and demands that the scoundrels be taken to the police station came from all sides. Mocking the public's indignation, one of the hooligans spat right in the face of a well-dressed man.

Not only the seat of government, but the entire country seemed to be sinking under a wave of crime. Reports about criminal incidents arrived 'from Arkhangelsk to Yalta', and even in the countryside, peasants showed a terrifying lack of respect for their superiors:

In the village N., a young noblewoman was calmly walking down the road when a hooligan, well known to everyone, approached and began to pester her, asking for her handkerchief. When she refused him, he threw her to the ground, held her down with his knee on her chest, took off her dress, and stripped her entirely. As a crowd gathered he shouted, 'Look, guys, at the *intelligentka*.' After this, he got up, hit her on the back of the head, and walked away as if nothing had happened.

If many poorer Russians appeared to be walking away from their own society, the rise in crime was not as dramatic as the papers would have their readers believe. The number of juvenile convictions rose steeply, from 1,113 in 1900 to 2,848 in 1910, but in absolute numbers it remained tiny, certainly if compared with the more than 51,000 young men and women convicted in 1910 in Germany, a country with less than half of Russia's population. Even relative to other age groups, the problem of youth crime appears less dramatic than was reported in the press: at no time before the War did the juvenile conviction rate exceed 5 per cent of the total.

The Science of Crime

While Russian observers believed that society could not long withstand the 'mighty floods of popular resentment that were barely restrained by the feeble dikes of civilization and a decaying state', the situation was not actually as desperate as perceived. Still, the mere perception of a dramatic rise in youth violence and anarchist threats matched the fears of the period all too well: a once-great civilization undermined by 'degenerate elements' from the lowest classes, overwhelmed by the forces of anarchic plebs alienated from a healthy, traditional way of life by the big city and the machine.

Just as the bourgeois ailments, neurasthenia and psychosis, had led to the rise of psychiatry, violence and crime committed by the most disadvantaged elicited their own scientific response focused on understanding, managing and preventing the problem. Criminology was born. The Italian anthropologist Cesare Lombroso (1835–1909) was the acknowledged father of this new discipline.

Born into a wealthy Jewish family in Genoa, Lombroso had studied literature, linguistics and archaeology but later chose to become an army doctor. During his service he was intrigued by the correlations between soldiers' discipline, their mental health and social conditions, and their heredity. His fascination led him to psychiatry, and having practised both as an academic and as director of an asylum, he published his magnum opus *L'Uomo delinquente* (*Criminal Man*, 1876, with several updated and augmented re-editions), which presented the best and most comprehensive statistical evidence ever assembled for factors leading to crime. Lombroso correlated the most diverse factors with incidence of crime: weather (everywhere in Europe most murders were committed in summer), geology and landscape, confession, birth rate, living conditions (the urban poor, unsurprisingly, led the charts), alcoholism and the price of alcoholic beverages (in France, every rise in the price of wine led to plummeting murder figures, and vice versa), immigration (bad news), education, income and public wealth (in Italy, most murders were committed in the richest cities), illegitimacy, working conditions.

While Lombroso held all these factors partly responsible for the rise of crime or implicated all of them, he believed that the central reason lay elsewhere: evolution could reverse as well as progress, and it would produce 'atavists', throwbacks to previous, more brutish stages of human development, a dangerous subclass of savages. These, Lombroso claimed, were at the heart of the problem: 'scientific examination ... [demonstrates] the existence of a type of human dedicated to crime by his innermost organization, of born criminals who form great battalions in ... the "army of crime".'

A kindly and intellectually conscientious man, Lombroso was a product of the nineteenth century. With pure, ardent faith in positivist science he fought for the dignified treatment of criminals, for social rehabilitation and abolition of the death penalty. Society's attitude to crime must be based on knowledge, he argued:

> The philosophy of penal law [we have inherited] from ancient time now causes us pity. Free will and vengeance are a very fragile foundation [for law] and a miserable goal. We know that whatever happens man always

and fatally obeys the strongest motive. We therefore believe that if society incontestably has a right to defend itself it is never worthy of society to wreak vengeance. Penal repression cannot and must not be dictated by anything else than scientifically proven usefulness.

The anthropologist relied on piles of statistics collected around the world and supplemented his data by measuring thousands of skulls of criminals and collating tens of thousands of biographical data to arrive at a definitive answer to his questions about hereditary crime. Following the early nineteenth-century physiologist Franz Josef Gall, Lombroso was convinced that activities in different centres of the brain would cause the organ to swell or shrink like a muscle that was developed or atrophied, and that such outgrowths would manifest themselves in the form of the skull. By measuring heads, he believed he would be able to create a strictly scientific typology of evil, incontrovertible proof for criminal tendencies in an individual. Apart from cranial measurements, the typology also included external signs such as large jaws, low forehead, unusually good eyesight, high cheekbones, a fleshy, flat or upturned nose, large ears, scanty growth of hair, insensitivity to pain, and unusually long arms. Born criminals, in effect, had to be contained, but could not be blamed. Atavism, hereditary alcoholism and epilepsy were all signs of decayed biological characteristics. It would be society's goal to eradicate the biological basis for this crime by sterilizing those who could only give birth to more misery, Lombroso argued. Civilization, he implied, was a fragile thing, based on discipline and education, all too easily jeopardized:

> What should we conclude if not that the most hideous and barbarous crimes have a physiological, atavistic point of departure. These animal instincts can be blunted for a while in man, thanks to [the influence of] education, of the environment, and the fear of punishment; but they are reborn suddenly under the influence of certain circumstances such as illness, weather, imitation [of peers], and an intoxication with sperm, the consequence of an overly long period of abstinence. It is because of this, no doubt, that it makes itself known at puberty... and in individuals who lead a life of celibacy or great solitude, such as priests, shepherds and soldiers.

In contrast to many others who were dedicated to creating a new morality based on race, heredity and science, Lombroso wrote without hatred. Nature itself was immoral, he believed, and culture was, after all, nothing but a flower on the dung heap of history: 'The criterion for merit does not

Criminal types: Jean-Paul Marat and Louise Michel are among the 'morally insane' revolutionaries on this illustration by Lombroso.

Fig. 7. Tipo comune (a lunga faccia) - Uxoricida.

Fig. 10. Tipo comune (a grande mascella) - Omicida.

Fig. 8. Tipo comune (a lunga faccia) - Omicida-ladro.

Fig II. Tipo comune (a grande mascella) - Assassino.

change if most virtues and vices are recognized as results of a molecular change... A diamond has no more reason to sparkle than coal, but which woman would cast them away because they are nothing but coal?' A Jew himself, Lombroso was sensitive to the stupidity and cruelty of prejudice, but scrupulously fair-minded. He also despised antisemites and argued they were inferior minds, acting from impulses still engrained in them since the Middle Ages.

Lombroso's method, he hoped, would lead not only to understanding crime, but also for enlightened, scientific policies and even a prevention of crime and delinquence at the very root: by diagnosing, classifying and perhaps weeding out likely offenders before they were even born. A whole generation of scholars extended his research (in the introduction to his *Nouvelles recherches de psychiatrie* Lombroso himself mentions twenty-eight scholars who had recently published books on the subject). At the intersection where they converged, anthropology, justice and psychiatry made the scientific treatment of *les aliénés* into an established scientific discipline, notably in Germany, where the biological origins of crime were enthusiastically taken up by eugenicists.

The scholar was fascinated by all types of deviance, from crime to madness, and even genius. The latter, he claimed in a weighty book, *L'uomo di genio in rapporto alla psichiatria* (1889, English translation, *Man of Genius*, London, 1891), was simply a lucky, fruitful form of insanity. Trawling a sea of literary sources (at times with remarkable credulity as to their factual accuracy) and drawing on research on mental illness, as well as on his professional experiences, to his surprise he 'found [in genius] several characteristics of degeneration which are the basis and the signals of almost all forms of congenital madness'. Geniuses, he concluded, were simply freaks of nature who had been endowed with one capacity at the expense of others: 'Just as giants pay the price for their height and their muscles by being sterile and of relatively feeble intelligence, the giants of thought pay through their psychoses for their great intellectual force.'

Genius and madness have long been associated, often accompanied by violence and exclusion. Their marriage is part of the stock repertoire of Romanticism, and during the late nineteenth century Edgar Allan Poe, Charles Baudelaire, Vincent van Gogh, Friedrich Nietzsche, Robert Schumann and Edvard Munch all dramatized psychological states and also suffered from mental illness. The experience of an uncertain rationality and the visionary horizons beyond became a part of art, as it had been a part of religion before.

While an element of alienation from society and tradition was inherent in the very idea of Romanticism, the nineteenth century had also shown abundant literary instances of insanity: from Lucia di Lammermoor and scores of other noble but hapless operatic heroines to Georg Büchner's desperate and murderous Woyzeck, from Dickens's Miss Havisham and William Blake's intricate and apocalyptic drawings to the protagonists in the stories of E. T. A. Hoffmann and the progressive derangement of Mussorgsky's Boris Godunov, to name but a few. At the turn of the twentieth century, a period permeated by phenomena like neurasthenia and sexual insecurity, by the dizzy sense of feeling the floods of change swirling around one's ankles every day, one might expect artists to give a more forceful expression to this fantastical disorientation than ever before. Instead a baffling quietness is spread over the theme of madness, and if it was discussed, it was mostly in German-speaking countries.

There are notable exceptions to this rule, of course. Nicolai Abelukhov, the anti-hero of Andrei Bely's novel *Petersburg*, roams around his city, terrified by his own violence and driven to irrational and destructive acts; Picasso's eye alighted on the marginal existences and emaciated limbs of circus artistes, before plunging into the world of African ornament that would become Cubism; the Futurists in Russia and Italy positively revered violence, crime and ecstasy, and the infamous Kurtz in Joseph Conrad's *Heart of Darkness* can be read as a study in insanity, like August Strindberg's hallucinatory *Dream Play* (1901).

The graphic work of the Austrian painter, print-maker and novelist Alfred Kubin (1877–1958) might also have been conceived as a series of illustrations to Ernst Wagner and Daniel Schreber's fantasies, so close was their intersection with their central images. Kubin knew neither of these cases, and created most of his graphic work before Wagner's crime and Schreber's publication. His etchings look like those of a latter-day Goya, a series of intoxicating, nightmarish visions in a wash of shadow and light. We have already encountered his *War*, an etching seemingly sprung from one of Ernst Wagner's sexual fantasies: the god of war as barbaric colossus, a mountain of helmet, chest, shield, testicles and devastating axe, with feet of clay heavy as houses, about to be plunged into the mass of tiny soldiers. It is a rare moment of masculine power in his pre-War work. In most of Kubin's etchings this force is on the wane. Men are thin, dried-up creatures, stooping, aged kings in front of hooded followers, bizarrely transformed and insubstantial. In one sheet, *Madness*, a bearded, pale-faced sufferer in a long shirt has his head chiselled open from behind by a shadowy, professorial ghost. Male power leads into the abyss. In retrospect, some of these graphic visions seem terribly prophetic: the monstrous and monstrously mustachioed walrus enthroned on a heap of skeletons; the strangely modernist tank entitled *Government*, ready to machine-gun all challengers; the ruined city across a churned-up landscape inhabited by tiny, isolated figures.

While the dominance of men was terrifying because of its mechanized violence, Kubin showed the erotic lure of women as perhaps even more terrifying and overwhelming. With the certainty of a dreamer, he combined the main forces of the period into images: sleek, black and engine-driven vehicles hurtle along an eight-lane highway leading directly between the thighs of a gigantic woman, into the darkness; a gigantic Salome with a huge mass of hair, her belly distended by monstrous fecundity, dances over a row of severed male heads; a female body with severed limbs is pierced by knives on a sheet entitled *An Eye for an Eye*; an insignificant and pitiable

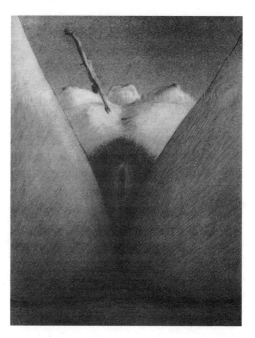

Size does matter: Kubin's Salto Mortale drastically illustrates male fears.

male figure with a tiny erection jumps head-first off a gigantic woman's thighs and into her vagina (one remembers Gustave Courbet's *L'origine du monde*), the most unequal of all unions.

In 1909 the painter Oskar Kokoschka, then in the middle of an affair with Alma Mahler, the famously seductive and capricious wife of court opera director Gustav Mahler, premiered his play *Mörder, Hoffnung der Frauen* (Murderer, Hope of Women). In this work a tribe of warring men meets a woman with a retinue of girls, an encounter that leads to cruel fighting, seduction, mutual mutilation and finally assassination, a bloody ritual of erotic ecstasy reminiscent of Stravinsky's *Sacre du printemps* in which all protagonists are gripped by an incurable fever which, the spectator learns, is the erotic impulse itself.

In prose, there are indications of the fear of radical expulsion and alienation beyond the merely conventional or political. Arthur Schnitzler's *Leutnant Gustl* finds himself abandoned to the night and to his fears, and blurts out a garbled stream of words as he expects the morning and his possible death in a duel; and in 1916 the most irreversible and cruel of transformations took place when the commercial traveller Gregor Samsa woke up in his Prague bed to find that during the night he had been changed into a huge black beetle. Kafka had arrived in literature.

One writer, in particular, obliquely made the theme of madness and violence his own: Robert Musil's 'Man Without Qualities' is Ulrich, the impassive chronicler of the world's follies and his own. His calm rationality is shadowed by another character, a counterpoint to impassive reason, the axe murderer Moosbrugger, who has brutally killed a prostitute and is awaiting execution. Musil is likely to have read about Ernst August Wagner as he was writing his monumental work, even if the direct inspiration for the figure of Moosbrugger was Christian Voigt, another deranged killer who was tried and condemned to death in 1911. As with the apaches in the popular imagination, the violent impulse personified by Moosbrugger obsesses several characters in the novel, including the protagonist Ulrich. The phenomenon of random violence fascinates them; the instinctual brutishness of Moosbrugger's force emerges like the antithesis of the nervous, constantly insecure thinking of those claiming to be rational.

Artists no longer treated madness as a convenient trope, a sentimental convention. It had come closer, grown more real. While the *fin de siècle* had gloried in its rotten sophistication, in the elegant decadence of Oscar Wilde and the perfumed unreality of Maurice Maeterlinck, decadence had reappeared in the hideous shape of its diseased and evil cousin, degeneration. With its thirsty cult of health and vigour and its permanently shattered nerves, the early twentieth century had no place for creatures like this, and those who admitted to being overly sensitive found themselves on the steep and slippery slope to being branded degenerates.

Who wants to be a degenerate? The refined nerves of the decadent poet gave him insights into mysteries. The freakish feats performed by the insane and by those tainted with the stigma of heredity had no such noble connotations. It was a time for artists to be vigorous and iconoclastic, pugilists of the pen and barbarians of the brush, raising ancient creative powers or looking into a future of machines and heroism. It was a time to become anarchists, Futurists, but not to succumb to the enfeebling whisperings of bad blood. Only a Thomas Mann could afford to describe, in his *Buddenbrooks* (1901), the history of his own family as a story of degeneration. His book shows a slow decline as one generation becomes less fit than the preceding one until the line is doomed to end with Hanno Buddenbrook, by all accounts a degenerate, a boy with an artistic bent who cannot stop dreaming of the oceanic soundscapes of his beloved Wagner operas, but is himself quite unsuitable for any practical task. Mann could write such a tale because his sense of personal superiority was too clear, too indestructible, to be impaired by his own story.

One real-life Hanno Buddenbrook, the morbidly sensitive Rainer Maria Rilke, even made himself advocate and bard of those who were overwhelmed by the modern world. His novel *Aufzeichnungen des Malte Laurids*

Brigge (1910) is one of the most disturbing artistic documents of incipient madness in the history of literature. Already in his *Stunden-Buch* (Book of Hours, 1903) he had described those who were lost on the seas of civilization:

> And there are people, flowering white, pale,
> and die, unmoved, of this heavy world.
> Nobody sees the gaping grimace
> to which the smile of a delicate race
> distends itself in nameless nights.

> They walk around, bared of their dignity by the strife
> of insipidly ministering to the meaningless
> their clothes are wilting away on them,
> and their beautiful hands are already old.
> The crowd does not consider sparing them,
> despite their being hesitant and weak,
> only shy dogs living in no fixed place,
> trot after them silently for a little while.

> They have been given a hundred torturers,
> and, screamed at by every strike of the hour,
> they circle forlornly around the hospitals
> and fearfully await admission day.

Popular Heroes

If there was surprisingly little artistic resonance among the avant-garde to the theme of insanity and radical marginalization, the place that the idea of alienation held in the imagination of the period can be deduced from the huge popularity enjoyed by a particular branch of popular fiction: the detective story. The famous 'man on the Clapham omnibus' or the woman in the Métro at the place de la Concorde did not know who Kubin was, and had never heard of Bely or Rilke. They read crime stories instead, intricate and effective romanticizations of outsiders and outcasts on either side of the law. Just as every period has its fixed tropes of insanity, it also has its very own popular heroes in stories of justice and redemption. The murder mystery and the crime story, creations of the nineteenth century, came into their own before the War. They were sold in their hundreds of thousands, often after being serialized in the biggest-selling magazines and newspapers of the day.

The Scottish doctor Arthur Conan Doyle knew and admired Cesare

Lombroso's work and used the same kind of deductive observation for his hero Sherlock Holmes, perhaps the most famous figure in crime fiction. Holmes, whose fictional cases were serialized by the *Strand Magazine* from 1887 to 1915, was not just a deductive reasoner. In a country with a healthy disrespect for institutional solutions and a great reverence for eccentric amateurs, he was a singular figure in the mould of Lombroso's genius. His all too active mind had to be calmed down with morphine or awakened with cocaine in between cases; he was a man oscillating between brilliance and disturbingly violent flashes of temper, to whom solving crimes was the ultimate intellectual challenge, as well as a necessary food for his overactive imagination. Little wonder, then, that earnest, clean-living Inspector Lestrade of Scotland Yard can do nothing more than arrive at the scene panting and puffing, to find that the great detective has made him look foolish once again. British crime writers have never placed much faith in the police. British crime was solved by gentlemen.

France's mystery novel hero Arsène Lupin was a very different creature. He too was a man of culture, brilliant and schooled in all arts. But he was not the detective. He was the king of burglars, stealing from the rich and giving to the deserving poor – a dashing, improbable creation:

> … the eccentric gentleman who operates only in the chateaux and salons, and who, one night, entered the residence of Baron Schormann, but emerged empty-handed, leaving, however, his card on which he had scribbled these words: 'Arsène Lupin, gentleman-burglar, will return when the furniture is genuine.' Arsène Lupin, the man of a thousand disguises: in turn a chauffeur, detective, bookmaker, Russian physician, Spanish bullfighter, commercial traveller, robust youth, or decrepit old man.

Gifted with humour, boundless ingenuity and a truly French disrespect for all authority, Lupin was not, in fact, solely the creation of his author, Maurice Leblanc (1864–1941), who even made his master criminal go head-to-head with the British icon in the unsubtly titled novel *Arsène Lupin contre Herlock Sholmes* (1908). Lupin had a real-life inspiration in one of France's popular heroes at the time, the anarchist Alexandre Marius Jacob (1875–1954), who became famous for his daring, imaginative crimes, as well as his unbusinesslike chivalry and wit.

Jacob, born into a poor Alsatian family, had joined the navy as a cabin boy at the age of twelve, had become involved in anarchist terrorism and was sentenced to prison for explosives offences. After his sentence, he could no longer find a job and so decided to serve the cause of anarchism in a more direct, less orthodox way. On 31 March 1899 he and two accomplices went to the Marseille office of the Mont de Piété, the pawnbrokers, arrested the leading cashier for embezzlement, impounded 400,000 francs as evidence, and then calmly delivered his prisoner to the Palais de la Justice. Before the confusion could be cleared, the 'inspector' and his two assistants had vanished. This was the first of many coups whose trademarks were cunning and style. Arrested, Jacob faked insanity and escaped to southern France, where he set up a gang, the *travailleurs de la nuit*. In the following years, stories

Gentleman-burglar: Marius Jacob, the real-life Arséne Lupin.

about his daring and most of all, meticulously planned, robberies filled the popular papers. He would steal only from the rich and would always give part of his profits to anarchist causes. When once, on burgling the house of a sea captain, he found that his victim was the French writer Pierre Loti, he put everything back in its place and left a note: 'Having entered here by mistake I could not take anything from someone who lives by his pen. All work deserves payment. PS: Enclosed ten francs for the broken glass and damaged shutters.'

Jacob's epic crusade against unjustly held private property finally ended when a policeman was fatally shot during a chase. Jacob was arrested in 1903. During the months leading up to his trial, he penned an impassioned justification of his acts, an anarchist interpretation of Darwinism: 'Since you primarily condemn me for being a thief it's useful to define what theft is. In my opinion theft is a need that is felt by all men to take in order to satisfy their appetites. This need manifests itself in everything: from the stars that are born and die like beings, to the insect in space, so small, so infinite that our eyes can barely distinguish it. Life is nothing but theft and massacre. Plants and beasts devour each other in order to survive.'

Instead of collaborating, men exploit one another, Jacob wrote.

> From top to bottom of the social scale everything is but dastardy on one side and idiocy on the other. How can you expect that convinced of these truths I could have respected such a state of things?

A liquor seller and the boss of a brothel enrich themselves, while a man of genius dies of poverty in a hospital bed. The baker who bakes bread doesn't get any; the shoemaker who makes thousands of shoes shows his toes; the weaver who makes stocks of clothing doesn't have any to cover himself with; the bricklayer who builds castles and palaces wants for air in a filthy hovel. Those who produce everything have nothing, and those who produce nothing have everything. ...

In a word, I found it hateful to surrender to the prostitution of work. Begging is degradation, the negation of all dignity. Every man has a right to life's banquet.

The right to live isn't begged for, it's taken.

Jacob's eloquence won him no sympathy from the judges and he was condemned to banishment for life. After seventeen escape attempts, he was finally released in 1927. Always faithful to his anarchist convictions, he led a quieter life now. When, in 1954, he found that illness and old age were overcoming him, he injected himself with an overdose of morphine. His parting letter, a final, characteristic gesture, ended: 'The linen has been washed, rinsed, dried, but not yet ironed. I'm too lazy. Forgive me. You will find two litres of rosé next to the bread basket. *À votre santé.*'

While the stylish and dignified master criminal Jacob was an ideal template for Arsène Lupin, France's other great crime figure, the wicked Fantomas (first appeared in 1910), was not designed to attract sympathies. A sadistic and evil killer, he incarnated popular fears and managed despite many attempts at his capture to escape his nemesis, the great Inspector Juve. Finally, only history itself could end the sinister career of the 'genius of crime'. His co-creator Marcel Allain simply sent him on the epic 1912 maiden voyage of the RMS *Titanic*.

German pulp fiction, incidentally, had no bestselling detectives and villains of its own. The taste here was for adventure stories in the Karl May mould, or for sentimental romances like those written by the immensely popular Hedwig Courts-Mahler, whose fame and fortune rested on 208 honest-but-poor-and-secretly-nobly-born-maid-finds-handsome-count-and-marries-him novels.

Those alienated by society were fighting both their own demons, and those who had condemned them to their isolation. But real cases like that of the psychotic killer Ernst Wagner were followed by the press with ardent enthusiasm.

The Wagner case is an example not only of the constituent parts of psychosis around 1910, but also of a remarkably enlightened scientific response to insanity. Despite his horrifying crimes, Wagner was declared insane and was not executed, but allowed to live out his life in peace, under medical supervision. The murderous schoolteacher even became a minor celebrity among psychiatrists. His doctor, Robert Gaupp, exhibited his articulate patient at one psychiatric conference after another

'I recognize that my crimes were the result of a severe mental illness, which is justly called "persecution mania",' wrote Ernst Wagner in a letter to Gaupp in 1920. 'I declare today, that I was never…"persecuted". Certain overheard words could be so interpreted as I did then – for there are coincidences and things without any logical correlation…but I would not have had to interpret them in this way. But one has the tendency to shift things which fill one's own head into the heads of others.' Wagner continued to correspond with his doctor and even sent him for publication a play he had written, entitled *Madness*. The rabid mind, it seemed, had become tender as a lamb: 'I would ask you to forgive me all feelings of hatred and rage which were alive in me with regard to your person,' the patient wrote to Gaupp. 'If you have the opportunity to visit me here and consider it worth your effort to speak with me…you shall be assured of a friendly welcome. With the expression of my highest esteem, your grateful and devoted Ernst Wagner.'

Wagner drew a civil service pension and pursued his literary work, as well as maintaining a voluminous correspondence with various literary and medical luminaries. He died of natural causes at the Winnetal asylum in April 1938. His body was cremated and his brain sent to the Kaiser Wilhelm Institut in Berlin for examination, though it was damaged in transport. It is still held in the collection of pathological specimens at Düsseldorf University.

15

1914:
Murder Most Foul

The [London] docks are enormous; one loses all sense of proportion when one hurtles along the rails for miles past the ships on
Albert Dock, straight past the long row of hulls prolonging itself as
if in a dream. And the Albert Dock is only one of those making up
London harbour. Here the modern world becomes *completely* fantastical. I have not had this sensation of the fairy-tale character of
our world with such immediacy since seeing the slaughterhouses in
Chicago.   – Count Harry Kessler, *Diary*, 6 June 1903

On 28 July 1914, all of Paris was talking murder, a particular, outrageous
murder which had been in the forefront of everybody's mind. Three
months earlier, on 16 March, a well-dressed woman had entered the offices
of *Le Figaro*, the country's leading conservative newspaper. She was
Henriette Caillaux, wife of Joseph Caillaux, France's minister of finance.
Having asked to be shown to the office of the editor-in-chief, Gaston
Calmette (the same Calmette, incidentally, who had written so savagely
about Stravinsky's *Sacre* a year earlier), she was told that the editor was out.
She agreed to wait, and when she entered his office about one hour later she
spoke a few words to Monsieur Calmette, pulled a revolver out of her fur
muff and shot him four times in the chest.

When Henriette Caillaux came to trial in July there was hardly a person in
France who did not know all the details of the year's most sensational news
story, particularly since minister Caillaux had been subjected to a hostile
media campaign for some months. Irresistibly, the tale around him and his
wife Henriette comprised not only a murder but a sordid affair, the fight for a
political career, and a war averted. No detail was left untold. Mme Caillaux
sold copies. During the trial itself, the *Figaro*, Calmette's former paper, even
went from eight to twelve pages to print verbatim reports from the courtroom.

It had all begun with the worst kind of cliché: with secret letters and furtive hotel visits by a married man and his lover, a charade worthy of a musical comedy. For Joseph Caillaux (1863–1944), the no longer youthful lover in the affair, this was a delicate situation. He was one of the new breed of technocrats who were pushing into positions of power, a financial expert who had been appointed finance minister for the first time at the age of thirty-six, an appointment which confirmed the self-made businessman in his high opinion of himself – one that few others shared. He was competent and daring, even his enemies had to admit, but he was a dandy, an arrogant, self-obsessed social climber. Being caught *in flagrante* would have been poison to his ambitions. He could be prime minister, president even. An affair could cost him the support he needed, Caillaux knew, and he had resolved the situation by divorcing his first wife and marrying Henriette. Her great charm made up for his lack of tact or humour, and the couple was popular in society. Nobody knew that they had been lovers. In 1911 Caillaux became prime minister, as he had planned.

1911 was a crisis year in Franco-German relations and in international politics – one of several points at which the world could have gone to war. Still resentful at the colonial understanding between France and Britain, in which the powers accorded each other a free hand in Egypt and Morocco respectively (leaving Germany out of the picture altogether), the German government had sent a gunboat to the Moroccan port of Agadir, asserting that they would not be ignored. Unknown to the Kaiser, the plan had been hatched months earlier by his foreign minister, Alfred von Kinderlen-Wächter, who had finally convinced the Supreme Warlord during a stay on the imperial yacht *Hohenzollern* as he was attending the Kiel regatta. There were already German firms in Morocco; German citizens lived there, and their interests and those of the state had to be protected at all costs. Wilhelm, who had been reluctant to antagonize his cousin George (or even the French) with such a gesture, agreed after some hesitation. Immediately a wireless telegraph signal was sent from the Admiralty to the imperial gunboat *Panther*, then off the coast of West Africa.

The German vessel changed course and prepared to meet destiny – an unequal encounter, since she was not the kind of ship the Kaiser would have chosen to represent his military might. This was the height of the Dreadnought race, during which ever bigger, ever newer, ever more devastating floating fortresses were launched in a bid for naval supremacy by all major powers. The *Panther* was no such fighting machine. It was slow, squat, and lightly armed with two 4-inch guns: a tomcat rather than a predator, ploughing asthmatically through the waves with its two stubby funnels and two masts. Its crew of 130 men included a brass band employed to demonstrate the splendour of German march music to native African villagers. Now its orders were to protect all Germans in Agadir from aggression from rebel tribes inland. It was an easy assignment – there were no Germans in Agadir. The sole specimen, a man named Wilberg, had been cabled that his presence was urgently required on the coast. Herr Wilberg had set out immediately from Mogador, 75 arduous miles away, where he had been stationed by a consortium of Hamburg investors.

Even as the *Panther* dropped anchor in the Bay of Agadir, Herr Wilberg, a strange figure in his white suit, was marching through the scorching heat, fighting off insects. He turned up four days after his rescuer had arrived and did his best to attract the attention of his countrymen on board. When they finally saw a white man on the beach, surrounded by local fishermen, they sent out a boat to collect him. The mission had been accomplished, the entire German population brought out of harm's way. The headlines of the German press were jubilant: 'Hurrah! A deed! ... Action at last, a liberating deed ... Again it is seen that the foreign policy of a great nation, a powerful state, cannot exhaust itself in patient inaction.'

Despite its modest dimensions, the *Panther* caused a first-rate storm. There were tense negotiations between Paris and Berlin, and the flame soon jumped the Channel. The British were determined to support France against any German claims to Morocco, the Germans warned the British to stay out of this fight, and Winston Churchill, the First Lord of the Admiralty, alerted the navy to a possible pre-emptive attack from the *Kriegsmarine*. All signs pointed to war. Then, suddenly, German chancellor Kinderlen pulled back from the brink. The negotiations with Paris would not touch on British interests in any way, he assured Lord Grey at the Foreign Office. It would be purely an affair between Germany and France.

When it became clear that Britain would not allow a partition of Morocco (Kinderlen's initial objective), the German chancellor understood that he had miscalculated. The calm but firm stance of the French and the unwavering British support were more than he had bargained for. He settled for French territories in equatorial Africa 'in compensation' for Germany's renouncing any claim to Morocco: 100,000 square kilometres of disease-ridden swamps and grasslands in the Congo, to be precise. For Germany this was a debacle. Having risked international war to assert influence in Morocco and to secure Moroccan territories, Berlin had to settle for tropical swamps without either use or prestige.

The French success at the negotiating table was owed to the shrewd but measured instruction of prime minister Caillaux, who had led the negotiations from Paris. Caillaux was a businessman who had invested money abroad, mainly in South America, and he was a realist. He knew that Germany had outstripped France, not only in terms of population, but also in engineering, manufacturing and exports. He knew that in peacetime France needed Germany more than Germany needed France, and that a war would not be winnable. He knew that he had to come to a peaceful arrangement with the irascible but powerful neighbour, and he thought that a stretch of African marshland was not too high a price to pay for peace and prosperity. This moderation would become his downfall.

In a society dominated by mass media, politics are what they are represented to be, and the conservative press in France was adamant that not Germany but France had been the loser in this conflict. Losing Alsace-Lorraine to Germany in 1871 still rankled in the French memory, and giving up more territory seemed simply out of the question. Caillaux lost his post in 1912 and was made finance minister one year later. At last, the Agadir affair seemed over.

The conservatives, however, had not forgiven Caillaux for what they saw as his treason. When Raymond Poincaré became French president in 1913, wheels were set in motion to destroy Caillaux for good. The two chief axes of this attack were Gaston Calmette, the chief editor of Le Figaro, and the first Madame Caillaux, who had approached him with a stack of compromising letters giving insights, not only into the political life of the minister of finance, but also into his personal affairs. In flagrant disregard of all journalistic conventions of the day, Calmette set about publishing this correspondence, beginning with the political material. The mighty minister Caillaux, he knew, was enjoying the last days of his career.

Calmette mounted a veritable campaign of character assassination against the minister. Within a few months, 138 articles and cartoons appeared in Le Figaro, all of them attacking or ridiculing the politician. The best, however, was still to come. Among the compromising material handed over by the minister's spiteful ex-wife were love letters he had sent to his then mistress, the second Madame Caillaux, who now took it upon herself to solve the matter in her husband's best interests. 'I'll smash in his face,' the minister had growled over dinner with his wife, as the first letter appeared in print. Henriette Caillaux began to be afraid that her husband would challenge the editor to a duel, that he might be killed, and that the secret of their early love would be exposed. Taking her husband's official limousine, she had the chauffeur drive her to a gun dealer's, where she tested a Browning revolver and bought it. Then she drove to the offices of Le Figaro, where she waited for the editor in his office. When he finally

Attractive assassin: Henriette Caillaux on her way to the trial.

arrived she simply asked: 'You know why I'm here, don't you?' then pulled out her revolver and emptied the cylinder. Four of the six bullets hit Calmette, injuring him fatally. The assassin stayed where she was, waiting for the police. For her husband she had left a simple note: 'I'll do it for you.'

The trial of Henriette Caillaux was a sensation. Having resigned from his office minutes after he heard of his wife's deed, Caillaux himself worked for her defence. The strategy he had devised in accordance with the star lawyer he had hired was very simple: women, the court heard, were weak, emotional creatures and easily overwrought. Seeing her husband so viciously attacked by the press had upset the fragile balance of her feminine mind and she had acted out of mistaken loyalty, a *crime de passion* in the noblest sense of the term. The defence worked perfectly, and on 28 July 1914 Henriette Caillaux was found not guilty of murder, but of a *crime de passion*. She walked out of the courtroom, and into her husband's arms, a free woman. France was titillated and scandalized at once. 'The jury has acquitted Mme Caillaux,' wrote the gossipy abbé Mugnier in his diary:

Ah! How the conservatives, how the Catholics will shout! They so love anticipating the Last Judgement, making rules, inventing sanctions! They love pain, love justice that causes suffering! No indulgence, no grandeur in forgiveness. One must expiate, they say. That good countess Armand told me, last Sunday, about the war: 'we really need to be punished.' This need to punish is in the blood of the faithful ... They take communion, go up to the Sacré-Coeur and to the eucharist, the benedictions, [but] these good offices only inspire desires for evil, for condemnation, the love of a vengeful god. Ah! This is ugly...

Austria has declared war on Serbia.

The public was not given any time to recover from this murderous excitement. On 31 July, three days after the Caillaux acquittal, another murder shook the country. Jean Jaurès, the great orator, main defender of Captain Dreyfus, president and heart of the Socialist Party, one of the most universally respected politicians in France, was gunned down in the café du Croissant in Paris and died soon afterwards. A nationalist had taken exception to his call for a general strike in protest at the next war which was looming on the horizon, just as it had done at Agadir three years earlier. These were the great crimes that exercised French public opinion in July 1914. As newspapers were overflowing with the latest on the murders of Calmette and Jean Jaurès, very few column inches were left for other murders such as that of Archduke Franz Ferdinand in faraway Sarajevo.

The shots fired at Gaston Calmette from Madame Caillaux's Browning became a national sensation, partly because they resonated strongly with the preoccupations and anxieties of the period. Many motifs were drawn together in these cases: the French worries about being strong enough to stand up to overbearing Germany; the rise of the technocrat (Caillaux) and the thrust of modern politics; the crucial role of mass media; the colonial background with its sordid deals; the naval arms race and the constant threat of escalation; the violent deeds glorified by the Futurists and the anxiety about rising violence in everyday life; and finally the fact that Mme Caillaux was not content to be a passive wife, but instead took the initiative in killing a powerful man. This was the perfect murder of the time.

The Vortex of Infinite Forces

Fifteen years had passed since the 1900 World Fair, fifteen years in which the world had changed radically. Some of these changes – the growing cities, the factory chimneys, the rail tracks and Dreadnoughts – were very obvious. Others were less apparent but all the more profound. The War would bring them to the surface and shake what was left of the old order. But the modern world was present even before the first German soldier crossed the Belgian border.

To the American writer Henry Adams, the sight of the silently powerful dynamos at the 1900 Fair had been a revelation. Their hidden velocity made them a symbol of a fundamental upheaval at the heart of civilization, he wrote:

Power leaped from every atom, and enough of it to supply the stellar universe showed itself running to waste at every pore of matter. Man could no longer hold it off. Forces grasped his wrists and flung him about as though he had hold of a live wire or a runaway automobile; which was very nearly the exact truth for the purposes of an elderly and timid single gentleman in Paris, who never drove down the Champs Elysées without expecting an accident, and commonly witnessing one; or found himself in the neighbourhood of an official without calculating the chances of a bomb. So long as the rates of progress held good, these bombs would double in force and number every ten years.

Impossibilities no longer stood in the way. One's life had fattened on impossibilities. Before the boy was six years old, he had seen four impossibilities made actual – the ocean-steamer, the railway, the electric telegraph, and the Daguerreotype; nor could he ever learn which of the four had most hurried others to come.

The rush of modernity caused danger (the accidents, the terrorist bombs), the anxious feeling of speeding along without control, of holding on to live wire, flung and 'whirled about in the vortex of infinite forces'.

Adams's elderly gentleman, timidly driving down the Champs-Elysées in his automobile and watching out anxiously, would have been born around 1840, and his grandmother might still have had memories of France before 1789, of the *ancien régime*. His grandchildren would witness the mushroom cloud disperse over Hiroshima and watch live on their televisions as the first man walked on the moon. The most important intellectual, scientific and emotional changes dividing these two worlds occurred in the years between 1900 and 1914. At the 1900 World Fair, Adams had declared the culture of the traditional principle of female fertility, the Virgin, dead, replaced by that of the Dynamo's surging power and generative force. In choosing these two emblems, he had also identified the two central motifs of change in the 1900s: machines and women, speed and sex.

The Dynamo...

The 1900s were nothing if not dynamic. Everything appeared bigger today than it had yesterday: cities, industrial production, railway networks, streets with automobiles hurtling along, high-rise buildings with stern façades, populations, media and entertainment, mass culture, speed records. Gripped between the steely jaws of industry and the emerging global market, millions were uprooted and forced to invent new identities in an unfamiliar world.

Despite this dynamism, the spectre of degeneracy and decline was a haunting, constant presence in European minds. Eugenicists warned about the decline of the race; conservative publicists foretold the end of civilization; empires anxiously eyed one another's military might. Never before had there been so much reason to be optimistic, and never before had people looked towards the future with stronger misgivings. The sheer speed of change made people weary, but while they were uncertain of what was to come, Europeans were also increasingly doubtful about the values and achievements of power. Unlike the Victorians, they no longer tacitly assumed that they were Christian soldiers marching onward to paradise.

The twentieth century began compromised. Its most visible expression, the 1900 Paris World Fair, was symptomatic of the lack of confidence in the aesthetics of a new world, of a need to cover up the manifestations of tomorrow in a cloak borrowed from yesterday. A miniature medieval Paris lured consumers with its swordfights, souvenirs and chocolate advertising, the historicist national pavilions sat by the banks of the Seine like a row of grotesquely overbred pedigree dogs, and the colonial exhibition suggested a harmonious world which every visitor who had read about the events in Africa in the morning paper knew to be a lie. More than ever before, the programme of the fair itself was questioned. It was, in fact, a political exercise, reflecting the anxieties and misgivings of a society undermined by the divisiveness of the Dreyfus trial and by the debate about depopulation, declining manliness, and the man-eating city.

Elsewhere, the century began with the Boer War and the death of Queen Victoria, two events that did much to shake the moral confidence of the world's greatest empire. The death of the old Queen marked the end of an era (Henry James feared that the 'wild waters' would break loose), but the sordid war against the Boers and the uncovering of the monstrous regime in the Congo did much to undercut any idea of the *mission civilisatrice* that white Europeans were supposed to fulfil in the world. Japan's victory in 1905 only reinforced a widespread sense that the great powers were acting out of doubtful motives, were often badly led, and that the European 'race' itself was in permanent decline. The eugenics movement was born out of this anxiety, but its plans to create a master race only served to emphasize and exaggerate the impression that Europe's societies were in a sorry state.

As social realities seemingly shifted with every new day, the previous guarantor of stability, Europe's old ruling caste, went into terminal decline, taking with it the traditional social order and its values. The descendants of the knights and princes of old had been defeated – not by invading armies but by refrigeration and steam turbines. The new ruling class, the bourgeoisie, brought its own, pragmatic, ideals, and even if industrialists liked to play at being country noblemen every now and then, the game was played strictly by capitalist rules. The stately piles they bought as playthings were equipped with electrical light and modern sanitation. Their fortunes and industry held the real power now, and a factory prettified with mock-Gothic turrets was still a factory.

In the fast-living and constantly expanding universe of the city, certainty became a rare commodity. The rule of the dynamo not only accelerated things, it apparently made them spin out of control. Newspapers were full of reports of car accidents, of street violence and suicides, and even the advertising sections whispered disquieting messages: Are you man enough? they asked of the men; Are you beautiful enough? of the women; Are you healthy enough to withstand the pressure? of both. Those uncertain were discreetly informed of the existence of tonics and healing apparatuses, of sanatoriums and patent medicines, of life insurances as the last remaining certainty in the quicksand of existence.

Industrial production was rapidly overtaking traditional manufacture. Food imports from around the globe had long outstripped the capacities of domestic farming, and identities were increasingly cast in an industrial mould. The great majority of people had become consumers who did not themselves produce the goods they needed, but who exchanged their labour or services for money in order to buy labour, services and prefabricated goods from others. New social realities were created as the swelling ranks of workers were organized in trade unions and socialist parties, creating a considerable political force whose goal was the revolution of societies, and a large part of the equally radical feminist movement originated with female industrial workers. Church attendance declined dramatically, while political parties and associations grew, and even sports became a focus of tribal identities, particularly among working-class football followers. These were the new tribes.

Much of this transformation had taken place in less than a generation, and as there were fewer traditional certainties to hold on to, members of European societies felt a need for new points of reference. New creeds used the vocabulary of science to satisfy the need to feel chosen and superior. Nationalists and racial thinkers 'proved' their own excellence and deduced from it a claim to political domination and a right to violence if necessary. A little more subtly, eugenicists argued that 'superior' white middle-class Europeans and Americans had not only the right but the urgent duty to determine whether other, 'inferior', people should be allowed to have offspring. The majority simply decided to amuse themselves. Where once

Christianity had projected images of belonging, duty and hope in people's minds, the projection screen of the early cinema and the façade of the department store now replaced the Church as dream-weaver. It was a secular, industrial world that was shown here, but it was pretty, affordable, and entertaining. Already by 1910, those who could afford it shopped themselves out of existential trouble.

Artists and intellectuals recognized the compromised, damaged aspect of their time and were obsessed by formulating a new aesthetic and a genuine morality, but they could not agree exactly what to base it on. Official Western culture – Christianity, the Enlightenment – appeared to have spawned the meaninglessness of consumer life, the cruelty of capitalism, the anonymity of the big city, the moral bankruptcy of society itself. Many creative minds agreed that a real basis for renewal – aesthetic as well as moral – could be found only outside of Christian civilization in Africa (Picasso, Braque, Gide), Oceania (the anthropologist Marcel Mauss), South America (the intellectual historian Aby Warburg), in the pioneer spirit of the United States (Adolf Loos, Henry Adams), or in the pre-Christian pagan

Speed and the disintegration of the self: Metzinger's racing cyclist fuses man, machine, and the crowd.

civilizations of Europe in the countryside (Bartók, Kodály, Kandinsky) or in classical antiquity (Nietzsche, already dead, or Freud, Hofmannsthal, Klimt, Strauss).

The Futurists were not interested in primitive civilizations. They used the achievements of civilization against itself. Their weapons (wielded exclusively in manifestos and early artistic happenings) were modern machines such as fast cars, huge turbines and big guns. Their propaganda consisted in snippets of daily life: in newspaper clippings and nonsensical sounds gleaned from street noise and the screeches of engines in factory halls and railway stations, in the attempt to catch all that was transitory and to find heroism in iconic moments connecting speed and technology. Their hero was not the noble soldier or missionary, but the racing pilot, the cyclist fusing muscle power and body into a fast machine: an early bionic man.

... and the Virgin

The growth of industrialized society and the shift in attitudes between the sexes, and about sex, came by stealth. It slipped under the bed sheets and into people's minds. Nobody had written the Little Red Book of this revolution; no one great battle was fought over it; no Bastille stormed. Often imperceptibly and by small increments, ideals and expectations about men and women lost their anchorage and were cast adrift.

Spearheaded by the suffragettes in Britain and by feminist writers such as Emmeline Pankhurst and Rosa Mayreder, the cause of women's liberation forced itself into the public debate. Sometimes there were no more than a handful of these courageous women, and their demonstrations seem perfectly innocuous today, but this was the dawn of the media age, and newspapers are always out to expose the remarkable, the scandalous, the strange. Women in cycling trousers, rioting campaigners and activists with short hair were sure to get their photos into the papers (whether or not they wanted to), and to be read about by millions around the Continent. They were often met with derision and even hatred, but they could no longer be ignored.

But there were also more subtle, less spectacular but no less pervasive changes. All over Europe, women were having fewer children year on year; all over the West, they were becoming more educated and many were earning their own money in factories, shops, and soon also in the professions. They were very obviously taking more decisions for themselves, because they chose not to risk too many pregnancies and to invest in the future of a smaller number of better-educated children. If we can believe the learned contemporary authors writing about this phenomenon, commentators were taken by surprise and, what is more, they took it personally. It had apparently not occurred to them that sinking birth rates were evidence of social competence and mutually agreed decisions made by couples – instead they wrote about the decline of men, the spectre of *la dépopulation*, as one of them put it. While France had reason to be worried about this, it was a phantom problem for countries such as Britain and Germany, where populations continued to grow despite a dip in birth rates, but the same concerns were raised here.

This exaggerated reaction points to another phenomenon of the time. As women grew more assertive and appeared to be assuming new roles, men were suddenly on the defensive. It was Freud who had written that his research showed man to be 'no longer master in his own house', and this was true in more ways than one. Their physical strength made useless by machines that could be operated by a child, and their position questioned by social change and sexual uncertainty, men retreated into an assertion of exaggerated ideas of manliness. There was more duelling between 1900 and 1914 than there had been in the thirty years before, there were more people in uniform in the streets, there were chaps with bigger moustaches, body builders with bigger muscles, battleships with bigger guns. There were racing cars and speed records, sporting heroes and endless advertising for electrical belts and other remedies for lost 'manly vigour'. Little wonder that the sinking of the sleek, fast, powerful *Titanic* in 1912 was such an emblem of disaster for the period. Freud might have understood this, had he not, after all, been a child of his time: he conveniently diagnosed suffragettes as suffering from penis envy.

Feminist writers were not afraid of dismissals such as this one and took the fight to their critics. Their own analysis of society exposed male anxiety and patriarchal power structures with the greatest ease. 'Modern man suffers from his intellectualism as from an illness,' Rosa Mayreder had written. 'To be masculine ... as masculine as possible ... that is the true distinction in their [men's] eyes; they are insensitive to brutality of defeat or the sheer wrongness of an act if only it coincides with the traditional canon of masculinity.' This analysis from a woman's perspective questioned the very certainties that men relied on most, and few male writers (George Bernard Shaw, Arthur Schnitzler and August Bebel among them) had the far-sightedness and the moral courage to acknowledge the need for radical change.

To many men, the twin spectres of declining birth rates and of suffragettes throwing stones and attacking politicians seemed to herald the end of civilization. A society of mannish women and effeminate men was an aberration, conservative critics warned, an enfeebled stock that could only be submerged by 'inferior races' which had retained their vitality and virility because they had remained untouched by the corrupting influences of modernity. While women were demanding societal changes from within, away from ideas of domination and violence and towards a life of co-operative dialogue, many male writers (as well as some female ones) saw this as the road to ruin and demanded a revival of the warrior spirit and the faith they recognized in earlier centuries.

This male–female conflict in ideology which had roots in the feminist agitation of the 1900s was also transposed into racist ideas. Antisemitism was also, importantly, an expression of male anxiety, based on the perception that 'unmanly' Jews were symbolically castrating gentiles by yoking them to machines and making them subject to capitalist manipulations. The orientalist fascination with African cultures was strongly influenced by the perceived sexual freedom men enjoyed within them, be it the idea of the endlessly potent pasha with a harem of submissive women or the perceived natural virility of sub-Saharan Africans whose supposed sexual prowess and pride was a recurrent motif in novels and in graphic art. To dominate the colonies gave proof of European manliness, and it was all the more disturbing to be forced to admit the excesses of colonial brutality which inconveniently pulled the reality of near-slavery and abuse out of the realm of the symbolic and into the political sphere. As European identities were questioned on the most basic level – in considering men and women and their relations – political and social questions developed strongly sexual connotations, oscillating between direct sexual anxiety about questions such as masturbation, homosexuality, potency and mental illness, and a metaphorical level at which different groups were substituted for the real object of anxiety. Sublimation and displacement were the technical terms Freud had proposed for these mechanisms, which he had observed in patients unwilling to confront their innermost desires.

Lost in Space-Time

As the reign of the dynamo began, time and space themselves – which Kant had called the 'categories of perception' – mutated into something strange. For Einstein they had fused into space-time, a mysterious continuum that would warp and expand as well as contract. Scientists were investigating space at the level of the atom and had stopped time altogether, photographing bullets in flight, breaking up sequences of movements into their constituent parts in photographs, capturing series of static moments and bringing them to life again on film. Distance had shrunk due to wireless telegraphy and the telephone, railway lines transformed seaside towns, which had seemed unreachably far away only a generation earlier, into popular holiday destinations for the masses. People went faster; further. The commuter and the garden suburb were made possible by new trains, and at the same time the world came to them in wired newspaper articles and even in photographs, in the movies, on gramophone records.

The single space and the unique moment ceased to exist. Just a few years earlier, an aria performed at the Metropolitan Opera had been imprinted only on the memories of those present, or else lost into the ether. Now it could be recorded, copied thousands of times and sent around the world, to be played and replayed at will. There were photographs of colonial atrocities in the Congo and the fighting in the Boer War, and part of the sensation of one of the first short movies ever made, the *Sortie de l'usine Lumière à Lyon*, 1895, was the novelty, the sheer amazement, of seeing ordinary working women leaving their factory, a fleeting moment captured one late afternoon in a French city in 1895 that could be replayed at will in Cape Town or in Oslo.

Artists responded to this new, less certain sense of being in the world. Picasso and Braque showed objects and faces from several points at once, giving the viewer an unsettling omnipresence in the depicted room; Giacomo Balla and Marcel Duchamp pressed movements through time into a single picture frame; novelists and playwrights such as Schnitzler and Strindberg blurred the space between reality and imagination, dream and waking. Life was 'more fragmented and faster-moving than in previous periods', the Cubist painter Fernand Léger wrote in 1913: 'a modern man registers a hundred times more sensory impressions than an eighteenth-century artist.'

Man and machine entered into a strange marriage, a fused, bionic body, a second creation. Frederick Taylor revolutionized industrial processes by describing the human body as a mechanism that must be employed with ideal efficiency. Human personality was nothing but a fiction masking a stream of sensory impressions, much like exposures of a camera, in Ernst Mach's analysis. The sculptor Jacob Epstein created his uncannily robotic *Rock Drill* in 1913, the painter Umberto Boccioni and other Italian Futurists were endlessly fascinated by the melding of flesh and steel which they expressed in sculptures that to us seem to come right out of *Star Wars*, and in the minds of psychiatric patients rose the spectre of the Great

Influencing Machine, directly controlling minds and emotions over great distances. The robotic self was becoming a reality. As the cinema projectionist and hero of Luigi Pirandello's 1915 novel *Shoot* commented of his relationship to his projector: 'I cease to exist. *It* walks now, upon my legs. From head to foot, I belong to it: I form part of its equipment.'

The loss of integrity of the self, of a personality with clearly defined borders and a solid core which people felt in their social experience was further amplified by science. Instead of building the solid basis predicted by the positivist nineteenth century, advanced research and theory dissolved all certainty. They smashed the very matter into empty atoms and swirling electrons, twisted and distended time and space, showed dark powers and invoked a lurking, invisible reality: living people could be made to look like skeletons by X-ray machines; the mysterious rays from uranium could fly through solid objects; telegraph signals were whizzing through the air unseen; electricity could be sent over great distances and could be made to tickle, turn on a light bulb, power a locomotive, even to kill. None of this accorded in any way with the limited range of direct experience that people could rely upon from their senses. According to experience, physics was and still is Newtonian, time and space were the same for everyone, objects were solid. But experience was wrong, a mere projection of the mind, which in itself was part social construct, part illusion. As science expanded human possibilities and vastly increased human knowledge about nature, it also sapped any sense of direction, of purpose. More knowledge went hand-in-hand with less reliance on perception, with a weaker sense of which direction to head in. More knowledge made the world a darker, less familiar place.

If scientific analysis made the world fall apart, philosophical reason poured acid over the remaining truths. William James trenchantly proclaimed that truth was simply what was useful. Bertrand Russell explained that the very term 'truth' was a misunderstanding, and others like Mauthner and Wittgenstein questioned whether language could be meaningful at all. Ernst Mach was adamant that there was no such thing as a self, while Freud believed that not only the self, but even its morality, were individual, narcissistic constructions. Against all this, only Henri Bergson's vitalism appeared to offer some sort of salvation for instinct and experience, but it, too, rested on a critique of 'spatial' values, the very quantifying mind that had proven such a powerful tool for constructing new things and administrating existing ones. The comforting certainties of German idealism, Kant's critical reason and Hegel's obsessively methodical world spirit, were broken on the wheel of uncertainty. Nietzsche remained, but his poetic language meant that he could be claimed by anyone, that his intentions were endlessly disputed, that there was no authoritative legacy to hang on to.

Avant-garde artists mirrored this dissolution of personal integrity and authoritative myth. Figures were splintered, heads were smashed into fragments and multiple perspectives existing simultaneously, none of them more authoritative than the other. The shrapnel of the exploding outside world pierced the figures shown; borders between self and environment had broken down. Musicians such as Gustav Mahler mirrored this feeling as they let melodies interrupt one another, vulgar military marches riding roughshod over exquisitely turned phrases, sentiment distorted by sentimentality or undermined by irony. Stravinsky's *Sacre* blurred musical structures into a series of atmospheric moments and vicious assaults, while Arnold Schönberg went even further by using the breakdown of form and tradition as a tool with which to split music into its smallest constituent parts.

The very basics of life – time and space, physical integrity and personal identity – had been robbed of their solidity by the tide of change sweeping across the West, and as tribes of consumers replaced the estates of old, the loss of authenticity, of uniqueness and of unquestioned selfhood was keenly felt.

The Cult of Unreason

The new world taking shape in the 1900s was a creature of reason, of experts and scientists, statisticians and engineers. Until this era, reason had demystified the world, tearing away the veils of superstition in the tradition of Descartes, Hume and Kant. Evidence and deduction had taken over from revelation, from faith.

Now reason no longer fulfilled this function. Philosophical reason had attacked its own constituent parts (language and perception) and echoed Nietzsche's description of truth as a 'mobile army of metaphors', constantly changing formation to meet its enemy. As the society of reason was hurtling into an uncertain future, rationality aroused suspicion and the feeling of vertigo described by so many witnesses elicited a strongly irrational response. if reason was not providing certainty but breaking it down, salvation must lie in instinct, in primeval forces, many intellectuals proclaimed. The result was a search for ancient certainties, for mystical truth, a fascination with the unconscious, a celebration of violence and spontaneous action and of war, an anxious manifestation of manliness and virile strength. As reason undermined the world, unreason – the timeless realm of instinct and inspiration, of impulse and irrationality – promised to remedy the widespread feeling of emotional and intellectual alienation.

Unreason has always had a role to play in Western history. It is the driving force behind the Greek tragedies, the spiritual goal of medieval mysticism, the sublime or the thing-in-itself of the Enlightenment. To the Romantics of the turn of the nineteenth century, it blossomed into the Blue Flower, the elusive ideal of all artistic and spiritual life. It was there in Coleridge's opium dreams, in Shelley's ecstatic verse, in Hölderlin's poetic search and madness, in Pushkin and in the Marquis de Sade. Now it became both a political force and a phenomenon of mass culture. Dreyfus-haters in France chose unreason in the face of irrefutable evidence to manifest their disgust with what they perceived as the degeneracy of modernity, while avant-garde artists were fascinated with the archaic instincts and aesthetics of pre-industrial and pre-Christian societies. Mystics like Madame Blavatsky and Rudolf Steiner attracted a substantial following by choosing spiritual vision over reasonable doubt; Kaiser Wilhelm had a famously short attention span and constantly wanted to *do something*. Unreason could be worshipped in many ways.

The prophet of this turn-of-the-century counter-culture had been Friedrich Nietzsche, whose celebration of Dionysian will and ultimate self-overcoming was read (wrongly perhaps) as gospel by a whole generation of young Europeans. Nietzsche famously denounced the morality of his day as a slave morality, and his indictment gained a new and powerful resonance. The sexual morality of the day condemned many young women to ignorance and nervous fear, while encouraging young men to find release in the arms of prostitutes, strictly separating lust from 'higher' feelings and dividing women into virgins and whores.

As the speed of change gathered momentum, reason and instinct seemed increasingly estranged. All instinct is ultimately sexual, and the battle lines were drawn along sexual frontiers: the relationship between men and women was being questioned socially as well as erotically, leaving men, in particular, anxious and bewildered and looking for solutions. The question of unreason was a sexual question.

It was Sigmund Freud's genius to recognize this at this time and to make the irrational and sexuality central to understanding psychology. Freud described the revolt of unreason at the individual level and his concept of the subconscious made reason little more than a metaphoricizing gloss over ungovernable lust, a buoy bobbing haplessly on a sea of unrecognized desires. This analysis and its artistic expression centred particularly on

Vienna, the capital of pathological sensitivity to questions of identity, to language and its pitfalls, to the limits of rationality. The canvases of Egon Schiele showed subjects falling prey to their impulses, exposing themselves and burying themselves in the loneliness of convulsive embraces. His works were often sexually explicit but never joyful — logbooks of inescapable erotic slavery. In nearby Prague, the young Franz Kafka began to narrate and investigate the dimension of the mythical in the personal, of deep structures at work under a seemingly everyday surface. Kafka's central myth was biblical, while Freud drew his inspiration from ancient Greece, but their projects resemble each other and have the same resonances at their cores.

To antisemites and prophets of race such as Guido von List, Houston Stewart Chamberlain or Edouard Drumont, a pseudo-scientific notion of descent and mystical deep structures simply denied the force of reason altogether. The highest race (representing, without exception, the writer's own ethnic group) was automatically right in all its actions and instincts. Its impulses were healthy and sanctioned by nature, its actions necessarily good. No argument could question this. These utopias constituted a true revolt against reason, which they identified with the 'soulless rush' of modernity, with degeneracy and an ominous, corrosive Jewish influence on culture. Rationality condemned itself; any argument against this utopia was further evidence of conspiracy. 'Jewish reason' had corrupted the world; 'inferior races' and 'degenerates' had undermined the alleged purity of the race. The goal was to return, by way of a violent cataclysm, to a primeval harmony with Destiny, to a primeval community based on a spiritual essence, the very antithesis of the modern tribes.

The revolt of unreason was a revolt against modernity itself. It held the idea of an ancient and immutable essence of man against the unstable identities of city folk, it articulated itself in the male backlash against early feminism, in violence and the cult of manliness, in reactionary politics. But it was not backward-looking in all its aspects: it also played an important role in Futurism, avant-garde art and 'scientific' racial theories, in mysticism, and in the careers of men as different as W. B. Yeats, James Joyce, Adolf Hitler and Mark Rothko. The cult of unreason was important to movements as seemingly incompatible as abstract modernism and fascism.

But we are getting ahead of ourselves. At the beginning of the book, I invited you to try a thought experiment, to imagine a plague of document-devouring bookworms depriving us of all information about the twentieth century after July 1914. Only this somewhat unlikely perspective can, I think, allow an understanding of this period which is so massively overshadowed by the events that followed and is too often treated as a hostage to historical inevitability, can give back to this period its open future. We all know what happened in August 1914 and how the War (and perhaps the second Thirty Years War, 1914–1945) marked and marred the face of the century, but in this book I have found it essential to keep this perspective out, to unravel the period from within, interpreting it not retrospectively but as it was viewed by those living through it. Nobody would interpret the 1990s exclusively from the vantage point of 9/11, blaming the world for not anticipating what was to come. Similarly, nobody should look at the years before 1914 expecting to find a prophetic awareness of the horrors and preoccupations of the future.

Before 1914, the process of being rushed into the age of industrial mass production dominated many people's lives, feelings and thoughts. In spite of Virginia Woolf's claim, nobody was already fully 'modern' around 1910 – nobody is today. Different periods and different ways of seeing the world coexist, not only in societies, but even in individuals. The modernist heroes of cultural history had their personal blind spots which showed them rooted in conventional culture: Schnitzler despised experimental painting (he gave a devastating account of a show including paintings by Viennese modernists and called Egon Schiele an 'affected charlatan') and thought little of avant-garde music; Picasso was indifferent to music and had never heard of Schnitzler; Stravinsky never visited a theatre without a profession- al reason, and his taste in paintings was decidedly conservative. Mentalities and identities have a way of interweaving across the generations, creating composite and fractured selves, and this in itself is an integral part of mod- ernism, notably dramatized by the fragmentary character of modernist art and philosophy.

The identities of the 'new' men and women of this time (an important rhetorical trope in contemporary literature) were always torn between old loyalties and new aspirations, between nostalgia and social reality. They were transitory and haunted by fragility, by decline, by impotence, and they were always struggling to catch up with the social realities changing around them. Change occurred too fast; rationality had outstripped experi- ence, people felt locked inside a runaway automobile like Henry Adams, or, with Max Weber, on a train whose points had not been set. The accelera- tion without direction made them dizzy. Vertigo was everywhere, cutting across cultural and ideological divides. Writers of the day spoke of them- selves and others not only as New Men and New Women, but also, in German-speaking countries, as *Übergangsmenschen*, people in transition. Nothing was the same any more, and nothing had yet settled into a new, fixed shape. Our own world and our intellectual and emotional horizons were shaped by these transitional people. Fear and exhilaration formed an extraordinary creative tension, the origin of almost every idea and social phenomenon that would come to dominate the twentieth century – socialism and fascism, nuclear physics and the theory of relativity, conceptual art and consumer society, mass media and democratization, feminism and psychoanalysis. In many ways the twentieth century merely played out the dreams and the nightmares arising in the creative ferment of 1900–1914.

In Robert Musil's novel *The Man Without Qualities* the protagonist Ulrich muses about the era he is living in:

Stuffed shirts: consumer identities.

Was there really a war in the Balkans or not? Some intervention was bound to be taking place; but he was not certain whether it was a war. So many things were moving humankind. The record height for aeroplanes had been raised once again; a proud affair. If he was not wrong it was now at 3,700 metres, and the man was called Jouhoux. A negro boxer had beaten a white champion and conquered the world title; Johnson was his name. The president of France was going to Russia; people were speaking of a danger for world peace. A newly-discovered tenor earned sums in South America which were unheard of even in North America. A terrible earthquake had hit Japan; the poor Japanese. In a word, a lot was going on, the times around the end of 1913 and the beginning of 1914 were momentous indeed.

Notes

1. **1900:** *The Dynamo and the Virgin*

page 7 *Sauvage, a schoolteacher:* Jean Sauvage, *Eine Reise nach Paris von Jean Sauvage, Oberlehrer*, Berlin, 1900, 2.

7 *'by tourist guides':* ibid., 3.

7 *'advertisements with me':* ibid., 16.

7 *'Bois de Vincennes':* ibid., 22.

8 *'Tendeur pour pantalons':* ibid., 25.

8 *'in advanced civilization':* quoted in: Frederic Mayer, *The Parisian Dream City*, St Louis, 1900, n.p.

10 *'has claimed victory':* ibid., 40.

10 *'to individual atoms':* ibid.

11 *'the most expressive':* Adams, 380.

13 *'have explained it':* J. de Maistre, *Trois Fragments sur la France*, in *Œuvres inédites du comte J. de Maistre*, Paris, 1870, 9. Translation by Theodore Zeldin.

13 *'and twentieth centuries':* Jacques Bertillon, *La dépopulation en France*, Paris, 1911, 7.

14 *'itself in plaster':* Eugène-Melchior de Vogüé, 'Sur la défunte exposition', *Revue des deux mondes*, November 1900, 396.

14 *La France juive:* Edouard Drumont, I, 6.

15 *'literal sense of the term':* René Gonnard, *La dépopulation*, Paris, 1898, 85.

15 *'life of tomorrow':* quoted in Winock, 35.

18 *'terrible... terrible disaster':* Maksim Gorky, *The Philistines*, 42.

19 *'an ocean liner':* Vogüé, 'Sur la défunte exposition', 394.

20 *'as far as possible sexless':* Adams, 11.

2. **1901:** *The Changing of the Guard*

25 *'Lamb of God':* quoted in Wilson, 472.

25 *'their own might':* Tuchman, 54–5.

27 'waters are upon us now': Edel, Leon ed., *Henry James's Letters*, vol. IV, 1895–1916, Cambridge, Mass., 1984, 184.

27 'pleasure and comfort': quoted after Cannadine, *The Decline*, 349.

31 'keeping it up': Oscar Wilde, *The Importance of Being Earnest*, Act I, Scene 1.

32 'had become accustomed': Lvov, quoted in Figes, *Natasha's Dance*, 49.

35 'ostentation, indeed presumption': Musil, 66–7.

36 'the cheapest hospice': quoted after MacDonough, *Prussia*, 124.

37 'with astonishing rapidity': in conversation with the author.

39 'boating with the Kaiser': quoted after Blackbourn, *History of Germany*, 366.

40 'ring of racing people': quoted after Cannadine, *The Decline*, 349.

41 'more reality than appearance': quoted after Giles MacDonough, *Prussia: the Perversion of an Idea*, London, 1995, 137.

41 'no sense of proportion': Spitzemberg, 528, 29 April and 20 May 1911.

3. **1902:** *Oedipus Rex*

46 'Dr Emil Fronz': *Weiner Zeitung*, 18 March 1902, 1.

49 *remembered of his youth:* Stefan Zweig, 92.

50 'warm, comfortable existence': ibid., 15–20.

50 'that of operetta': Bruno Bettelheim, 'La Vienne de Freud', in *Vienne, 1880–1938*, exhibition catalogue, Paris, 1986, 33.

51 *The Daisy Chain:* more commonly translated, after the film by Max Ophuls, *La Ronde*.

54 'into [self-]reproach': quoted in Gay, *Freud*, 92.

54 *prevent facts from existing:* Gay, *Freud*, 52.

54 'during the night': Sigmund Freud, *The Interpretation of Dreams*, New York, 1911, 189.

55 'in normal functioning': ibid.

55 'to this day': ibid., 308.

57 'interested in that': Schnitzler, *Fräulein Else*, 113.

58 'life passes you by': Schnitzler, *Ruf des Lebens*, Act I, Scene 1.

58 'a coherent way': Hugo von Hofmannsthal, 'Ein Brief', in: *Der Brief des Lord Chandos*, Stuttgart, 2000, 50.

58 *alone, and silent:* ibid., 50–1.

59 'of psychological anaylsis': Ernst Mach, *The Anaylsis of Sensations* (1897). Translation by C. M. Williams and Sydney Waterlow.

61 'every cliché killed': Karl Kraus, *Die Fackel*, 319–320, 31 March 1911, 19.

61 'funeral orations for it': Hermann Bahr, 'Die Moderne', in *Die Wiener Moderne*, Stuttgart, 1981, 189.

63 'material it is in itself': Adolf Loos, *Ins Leere gesprochen*, Paris/Zurich, 1921, 136.

63 'be entirely different': ibid., 159.

64 *'stuck in the past'*: Adolf Loos, *Ornament und Verbrechen*, in Ulrich Conrads, *Programme und Manifeste zur Architektur des 20. Jahrhunderts*, Braunschweig, 1981, 16.

64 *'can be beautiful'*: Otto Wagner, *Die Baukunst unserer Zeit*, Vienna, 1914, 44.

69 *'majority in parliament'*: Freud to Fliess, 11 March 1902, *Freud–Fliess*, 501 2.

70 *'for the apocalypse'*: Karl Kraus, in *Die Fackel*, 10 July 1914.

4. 1903: *A Strange Luminescence*

75 *'It was over'*: Thomas Mann, *Der Zauberberg*, 297–8, transl. PB.

76 *'faint, fairy lights'*: Marie Curie, Autobiographical Notes, in *Pierre Curie*, translated by C. & V. Kellog, New York, 1923, 186–7.

77 *'origin of one of us'*: quoted in Rosalynd Pflaum, *Grand Obsession: Madame Curie and Her World*, Doubleday, New York: Macmillan, 1989, 74.

78 *'the new discoveries'*: Pierre Curie, Nobel Prize lecture, in *Nobel Lectures*, 'Physics 1901–2', Amsterdam: Elsevier, 1967, 74.

78 *'companion of my life'*: quoted in Vincent Cronin, *Paris on the Eve*, London: HarperCollins, 1989, 222.

81 *'sixth place of decimals'*: quoted in Teich and Porter, 245.

84 *'constitutes true duration'*: Henri Bergson, *Essai sur les données immédiates de la conscience*, Paris: Daus, 1909, 51.

84 *'man who runs'*: Henri Bergson, *Matter and Memory*, London: Allea, 1911, 208–9.

84 *'itself varnished too'*: Joseph Conrad, *Heart of Darkness*, London, 1902, 89.

85 *'points of view'*: José Ortega y Gasset, 'Adám en el Paraiso', in *Obras Completas*, 1910, I, 471. Quoted in Kern, *Culture of Space and Time*, 151.

86 *'and so forth'*: Patrick Brantlinger, in Teich and Porter, 108.

87 *'boulevard Montmartre, Paris'*: *Le Matin*, 13 March 1910.

88 *'this thing you know'*: quoted in Simon, *Dark Light*, 237.

88 *'a legal crime'*: ibid., 238–9.

89 *'to these things'*: Wells, *A World Set Free*, London, 1914, 16.

90 *'fan-like humped body'*: Wells, *The War in the Air*, London, 1898, 47.

91 *'What a career'*: *Le Figaro*, 6 November 1906.

91 *'strength or certainty'*: quoted in Conrad, *Modern Times*, 83.

5. 1904: *His Majesty and Mister Morel*

92 *'poured into the village'*: quoted in John Bierman, *Dark Safari: The Life behind the Legend of Henry Morton Stanley*, New York, 1990, 281.

93 *'drilled into soldierhood'*: Casement and O'Sullivan, 68ff.

93 *'given to me'*: ibid., 72.

95 'with passionate emphasis': Morel et al., *E. D. Morel's History*, 28–9.

96 'King for a croniman': ibid., 41–2.

97 'production of india-rubber': Casement, 87.

98 'in that institution': ibid., 99.

98 'poor, poor people': Casement and O'Sullivan, 17.

99 'Infamous shameful system': ibid., 263.

100 'more than 5 years': John Harris, unpublished MS, quoted in Louis 'Sir John Harris', 833.

102 'Boers to do it': Der Floh, 8 June 1902, 2.

102 'people of heroes': Arbeiterzeitung, 7 June 1902, 1.

102 'entirely in… [the Jews'] hands': quoted after Judd and Surridge, 242.

103 'white man's war': quoted after Judd and Surridge, 154.

103 'yes, in capacity': Webb, 232.

104 'mighty German Kaiser': Bundesarchiv Potsdam, *Akten des Reichskolonialamtes*, RKA, 10.01 2089, Bl. 23, MS copy of the proclamation to the Herero and the additional order to the Kaiserliche Schutztruppe, 2 October 1904.

105 'killed them with bayonets': J. De Bruijn and H. Colijn, *De slag om Tjakra Negara. Een verslag in drie brieven*. Amsterdam, VI uitgeverij, 1998, 34.

106 'old wives' tales': quoted after Hochschild, 240.

106 'seen in the Congo': ibid., 238.

107 'too large a subject': ibid., 247.

108 'sacrifices in the Congo': ibid., 259.

110 'develop his estate': Joseph Chamberlain, quoted in J. L. Gavin and Julian Amery, *The Life of Joseph Chamberlain*, London, 1932–51, I, 27.

112 'Cowboys and Indians' were introduced: Bernard Potter, 66.

114 'lowest order of humanity': *Plakate in Frankfurt, 1880–1914*, Exhibition, Historisches Museum Frankfurt, 1986.

114 'youth was in it': Loti, *Aziyadé*, 7.

115 'more individual freedom': Spitzemberg, 434.

116 was specifically colonial: Sauvage, *Eine Reise von Jean Sauvage, Oberlehrer*, Berlin, 1900, 65.

118 'now and then': Bely, 101.

120 'could deepy admire': quoted after Hochschild, 289.

121 'was the Congo': ibid., 287.

6. **1905:** *In All Fury*

122 'among them children': Witte, 402.

124 'realised by experience': quoted in Figes, *Tragedy*, 95.

125 'that I know of': quoted in Figes, *Tragedy*, 66.

126 'more obstinate character': quoted in Engel, 82.

127 'as lavatory attendants': quoted in Figes, *Tragedy*, 113.

127 'a common business': M. B., 'Peterburgskie trushchoby', 31 October 1913. Quoted in Neuberger, *Hooliganism: Crime, Culture and Power in St Petersburg, 1900–1914*, Berkeley: University of California Press, 1993.

127 'resembled human beings': Svirskii, 'Peterburgskie khuligany', 250. Quoted in Neuberger, *Hooliganism*.

128 'revolution will break out': Witte, 397.

128 'noted for free thinking': quoted after Harcave, 11.

130 'governor-general of Finland': Witte, 372.

130 'than of men': ibid., 364.

130 'promoted his advancement': ibid., 365.

130 'a rough manner': ibid., 98–9.

131 'Russia is happy': ibid., 374.

131 'against the Jews': ibid., 377.

131 'become extreme revolutionaries': ibid., 379.

131 'buy his way out': ibid., 378.

133 'exterminate our enemies': Piotr Zaichnevsky, quoted after Figes, *Tragedy*, 132.

135 'about the navy': Witte, 382.

135 'certain of victory': ibid., 385.

136 'beat them with icons': Figes, *People's Tragedy*, 170.

136 'the highest authority': ibid., 170.

137 'let us build jails': ibid., 173.

138 'powers that be': A. M. Buiko, quoted after Salisbury, *Black Snow*, 105.

140 'purpose in going': quoted in Salisbury, *Black Snow*, 120.

141 'open fire on us': quoted in Salisbury, *Black Snow*, 121.

141 'through his teeth': quoted in Figes, *People's Tragedy*, 177.

142 'of innocent blood': ibid., 127.

142 'pogromshchik by conviction': Witte, 404.

143 'are absolutely terrified': quoted after Salisbury, *Black Snow*, 130–1.

143 'to enact laws': Witte, 468.

146 'of whatever variety': ibid., 479.

146 'his personal enemies': ibid., 480, 481.

147 'everyone was asking for': quoted in Figes, 191.

147 'shipping transport grease': Salisbury, *Black Snow*, 174.

148 settling of accounts began: ibid., 167.

148 'to be preserved': quoted in Salisbury, 166–7.

150 'and again dispersed': Bely, 51.

150 'oceans of blood': ibid., 65.

152 *'scroll spells Death'*: quoted in Salisbury, *Black Snow*, 193.

152 *'generally joyless existence'*: Zdanevich and Larionov, 'Why We Paint Ourselves', 83. Quoted in Neuberger, *Hooliganism*.

152 *'to rearrange life'*: quoted in Vladimir Markov, *Russian Futurism*, Berkeley: University of California Press, 1968, 9.

152 *'all yours, yours'*: Livshits, *The One and a Half-Eyed Archer*, 42. Quoted in Neuberger, *Hoolganism*.

153 *'will of the Board'*: Bryusov, 'Republic of the Southern Cross', in *The Republic of the Southern Cross, and other stories*, G. Constable, London, 1918.

154 *'and bury him'*: Andreyev, 41.

154 *'way any longer'*: Witte, 474.

7. **1906**: Dreadnought *and Anxiety*

155 *'wine and of flowers'*: *Manchester Guardian*, 12 February 1906, 1.

156 *'as the English'*: quoted in Massie, 151.

157 *'habitually called "home"'*: ibid., 26.

157 *'got his balance'*: ibid., 28.

157 *'of the ladies'*: ibid., 153–4.

158 *'for the navy'*: ibid., 157.

159 *'on the water'*: ibid., 162.

159 *'equal to English'*: ibid., 166.

160 *'present time is England'*: ibid., 172.

161 *'fainted at the sight'*: ibid., 410.

161 *'the revolver tracks'*: ibid., 399.

161 *'takes four years'*: ibid., 406.

163 *'be pea shooters'*: ibid., 471.

163 *'would be HELL'*: ibid., 472.

164 *'were considered imbeciles'*: Zeldin, *Conflicts in French Society*, 896.

164 *'of male pride'*: ibid., 881.

165 *'not a man'*: ibid., 898.

165 *'an effiminate man'*: Marcel Proust, *Correspondance*, 6–8 November 1920, ed. Philip Kolt, Paris, 1970.

166 *'termination of the affair'*: Wythe Williams, *The Tiger of France: Conversations with Clemenceau*, New York: Ovell, Sloan and Pearce, 1949, 82.

166 *'ideal of justice'*: quoted by Richard Cohen, *By the Sword*, New York: Random House, 2002, 183.

167 *'reservist beer mugs'*: C. Berg and U. Hermann, *Industriegesellschaft und Kulturkrise*, Munich, 1991, 13.

167 *'follow orders immediately'*: H. F. Kahle, *Grundzüge einer evangelischen Volkserziehung*, Breslau, 1890.

168 *'and other Russians'*: Hans Kohn 'Rückblick auf eine gemeinsame Jugend', in Tramer ed., *Robert Weltsch*, Tel Aviv, 1961, 115.

168 *'Dr. von Staat'*: Thomas Mann, *Betrachtungen eines Unpolitischen*, Frankfurt/M, 1983, 247.

170 *by his cabinet:* Clark, *Wilhelm II*, 162.

170 *'ordered them to do so'*: ibid., 163.

171 *'askance at a German'*: ibid., 169.

171 *'holds a dagger'*: *Daily Telegraph*, 28 October 1908.

171 *'this is a madhouse'*: Spitzemberg, 489.

172 *'hitherto been unquestioned'*: quoted after Clark, *Wilhelm II*, 172–3.

172 *'made in public'*: ibid., 167.

172 *'routine of life'*: quoted in Massie, 666.

172 *'out of the question'*: ibid., 669.

173 *'my only bosom friend'*: ibid., 667.

173 *'radiance in my life'*: ibid., 667.

173 *'arm around him'*: Witte, 457.

173 *'would not suffer it'*: quoted in Massie, 669.

174 *'his good nose'*: quoted in Massie, 131.

175 *'with your peculiarities'*: quoted in Massie, 672.

176 *'in the dark'*: *Die Zukunft*, 17 November 1906.

176 *'already warm enough'*: ibid., 13 April 1907.

178 *'of such sinners'*: Spitzemberg, 472.

178 *'to the music'*: quoted after Massie, 690.

179 *'a third one'*: Magnus Hirschfeld, *Berlins drittes Geschlecht*, Berlin, 1904, 6.

179 *'profound psychological shock'*: ibid., 39.

180 *'less than fifteen times'*: quoted in Caroline Daley, 'Sandow, the Strongman of Eugenics', *Australian Historical Studies*, 120, 2, 234.

181 *'see his passport'*: quoted in Massie, 630.

181 *'subject of the Kaiser'*: quoted in Massie, 637.

182 *'passage of the seas'*: Erskine Childers, *The Riddle of the Sands*, London, 1903, 90.

182 *'the English shores'*: quoted in Massie, 633.

184 *'something of beauty'*: Nordau, *Degeneration*, 7.

184 *'and frizzy images'*: ibid., 228.

184 *'the lowest level'*: ibid., 119–22.

185 *'under his thumbs'*: ibid., 544, 556–7.

186 *'their own guilt'*: Nordau, *Sandow Paper*, 1:20.

186 *'proclaim their Jewishness'*: Nordau, *Jüdische Turnerzeitung*, 1900, II, 12.

186 *'diseased organic processes'*: Nordau, *Degeneration*, 416.

188 *'become entirely superfluous'*: Mayreder, *Kritik der Weiblichkeit*, 109–10.

188 *'canon of masculinity'*: ibid., 122.

8. 1907: *Dreams and Visions*

189 *'rise inside you'*: Ernst Stadler, *Dichtungen*, ed. K. L. Schneider, 2 vols. (Hamburg, 1954), vol. I, 120; a poem from around 1910.

192 *'absolute masculine activity'*: Mayreder, 12.

192 *'they were raped'*: Lida Gustava Heymann, 'Weiblicher Pazifismus', in Gisela Brinker-Gabler (ed.), *Frauen gegen den Krieg*, Frankfurt/M, 1980, 65.

193 *'like bloody snowflakes'*: Suttner, *Maschinenzeitalter*, 54.

194 *'in their development'*: quoted in Geiss, *Julikrise und Kriegsausbruch 1914*, Hannover, 1963, nos. 319, 346.

194 *'the whole world'*: quoted in Tuchman, 237.

195 *'aegis of Russia'*: ibid., 257–8.

195 *'our time, is enormous'*: Andrew D. White, *Autobiography*, New York, 1922, 260.

196 *'exhaustion and ruin'*: quoted in Tuchman, 258.

196 *'been carfully eliminated'*: ibid., 261.

196 *'chilled to the bone'*: ibid., 264.

199 *'all this novelty'*: Franziska von Reventlow, *Herrn Dames Aufzeichnungen*, in *Gesammelte Werke*, Munich, 1925, 194.

200 *'made of glass'*: ibid.

200 *'in the middle'*: ibid.

201 *'towards the heavens'*: *Münchner Post*, 2 August 1888.

204 *'coloured by it'*: Martin Buber, *Drei Reden über das Judentum*, Frankfurt/M, 1911, 12–13.

208 *'a clammy hell'*: Schorske, *Vienna*, 251.

209 *'a cotswold ewe'*: quoted in Peter Washington, *Blavatsky*, 41.

211 *'Thousand kisses, darling'*: ibid., 123.

211 *'and political tendencies'*: Edward Carpenter, *The Intermediate Sex*, London, 1908, 114–15.

212 *'wearer [and] sex maniac'*: George Orwell, *The Road to Wigan Pier*, London, 1937.

215 *'extra-sensory capabilities'*: quoted in Wolfgang G. Vögele, *Der andere Rudolf Steiner. Augenzeugenberichte, Interviews, Karikaturen*, Dornach, 2005, 49ff.

215 was *'murdering souls'*: Ellen Key, *Das Jahrhurdert des Kindes*, Berlin, 1908, 124.

9. **1908:** *Ladies with Rocks*

220 '*anywhere in the world*': quoted in Andrew Rosen, *Rise up, Women!*, 104–5.

220 '*Simply indifferent*': ibid., 105.

220 '*to human society*': ibid., 97.

222 '*is always untidy*': Saltonstall, quoted in Liddington, 87–8, 101–2.

222 '*up in poverty*': quoted in Liddington and Norris, 32.

223 '*communal outdoor closets*': Liddington, 30–1.

224 '*silently, Mother's side*': ibid., 34.

225 '*manly or just*': ibid., 151.

225 '*freedom really means*': ibid., 48.

225 '*bear the consequences*': ibid., 49.

226 '*matter so much*': ibid., 87.

227 '*barrage of press cuttings*': ibid., 48.

229 '*name was mud*': ibid., 241.

229 '*by Big Ben*': ibid., 238.

229 '*Signed, Leonora Cohen*': ibid, 139.

233 '*and the cooking*': quoted after Stites, *Women's Liberation Movement*, 208–9.

234 '*for me to do*': ibid., 231–2.

237 '*its very foundations*': Anita Augspurg, *Ehe?: Zur Reform der sexuellen Moral*, Berlin, Internationale Verlagsgesellschaft, 1911, 19.

237 '*and the family*': quoted in Allen, 53.

238 '*a men's state*': Heymann and Augspurg, 36.

238 '*consternation in Munich*': ibid., 45.

239 '*the only option*': quoted in Christiane Henke, *Anita Augspurg*, Reinbeck, 2000, 58.

239 '*your husband's signature*': Anita Augspurg, 'Ein typischer Fall der Gegenwart', in: *Zeitschrift für Frauenstimmrecht*, 1905, 81.

239 '*on all women*': Anita Augspurg, 'Sittlichkeit und Rechtsschutz', in *Die Zeit*, 469, 1903, 312.

239 '*destroying our race*': Anita Augspurg, *Ehe?*, 19.

240 '*chance of success*': Bebel, *Frau im Sozialismus*, 35.

241 '*of stupidity begins*': ibid, 2.

241 '*our sexual misery*': Grete Meisel-Hess, *Die sexuelle Krise*, 397; transl. Harriet Anderson, *Utopian Feminism*, New Haven, 1992, 182.

241 '*of this society*': ibid., 182–4.

243 '*of former circumstances*': ibid., 103.

243 '*to normative violence*': Mayreder, 90.

243 '*first social order*': ibid., 109–10.

243 '*canon of masculinity*': ibid., 122.

243 *'they are supposed to be'*: ibid., 199.

243 *'influences are on the increase'*: ibid., 105.

243 *'destruction of masculinity'*: ibid., 106.

243 *'nervous exhaustion'*: ibid., 118.

245 *'not as individuals'*: Otto Weininger, *Geschlecht und Charakter*, Vienna, 1923, 402.

245 *'most of them puny-looking'*: Stites, *Women's Liberation*, 208.

10. **1909**: *The Cult of the Fast Machine*

255 *'albatross with his airplanes'*: Uzanne, *La Locomotion*, 244, translation in Kern, *Culture of Time and Space*, 128.

255 *around the turn of the century*: Kern, *Culture of Time and Space*, 110.

256 *'out of phase with his own'*: Mirbeau, *La 628 E-8*, 7, translation in Kern, *Culture of Time and Space*, 113.

256 *to drive around the globe*: Deutsche Zeitung, Nr. 46, 21 March 1902, 1.

257 *new automobile fad, le camping*: Deutsche Revue, July 1912, July 1910, July 1906.

259 *'fails to evoke'*: quoted after Kern, *Culture of Time and Space*, 118.

260 *'grown men points'*: H. G. Wells, *Selected Short Stories*, London, 1927, 86.

260 *'Anaemic cockneymen'*: ibid., 105.

260 *'a minute will reverse'*: T. S. Eliot, 'The Love Song of J. Alfred Prufrock'.

261 *'crushed under the wheels'*: Vladimir Mayakovsky, originally published in *Nov'*, 16 November 1914; here translated by Helen Segall in *The Ardis Anthology of Russian Futurism*, ed. Carl Proffer and Ellendea Proffer, Ann Arbor, Mich., 1980, 187–8.

264 *'part of its equipment'*: Pirandello, *Quaderni di Serafino Gubbio operatore*, Engl. translation, New York, 1926, 86.

264 *'which are also falling'*: Pierre Loti, *Quelques aspects*, 2–3.

265 *'brain-working household'*: Beard and Rockwell, 23.

266 *the years of the Kaissereich, imperial Germany*: Radkau, *Das Zeitalter der Nervosität*.

266 *'heart race every day'*: quoted after Radkau, 102–3.

266 *'back and arms'*: ibid., 189.

267 *56 students and eleven farmers*: ibid., 215.

267 *'my poor girls'*: ibid., 229.

267 *'slit his throat'*: ibid., 212.

268 *'largely done by neurasthenes'*: ibid., 263.

269 *'neurasthenia, phobias, etc.'*: Ernest Monin, *Les troubles nerveux de cause sexuelle*, Paris, 1890, 19–20.

270 *'battlefield of the neurasthenic'*: Radkau, 146.

270 'a perverse sadist': ibid., 159.

270 'the Russian illness': P. I. Kovalevskii, 'Folie du doute', *Arkhiv psikhiatrii, neirologii i sudebnoi psikhopatologii*, 1886, 8, 38, transl. Laura Goering, 'Russian Nervousness: Neurasthenia and National Identity in Nineteenth-Century Russia', *Medical History*, 2003, 17, 23–16.

270 'devastate the nervous system': P. I. Kovalevskii, *Nervnye bolezni nashego obshchestva*, Khartov, 1894, 42, transl. Laura Goering.

271 'for our sins': S. T. Aksatov, 'Yapiski ob uzhen'e ryby' in *Sobranie sochinenii v 4kb tomakh*, Moscow, 1954 (reprint), transl. Laura Goering.

271 'degeneration is its fate': P. I. Kovalevskii, *Vyrozhdenie I vozrozhdenie*, St Petersburg, 1903, 16, transl. Laura Goering.

271 'concerts and fashionable brasseries': quoted in Christopher E. Forth, 'Neurasthenia and Manhood in fin-de-siècle France', in M. Gijswijt Hofstra and Roy Porter, eds, *Cultures of Neurasthenia, From Beard to the First World War*, Amsterdam/New York, 2001, 347.

271 'firmness of character': ibid., 339.

272 'they kill us': ibid., 335.

273 'designated as hysteria': Nordau, *Degeneration*, 1895, reprint Nebraska, 1993, 15.

273 'chambers with patients': quoted by Chandrak Segoopta, 'A Mob of Incoherent Symptoms', in M. Gijswijt Hofstra and Roy Porter, eds, *Cultures of Neurasthenia, From Beard to the First World War*, Amsterdam/New York, 2001, 103.

273 'in idle damsels': Thomas Clifford Allbutt, *A System of Medicine*, London, 1905–11, 741.

274 'new impressions, new images': Radkau, *Nervosität*, 277.

274 'no longer be changed': ibid., 278.

274 'at work in all of us': ibid., 281.

274 'in nervous haste': ibid., 275.

274 'the fleet project': ibid., 286.

274 the Latin verb amare: ibid., 317.

275 '"forceful" and "limp"': ibid., 264.

11. **1910**: *Human Nature Changed*

277 'with a coloured photograph': Clive Bell, 'The English Group', *Second Post-Impressionist Exhibition*, catalogue, London, Grafton Galleries, 1912.

277 'human character changed': Virginia Woolf, *Collected Essays*, London: Hogarth Press, 1966, 4 vols, vol. I, 320.

278 'human race to change': ibid., 320.

278 'conduct, politics, and literature': ibid., 321.

278 *'a waste of energy'*: ibid., 324.

279 *'concealment and conversation'*: ibid., 335.

279 *'the fragmentary, the failure'*: ibid., 337.

280 *'and for how long'*: quoted in Nicholson, 33.

281 *'last degradation of art'*: William Blake Richmond, 'Post Impressionists', *Morning Post*, 16 November 1910, 5; reprinted in J. B. Bullen, 115; 'The Post Impressionists at the Grafton Galleries', *The Academy*, 3 December 1910, 547; Laurence Binyon, 'Post Impressionists', *Saturday Review*, 12 November 1910, 609–10, reprinted in Bullen, 111; A. J. Finberg, 'Art and Artists', *The Star*, 14 December 1910, reprinted in Bullen, 137; 'New Art that Perplexes London', *The Literary Digest*, 10 December 1910, 1094; Robert Morley, letter to the *Nation*, December 1910, 406; Ebenezer Wake Cook, 4, reprinted in Bullen, 119–20.

281 *'pain and evil'*: Julius Meier-Graefe, *Modern Art*, London, 1908, 60, 62.

284 *'influence on the psyche'*: Marinetti, *Futurist Manifesto*.

287 *'It was superb acting'*: Adolf de Meyer and Jennifer Dunning, *L'après-midi d'un faune*, Dance Books, London, 87.

287 *'accepted by the true public'*: Gaston Calmette, *Le Figaro*, 20 May 1912.

288 *'cause a scandal'*: 'Early Years', in Minna Lederman, ed., *Stravinsky in the Theatre*, New York, 1949, 128–9.

289 *le massacre du printemps*: Gaston Calmette, *Le Figaro*, 31 May 1913.

289 *'to be reborn'*: quoted in Gerard Guicheteau, *Les années radieuses: 1909–1914*, Paris: Payard, 2005, 317.

290 *'in terms of pathology'*: quoted in Hepp, *Avantgarde*, 110.

298 *'of my entire being'*: Gide, *Si le grain ne meurt*, 287.

300 *'I am afraid'*: Eysoldt to Hofmannsthal, 1903, in L. Fiedler, ed., *Der Sturm Elektra*, Vienna: Residenz Verlag, 2001, 9.

300 *'bloody furor with syle'*: ibid., 37.

301 *'see the light I radiate'*: Strauss, *Elektra*, 53.

301 *'temples and palaces'*: ibid., 5.

302 *'perverted by these "modernizers"'*: Fiedler, *Sturm Elektra*, 42.

302 *'façade of the educated person'*: ibid., 45.

306 *'purpose willed by God'*: Max Weber, *Protestant Ethic*, transl. Talcott Parsons, New York: Scribner's, 1930, 177.

12. **1911**: *People's Palaces*

312 *'hero-cripple's corpse'*: Joseph Medill Patterson, 'The Nickelodeons', *The Saturday Evening Post*, 23 November 1907.

312 *'conquering the world'*: R. Doumic, 'L'Age du Cinéma', *Revue des deux mondes*, 16, 15 August 1913, 919–20.

315 *'twenty-four hours of vomiting'*: Robert Gottlieb, 'The Drama of Sarah Bernhardt', *New York Review of Books*, vol. 54, no.8, 10 May 2007.

317 *'threaten us from on high'*: Mugnier and d'Hendecourt, 192.

317 *'universal mummery will reign'*: Louis Haugmard, 'L'Esthétique' du cinématographe, quoted in Williams, *Dream Worlds*, 83.

321 *'with their irislescent pencils'*: quoted in Williams, 88.

321 *'a palace rather than a shop'*: ibid., 93.

323 *'they honour it greatly'*: ibid., 98.

323 *'the results of industrialism'*: ibid., 98.

325 *'a demon were after him'*: Upton Sinclair, *The Jungle*, New York: Doubleday, 1906, 52.

325 *'colours, cuisine and music'*: quoted in Williams, 61.

326 *'it is a cemetery'*: ibid., 62–3.

326 *'Simply: Menier Chocolate'*: ibid., 63.

327 *'go without advertisements'*: ibid., 64.

327 *'used to be very remote'*: quoted in Williams, 103.

329 *'suspiciously unsolid age'*: Zweig, 51–2.

331 *'twelve-year-old boy to his neighbour'*: Ostwald, *Dunkle Winkel in Berlin*, 22–3.

332 *'into our empirical reality'*: Georg Simmel, 'Der Fragmentcharakter des Lebens', in *Logos. Internationale Zeitschrift für Philosophie der Kultur*, year VI, no. I, 29–40, Tübingen: J. C. B. Mohr, 1916–17, 29.

13. **1912:** *Questions of Breeding*

334 *'evolution of the human race'*: Hugo Ribbert, *Heredity, Disease and Human Evolution*, New York, 1918, 214.

339 *'inhabitants of the earth'*: Francis Galton, *Hereditary Genius*, London, 1892, 3.

339 *'her abler races'*: ibid., 4.

339 *'highly-bred varieties'*: Francis Galton, *Macmillan's Magazine*, vol. 11, April 1865, 166.

339 *'too heavy for their powers'*: ibid.

340 *'the machine and the abyss'*: Jack London, *The People of the Abyss*, London: Nelson, 1904, 328.

340 *'often they destroy it'*: Gillham, *A Life of Sir Francis Galton*, Oxford, 2001, 325.

340 *'providently, quickly, and kindly'*: Francis Galton, 'Eugenics: its definition, scope and forms' in *Nature*, 64 (1901), 50.

341 *'should certainly be killed'*: Virginia Woolf, *The Diary of Virginia Woolf*, vol. I, 1915–1919, London, 1979, 13.

341 *'all previous civilizations'*: quoted in Gillham, 330.

341 'not a eugenic marriage': ibid., 335.

343 'create happy families': Ernst Haeckel, *Die Lebenswunder*, Stuttgart, 1904, chapter 17, paragraph IV.

343 'for all society': ibid.

344 'pave new roads': Wilhelm Schallmayer, *Vererbung und Auslese in ihrer soziologischen und politischen Bedeutung*, 2d ed., Jena: Gustav Fischer, 1910, 380–1.

344 'for human development': ibid., 242.

344 'burden of useless individuals': Wilhelm Schallmayer, 'Geleitwort', *Eugenik* 1 (1930), n.p.

344 'struggle for survival is diminished': Wilhelm Schallmayer, 'Kultur und Entartung', 483–4.

344 'exactly the same result': Schallmayer, rcv. of *Rassenverbesserung, Malthusianismus und Neumalthusianismus*, by Johannes Rutgers, 832.

345 'small dose of morphine': Alfred Ploetz, *Die Tüchtigkeit unserer Rasse und der Schutz der Schwachen*, Berlin, 1895, 144.

345 'friend and redeemer': Theodor Fritsch, *Vom neuen Glauben*, Leipzig, 1914.

345 'one's own sympathy': Alexander Tille, *Von Darwin zu Nietzsche*, Leipzig, 1895, 214.

346 'a hundred voices in history': Emile Laurent, *Le criminel aux points de vue anthropologique, psychologique et social*, Paris: Vigot, 1908, 242.

347 'vice-infected conceptions': Servier, Dr, La peine de mort remplacée par la castration, *Archives d'anthropologie criminelle*, Paris, 1901, 16, 130–1.

348 'all of us would prefer death': Paul Robin, 'La prudence procréatrice', *La Régénération*, 1902, n.p.

348 'organization of public decline': Paul Robin, *Rapport présenté par M. Laurent Ctly au vu de la Commission d'enquête sur l'orphelinat Prévost à Cempuis*, 1895, 162–3.

348 'than artificial sterilization': Paul Robin, *Le néo-malthusianisme*, 1905.

348 'or to eat an apple': Paul Robin, 'La vrai morale sexuelle. Le néo-malthusianisme', in *Régénération*, no. 17, October 1902.

349 'veritable regenerator of humankind': Paul Robin, 'Dégénérascence de l'espéce humaine, causes et remédes', in *Bulletin de la Société d'anthropologie de Paris*, 1895.

350 'altogether inferior to whites': Theodore Roosevelt, in Morrison and Elting, eds, *The Letters of Theodore Roosevelt*, 2 vols., Cambridge, MA: Harvard University, 1951, V, 226.

350 'disgraced his ancestors': N. K. Mikhailovskii, *Polnoe sobranie sochinenii*, vol. 1, 5th ed., 459. Quoted in Vucinich, 333.

351 'eagerly searched for them': Petr Kropotkin, *Mutual Aid*, quoted in Vucinich, 347–8.

352 *'doomed to decay'*: Kropotkin, conclusion.

352 *'politics in our time'*: Gillham, *A Life of Sir Francis Galton*, 346.

352 *'those who survive are fit'*: ibid., 347.

352 *'most difficult question'*: ibid.

352 *'rise up to bless us'*: ibid., 331.

353 *'the Japanese as a nation'*: ibid., 332.

353 *'earthquake of the age'*: Gottfried Benn, 'Nietzsche nach 50 Jahren', in *Gesammelte Werke in der Fassung der Erstdrucke*. Frankfurt/M, 1989, III, 496.

353 *'he knows Greek'*: Bertrand Russell, *History of Western Philosophy*, London, 1946, 687.

354 *'putting it mildest, exploitation'*: Friedrich Nietzsche, *Beyond Good and Evil*, German 1886, translation in *Complete Works*, London, 1909–13, 202.

354 *'degenerate and parasitical'*: Friedrich Nietzsche, *Ecce Homo*, Die Geburt der Tragödie, section 4.

354 *'antisemites shot'*: Letter to Franz Overbeck, January 1889.

355 *'a perfect lion'*: Rudolf Steiner, *Gesamtausgabe*, vol. 53, 76.

355 *'a race is thrown back'*: ibid., vol. 300/2, 1975, 282.

356 *'woolly hair and so on'*: ibid., vol. 121, 107.

356 *'Jewish way of thinking'*: ibid., vol. 32, 152.

357 *'hollowness and putrification'*: List, *Geheimnis der Runen*, 56, emphasis original.

357 *'in a national soil'*: ibid., 185.

357 *'toward Aryo-Germanism'*: quoted in Hamann, *Vienna*, 208.

358 *'from the ancient past'*: ibid., 216.

358 *'harmony with the cosmos'*: Hugo Ribbert, *Heredity, Disease and Human Evolution*, New York, 1918, 214, 237.

358 *'the lowest human species'*: Bartholomaeus von Carneri, *Sittlichkeit und Darwinismus*, Vienna, 1871, 29.

14. **1913:** *Wagner's Crime*

362 *'the greatest German dramatist'*: Neuzner, *Wagner*, 59.

362 *'even for two days'*: ibid., 38.

362 *'an educated man'*: ibid., 66–7.

363 *'wished the duchess were young'*: ibid., 39.

363 *'suffers from their sex'*: ibid., 40–1.

363 *'know the best by far'*: ibid., 43.

363 *'I can only smile'*: ibid., 86.

364 *'father is no longer alive'*: ibid., 141.

364 *'degeneration of every kind'*: ibid., 92.

364 'to anaylse [this] a little': ibid., 107.

364 'will not finish with me': ibid., 87.

364 'the longest comet's tail': ibid., 112.

365 'its elements create connections': ibid., 97.

365 'one gram heavier than before': ibid., 93.

365 'who are pitied themselves': ibid., 91.

365 'a horn named paranoia': ibid., 102.

367 'quite simply reversed': Schreber, Denkwürdigkeiten, 192.

367 'submitting to sexual intercourse': ibid., 26.

368 'this, however, is the question': ibid., 130.

370 'genitalia of the machine': quoted in Sass, 217.

372 'last rebels against industrial discipline': quoted in Winock, La belle époque, 180.

372 'exasperated by the recent crimes': ibid.

373 'price for your victory': Le Matin, 10 March 1912.

374 'Long live anarchy': quoted in Alphonse Boudard, Les Grands Criminels, Paris: Le Livre de Poche, 1990, 35–6.

374 'knives and other weapons': S-i, 'Pogibaiushchie deti', Petersburgskii listok, 19 April 1901, quoted in Neuberger, Hooliganism.

374 'tavern and café waiters': Narskii, 'Khuligan', Petersburgskii gazeta, 30 June 1903, quoted in Neuberger, Hooliganism.

375 'a well-dressed man': Petersburgskii listok, 'Vozmutitel'nyi fakt', 28 May 1905, quoted in Neuberger, Hooliganism.

375 'nothing had happened': V. Ivanov, Chto takoe khuliganstvo?, Orenburg, 1915, 8, quoted in Neuberger, Hooliganism.

375 'a decaying state': quoted in Hans Rogger, 'Russia in 1914', Journal of Contemporary History, vol. 1, no. 4 (1966), 95.

376 'the "army of crime"': Charles Letourneau, introduction, in Lombroso, L'Uomo Delinquente, iv.

377 'scientifically proven usefulness': ibid., iii.

377 'priests, shepherds and soldiers': ibid., 665–6.

378 'nothing but coal': ibid., xix–xx.

379 'forms of congenital madness': ibid., xix.

379 'great intellectual force': ibid., xx.

383 'await admission day': Rainer Maria Rilke, Werke, 102.

384 'decrepit old man': Maurice Leblanc, 'L'Arrestation d'Arsène Lupin', Je sais tout, no. 6, 15 juillet 1905.

385 'broken glass and damaged shutters': Bernard Thomas, Jacob: Alexandre Marius, Paris, 1970, 273.

386 'isn't begged for, it's taken': Marius Jacob, 'Pourquoi j'étais cambrioleur', in Jean Maitron, Histoire du mouvement anarchiste en France, Paris: Societé Universitaire d'Editions et de Librairie, 1951.

386 *'A votre santé'*: quoted in Thomas, 357.
387 *'the heads of others'*: quoted in Neuzner, 74.
387 *'grateful and devoted Ernst Wagner'*: ibid., 75.

15. **1914**: *Murder Most Fowl*

390 *'in patient inaction'*: quoted in Massie, 728.
393 *'declared war on Serbia'*: Mugnier and d'Hendecourt, *Journal*, 264–5.
394 *'hurried others to come'*: Adams, 494.
399 *'canon of masculinity'*: Mayreder, 122.
401 *'an eighteenth-century artist'*: Fernand Léger, quoted in Kern, *Culture of Time and Space*, 118.
402 *'part of its equipment'*: Pirandello, *Shoot*, quoted in Kern, *Culture of Time and Space*, 119.
407 *'were momentous indeed'*: Musil, 359.

Bibliography

Primary Sources

NEWSPAPERS AND MAGAZINES

Arbeiterzeitung (Austria-Hungary)
L'assiette au beurre (France)
Die Bombe (Austria-Hungary)
Daily Mail (Britain)
Daily Telegraph (Britain)
Le Figaro (France)
L'Illustration (France)
Je sais tout! (France)
Kreuzzeitung (Germany)
Macmillan's Magazine (Britain)
Manchester Guardian (Britain)
Neue Freie Presse (Austria-Hungary)
Neue Zeitung (Austria-Hungary)

New York Times (USA)
Novoe Vremia (Russia)
Pester Lloyd (Austria-Hungary)
Le petit journal (France)
Revue des deux mondes (France)
Sanktpeterburgskija vedomosti (Russia)
Simplicissimus (Germany)
The Times (Britain)
Das Vaterland (Austria-Hungary)
Volksblatt (Austria-Hungary)
Die Weltbühne (Germany)
Wiener Zeitung (Austria-Hungary)
Die Zukunft (Germany)

BOOKS

Adams, Henry Cabot Lodge. *The Education of Henry Adams; An Autobiography*. Boston and New York: Houghton Mifflin, 1918
Aleramo, Sibilla. *Una donna: romanzo*. Milano: Feltrinelli, 1983
Andreyev, Leonid, and Herman Bernstein. *The Seven Who Were Hanged. A Story*. New York: J. S. Ogilvie, 1909
Anonyma. *Journal d'une jeune petite-bourgeoise*. MS [unpublished]. 1911–16. Bibliothèque de l'histoire de Paris, MJCP 4111
Apollinaire, Guillaume. *A propos d'art nègre, 1909–1918*. Toulouse: Toguna, 1999
——, and Lionel Abel. *The Cubist Painters; Aesthetic Meditations, 1913, The Documents of Modern Art*. New York: Wittenborn, 1944

——, Filippo Tommaso Marinetti and Pasquale Aniel Jannini. *Lettere a F. T. Marinetti: con il manoscritto del manifesto Antitradizione futurista*. Milano: All'insegna del pesce d'oro, 1978

——, and Garnet Rees. *Alcools*. London: Athlone Press, 1975

Artsybashev, M., and Percy E. Pinkerton. *Sanine*. New York: B. W. Huebsch, 1922

Asenijeff, Else. *Aufruhr der Weiber und das dritte Geschlecht*. Leipzig: Dr Brandstetter, 1898

——. *Tagebuchblätter einer Emancipierten*. Leipzig: Hermann Seemann Nachf., 1902

Augspurg, Anita. *Fraueunstimmrecht!*. Munich: Reinhardt, 1912

Avenel, Georges Vicomte de. *Le méchanisme de la vie moderne*. Paris: Colin, 1902

Bahr, Hermann. *Buch der Jugend*. Wien: H. Heller, 1908

Baldacci, Paolo, Philippe Daverio, Galleria Philippe Daverio, Agenzia d'arte moderna Paolo Sprovieri and Philippe Daverio Gallery. *Futurism, 1911–1918: Works by Balla, Boccioni, Carrà, Severini, Prampolini, Depero, Sironi, Marinetti*. Milano, New York: Philippe Daverio, 1988

Barbellion, W. N. P. *The Journal of a Disappointed Man*. New York: Gordon Press, 1974

Barrès, Maurice. *Les diverses familles spirituelles de la France*. Paris: Emile-Paul frères, 1917

——. *Le Culte du moi*. Paris: Plon, 1966

Bäumer, Gertrud, et al. *Frauenbewegung und Sexualethik*. Heilbronn: E. Sulzer, 1909

Bazin, René. *La terre qui meurt*. Paris: Calmann Lévy, 1899

Beard, George Miller. *American Nervousness: Its Causes and Consequences, a Supplement to Nervous Exhaustion (Neurasthenia)*. New York: Arno Press, 1972

——, and Alphonse David Rockwell. *A Practical Treatise on the Medical and Surgical Uses of Electricity*. New York: W. Wood, 1881

——, Alphonse David Rockwell, Carrie Chapman Catt, and National American Woman Suffrage Association Collection (Library of Congress). *Sexual Neurasthenia 'Nervous Exhaustion'. Its Hygiene, Causes, Symptoms, and Treatment, with a Chapter on Diet for the Nervous*. New York: E. B. Treat, 1884

Bebel, August. *Die Frau und der Sozialismus*. Berlin, 1973

Bely, Andrei. *Peterburg; roman v vosmi glavakh*. Letchworth (Herts.): Bradda Books, 1967

Bennett, Cyril. *The Modern Malady; or, Sufferers from 'Nerves'*. London: E. Arnold, 1890

Bertillon, Jacques. *La dépopulation de la France.* Paris: F. Alcan, 1911

Blasco Ibáñez, Vicente. *La barraca.* New York, 1910

——. *La catedral,* Valencia: Prometeo sociedad editorial, (1903) 1916

——. *Los cuatro jinetes del Apocalipsis.* 2d ed. Valencia: Prometeo, 1916

Blum, Léon. *Du mariage.* Paris: Ollendorff, 1907

Blunt, Wilfrid Scawen. *My Diaries, Being a Personal Narrative of Events, 1888–1914.* London: M. Secker, 1919

Bölsche, Wilhelm. *Das Liebesleben in der Natur; eine Entwicklungsgeschichte der Liebe.* Jena: E. Diederichs, 1909

Bryusov, Valery Yakovlevich. *Rasskazy i povesti. Erzählungen und Novellen, Slavische Propyläen, Bd. 49.* München: W. Fink, 1970

——. *Zerkalo tëieneœi: stikhi 1909–1912.* Moskva: Skorpion, 1912

Bunin, Ivan Alekseevich, and Isabel Florence Hapgood. *The Village.* New York: A. A. Knopf, 1923

Carito, Diomede. *La neurastenia e la vita moderna.* Napoli: E. Prass, 1903

Carneri, Bartholomaeus (Ritter von). *Sittlichkeit und Darwinismus. Drei Bücher Ethik.* Wien: Wilhelm Braumüller, 1871

Casement, Roger. *The Crime Against Europe.* Philadelphia: The Celtic Press, 1915

——, and Michael O'Sullivan. *The Eyes of Another Race: Roger Casement's Congo Report and 1903 Diary.* Dublin: University College Dublin Press, 2003

——, Angus Mitchell, and Irish Manuscripts Commission. *Sir Roger Casement's Heart of Darkness: the 1911 Documents.* Dublin: Irish Manuscripts Commission, 2003

——, and Roger Sawyer. *Roger Casement's Diaries: 1910: the Black and the White.* London: Pimlico, 1997

Chamberlain, Houston Stewart. *Die Grundlagen des neunzehnten Jahrhunderts.* München: F. Bruckmann, 1900

Congo Free State, Louis Hébette, Lambert Petit, and Belgium. *Les codes du Congo, suivis des décrets; ordonnances et arrêtés complémentaires, mis en ordre et annotés d'après leur concordance avec les codes et les textes du droit belge utiles à leur interprétation, et précédés des traités et autres actes internationaux, ainsi que des lois et actes législatifs belges relatifs à l'état indépendant.* Bruxelles: Ve F. Larcier, 1892

Conrad, Joseph. *Heart of Darkness.* Harmondsworth: Penguin, 1973

Dohm, Hedwig, et al. *Ehe? Zur Reform der sexuellen Moral.* Berlin: 1911

Drumont, Edouard Adolphe. *La France juive: essai d'histoire contemporaine.* Paris: C. Marpon & F. Flammarion, 1887

Dudgeon, Jeffrey, and Roger Casement. *Roger Casement: the Black Diaries; With a Study of His Background, Sexuality and Irish Political Life.* Belfast: Belfast Press, 2002

Durkheim, Emile. *La sociologie, La science française.* Paris: Larousse, 1915

——. *Le suicide; étude de sociologie, Bibliothèque de philosophie contemporaine.* Paris: F. Alcan, 1897

Forel, August. *Die sexuelle Frage. Eine naturwissenschaftliche; psychologische, hygienische und soziologische Studie für Gebildete.* Munich, Ernst Reinhardt, 1905

Frenssen, Gustav. *Peter Moors fahrt nach Südwest, ein feldzugsbericht.* Berlin: G. Grote'sche Verlagsbuchhandlung, 1906

Freud, Sigmund. *Letters of Sigmund Freud, 1873–1939.* London: Hogarth Press, 1961

——. *Vorlesungen zur Einführung in die Psychoanaylse.* Frankfart/M: S. Fischer, 1966

——. *Zur Psychopathologie des Alltagslebens (Vergessen, Versprechen, Vergreifen): nebst Bemerkungen über eine Wurzel des Aberglaubens.* Berlin: S. Karger, 1901

——. *Die Traumdeutung.* Leipzig: F. Deuticke, 1900

——, Lou Andreas-Salomé and Ernst Pfeiffer. *Correspondance de Lou Andreas Salomé.* Paris: Gallimard, 1970

——, J. Moussaieff Masson and Michael Schroter. *Briefe an Wilhelm Fliess, 1887–1904.* Ungekürzte Ausg. ed. Frankfurt am Main: S. Fischer, 1986

Fritsch, Theodor. *Handbuch der Judenfrage. Eine Zusammenstellung des wichtigsten Materials zur Beurteilung des jüdischen Volkes.* Hamburg: Hanseatische Druck- u. Verlags-Anst., 1907

Gide, André. *Les nourritures terrestres.* Paris: Editions de la Nouvelle revue française., 1918

——. *Si le grain ne meurt.* Paris: Gallimard, 1929

Gilman, Charlotte Perkins. *The Yellow Wallpaper.* 1st ed. New York: Feminist Press, 1973

Gippius, Z. N., and Aleksandr Nikolaevich Nikoliukin. *Dnevniki.* Moskva: NPK 'Intelvak', 1999

Gorky, Maksim. *Razskazy.* S.-Peterburg: Izdanie Tovarishchestva 'znanie', 1903

——, and I. Bocharova. *Detstvo.* Moskva: Khudozh. lit-ra, 1966

——, Leonid Andreyev and Peter Yershov. *Letters of Gorky and Andreev, 1899–1912.* London: Routledge and K. Paul, 1958

Haeckel, Ernst. *Der Kampf um den Entwicklungs-Gedanken. 3 Vortr. (etc.)* Berlin: Reimer, 1905

——. *Die Natur als Künstlerin.* Berlin, 1913

——. *Die Welträthsel. Gemeinverständliche Studien über monistische Philosophie.* Bonn: Strauss, 1899

Hauptmann, Gerhart. *Gesammelte Werke.* Berlin: S. Fischer, 1913

Heymann, Lida Gustava, and Anita Augspurg. *Erlebtes, Erschautes; deutsche Frauen kämpfen für Freiheit Recht und Frieden 1850–1940.* Meisenheim am Glan: A. Hain, 1972

Hirschfeld, Magnus. *Berlins drittes Geschlecht*. Berlin: Seemann, 1904

Hofmannsthal, Hugo von, Harry Kessler and Hilde Burger. *Briefwechsel, 1898–1929*. Frankfurt am Main: Insel Verlag, 1968

James, William. *The Principles of Psychology*. Cambridge, MA: Harvard University Press, 1981

——. *The Varieties of Religious Experience*. New York: Longmans, Green, 1916

——. *Pragmatism*. Cambridge, MA: Harvard University Press, 1979

——. *The Meaning of Truth*. Cambridge, MA and London: Harvard University Press, 1979

Jarry, Alfred. *Le Surmâle: roman moderne*. Paris: E. Losfeld, 1977

Jaurès, Jean, Eric Cahm and Madeleine Rebérioux. *Les temps de l'affaire Dreyfus, 1897–1899*. Paris: Fayard, 2000

——, and Madeleine Rebérioux. *La classe ouvrière*. Paris: F. Maspero, 1976

Jerusalem, Else. *Der heilige Skarabäus*. Berlin: Fischer, 1909

Jong van Beek en Donk, Cécile de. *Hilda van Suylenburg*. Amsterdam: Scheltema & Hokema, 1897

Kessler, Harry, Roland Kamzelak, Ulrich Ott, Hans-Ulrich Simon, Werner Volke and Bernhard Zeller. *Das Tagebuch 1880–1937*. Stuttgart: Cotta, 2004

Klemperer, Victor. *Curriculum vitae: Jugend um 1900*. Berlin: Siedler, 1989

——. *Philistines*. Transl. Andrew Upton. London: Faber & Faber, 2007

Krafft-Ebbing, R. von. *Psychopathia sexualis: mit besonderer Berücksichtigung der conträren Sexualempfindung: eine klinisch-forensische Studie*. Stuttgart: Verlag von F. Enke, 1898

Kuzmin, M. A. *Nezdeshnie vechera*. New York: Russica Publishers, 1979

——, N. A. Bogomolov and S. V. Shumikhin. *Dnevnik 1905–1907*. Sankt-Peterburg: Izd-vo Ivana Limbakha, 2000

——. *Dnevnik 1908–1915*. Sankt-Peterburg: Izd-vo Ivana Limbakha, 2005

——, John E. Malmstad and Vladimir Markov. *Sobrani stikhov, Gesammelte Gedichte, Centrifuga*. Munich: W. Fink, 1977

——, and Vladimir Markov. *Tretiakniga rasskazov, Modern Russian literature and culture, studies and texts*. Berkeley: Berkeley Slavic Specialties, 1984

——, Vladimir Markov and Friedrich Scholz. *Proza, Modern Russian literature and culture, studies and texts*. Berkeley: Berkeley Slavic Specialties, 1984

Lange, Helene, Gertrud Bäumer, Robert Wilbrandt, Lisbeth Wilbrandt and Josephine Levy-Rathenau. *Handbuch der Frauenbewegung*. Berlin: W. Moeser, 1901

List, Guido (von). *Die Armanenschaft der Ariogermanen*. Leipzig, Vienna, 1908

——. *Das Geheimnis der Runen*. Leipzig, Vienna, 1908

Lombroso, Cesare. *L'homme de génie*. Paris: F. Alcan, 1887

——. *L'uomo delinquente*. Turin: Bocca, 1897

London, Jack. *The People of the Abyss*. New York: Macmilllan, 1903

Loti, Pierre. *Au Maroc.*, 6th ed., Paris: Calmann-Lévy, 1890

——. *Aziyadé; extrait des notes et lettres d'un lieutenant de la marine anglaise.* 32nd ed., Paris: Calmann-Lévy, 1897

——. *Jérusalem.* Paris: Nelson, 1914

——. *Les désenchantées, roman des harems turcs contemporains.* 44th ed., *Bibliothèque contemporaine.* Paris: Calmann-Lévy, 1906

——. *L'Inde (sans les Anglais).* Paris: Calmann-Lévy, 1903

——. *Quelques aspects du vertige mondial.* Paris: E. Flammarion, 1917

——. *Turquie agonisante.* Nouv. ed., rev. et considérablement augm. Paris: Calmann-Lévy, 1913

Ludovici, Anthony. *Who Is to Be Master of the World.* London, 1909

MacDonnell, John de Courcy. *King Leopold II., His Rule in Belgium and the Congo.* London, Paris, New York and Melbourne: Cassell, 1905

Mach, Ernst. *Die Mechanik in ihrer Entwickelung historisch-kritisch Dargestellt.* 5th ed., *Internationale wissenschaftliche Bibliothek. LIX. Bd.* Leipzig: F. A. Brockhaus, 1904

——. *Die Prinzipien der Physikalischen Optik; historisch und erkenntnispsychologisch entwickelt.* Leipzig: J. A. Barth, 1921

Mann, Heinrich. *Der Untertan.* Ungekürzte Ausg., 24. Aufl., 511th bis 540th ed. Berlin: Aufbau-Verlag, 1982

Mann, Thomas. *Der Zauberberg.* Frankfurt/M: Fischer-Bücherei, 1967

Marinetti, Filippo Tommaso, and Günter Berghaus. *Critical writings.* New York: Farrar Straus and Giroux, 2006

Mayreder, Rosa Obermayer. *Zur Kritik der Weiblichkeit: Essays.* Jena: Eugen Diederichs, 1905

——, and Harriet Anderson. *Tagebücher 1873–1937.* Frankfurt am Main: Insel, 1988

Meisel-Hess, Grete. *Weiberhass und Weiberverachtung.* Wien: Perles, 1904

——. *Die Sexuelle Krise; eine sozialpsychologische Untersuchung.* Jena: E. Diederichs, 1909

——. *Das Wesen der Geschlechtlichkeit. Die sexuelle Krise in ihren Beziehungen zur sozialen Frage, zum Krieg (etc.).* Jena: Diederichs, 1916

Merezhkovsky, Dmitry Sergeyevich, E. G. Domogaëtìskaëia, E. A. Pevak, I. L. Anastaseva and Dmitry Sergeyevich Merezhkovsky. *Bylo i budet: dnevnik 1910–1914; Nevoennyi dnevnik: 1914–1916 Simvoly vremeni.* Moskva: Agraf, 2001

——, D. M. Magomedova and A. L. Sobolev. *Smert bogov: Ulian Otstupnik.* Moskva: 'Khudozh lit-ra', 1993

——, Oleg Nikolaevich Mikhaëilov and Z. N. Gippius. *14 dekabria: roman.* Moskva: Moskovskiæi rabochiæi, 1990

Mirbeau, Octave. *La 628-E 8.* Paris: Union générale d'éditions, 1977

Morel, E. D. *The British Case in French Congo; the Story of a Great Injustice, Its Causes and Its Lessons.* London: W. Heinemann, 1903

——. *The Congo Slave State. A Protest Against the New African Slavery; and an Appeal to the Public of Great Britain, of the United States, and of the Continent of Europe.* Liverpool: J. Richardson & Sons Printers, 1903

——. *Great Britain and the Congo; the Pillage of the Congo Basin.* London: Smith Elder & Co., 1909

——. *Truth and the War.* London: National Labour Press, 1916

——, William Roger Louis and Jean Stengers. *E. D. Morel's History of the Congo Reform Movement.* Oxford: Clarendon P., 1968

——, and Robert E. Park. *The Treatment of Women and Children in the Congo State, 1899–1904.* Boston, Mass., 1904

Mugnier, Marcel Billot, and Jean d'Hendecourt. *Journal de l'abbé Mugnier: 1879–1939.* Paris: Mercure de France, 1985

Musil, Robert, and Adolf Frisé. *Der Mann ohne Eigenschaften: Roman.* Neu durchgesehene und verb. Aufl. ed. Reinbek bei Hamburg: Rowohlt, 1981

Noailles, Anna Elisabeth de Brancovan, Maurice Barrès and Claude Mignot-Ogliastri. *Anna de Noailles–Maurice Barrès: correspondance, 1901–1923.* Paris: L'Inventaire, 1994

Nordau, Max Simon. *Entartung.* Berlin: C. Duncker, 1892

Ostwald, Hans. *Berliner Cafés.* Berlin: Seemann, 1906

——. *Dunkle Winkel in Berlin.* Berlin: Seemann, 1904

Pelletier, Madeleine. *Dieu, la morale, la patrie: idéologie d'hier.* Paris: V. Giard et E. Brière, 1910

——. *L'émancipation sexuelle de la femme.* Paris: M. Giard et E. Brière, 1911

Pirandello, Luigi. *Quaderni di Serafino Gubbio operatore: romanzo.* Milano: A. Mondadori, 1974

Proust, Marcel, and Marc van Dongen. *A la recherche du temps perdu.* Paris: Gallimard, 1947

Rathenau, Walther, and H. Pogge von Strandmann. *Tagebuch 1907–1922.* Düsseldorf: Droste Verlag, 1967

Ratzenhofer, Gustav. *Positive Ethik. Die Verwirklichung des Sittlich-Seinsollenden.* Leipzig: Brockhaus, 1901

Richet, Charles Robert, and Bertha von Suttner. *Die Vergangenheit des Krieges und die Zukunft des Friedens.* Wien: Österreichische Friedensgesellschaft, 1909

Rilke, Rainer Maria. *Sämtliche Werke in 7 Bänden,* ed. Ernst Zinn, Frankfurt/Main: Rilke Archiv, 1955–97

Robertson, Morgan. *Futility.* New York: M. F. Mansfield, 1898

Robin, Paul. *Le néo-malthusianisme: la vraie morale sexuelle, le choix des procréateurs.* Paris: Librairie de 'Régénération', 1905

Sandow, Eugen. *Body-Building or, Man in the Making: How to Become Healthy & Strong: Containing Sets of Exercises and Special Photos of Mr. Sandow and Family.* London: Gale & Polden, 1904

——. *Strength and Health*. New York City: Richard K. Fox, 1912

Schnitzler, Arthur. *Der Weg ins Freie; Roman*. Berlin: S. Fischer, 1908

——. *Professor Bernhardi: Komödie in fünf Akten*. 2. Aufl. ed. Berlin: S. Fischer, 1912

——. *Reigen; zehn Dialoge geschrieben Winter 1896–97*. Berlin, Wien: B. Harz, 1914

——, and Konstanze Fliedl. *Briefwechsel 1891–1931*. Wien: Europaverlag, 1992

——, Therese Nickl and Heinrich Schnitzler. *Jugend in Wien. Eine Autobiographie*. Wien, München, Zurich: Molden, 1968

——. *Leutnant Gustl; Fräulein Else*. Frankfurt am Main: S. Fischer, 1981

——, Werner Welzig, Peter Michael Braunwarth and Österreichische Akademie der Wissenschaften. Kommission für Literarische Gebrauchsformen. *Tagebuch*. Wien: Verlag der Österreichischen Akademie der Wissenschaften, 1981

Simmel, Georg. *Der Konflikt der modernen Kultur: ein Vortrag*. München: Duncker & Humbolt, 1918

——. *Deutschlands innere Wandlung*. Strassburg: K. J. Trübner, 1914

——. *Philosophie des Geldes*. Leipzig: Duncker & Humbolt, 1900

——. *Sozologie. Untersuchungen über die Formen der Vergesellschaftung*. Leipzig: Duncker & Humbolt, 1908

——, and Klaus Christian Köhnke. *Briefe 1880–1911*. 1. Aufl. ed. Frankfurt am Main: Suhrkamp, 2005

——, and Otthein Rammstedt. *Gesamtausgabe*. 1. Aufl. ed. Frankfurt am Main: Suhrkamp, 1989

Sorel, Georges. *Réflexions sur la violence*. 3rd ed. Paris: M. Riveère, 1912

Spitzemberg, Hildegard von Varbüler. *Das Tagebuch der Baronin Spitzemberg, geb. Freiin v. Varbüler*. Göttingen: Vandenhoeck & Ruprecht, 1960

Stöcker, Helene. *Die Liebe und die Frauen*. Minden, [1906]

Strauss, David, Friedrich. *Der alte und der neue Glaube. Ein Bekenntniß*. Bonn: Strauß, 1873

Suttner, Bertha von. *Aus der Werkstatt des Pazifismus*. Leipzig und Wien: H. Heller, 1912

——. *Das Maschinenzeitalter: Zukunftsvorlesungen über unsere Zeit*. Düsseldorf: Zwiebelzwerg, 1983

——. *Die Barbarisierung der Luft, Internationale Verständigung; Heft 6*. Berlin: Verlag der 'Friedens-Warte', 1912

——. *Die Waffin nieder!* Dresden und Leipzig: E. Pierson, 1899

——. *Memoiren von Bertha von Suttner*. Stuttgart, Leipzig: Deutsche Verlags-Anstalt, 1919

Taylor, Frederick Winslow. *The Principles of Scientific Management*. New York, London: Harper & Brothers, 1911

Tille, Alexander. *Von Darwin bis Nietzsche. Ein Buch Entwicklungsethik*. Leipzig: Naumann, 1895

Timofeev, P. *Chem zhivet' zavodskii rabochii.* St Petersburg, 1909

Unamuno, Miguel de, and Warner Fite. *Mist: a Tragicomic Novel.* Urbana: University of Illinois Press, 2000

Uzanne, Octave. *La locomotion à travers l'histoire et les moeurs.* Paris: P. Ollendorff, 1900

——. *Vingt jours dans le Nouveau monde.* Paris: May & Motteroz, 1893

Vaihinger, Hans. *Die Philosophie des Als Ob.* Aalen: Scientia, 1986

Webb, Beatrice Potter. *The Diary of Beatrice Webb.* Cambridge, Mass.: Belknap Press of Harvard University Press, 1982

Wells, H. G. *The First Men in the Moon.* London: G. Newnes, 1901

——. *The Invisible Man, a Grotesque Romance.* New York and London: Harper & Brothers, 1897

——. *The Island of Doctor Moreau.* London: W. Heinemann, 1896

——. *Kipps; a Monograph.* New York: C. Scribner's Sons, 1905

——. *Socialism and the Family.* London: A. C. Fifield, 1906

——. *The Time Machine, an Invention.* New York: H. Holt, 1895

——. *The War that Will End War.* New York: Duffield, 1914

——. *The Wheels of Chance; a Bicycling Idyll.* New York, London: The Macmillan Company, 1896

Whitman, Sidney. *Things I Remember; the Recollections of a Political Writer in the Capitals of Europe.* London, New York: Cassell, 1916

Witte, Sergei, and Sidney Harcave. *The Memoirs of Count Witte.* Armonk, N.Y.: M. E. Sharpe, 1990

Wolzogen, Ernst von. *Das dritte Geschlecht.* Berlin: Eckstein, [1903]

Woolf, Virginia. *The Diary of Virginia Woolf.* New York: Harcourt Brace Jovanovich, 1977

——, and Mitchell Alexander Leaska. *A Passionate Apprentice: the Early Journals, 1897–1909.* San Diego: Harcourt Brace Jovanovich, 1990

——, Nigel Nicolson and Joanne Trautmann Banks, eds. *The Letters of Virginia Woolf.* New York: Harcourt Brace Jovanovich, 1977

Wunberg, Gotthart, and Johannes J. Braakenburg. *Die Wiener Moderne: Literatur, Kunst und Musik zwischen 1890 und 1910.* Stuttgart: Reclam, 1981

Zweig, Stefan. *Die Welt von Gestern, Erinnerungen eines Europäers.* Frankfurt a. M.: Suhrkamp, 1947

Secondary Literature

ARTICLES

Alaimo, Kathleen. Adolescence, Gender, and Class in Education Reform in France: The Development of Enseignement Primaire Supérieur, 1880–1910, in: *French Historical Studies*, vol. 18, no. 4 (Autumn 1994), pp. 1025–55

Albisetti, James C. Could Separate Be Equal? Helene Lange and Women's Education in Imperial Germany, in: *History of Education Quarterly*, vol. 22, no. 3, Special Issue: Educational Policy and Reform in Modern Germany (Autumn 1982), pp. 301–17

Allen, Ann Taylor. Feminism, Social Science, and the Meanings of Modernity. The Debate on the Origin of the Family in Europe and the United States, 1860–1914, in: *The American Historical Review*, vol. 104, no. 4 (Oct. 1999), pp. 1085–113

Allen, Garland. Genetics, Eugenics and Society: Internalists and Externalists in Contemporary History of Science, in: *Social Studies of Science*, vol. 6, no. 1 (Feb. 1976), pp. 105–22

Aschheim, Steven E. Nietzschean Socialism – Left and Right, 1890–1933, in: *Journal of Contemporary History*, vol. 23, no. 2, Bolshevism and the Socialist Left (Apr. 1988), pp. 147–68

——. Max Nordau, Friedrich Nietzsche and Degeneration, in: *Journal of Contemporary History*, vol. 28, no. 4 (Oct. 1993), pp. 643–57

Badash, Lawrence. The Completeness of Nineteenth-Century Science, in: *Isis*, vol. 63, no. 1 (Mar. 1972), pp. 48–58

Bassin, Mark. Geographical Determinism in Fin-de-siècle Marxism: Georgii Plekhanov and the Environmental Basis of Russian History, in: *Annals of the Association of American Geographers*, vol. 82, no. 1 (Mar. 1992), pp. 3–22

Best, Geoffrey. Peace Conferences and the Century of Total War: The 1899 Hague Conference and What Came After, in: *International Affairs*, vol. 75, no. 3 (Jul. 1999), pp. 619–34

Blessing, Werner K. The Cult of Monarchy, Political Loyalty and the Workers' Movement in Imperial Germany, in: *Journal of Contemporary History*, vol. 13, no. 2, Special Issue: Workers' Culture (Apr. 1978), pp. 357–75

Bowman, William D. Regional History and the Austrian Nation, in: *The Journal of Modern History*, vol. 67, no. 4 (Dec. 1995), pp. 873–97

Brown, M. Craig, and Barbara D. Warner. Immigrants, Urban Politics, and Policing in 1900, in: *American Sociological Review*, vol. 57, no. 3 (Jun. 1992), pp. 293–305

Brush, Stephen G. Irreversibility and Indeterminism: Fourier to Heisenberg, in: *Journal of the History of Ideas*, vol. 37, no. 4 (Oct.–Dec. 1976), pp. 603–30

Chickering, Roger. A Voice of Moderation in Imperial Germany: The 'Verband für internationale Verständigung' 1911–1914, in: *Journal of Contemporary History*, vol. 8, no. 1 (Jan. 1973), pp. 147–64

Clarke, I. F. Forecasts of Warfare in Fiction 1803–1914, in: *Comparative Studies in Society and History*, vol. 10, no. 1 (Oct. 1967), pp. 1–25

Cooper, Sandi E. Pacifism in France, 1889–1914: International Peace as a

Human Right, in: *French Historical Studies*, vol. 17, no. 2 (Autumn 1991), pp. 359–86

Danius, Sara. The Aesthetics of the Windshield: Proust and the Modernist Rhetoric of Speed, in: *Modernism*, vol. 8, no. 1 (2001), pp. 99–126

Devons, S. Rutherford and the Science of His Day, in: *Notes and Records of the Royal Society of London*, vol. 45, no. 2 (Jul. 1991), pp. 221–42

Dickinson, Edward Ross. Reflections on Feminism and Monism in the Kaiserreich, 1900–1913, in: *Central European History*, vol. 34, no. 2, pp. 191–230

Dikotter, Frank. Race Culture: Recent Perspectives on the History of Eugenics, in: *The American Historical Review*, vol. 103, no. 2 (Apr. 1998), pp. 467–78

Drouard, Alain. Aux origines de l'eugénisme en France: le néo-malthusianisme (1896–1914), in: *Population* (French Edition), 47e Année, no. 2. (Mar.–Apr. 1992), pp. 435–59

Eddie, Scott M. Agricultural Production and Output per Worker in Hungary, 1870–1913, in: *The Journal of Economic History*, vol. 28, no. 2. (Jun. 1968), pp. 197–222

——. The Changing Pattern of Landownership in Hungary, 1867–1914, in: *The Economic History Review*, New Series, vol. 20, no. 2 (Aug. 1967), pp. 293–310

Eklof, Ben. The Adequacy of Basic Schooling in Rural Russia: Teachers and Their Craft, 1880–1914, in: *History of Education Quarterly*, vol. 26, no. 2 (Summer 1986) pp. 199–223

Engelstein, Laura. Holy Russia in Modern Times: An Essay on Orthodoxy and Cultural Change, in: *Past and Present*, no. 173 (Nov. 2001), pp. 129–56

Evans, Richard J. In Search of German Social Darwinism: The History and Historiography of a Concept, in: *Medicine and Modernity Public Health and Medical Care in Nineteenth and Twentieth-Century Germany*, ed. Manfred Berg and Geoffrey Cocks (Washington, 1997), pp. 55–79

——. Prostitution, State and Society in Imperial Germany, in: *Past and Present*, no. 70 (Feb. 1976), pp. 106–29

Field, Geoffrey G. Nordic Racism, in: *Journal of the History of Ideas*, vol. 38, no. 3 (Jul.–Sep. 1977), pp. 523–40

Fishman, Sterling. Suicide, Sex, and the Discovery of the German Adolescent, in: *History of Education Quarterly*, vol. 10, no. 2 (Summer 1970), pp. 170–88

Gentile, Emilio. The Struggle for Modernity: Echoes of the Dreyfus Affair in Italian Political Culture, 1898–1912, in: *Journal of Contemporary History*, vol. 33, no. 4 (Oct. 1998), pp. 497–511

Gillis, John R. The Evolution of Juvenile Delinquency in England 1890–1914, in: *Past and Present*, no. 67 (May 1975), pp. 96–126

——. Conformity and Rebellion: Contrasting Styles of English and German Youth, 1900–33, in: *History of Education Quarterly*, vol. 13, no. 3 (Autumn 1973), pp. 249–60

Godsey, William D., Jr. Quarterings and Kinship: The Social Composition of the Habsburg Aristocracy in the Dualist Era, in: *The Journal of Modern History*, vol. 71, no. 1 (Mar. 1999), pp. 56–104

Good, David F. The Economic Lag of Central and Eastern Europe: Income Estimates for the Habsburg Successor States, 1870–1910, in: *The Journal of Economic History*, vol. 54, no. 4 (Dec. 1994), pp. 89–91

Graham, Loren R. Science and Values: The Eugenics Movement in Germany and Russia in the 1920s, in: *The American Historical Review*, vol. 82, no. 5 (Dec. 1977), pp. 1133–64

Hagboldt, Peter. Der Kampf des jungen Menschen im neueren deutschen Drama, in: *Modern Philology*, vol. 28, no. 3 (Feb. 1931), pp. 337–52

Herman, Sondra R. Loving Courtship or the Marriage Market? The Ideal and its Critics 1871–1911, in: *American Quarterly*, vol. 25, no. 2 (May 1973), pp. 235–52

Holt, Niles R. Ernst Haeckel's Monistic Religion, in: *Journal of the History of Ideas*, vol. 32, no. 2 (Apr.–Jun. 1971), pp. 265–80

Hooker, Lynn. Modernism on the Periphery: Béla Bartók and the New Hungarian Music Society of 1911–1912, in: *The Musical Quarterly*, vol. 88 (2004), pp. 274–319

Hurd, Madeleine. Education, Morality, and the Politics of Class in Hamburg and Stockholm, 1870–1914, in: *Journal of Contemporary History*, vol. 31, no. 4 (Oct. 1996), pp. 619–50

Hyde, William J. The Socialism of H. G. Wells in the Early Twentieth Century, in: *Journal of the History of Ideas*, vol. 17, no. 2 (Apr. 1956), pp. 217–34

Jarausch, Konrad H. Students, Sex and Politics in Imperial Germany, in: *Journal of Contemporary History*, vol. 17, no. 2, Sexuality in History (Apr. 1982), pp. 285–303

Karl, Willibald. Students and the Youth Movement in Germany: Attempt at a Structural Comparison, in: *Journal of Contemporary History*, vol. 5, no. 1, Generations in Conflict (1970), pp. 113–27

Kevles, Daniel J. Genetics in the United States and Great Britain, 1890–1930: A Review with Speculations, in: *Isis*, vol. 71, no. 3 (Sep. 1980), pp. 441–55

Killen, Andreas. From Shock to Schreck: Psychiatrists, Telephone Operators and Traumatic Neurosis in Germany, 1900–26, in: *Journal of Contemporary History*, vol. 38, no. 2 (Apr. 2003), pp. 201–20

Kocka, Jurgen. The Middle Classes in Europe, in: *The Journal of Modern History*, vol. 67, no. 4 (Dec. 1995), pp. 783–806

Lambert, Nicholas A. British Naval Policy, 1913–1914: Financial Limitation and Strategic Revolution, in: *The Journal of Modern History*, vol. 67, no. 3 (Sep. 1995), pp. 595–626

Lamberti, Marjorie. Elementary School Teachers and the Struggle against Social Democracy in Wilhelmine Germany, in: *History of Education Quarterly*, vol. 32, no. 1 (Spring 1992), pp. 73–97

Lenman, Robin. Painters, Patronage and the Art Market in Germany 1850–1914, in: *Past and Present*, no. 123 (May 1989), pp. 109–40

Le Rider, Jacques. 'Vielleicht ist eine der wichtigsten Entstehungsbedingungen der Frauenbewegung in Veränderungen innerhalb des männlichen Geschlechtes zu suchen.' Rosa Mayreder und die Krise der modernen Männlichkeit, in: *Mitteilungen des Instituts für Wissenschaft und Kunst*, 44 (1989), pp. 12–16

Louis, William Roger. Sir John Harris and 'Colonial Trusteeship', in: *Bulletin des Séances de l'Académie Royale des sciences d'Outre Mer*, 3 (1968), pp. 832–56

MacLeod, Roy. The 'Bankruptcy of Science' Debate: The Creed of Science and Its Critics, 1885–1900, in: *Science, Technology, & Human Values*, vol. 7, no. 41 (Autumn 1982), pp. 2–15

Maura, J. Romero. Terrorism in Barcelona and Its Impact on Spanish Politics 1904–1909, in: *Past and Present*, no. 41 (Dec. 1968), pp. 130–83

Moran, Jeffrey P. 'Modernism Gone Mad': Sex Education Comes to Chicago, 1913, in: *The Journal of American History*, vol. 83, no. 2 (Sep. 1996), pp. 481–513

Morris, A. J. A. The English Radicals' Campaign for Disarmament and the Hague Conference of 1907, in: *The Journal of Modern History*, vol. 43, no. 3 (Sep. 1971), pp. 367–93

Mosse, George L. Max Nordau, Liberalism and the New Jew, in: *Journal of Contemporary History*, vol. 27, no. 4 (Oct. 1992), pp. 565–81

——. Nationalism and Respectability: Normal and Abnormal Sexuality in the Nineteenth Century, in: *Journal of Contemporary History*, vol. 17, no. 2, Sexuality in History (Apr. 1982), pp. 221–46

Nord, Philip. The Welfare State in France, 1870–1914, in: *French Historical Studies*, vol. 18, no. 3 (Spring 1994), pp. 821–38

Nye, Robert A. Honor, Impotence, and Male Sexuality in Nineteenth-Century French Medicine, in: *French Historical Studies*, vol. 16, no. 1 (Spring 1989), pp. 48–71

——. Degeneration, Neurasthenia and the Culture of Sport in Belle Epoque France, in: *Journal of Contemporary History*, vol. 17, no. 1, Decadence (Jan. 1982), pp. 51–68

Offen, Karen. Depopulation, Nationalism, and Feminism in Fin-de-Siècle France, in: *The American Historical Review*, vol. 89, no. 3 (Jun. 1984), pp. 648–76

Paul, Diane. Eugenics and the Left, in: *Journal of the History of Ideas*, vol. 45, no. 4 (Oct.–Dec. 1984), pp. 567–90

Paul, Harry W. The Issue of Decline in Nineteenth-Century French Science, in: *French Historical Studies*, vol. 7, no. 3 (Spring 1972), pp. 416–50.

Payne, Stanley G. Spanish Conservatism 1834–1923, in: *Journal of Contemporary History*, vol. 13, no. 4, A Century of Conservatism (Oct. 1978), pp. 765–89

Pellew, Jill. The Home Office and the Aliens Act, 1905, in: *The Historical Journal*, vol. 32, no. 2 (Jun. 1989), pp. 369–85

Perrie, Maureen. The Russian Peasant Movement of 1905–1907: Its Social Composition and Revolutionary Significance, in: *Past and Present*, no. 57 (Nov. 1972), pp. 123–55

Reagin, Nancy. The Imagined Hausfrau: National Identity, Domesticity, and Colonialism in Imperial Germany, in: *The Journal of Modern History*, vol. 73, no. 1 (Mar. 2001), pp. 54–86

Repp, Kevin. 'More Corporeal, More Concrete': Liberal Humanism, Eugenics, and German Progressives at the Last Fin de Siècle, in: *The Journal of Modern History*, vol. 72, no. 3 (Sep. 2000), pp. 683–730

Rohl, J. C. G. Admiral von Muller and the Approach of War, 1911–1914, in: *The Historical Journal*, vol. 12, no. 4 (Dec. 1969), pp. 651–73

Rothenberg, Gunther E. Nobility and Military Careers: The Habsburg Officer Corps, 1740–1914, in: *Military Affairs*, vol. 40, no. 4 (Dec. 1976), pp. 182–6

Rupp, Leila J. Sexuality and Politics in the Early Twentieth Century: The Case of the International Women's Movement, in: *Feminist Studies*, vol. 23, no. 3 (Autumn 1997), pp. 577–605

Sayer, Derek. The Language of Nationality and the Nationality of Language: Prague 1780–1920, in: *Past and Present*, no. 153 (Nov. 1996), pp. 164–210

Schneider, William. Toward the Improvement of the Human Race: The History of Eugenics in France, in: *The Journal of Modern History*, vol. 54, no. 2, Sex, Science, and Society in Modern France (Jun. 1982), pp. 268–91

Sclove Richard E. From Alchemy to Atomic War: Frederick Soddy's 'Technology Assessment' of Atomic Energy, 1900–1915, in: *Science, Technology, & Human Values*, vol. 14, no. 2 (Spring 1989), pp. 163–94

Sell, Friedrich Carl. Intellectual Liberalism in Germany about 1900, in: *The Journal of Modern History*, vol. 15, no. 3 (Sep. 1943), pp. 227–36

Soffer, Reba N. The Revolution in English Social Thought, 1880–1914, in: *The American Historical Review*, vol. 75, no. 7 (Dec. 1970), pp. 1938–64

Soloway, Richard. Counting the Degenerates: The Statistics of Race Deterioration in Edwardian England, in: *Journal of Contemporary History*, vol. 17, no. 1, Decadence (Jan. 1982), pp. 137–64

Stearns, Peter N. Girls, Boys, and Emotions: Redefinitions and Historical

Change, in: *The Journal of American History*, vol. 80, no. 1 (Jun. 1993), pp. 36–74

Stevenson, David. Militarization and Diplomacy in Europe before 1914, in: *International Security*, vol. 22, no. 1 (Summer 1997), pp. 125–61

Stone, Norman. Army and Society in the Habsburg Monarchy, 1900–1914, in: *Past and Present*, no. 33 (Apr. 1966), pp. 95–111

Strong, Bryan. Ideas of the Early Sex Education Movement in America, 1890–1920, in: *History of Education Quarterly*, vol. 12, no. 2 (Summer 1972), pp. 129–61

Sumida, Jon Tetsuro. Sir John Fisher and the Dreadnought: The Sources of Naval Mythology, in: *The Journal of Military History*, vol. 59, no. 4 (Oct. 1995), pp. 619–37

Teal, Laurie. The Hollow Women: Modernism, the Prostitute, and Commodity Aesthetics, in: *Differences*, vol. 7, no. 3 (1995), pp. 80–109

Thompson, Alastair. Honours Uneven: Decorations, the State and Bourgeois Society in Imperial Germany, in: *Past and Present*, vol. 144 (Aug. 1994), pp. 171–204

Thurston, Robert W. Police and People in Moscow, 1906–1914, in: *Russian Review*, vol. 39, no. 3 (Jul. 1980), pp. 320–38

Trommler, Frank. Working-Class Culture and Modern Mass Culture before World War I, in: *New German Critique*, no. 29, The Origins of Mass Culture: The Case of Imperial Germany (1871–1918) (Spring–Summer 1983), pp. 57–70

Tschebotarieff Bill, Valentine. The Morozovs, in: *Russian Review*, vol. 14, no. 2 (Apr. 1955), pp. 109–16

Walkin, Jacob. Government Controls Over the Press in Russia, 1905–1914, in: *Russian Review*, vol. 13, no. 3 (Jul. 1954), pp. 203–9

Weikart, Richard. Darwinism and Death: Devaluing Human Life in Germany 1859–1920, in: *Journal of the History of Ideas*, vol. 63, no. 2 (Apr. 2002), pp. 323–44

Williams, John Alexander. Ecstasies of the Young: Sexuality, the Youth Movement, and Moral Panic in Germany on the Eve of the First World War, in: *Central European History*, vol. 34 (2001), no. 2, pp. 163–89

Winkler, Allan M. The 'Atom' and American Life, in: *The History Teacher*, vol. 26, no. 3 (May 1993), pp. 317–37

Wolff, Larry. Dynastic Conservatism and Poetic Violence in Fin-de-Siècle Cracow: The Habsburg Matrix of Polish Modernism, in: *The American Historical Review*, vol. 106, no. 3 (Jun. 2001), pp. 735–64

Wucherpfennig, Wolf. The 'Young Viennese' and Their Fathers. Decadence and the Generation Conflict around 1890, in: *Journal of Contemporary History*, vol. 17, no. 1, Decadence (Jan. 1982), pp. 21–49

BOOKS

Allen, Ann Taylor. *Feminism and Motherhood in Western Europe 1890–1970*. New York: Palgrave, 2005

Anderson, Bonnie S., and Judith P. Zinsser. *A History of Their Own: Women in Europe from Prehistory to the Present*. New York: Oxford University Press, 2000

Anderson, Harriet. *Utopian Feminism: Women's Movements in fin-de-siècle Vienna*. New Haven: Yale University Press, 1992

Antiseri, Dario. *Popper's Vienna*. Aurora, Colo.: Davies Group Publishers, 2006

Arenzon, E. *Savva Mamontov, Rossii slavnye imena*. Moskva: 'Russkaëïa kniga', 1995

L'art russe dans la seconde moitié du XIXe siècle: en quéte d'identité (exhibition catalogue), Musée d'Orsay, Paris, 19 septembre 2005–8 janvier 2006. Marie-Pierre Salé et Édouard Papet, eds. Paris: Musée d'Orsay: Réunion des musées nationaux, impr. 2005

Aschhelm, Steven E. *The Nietzsche Legacy in Germany 1890–1990*. Berkeley, UCP, 1992

August, Thomas G. *The Selling of the Empire: British and French Imperialist Propaganda, 1890–1940*. Westport, Conn.: Greenwood Press, 1985

Bedwell, Carol E. B. *The Parallelism of Artistic and Literary Tendencies in Germany 1880–1910*. Diss., Indiana University, 1962

Beliëu, H. M., M. P. Bossenbroek and Gert Jan van Setten. *In de vaart der volken: Nederlanders rond 1900*. Amsterdam: B. Bakker, 1998

Berglar, Peter. *Walther Rathenau: ein Leben zwischen Philosophie und Politik*. Graz: Styria, 1987

Berlage, Andreas. *Empfindung, Ich und Sprache um 1900: Ernst Mach, Hermann Bahr und Fritz Mauthner im Zusammenhang*. Frankfurt am Main; New York: P. Lang, 1994

Blackbourn, David. *Populists and Patricians: Essays in Modern German History*. London; Boston: Allen & Unwin, 1987

——. *History of Germany, 1780–1918: the long Nineteenth Century*. Malden, MA: Blackwell, 2003

——, and Geoff Eley. *The Peculiarities of German History: Bourgeois Society and Politics in Nineteenth-Century Germany*. Oxford; New York: Oxford University Press, 1984

——, and Richard J. Evans. *The German Bourgeoisie: Essays on the Social History of the German Middle Class from the Late Eighteenth to the Early Twentieth Century*. London; New York: Routledge, 1991

Blanchard, Pascal, and Sandrine Lemaire, eds. *Culture coloniale: la France conquise par son empire, 1871–1931.* Paris: Éd. Autrement, 2002

Bland, Lucy. *Banishing the Beast: Sexuality and the Early Feminists.* New York: New Press, 1995

Bonnell, Victoria E. *Roots of Rebellion: Workers' Politics and Organizations in St. Petersburg and Moscow, 1900–1914.* Berkeley: UCP, 1983

———. ed. and trans. *The Russian Worker: Life and Labor under the Tsarist Regime.* Berkeley: UCP, 1983

Boorstin, Daniel J. *The Americans – The Democratic Experience.* New York: Vintage, 1974

Borscheid, Peter. *Das Tempo-Virus: eine Kulturgeschichte der Beschleunigung.* Frankfurt am Main; New York: Campus, 2004

Bossenbroek, M. P. *Holland op zijn breedst: Indië en Zuid-Afrika in de Nederlandse cultuur omstreeks 1900.* Amsterdam: Bert Bakker, 1996

———. *Van Holland naar Indië het transport van koloniale troepen voor het Oost-Indische leger, 1815–1909.* Amsterdam: Bataafsche Leeuw, 1986

Boyd, Kelly. *Manliness and the Boys' Story Paper in Britain: A Cultural History, 1855–1940.* Basingstoke: Palgrave Macmillan, 2003

Bradley, Joseph. *Muzhik and Muscovite: Urbanization in Late Imperial Russia.* Berkeley: University of California Press, 1985

Brandstätter, Horst, and Bernd Neuzner. *Wagner–Lehrer, Dichter, Massenmörder.* Frankfurt/M: Eichborn, 1996

Brenner, Wolfgang. *Walther Rathenau: Deutscher und Jude.* München: Piper, 2005

Brooks, Jeffrey, *When Russia learned to Read: Literary and Popular Literature, 1861–1917.* Princeton: PUP, 1985

Brower, Daniel R. *The Russian City Between Tradition and Modernity, 1850–1900.* Berkeley: University of California Press, 1990

Brumfield, William Craft. *The Origins of Modernism in Russian Architecture.* Berkeley: University of California Press, 1991

Burrow, J. W. *The Crisis of Reason: European Thought, 1848–1914.* New Haven: Yale University Press, 2000

Bushnell, John. *Mutiny Amid Repression: Russian Soldiers in the Revolution of 1905–1906.* Bloomington: Indiana University Press, 1985

Cain, Peter, and A. G. Hopkins. *Gentlemanly Capitalism and British Imperialism: the New Debate on Empire.* London: Longman, 1999

Calvesi, Maurizio, Claudia Salaris, Gino Agnese and Italy. Ministero per i beni culturali e ambientali. *Marinetti e il futurismo.* Roma: Edizioni De Luca, 1994

Cannadine, David. *The Decline and Fall of the British Aristocracy.* New Haven, Conn.: Yale University Press, 1990

——. *Ornamentalism: How the British Saw Their Empire*. Oxford; New York: Oxford University Press, 2001

Carlino, Marcello, and Francesco Muzzioli. *La letteratura italiana del primo Novecento (1900–1915)*. Roma: La Nuova Italia Scientifica, 1986

Charle, Christophe, *Paris fin de siècle : Culture et politique*. Paris, Seuil, 1998

——. *La crise des sociétes impériales: Allemagne, France, Grande-Bretagne, 1900–1940: essai d'histoire sociale comparée, L'univers historique*. Paris: Seuil, 2001

Clark, Christopher M. *Iron Kingdom: the Rise and Downfall of Prussia, 1600–1947*. Cambridge, Mass.: Belknap Press of Harvard University Press, 2006

——. *Kaiser Wilhelm II*. Harlow, England; New York: Longman, 2000

Clifford, James. *The Predicament of Culture: Twentieth-Century Ethnography, Literature, and Art*. Cambridge, Mass.: HUP, 1988

Clowes, E. W., S. D. Kassow and J. L. West, ed. *Between Tsar and People: Educated Society and the Quest for Public Identity in Late Imperial Russia*. Princeton: PUP, 1991

Confino, Michael. *Société et mentalités collectives en Russie sous l'Ancien Régime*. Paris: Institut d'études slaves, 1991

Connaughton, R. M. *Rising Sun and Tumbling Bear: Russia's War with Japan*. London; New York, N.Y.: Cassell, 2004

Conrad, Peter. *Modern Times, Modern Places*. 1st American ed. New York: Knopf, 1999

Cossick, G. et al., eds. *Cathedrals of Consumption*. Aldershot: Ashgate, 1999

Daniels, Roger. *Coming to America – A History of Immigration and Ethnicity in American Life*. New York: Harper Perennial, 1991

De Maria, Luciano, and Laura Dondi. *Marinetti e i futuristi*. 1st ed. Milano: Garzanti, 1994

Delathuy, A. M. *De Kongostaat van Leopold II: het verloren paradijs, 1876–1900*. Antwerpen: Standaard, 1988

Di Gregorio, Mario A. *From Here to Eternity: Ernst Haeckel and the Scientific Faith*. Göttingen: Vanderhoek and Ruprecht, 2005

Doetry, Martin. *Übergangsmensche: die Mentalität der Wilhelminer und die Krise des Kaiserreichs*. Weinheim: Juventa, 1986

Dunant, Sarah, and Roy Porter. *The Age of Anxiety*. London: Virago, 1996

Eksteins, Modris. *Rites of Spring: The Great War and the Birth of the Modern Age*. New York: Doubleday, 1990

Engel, Barbara Alpern. *Between the Fields and the City: Women, Work, and Family in Russia, 1861–1914*. Cambridge, England; New York: Cambridge University Press, 1994

Engelstein, Laura. *The Keys to Happiness: Sex and the Search for Modernity in fin-de-siècle Russia*. Ithaca: Cornell University Press, 1992

——. *Moscow, 1905: Working-Class Organization and Political Conflict.* Stanford, Calif.: Stanford University Press, 1982

Evans, Martin. *Empire and Culture: the French Experience, 1830–1940.* Houndmills, Basingstoke, Hampshire; New York: Palgrave Macmillan, 2004

Evans, Richard J., ed. *The German Working Class, 1888–1933.* London: Croom Helm, 1982

Ferro, Marc, ed. *Le livre noir du colonialisme: XVIe–XXIe siècle, de l'extermination à la repentance.* Paris: Hachette Littératures, 2004

Figes, Orlando. *Natasha's Dance: a Cultural History of Russia.* New York: Metropolitan Books, 2002

——. *A People's Tragedy: the Russian Revolution, 1891–1924.* New York, N.Y.: Penguin Books, 1998

Fisher, David James. *Romain Rolland and the Politics of Intellectual Engagement.* Berkeley: University of California Press, 1988

Forth, Christopher E. *The Dreyfus Affair and the Crisis of French Manhood.* Baltimore: Johns Hopkins University Press, 2004

Fröhlich, Michael. *Das Kaiserreich: Portrait einer Epoche in Biographien.* Darmstadt: Primus, 2001

——. *Imperialismus: deutsche Kolonial- und Weltpolitik, 1880–1914.* Originalausg. ed., *Deutsche Geschichte der neuesten Zeit vom 19. Jahrhundert bis zur Gegenwart.* München: Deutscher Taschenbuch Verlag, 1994

Fromkin, David. *Europe's Last Summer. Who Started the Great War in 1914?* New York: Knopf, 2004

Gay, Peter. *The Bourgeois Experience: Victoria to Freud.* New York: Oxford University Press, 1984

——. *Freud: a Life for Our Time.* New York: Norton, 2006

——. *Schnitzler's Century: the Making of Middle-Class Culture, 1815–1914.* 1st ed. New York: Norton, 2002

Gillham, Nicholas Wright. *A life of Sir Francis Galton.* Oxford: OUP, 2001

Girardet, Raoul. *L'idée coloniale en France de 1871 à 1962.* Paris: La Table Ronde, 1972

Gosudarstvennyï Ermitazh (Russia), Museum Folkwang Essen., and Gosudarstvennyï muzeæi izobrazitelnykh iskusstv imeni A. S. Pushkina. *Morozov, Shchukin: the collectors: Monet to Picasso: 120 masterpieces from the Hermitage, St. Petersburg, and the Pushkin Museum, Moscow.* Bonn: Bild-Kunst, 1993

Haferkamp, Hans, and Neil J. Smelser, eds. *Social Change and Modernity.* Berkeley: University of California Press, 1991

Hamann, Brigitte, *Hitler's Vienna – A Dictator's Apprenticeship.* Oxford: OUP, 1999

——. *Bertha von Suttner: a Life for Peace.* Syracuse, N.Y., Syracuse University Press, 1996

Hamm, Michael F., ed. *The City in Late Imperial Russia.* Bloomington, Ind., 1986

Harcave, Sidney. *Count Sergei Witte and the Twilight of Imperial Russia: a Biography.* Armonk, N.Y.: M. E. Sharpe, 2004

Harrison, Thomas. *1910: The Emancipation of Dissonance.* Berkeley: University of California Press, 1996

Haumann, Heiko. *Kapitalismus im zaristischen Staat 1906–1917: Organisationformen, Machtverhältnisse u. Leistungsbilanz im Industrialisierungsprozess.* Königstein/Ts.: Hain, 1980

Heller, Karl Daniel. *Ernst Mach; Wegbereiter der modernen Physik. Mit ausgewählten Kapiteln aus seinem Werk.* Wien, New York: Springer-Verlag, 1964

Hepp, Corona. *Avantgarde: Moderne Kunst, Kulturkritik und Reformbewegungen nach der Jahrhundertwende.* Munich: DTV, 1992

Hobsbawm, Eric. *The Age of Empire 1875–1914.* New York: Vintage, 1989

Hochschild, Adam. *King Leopold's Ghost: A Story of Greed, Terror and Heroism in Colonial Africa.* New York: Houghton Mifflin, 1999

Hofer, Hans-Georg. *Nervenschwäche und Krieg. Modernitätskritik und Krisenbewältigung in der österreichischen Psychiatrie (1880–1920).* Wien: Böhlau, 2004

Hughes, Robert. *The Shock of the New.* Rev. ed. New York: Knopf, 1991

Humphries, Stephen. *Hooligans or Rebels? An Oral History of Working-Class Childhood and Youth, 1889–1939.* Oxford: OUP, 1981

Hüppauf, Bernd-Rüdiger. *Expressionismus und Kulturkrise.* Heidelberg: C. Winter, 1983

Inglis, Brian. *Roger Casement.* Belfast: Blackstaff Press, 1993

Jauss, Hans Robert. *Die Epochenschwelle von 1912: Guillaume Apollinaire, 'Zone' und 'Landi Rue Christine', Sitzungsberichte der Heidelberger Akademie der Wissenschaften; Jahrg. 1986, Bericht 1.* Heidelberg: C. Winter, 1986

Johnson, Eric A. *Urbarnization and Crime, Germany 1871–1914.* Cambridge: CUP, 1995

Johnston, William M. *The Austrian Mind – An Intellectual and Social History 1848–1938.* Berkeley, UCP, 1962

Joll, James. *Europe since 1870 – An International History.* London: Weidenfeld and Nicolson, 1973

Judd, Denis. *Eclipse of Kings: European Monarchies in the Twentieth Century.* New York: Stein and Day, 1976

——. *Empire: the British Imperial Experience from 1765 to the Present.* New York: Basic Books, 1997

——. *The Lion and the Tiger: the Rise and Fall of the British Raj, 1600–1947*. Oxford; New York: Oxford University Press, 2004

——, and Keith Terrance Surridge. *The Boer War*. 1st Palgrave Macmillan ed. New York: Palgrave Macmillan, 2003

Kanigel, Robert. *The One Best Way: Frederick Winslow Taylor and the Enigma of Efficiency*. New York: Viking, 1997

Kasson, John F. *Houdini, Tarzan, and the Perfect Man: the White Male Body and the Challenge of Modernity in America*. 1st ed. New York: Hill and Wang, 2001

Kassow, Samuel D. *Students, Professors, and the State in Tsarist Russia*. Berkeley: University of California Press, 1989

Kayali, Hasan. *Arabs and Young Turks: Ottomanism, Arabism, and Islamism in the Ottoman Empire, 1908–1918*. Berkeley: University of California Press, 1997

Kean, Beverly Whitney. *All the Empty Palaces: the Merchant Patrons of Modern Art in Pre-Revolutionary Russia*. New York: Universe Books, 1983

Kern, Stephen. *Anatomy and Destiny: a Cultural History of the Human Body*. Indianapolis: Bobbs-Merrill, 1975

——. *The Culture of Love: Victorians to Moderns*. Cambridge, Mass.: Harvard University Press, 1992

——. *The Culture of Time and Space, 1880–1918*. Cambridge, Mass.: Harvard University Press, 2003

Klejman, Laurence and Florence Rochefort. *L'égalité en marche – le féminisme sous la Troisième République*. Paris: Presses de la Fondation Nationale des Sciences Politiques, 1989

Kohut, Thomas August. *Wilhelm II and the Germans: a Study in Leadership*. New York: Oxford University Press, 1991

Kovtun, E. F. *Mikhail Larionov: 1881–1964, Velikie mastera zhivopisi*. Sankt-Peterburg: Avrora, 1998

Landes, David S. *The Unbound Prometheus: Technical Change and Industrial Development in Western Europe from 1750 to the Present*. Cambridge; New York: Cambridge University Press, 2003

Lears, T. J. Jackson. *No Place of Grace. Antimodernism and the Transformation of American Culture 1880–1920*. New York: Pantheon, 1981

Liauzu, Claude. *L'Islam de l'Occident: la question de l'Islam dans la conscience occidentale, Collection Mémoires et identités*. Paris: Arcantère, 1989

——. *Race et civilisation: l'Autre dans la culture occidentale: anthologie historique*. Paris: Syros-Alternatives, 1992

——. *Violence et colonisation: pour en finir avec les guerres de mémoires*. Paris: Editions Syllepse, 2003

——, and Leila Blili. *Colonisation, droit d'inventaire, Collection Les enjeux de l'histoire*. Paris: Colin, 2004

Liddington, Jill. *Rebel Girls: Their Fight for the Vote*. London: Virago, 2006

——, and Jill Norris. *One Hand Tied Behind Us: the Rise of the Women's Suffrage Movement*. London: Virago, 1978

Loeffler, Hans F. *Walther Rathenau: ein Europäer im Kaiserreich*. Berlin: Berlin Verlag A. Spitz, 1997

Long, Kathleen P. *High Anxiety: Masculinity in Crisis in Early Modern France*. Kirksville, Mo.: Truman State University Press, 2001

Löther, Rolf. *Wegbereiter der Genetik: Gregor Johann Mendel und August Weismann*. Frankfurt/Main: Harri Deutsch, 1990

Lukacs, John. *Budapest 1900: a Historical Portrait of a City and Its Culture*. London: Weidenfeld & Nicolson, 1989

Malcolm, Noel. *Bosnia: a Short History*. New York: New York University Press, 1994

Malmstad, John E., and N. A. Bogomolov. *Mikhail Kuzmin: a life in art*. Cambridge, Mass.: Harvard University Press, 1999

Manning, Roberta Thompson. *The Crisis of the Old Order in Russia: Gentry and Government*. Princeton, N.J.: Princeton University Press, 1982

Marks, Patricia. *Bicycles, Bangs, and Bloomers: the New Woman in the Popular Press*. Lexington, KY: University Press of Kentucky, 1990

Massie, Robert K. *Dreadnought: Britain, Germany, and the Coming of the Great War*. New York: Ballantine Books, 1992

Matich, Olga. *Erotic Utopia: the Decadent Imagination in Russia's fin-de-siècle*. Madison, Wis.: University of Wisconsin Press, 2005

Maynes, Mary Jo. *Taking the Hard Road. Life Course in French and German Workers' Autobiographies in the Era of Industrialization*. Chapel Hill: University of North Carolina Press, 1995

Meysels, Lucian O. *In Meinem Salon ist Österreich – Berta Zuckerkandl und ihre Zeit*. Vienna: Herold, 1984

Miller, Arthur I. *Einstein Picasso: Space, Time, and the Beauty That Causes Havoc*. New York: Basic Books, 2001

Miller, Manu von. *Sonja Knips und die Wiener Moderne: Gustav Klimt, Josef Hoffmann und die Wiener Werkstätte gestalten eine Lebenswelt*. 1. Aufl. ed. Wien: Christian Brandstätter, 2004

Morton, Frederic. *A Nervous Splendor: Vienna, 1888/1889*. Harmondsworth: Penguin Books, 1980.

——. *Thunder at Twilight: Vienna 1913/1914*. New York, 1990

Mosse, George L. *The Crisis of German Ideology: Intellectual Origins of the Third Reich*. New York: Schocken Books, 1981

——. *The Culture of Western Europe: the Nineteenth and Twentieth Centuries, an Introduction*. Chicago: Rand McNally, 1961

——. *German Jews Beyond Judaism*. Bloomington; Cincinnati: Indiana University Press, 1985

——. *Germans and Jews; the Right, the Left, and the Search for a 'Third Force' in pre-Nazi Germany.* 1st ed. New York: H. Fertig, 1970

——. *Masses and Man: Nationalist and Fascist Perceptions of Reality.* Detroit: Wayne State University Press, 1987

——. *The Nationalization of the Masses; Political Symbolism and Mass Movements in Germany from the Napoleonic Wars through the Third Reich.* New York: H. Fertig, 1975

Nicholson, Virginia. *Among the Bohemians – Experiments in Living 1900–1939.* London: Penguin, 2002

Noble, Iris. *Emmeline and Her Daughters: the Pankhurst Suffragettes.* New York: J. Messner, 1971

Nora, Pierre. *Les Lieux de mémoire, Bibliothèque illustrée des histoires.* Paris: Gallimard, 1984

Nuhn, Walter. *Feind überall: Guerillakrieg in Südwest. Der große Nama-Aufstand 1904–1908.* Bonn: Bernhard & Graefe-Verlag, 2000

Nye, Robert A. *Crime, Madness, and Politics in Modern France: The Medical Concept of National Decline.* Princeton: UPP, 1984

Padfield, Peter. *The Great Naval Race: the Anglo-German Naval Rivalry, 1900–1914.* London: Hart-Davis MacGibbon, 1974

Patton, Anthony. *Mikhail Larionov and the Russian Avant-Garde.* Princeton, N.J.: Princeton University Press, 1993

Pearson, Geoffrey. *Hooligan: A History of Respectable Fears.* London: Macmillan, 1983

Perkin, Harold James. *The Rise of Professional Society: England since 1880.* London, New York: Routledge, 1989

Pinner, Felix. *Emil Rathenau und das elektrische Zeitalter, European business.* New York: Arno Press, 1977

Pipes, Richard. *The Russian Revolution.* 1st Vintage Books ed. New York: Vintage Books, 1991

Pluchon, Pierre. *Histoire de la colonisation française.* Paris: Fayard, 1991

Porter, Bernard. *The Absent-Minded Imperialists: Empire, Society, and Culture in Britain.* Oxford, England; New York: Oxford University Press, 2004

——. *Critics of Empire: British Radical Attitudes to Colonialism in Africa 1895–1914.* London: St Martin's Press, 1968

——. *The Lion's Share: a Short History of British Imperialism, 1850–1970.* London; New York: Longman, 1975

Porter, Roy. *Madness: a Brief History.* Oxford; New York: Oxford University Press, 2002

Rabinbach, Anson. *The Human Motor.* New York: Basic Books, 1990

Radkau, Joachim. *Das Zeitalter der Nervosität: Deutschland zwischen Bismarck und Hitler.* München: Hanser, 1998

——. *Max Weber: die Leidenschaft des Denkens.* München: Hanser, 2005

——. *Technik in Deutschland: vom 18. Jahrhundert bis zur Gegenwart.* 1. Aufl. ed., *Neue historische Bibliothek.* Frankfurt am Main: Suhrkamp, 1989

Reid, B.L. *The Lives of Roger Casement.* New Haven: Yale University Press, 1976

Richards, Thomas. *The Commodity Culture of Victorian England: Advertising and Spectacle, 1851–1914.* London: Verso, 1990

Rioux, Jean-Pierre, and Jean-François Sivinelli, eds. *La culture de masse en France de la belle époque à aujourd'hui.* Paris: Fayard, 2002

Roberts, Brian. *Cecil Rhodes: Flawed Colossus.* 1st American ed. New York: Norton, 1988

Robinson, Geroid Tanquary. *Rural Russia under the Old Régime; a History of the Landlord–Peasant World and a Prologue to the Peasant Revolution of 1917.* New York: Macmillan, 1949

Röhl, John C. G. *Germany Without Bismarck; the Crisis of Government in the Second Reich, 1890–1900.* Berkeley: University of California Press, 1967

——. *The Kaiser and His Court: Wilhelm II and the Government of Germany.* Cambridge; New York: Cambridge University Press, 1994.

——. *Wilhelm II: the Kaiser's Personal Monarchy, 1888–1900.* New York: Cambridge University Press, 2004

——. *Young Wilhelm: the Kaiser's Early Life, 1859–1888.* Cambridge, U.K.; New York, N.Y.: Cambridge University Press, 1998

——, and Elisabeth Müller-Luckner. *Der Ort Kaiser Wilhelms II. in der deutschen Geschichte, Schriften des Historischen Kollegs. Kolloquien; 17.* München: R. Oldenbourg, 1991

Rosen, Andrew. *Rise Up, Women! The Militant Campaign of the Woman's Social and Political Union 1903–1914.* London: Routledge, 1974

Rosenblum, Robert, Maryanne Stevens, Ann Dumas, Royal Academy of Arts (Great Britain) and Solomon R. Guggenheim Museum. *1900: Art at the Crossroads.* New York: Harry N. Abrams, 2000

Russkij avangard 1910–1920-h godov v evropejskom kontekste Gosudarstvennyj institut iskusstvoznaniâ Ministerstva kultury Rossijskoj Federacii, komissiâ po izučeniû iskusstva avangarda 1910–1920-h godov. Moskva: Nauka, 2000

Salisbury, Harrison E. *Black Night White Snow: Russia's Revolutions 1905–1917.* 1st ed. Garden City, N.Y.: Doubleday, 1978

Sass, Louis A. *Madness and Modernism. Insanity in the Light of Modern Art, Literature, and Thought.* New York: Basic Books, 1992

Sassoon, Donald. *The Culture of the Europeans from 1800 to the Present.* London: HarperCollins, 2006

Schorske, Carl. *Fin-de-Siècle Vienna: Politics and Culture.* New York: Random House, 1980

Schwarz, Solomon M., and Inter-university Project on the History of the Menshevik Movement. *The Russian Revolution of 1905; the Workers' Movement and the Formation of Bolshevism and Menshevism*. Chicago: University of Chicago Press, 1967

Schweiger, Werner J. *Aufbruch und Erfüllung: Gebrauchsgraphik der Wiener Moderne 1897–1918*. Wien: Edition C. Brandstätter, 1988

Scull, Andrew. *Social Order/Mental Disorder: Anglo-American Psychiatry in Historical Perspective*. Berkeley: University of California Press, 1989

Seigel, Jerrold. *The Private Worlds of Marcel Duchamp: Desire, Liberation, and the Self in Modern Culture*. Berkeley: University of California Press, 1995

Seregny, Scott Joseph. *Russian Teachers and Peasant Revolution: the Politics of Education in 1905*. Bloomington: Indiana University Press, 1989

——, and Rex A. Wade. *Politics and Society in Provincial Russia: Saratov, 1590–1917*. Columbus: Ohio State University Press, 1989

Sieg, Ulrich. *Jüdische Intellektuelle im Ersten Weltkrieg: Kriegserfahrungen, weltanschauliche Debatten und kulturelle Neuentwürfe*. Berlin: Akademie Verlag, 2001

——. *Deutschlands Prophet. Paul de Lagarde und die Ursprünge des modernen Antisemitismus*. Munich: Carl Hanser, 2007

Simon, Linda. *Dark Light: Electricity and Anxiety from the Telegraph to the X-Ray*. San Diego: Harcourt Brace, 2004

Sprengel, Peter, Gregor Streim and Barbara Noth. *Berliner und Wiener Moderne: Vermittlungen und Abgrenzungen in Literatur, Theater, Publizistik, Literatur in der Geschichte, Geschichte in der Literatur*. Wien: Böhlau, 1998

Stansky, Peter. *On or About December 1910: Early Bloomsbury and Its Intimate World*. Cambridge, Mass.: Harvard University Press, 1996

Steinberg, Mark D. *Moral Communities: The Culture of Class Relations in the Russian Printing Industry 1867–1907*. Berkeley: University of California Press, 1992

Steltzer, Hans Georg. *Die deutsche Flotte: ein historischer Überblick von 1640 bis 1918*. Frankfurt am Main: Societäts-Verlag, 1989

——. *Die Deutschen und ihr Kolonialreich*. Frankfurt am Main: Frankfurter Societäts-Verlag, 1984

Stengers, Jean. *Congo, mythes et réalités: 100 ans d'histoire*. Paris: Duculot, 1989

——, and Anne van Neck. *Histoire d'une grande peur, la masturbation*. Paris: Le Plessis-Robinson France, 1998

Stites, Richard. *Russian Popular Culture: Entertainment and Society since 1900*. Cambridge; New York, N.Y.: Cambridge University Press, 1992

——. *The Women's Liberation Movement in Russia: Feminism, Nihilism, and Bolshevism, 1860–1930*. Princeton, N.J.: Princeton University Press, 1978

Stone, Dan. *Breeding Superman: Nietzsche, Race, and Eugenics in Edwardian and Interwar Britain*. Liverpool: Liverpool University Press, 2002

Stone, Norman. *Europe Transformed, 1878–1919.* Oxford, UK; Malden, Mass.: Blackwell, 1999

Streibel, Robert, ed. *Eugenie Schwarzwald und ihr Kreis.* Vienna: Picus, 1996

Surh, Gerald Dennis. *1905 in St. Petersburg: Labor, Society, and Revolution.* Stanford, Calif.: Stanford University Press, 1989

Teich, Mikuláš and Roy Porter, eds. *Fin de Siècle and Its Legacy.* Cambridge: CUP, 1990

Tichy, Marina. *Alltag und Traum: Leben und Lektüre der Wiener Dienstmädchen um die Jahrhundertwende.* Wien: H. Böhlau, 1984

Torgovnick, Marianna. *Gone Primitive: Savage Intellects, Modern Lives.* Chicago: UCP, 1990

Tuchman, Barbara W. *The Proud Tower – Portrait of the World before the War.* New York: Ballantines, 1996 (1962)

Ullrich, Volker. *Die nervöse Grossmacht 1871–1918: Aufstieg und Untergang des deutschen Kaiserreichs.* Frankfurt: Fischer, 1999

Valkenier, Elizabeth Kridl. *Valentin Serov: Portraits of Russia's Silver Age.* Evanston, Ill.: Northwestern University Press, 2001

van den Toorn, Pieter C. *Stravinsky and The Rite of Spring.* Berkeley: University of California Press, 1987

Verner, Andrew M. *The Crisis of Russian Autocracy: Nicholas II and the 1905 Revolution.* Princeton, NJ.: Princeton University Press, 1990

Vucinich, Alexander. *Darwin in Russian Thought.* Berkeley: University of California Press, 1988

Warner, Sam Bass, Jr. *The Urban Wilderness: A History of the American City.* Berkeley: University of California Press, 1995

Weikart, Richard. *From Darwin to Hitler: Evolutionary Ethics, Eugenics, and Racism in Germany.* New York: Palgrave Macmillan, 2004

Weiss, Sheila Faith. *Race Hygiene and National Efficiency: The Eugenics of Wilhelm Schallmayer.* Berkeley: University of California Press, 1987

Wesseling, H. L. *Certain Ideas of France: Essays on French History and Civilization.* Westport, Conn.: Greenwood Press, 2002

———. *Divide and Rule: the Partition of Africa, 1880–1914.* Westport, Conn.: Praeger, 1996

———, and Diane Webb. *The European Colonial Empires, 1815–1919.* 1st ed. Harlow, England; New York: Pearson/Longman, 2004

Williams, Rosalina H. *Dream Worlds. Mass Consumption in Late Nineteenth-Century France.* Berkeley: UCP, 1982

Wilson, A. N. *The Victorians.* London: Arrow, 2003

Winock, Michel. *La Belle Epoque – France de 1900 à 1914.* Paris: Perrin, 2002

Yablonskaya, Miuda Naumovna. *Women Artists of Russia's New Age, 1900–1935.* London: Thames and Hudson, 1990

Zeldin, Theodore. *Conflicts in French Society: Anticlericalism, Education and Morals in the Nineteenth Century: Essays*. London: Allen & Unwin, 1970

——. *France, 1848–1945*. Oxford: Clarendon Press, 1973

——. *The French*. 1st Vintage Books ed. New York: Vintage Books, 1984

Zelnik, E., ed. and trans. *A Radical Worker in Tsarist Russia: The Autobiography of Semen Ivanovich Kanatchikov*. Stanford: SUP, 1986

Index

Page numbers in *italic* refer to illustrations